Christian Martyrs under Islam

Christian Martyrs under Islam

RELIGIOUS VIOLENCE
AND THE MAKING OF THE MUSLIM WORLD

Christian C. Sahner

PRINCETON UNIVERSITY PRESS
Princeton & Oxford

Published by Princeton University Press,
41 William Street, Princeton, New Jersey 08540

In the United Kingdom: Princeton University Press,
6 Oxford Street, Woodstock, Oxfordshire OX20 1TR

press.princeton.edu

ISBN 978-0-691-17910-0

Library of Congress Control Number: 2017956010

British Library Cataloging-in-Publication Data is available

Editorial: Fred Appel and Thalia Leaf
Production Editorial: Debbie Tegarden
Text Design: Leslie Flis
Jacket Design: Leslie Flis
Jacket art: *Crucifixion with Two Thieves*, by permission of Saint Catharine's Monastery, Sinai, Egypt. Photograph courtesy of Michigan-Princeton-Alexandria Expeditions to Mount Sinai
Production: Jacquie Poirier
Publicity: Katie Lewis
Copyeditor: Elisabeth Graves

This book has been composed in Miller

Printed on acid-free paper. ∞

Printed in the United States of America

1 3 5 7 9 10 8 6 4 2

For my parents.

[Jesus said to the crowd:] “But before all this occurs, they will arrest and persecute you, delivering you over to synagogues and prisons, and they will have you led before kings and governors because of my name. This will be the time for you to testify. Remember, you are not to prepare your defense beforehand, for I myself shall give you a mouth and a wisdom, which none of your opponents will be able to resist or refute. You will be betrayed even by parents, brothers, kinsmen, and friends, and they will put some of you to death. You will be hated by all because of my name, but not a hair on your head will perish. By your perseverance you will gain your souls.”

—Luke 21:12–19

Do not call those who are slain in the way of God “dead.” Nay, they are living, only you perceive it not.

—Qur’an *al-Baqara* 2:154

Contents

Preface

Some readers may open this book seeking answers about the tumult that currently roils the Middle East. I hope that it is interesting and useful for them. My goal, however, has never been to write a history that connects past and present. Indeed, aside from these brief words of introduction (and a few scattered thoughts in the conclusion), this book does not engage in comparisons between religious violence in the early Islamic era and violence today. Such comparisons are legitimate—as much for the similarities they reveal as the differences. But that is an exercise best left to another writer for another time.

Research on this book started in 2011, just as the movement of popular protest known as the "Arab Spring" was beginning to sweep across the region. In the years since, this moment of optimism has given way to political bedlam and sectarian conflict. Especially notable has been the rise of the Islamic State and its persecution of ancient Christian communities and other minorities in Syria and Iraq. To watch these events unfold has been to hear distant echoes of a medieval world I encountered through my research: mass enslavement, burdensome taxes, forced conversions, crucifixions, and still worse. Although the Islamic State alleged to revive the traditions of the early caliphate, it was clear that it often misinterpreted, exaggerated, and twisted these to suit its modern agenda. I also observed Christians reviving the practices of their early medieval forebears, venerating the victims of recent religious violence as saints and martyrs.

It is important to acknowledge these symbolic parallels up front. At the same time, this book aspires to tell another story: to provide the first comprehensive history of Christian martyrdom in the formative centuries after the rise of Islam, a phenomenon that is largely unknown to the public as well as many academic specialists. More broadly, it aims to explore how violence configured relations between the early Muslims and their Christian subjects, the role that coercion and bloodshed did or did not play in the initial spread of Islam, and the manner in which Christians came to see themselves as a beleaguered minority in the new Muslim cosmos. These are central questions for the study of early Islam and Middle Eastern Christianity more broadly, yet finding clear answers to them can be surprisingly difficult.

In the pages to come, I suspect that readers of all religious and political stripes will find some points to cheer and others to contest. As a historian, my only goal is to represent the past as accurately as possible, not on the basis of personal conviction but on reasoned analysis and balanced treatment of the evidence. I will consider this book a success if it manages to spur others to learn more about the rich history of Middle Eastern Christians, especially their relationship with Muslims. In these troubled times, it is necessary to remember that peace has defined this relationship across the ages to a much greater extent than bloodshed.

Acknowledgments

This book began as a doctoral dissertation in the Department of History at Princeton University. While there, I could not have asked for better advisers than Peter Brown and Michael Cook, fine scholars and even finer mentors. In addition to shepherding the thesis to completion, they read and critiqued drafts of the revised book manuscript. John Haldon and Robert Hoyland assessed the original dissertation and have provided support ever since.

Garth Fowden, Elizabeth Key Fowden, Luke Yarbrough, and two anonymous reviewers from Princeton University Press read drafts of the entire book, saving me from countless errors and proposing changes that clarified my own muddled thoughts. Uriel Simonsohn read chapters 1 and 2; Maribel Fierro read chapter 3; Mathieu Tillier and Andrew Marsham read chapter 4; and Philip Wood read chapter 5. Their feedback has helped strengthen the final product in countless ways. Over the years, I also profited from the questions and criticisms of audiences at Université Saint-Joseph, Beirut, Toruń, Vienna, Paris, Warsaw, Münster, Princeton, Notre Dame, New York University, Beersheba, Baylor, Oxford, and Cambridge. Needless to say, all remaining mistakes are my own. An earlier version of chapter 2 appeared in the *Journal of the American Oriental Society* 136 (2016), which is reproduced here with the generous consent of the editors.

I would like to acknowledge the following teachers and colleagues who contributed to the completion of this book in ways both big and small: Sean Anthony, David Bertaina, André Binggeli, Betsy Brown, the late Patricia Crone, the late Slobodan Ćurčić, the late Robert Gabriel, George Kiraz, Mustafa Mahfuz, Emmanuel Papoutsakis, Helmut Reimitz, Michael Reynolds, Peter Sarris, John Slight, Stephen Shoemaker, Kenneth Wolf, and Fritz Zimmermann. Various individuals helped me procure photos, and they are gratefully acknowledged in the captions. I would especially like to thank Fr. Justin Sinaites for obtaining high-resolution photos from St. Catherine's Monastery, Mt. Sinai. Thanks go to Shane Kelley for producing the fine maps.

Over the years, my research benefited from the support of the following academic institutions: in Oxford, the Rhodes Trust; in Princeton, the Department of History, the Seeger Center for Hellenic Studies, the Group for the Study of Late Antiquity, the Center for the Study of Religion, and the Program in Near Eastern Studies in conjunction with the U.S. Department of Education; in Beirut, the Institut français du Proche-Orient; in Amman, the American

Center for Oriental Research; and in New York, the Harry Frank Guggenheim Foundation. I would especially like to thank the Master and Fellows of St John's College, Cambridge, where I spent two blissful years as a research fellow, with ample time to complete this project and explore new ones. I am also grateful for the support of my new colleagues in the Faculty of Oriental Studies and St Cross College, Oxford. Thanks also go to Fred Appel, Debbie Tegarden, Elisabeth A. Graves, and the staff of Princeton University Press for expertly guiding this book to publication.

A scholar is only as good as the intellectual company he or she keeps. Given this, I consider myself lucky to have become friends with Thomas Carlson, Simon Fuchs, Nick Marinides, Jacob Olidort, Jack Tannous, Lev Weitz, and Luke Yarbrough. They have been constant fonts of ideas and encouragement during our time at Princeton and beyond. I am particularly grateful to Thomas, Nick, and Lev for their help in checking translations at the end.

Many other friends have made these past years of study and writing so fruitful and happy. Between Maplewood, Princeton, Oxford, New York, Cambridge, Damascus, and Beirut, there are too many to name, but I trust that they know who they are and are aware of my affection for them. Last, it remains to thank my family—Dad, Mom, Duncan, Elizabeth, and Tom, who have buoyed me with their love and support at every turn.

The Oriental Institute
University of Oxford
November 2017

Abbreviations

The following abbreviations appear in the footnotes of this book. For full references, see the bibliography.

BHG = Halkin, François, ed. *Bibliotheca hagiographica graeca*
BHO = Peeters, Paul, ed. *Bibliotheca hagiographica orientalis*
BS = *Bibliotheca sanctorum*
BSO = *Bibliotheca sanctorum orientalium*
CE = Atiya, Aziz S., ed. *The Coptic Encyclopedia*
CMLT = Combefis, Franciscus, ed. *Christi martyrum lecta trias*
CMR, i = Thomas, David, and Barbara Roggema, eds. *Christian-Muslim Relations: A Bibliographical History. Volume 1 (600–900)*
CMR, ii = Thomas, David, and Alex Mallett, eds. *Christian-Muslim Relations: A Bibliographical History. Volume 2 (900–1050)*
CSM = Gil, Ioannes, ed. *Corpus scriptorum Muzarabicorum*
*EI*² = Bearman, Peri, et al., eds. *The Encyclopaedia of Islam. Second Edition*
*EI*³ = Fleet, Kate, et al., eds. *Encyclopaedia of Islam Three*
EIr = Yashater, Ehsan, ed. *Encyclopædia Iranica*
EQ = McAuliffe, Jane Dammen, ed. *Encyclopaedia of the Qurʾān*
GCAL = Graf, Georg, ed. *Geschichte der christlichen arabischen Literatur*
PG = Migne, J. P., ed. *Patrologia Cursus Completus, Series Graeca*
PMBZ = *Prosopographie der mittelbyzantinischen Zeit*
Q = The Qur'an
SPSH = Papadopoulos-Kerameus, Athanasios, ed. *Syllogē Palaistinēs kai Syriakēs hagiologias*

A Note to Readers

Comprehensive bibliography on each martyr may be found in the first footnote of the relevant section.

Translations from Arabic, Greek, Syriac, and Latin are by me unless otherwise noted. Translations from Armenian and Georgian are acknowledged in the footnotes.

The following abbreviations are used throughout: Ar. (Arabic), Eng. (English), Fr. (French), Gk. (Greek), It. (Italian), Lat. (Latin), Syr. (Syriac), Arm. (Armenian), Geo. (Georgian), M.P. (Middle Persian), N.P. (New Persian), Turk. (Turkish).

This book employs an Arabic transliteration system adapted from *The Encyclopaedia of Islam. Second Edition,* with two main exceptions: the letter *jīm* is rendered with a *j* instead of a *dj,* and the letter *qāf* is rendered with a *q* instead of a *ḳ.*

The book employs a Syriac transliteration system adapted from J. F. Coakley's proposed guidelines for the Library of Congress, available at http://www.loc.gov/catdir/cpso/roman_proposal_111104.html.

Greek transliteration follows standard Romanization practice, with long vowels represented by macrons (*ēta, ē; ōmega, ō*).

All dates are given according to the Anno Domini calendar and, when known and/or relevant, also according to the Hijrī calendar, which commences in AD 622.

Maps

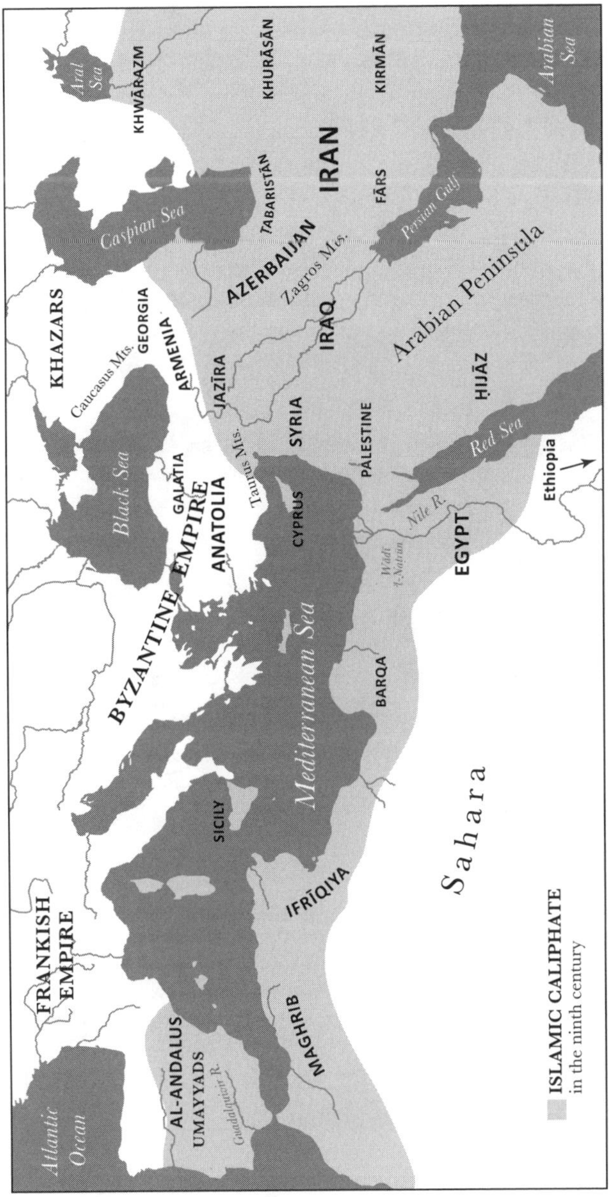

Map 1. Regions of the early Islamic caliphate.

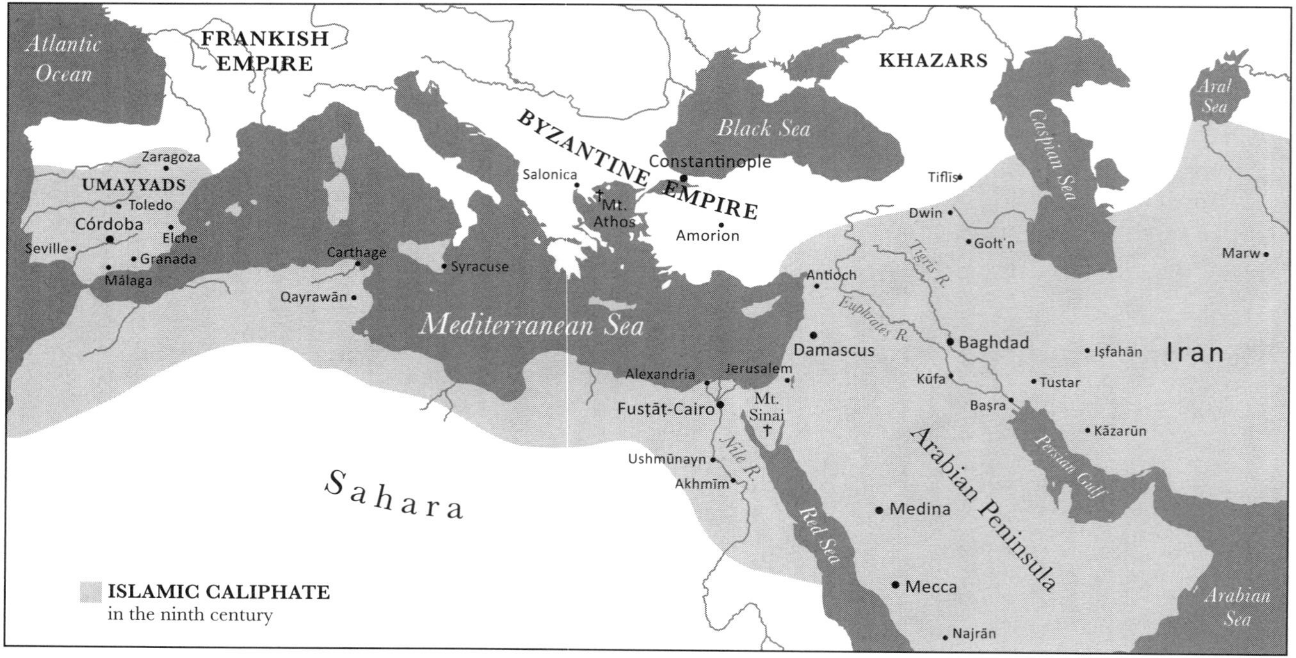

Map 2. Cities of the early Islamic caliphate.

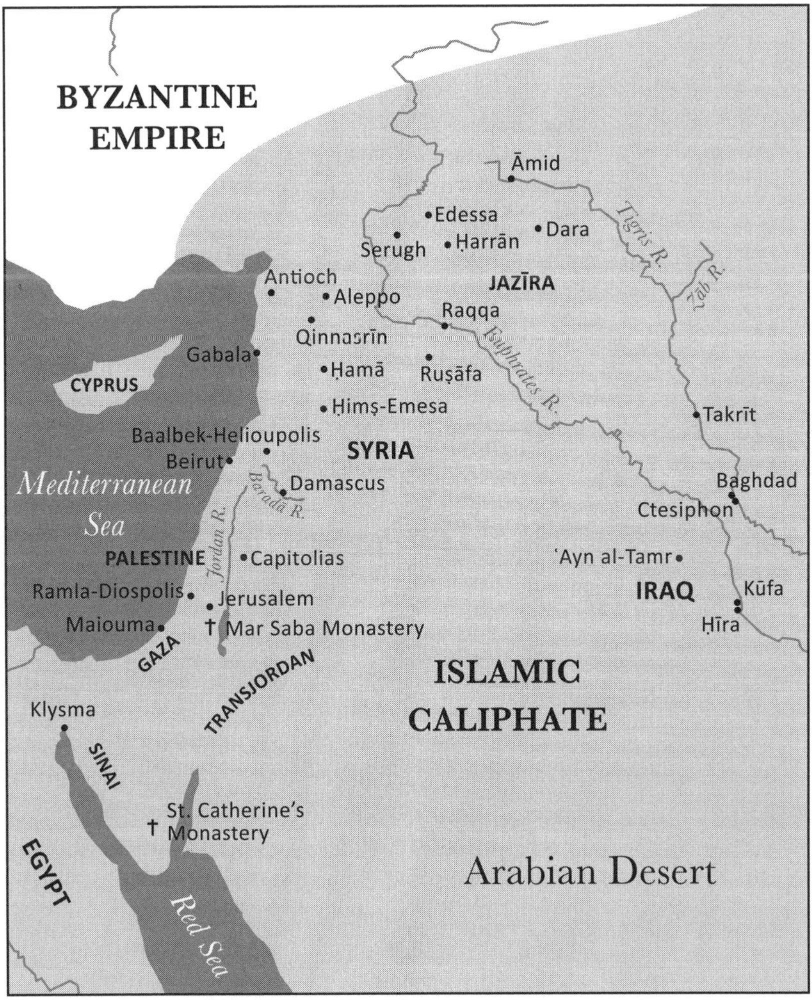

Map 3. Syria and Mesopotamia in the early Islamic period.

Christian Martyrs under Islam

INTRODUCTION

Christian Martyrs under Islam

The early Islamic period is one of the greatest watersheds in human history. In a matter of a few generations, Muslim armies emerged from the Arabian Peninsula and established a caliphate stretching from the Atlantic Ocean to the Punjab. Today, we regard these areas as the heartlands of the "Muslim world." But in the early centuries after the conquests, the situation was radically different. Muslims formed a demographic minority in many areas under their control. In places such as Egypt, Palestine, and Syria, the so-called Muslim world was in fact a majority-Christian world and would remain so for centuries to come.[1] This book seeks to explain the earliest stages of a long-term process whereby the predominantly Christian Middle East of late antiquity became the predominantly Islamic region of today. In particular, it explores the role of religious violence in the process of de-Christianization, as well as how Christians adopted the mentality of a minority through memories of violence.

To tell the story, this book investigates a neglected group of Christian martyrs who died at the hands of Muslim officials between the seventh and ninth centuries AD. They were known by their contemporaries as "new martyrs" or "neomartyrs."[2] Despite the name, there was nothing new about martyrdom itself. Since the first century, Christians had been celebrating as saints members of their community who died witnessing to their faith.[3] All but one of Christ's apostles were martyred, and many luminaries of the early church died

[1] Despite this, there is sometimes a tendency in the literature to refer to Christians in the medieval Middle East as "minorities"; e.g., Bennison, *Great Caliphs*, 122–33 (though cf. 94, which acknowledges the Christian majority). But as one prominent sociologist has noted, "A social minority need not be a mathematical one. A minority group is a subordinate group whose members have significantly less control or power over their own lives than do the members of a dominant or majority group." This certainly fits the Christians of the postconquest Middle East; see Schaefer, *Racial and Ethnic Groups*, 5–6. On the long-term demography of Christianity in the region, see Fargues, "Demographic Islamization."

[2] On the term *new martyr*, see Sahner, "Old Martyrs, New Martyrs," 94–97; on the term *martyr* in various eastern Christian languages, see Peeters, "Traductions orientales du mot Martyr."

[3] Frend, *Martyrdom and Persecution*; Musurillo, *Acts of the Christian Martyrs*; Bowersock, *Martyrdom and Rome*; Boyarin, *Dying for God*; De Ste. Croix, *Christian Persecution, Martyrdom, and Orthodoxy*.

under violent circumstances, including figures such as Ignatius of Antioch (d. ca. 108), Polycarp of Smyrna (d. ca. 155), and Cyprian of Carthage (d. 258). Martyrdom waned with the conversion of the emperor Constantine to Christianity in the early fourth century. Suddenly, the very state that had once committed itself to persecuting Christians was now committed to defending them. While the pace of martyrdom may have slowed inside the Roman Empire, bloodshed carried on outside Rome's borders. In Sasanian Iraq and Iran, for example, Syriac-speaking Christians who ran afoul of the Zoroastrian authorities were killed and remembered as saints.[4] What is more, although pagan-on-Christian violence declined inside Rome, the acid rivalry among competing Christian sects gave rise to new martyr cults within the "schismatic churches" of the empire. These included Donatist martyrs in North Africa and (West Syrian) Miaphysite martyrs in northern Mesopotamia and the Levant.[5]

With the rise of Islam, Christians once again found themselves living and dying under what many regarded as a hostile, pagan state. This was a jarring experience, especially for those in the former provinces of the Byzantine Empire, where Christianity had enjoyed imperial patronage for more than three hundred years. In a sense, the Arab conquest thrust these Christians back into a pre-Constantinian way of doing things. They embraced resources in their own tradition, in turn, to make sense of their new predicament, and the most powerful of these was martyrdom. In places as diverse as the Iberian Peninsula, Egypt, Syria, Armenia, and Georgia, local churches began to venerate Christians who had died at the hands of the Umayyad and ʿAbbasid states. The term *new martyr* was intended to emphasize a sense of continuity between the sufferings of the present day and those of the golden age before the conversion of Constantine.[6] But unlike the classical martyrs—many of whom were killed for shirking what hagiographers portrayed as a timeless paganism—the new martyrs were executed for reneging on a faith and culture that truly surrounded them and which some had even embraced. Thus, the "outsider"—the Muslim—is as visible and real in the martyrologies of the period as the Christians themselves. These martyrs were a varied group, including monks, soldiers, shopkeepers, village priests, craftsmen, princes, and bishops. They were women and men, young and old, peasants and nobles. Although capital punishment disproportionately affected certain groups, especially the clergy, martyrs hailed from across the social spectrum of the early medieval Middle East.

[4] Brock, *Guide to the Persian Martyr Acts*; Payne, *State of Mixture*; Smith, *Constantine and the Captive Christians of Persia*.

[5] Tilley, *Donatist Martyr Stories*; Chabot, *Chronicon anonymum Pseudo-Dionysianum*, ii, 21–23, 32–36, with the term *new martyrs* (Syr. *sāhdē hadtē*) at 33.

[6] Sahner, "Old Martyrs, New Martyrs."

Seen from this perspective, there were three main types of martyrs in the Umayyad and early ʿAbbasid periods (for the purposes of this book, defined as ca. AD 660–860, between the first recorded martyrdom after the accession of the Umayyads, which occurred in Damascus, and the last substantial burst of martyrdoms, which occurred in Córdoba).[7] The first and most numerous were Christian converts to Islam who then returned to Christianity. Because apostasy came to be considered a capital offense under Islamic law, they faced execution if found guilty. The second group was made up of Muslims who converted to Christianity without any prior affiliation with their new religion. The third consisted of Christians who slandered the Prophet Muḥammad, usually before a high-ranking Muslim official. Along with these, there were smaller numbers of Christians who were executed for refusing forced conversion, who were killed fighting the Arabs in times of war, or who died as a result of random, nonreligious violence.

There are roughly 270 new martyrs from the early Islamic period if we compile all the saints mentioned in hagiography, liturgical calendars, and chronicles. This figure, however, is slightly misleading because it includes many saints who died within larger groups and therefore are poorly differentiated from one another in the historical record. These include the Sixty Martyrs of Gaza, a group of Byzantine soldiers executed following the Arab conquest of Palestine in the late 630s;[8] the Sixty Martyrs of Jerusalem, a cohort of Byzantine soldiers killed during a pilgrimage to the Holy Land in 724/725; the Twenty Martyrs of Mar Saba, who were massacred during a Bedouin raid on their monastery in 788/797; the Forty-Two Martyrs of Amorion, a company of Byzantine soldiers who were captured in an Arab attack on Anatolia in 838 and executed in Iraq in 845;[9] and the forty-eight voluntary martyrs of Córdoba, who were executed for blasphemy and apostasy in the capital of Umayyad

[7]For George the Black, one of the earliest neomartyrs, see chapter 1, sec. II; for the Córdoba martyrs, the last of the group martyrs, see esp. chapter 1, sec. IV, and chapter 3, sec. IV.

[8]Delehaye, "Passio sanctorum sexaginta martyrum"; with discussion in *CMR*, i, 190–92; Pargoire, "LX soldats martyrs"; Guillou, "Prise de Gaza."

[9]The Forty-Two Martyrs of Amorion will not be dealt with extensively in this book. Despite the existence of rich hagiographic traditions (see *CMR*, i, 630–32, 636–41, 676–78, 845–47), all of these texts were composed in Byzantium, not the caliphate. Furthermore, although the martyrs were eventually killed in Baghdad, they were captured in Byzantium. The cult of the Forty-Two Martyrs spread among Christians in the caliphate (see Peeters, "Rabban Sliba," 177; Nau, "Martyrologe et douze ménologes," 73), but it was largely a Byzantine affair. Occasional reference will be made to "Recension G" of the *Passion of the Forty-Two Martyrs*, composed between 845 and 846, immediately after the martyrs' death. Its author is Michael Synkellos, a monk of Mar Saba and a priest of the Jerusalem patriarchate who spent his later years in Constantinople. Of all the recensions of the text, it comes closest to offering a "non-Byzantine" view of the incident. For text, see Vasil'evskii and Nikitin, *Skazaniia o 42 Amoriiskikh muchenikakh i tserkovnaia sluzhba im*, 22–36; for discussion, see *CMR*, i, 630–32.

al-Andalus between 850 and 859. If we remove these saints from the overall tally, the total number of individual martyrs shrinks to around forty.

Some may question whether we can draw broad conclusions about a topic as vast as "the making of the Muslim world" from such a slender base of evidence. Indeed, we should not underestimate the difficulty of reconstructing an entire period on the basis of the somewhat limited body of sources that survive to the present. The challenge is doubly formidable considering the accumulated debris of legend that surrounds many martyrs and which can make it hard to obtain a clear picture of their life and times. In the pages to come, I will explain why so many saints' *lives* are historically plausible and therefore why we should treat them as useful sources of information for the whole of early Islamic society. Yet the difficulties must be soberly acknowledged at the outset. Here, it is important to note that history furnishes other examples of how Christians behaved when confronted by the dominion of an alien faith, and these offer helpful comparisons for assessing the early medieval evidence.

We have already met the so-called Persian Martyrs, who were executed by the Sasanians between the fourth and seventh centuries. They present an especially useful comparison with the neomartyrs not only because of their chronological and geographic proximity to each other but also because Christians in both periods reacted to the threat of state violence in similar ways. Indeed, stories of Zoroastrian converts to Christianity and Christian blasphemers against Zoroastrianism could often be retold with Muslim and Christian characters instead without losing their narrative logic. This is not only the result of their common literary heritage. It is also the result of the somewhat consistent manner in which Christian communities in the premodern Middle East reacted when confronted by a similar array of religious, cultural, and social pressures at the hands of non-Christian sovereigns. In other words, there was often a predetermined script that both martyrs and biographers followed when confronted by state violence.

The parallels are even more striking with the Christian martyrs of the early Ottoman period—also commonly known as "neomartyrs"—who were revered across the Balkans and much of Anatolia.[10] Despite the historical chasm separating the two groups, their biographies are shockingly similar: tales of Christians executed after refusing to convert to Islam or, having already converted, apostatized from Islam and returned to Christianity. The parallels between the two cohorts of saints—which have not been noticed by scholars but which merit thorough study in their own right—are not merely the result of a com-

[10] Vaporis, *Witnesses for Christ*; Krstić, *Contested Conversions to Islam*; Greene, *History of the Greeks*, 74, 146–51.

mon literary heritage. They are also the result of shared demographic realities between the early Islamic caliphate and the early Ottoman Empire, both postconquest societies in which culturally Byzantine Christians found themselves living under Muslim ruling minorities. In these worlds, Christians and Muslims could rub shoulders in remarkably similar ways, living in a state of official competition that was offset by many deep cultural, religious, and linguistic similarities. Perhaps inevitably, these worlds produced similar kinds of violence, which Christians commemorated in similar ways, namely, by writing martyrologies. So, when someone reads the *lives* of the Umayyad and ʿAbbasid neomartyrs and asks of these harrowing, sometimes theatrical tales whether they represent pure fiction or contain elements of psychological reality, the parallels to earlier and later generations of apostates and blasphemers should instill some confidence in the plausibility of the evidence. Put simply, the sources report the kinds of information we might expect to find when Christians existed under non-Christian powers in the premodern Middle East.

The use of capital punishment against Christians was an important feature of early Islamic history, but it was limited in its scope and aimed at two specific goals. The first was to establish the primacy of Islam and the Islamic character of the state at a moment when Muslims were dramatically outnumbered by their non-Muslim subjects. In this world, public executions had a performative function and were designed to instill obedience in the massive and potentially recalcitrant non-Muslim population. The second was to forge boundaries between groups at a time of unprecedented social and religious mixing. Indeed, Muslims and Christians interacted with each other in the most intimate of settings, from workshops and markets to city blocks and even marital beds. Not surprisingly, these interactions gave rise to overlapping practices, including behaviors that blurred the line between Christianity and Islam. To ensure that conversion and assimilation went exclusively in the direction of Islam, Muslim officials executed the most flagrant boundary-crossers, and Christians, in turn, revered some of these as saints.

Thus, contrary to the common impression in popular culture today that Islam won converts principally by the sword, the historical record suggests a more complex picture. Capital punishment—while real and occasionally ferocious—was also a remarkably bureaucratic phenomenon that followed established rules and relied on state institutions. Private, nonstate violence against non-Muslims was not a major feature of the postconquest period, nor was forced conversion. On balance, the Umayyads and ʿAbbasids were not much interested in persecuting Christians, at least systematically. In fact, the state took a rather laissez-faire attitude toward the governance of *dhimmīs* (the protected non-Muslim subjects of the Islamic state, also including Jews and

Zoroastrians). It allowed them to live as they wished provided they paid the *jizya* (the poll tax imposed on non-Muslims in commutation for military service) and accepted their subordination as laid down by the law.

By and large, relations between Muslims and Christians in the early period were characterized by a peaceful but begrudging form of coexistence. The two groups—themselves internally diverse—shared the same cities, spoke the same languages, and as time went on, increasingly shared many of the same relatives and friends. Indeed, the firm distinction between the Arab Muslim ruling class and the non-Muslim subject population began to dissolve over time as the ranks of the Muslim community swelled with non-Arab converts. This is not to discount the fact that the Islamic empire was forged in the cauldron of conquest, which, like all wars, imposed suffering and deprivation on native populations, including Christians. It is also not to discount the fact that Muslims and Christians made antagonistic and mutually exclusive claims about the nature of God or that Muslims enjoyed privileged access to political, social, and economic power, which they used to marginalize their competitors. Rather, it is to point out that violent episodes such as martyrdom occurred against a backdrop of what Arabs today call *ʿaysh mushtarak*, or a "common way of life," not against a backdrop of constant hostility.

One of the great advantages of the sources is the ability to track the ebb and flow of religious and cultural change in the postconquest Middle East. Through these texts, we can gain a clearer picture of when conversion may have accelerated, where violence against Christians was most intense, and how the Middle East first took on the guise of the Islamic society that we know today. Here, the first fifty years of ʿAbbasid rule emerge as the single most important period in what this book calls "the making of the Muslim world." It was at this time that Muslims and Christians began interacting with each other as members of a shared, increasingly integrated society, rather than as rulers and subjects in a divided, socially stratified world, as they had done in the immediate wake of the conquests. The traditional distinctions between Muslims and Christians—as Arabs and non-Arabs, soldiers and peasants, city-dwellers and villagers—were disappearing in the early ʿAbbasid period. This was due to the large numbers of non-Muslims converting to Islam, increasing Muslim settlement of the countryside, and practices such as slavery and intermarriage, which brought conquerors and conquered into ever greater proximity. This muddled world generated new anxieties about social and religious differentiation, which led to higher rates of state violence. These may be seen in the larger number of martyrdom incidents in the ʿAbbasid period, as well as the impulse of Christian writers to commemorate these incidents in literary form. The martyrologies testify to the creation of a Christian identity in the early medieval Middle East grounded in memories of bloodshed, antagonism toward Islam, and hostility to Christians who switched sides. Thus, this book aspires to provide not just a history of a specific historical and literary phenomenon—martyrdom—but also a history of the wider society that generated violence and texts alike, one that was in the process of becoming "Muslim."

Finally, Christians were not the only victims of state violence in the early Islamic period. Jews, Zoroastrians, and others felt the anger of the Muslim authorities for a similar range of offenses, including apostasy and blasphemy. Yet it is significant that these groups did not respond to the violence by creating martyrs. Indeed, it would be impossible to write a comparable book about the phenomenon of Jewish or Zoroastrian "martyrdom" under Islam. The disparity points to the fact that in this period, at least, "martyrdom" was a uniquely Christian idea and practice. As we have seen, the inclination toward martyrdom had deep roots in Christian antiquity. It drew its most profound inspiration from the figure of Jesus himself, who preached a message of finding strength through weakness and achieving victory through defeat. Such ideals were not nearly as pronounced in late ancient Judaism or Zoroastrianism. For this reason, the book is focused on relations between Muslims and Christians specifically, as opposed to Muslims and non-Muslims more broadly. It makes occasional comparisons with the experiences of Jews and Zoroastrians, but a thorough study of these similarities and differences will have to wait for another time.

I. HAGIOGRAPHY AS A TOOL FOR SOCIAL HISTORY

This book is not simply a study of violence against Christians. It is also a study of how Christians remembered this violence in literary forms and used texts to construct social identities.[11] The *lives* of the martyrs were written in practically every corner of the nascent caliphate where Muslims and Christians lived side by side. Given the demographic realities of the seventh, eighth, and ninth centuries, this meant practically every region under Muslim control west of Iran. The evidence survives in a polyphony of ancient and medieval languages, including Greek, Arabic, Latin, Armenian, Georgian, Syriac, and Ethiopic. Many of these texts have been studied individually over the years,[12] but they are little known outside a small circle of academic

[11] For this approach in an earlier period, see Castelli, *Martyrdom and Memory.*

[12] The brilliant Belgian Bollandist Fr. Paul Peeters (d. 1950) did the most to advance the field in the early twentieth century through a series of editions, translations, and studies of sources in Arabic, Georgian, and Geʿez. Despite his erudition, Peeters never synthesized his findings in a

specialists.[13] Indeed, as Sidney Griffith has recently put it, the Christian martyrs represent a "little-studied chapter of early Islamic history."[14] What is more, the texts have never been knitted together to tell a general history of Christian martyrdom under Islam or to gain insights into the development of Islamic civilization more broadly. This book attempts to accomplish both of these things.

When it comes to writing social and religious history, medieval hagiography is a rich but perilous source. Over the years, many scholars have dismissed it as a collection of tall tales and scurrilous lies, in some instances refusing to even entertain the idea that it may contain useful historical information. The early twentieth-century German medievalist Bruno Krusch summed up this view when he referred to a famous work of Merovingian hagiography as "kirchliche Schwindelliteratur."[15] Thankfully, Krusch's opinion is rarely stated so bluntly today, but there are still plenty of scholars who approach hagiography with comparable reserve. The most prominent of these in recent years has been Candida Moss, who regards most of the early Christian martyr texts as essentially fabricated (and on the basis of this, seeks to counter contemporary Christians who, she believes, abuse the mantle of martyrdom for political gain—a political interpretation in its own right that often colors her reading of the evidence).[16]

Despite the prevailing skepticism in some corners, the study of late antique and medieval saints' *lives* has undergone a renaissance over the past forty years.[17] Indeed, scholars have used hagiography as a tool for social history and, in particular, for understanding issues such as identity formation, conceptions of the holy, the relationship between church and state, and Christianization.[18] What is more, scholars have discovered that hagiographic texts are not simply collections of pious myths. Rather, hagiography is often filled with historical

---

single article or book on the neomartyrs; for more on his life and work, see Devos, "R. P. Paul Peeters."

[13] For the key synthetic studies, see Zayyāt, "Shuhadāʾ al-naṣrānīya"; Hoyland, *Seeing Islam*, 336–86; Griffith, "Christians, Muslims, and Neo-martyrs"; Vila, "Christian Martyrs." See also *CMR*, i; *CMR*, ii; Shoemaker, *Three Christian Martyrdoms*, xi–xliii.

[14] Griffith, "Manṣūr Family," 44.

[15] Krusch, "Zur Florians- und Lupus-Legende," 559, cited in Kreiner, *Social Life of Hagiography*, 3.

[16] Moss, *Myth of Persecution*. For similar statements of the problem, see Mango, "Saints," 265–66; Kazhdan and Talbot, "Hagiography," 897; more broadly, Harvey, "Martyr Passions and Hagiography."

[17] E.g., Brown, "Rise and Function of the Holy Man"; Brown, *Cult of the Saints*; Bartlett, *Why Can the Dead Do Such Great Things?*

[18] Patlagean, "Ancienne hagiographie byzantine et histoire sociale"; Lifshitz, "Beyond Positivism and Genre"; Geary, "Saints, Scholars, and Society"; Kaplan and Kountoura-Galaki, "Economy and Society in Byzantine Hagiography."

details that can be corroborated using outside sources. These, in turn, can instill confidence that a given text may describe real events and people, though dramatizing these elements to suit the conventions of the genre. Of course, there are many saints' *lives* in which thick layers of fantasy obscure any underlying reality. But whether it is from Merovingian Gaul, Sasanian Iran, or ʿAbbasid Syria, hagiography often offers a tantalizing, three-dimensional glimpse of real and imaginary worlds that historians would not be able to gaze at otherwise.

Even when we do not possess corroborating evidence to verify the claims made in hagiography, it is important to remember that saints' *lives* were successful as a form of literature precisely because they portrayed a world that was in some sense familiar and comprehensible to their readers. Thus, it may be beyond the power of most scholars to ascertain whether a saint lived and died exactly as a biography claims. But taking them judiciously and on a case-by-case basis, we can often trust hagiographic sources to provide a snapshot of a saint's world not completely divorced from his or her reality or that of the biographer. This is especially true if we can manage to establish when a text's author lived.

Herein lies the great challenge for social historians who wish to exploit hagiographic sources: How can we determine the gap between the life of a Christian killed by Muslim officials and his or her afterlife as a saint—or to put it more succinctly, the chasm between record and representation? The earliest academics who studied hagiography were focused on these very questions. The Bollandists—the famous Jesuit order founded in the wake of the Reformation with the mission of studying hagiography—were interested in using the sources to establish the veracity of saints' cults in the life of the contemporary church. The most prolific of the twentieth-century Bollandists was the Belgian scholar Hippolyte Delehaye (d. 1941), who produced many learned studies of ancient and medieval hagiography. His main interest was in recovering positive data about saints—the "what, where, and when" of their *lives*—rather than in understanding the texts as a genre of literature.[19] Over the past fifty years, a new cohort of scholars has emerged that has been less interested in establishing biographical facts than in understanding the milieu in which saints' *lives* were written. Indeed, historians have recently shown how hagiography is often more useful for grasping the priorities of its authors than those of the saints themselves.[20]

[19] Delehaye, *Légendes hagiographiques*; Delehaye, *L'œuvre des Bollandistes*; cf. Sullivan, "Jean Bolland (1596–1665) and the Early Bollandists."

[20] Debié, "Writing History as 'Histories' "; Kreiner, *Social Life of Hagiography*; Payne, *State of Mixture*.

It is important to remember just how ubiquitous saints' *lives* were across the late antique and medieval worlds. Practically every Christian society in premodern times (and many thereafter) produced hagiography.[21] The genre was so widespread, in fact, that pagans, Jews, Manichaeans, Zoroastrians, and Muslims also produced biographies of holy men and women.[22] The cult of the saints was very popular more generally, and Christians from Ireland to Iran undertook local and long-distance pilgrimage to revere their martyred heroes. As a result, they were often intimately familiar with the details of their *lives*, whether they encountered these in manuscripts—like the monks and priests who had ready access to texts in monastic libraries—or heard them recounted aloud—like the peasants who visited saints' shrines on their feast days.[23]

Given how universal the veneration of saints was in late antiquity and the Middle Ages, we can approach hagiography with a common set of questions regardless of where we find it: What were the goals of hagiographers, and how did their audiences react to their works? To borrow the apt phrase of Richard Payne, hagiographers were nothing short of the "anonymous architects of Christian communities" across the late antique and medieval worlds.[24] The texts they composed played a central role in configuring the identity of their readers. After all, to write a saint's *life* was to make an argument for a particular social, spiritual, and cultural ideal—to provide a vivid portrait of the "angelic life" (Gk. *bios angelikos*) to readers hungry for instruction and eager for saintly perfection.

Hagiography offered sound advice on a range of expected themes: prayer, charity, obedience, chastity, and sin. But it also provided advice on a range of social and political concerns: How should Christians interact with members of other religions? What were the duties of a Christian to his or her family, clergy, and king? What were the obligations of the rich to the poor? How should Christians spend their money? What were the virtuous ways of engaging in war? There are countless other questions about everyday life that late antique and medieval hagiography sought to address. For the scholar, the texts that strove to answer these questions are a boon because they amplify the kinds of low-volume but important conversations that are usually muted to

[21] For the eastern Mediterranean, see Efthymiadis, *Research Companion to Byzantine Hagiography. Volume I* and *Research Companion to Byzantine Hagiography. Volume II*; for the European Reformation, see Gregory, *Salvation at Stake*; for the Christians of the Ottoman Empire, see Vaporis, *Witnesses for Christ*.

[22] Pagans and Christians: Miller, *Biography in Late Antiquity*. Jews: Dan, "Hagiography." Manichaeans: Sundermann, "Mani," *EIr*. Zoroastrians: Choksy, "Hagiography and Monotheism"; Cereti, "Myths, Legends, Eschatologies," 264–69. Muslims: Renard, *Friends of God*.

[23] Efthymiadis and Kalogeras, "Audience, Language and Patronage."

[24] Payne, *State of Mixture*, 19.

modern ears. Thus, Bruno Krusch's characterization of a saint's *life* as *kirchliche Schwindelliteratur* misses the point of the genre completely: even in its most fanciful forms, late antique and medieval hagiography makes powerful statements about the social priorities of long-lost worlds.

This book approaches the Christian martyrologies of the early Islamic period with a posture of critical positivism. It is "positivistic" because it does not prima facie discount the historical claims of the sources simply because they appear in hagiographic narratives. Rather, it takes these claims seriously by constantly testing them against outside evidence, mainly in the form of contemporary Muslim texts. It can be extremely difficult to verify the existence of a given martyr by name (virtually no martyrs are mentioned individually by Muslim authors), but more often than not, hagiography does contain the kinds of corroborating details that instill confidence in elements of a story, including places, dates, and minor characters of historical importance. When such details do not exist, it is still possible to compare the sources with more general legal and historical accounts of Muslim-Christian interactions. These, in turn, reveal that the martyrs' *lives* often adhered to recognizable patterns of behavior spread across postconquest society, which were shaped, in turn, by common legal, economic, and social norms. Thus, while we may not be able to say whether a given martyrology is "factual," we can usually establish whether individual elements of a text are "plausible" (readers wishing to understand how Christian hagiography can be read alongside Muslim texts for the purposes of verification should turn to appendix 1, which contains several methodological case studies).

At the same time, the posture of the book is "critical" in the sense that it is not purely interested in what saints' *lives* say about events and people. It is also interested in what the sources reveal about their authors and readers. Thus, it tempers methodological openness to the existence of historical data with sensitivity to the roles rhetoric, symbol, and motif play in presenting this information. Miracles, polemic, and fantasy—all stock features of hagiography in late antiquity and the Middle Ages—fill the texts, as one would expect. But they are not enemies of the historian; in fact, they can be assets to help us grasp how biographers represented the past to their readers and repackaged it in literary forms to suit the concerns and expectations of the present (these themes are dealt with throughout the book, though most especially in chapter 5).

Thus, to be clear, this book does not reject more text-centered approaches to hagiography, such as those that insist on the cultural function and meaning of the stories. Rather, this book charts a clear course between two competing impulses: literalism and skepticism. A hermeneutic of literalism falls short because it takes the claims of hagiography too seriously and, in the process, fails to appreciate the literary dimensions of the genre. A hermeneutic of skepticism, meanwhile, is usually deficient because it treats the claims of hagiography too lightly and, in the process, fails to notice their grounding in real social, political, and cultural contexts. Both approaches have something to teach us when it comes to reading late antique and medieval saints' *lives*, but only when they are combined together can we realize the potential of what the sources have to say.

II. THE LIVES OF THE MARTYRS: AN OVERVIEW

If this combination of approaches does succeed, the *lives* of the martyrs emerge as some of the richest, most revealing bodies of evidence about relations between Christians and Muslims in the early Islamic period. They throw light on an array of important but poorly understood questions of deep concern to any scholar of the premodern Middle East: What motivated Christians to convert to Islam? Why did recent converts sometimes return to Christianity? Did Muslims ever apostatize from Islam? What was it like to grow up in a religiously mixed family? When and why did blasphemy first become a capital offense under Islamic law? Did the early caliphs faithfully implement Qurʾanic punishments in everyday life? How did the Umayyads and the ʿAbbasids discipline religious dissidents? How did the spread of Islam destabilize and reconfigure internal relations within the churches of the greater Middle East? Did some Christian denominations experience higher levels of violence than others? Did certain periods witness increased tensions within and between communities?

These are central questions to any scholar of the early Islamic period. Yet the traditional body of evidence that historians have used to answer these questions—much of it written in Arabic by medieval Muslim authors—provides unsatisfying answers. The problem is not only that many Arabic Muslim sources were written down centuries after the events they purport to describe, presenting a latter-day *Heilsgeschichte*, as Patricia Crone and Michael Cook noted in their pathbreaking 1977 book *Hagarism: The Making of the Islamic World*.[25] It is also that these sources take little interest in the affairs of non-Muslims. Indeed, if the great Muslim annalist al-Ṭabarī (d. 310/923) were all we relied upon to understand the shape of Middle Eastern society in the post-conquest period, we would come to the erroneous conclusion that nearly ev-

[25] Crone and Cook, *Hagarism*; building on Wansbrough, *Quranic Studies*; Wansbrough, *Sectarian Milieu.*

eryone in this world had already converted. Yet this was not the case. As Peter Brown put it:

> Jews and Christians, Persians and East Romans were allotted "walk-on" parts [in early Muslim historiography] but little more. The immensely rich but inward-looking Arabic historical tradition virtually ignored the intimacy and complexity of the relations between the Arabs and the other cultures of the Near East.[26]

Islamic historian R. Stephen Humphreys came to a similar conclusion about one significant corner of the early Muslim empire, noting: "In general, the Arabic Muslim chronicles and biographical compendia maintain a frustrating silence about the Christians of Syria and the Jazīra."[27] Of course, medieval Muslim historians had a vested interest in downplaying the diversity of the world in which they lived, which consisted of not only Christians from many denominations but also Zoroastrians, Jews, Manichaeans, Buddhists, polytheists, and others.[28] Not only were Muslim authors relatively unconcerned about the affairs of the subject population (whom they viewed as religiously and socially backward, by and large), but they were also committed to telling a story of Muslim triumph that discounted the importance of these communities in their shared cosmos. To admit that the major portion of the population in the Islamic heartlands of Egypt, Palestine, and Syria was in fact non-Muslim—and would remain so even until the time of the Crusades, as some scholars believe[29]—ran counter to the favored story line. Put succinctly, the mainstream sources provide a portrait of a homogeneous Muslim society that later writers wished to imagine. They do not provide a faithful snapshot of the diverse society as it actually was.

[26] Brown, *Rise of Western Christendom*, 301; see also Papaconstantinou, "Between *Umma* and *Dhimma*," 129.

[27] Humphreys, "Christian Communities," 48.

[28] Zoroastrians were the second-largest non-Muslim community in the early caliphate, yet their experiences under Islamic rule are poorly researched, especially in comparison with those of Christians and Jews; see Choksy, *Conflict and Cooperation*; Morony, "Madjūs," *EI²*, v, 1110–18; Daryaee, "Zoroastrianism under Islamic Rule"; also Crone, *Nativist Prophets*; Savant, *New Muslims of Post-conquest Iran*.

[29] The most influential work on conversion remains Bulliet, *Conversion to Islam*, which argues that most regions crossed the threshold of a Muslim numerical majority in the ninth or tenth century. Other studies have pushed this estimate later, including for Palestine: Cahen, "First Crusade," 7; Ḥitti, "Impact of the Crusades," 212; Gil, *History of Palestine*, 170–72; Ellenblum, *Frankish Rural Settlement*, 20–22; Avni, *Byzantine-Islamic Transition*, 331–37. For Egypt: Friedmann, "Conversion of Egypt to Islam"; El-Leithy, "Coptic Culture"; Sijpesteijn, *Shaping a Muslim State*, 107. On general population estimates for Muslims in the very early period, see Tannous, "Syria," 480; Carlson, "Contours of Conversion."

Christian sources from the early Islamic period, not least of them hagiography, pose their own methodological risks. Not only are these texts filled with literary motifs, but they are also overtly hostile to the new religion and ruling class. What is more, they often misunderstand the events and peoples they discuss, much as early Muslims sometimes misunderstood non-Muslims. Furthermore, the dating of these sources can be just as contested as that of their counterparts on the Islamic side. Therefore, this book attempts to balance the evidence from martyrologies with information culled from Muslim sources. These include chronicles (Ar. *tārīkh*, pl. *tawārīkh*), as well as early traditions (Ar. *ḥadīth*, pl. *aḥādīth*) and law (Ar. *fiqh*). By combining Christian and Muslim sources in this way, this book aspires to convey a robust and balanced picture of issues scholars usually examine from only one angle or another, including conversion, apostasy, blasphemy, and the judicial system.

Genres

We have already discussed the promise and peril of using hagiographic sources to tell social history. In light of this, how do we know what we know about the martyrs? Information about the saints of the seventh, eighth, and ninth centuries comes in a variety of forms.[30] The single largest and most important texts are *lives*, or *vitae* to use the common Latin term: stand-alone biographies written independently of larger historical or literary works.[31] Some of these biographies run for as much as forty pages in modern printed editions; others, for as little as four pages.[32] Only in the case of the martyrs of Córdoba (Lat., d. 850–59) does a voluminous dossier about one group of saints survive from the pens of multiple contemporary authors.

The second most important genre is liturgical calendars, known by their Greek name as *synaxaria*.[33] Such calendars detail the feasts celebrated in the

[30] For an overview of the different forms of hagiographic writing, see Hinterberger, "Byzantine Hagiography and Its Literary Genres."

[31] Detoraki, "*Passions* of the Martyrs," esp. 81–84.

[32] E.g., the *Passion of the Twenty Martyrs of Mar Saba*, *SPSH*, i, 1–41; versus the *Passion of the Twenty Martyrs of Gaza*: Delehaye, "Passio sanctorum sexaginta martyrum," 300–303.

[33] The most significant were the *Synaxarium of Constantinople*, compiled in Greek in the tenth–eleventh centuries—Delehaye, *Synaxarium*, esp. 72–74, 98 (Michael of the Zobē Monastery, d. ca. 780–90, abbot killed by Muslims inside Byzantium, not discussed in this book), 105–6, 310–12, 434 (Theophilus the New, d. ca. 780–90, Byzantine naval commander captured by the Arabs, not discussed); Kazhdan, "Constantinopolitan Synaxarium as a Source for Social History"; Luzzi, "Synaxaria"—and the *Synaxarium of Alexandria*, compiled in Arabic in the fourteenth century—Basset, "Synaxaire arabe jacobite" (1909), 175, 360, 376; (1915), 797–98; (1922), 845–47; (1923), 1120–23, 1296–97 (henceforth, all references to Basset, "Synaxaire arabe jacobite," will follow the continu-

course of the church year. In some instances, they identify a saint with a single line of information.[34] In other instances, they provide a longer biography, running up to three pages in certain cases. Some of these saints are known exclusively through *synaxaria*, while others were the subject of independent biographies and therefore can be cross-checked using sources outside the liturgy.

The third most important source is chronicles. Unlike hagiography, chronicles do not always make clear whether a given Christian was venerated as a martyr. Indeed, most victims of religious violence in this period were not considered saints.[35] Despite this, chronicles sometimes do mention martyrs and their cults. Some of these "pseudo-hagiographies" appear in the course of longer historical works, as with Cyrus of Ḥarrān, whose biography fills the final fragmentary pages of the *Chronicle of Zuqnīn*.[36] Others appear as incidental references in the chronicles of famous writers such as Theophanes Confessor (Gk., d. 818), Łewond (Arm., fl. eighth–ninth centuries), Thomas Artsruni (Arm., d. ca. 904–8), and Michael the Syrian (Syr., d. 1199).[37]

Finally, information about the martyrs comes from a range of miscellaneous texts. One of the very earliest references to a new martyr appears in the *Narrationes* of Anastasius of Sinai (Gk., d. ca. 700), a collection of edifying anecdotes that the author gathered during his travels around the eastern Mediterranean.[38] Miracle collections—especially those associated with the shrine of Saint George at Diospolis in Palestine—also provide information about

ous pagination given in brackets in the print edition); Hoyland, *Seeing Islam*, 367–69; Coquin, "Editions of the Synaxarion," *CE*, vii, 2172–73; Atiya, "List of Saints," *CE*, vii, 2173–90.

[34] For liturgical texts with brief references to new martyrs, see Nau, "Martyrologe et douze ménologes," 73; Peeters, "Rabban Sliba," 169 (George, patriarch of Baghdad, d. unknown, not discussed in this book), 174 (Elias of Beth Qūsaynā, d. unknown, not discussed), 177, 180; Sauget, *Synaxaires melkites*, 310–11, 332–34, 344–45 (Rizqallāh of Tripoli, d. ca. 1360s, not discussed), 366–67, 377–78 (Ephrem, neomartyr of Damascus, d. unknown, not discussed), 380–83, 411–14, 427–29 (Isaac of Ḥamā, d. unknown, not discussed); Garitte, *Calendrier palestino-géorgien*, 44/126–27, 44/131–32, 45/136, 47/144, 48/151, 54/172, 55/179–80, 59/196, 59/197, 60/198–99, 64/213–14, 92/340, 98/363–64, 105/393, 110/410.

[35] E.g., Chabot, *Chronicon ad annum Christi 1234*, i, 245 (for an account of Muslims killing Christians but without reference to martyrdom); cf. Tritton, *Non-Muslim Subjects*, 127.

[36] Harrak, "Martyrdom of Cyrus"; see also the martyrdom of Arčʻil (d. 786) in the *Royal Georgian Annals*: Thomson, *Rewriting Caucasian History*, 251–55.

[37] Theophanes on the women martyrs of Ḥimṣ (d. 779/780): de Boor, *Chronographia*, i, 452–53. Łewond on Hamazasp and Sahak (d. 786): Arzoumanian, *History of Lewond*, 144–47. Thomas Artsruni on various Armenian martyrs killed under Bughā al-Kabīr (d. ca. 851–52): Thomson, *House of Artsrunikʻ*, 206–7, 249–55. Michael the Syrian on ʻAbdūn of Takrīt (d. 820): Chabot, *Chronique*, iii, 48–49 (Fr.); iv, 506–7 (Syr.). Cf. Abbeloos and Lamy, *Chronicon*, iii, 183–84.

[38] Binggeli, "Anastase le Sinaïte," 251–52 (Gk.), 566–67 (Fr.), with other stories involving Muslims: 219–20, 225–28, 230–31 (Gk.); 531–32, 538–42, 545–46 (Fr.). For Anatasius on Islam, see Griffith, "Anastasios of Sinai, the *Hodegos*, and the Muslims."

martyrs,[39] as do sermons, apologetic works, and polemical treatises.[40] Our understanding of individual martyrs varies widely from one saint to the next: Some individuals are known thanks to a single reference in one text; others star in multiple biographies written across a variety of genres and languages. With notable exceptions (see appendix 1), Muslim sources are silent about individual martyrs, though they can help us reconstruct the general historical and legal setting in which the martyrdoms took place.

Languages

One of the most striking features of the *lives* of the new martyrs is their linguistic diversity.[41] Greek continued to be used as a language of hagiography in greater Syria until the eleventh century.[42] This was especially true in the Chalcedonian monasteries of Palestine, such as Mar Saba, whose monks produced an outsized share of the texts discussed in this book (the topic of chapter 5).[43] So vital was their Hellenic culture that Cyril Mango famously described Muslim-controlled Palestine as the single most active center of Greek literary production in the eighth century.[44] As Greek waned, it was replaced by Arabic in many Christian communities of the Middle East.[45] In general, the very earliest Christian Arabic texts can be dated to the mid-eighth century, though recent research has suggested that an Arabic translation of the Bible may have existed before Islam, though this is a matter of major debate.[46] If this is true, it

[39] Aufhauser, *Miracula*, 65–89, 90–93; see also the later Latin translations: Braida and Pelissetti, *Rawḥ al-Qurašī*, 81–91 (It. trans.), 129–38 (Lat. text).

[40] The account of the martyrdom of Pachomius (alias Joachim, Malmeth) in Vat. Gk. 1130 (16–17th c.) describes itself as a *logos historikos* of Gregory of Decapolis (d. 842). On the disputed authorship of this text, see now Binggeli, "Converting the Caliph," 92–93 n. 58. Two famous apologetic treatises that mention the martyrs are the *Indiculus luminosus* of Paulus Alvarus (*CSM*, i, 270–315) and the *Apologeticus martyrum* of Eulogius (*CSM*, ii, 475–95).

[41] On language change more generally, see Wasserstein, "Why Did Arabic Succeed Where Greek Failed?"; Hoyland, "Why Did Aramaic Succeed Where Greek Failed?"; Papaconstantinou, "Hellenism and *Romanitas*."

[42] See the reworking of the *Passion of the Sixty Martyrs of Jerusalem* (d. 725) in the eleventh century by Simeon of the monastery of Quarantine near Jericho: *SPSH*, i, 136–63; Flusin, "Palestinian Hagiography," 216, 218.

[43] Griffith, "Aramaic to Arabic."

[44] Mango, "Greek Culture in Palestine"; cf. Blake, "Littérature grecque en Palestine"; Cavallo, "Cultura greca in oriente"; Johnson, "Social Presence of Greek"; Mavroudi, "Greek Language and Education under Early Islam."

[45] Griffith, "Greek into Arabic"; Griffith, "Monks of Palestine and the Growth of Christian Literature in Arabic"; Griffith, "Stephen of Ramlah"; Griffith, "Church of Jerusalem and the 'Melkites'"; Levy-Rubin, "Arabization versus Islamization."

[46] Kashouh, *Arabic Versions of the Gospels*, 143–71 (on Vat. Ar. 13, copied in the ninth century,

would mean that the Christian scriptures constitute the oldest book written in Arabic, not the Qur'an as is usually thought. Hagiography was among the very earliest Christian Arabic writings.[47] Again, the Melkite monasteries of the Holy Land played a leading role in their production, as did monastic communities farther north near Antioch.[48]

The main example of Latin hagiography from the period is the *lives* of the Córdoba martyrs. In al-Andalus, Latin remained an important language for educated Christians until at least the late ninth century, and there is evidence of high-level knowledge of Latin surviving into the tenth century and beyond.[49] Indeed, the Córdoba martyr acts are among the finest (and most complex) examples of Latin prose composition in al-Andalus before it was finally eclipsed by Arabic and Romance.[50]

Armenian and Georgian authors also produced *lives* of neomartyrs.[51] Due to the peculiar circumstances of Arab rule in the Caucasus, these sources tend to convey similar kinds of information, focusing on the violence that arose there amid the political disputes between the Muslim conquerors and the indigenous Christian nobility. In addition to composing new texts, Georgian monks also played an important role in translating old texts.[52] For example, many saints' *lives* that were first written in Greek and Arabic in the Levant were later translated into Georgian, and in certain instances, the only versions that survive today are the Georgian copies.[53] Even when it is not clear what

probably at Mar Saba but, according to Kashouh, possibly based on a pre-Islamic *Vorlage* or a *Vorlage* written at the very beginning of Islam at a site such as Ḥīra, Najrān, or Baṣra); for an opposing view, see Griffith, *Bible in Arabic*, esp. 41–53.

[47] Swanson, "Arabic Hagiography"; see also *GCAL*, i, 487–555.

[48] For Sinai, see Binggeli, "Hagiographie du Sinaï"; for Antioch, see Zayyāt, "Vie du patriarche melkite."

[49] Sahner, "From Augustine to Islam."

[50] Banniard, *Viva voce*, 423–84; Wright, *Late Latin and Early Romance*, 145–207; Wright, "End of Written Ladino"; Aillet, *Mozarabes*, 133–246.

[51] Vacca, "Creation of an Islamic Frontier in Armīniya," 195–203. A revised version of this work has just appeared as Vacca, *Non-Muslim Provinces under Early Islam*.

[52] Peeters, *Tréfonds oriental*, 155–64; Samir, "Plus anciens homélaires géorgiens"; Mgaloblishvili, "Georgian Sabaite (Sabatsminduri) Literary School"; Griffith, "Aramaic to Arabic," 30–31; Nanobashvili, "Literary Contacts"; Johnson, "Social Presence of Greek," 81–84.

[53] The *Life of Peter of Capitolias* (d. 715), written first in Greek (Peeters, "Passion de S. Pierre") and the *Life of Romanus* (d. 780), written first in either Greek or Arabic (Peeters, "S. Romain le néomartyr"). English translations of both are now available in Shoemaker, *Three Christian Martyrdoms*. See also the Georgian translations of the *Passion of the Twenty Martyrs of Mar Saba* and the *Life of Anthony*, written in Greek and Arabic, respectively, and surviving in their original languages as well as later Georgian translations: Blake, "Deux lacunes comblées"; Kipshidze, "Zhitie i muchenichestvo sv. Antoniia Ravakha"; Peeters, "Autobiographie de S. Antoine." The manuscript containing the Georgian translation of the *Life of Anthony* (Iviron, Passionary 57) also contains the *Life of Abo of Tiflīs* and the *Life of Michael of Mar Saba*, both new martyrs: Wardrop,

the original language of a text may have been,[54] the existence of Georgian translations from the ninth and tenth centuries underlines the close connections among different Christian communities in the early medieval Middle East and central Asia.[55] Martyrologies and their authors traveled from place to place, as evidenced by the many Georgian sources that survive in institutions such as St. Catherine's Monastery in the Sinai,[56] as well as the accounts of individual martyrs who traveled between Palestine and the Iberian Peninsula.[57] Although Ethiopic preserves far fewer translations than Georgian, it played a similar role in disseminating hagiography originally written in Coptic and Arabic in Egypt.

The final language of martyrology-writing was Syriac. A prestige dialect of Aramaic associated with the city of Edessa, Syriac was one of the most important Christian languages of late antiquity and continued to be used long after the Arab conquest.[58] Despite this, Syriac speakers produced no stand-alone biographies of martyrs that survive to the present. There are a few quasi-exceptions—including the *Life of Cyrus of Ḥarrān*, which appears as an epilogue in the *Chronicle of Zuqnīn*, and the *Passion of the Sixty Martyrs of Jerusalem*, which may have been written in Aramaic before being translated into Greek[59]—but the overall absence of martyrs' *lives* in Syriac is noteworthy. It is especially striking given that Syriac speakers of all denominations (West Syrian, East Syrian, etc.) continued to pen saints' *lives* after the conquests, including of pre-Islamic saints and nonmartyr saints who lived under Islam. The

"Georgian Manuscripts," 603; Blake, *Catalogue des manuscrits géorgiens*, 318. On hagiography-writing in Armenian and Georgian more generally, see Cowe, "Armenian Hagiography"; Martin-Hisard, "Georgian Hagiography."

[54] This is especially true of the *Life of Michael of Mar Saba*: Peeters, "Passion de S. Michel"; Blanchard, "Martyrdom of Saint Michael"; Griffith, "Michael, the Martyr"; and chapter 3, sec. II.

[55] On the presence of Georgians in the Holy Land more generally, see Janin, "Géorgiens à Jérusalem"; Mgaloblishvili, "Unknown Georgian Monastery in the Holy Land"; Avni, *Byzantine-Islamic Transition*, 126. The *life* of the martyr Constantine-Kakhay describes the journey of one pilgrim from Georgia to Palestine: Abashidze and Rapp, "Kostanti-Kaxay," 150–51.

[56] Sinai Geo. N. 3 and Sinai Geo. O. 11, with the *Life of Abo of Tiflīs*: Garitte, *Catalogue des manuscrits géorgiens littéraires du Mont Sinaï*, 42–43; *CMR*, i, 336.

[57] See chapter 5, sec. III.

[58] On the history of Syriac in late antiquity and the early Islamic period, see Hoyland, "Why Did Aramaic Succeed Where Greek Failed?"; on hagiography-writing in Syriac, see Brock, "Syriac Hagiography."

[59] Papadopoulos-Kerameus, "Muchenichestvo shestidesiati novykh sviatykh muchenikov postradavshikh," 7; the author of the text states that he first "read about the Sixty Martyrs in the Syrian language [Gk. *syristi*]"; cf. Peeters, *Tréfonds oriental*, 21. Such references to the "Syrian language" usually mean the local dialect known as Christian Palestinian Aramaic; see Griffith, "Aramaic to Arabic," 16–24. For more on the history and languages of this text, see Auzépy, *Hagiographie et l'iconoclasme*, 196.

absence of Syriac is a complicated issue connected to Christian sectarian identity and will be addressed more thoroughly in chapter 5.

Authors and Dates

Nearly all martyrologies were composed by monks and priests, who wrote for the spiritual edification of their brethren and the lay faithful they served.[60] As we shall see in the coming chapters, their general goal was to discourage conversion to the Muslim faith and assimilation into Arabic culture by showcasing models of resistance to both forces. Thus, we must be careful not to automatically conflate the views of the clerical authors with those of the laity they served, even if it is exceptionally difficult to disentangle them. We are fortunate to know several of the biographers by name. Eulogius of Córdoba and Stephen Manṣūr of Mar Saba are the only authors known to have produced multiple martyrologies in this period.[61] We know about others because they mention themselves in their own compositions, such as the Georgian churchman John Sabanisdze and the Armenian monk Abraham, who composed biographies of Abo of Tiflīs and Vahan of Gołt'n, respectively.[62] Still others left only their names,[63] while the vast majority of works are anonymous.

The matter of authorship raises the thornier question of when martyrologies were written. Here it is difficult to make generalizations about the corpus as a whole, since dating varies widely from one text to another. Some martyrologies—including the *passions* of Cyrus, Abo, Vahan, and the Córdoba martyrs—claim to have been written only a few years after the events they describe. In many instances, however, there is no concrete information to help

[60] For an overview, see Hinterberger, "Byzantine Hagiographer and His Text."

[61] For the *Life of Eulogius* by Paulus Alvarus, written ca. 859, see *CSM*, i, 330–43; Eng. trans. in Sage, *Paul Albar*, 190–214. The first complete English translation of his works by Kenneth Wolf will soon appear with Liverpool University Press. On Stephen and the confusion surrounding his biography, see Auzépy, "Étienne le Sabaïte et Jean Damascène"; Johnson, "Social Presence of Greek," 73–74. Stephen was responsible for the *Passion of the Twenty Martyrs of Mar Saba* and the *Life of Romanus* and also possibly the *Life of Bacchus*; *CMR*, i, 597, regards the author of this text as "Stephen the Deacon," who also wrote the *Life of Stephen the Younger* (d. 764/765), the first martyr of Byzantine iconoclasm. This would place the *Life of Bacchus* in Constantinople, not Palestine.

[62] Shurgaia, *Martirio di Abo*, 77–85; Gatteyrias, "Martyre de saint Vahan," 212–13.

[63] E.g., Cyrus of Ḥarrān by Joshua the Stylite: Harrak, *Chronicle of Zuqnīn*, 4–8. The Greek version of the *Life of Michael of Mar Saba* by Basil of Emesa: Blanchard, "Martyrdom of Saint Michael," 149; Peeters, "Passion de S. Michel," 80 n. 2. On a Sabaite monk named Basil who was present for the sack of the monastery in the late eighth century: *SPSH*, i, 2; Swanson, "Christian al-Maʾmūn Tradition," 81. George-Muzāḥim by Mena: *CMR*, ii, 460–63. Christopher of Antioch by Ibrāhīm b. Yuḥannā ʾl-Anṭākī: Zayyāt, "Vie du patriarche melkite."

assess when they were composed. That being said, it is not impossible to derive a general sense of the temporal distance between a martyr and his or her biographer by examining extraneous information in the text, including references to places, dates, secondary characters, and outside events. A writer who knows a martyr's world very intimately—such as the author of the *Life of Peter of Capitolias* (d. 715)—probably penned the work shortly after the martyr's death, in this instance, in a monastery not far from Capitolias, possibly Mar Saba.[64] By contrast, an author who knows a martyr's world poorly or who plainly fills the text with fictional elements—such as Basil of Emesa, to whom the Greek *Life of Michael of Mar Saba* (as contained in the *Life of Theodore of Edessa*) is ascribed—probably did not compose his work in close proximity to the incident it describes.

In addition to clues in the texts, there is information about dating to be gleaned from the manuscripts. Here again, it is difficult to make generalizations on the basis of material evidence, since dating varies so significantly from one martyrology to another. With the possible exception of the *Life of Cyrus*, there are no autographs of martyrs' *lives* from the early period. The oldest manuscripts were written in Arabic and Greek and come from the ninth and tenth centuries.[65]

One such manuscript—Paris Coislin 303—is especially interesting since it contains the only known copies of several Greek martyrologies, including the *passions* of the Sixty Martyrs of Jerusalem (d. 724/725), Elias of Helioupolis (d. 779; see Figure I.1), and the Twenty Martyrs of Mar Saba (d. 788/797).[66] According to André Binggeli, the manuscript was copied in Constantinople in the tenth century on the basis of an older manuscript from Jerusalem.[67] Interestingly, some of the texts in the manuscript seem to draw on older Aramaic *Vorlage* (such as the *Passion of the Sixty Martyrs*) or were possibly written by bilingual Greek/Aramaic speakers (the *Life of Elias*). These texts, however, never became popular in the imperial capital, and the cults they were meant to promote never became widespread in Byzantium at large. There are also a number of very early manuscripts in Georgian that contain original Georgian compositions as well as translations from Greek and Arabic, many of which date to the tenth century.[68]

[64] See chapter 3, sec. III.

[65] E.g., Sinai Ar. 542 (9th c.), with the *Life of ʿAbd al-Masīḥ*: Binggeli, "Hagiographie du Sinaï," 175–77; Sinai Ar. 513 (10th c.), with the *Life of Anthony*: *CMR*, i, 500.

[66] Devreese, *Fonds Coislin*, 286–88.

[67] Binggeli, "Réception de l'hagiographie palestinienne à Byzance." I am grateful to André Binggeli for sharing a draft of this article with me in advance of its publication.

[68] E.g., Iviron Geo. 8 (10th c.), with the *Life of Romanus*: *CMR*, i, 392; Iviron Geo. 57 (10th c.), with the *lives* of Anthony, Abo, and Michael: see n. 53 above; and Sinai Geo. 11 (10th c.), with the

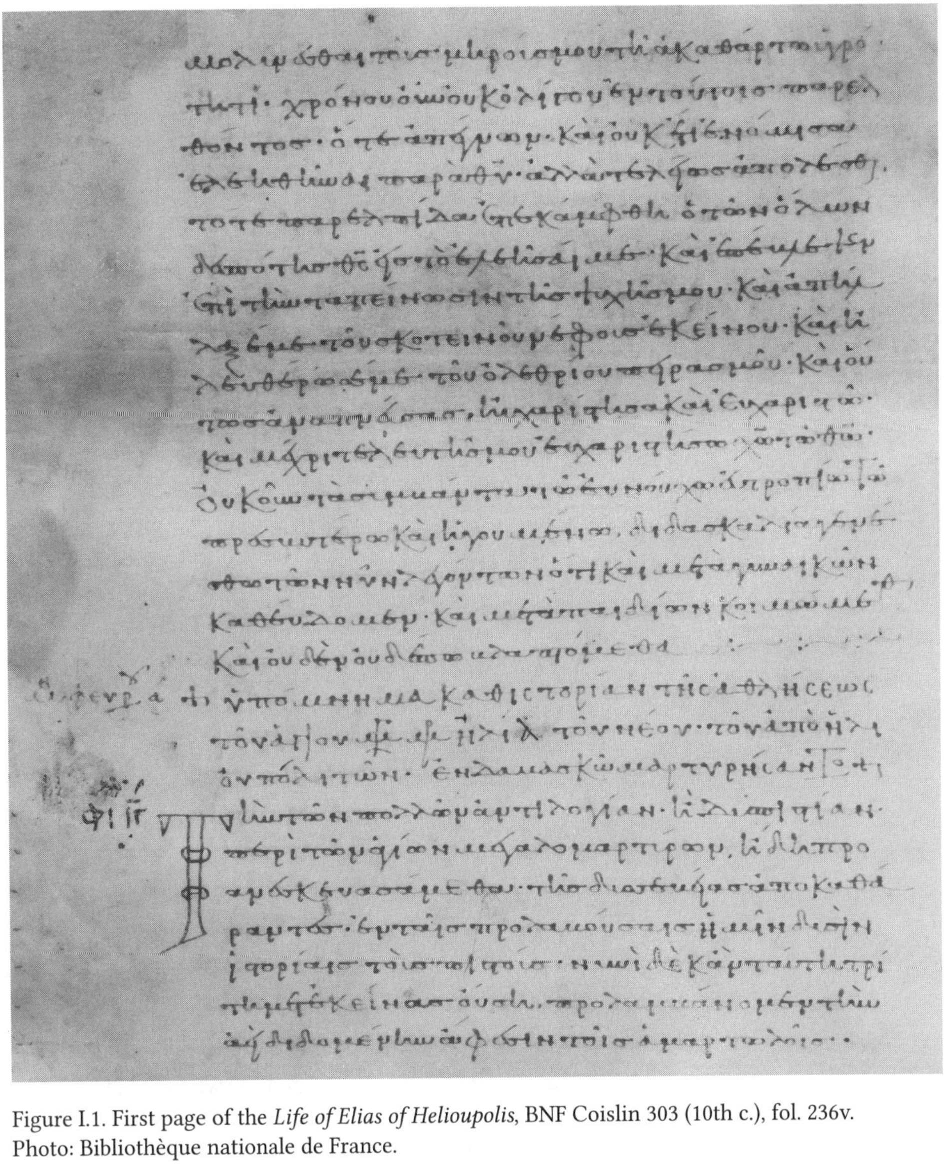

Figure I.1. First page of the *Life of Elias of Helioupolis*, BNF Coislin 303 (10th c.), fol. 236v. Photo: Bibliothèque nationale de France.

Thus, even with our earliest sources, we face a chasm of at least a century between the date of a martyrdom and the copying of the surviving manuscript. The most problematic manuscript tradition of all is that of the Córdoba martyr

Life of Abo: see n. 56 above. Along with these, there are many late Georgian and Armenian manuscripts, e.g., *CMR*, i, 282, 421, 720.

acts, which seem to have been lost between 884 and the mid-sixteenth century, when they were "rediscovered" by the bishop and inquisitor Pedro Ponce de León. After being studied by Ambrosio de Morales, they disappeared again and have never resurfaced. Thus, Morales's 1574 edition—which shows signs of linguistic tampering—has served as the basis for all research on the Córdoba martyrs until today.[69]

How we interpret the *lives* of the new martyrs depends on when we date such texts. Were most written shortly after the martyrdoms they recount, or were they products of much later periods? Here again, it would be imprudent to make sweeping generalizations about the corpus as a whole. It is simply too diverse linguistically, geographically, and confessionally to make a definitive statement one way or another. In the course of the following pages, each text will be assessed on its own to determine when it may have been written. Suffice it to say, it is my reasoned opinion that many martyrologies were products of the world they describe—and to a much greater extent than other genres of hagiographic literature, such as the early Christian *lives* that Candida Moss and other skeptical scholars regard as fabricated. Though they may have been written at a remove of several years or decades from the incidents they recount, I believe that they can tell us something useful about the world in which the martyrs lived and the one in which their biographers wrote. This is especially true when they are controlled with outside sources and read in accordance with the methodological principles outlined above.

III. TOLERANCE AND INTOLERANCE IN MEDIEVAL ISLAM

This is the first book-length study of Christian martyrdom in the early Islamic period. As such, it seeks to explore a relatively unknown aspect of the broader transition from late antiquity to the Islamic Middle Ages.[70] Historians once argued that the rise of Islam violently disrupted the rhythms of life in the late ancient Near East. Over the past decades, however, a new symphony of literary and archaeological evidence has emerged that has changed the way we see the

[69] Morales, *Eulogii Cordubensis*; Colbert, *Martyrs of Córdoba*, 435–53; Wolf, *Christian Martyrs*, 36–47. However, early manuscripts of Paulus Alvarus's *Indiculus luminosus* do survive to the present: *CMR*, i, 648.

[70] See esp. Brown, *World of Late Antiquity*, 189–203; Cameron et al., *Byzantine and Early Islamic Near East*; Fowden, *Empire to Commonwealth*; Fowden, *Before and after Muḥammad*; Sizgorich, *Violence and Belief*; Al-Azmeh, *Emergence of Islam in Late Antiquity*; Bowersock, *Crucible of Islam*; etc. On the "long late antiquity," which makes room for Islam, see Bowersock, Brown, and Grabar, *Late Antiquity*; Rousseau, *Companion to Late Antiquity*; Johnson, *Oxford Handbook of Late Antiquity*; Cameron, "Long Late Antiquity"; Marcone, "Long Late Antiquity?"

period.[71] Far from marking a rupture with the past, the first two centuries of Islamic history have come to be seen as an extension of late antiquity—if not its triumphant denouement. This is especially true if we regard Muḥammad and the early caliphs as heirs to the Constantinian revolution—especially that distinctive marriage of empire and monotheism that Constantine brought about through his conversion in the fourth century. A by-product of this revolution was the use of state power to promote right belief and purge wrong belief. It is this violent by-product, especially in its Islamic context, that constitutes the subject of the present book.

This book also focuses on the history of Muslim-Christian relations. Despite the many exemplary works on this topic over the years, it is a subject that has traditionally lacked a vigorous engagement with social history. This is particularly true in comparison with the study of medieval Judaism, in which the documents of the Cairo Geniza have helped scholars reconstruct the daily life of Jews in the Middle East with unparalleled richness and humanity.[72] When it comes to Christians, we have a clear picture of what was at stake in intellectual encounters at the top of society—especially in the realm of theological dialogue and debate with Muslims.[73] We also have a clear picture of how Muslims used legal categories to regulate their contact with non-Muslims, especially in the form of the so-called Pact of ʿUmar (Ar. *ʿahd ʿumar, al-shurūṭ al-ʿumarīya*).[74] But we do not have the same grasp of what was happening on the ground.[75] This book attempts to begin filling this gap.

Amid this, it is surprising to observe that until now, there has been no book-length study of Christian martyrdom in the early Islamic period.[76] There is also no general account of anti-Christian violence under Islam comparable to the voluminous literature on Christian persecution in the Roman Empire.[77]

[71] See especially Pentz, *Invisible Conquest*; Piccirillo, *Mosaics of Jordan*; Schick, *Christian Communities*; Walmsley, *Early Islamic Syria*; Sijpesteijn, "Landholding Patterns"; Evans and Ratliff, *Byzantium and Islam*; Khalek, *Damascus*; King, "Why Were the Syrians Interested in Greek Philosophy?"; Tannous, "Qenneshre and the Miaphysite Church"; Avni, *Byzantine-Islamic Transition*, 311–19.

[72] Goitein, *Mediterranean Society*.

[73] See the collected essays in Griffith, *Beginnings of Christian Theology in Arabic*; Griffith, *Church in the Shadow of the Mosque*; and Samir, *Foi et culture en Irak*, among many others.

[74] Tritton, *Non-Muslim Subjects*; Fattal, *Statut légal*; Levy-Rubin, *From Surrender to Coexistence*.

[75] This is beginning to change; see esp. Robinson, *Empire and Elites*; Tannous, "Syria"; Hoyland, *In God's Path*.

[76] There are several popular accounts of the plight of Christians in the contemporary Middle East, including Dalrymple, *From the Holy Mountain*; Sennott, *Body and the Blood*; Russell, *Heirs to Forgotten Kingdoms*, esp. 215–60.

[77] For more, see n. 3 above. And on the legal dimensions of Roman persecution of Christians, see Sherwin-White, "Early Persecutions and Roman Law"; De Ste. Croix, "Aspects of the 'Great'

Despite the novelty of the topic, this book enters a long-running debate about the question of "tolerance" and "intolerance" in premodern Islam. It is a debate that has gripped academic specialists and the general public alike, and here, it is possible to discern two broad views. At one end of the spectrum lies what I will call the "apologetic thesis," which stresses the essential tolerance of medieval Muslim rulers toward the non-Muslim subject population. It tends to highlight verses in the Qurʾan that describe the People of the Book positively (e.g., Q. *al-Baqara* 2:62 etc.), regarding these as normative for how Muslims and non-Muslims interacted throughout history; it suggests that medieval caliphs granted "freedom of religion" to Christians and Jews; it downplays the legal strictures associated with the *dhimmī* regime; it celebrates moments of *convivencia* between Muslims and others, especially in mixed areas such as al-Andalus; and it contrasts the allegedly secure status of non-Muslims in the medieval Middle East with the precarious state of Jews and other minorities in Europe at the same time.[78] At the other end of the spectrum is the "lachrymose thesis," famously championed by the Egyptian Jewish writer Bat Ye'or (née Gisèle Littman). For Bat Ye'or (and her even more strident followers, such as Robert Spencer), non-Muslims were the despised second-class citizens of states committed to their gradual eradication, a view she believed was spelled out in the Qur'an itself (e.g., Q. *al-Māʾida* 5:51, *al-Tawba* 9:29, etc.) and developed with zeal and vigor across the ages. Indeed, her books—which have been influential in popular as well as academic settings—consider the *longue durée* of Christian and Jewish decline in the Near East from the time of the conquests to the present as a consequence of what she calls "dhimmitude," or the state of living as a subjugated minority.[79]

Needless to say, both of these views have serious flaws. The "apologetic thesis" reads into the Qurʾan anachronistic ideas of religious freedom that are borrowed from modern culture.[80] It also whitewashes the sometimes troubled history of interreligious relations in the premodern period in the interest of

Persecution"; De Ste. Croix, "Why Were the Early Christians Persecuted?"; Barnes, "Legislation against the Christians."

[78] For example, Menocal, *Ornament of the World*; Morrow, *Covenants of the Prophet Muhammad*; and Alkhateeb, *Lost Islamic History*, among others. For discussion of the historiography of "tolerance" in medieval al-Andalus, see Akasoy, "*Convivencia* and Its Discontents"; Soifer, "Beyond *Convivencia*"; Fernández-Morera, *Myth of the Andalusian Paradise*.

[79] Bat Ye'or, *Dhimmi*; Bat Ye'or, *Decline of Eastern Christianity*; Bat Ye'or, *Islam and Dhimmitude*. See also Spencer, *Truth about Muhammad*; Spencer, *Religion of Peace?* I borrow the term *lachrymose* from Cohen, *Under Crescent and Cross*, 3–14, which focuses on the treatment of Jews; cf. Lewis, *Semites and Anti-Semites*, 117–39.

[80] With special attention to the famous verse Q. *al-Baqara* 2:256, "There is no compulsion in religion [*lā ikrāha fī ʾl-dīn*]"; cf. Crone, "No Compulsion in Religion." On the late antique context, see now Leppin, "Christianity and the Discovery of Religious Freedom."

making medieval Islam seem much more open-minded and liberal than it really was. In the process, it overlooks the manner in which premodern Muslim states did often marginalize non-Muslims, whether by imposing heavy taxes on them, criminalizing apostasy, barring them from public service, prohibiting the construction of new churches and synagogues, mandating the wearing of humiliating clothing, or enslaving native populations (parallels to which are easy to find in other medieval societies outside the Middle East). The "lachrymose thesis" goes in the opposite direction by downplaying the abundant evidence of peaceful coexistence in the medieval Middle East. At its most extreme manifestations, it does so in order to discredit Islam in the present by tethering it to a history of supposed intolerance in the past. Perhaps inadvertently, the "lachrymose thesis" commits a second error by stripping non-Muslims of historical agency. Indeed, "dhimmitude" and concepts like it treat non-Muslims as hapless victims of persecution rather than as agents with the capacity for independent action, whether resistance or accommodation.

This book attempts to tread a careful path between these two views. As martyrologies and other medieval sources make clear, Muslim-Christian relations were not always irenic. In fact, they could be extremely tense, occasionally spilling over into violence. When this did take place inside the caliphate, the violence almost always went in one direction: from Muslims to Christians and not the other way around.[81] On the other hand, social and religious conflict usually took place against a backdrop of peaceful relations between communities. It is for this reason that hagiographers, chroniclers, and other medieval writers recorded bloodshed in the first place: not because it was ordinary but precisely because it was extraordinary.

IV. ORGANIZATION OF THE BOOK

This book is divided into five main sections. Chapter 1, "Converting to Islam and Returning to Christianity," profiles the largest group of new martyrs, those who began life as Christians, became Muslims, and then reverted to Christianity. Among these, there were several subgroups, including Christians who converted to Islam as slaves or prisoners, Christians who converted under disputed or contingent circumstances, and martyrs who were brought up in religiously mixed families. Because of the contingent nature of this process, conversions could also be undone, leading to sizable numbers of apostates over the course of the seventh, eighth, and ninth centuries.

[81] A notable exception to this involves the non-Muslim revolts discussed in chapter 4.

Chapter 2, "Converting from Islam to Christianity," follows the preceding chapter by exploring a small and neglected group of martyrs who converted from Islam to Christianity. The chapter shows that religious change in the postconquest Middle East did not go in one direction—from the church to the mosque—by highlighting a group of martyrs who moved from the mosque to the church. After surveying the evidence of true apostasy in legal, liturgical, and historical literature, it discusses a convert who is said to have been a member of the Prophet's tribe of Quraysh. It then profiles two Muslim martyrs from the Caucasus and a collection of apostates from Iraq, Iberia, and Egypt. The last section investigates a curious cluster of legends about the conversion of caliphs and other high-ranking Muslims to Christianity. It argues that these expressed contemporary hopes for a second "Constantinian moment," when a new pagan ruler would convert to Christianity and restore the church's standing in the Middle East. These and other texts show how Islamization could be a fragile process, even in a world in which Muslims enjoyed privileged access to political and social power.

Chapter 3, "Blaspheming against Islam," investigates the third major group of martyrs, those who were executed after disparaging the Prophet. It begins with a brief overview of the evolution of antiblasphemy laws in Islam, arguing that prohibitions against blasphemy were very slow to coalesce throughout the classical period. It then examines a number of Christians who were killed for blasphemy in Egypt and the Levant, including Peter of Capitolias, whose exceptionally detailed biography has been largely unstudied until now. The final section examines the abundant evidence for blasphemy in Córdoba, the capital of al-Andalus, where forty-eight Christians were martyred between 850 and 859. It suggests that the Christians most likely to blaspheme were those who were closest to Muslims, including members of religiously mixed families, servants of the Muslim court, and individuals in religiously mixed workplaces. On the basis of this evidence, it proposes that blasphemy emerged as a specific form of Christian protest against Islamization and Arabization at a time when the number of Muslim religious scholars in al-Andalus was on the rise and debate between members of the two religions was intensifying. This, in turn, sensitized Christians at all levels of society to the differences between the two faiths, thereby encouraging them to disparage Islam ever more effectively.

Chapter 4, "Trying and Killing Christian Martyrs," investigates how the *lives* of the martyrs represent judicial procedure and criminal punishments. It argues that the state was dependent on private networks of informants—including relatives and friends—to root out apostates and blasphemers. It then shows how state officials could be exceptionally cautious in prosecuting religious criminals but, once they established their guilt, how they could be exceptionally brutal in punishing them. It suggests that the state used specific punishments derived from the Qur'an (esp. Q. *al-Mā'ida* 5:33, the "*Ḥirāba* Verse") at an early date, along with other controversial punishments that were hotly debated by Muslim jurists. The most important of these was the burning of corpses. The chapter suggests that the state developed a coherent approach for punishing a wide array of religious dissidents, as evidenced by the striking parallels between the executions of Christian martyrs and Muslim heretics, especially the leaders of Shīʿī and Khārijī revolts. It concludes by arguing that violence was limited in its scope and aimed at two specific goals: securing Muslims' place at the top of the religiously mixed society they ruled and countering a widespread culture of boundary-crossing. Indeed, the need to contain potential unrest and clamp down on perceived lawlessness seems to have underlain much of the state's brutality.

Chapter 5, "Creating Saints and Communities," considers what hagiography meant as a genre of literature in the postconquest period. It investigates the rhetorical goals of these texts, arguing that many were written by monks and priests to discourage conversion to Islam and to condemn Christians who were drawn too closely to Arab culture. It then suggests that the martyrologies enshrined the views of one side of an intra-Christian debate about the threats of Islamization and Arabization. Developing a thesis first introduced by historians of the Córdoba martyrs, it proposes that hagiographers across the Middle East were advocates of a "rejectionist" tendency that looked warily upon the religion and culture of the conquerors. These "rejectionists," in turn, encouraged Christians to preserve their identity by quarantining themselves from Muslims and, when necessary, by taking public stands against Islam through acts of blasphemy. The views of their ideological opponents, the "accommodationists," do not survive explicitly, though judging from the complaints of the "rejectionists," it seems that they held more permissive attitudes toward Islamization and Arabization and more readily went with the tides of change. Furthermore, it seems that they saw greater benefit in making peace with Muslims than in protesting against them through behaviors like martyrdom. The chapter concludes by imagining how these two orientations—if they ever existed as such—may have mapped onto certain social and confessional categories. These include distinctions between urban and rural communities, secular clergy and monks, and Melkite, West Syrian (Miaphysite), and East Syrian churches. The chapter explains how and why Melkites—the Chalcedonian Christians of the Middle East who remained in communion with

Constantinople after the conquests—took to martyrology-writing more enthusiastically than their rivals in other denominations, arguing that this had to do with their fall from grace after hundreds of years of imperial patronage.

The conclusion considers the chronology of the martyrdoms as a way of measuring the pace of Islamization and Arabization in the postconquest period. It suggests that the apparent surge in violence between 750 and 800 may have come about as Muslims and Christians began interacting with each other for the very first time as members of a shared society, rather than as rulers and subjects in a divided world, as they had done for much of the immediate post-conquest period. This, in turn, destabilized relations between the two communities, giving rise to new anxieties about social and religious differentiation. The final pages consider the legacy of the martyrs from the Middle Ages to the present, as well as the role martyrs played in the process of community formation for various emergent sects in the early medieval period, Christian and Muslim alike. Appendix 1 presents information about the neomartyrs contained in Muslim texts, while appendix 2 offers a glossary of key names and concepts.

1

Converting to Islam and Returning to Christianity

Let us begin this chapter with a story that illustrates how conversion is usually thought to have worked in the early Islamic period. The anecdote comes from the *Chronicle of Zuqnīn*, a historical work completed around 775 in a monastery near Āmid in northern Mesopotamia.[1] The author of the chronicle, a Syriac-speaking monk known as Joshua the Stylite, lamented the perceived uptick in conversions in his day. Burdened by heavy taxes and the harassment of the ʿAbbasid authorities, Christians were "turn[ing] to Islam [Syr. *ḥanpūtā*] faster than sheep rushing to water." In packs of "twenty, thirty, one hundred, two hundred, and three hundred" at a time, they descended on the Muslim prefects in Ḥarrān, where they "renounced Christ, baptism, the Eucharist, and the Cross." The desire to convert transcended social and economic classes. "This was done not only by the young," the chronicler bemoaned, "but also by adults, the elderly . . . even by senior priests and so many deacons they cannot be counted."[2] Although the *Chronicle of Zuqnīn* is a Christian eyewitness to the events of the early ʿAbbasid period, it reinforces an impression left by medieval Muslim sources, too. That is, the eighth century was a time of rapid religious change, but this change usually went in one direction: from the church to the mosque.

From a historical perspective, this impression is not entirely inaccurate. Sometime during or shortly after the Crusades, scholars surmise, the Middle East went from being a predominantly Christian world (with large numbers

[1] Chabot, *Chronicon anonymum Pseudo-Dionysianum*, ii, 381–92, esp. 383 ("sheep"), 385 (mass conversions), 388 (renunciation of beliefs), 389 (priests and deacons); see trans. in Harrak, *Chronicle of Zuqnīn*, 321–27. For discussion, see Harrak, "Christianity in the Eyes of the Muslims." On the term *ḥanpūtā* for Islam, see de Blois, "*Naṣrānī* (Ναζωραῖος) and *Ḥanīf* (ἐθνικός)," 23; generally Penn, *Envisioning Islam*, 53–101. On the economic conditions in the Jazīra at this time, see Dennett, *Conversion and the Poll Tax*, 43–48; Cahen, "Fiscalité, propriété, antagonismes sociaux."

[2] The prefects also told the Christians, "You are Godless and you are holding on, as if to a spider's web," a possible allusion to Q. *al-ʿAnkabūt* 29:41: Harrak, "Christianity in the Eyes of the Muslims," 343–47.

of Jews, Zoroastrians, Manichaeans, and pagans) to one whose majority population practiced Islam.[3] This was an uneven process, probably invisible to most who lived through it, and shaped by the vicissitudes of conquest and the varying fortunes of missionaries. It was also a process of remarkable regional diversity, for just as some areas crossed the threshold of a Muslim numerical majority early on, others held out for centuries, including parts of Upper Egypt, the mountains of Lebanon, and much of northern Mesopotamia, which remained predominantly Christian into the twentieth century.[4] Despite this, conversion to Islam should not be regarded as the only religious option in the early period. While it is undeniable that most of the region's Christians (and non-Muslims) converted to Islam gradually, there were many who chose to convert in less "popular" directions. These included Christians who embraced Islam but regretted their decision and returned to their original faith, the children of religiously mixed marriages who spurned their fathers' Islam and adopted their mothers' Christianity, and a small but significant group of Muslims from Muslim backgrounds who converted to Christianity. They constitute the focus of this and the next chapter.

Normally, such unconventional forms of conversion are invisible in Muslim sources. By and large, these texts paint a triumphalist portrait of Islamization as an irreversible process, one that was well on its way by the early ʿAbbasid period.[5] Basing their research on these sources, too, some modern scholars have implicitly accepted the master narrative.[6] Even among those who have not, many have concentrated their research on the question of when the Middle East first became predominantly Muslim, as if this benchmark were intrinsically important for understanding the shape of a society or were a foregone conclusion in the early period itself. The truth is that the demographic tipping point between Muslims and non-Muslims is almost impossible

[3]For the most important studies, see Arnold, *Preaching of Islam*; Dennett, *Conversion and the Poll Tax*; Bulliet, *Conversion to Islam*; Gervers and Bikhazi, *Conversion and Continuity*; Fiey, "Conversions à l'Islam"; Wasserstein, "Conversion and the *Ahl al-dhimma*"; Peacock, *Islamisation.*

[4]For greater Syria, see Levtzion, "Conversion to Islam in Syria and Palestine"; Schick, *Christian Communities*, 139–58; Levy-Rubin, "Case of Samaria"; Humphreys, "Christian Communities"; Carlson, "Contours of Conversion." For Egypt, see Lapidus, "Conversion of Egypt"; Brett, "Spread of Islam in Egypt and North Africa"; Little, "Coptic Conversion to Islam"; Friedmann, "Conversion of Egypt to Islam"; Lev, "Persecutions and Conversion"; Frantz-Murphy, "Conversion in Early Islamic Egypt"; El-Leithy, "Coptic Culture"; Sijpesteijn, *Shaping a Muslim State*, 165–67. For the Iberian Peninsula, see Glick, *Islamic and Christian Spain*, 21–24; Epalza, "Mozarabs"; Penelas, "Conversion to Islam"; Fernández Félix and Fierro, "Cristianos y conversos."

[5]For an exemplary anecdote, see al-Ṭabarī, *Annales*, ii, 1024, on the alleged conversion of fifty thousand non-Muslims to escape the *kharāj*.

[6]E.g., for older views that Egypt converted in the ninth century, see Lapidus, "Conversion of Egypt."

to know. Scholars of the medieval period lack the kind of reliable demographic data that could shed definitive light on the question, comparable to what we can glean from tax registers or censuses of later periods.[7] Attempts to deduce such data from premodern sources have been met with mixed success—most notably, Richard Bulliet's groundbreaking 1979 study *Conversion to Islam in the Medieval Period: An Essay in Quantitative History*, which proposed conversion curves for different regions of the medieval Middle East on the basis of onomastic information in biographical literature (*ṭabaqāt*).[8]

Bulliet's approach was creative and remains broadly influential nearly forty years after its publication. Despite this, it has had the practical effect of narrowing research on conversion to a cluster of broadly empirical questions, such as when conversion to Islam took place and how many individuals converted. Along the way, other basic questions related to the process of conversion have received less attention: How did converts relate to their old and new communities? How did relatives, friends, and neighbors perceive the conversion of their loved ones? How did conversion affect an individual's political, social, and cultural identities? How did different kinds of literary sources represent the experience of religious change? Was conversion a discrete moment in time or a drawn-out process that lasted for many years, if not for generations?[9]

One way we can begin to answer these questions is by consulting the Christian martyrologies of the early Islamic period (a type of evidence whose usefulness Bulliet has doubted, unjustifiably so in my opinion).[10] Many of these texts recount the stories of apostates who were executed for leaving Islam. Their motivations were varied, but in each case, we can see how the process of Islamization was neither absolute nor inevitable in the early years. Rather, the Middle East during the seventh, eighth, and ninth centuries was an intensely competitive world in which confessional costume changes were common. In this chapter, I wish to explore the nature of conversion in the

[7] On the unreliability of demographic data for the premodern Middle East more generally, see Ayalon, "Population Estimates"; for the religious census of Ottoman Syria and Palestine from 1870–71, see Grehan, *Twilight of the Saints*, 29–41.

[8] Bulliet, *Conversion to Islam*, with critiques in Morony, "Age of Conversions"; Christys, *Christians in al-Andalus*, 3; Harrison, "Behind the Curve." For Bulliet's subsequent writings on conversion, see Bulliet, "Conversion Stories in Early Islam"; Bulliet, "Conversion-Based Patronage and Onomastic Evidence"; Bulliet, "Conversion and Law"; Bulliet, "Conversion Curve Revisited."

[9] Uriel Simonsohn has begun to tackle these questions in a group of stimulating articles: e.g., Simonsohn, "Halting between Two Opinions"; Simonsohn, "Conversion to Islam"; Simonsohn, "Conversion, Apostasy, and Penance"; Simonsohn, "Jewish Apostates and Their Spouses."

[10] Bulliet, "Conversion Curve Revisited," 72: "Such testimonies and anecdotes [dealing with individual or group conversions] do exist, but they are too few and far between, not to mention too infected by hagiographical distortion, to constitute a convincing body of evidence."

early medieval Middle East by focusing on the first half of these convert martyrs, who began their lives as Christians, embraced Islam, and then returned to Christianity. I will also focus on martyrs from religiously mixed families, leaving the matter of "true apostates"—that is, Muslim converts to Christianity—to chapter 2.

The central argument of these two chapters may be summarized as follows: there were many forms of conversion in the early medieval Middle East other than the monolithic form of conversion that most scholars investigate today. Even if the number of apostates paled in comparison with the number of those who converted and remained Muslims, their paths in and out of Islam can tell us a great deal about how conversion worked more generally, especially the myriad social, spiritual, economic, and political pressures that powered religious change in the period. In a sense, we can understand the long-term, large-scale conversion of the Middle East better by investigating those exceptional moments when this process was undermined or reversed. For this reason, these two chapters present several case studies designed to highlight alternative models of conversion in the early medieval Middle East. These include apostasy from Islam in the context of slavery; conversion to Islam in contested circumstances, such as intoxication or financial disputes; apostasy within religiously mixed families; conversion due to alleged supernatural experiences; and apostasy caused by Muslims losing contact with Muslim communities and institutions.

These models accord well with much recent theoretical literature that has stressed the complexity and diversity of motivations behind conversion, as well as the variety of ways in which conversion can be represented and instantiated.[11] Thus, this chapter and the next investigate conversion in the context of spiritual excursions (Anthony al-Qurashī, Ibn Rajāʾ), social encounters with the religious other (ʿAbd al-Masīḥ, Elias), and cultural dislocation (Vahan, Abo). They also show how converts signaled their shift in allegiances by changes in appearance (Dioscorus), administrative status (Cyrus), social groups (George the Black), and naming (Bacchus) and by redefining their ties with broader family networks (Aurea). Above all, they reveal the importance of narrative in portraying the experience of conversion, particularly how authors represented conversion using literary devices that were intelligible and persuasive in the eyes of their readers.[12]

[11] Rambo and Farhadian, *Oxford Handbook of Religious Conversion*, esp. 1–22; and for late antiquity and the early Islamic period, Papaconstantinou, "Introduction."

[12] On the role of stories in conversion, see Stromberg, "Role of Language"; Hindmarsh, "Narrative and Autobiography."

I. RELIGIOUS CHANGE IN THE POSTCONQUEST MIDDLE EAST: AN OVERVIEW

To understand what compelled martyrs to convert and revert, we must step around one popular image of conversion that is based on the experiences of famous figures such as Paul of Tarsus, Augustine of Hippo, the Protestant Christians of the Second Great Awakening, and Malcolm X. This model understands conversion as an outward manifestation of a changing emotional, spiritual, or intellectual reality. Though this may describe some conversions in premodern times, it is inadequate for understanding what I would regard as the majority of conversions in the early Islamic period. In this world, conversion hinged not only on spiritual convictions but also on an array of social and political factors detached from questions of high theology. In fact, the line between religious conversion and cultural assimilation was often very blurry. For this reason, Arthur Darby Nock famously distinguished between the process of "conversion" and that of "adhesion," in other words, a wholesale change of heart and practice and a kind of fence-sitting in which religious change was more cultural than creedal.[13] Nock's model has been hotly debated ever since. Recently, for instance, Linford Fisher has argued that it is better to speak about religious "engagement" or "affiliation" among Native American Christians in the colonial period rather than outright "conversion"—a distinction that holds for the early Islamic period, too.[14]

The issue of religious change in the early medieval Middle East raises a more fundamental question that scholars tend to overlook when discussing conversion: What kind of Islam were these converts embracing, and what kind of Christianity were they leaving behind?[15] When we think back to the seventh, eighth, and ninth centuries, it is important to recall that "Islam" and "Christianity" meant something very different than they do today. Levels of lay catechesis were very inconsistent, and in the cities and villages of Egypt, Palestine, Syria, and Iraq where Muslims and Christians first rubbed shoulders, it was not always clear in practice where one community ended and the other one began. The problem of overlapping beliefs was compounded by deep social and cultural similarities between the two

[13] Nock, *Conversion*, esp. 7.

[14] Fisher, *Indian Great Awakening*, esp. 8.

[15] On the porosity of the Muslim community at this time, see Donner, *Muhammad and the Believers*; Shoemaker, *Death of a Prophet*.

populations, especially as the ranks of the Muslim community swelled with converts from non-Arab backgrounds.[16]

As Jack Tannous has shown, early medieval sources are filled with vivid reports about the state of mixture on the ground: recent converts who demanded baptism for their Muslim children, individuals who recited pagan poetry from the pulpits of the mosques because they confused it with the sound of the Qurʾan, caliphal missions to catechize converts who had no idea how to pray, and Muslims who sought spiritual counsel at the feet of Christian holy men.[17] Political leaders and religious scholars were often the first to take issue with the resemblance between groups and their practices. Muḥammad b. ʿAlī (d. 125/743), for instance, the father of the first ʿAbbasid caliph, denounced his Khārijite opponents in the Jazīra as "Muslims who behave like Christians" (*wa-muslimūn fī akhlāq al-naṣārā*).[18] The *Chronicle of Zuqnīn* describes the efforts of an ʿAbbasid governor in Mosul to ferret out suspicious Muslims "who took [Syrian] wives, sired Syrian [*sūryāyē*] children, mingled with Syrians, and were even indistinguishable from Aramaeans [*arāmāyē*]."[19] The annalist al-Ṭabarī hints at the existence of similar problems in Ctesiphon (al-Madāʾin), the old Sasanian capital on the banks of the Tigris, where a "Muslim" was regarded as anyone who "prays as we do, who prays [while] facing the [proper] direction as we do, and eats meat ritually butchered as we do"—a minimalist definition that falls well short of an orthodox Muslim by the standard of later periods.[20]

There were many reasons to stay put within the Muslim fold, but conversion did not always instill a deep sense of attachment to other Muslims or necessarily impart a rigorous understanding of Islamic belief and practice (if such things even existed at the start). In fact, as Nehemia Levtzion put it, a good many converts entered the Muslim community through a process of "passive adhesion to Islam"—brought about by the mass conversion of an Arab tribe, for instance, not after a process of spiritual deliberation.[21] This is not to say that converts were insincere about their beliefs or motivated purely by material concerns—far from it. As Patricia Crone argued, there was no greater proof of the truth of the Muslim God than the riches and power He bestowed on the *umma* throughout

[16] This culture carried on for centuries: e.g., Grehan, *Twilight of the Saints*, esp. 63, 72, 164, 177–87, 190–96.

[17] Tannous, "Syria," 407–29.

[18] *Akhbār al-dawla al-ʿabbāsīya*, 206.

[19] Chabot, *Chronicon anonymum Pseudo-Dionysianum*, ii, 256; discussion in Penn, *Envisioning Islam*, 142–43.

[20] al-Ṭabarī, *Annales*, i, 2020; discussion in Choksy, *Conflict and Cooperation*, 74–75.

[21] Levtzion, "Comparative Study of Islamization," 20; for the Arabian Peninsula, see now Munt, "Seventh-Century Arabia."

the conquests, a truth that would have been easy for prospective converts to grasp.[22] Rather, it is to say that the early Islamic period was a time of experimentation about what it meant to be a Muslim, and it is against this backdrop that we must study the surprising phenomenon of apostasy.

One major reason for the porosity of the early Muslim community was its low barrier for entry. Conversion to Islam was a straightforward procedure, especially in contrast to the complicated rites of initiation in late antique Christianity.[23] Then, as today, converting to Islam involved the recitation of the double *shahāda*, "There is no god but God, Muḥammad is the messenger of God," usually but not necessarily in the company of a witness.[24] In the early generations, non-Arab converts became Muslims by also becoming clients of an Arab tribe, and therefore, they had to secure an Arab Muslim patron to sponsor them, a practice known as *walāʾ al-islām*.[25] Converts, in turn, served this patron as clients (Ar. *mawālī*). Gradually, this requirement was waived as the number of non-Arabs in the Muslim community increased. Indeed, already by the early ʿAbbasid period, Muslims of non-Arab or mixed ancestry probably outnumbered purebred Arab Muslims.[26]

Although it may have been easy to join the Muslim community, over time, it became exceptionally hard to leave it.[27] The Qurʾan does not approve of apostasy, but at the same time, it makes no provision for the execution of apostates. In fact, it could be surprisingly lenient toward those who reneged on Islam, as in Q. *al-Baqara* 2:109, which urges forgiveness of individuals who depart the Muslim community without any clear expectation of their returning. There are even notable examples of early Muslims who apostatized and were not killed, including the Prophet's Companion ʿUbaydallāh b. Jaḥsh, who took part in the first *hijra* to Ethiopia in 7 BH/614–15 and then converted to

[22] Crone, "Islam, Judeo-Christianity and Byzantine Iconoclasm," 60–61 n. 5; Crone, *Nativist Prophets*, 14.

[23] See now Schwartz, *Paideia and Cult*.

[24] Kister, "*Illā bi-ḥaqqihi*."

[25] In contradistinction to *walāʾ al-ʿitāqa*, patronage through manumission, not conversion. For an overview, see Crone, "Mawlā," *EI*², vi, 874–82; also Crone, *Slaves on Horses*; Bernards and Nawas, *Patronate and Patronage*. On conversion without *walāʾ* in al-Andalus, see Fierro, "Árabes, berbéres, muladíes," 51–52. On the institution of *walāʾ* as represented in a Christian martyrology, see nn. 112–13 below.

[26] On tensions between Arab and non-Arab Muslims, see Goldziher, *Muslim Studies*, i, 98–136; Bashear, *Arabs and Others*; Agha, *Revolution which Toppled the Umayyads*; Crone, *Nativist Prophets*, 1–27.

[27] The best overview of legal attitudes toward apostasy in the medieval period is Friedmann, *Tolerance and Coercion*, 121–59; also Heffening, "Murtadd," *EI*², vii, 635–36; Hallaq, "Apostasy," *EQ*, i, 119–22; Griffel, "Apostasy," *EI*³ (2007), i, 131–34; Peters and de Vries, "Apostasy in Islam"; Kraemer, "Apostates, Rebels and Brigands," 36–48; Griffel, *Apostasie und Toleranz*; Cook, "Apostasy from Islam."

Christianity and never returned.[28] This more lenient attitude is also attested in precanonical *ḥadīth* collections, including the *Muṣannaf* of ʿAbd al-Razzāq al-Ṣanʿānī (d. 211/827), which portrays apostates as going free despite not having returned to Islam.[29] It did not take long for this liberal attitude to give way to fierce opposition. The change was owed to several factors, among them the experience of the Ridda Wars (ca. 11–12/632–33), when numerous Arab tribes "apostatized" following Muḥammad's death, refusing to pay taxes to his successor, Abū Bakr. In the wake of this tumult, a strong consensus emerged that apostasy was inadmissible and should be punished by death. In later periods, the only serious debate surrounded the levels of punishment for women and minors who had apostatized (Ḥanafīs and Shāfiʿīs believed that they should be imprisoned, not killed), as well as for apostates who were Muslim by birth versus those who had converted from non-Muslim backgrounds.[30] Taken as a whole, the medieval tradition spoke with a unified, unambiguous voice on the matter. As a *ḥadīth* narrated by the Companion Ibn ʿAbbās (d. 68/688) put it: "Kill anyone who changes his religion!" (*man baddala dīnahu fa-ʾqtulūhu*).[31]

One of the most troubling forms of apostasy for early Muslims was conversion to and away from Islam, what we might call "flip-flopping" today. The Qurʾan refers to flip-floppers as *munāfiqūn*, a term of Ethiopic origin, usually translated as "hypocrites" or "dissenters."[32] In the words of Q. *al-Nisāʾ* 4:137, "Lo, those who believe then unbelieve [*āmanū thumma kafarū*], believe then unbelieve, only to increase in their unbelief: God has never forgotten them and will not guide them on the path [of righteousness]!" Flip-floppers were also referred to using the term *mudhabdhabūn* (Q. *al-Nisāʾ* 4:143), from the Arabic root for "wavering" or "vacillating."[33] Muslim jurists of the period puzzled over

[28] Ibn Hishām, *Sīra*, ii, 362; Guillaume, *Life of Muḥammad*, 527.

[29] ʿAbd al-Razzāq, *Muṣannaf*, x, 171, no. 18713.

[30] Women and children: Abū Bakr al-Khallāl, *Aḥkām*, 428–30. For different rulings on apostates from Muslim and non-Muslim backgrounds, see chapter 2, sec. I; see also Kamali, *Freedom of Expression*, 218.

[31] The *ḥadīth* is widely attested; e.g., Abū Dāwūd, *Sunan* (2009), vi, 406, no. 4351; Abū Bakr al-Khallāl, *Aḥkām*, 415; Friedmann, *Tolerance and Coercion*, 146–48.

[32] Brockett, "al-Munāfiḳūn," *EI²*, vii, 561–62; Adang, "Hypocrites and Hypocrisy," *EQ*, ii, 468–72. The word derives from the Ethiopic root *n-f-q*, "to tear off, rend, divide," specifically the active participle *manāfəq*, "heretic, schismatic, hypocrite"; see Leslau, *Dictionary of Geʿez*, 388; Jeffery, *Foreign Vocabulary of the Qurʾān*, 272.

[33] Muqātil b. Sulaymān (d. 150/767) explains that the *mudhabdhabūn* were allies neither of the Believers nor of the Jews during the Prophet's time in Medina, sitting on the fence politically and religiously: Muqātil b. Sulaymān, *Tafsīr*, i, 417. Al-Zamakhsharī (d. 538/1144) states, "Satan and the wind blow [the *mudhabdhabūn*] between belief and unbelief": al-Zamakhsharī, *Kashshāf*, i, 579–80. The term was also used by medieval Christians to condemn their coreligionists who were in the habit of using Muslim creedal formulas to disguise their Christian beliefs: Griffith, "First

how to deal with converts who returned to their former religions.[34] Likewise, contemporary Christian clergy offered succor to returnees, even developing rituals to reintegrate ex-Muslims into the Christian fold.[35]

Christian literary sources also provide portraits of this peculiar form of reconversion. Anastasius of Sinai, for example, mentions a young man named Moses who hailed from the port city of Klysma (Ar. al-Qulzum) at the northern end of the Gulf of Suez.[36] Moses's father died when he was only five, sending the boy into an unpredictable cycle of conversion and apostasy, which Moses blamed on the influence of a demon. Anastasius does not state whether he was ever punished for his flip-flopping, though in later generations, many like him were indeed killed. Theophanes also mentions that the caliph al-Mahdī dispatched a general named Mouchesia to Syria in order to convert Christians and destroy churches around 779–80.[37] When this general reached Emesa (Ar. Ḥimṣ), he announced that he would not force anyone to become Muslim except for those who had already apostatized from Islam and returned to Christianity. Many of these flip-floppers yielded to the pressure and went back, while others refused to convert and were killed. These included the wife of an unnamed archdeacon and the wife of a nobleman called Hesios.

Michael the Syrian recounts a persecution (Syr. *rdūpyā*) that took place in the late 830s or early 840s in Serugh in northern Mesopotamia, where a Muslim strongman rounded up a group of apostates who had gone back to Christianity.[38] Many of the captured yielded to this man's tortures and embraced Islam, but one woman refused. News of the incident reached a judge

Christian *Summa Theologiae* in Arabic," 22. There is also the legend of a pre-Islamic ascetic named Kursuf who spent three hundred years fasting and the encountered a beautiful woman and gave up his ascetic ways. He then lost faith until God forgave him. In recounting this story, the Prophet Muḥammad called Kursuf a *mudhabdhab* for his vacillations: Aḥmad b. Ḥanbal, *Musnad* (1969), v, 163–64.

34 Abū Bakr al-Khallāl, *Aḥkām*, 421–24; al-Shāfiʿī, *Kitāb al-umm*, ii, 568–78; Kraemer, "Apostates, Rebels and Brigands," 40 n. 22; Friedmann, *Tolerance and Coercion*, 143–44.

35 For example, Jacob of Edessa (d. 708) states that Christian converts from Islam did not need to be rebaptized but did need to perform penance: Vööbus, *Synodicon*, i, I, 253 (Syr.); i, II, 231–32 (Eng.). On the various rites of abjuration, see chapter 2, sec. I.

36 Binggeli, "Anastase le Sinaïte," 233–34 (Gk.), 548–49 (Fr.). For discussion, see Flusin, "Démons et Sarrasins," 409; Hoyland, *Seeing Islam*, 100–101; Tannous, "Syria," 447–48; Simonsohn, "Halting between Two Opinions," 346. On Klysma, see Yāqūt, *Muʿjam al-buldān*, iv, 387–88. On the role of demons in conversion to Islam according to Christian sources, see Reinink, "Doctrine of the Demons." On another Egyptian convert who flipped-flopped in and out of Islam, see Ibn ʿAbd al-Ḥakam, *Futūḥ Miṣr*, 168–69.

37 de Boor, *Chronographia*, i, 452–53; Mango and Scott, *Theophanes*, 624–25. For discussion, see Peeters, "Glanures martyrologiques," 104–9; Todt, "Griechisch-orthodoxe (Melkitische) Christen," 65–66. Theophanes refers to the women as *noubitissai*, which Peeters interprets as a Syriac or Arabic corruption of the Greek *neophōtistai*, or "newly baptized."

38 Chabot, *Chronique*, iii, 97 (Fr.); iv, 534–35 (Syr.).

in neighboring Raqqa, who summoned the woman to explain what had happened. Upon hearing the story, the judge was so furious that he had the Muslim vigilante thrown in jail (a rare example of a Muslim official siding with an apostate over her accuser). There were also flip-floppers among the martyrs of Córdoba, including Felix, who was executed in June 853.[39] According to Eulogius, Felix had been born into a Christian family but "wavered in faith due to some diabolical pretext" (Lat. *occasione diaboli in fide uaccillans*) and converted to Islam. Later, he regretted his decision and returned to Christianity, at which point he married Liliosa, a fellow martyr born to Muslims but who had practiced Christianity in secret. It is not clear why these converts wavered in their commitments to Islam: Was it the result of changing convictions, economic incentives, or social circumstances? In most instances, we cannot tell, but what is clear is that the Muslim authorities strove to suppress this behavior through the law and, failing that, relied on capital punishment to stamp it out.

II. COERCION, CAPTIVITY, AND CONVERSION

The early Muslim community did not gain converts at swordpoint, at least not usually. In fact, Q. *Yūnus* 10:99–100 condemns forced conversion in no uncertain terms, stating, "So can you [O Prophet] compel people to believe? No soul can believe except by God's will!"[40] If anything, the earliest Muslims were rather ambivalent about winning converts at all. Their hesitation owed to several factors, some ideological, others practical. For one, many early Muslims saw their religion as a special monotheism for the Arab people, and therefore, as we have seen, converts had to both embrace the Muslim faith and become clients of an Arab tribe. Naturally, tribal leaders looked warily upon non-Arabs who embraced the new religion.[41] Such elites, who maintained a monopoly on power through much of the Umayyad period, despised the *mawālī* as second-class citizens and strove to distinguish themselves from non-Arabs through legal and financial means. A second factor that made the early Muslims ambivalent about proselytizing was the practical knowledge that non-Muslims kept the state afloat through their tax contributions, namely, the *jizya* and the *kharāj* (though it is unclear how early and how consistently these taxes were levied, as well as their precise significance in the earliest

[39] *CSM*, ii, 417.

[40] That is not to say that forced conversion never happened: e.g., Sijpesteijn, *Shaping a Muslim State*, 107; cf. Crone, "No Compulsion in Religion." Perhaps the most famous example of large-scale forced conversion in the medieval period was under the Almohads of the Maghrib in the twelfth century; see Fierro, "Conversion, Ancestry and Universal Religion."

[41] See n. 26 above.

period).[42] When these non-Muslims converted, the state lost a key source of revenue—though Muslims paid heavy taxes, too. Therefore, efforts to convert non-Muslims were not always as energetic as the universalist and egalitarian rhetoric of the Muslim community seemed to imply.[43] Similarly, the Umayyads are well known to have continued taxing converts as if they were still non-Muslims, a practice closely associated with the notorious governor of Iraq, al-Ḥajjāj b. Yūsuf (d. 95/714) before it was abolished by the caliph ʿUmar b. ʿAbd al-ʿAzīz (r. 99–101/717–20).[44]

There was one form of coercion that did supply the early Muslims with large numbers of converts, and this was slavery. During the first two centuries, the *umma* grew tremendously thanks to the influx of slaves from non-Arab backgrounds, many of whom were captured in war.[45] They formed part of the initial cohort of converts whom Richard Bulliet has called "the innovators"—individuals of low social standing who had little to lose by jettisoning their old religions and much to gain by embracing the religion of the conquerors, especially if this opened a path to manumission.[46] We can catch a glimpse of the massive influx of Christian slaves from Byzantium in a pair of Greek inscriptions that commemorate two Arab invasions of Cyprus in the 650s.[47] The inscriptions claim that 120,000 were carried off in the first raid and 50,000 in the second. These figures should not be taken at face value, of course, but they do convey a sense of the magnitude of the plunder, as well as the vast number of potential converts entering Muslim society. For those who did not convert, the sudden influx of captives from Byzantium also contributed to a demographic shift among the Christian sects of the region, leading to a "re-Chalcedonization" of Syria and parts of Mesopotamia, as Muriel Debié has argued (discussed at greater length in chapter 5).[48]

[42] Dennett, *Conversion and the Poll Tax*; read with Papaconstantinou, "Administering the Early Islamic Empire."

[43] Marlow, *Hierarchy and Egalitarianism*.

[44] Wellhausen, *Arab Kingdom*, 279–86, 308–9; Gibb, "Fiscal Rescript of ʿUmar II"; Blankinship, *Jihâd State*, 86–89; Hawting, *First Dynasty*, 69–70. See also the legal discussion of whether it is permissible to impose the *jizya* on recent converts, especially in rural areas: Abū Bakr al-Khallāl, *Aḥkām*, 96–98.

[45] Crone, *Slaves on Horses*, 50–51; Wasserstein, "Conversion and the *Ahl al-dhimma*," 186. On whether it was permissible to forcibly convert prisoners of war, see Friedmann, *Tolerance and Coercion*, 115–20. Friedmann remarks that the Qur'an and medieval *fiqh* are much more concerned with whether it is lawful to kill prisoners than whether it is lawful to convert them.

[46] Bulliet, *Conversion to Islam*, 41–42; see also Fierro, "*Mawālī* and *Muwalladūn* in al-Andalus," 229–30.

[47] Feissel, "Bulletin épigraphique," 380; discussion in Crone, *Nativist Prophets*, 7; Hoyland, *In God's Path*, 93. For background on deportation and slavery more broadly, see Shahbazi, Kettenhofen, and Perry, "Deportations," *EIr*, vii, 297–312; Charanis, "Transfer of Population."

[48] Debié, "Christians in the Service of the Caliph," 63–64; see also Tannous, "In Search of Monothelitism," 34.

Events like these created a massive pastoral crisis for Christian leaders in the Middle East. Anastasius of Sinai, for example, wrestled with how to properly care for Christian slaves who toiled under Muslim masters. In one particularly poignant petition, Anastasius was asked whether it was still possible for a Christian slave to achieve salvation if his owner barred him from attending church.[49] Some clergy even seem to have ministered to captive Christians, such as the Galatian priest and martyr Romanus, who was executed by the caliph al-Mahdī in 780 for trying to reconvert Byzantine prisoners who had become Muslims while in captivity.[50] At a moment when Christians were at risk of abandoning their faith because of pressure from their masters, priests such as Anastasius and Romanus strove to provide practical advice that would help their flocks resist the new religion.

George the Black

There are several martyrs whose deaths resulted from circumstances such as these. The earliest known neomartyr of all, George the Black, died in Damascus sometime in the 650s or 660s.[51] Our oldest information about George comes from the *Narrationes* of Anastasius of Sinai, though his cult may have carried on into early modern times.[52] The Rūm Orthodox patriarch of Antioch, Macarius b. al-Zaʿīm (r. 1647–72), mentioned George and the existence of his tomb outside Damascus a millennium after his death. It is not clear whether Macarius obtained his information independently or from an Arabic translation of Anastasius's *Narrationes* that was produced in Antioch at this time.[53]

According to Anastasius, George was born to a Christian family—perhaps in Syria or across the border in Byzantium—but was taken captive by Muslims at a young age. He renounced the faith of his birth when he was only eight

[49] Anastasius of Sinai, *Quaestiones et responsiones*, 139–40; see also Haldon, "Anastasius of Sinai," 131; Papaconstantinou, "Saints and Saracens," 324–28; more generally, now Papadogiannakis, "Anastasius of Sinai."

[50] Peeters, "S. Romain le néomartyr," 423–24; Shoemaker, *Three Christian Martyrdoms*, 184–87.

[51] Binggeli, "Anastase le Sinaïte," 252 (Gk.), 567 (Fr.). For discussion, see Flusin, "Démons et Sarrasins," 387, 403–4; Schick, *Christian Communities*, 175; Hoyland, *Seeing Islam*, 100, 351–52; Tannous, "Syria," 448–49; Papaconstantinou, "Saints and Saracens," 326. The precise dating of the martyrdom is unclear. Anastasius remarks that George's *passion* "is told even now around Damascus," indicating that it occurred some significant time before Anastasius recorded the event, possibly in the 650s or 660s.

[52] The first to be labeled a "new martyr" was technically Euphemia of Damascus, who was not killed for her transgressions: Binggeli, "Anastase le Sinaïte," 251 (Gk.), 566 (Fr.).

[53] Bīṭār, *al-Qiddīsūn al-mansīyūn*, 537–38; on Latakia 41 (written ca. 1716), see *al-Makhṭūṭāt al-ʿarabīya*, 108–9; on the Arabic translations of Anatasius of Sinai, see *GCAL*, i, 376. I am grateful to Fr. Elia Khalifeh for helping me identify this manuscript.

years old. When he became an adult, however, he once again became a Christian, worshipping in secret for fear that his Muslim master would discover and punish him. George was eventually betrayed by another slave, a fellow convert from Christianity to Islam, whom Anastasius calls a "Christ-hating apostate" (Gk. *apostatēs misochristos*).[54] This man notified their master of George's secret one day while the master was praying in a mosque. The master, in turn, summoned George to explain what had happened. He urged the martyr to exonerate himself by performing the Muslim prayers at his side, but when George refused, he had him cut in half.

George's conversion came about as a result of two factors that affected many Christian slaves in the years after the Arab conquest: pressure to practice Islam from their Muslim masters coupled with the absence of Christian authority figures with whom to maintain strong connections. The average Christian facing these challenges probably went the way of the "Christ-hating apostate" and converted. For whatever reason, George did not. We can imagine several reasons why this may have been the case, including the presence of other Christian slaves in the master's household or even Christian wives and concubines. Anastasius does not elaborate on this part of the story. We do know, however, that the Christians of Damascus buried George's remains in a memorial chapel (Gk. *en tini pro tēs poleōs idiazonti mnēmeiō*), which may point to the existence of a group of locals who nurtured his return to Christianity, kept his conversion a secret, and helped to promote his cult after his death. Whatever the case may be, George the Black and his apostate betrayer represent two responses to a common predicament in seventh-century Syria: Christian slaves could either resist the pressure to convert, thereby angering their masters, or assimilate into the religion and culture of their masters by joining Islam.[55]

Vahan of Gołtʿn

Christian slaves were not exclusively culled from the lower classes. Christians from aristocratic families were also captured, converted, and pressed into the service of Muslim masters. One of the most interesting of these was heir to a princely dynasty in his native Armenia: Vahan, son of Khusraw, the heir of the

[54] For more on this character, see chapter 5, sec. I.

[55] See the later example of Joseph Hazzāyā, the son of a Zoroastrian priest who was captured by Muslims and sold into slavery. His Muslim master had him circumcised and made him convert to Islam. Three years later, Joseph was sold to a Christian and baptized. He later entered the monastery where he had been baptized and became the abbot. For more, see Penn, *Envisioning Islam*, 176. For a precise legal parallel to George the Black, see Abū Bakr al-Khallāl, *Aḥkām*, 41–43.

local aristocratic house of Gołt'n, who was executed for apostasy in Ruṣāfa in 737.[56] His *life* survives in several medieval Armenian manuscripts, though the text claims to have been written in the immediate aftermath of the saint's death in the mid-eighth century.

Unlike in Egypt or Syria, where Muslim control was relatively undisputed from the time of the conquests, the capture of Armenia (Ar. Armīniya) during the 640s and 650s gave way to decades of tenuous, indirect rule.[57] The Umayyads governed Armenia as a quasi-independent tributary state with the help of local Christian families, much as the Sasanians and Byzantines had done before them. Umayyad control was so fragile, in fact, that no Arab troops and no Arab governors were permanently stationed in Armenia for much of the seventh century, in what Chase Robinson (speaking about a different region of the caliphate) has called an "Indian summer of *de facto* autonomy" before the Marwānids restored direct power.[58] Not surprisingly, this arrangement encouraged local rebellions. In the midst of these, Armenia also succumbed to several Byzantine and Khazar invasions, which finally prompted the Umayyads to reassert control in the early eighth century. The caliph ʿAbd al-Malik b. Marwān (r. 65–86/685–705) did so by ordering a general suppression of the Armenian aristocrats, a campaign that set the stage for Vahan's martyrdom.

According to his biography, Vahan's father was killed in 701 when the Muslim authorities locked a group of Armenian noblemen inside churches in Naxčawan and Gołt'n and set them ablaze. The incident is mentioned in a range of Armenian, Arabic, Greek, and Syriac chronicles and stands out as a singularly violent moment in the early Muslim-Christian encounter in the Caucasus.[59] As a result, Vahan, aged four, was orphaned and sent to Damascus in chains. Many of the Armenian prisoners who traveled with him were sold in the markets, but since Vahan was the son of a prince, he was handed over directly to the Umayyad court.[60] There, he converted to Islam, was renamed "Vahab" (Ar. Wahb?), and trained to serve as a scribe in the Umayyad *dīwān*. When ʿUmar b. ʿAbd al-ʿAzīz came to power in 99/717, he released the Arme-

[56] Gatteyrias, "Martyre de saint Vahan." For discussion, see *CMR*, i, 281–83; *BHO*, 267–68; Bayan, "Synaxaire arménien," 214–18; Hoyland, *Seeing Islam*, 373–75; Vacca, "Creation of an Islamic Frontier in Armīniya," 197–98. For further references in two Armenian chronicles, see Maksoudian, *History of Armenia*, 109; Thomson, *House of Artsrunik'*, 314–15.

[57] Canard, "Armīniya," *EI²*, i, esp. 635–38; Schütz, "Christian Enclave"; Garsoïan, "Rise of the Bagratuni"; Hoyland, *In God's Path*, 87–90, 111–15, 154–57; and especially the excellent dissertation of Vacca, "Creation of an Islamic Frontier in Armīniya"—now in book form as Vacca, *Non-Muslim Provinces under Early Islam*.

[58] Robinson, *Empire and Elites*, 57.

[59] Vacca, "Fires of Naxčawan."

[60] On hostage-taking in this period, see Vacca, "Creation of an Islamic Frontier in Armīniya," 130–33.

nian prisoners, apparently to make amends for their unjust capture years before.[61] By that time, however, Vahan had become "well versed in their sciences and law" and even developed "a strong and subtle eloquence", presumably in the Arabic language. Naturally, the caliph was hesitant to emancipate this valuable captive, but he was persuaded to do so on the condition that Vahan return to Armenia and administer his ancestral domains, presumably as an Umayyad vassal.[62]

ʿUmar died soon after Vahan's return to Armenia (ca. 101/720). Despite attempts to recall him to Damascus, Vahan remained in his native land and began practicing Christianity. As an apostate returning to the church, he did not have to undergo baptism a second time, but he cried so much in repentance, his biographer states, that his tears "functioned like a second baptismal pool."[63] Vahan then embraced the monastic life. Throughout this process, he was haunted by memories of his life as a Muslim. Therefore, he plotted a journey south to confront his former captors and friends. Vahan eventually reached the city of Ruṣāfa in the eastern desert of Syria, where the court of the caliph Hishām (r. 105–25/724–43) was then based.[64] There, he renounced Islam in public and was killed.

As with Anastasius's account of George the Black, the *Life of Vahan* reveals how a residual childhood Christianity might survive the pressures of captivity among Muslims. We lack information about what Vahan actually believed while he was serving in the court—as well as whether he might have been surrounded by other Christian slaves who sustained his faith in secret. But we do have a good idea of why Vahan abandoned Islam when he returned to Armenia. His sudden dislocation from Syria to the Caucasus seems to have reinvigorated his Christian faith. There were no doubt social and political advantages to being a Christian in this environment, especially if Vahan was returning to Armenia to rule his father's ancestral domains, as seems likely. But it is also hard to escape the impression that on a human level, the move must have induced a

[61] The sympathetic portrayal of ʿUmar b. ʿAbd al-ʿAzīz is consistent with the Armenian historical tradition more broadly: Gero, *Byzantine Iconoclasm*, 132–33, 138.

[62] For Vahan's release and return to Armenia, see Gatteyrias, "Martyre de saint Vahan," 188–91. The text is unclear about ʿUmar's motivations. In general, the Umayyads were eager to invite emigrants back to their homes in Armīniya; see Vacca, "Creation of an Islamic Frontier in Armīniya," 123. If Vahan was indeed sent back to Armenia to rule in the place of his Umayyad masters, that would mirror the later Ottoman practice known as *devşirme*, in which Christian boys from the Balkans were taken to Constantinople, where they converted to Islam and were enrolled in the Janissary corps. Later, many were sent back to their original communities to serve as Ottoman officials: Lowry, *Shaping of the Ottoman Balkans*, 1–14.

[63] The motif appears several times in the text: Gatteyrias, "Martyre de saint Vahan," 190, 194, 205 (baptism in blood).

[64] On Vahan in Ruṣāfa, see Fowden, *Barbarian Plain*, 183.

feeling of cultural whiplash: just as a young Christian was likely to abandon his or her religion in captivity among Muslims, a slave could also lose his or her adopted Islamic faith by returning to an old Christian world. In other words, dislocation cut both ways. The company of Arab princes in Damascus could make a Muslim of a Christian hostage, but the company of Christian clergy and nobles in Armenia could also make a Christian martyr of a Muslim courtier. It was a matter of religious faith as much as social belonging.

The Martyrs of Syracuse

If the absence of Christian parents made it easier for young slaves to become Muslims, then the presence of Christian parents could also help children withstand the pressures to convert in captivity. A good example involves two little-known saints, Anthony and Peter, brothers who were martyred sometime between 875 and 886, probably in the Aghlabid capital of Qayrawān in Tunisia.[65] The *Synaxarium of Constantinople* contains a brief biography of the brothers on September 23, though no other hagiographic traditions about them survive. Anthony and Peter were born into a Christian family in Syracuse in Sicily, where they were captured during one of the frequent Arab raids on the island. Muslim marauders and slave traders were a major nuisance at this time and inspired other hagiographic works. The most famous of these is the Greek *Life of Elias the Younger* (d. 903), another young Sicilian who was captured and brought to Muslim North Africa (though not martyred like the two brothers).[66] Along with their father and his companion Andrew, Anthony and Peter were pressed into the service of the Aghlabid court. The *amīr* at the time ordered them "to be educated with Hagarene doctrines," but they continued to practice Christianity in secret. Because of their intelligence and virtue, we are told, Anthony and Peter rose to prominent positions at court, which seems consistent with the Aghlabid practice of elevating Christians or ex-Christians to high-ranking government offices (indeed, there may be echoes of the martyrs in Muslim accounts of a Christian official named Sawāda who was killed by

[65] Delehaye, *Synaxarium*, 72–74; see further, *PMBZ*, ii, I, 217 (Andrew), 276 (Anthony); ii, III, 68–69 (John); ii, V, 373 (Peter); Amari, *Musulmani di Sicilia*, i, 375–76. The author of the *life* states that the martyrs died during the reign of the Byzantine emperor Basil I (r. 867–86). The author also identifies the *amīr* who executed the martyrs as "Abrachēn," almost certainly a Greek transliteration of the Arabic name "Ibrāhīm" (= Ibrāhīm II, r. 261–89/875–902). Given the overlap between the reigns of Basil and Ibrāhīm, the most plausible window for the martyrdom is 875–86. For a later Sicilian martyrdom and extensive discussion of the historical context, see now Mandalà, "Martyrdom of Yūḥannā."

[66] Rossi Taibbi, *Vita di Sant 'Elia il Giovane.*

Ibrāhīm II after refusing to convert to Islam).[67] Anthony was named *genikos*, and Peter was named *sakellarios*, probably referring to high-ranking financial and administrative roles. The *amīr* at the time of their martyrdom, Abū Isḥāq Ibrāhīm II (r. 261–89/875–902)—a man renowned for his violence, according to Muslim sources[68]—eventually discovered their secret and had them tortured and killed.

In a sense, the story of Anthony and Peter contains themes we have already encountered in the biographies of George and Vahan. Like George, they were child captives of apparently low social standing who were forced to convert to Islam. Like Vahan, they were compelled to serve as high-ranking officials of the Muslim state. Interestingly, unlike either George or Vahan, Anthony and Peter remained with their father during their time in captivity. Indeed, John was killed alongside his sons by having his throat slit and his body burned. If there is a significant difference among the three martyrdoms, it is that the continued presence of a Christian parent ensured that the boys never lost complete contact with their Christian roots. Rather, the author of the story implies that, unlike George and Vahan, who are portrayed as rediscovering their Christianity after long stretches of unbelief, the family kept practicing Christianity in private despite embracing Islam in public. Whatever their differences, these martyrs show how conversion and reversion could occur in circumstances of great personal vulnerability, such as when children were forcibly separated from their families and forced to practice the religion of their captors. For many non-Muslims in the early Middle Ages, conversions held out the hope of improving an otherwise miserable lot, and indeed, freed slaves and their descendants quickly found their way into the highest echelons of Muslim society.[69] There must have been some like George, Vahan, Anthony, and Peter, however, who resisted the pressure and left Islam.

III. CONTESTED CONVERSIONS TO ISLAM

Not all conversions in the early Islamic period were as clear-cut. In fact, more than a few martyrs seem to have entered Islam fully without realizing it, at

[67] In 278/891–92, Ibrāhīm II offered administration of the financial department (*dīwān al-kharāj*) to Sawāda on the condition that he convert to Islam. Sawāda refused and, according to Muslim sources, was cut in half and crucified in punishment: Talbi, *Émirat aghlabide*, 286; Mandalà, "Political Martyrdom," 157 n. 19.

[68] Nef, "Violence and the Prince," which does not mention this episode; for more on the reign of Ibrāhīm II, see Talbi, *Émirat aghlabide*, 271–322.

[69] See the example of the poet Abu Nuwās (d. ca. 200/815), in Crone, *Nativist Prophets*, 10–11.

least if their biographies are to be believed.[70] This subset of martyrologies can tell us a great deal about how hagiographers used literary devices to represent conversion. More than this, they testify to the high degree of social and cultural porosity in the Middle East in the generations after the conquests.

ʿAbd al-Masīḥ

A particularly interesting example of contingent conversion is that of ʿAbd al-Masīḥ al-Ghassānī, an abbot of Mt. Sinai who was executed for apostasy in Palestine and whose *life* was later written in Arabic.[71] The date of his execution is a matter of dispute: most scholars have favored Sidney Griffith's argument for the 860s, which he made on the basis of the regnal years of a Jerusalem patriarch named "John" mentioned in the text, whom Griffith identified as John VI (r. 839–43). Griffith also argued that a later date was consistent with what we know about the broader efflorescence of Christian Arabic literature during the ninth century.[72] André Binggeli, however, has recently argued that the martyrdom took place earlier, sometime in the eighth century.[73] According to his view, the patriarch mentioned in the text is not John VI but John V (r. 705–35). If we posit several decades between ʿAbd al-Masīḥ's encounter with the patriarch and his martyrdom, that would mean he died sometime in the 740s or 750s. Binggeli's argument also rests on observations about the Muslim tax regime described in the text, which could only reflect the situation in the eighth century, not in the ninth. Finally, Binggeli points to an important detail in the preface of a tenth- or eleventh-century copy of ʿAbd al-Masīḥ's *life* in British Museum Or. 5019, which states that he was martyred "during the reign of the Umayyads" (Ar. *fī mulk al-umawīya*).[74] It is difficult to say when the biography itself was composed (the earliest manuscript, Sinai Ar. 542, dates to the ninth century), though Binggeli's observations, coupled with the parallels between this *life* and other eighth-century martyrdoms, recommends a dating

[70] I borrow the title of this section from Krstić, *Contested Conversions to Islam*; see also Sizgorich, "Accidental Conversion."

[71] For the version in Sinai Ar. 542, see Griffith, "ʿAbd al-Masīḥ"; with corrections and modifications of the Arabic text in Swanson, "ʿAbd al-Masīḥ"; and a new English translation in Lamoreaux, "Hagiography," 123–28. For references in liturgical calendars, see Sauget, *Synaxaires melkites*, 366–67. For discussion, see *CMR*, i, 684–87; *GCAL*, i, 516–17 (which wrongly claims that the *life* was first written in Greek); Schick, *Christian Communities*, 177; Hoyland, *Seeing Islam*, 381–83; Griffith, "Christians, Muslims, and Neo-martyrs," 187–93; Vila, "Christian Martyrs," 140–60; Chrysostomides, "Religious Code-Switching," 127.

[72] Griffith, "ʿAbd al-Masīḥ," 351–59.

[73] Binggeli, "Hagiographie du Sinaï," 175–77.

[74] Zayyāt, "Shuhadāʾ al-naṣrānīya," 463.

of the incident itself to the mid-eighth century. In general, the text is surprisingly straightforward for a work of hagiography, giving it an aura of historical plausibility.

Born Qays b. Rabīʿ b. Yazīd, the martyr who would later become "ʿAbd al-Masīḥ" hailed from the city of Najrān in southwestern Arabia (a major hub of Christianity in late antiquity, where another group of martyrs famously perished during the 520s[75]) or was descended from Najrānī Christians who had relocated to Syria or Iraq.[76] As Harry Munt has recently shown, Islamic traditions about the expulsion of non-Muslims from the Arabian Peninsula are historically speaking overblown, and indeed, there is evidence of a Christian community carrying on at Najrān until the fourth/tenth century.[77] Ultimately, it is impossible to say where ʿAbd al-Masīḥ grew up, though it is clear that he came from an Arabic-speaking, tribal, and Christian milieu. As a youth, Qays was reportedly very pious, so pious, in fact, that he decided to embark on a pilgrimage to Jerusalem. He was twenty years old at the time. He reportedly set out with a group of Muslim friends who were also "among the people of Najrān." The text does not state why, but Qays never reached the Holy Land. Instead, he traveled with his friends—who "constantly beguiled and misled him"—to the frontier between the caliphate and Byzantium. There, they waged *jihād*, "fighting, killing, plundering, and burning" for the next thirteen years. Qays also lived as a Muslim, for "he trampled every sacred thing as they did and prayed alongside them."[78]

When Qays turned thirty-three,[79] he decided to spend the winter in Baalbek (Gk. Helioupolis), the great Roman city in the Biqāʿ Valley of Lebanon. While there, Qays came across a Christian priest who was reading the Gospel. Curious, he asked what the man was reading, and the priest responded by reciting the following verse aloud: "Whoever loves his mother or father or brother or anything more than me is not worthy of me" (see Matthew 10:37; Luke 14:26). In a scene reminiscent of Athanasius's *Life of Anthony* (as well as the *Confessions* of Saint Augustine), upon hearing these words, Qays burst into tears and begged the priest for forgiveness.[80] He explained how he had joined "the

[75] Beaucamp, Briquel-Chatonnet, and Robin, *Juifs et chrétiens en Arabie*; Sizgorich, "Martyrs of Najrān."

[76] There is a village in the southern Ḥawrān in Syria that was also called "Najrān," and Griffith speculates that this may have been where Najrānī Christians resettled after being expelled from the Arabian Peninsula: Griffith, "ʿAbd al-Masīḥ," 355 n. 81; Dussaud, *Topographie*, 378; see also Lecker, "Najrānī Exiles."

[77] Munt, "Non-Muslims in the Early Islamic Ḥijāz," esp. 259; Fattal, *Statut légal*, 34–36.

[78] Griffith, "ʿAbd al-Masīḥ," 362.

[79] That is, the traditional age given for Jesus at the time of his crucifixion.

[80] White, *Early Christian Lives*, 9; Augustine of Hippo, *Confessions*, 152–53.

enemies" of the Gospel and abandoned Christianity. Upon receiving his absolution, Qays sold his horse and weapons, distributed his money to the poor, and embarked for Jerusalem. From there, he headed to Mar Saba Monastery and became a monk. He continued to Mt. Sinai, where he rose to the rank of *hēgoumenos*, or abbot. At this point, he adopted the name "ʿAbd al-Masīḥ," meaning "Servant of Christ." Years later, while tending to the monastery's financial business in Ramla, ʿAbd al-Masīḥ encountered his old Muslim companions.[81] He announced his conversion to Christianity before the authorities and, after refusing to repent of apostasy, was executed.

The key scenes in the *Life of ʿAbd al-Masīḥ* are his conversion to Islam and his reversion to Christianity. As the text presents it, the martyr's embrace of Islam was rather frivolous: what began as a pilgrimage to the Christian holy sites of Jerusalem somehow morphed into thirteen years of holy war against the Byzantines. It seems that the hagiographer omitted certain details of the story, perhaps in the interest of whitewashing a controversial moment in the *life* of the saint, but the vagueness surrounding his conversion is striking. The text never states that Qays recited the *shahāda* in the company of his Muslim friends, as Islamic law theoretically required, or that he formally renounced Christianity in the way many apostates were expected to do, as we see in the *Chronicle of Zuqnīn*.[82] All the text states is that Qays prayed alongside his Muslim companions (Ar. *wa-ṣallā maʿahum*). It is clear from Qays's emotional return to Christianity years later, however, that he had undergone some kind of religious change, but the nature of this change is left tantalizingly unclear.

As with all hagiography, we should not take the *Life of ʿAbd al-Masīḥ* at face value. Its portrayal of the martyr's conversion is heavily influenced by the agenda of the author. This author was determined to disparage Islam by making ʿAbd al-Masīḥ's conversion appear thoughtless and insignificant. By contrast, the author was determined to portray ʿAbd al-Masīḥ's return to Christianity as heartfelt and sincere, thereby making Christianity seem more legitimate than Islam. For this author—most likely a monk from Mt. Sinai writing within several years of the saint's death—Islam was a false faith that people embraced in the pursuit of worldly thrills, while Christianity was a real faith that people stuck to because of spiritual conviction.

Polemics aside, it is worth thinking more about the dichotomy between the Muslim and Christian phases of the martyr's life. Qays was a young man when he set out for Jerusalem. His biographer would have us believe that he followed his Muslim friends to the borderlands with Byzantium as a result of deception, perhaps also in a fit of adolescent enthusiasm or a desire to be part of the "in

[81] On Ramla in this period, see Avni, *Byzantine-Islamic Transition*, 159–90.
[82] Chabot, *Chronicon anonymum Pseudo-Dionysianum*, ii, 390.

crowd." Perhaps he joined them as a soldier of fortune. Indeed, Qays may have been taking part in the raids (Ar. *ṣawāʾif*) that the Umayyads and ʿAbbasids often launched inside Byzantine territory during the summer months.[83] These were aimed at collecting booty and slaves as much as symbolically cowing the great enemy on the other side of the frontier.

Despite the ideological dimension of these raids, Christians are well known to have taken part in them. As Wadād al-Qāḍī has recently shown, early Muslim armies included large numbers of non-Muslim Arabs who were content to fight under the banner of Islam without necessarily converting.[84] This seems to have been the case especially along the frontier.[85] What makes the account of Qays unique, therefore, is precisely how participating in *jihād* led to his conversion. His conversion is so striking, in fact, that it may help contextualize a spurious-seeming motif that pops up elsewhere in early Muslim literature, in which Christian monks are shown converting to Islam and then waging *jihād* against the Byzantines.[86]

It is useful to remember that Qays's companions probably hailed from the same Arab tribe to which he belonged. In this period, it was not uncommon to find different branches of the same tribe practicing Christianity and Islam. Therefore, in Qays and his friends, we can observe the uneven and surging front of Islamization in the Umayyad period, a process that left people bound together by tribal genealogy but not necessarily by belief. The text underlines this point by invoking certain biblical passages—for example, Matthew 10:37 and Luke 14:26—that emphasize the superiority of spiritual commitments over those of the family. It was also a time when Christian Arabs were increasingly expected to convert to Islam, as evidenced by the stories of the martyrdom of tribal leaders discussed in appendix 1.

Cyrus of Ḥarrān

If ʿAbd al-Masīḥ's conversion was shrouded in mystery, then the circumstances surrounding the conversion of Cyrus of Ḥarrān are even more ambigu-

[83] Brooks, "Byzantines and Arabs"; Bonner, "Arab-Byzantine Frontier"; Haldon and Kennedy, "Arab-Byzantine Frontier."

[84] al-Qāḍī, "Non-Muslims in the Muslim Conquest Army"; see also Khuraysāt, "Dawr al-ʿarab al-mutanaṣṣira fī ʾl-futūḥāt"; Abū Bakr al-Khallāl, *Aḥkām*, 232–34. On the legal discourse concerning whether it is permissible to accept aid from non-Muslims, see Yarbrough, "I'll Not Accept Aid from a *Mushrik*."

[85] Friedmann, *Tolerance and Coercion*, 36; cf. Fattal, *Statut légal*, 232–36.

[86] E.g., Ibn Qutayba, *ʿUyūn al-akhbār*, ii, 297; Ibn ʿAbd Rabbih al-Andalusī, *al-ʿIqd al-farīd*, iii, 167; Abū Nuʿaym al-Iṣfahānī, *Ḥilyat al-awliyāʾ*, vi, 6–7. For discussion, see Sahner, "Monasticism of My Community Is Jihad," 30–31.

ous. Cyrus's *life* constitutes the final section of the *Chronicle of Zuqnīn* and appears within the longer discourse on apostasy with which we began this chapter. The text was probably written within a few years of Cyrus's death, and centuries later, Michael the Syrian included a summary of his *life* in his chronicle. The manuscript leaves containing the *Life of Cyrus*, now housed at the British Library, are heavily damaged, though Amir Harrak's impressive reconstruction can help us assemble a clearer picture of what may have taken place.[87]

Cyrus seems to have been born into a noble Christian family in Ḥarrān sometime in the early to mid-eighth century. His father was reportedly a priest. Cyrus seems to have taken part in an unnamed intra-Muslim conflict. Harrak surmises he may have been an ally of the embattled caliph Marwān b. Muḥammad (r. 127–32/744–50), whose loss at the battle of the Zāb River in 132/750 paved the way for the collapse of the Umayyad dynasty and the victory of the ʿAbbasids.[88] In fact, Harrak speculates that Cyrus may have been a commander of a unit of Christian cavalrymen (Syr. *rīsh farāshē*) at the Zāb.[89]

After toppling the Umayyads, the ʿAbbasids designated Ḥarrān as the administrative capital of the Jazīra (northern Mesopotamia), entrusting it to a governor named Ḥumayd b. Qaḥṭaba al-Ṭāʾī.[90] As the story goes, an unnamed group of locals slandered Cyrus to this official, claiming that he had converted to Islam and then returned to Christianity. Their motivation in doing this is unclear. Harrak speculates that Cyrus's Umayyad loyalties may have posed a threat in a world now run by the ʿAbbasids and that a pro-ʿAbbasid party may have been intent on taking revenge against old Umayyad partisans. Regardless of what caused the grudge, their accusation hinged on the claim that Cyrus had registered himself on the public rolls (Syr. *dūpṭīkīn*, from Gk. *diptycha*) as a Muslim.[91] These may have been the records of the *dīwān*, the official list of Muslims entitled to a share of the government's revenues—in this period,

[87] Harrak, "Martyrdom of Cyrus." For Michael the Syrian, see Chabot, *Chronique*, ii, 527 (Fr.); iv, 476 (Syr.). For a reference in a liturgical calendar, see Peeters, "Rabban Sliba," 151, 180. For discussion, see *BS*, iv, 1; Fattal, *Statut légal*, 165–66; Fiey, *Chrétiens syriaques*, 28; Fiey, *Saints syriaques*, 61; Griffith, *Church in the Shadow of the Mosque*, 148–49; Penn, *Envisioning Islam*, 174–76, which comments that this section of the *Chronicle of Zuqnīn* is unusual among Syriac sources for its intense hostility to Islam.

[88] Harrak, "Martyrdom of Cyrus," 302–7.

[89] On non-Muslims serving in Muslim armies in the early period, see n. 84 above.

[90] al-Ṭabarī, *Annales*, iii, 120.

[91] A process mentioned elsewhere in the *Chronicle of Zuqnīn*: Chabot, *Chronicon anonymum Pseudo-Dionysianum*, ii, 392; with comment in Harrak, *Chronicle of Zuqnīn*, 329 n. 9. Christians were massacred along with Umayyad family members at Nahr Abī Fuṭrus in Palestine in 132/750. This provides corroborating evidence of how Christian allies of the Umayyads also became targets during the ʿAbbasid Revolution: Robinson, "Violence of the Abbasid Revolution," 237–38.

probably meaning taxes, but in earlier periods, the conquest booty.[92] Cyrus denied that he had registered himself as a Muslim. Upon realizing this error, he tried instead to register himself for the *jizya*, the poll tax imposed on non-Muslims, thereby establishing himself as a Christian in the eyes of the law.[93] Initially confused, a Muslim judge refused to let him do this: Cyrus could be a Muslim or a Christian but not both at the same time. Pressuring him to embrace Islam, the judge proclaimed: "[Come up here] now and pray and confess that God is one and He has no [companion and Muḥammad is the servant] of God and His messenger [*wa-rasūlā*] and prophet, and that he is the [seal of the prophets]!"[94]

The judge tried to entice Cyrus with offers of power and riches, but he refused. The judge also goaded Cyrus by reminding him that everyone in the area was rushing to convert to Islam, even the elderly and the priests. The saint countered, proclaiming that if only these wayward Christians understood that "[through their backsliding, they were destroying their souls, they would have never converted]." At his wit's end, the judge had Cyrus thrown into prison. The saint languished there for a time but managed to escape to Edessa, where he found safe haven. Despite this, he felt an urge to confront his tormenters, so just as Vahan returned to Syria and ʿAbd al-Masīḥ returned to Palestine to be martyred, Cyrus eventually headed back to Ḥarrān, where a new governor had him tried and executed in 769.[95]

Did Cyrus actually convert to Islam? This is the central question of his *life*, though the author of the *Chronicle of Zuqnīn* goes to great lengths to portray his "conversion" as coerced and bureaucratic—and therefore inauthentic. Instead, he attributes Cyrus's "conversion" to the calumny of his Muslim enemies, who signed his name on the public rolls so as to embroil him in a legal trap. Michael the Syrian offers a slightly different perspective on what happened when he states that Cyrus converted because of "some illness" (Syr. *ḥashā medem*), not mentioning a Muslim plot.[96] Whether we believe the *Chron-*

[92] However, there is evidence elsewhere in the *Chronicle of Zuqnīn* that the *dīwān* was being abolished at this time, at least in the Jazīra; see Chabot, *Chronicon anonymum Pseudo-Dionysianum*, ii, 381. I thank Luke Yarbrough for suggesting this interpretation.

[93] In Syriac, *gzītā*; for more, see Harrak, "Arabisms," 475.

[94] Here and below, words in English in square brackets indicate Harrak's reconstruction of the damaged text.

[95] The circumstances of Cyrus's actual execution are known only through the *Chronicle of Michael the Syrian*; the folios containing these details in the *Chronicle of Zuqnīn* are damaged beyond repair.

[96] Chabot (*Chronique*, ii, 527) and Harrak ("Martyrdom of Cyrus," 298) both favor "passion" as a translation for *ḥashā*; cf. Payne Smith, *Compendious Syriac Dictionary*, 160. I have chosen "illness" because it captures the involuntarily aspect of the conversion that Michael clearly wished to convey.

icle of Zuqnīn that outsiders were at fault or the *Chronicle of Michael the Syrian* that Cyrus's illness was responsible, we can detect the outlines of a campaign to exonerate Cyrus of any wrongdoing. Given that he was later considered a saint, perhaps he had to be portrayed as a victim of an insidious power outside himself. In fact, one is tempted to imagine that the historical Cyrus may have been a more willing convert to Islam than his hagiography lets on. Could it be that Cyrus actually became a Muslim of his own free will, only to return to Christianity and be killed? If this is so, we can imagine how and why later biographers may have wished to airbrush the incident so as to burnish his credentials as a martyr.

At the same time, it is not inconceivable that Cyrus did actually convert without realizing it. We know from other hagiographic texts of the period—including the *lives* of ʿAbd al-Masīḥ and Elias of Helioupolis—that contingent conversions were not uncommon (or at least Christian authors strove to portray conversions to Islam as contingent). Such contested conversions seem to have been the unintended side effect of the process of conversion to Islam more broadly, which could be loose and ambiguous in comparison with standard forms of Christian conversion in late antiquity. While converts may have been moved by interior convictions, the manner in which they instantiated their conversions was through a set of public gestures that were open to interpretation and dispute. These included adopting new Muslim names, trading one set of taxes for another, or, as we see in the *Life of Cyrus*, registering oneself in a different set of government records. This accords well with much sociological research on conversion, which emphasizes the importance of changes to physical appearance, naming, and political status in order to embody a new religious identity.[97]

To make an analogy to Muslim theology and law, conversion to Islam in this period was often a *ẓāhirī* (exterior, literal), not a *bāṭinī* (interior, private), process. That is, religious change was represented through outward signs of membership in a new community but not necessarily through outward signs of new faith. The historian al-Narshakhī (d. 348/959) highlighted this problem in his history of Bukhāra in Transoxania, remarking on the Zoroastrian converts of the city at the time of the Arab conquest "who accepted Islam on the outside [NP. *bi ẓāhir*] but worshipped idols in private [*bi bāṭin*]."[98] Along these lines, M. J. Kister once noted that converts to Islam before the Ridda Wars used to recite a single *shahāda*—"There is no god but God"—but in later periods were forced to recite a double *shahāda*—"There is no god but God, Muḥammad is the messenger of God" (and sometimes also renounce their old beliefs). They

[97] Rambo and Farhadian, *Oxford Handbook of Religious Conversion*, 8.
[98] al-Narshakhī, *Tārīkh-i Bukhārā*, 57.

did so once it became clear that people were converting to Islam without actually professing the most distinctive element of Islamic monotheism, that is, belief in the revelation of the Prophet Muḥammad.[99] Once again, we are reminded of al-Ṭabarī's comment concerning what made a "Muslim" in seventh-century Ctesiphon: "whoever prays as we do, who prays [while] facing the [proper] direction as we do, and eats meat ritually butchered as we do."[100] There is nothing in this formulation to suggest orthodox Muslim belief, at least by the standards of later periods; rather, the concern is for acting in accordance with a set of outward markers of identity that could easily be confused with those of another religion.

Such a gap between action and belief can also help us understand why Cyrus may have taken on the appearance of a Muslim in public without necessarily assenting to Islam in private. This is especially true if we consider that the text's author was determined to discredit conversion to Islam by prying apart categories of "real belief" and "outward belonging." Here, we should recall Richard Bulliet's comment that many conversions in the postconquest period were "social conversions"—that is, changes in religion that also entailed the wholesale renunciation of old identities and communities.[101] As we can see in the case of Cyrus, however, some conversions may have been more akin to wardrobe changes: quickly executed, easily reversed, and sometimes difficult to detect. This may have been a special problem in a place such as Ḥarrān, the notorious last bastion of paganism in the Islamic Middle East, a fact that is mentioned in the *Life of Cyrus* several times.[102] Because of its great mix of peoples, conversion and social porosity may have been features of everyday life in Ḥarrān to a greater extent than in other, more homogeneous corners of the caliphate. This, in turn, may have set the stage for Cyrus's apostasy and death.

Elias of Helioupolis

The most dramatic case of disputed conversion in the early Islamic period is that of Elias of Helioupolis,[103] who was executed for apostasy in Damascus

[99] Kister, "*Illā bi-ḥaqqihi*"; on this phenomenon in later periods, see Chrysostomides, "Religious Code-Switching," 118–21.

[100] al-Ṭabarī, *Annales*, i, 2020.

[101] Bulliet, *Conversion to Islam*, 33–42.

[102] Harrak, "Martyrdom of Cyrus," 318, lines 34–35, 38; for comparison, see the *Book of Governors* of Thomas of Marga, in which a monk coaxes a demon from a Muslim woman that then announces its intention to go to Ḥarrān (in Arabic, no less!): Budge, *Book of Governors*, i, 288 (Syr.); ii, 517 (Eng.).

[103] *SPSH*, i, 42–59; also *CMLT*, 155–222; McGrath, "Elias of Heliopolis" (Eng. trans.). For discus-

in 779, a decade after Cyrus's martyrdom.[104] His biography was written in a very simple Greek style—linguistic features of which suggest that the author may have been a native speaker of a Semitic language such as Aramaic or Arabic—and survives in a unique manuscript now housed at the Bibliothèque Nationale in Paris. This manuscript, Coislin 303, was copied in Constantinople in the tenth century and contains several other martyrologies of Syro-Palestinian origin, as discussed in the introduction.[105] We know very little about the origins of the text: in the preface, its anonymous author states that he wrote two other accounts (Gk. *dusin historiais*), though he provides no clues about their contents.[106] The text was probably written near Damascus shortly after the events it describes. A collection of miracles follows the account of the martyrdom, and given the somewhat rough transition from the first section to the second, it seems that the text as it survives today was written in two phases.[107]

Unlike other new martyr cults from the region, that of Elias does not seem to have spread much beyond the borders of the caliphate. None of the Byzantine *synaxaria* mention him; his *life* does not refer to any Byzantine emperors or bishops (as was customary with other Levantine saints who became popular abroad[108]); and the only reference to a cult beyond the *life* itself is an entry in the Melkite Palestinian Georgian calendar of the tenth century.[109] In other

sion, see *CMR*, i, 916–18; *BHG*, i, 177; *BS*, iv, 1046–47; *BSO*, i, 754; *PMBZ*, i, I, 474–77; Bréhier, "Chrétiens de Palestine," 70–71; Hoyland, *Seeing Islam*, 363–65; Vila, "Christian Martyrs," 266–78; Foss, "Byzantine Saints," 107–9; Tannous, "Syria," 449; Chrysostomides, "Religious Code-Switching," 122–23; Sizgorich, "Dancing Martyr."

[104] The date of Elias's execution is a matter of dispute: the author states that he died in the year 6287. According to the Byzantine *anno mundi* system, this would correspond to AD 779; according to the Alexandrian *anno mundi* system, however, this would correspond to AD 795. The text seems to offer a solution when it states that the governor of Damascus at the time of the martyrdom was named Muḥammad and was a cousin of the caliph al-Mahdī. Given that al-Mahdī reigned as caliph from 158/775 until 169/785, 779 would appear to be the more likely date; see *SPSH*, i, 51; Grumel, *Chronologie*, 249–50.

[105] Binggeli, "Réception de l'hagiographie palestinienne à Byzance."

[106] *SPSH*, i, 42.

[107] *SPSH*, i, 53–59 (§§ 18–26); cf. McGrath, "Elias of Heliopolis," 102 n. 52.

[108] Notably the *Life of Bacchus*; e.g., *CMLT*, 61, 66 (mention of Irene and Constantine IV), 79–80 (reference to dialect among "the people of Constantinople").

[109] Garitte, *Calendrier palestino-géorgien*, 48, 151. Several scholars have claimed that Elias of Helioupolis also appears in the thirteenth-century Miaphysite calendar of Rabban Ṣlībā (Peeters, "Rabban Sliba," 174 n. 18; cf. McGrath, "Elias of Heliopolis," 86; Fiey, *Saints syriaques*, 73) under the name "Elias, a new martyr [Syr. *sāhdā ḥadtā*] from Beth Qūsaynā," but they cannot be the same person. Beth Qūsaynā was near the village of Ḥaḥ, the hometown of Rabban Ṣlībā, forty miles northeast of Mārdīn (see Joseph, *Beth Qustan*). Elias the martyr was born in Helioupolis and died in Damascus. This discrepancy undermines McGrath's claim that Elias may have been a Miaphysite or was commemorated in the Miaphysite church. He was clearly a Melkite.

words, the cult of Elias was a local Syrian affair. One of the most striking features of the text is also its focus on the laity: monks and priests, who are usually the stars of the martyrologies, are all but invisible in the *Life of Elias*. This, coupled with its simple literary style, may indicate that it was written by and for subelites. Indeed, it is the only martyrdom narrative from the period with such a clear interest in the life of the laity.

According to the text, Elias was around ten years old when he set out from his native Helioupolis (Ar. Baalbek) for Damascus. The year was 769, and he was accompanied by his mother and brothers. While in Helioupolis, Elias had trained as a carpenter, manufacturing wooden plows for farmers. Helioupolis, where the martyr ʿAbd al-Masīḥ had also undergone his conversion to Christianity decades earlier, was no backwater in the early ʿAbbasid period.[110] By the same token, it was also not a suitable home for an ambitious Christian family. A big city such as Damascus, by contrast, was a place where a rural family could make its fortune and "live more easily," as the text puts it.[111]

Upon arriving in the former Umayyad capital, Elias found work making camel saddles in the shop of a "certain man of the Syrian race" (Gk. *tina syron men onta tō genei*), a Christian who was probably a native speaker of an Aramaic dialect. Eventually, this man decided to convert to Islam under the patronage of the workshop's owner, a wealthy Arab Muslim (though the latter's religion is never stated explicitly). The *life* describes the Syrian as a *parasitos* of the Arab, meaning "one who clings," possibly a Greek translation of the Arabic term *mawlā*, or "client."[112] As is well known from Islamic law, non-Arab converts in this period had to secure the patronage of Arab Muslims if they wished to integrate into Muslim society. Thus, the *Life of Elias* provides an interesting image of the institution of *walāʾ* from a Christian perspective, a portrait we can find in other texts from the eighth century, including the *Chronicle of Zuqnīn*.[113]

One night, the son of this wealthy Arab decided to throw a birthday party for his own infant son and called upon Elias to serve as an attendant. The Muslims of Damascus heckled Elias throughout the night, asking why he was not a Muslim and inviting him to convert and join them as an equal. Elias managed to deflect their taunts, and the guests soon relented, allowing him to

[110] Griffith, "ʿAbd al-Masīḥ," 362–64. The relics of the martyr Vahan were also rumored to have been sent to Helioupolis: Gatteyrias, "Martyre de saint Vahan," 210–11. On Christians in this region in the early ʿAbbasid period, see Cobb, *White Banners*, 112–15. The inventor of Greek fire in this period was reportedly a Christian from Helioupolis: Hoyland, *Theophilus*, 168.

[111] *SPSH*, i, 45.

[112] *SPSH*, i, 45.

[113] Chabot, *Chronicon anonymum Pseudo-Dionysianum*, ii, 390; cf. Harrak, "Arabisms," 478.

celebrate with them regardless of his religion. One of the guests even managed to coax the young Christian onto the dance floor. This person then furtively loosened the boy's belt, allegedly to allow him freer movement as he danced (possibly in a veiled attempt at sexual seduction). But in the process of stripping away this belt, the Muslim removed what was also regarded as a public marker of his Christian faith—in effect, converting Elias to Islam without his realizing what had happened.[114]

The next morning, with the "dinner of the wicked plot" complete and the guests still nursing their headaches, Elias departed to pray. One bleary-eyed partygoer noticed him leaving and asked where he was going. Elias explained that he was headed to church, but the guest stared at him in bewilderment and asked, "Did you not deny your faith last night?"[115] Suddenly realizing what had happened, Elias rushed away in haste and fear: the accidental Muslim was now the accidental apostate, and he sensed that he was in grave danger of arrest. Elias immediately sought the advice of his employer, the Syrian foreman who had converted to Islam. At first, this man assured Elias that no harm would befall him, but he advised him to lie low and wait for the storm to pass. In the meantime, Elias's family approached the foreman in search of what they claimed to be the boy's unpaid wages. Insulted by this request, the foreman threatened to expose the boy's apostasy if they did not relent. Sensing danger on all sides, Elias returned to Helioupolis. Eight years later, now around twenty, he came back to Damascus expecting memories of his crime to have disappeared. Old grudges, however, die hard, so when Elias bumped into the foreman and again raised the matter of his unpaid wages, the foreman flew into a rage and handed him over to the authorities. After a lengthy trial and torture, Elias was executed for apostasy.

As with the *Life of Cyrus*, the key question is whether Elias actually converted to Islam. Again, one wonders whether there is a gap between the Elias of hagiography and the Elias of history, specifically whether a genuine conversion was made to appear coerced and accidental. The story is so dramatic and filled with hagiographic motifs that it is easy to imagine how it might have been written to portray a real convert as the unwitting victim of a Muslim plot. Regardless, the fact that Elias could be perceived as converting simply by removing an article of clothing reveals something important about how religious identity was signaled in public settings and how this identity, in turn, could be gravely misunderstood.

[114] Banquet scene: *SPSH*, i, 45–46.

[115] On the question of conversion while intoxicated, see Ibn Qudāma, *Mughnī*, xii, 148–50; for an Ottoman example, see Krstić, *Contested Conversions to Islam*, 146–47, 210.

It is well known that Muslims and non-Muslims sometimes struggled to differentiate themselves from one another. This was especially true in places such as Egypt and Syria, where Muslims remained a demographic minority for generations after the conquests. We can sense the risks and anxieties this provoked in a *ḥadīth* made famous by M. J. Kister: "Whoever imitates a people is one of them" (Ar. *man tashabbaha bi-qawm fa-huwa minhum*).[116] One way Muslims resisted the threat of imitation was by embracing practices perceived as opposite to those of Christians and other non-Muslims. Thus, a related group of *ḥadīth* exhorted Muslims to "do things differently" than those around them (*khālifūhum*).[117] This applied to a range of quotidian concerns, including dress, hairstyles, handshaking, and horseback riding. These behaviors formed the basis of the "Pact of ʿUmar" (Ar. *ʿahd ʿUmar*), laws that were allegedly based on the peace agreements contracted by ʿUmar b. al-Khaṭṭāb (r. 13–23/634–44) and the Christians of the Near East during the conquests. To read the *shurūṭ* and the *ḥadīth* alongside the *Life of Elias* is to realize the common dilemma to which they all respond: the superficial similarity of Muslims and non-Muslims in a world in which Muslims constituted a minority and in which a growing number of Muslims were themselves converts from non-Muslim non-Arab backgrounds.

This created an environment in which religious and ethnic identities were often overlapping. Not surprisingly, community leaders on both sides of the divide strove to disentangle their flocks, lest they lose all sense of distinctiveness in this soup of similarity. As Thomas Sizgorich remarked, what the *Life of Elias* attempts to do is not merely to valorize martyrdom but to warn its readers about "social promiscuity, the creeping dangers of family affection, perilous intercommunal friendships, and deadly seductions."[118] The Greek *life* of the latter-day saint Lazarus of Mt. Galesion (d. 1053) sums up these same concerns by advising its readers, "Do not make friends with the Saracens," mirroring the famous words of the Qur'an, "Do not take Jews and Christians as friends" (Q. *al-Māʾida* 5:51).[119]

The *Life of Elias* revolves around the removal and replacement of the martyr's belt: just as Elias allegedly became a Muslim when his belt was taken off, he later affirmed his Christian belief by refastening his belt in prison.[120] The Greek term here is *zōnē*, which is related to the Syriac word *zūnārā* and the

[116] Kister, "Do Not Assimilate Yourselves."

[117] Zayyāt, "Simāt al-naṣārā"; Noth, "Problems of Differentiation"; Levy-Rubin, *From Surrender to Coexistence*, 58–98; Yarbrough, "Origins of the *Ghiyār*."

[118] Sizgorich, "Accidental Conversion," 172–73.

[119] Greenfield, *Life of Lazaros*, 104.

[120] *SPSH*, i, 53–54.

Arabic *zunnār*.[121] Many recensions of the Pact of ʿUmar mention the *zunnār* alongside the *minṭaqa*, a special belt that only Muslims were supposed to wear.[122] The history of the *zunnār* is complicated and hotly debated: long ago, A. S. Tritton noted that monks in late antiquity wore girdles around their waists and therefore, after the conquests, the *zunnār* became the distinguishing article of clothing for Christians par excellence.[123] More recently, Milka Levy-Rubin has traced the origins of the *zunnār* to the religiously affiliated belts that Jews and Zoroastrians had to wear in the Sasanian Empire.[124] Mark Cohen has also argued that the *zunnār* was an ambiguous symbol in early Islamic society, for it had once been a prestige object for Christians, as in the relic of the cincture of the Virgin Mary.[125] After Islam, however, the *zunnār* was transformed into a symbol of Christians' subordination under the new regime.

Given its importance in Islamic law, it is no surprise that the removal of the *zunnār* was interpreted as the supreme gesture of conversion. The *Chronicle of Zuqnīn*, for example, mentions a deacon in Edessa who removed his belt and prayed in the direction of Mecca as the final gesture of his apostasy away from Christianity.[126] By the same token, refastening the *zunnār* was one way in which individuals signaled their conversion to Christianity, as we see with the martyr Dioscorus and the Muslim convert Ibn Rajāʾ.[127] Zoroastrian converts could also signal their apostasy from Islam by refastening their sacred girdle, known in Middle Persian as the *kustīg*.[128]

The removal and replacement of the *zunnār* was a symptom of a much bigger problem. Elias did not "convert" to Islam in the light of day by uttering the *shahāda* before Muslim witnesses.[129] His "conversion" took place during a

[121] Tritton, "Zunnār," *EI²*, xi, 571–72; Stillman, Stillman, and Majda, "Libās," *EI²*, v, 736; Fattal, *Statut légal*, 97–98.

[122] ʿUmar b. ʿAbd al-ʿAzīz forbade the Christians of Syria from wearing the *minṭaqa*: ʿAbd al-Razzāq, *Muṣannaf*, vi, 61, no. 10004.

[123] Tritton, *Non-Muslim Subjects*, 115–26. The impression is confirmed by the fact that some Jews saw the *zunnār* as being exclusively for Christians: Goitein, *Mediterranean Society*, iv, 398 n. 70; and some Christians were given nicknames connected to the *zunnār*, e.g., "Ibn Zanānīrīya": al-Nābulusī, *Sword of Ambition*, 63, 219.

[124] Levy-Rubin, *From Surrender to Coexistence*, 90–91, 154–57.

[125] Cohen, "Origins of the Distinctive Dress Regulation"; Cohen, *Under Crescent and Cross*, 62–64. I am grateful to Mark Cohen for sharing his unpublished article with me.

[126] Chabot, *Chronicon anonymum Pseudo-Dionysianum*, ii, 391. For discussion, see Harrak, "Christianity in the Eyes of the Muslims," 342–43; cf. Zayyāt, "Simāt al-naṣārā," 200–216.

[127] Dioscorus: Basset, "Synaxaire arabe jacobite" (1922), 846; Ibn Rajāʾ: Atiya, Abd al-Masih, and Burmester, *History of the Patriarchs*, 106.

[128] Choksy, *Conflict and Cooperation*, 41, 89; cf. Choksy, *Purity and Pollution*, 54–55, 62–67; Kiel and Skjærvø, "Apostasy and Repentance."

[129] Compare the "conversion" of Rudericus of Córdoba (d. 857), a priest who tried to intervene in a dispute between his two brothers, one of whom was a Christian and the other a Muslim. The

nighttime party pulsing with alcohol and song. There, wealthy Arab Muslims rubbed shoulders with poor Aramaic-speaking Christians, who served them food and drink. One wonders whether Elias, a child from a small agricultural city, was unprepared for the challenges he faced in Damascus. Furthermore, one is tempted to see Elias and his family as examples of peasants who fled the land during the Umayyad and early ʿAbbasid periods, whose clashes with the Muslim authorities are well documented in Arabic sources.[130] These were *mawālī* and non-Muslims who abandoned their farms to escape the crippling tax burden imposed on them by the state. They often flocked to Muslim cities and if they found work, settled there permanently—a trend reflected in early *ḥadīth* about how to cope with non-Muslims living inside the garrison cities (Ar. *amṣār*), which were supposed to be *dhimmī*-free.[131] We know from Muslim sources that the authorities also returned peasants to their lands, lest their tax base contract. Other Christian peasants, however, managed to stay put and made a life for themselves in Muslim metropoles. Still, even if they succeeded in eking out a living in the city, many probably remained naive about how to navigate the urban jungles in which they lived. Here, the constant mixing of Muslims and Christians undermined religious and ethnic markers that had been forged in more homogeneous areas in the countryside.

Failing to master the rules of engagement in the cities could be disastrous for such lay Christians, as Elias learned. His experience also underscores a point that will surface in other martyrdom stories later: the machinery for punishing apostasy tended not to engage unless activated by another conflict—usually of a social or economic nature—that superimposed onto it. In other words, religious infractions were usually not enough to get an apostate in trouble with the authorities; it took another dispute to throw gasoline on the flames and generate a real conflagration.

IV. CONVERSION AND RELIGIOUSLY MIXED FAMILIES

Although outright conversion was the most powerful engine of Islamization in the postconquest period, another important accelerator of change was

brothers turned on him and beat him ferociously. When Rudericus recovered several days later, he found that his Muslim brother had notified the authorities that he had converted; see *CSM*, ii, 488–90.

[130] Dennett, *Conversion and the Poll Tax*, 35, 40; Crone, *Slaves on Horses*, 51–52; Crone, *Nativist Prophets*, 13. This mirrors the practice of *anachōrēsis* in ancient Egypt, in which peasants sought to escape the crippling fiscal burdens of the state by fleeing from their villages to the desert; see Posener, "L'ἀναχώρησις dans l'Égypte pharaonique."

[131] ʿAbd al-Razzāq, *Muṣannaf*, vi, 59–60.

marriage between Muslims and non-Muslims (and so it remains today).[132] We can uniquely observe this fascinating but poorly understood phenomenon through Christian hagiography. Intermarriage was once very common in the Middle East, especially during periods in which Islam constituted a minority faith. In some ways, it was a demographic inevitability that Muslims would intermarry and procreate with the conquered peoples; and as Simon Barton recently remarked in the case of al-Andalus, it was also a shrewd strategy aimed at legitimizing Muslim rule by integrating themselves with the subject population.[133] The laws governing religiously mixed unions were clear, at least on the Muslim side: Muslim men were free to marry up to four women from the People of the Book (cf. Q. *al-Māʾida* 5:5), but under no circumstances could Muslim women marry non-Muslim men.[134] This prohibition seems to have been honored for the most part, since there are remarkably few examples of marriages between Muslim women and non-Muslim men in historical sources of the period.[135]

There were several problems with this type of union.[136] For one, it violated the pre-Islamic Arab concept of *kafāʾa*, that is, compatibility between husband and wife, in which a woman was discouraged from marrying a man of lower social standing (e.g., a slave, a man from an inferior tribe, etc.). The second problem is related to the Muslim perception of marriage as a form of female enslavement. If a woman is bound to her husband as a slave is to a master, then it is unacceptable for her to be subordinate to a member of an infidel faith. These specific rules were not necessarily consolidated at the beginning of Islamic history, of course, but over time, they reflected medieval Islam's more general disposition toward social and political dominance. As the Prophet is alleged to have said: "Islam is exalted and nothing is exalted above it" (Ar. *al-islām yaʿlūw wa-lā yuʿlā*).

If a father or both parents converted to Islam after the children were born, Islamic law automatically regarded their offspring as Muslims—provided their

[132] Schacht, *Introduction to Islamic Law*, 132; Fattal, *Statut légal*, 129–37; Shatzmiller, "Women's Conversion"; Nirenberg, *Communities of Violence*, 127–65; Friedmann, *Tolerance and Coercion*, 160–93; El-Leithy, "Coptic Culture," 91–97, 217–41; Tannous, "Syria," 524–41; Safran, *Defining Boundaries*, 103–6, 125–67; Barton, *Conquerors, Brides, and Concubines*; Simonsohn, "Communal Membership despite Religious Exogamy." On the role of intermarriage in Islamization today, see Fargues, "Demographic Islamization," 114.

[133] Barton, *Conquerors, Brides, and Concubines*, 17.

[134] Friedmann, *Tolerance and Coercion*, 162–64; cf. Abū Bakr al-Khallāl, *Aḥkām*, 167–68.

[135] Among the martyrs, the only examples are Walabonsus and Maria of Córdoba, who were born to a Christian father and a Muslim mother who converted to Christianity; see *CSM*, ii, 412; and n. 181 below. On what to do if a *dhimmī* commits adultery with a Muslim woman, see Abū Bakr al-Khallāl, *Aḥkām*, 264–67.

[136] Friedmann, *Tolerance and Coercion*, 161–62; Tsafrir, "Attitude of Sunnī Islam," 331; Ali, *Marriage and Slavery*, esp. 29–64, 164–86.

parents' conversion took place before they reached the age of legal majority (seven or ten years old depending on the *madhhab* in question). If their parents' conversion took place after, however, they were free to choose their religion.[137] In a striking break with the law's normally uncompromising opposition to apostasy, scholars such as Abū Ḥanīfa (d. 150/767) ruled that apostates who had first entered Islam because of a parent's conversion should not necessarily be executed for their crime. Rather, they should be spared death because of the presumed weakness of their Muslim faith, which had been imposed on them in childhood and not chosen freely in adulthood.[138]

While Islamic law provided relatively clear guidelines about religiously mixed marriages, it offered little advice about how religiously mixed households should be run. We can sense the regular dilemmas such families faced in the *responsa* of Aḥmad b. Ḥanbal (d. 241/855) as redacted by Abū Bakr al-Khallāl (d. 311/923).[139] For instance, Ibn Ḥanbal was asked whether a Christian woman who had died bearing the child of a Muslim man should be buried in a Christian or Muslim cemetery. He was also asked who was responsible for betrothing a Christian girl to her Muslim husband—her Christian father or her Muslim brother; whether Muslim and Christian children inherited equally from their Christian parents; and whether a Muslim son was entitled to take part in the funeral of his non-Muslim mother.[140] These queries—echoed in other early legal sources[141]—reveal a world of the most intimate kinds of mixing, in which families bound together by blood might also find themselves divided by religion.

For their part, Christian clergy frowned upon intermarriage, following Saint Paul's famous warning against "being bound together with the unbelievers" (2 Corinthians 6:14). At the same time, Christians were subjects of a land they did not rule and, therefore, had to accept the marriage of Christian women to Muslim men as a melancholy fact of life. Still, prominent Christian leaders such as the West Syrian bishop Jacob of Edessa (d. 708) tried to limit religiously mixed marriages and failing this, strove to keep the Christian wives of Muslim men inside the church. In a telling exchange from Jacob's canons, we learn that it was customary among some clergy to bar such women from

[137] Abū Bakr al-Khallāl, *Aḥkām*, 39–41. See also Fernández Félix, "Children on the Frontiers," 62–65; Zorgati, *Hybrid Identities*, 48–74.

[138] Friedmann, *Tolerance and Coercion*, 134.

[139] On these *responsa*, see now Al Sarhan, "Responsa of Aḥmad Ibn Ḥanbal."

[140] Abū Bakr al-Khallāl, *Aḥkām*, 149, 151 (betrothal), 218–20 (funerals), 220–23 (cemeteries), 331–32 (inheritance).

[141] ʿAbd al-Razzāq, *Muṣannaf*, iii, 528 (cemeteries); vi, 24–27 (inheritance), 36–38 (funerals); x, 344–50 (inheritance).

Communion.[142] Jacob, however, urged his petitioner Addai to admit these women to the Eucharist, believing that it was better to bend the rules and preserve these women as Christians than to slavishly follow the rules and cast them out, thereby increasing the risk of their becoming Muslims.

Bacchus

One of the most detailed portraits of a religiously mixed family is the *life* of the martyr Bacchus, who was executed for apostasy in 787–88 (Figure 1.1). The text survives in several Greek manuscripts, the earliest of which dates to the late ninth or early tenth century. According to its editors, Stephanos Efthymiadis and André Binggeli, the surviving recension is a product of Constantinople, not Palestine.[143] An earlier version of the text was probably composed inside the caliphate—perhaps at Mar Saba—shortly after the martyr's death, and this version served as the basis of the one written in the imperial capital.[144] Indeed, the feast of Bacchus is recorded in the *Synaxarium of Constantinople*, as well as the Melkite Syriac calendar edited by Binggeli and the Palestinian Georgian calendar edited by Garritte, suggesting that he was venerated by the Melkites of Syro-Palestine as well.[145] Thus, we see in Bacchus an unusual example of a Syrian neomartyr who won admirers on both sides of the imperial frontier (unlike the contemporary Elias of Helioupolis, whose cult was firmly anchored in the Levant).[146]

[142]For Syriac text and translation, see Tannous, "Syria," 470 n. 1120. Compare the matter of whether it is permissible for Christians to eat meat slaughtered by Muslims, addressed by Athanasius of Balad (d. 687): Nau, "Littérature canonique," 128–30; and more generally, Freidenreich, *Foreigners and Their Food.* See also Armenian discussions of intermarriage and food from the 760s: Mardirossian, "Synode de Partaw," 124, 126; Vacca, "Creation of an Islamic Frontier in Armīniya," 161.

[143]*CMLT*, 61–154; with a new edition and translation being prepared by Binggeli and Efthymiadis; for a shorter version of the text and Byzantine hymnography, see Dēmētrakopoulos, "Hagios Bakchos." For discussion, see *CMR*, i, 597–99; *BHG*, i, 75; *BS*, ii, 688; *BSO*, i, 331; *PMBZ*, i, I, 236–38; Bréhier, "Chrétiens de Palestine," 71–72; Schick, *Christian Communities*, 176; Hoyland, *Seeing Islam*, 346; Griffith, "Christians, Muslims, and Neo-martyrs," 196–98; Vila, "Christian Martyrs," 287–96; Swanson, "ʿAbd al-Masīḥ," 117–18; Foss, "Byzantine Saints," 116–17; Tannous, "Syria," 537–40; Chrysostomides, "Religious Code-Switching," 123–25 (this and the prior work consult the version in Dēmētrakopoulos). For more on the text's origins in Constantinople, see Flusin, "Palestinian Hagiography," 216; Binggeli, "Réception de l'hagiographie palestinienne à Byzance."

[144]See especially the section in praise of Jerusalem: *CMLT*, 104–5.

[145]Delehaye, *Synaxarium*, 310–12 (December 15); Binggeli, "Calendrier melkite de Jérusalem," 191; Garitte, *Calendrier palestino-géorgien*, 59, 197 (April 11), possibly also 110, 410 (December 15, "Bacchus the Neomartyr"), 111, 414–15 ("Bacchus the Monk").

[146]Like Peter of Capitolias (d. 715); see chapter 3, sec. III.

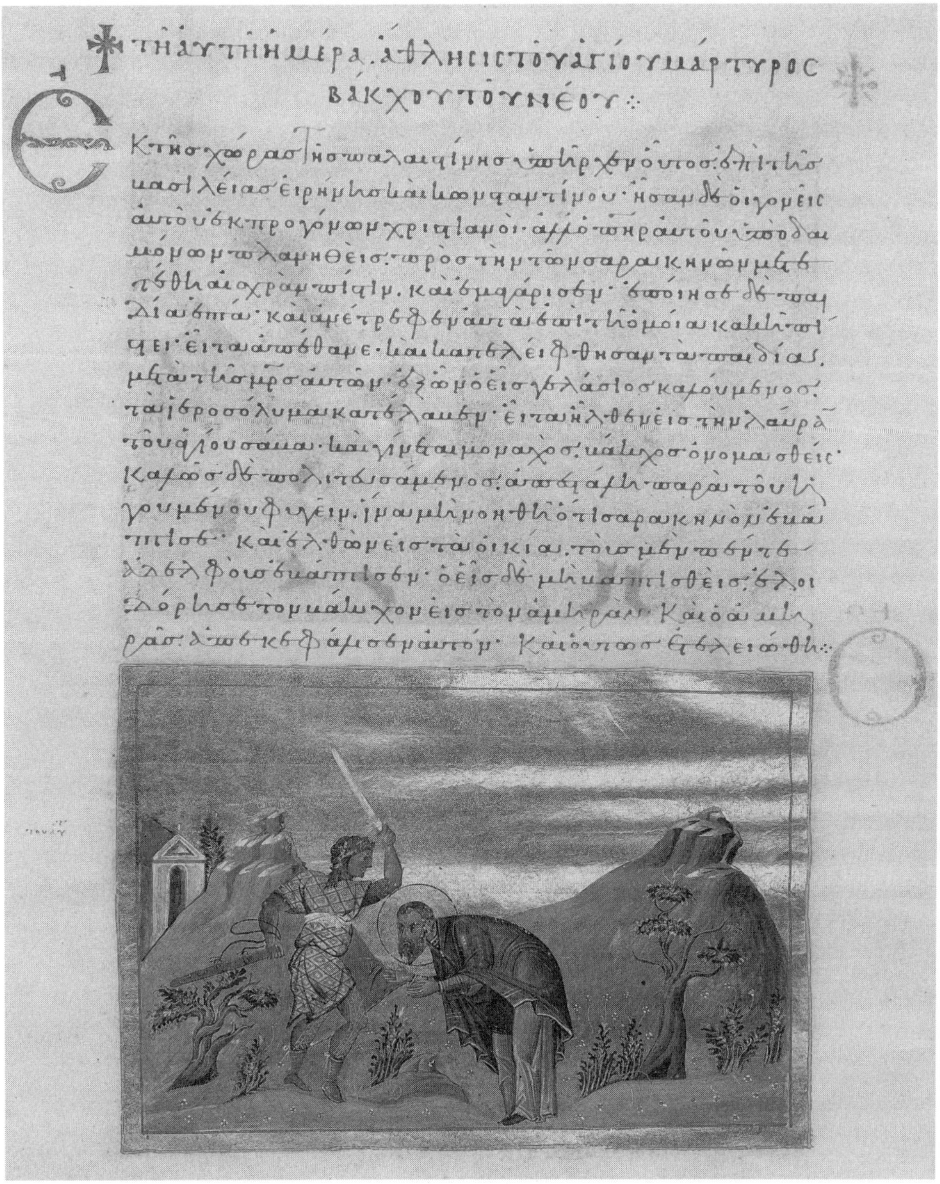
ΤΗ ΑΥΤΗ ΗΜΕΡΑ. ΑΘΛΗΣΙΣ ΤΟΥ ΑΓΙΟΥ ΜΑΡΤΥΡΟΣ
ΒΑΚΧΟΥ ΤΟΥ ΝΕΟΥ

Figure 1.1. Bacchus, *Menologion of Basil II*, Vat. Gr. 1613 (11th c.), fol. 253r. Photo: Biblioteca Apostolica Vaticana.

According to his *life*, Bacchus was born in the city of Maiouma, just north of Gaza along the coast of Palestine. His parents were Christians, but sometime after his birth, it seems, his father converted to Islam. As the text puts it:

> Having been ensnared by satanic baits and attracted by their wicked counsels, he abandoned the sacred religion of the Christians and came into the foul religion of the Hagarenes. He mingled with the pagans [Gk. *migeis en tois ethnesi*] and learned to perform their rites.[147]

Bacchus's mother remained a Christian, as was her right under the law. The couple had seven children, and when they came of age, they were duly betrothed to Muslim spouses. Bacchus's mother grieved deeply for her husband's loss and for that of her children. "She used to frequent the churches of the Christians in secret," the text tells us, "beseeching God to be separated from her husband's filthy intercourse [*tēs musaras chōristhēnai tou andros epimixias*] and to be joined with the church of the Christians."[148] She would even anoint her children with holy oil she received at nearby churches, marking them as a "foretaste . . . of the divine baptism."[149]

Her third child was a boy with the Arab name of "Ḍaḥḥāk" (Gk. Dachak), which the Greek biographer correctly translates as "Gelasios," meaning "Jester," or "the one who laughs."[150] Ḍaḥḥāk refused to marry when he came of age and expressed his desire to convert to Christianity instead. This seems to have been his lifelong wish, but Ḍaḥḥāk was not free to act upon it for fear of his Muslim father. Therefore, he worshipped as a Christian in secret, "like a spark that lays unseen in a pile of ash, waiting for its time to be revealed."[151] Ḍaḥḥāk was greatly relieved when his father eventually died. The text portrays this man in the grimmest of terms: "Having carried on in his filthy mania and having lived [his life] in the Hagarene way, he was torn from life and died in his own madness."[152] The father's demise gave Ḍaḥḥāk the chance to finally pursue his dream of becoming a Christian. His mother rejoiced when he told her his plans and blessed him as he headed to Jerusalem to be baptized. Upon reaching the holy city, Ḍaḥḥāk went straight to the Church of the Holy Sepulcher, where he beseeched God "not to loathe me, a stranger."[153] Wild-eyed and streaked with tears, Ḍaḥḥāk caught the attention of a visiting monk from Mar Saba. At

147 *CMLT*, 66–67.
148 *CMLT*, 67.
149 *CMLT*, 67–68.
150 *CMLT*, 69.
151 *CMLT*, 70.
152 *CMLT*, 70–71.
153 *CMLT*, 75.

first, the monk chastised the young Muslim for having entered a Christian holy site. But upon learning Ḍaḥḥāk's story, he took pity on him and brought him to the monastery.

The abbot of Mar Saba greeted Ḍaḥḥāk warmly and said that he would baptize him immediately. But he also expressed fear of what might happen to his community if the Muslim authorities discovered their plan. As the abbot proclaimed:

> My most beloved: know what sort of risk hangs over anyone who dares to do such a thing! Throughout their dominion, a proclamation [*diēggeltai kērugma*] has been issued stating that if anyone is apprehended for causing someone to apostatize from the religion of the Hagarenes and leading him to his own faith, he shall be condemned to death by the sword, while any domicile and church related to him shall be consigned to the flames![154]

Acknowledging the danger he posed to the monks, Ḍaḥḥāk relented. But the abbot was so moved by his constancy that he spirited him away to a "suitable hidden place in the monastery," baptizing him there in secret. He bestowed on Ḍaḥḥāk the Christian name of Bacchus.[155] The future martyr was eighteen years old when this took place.

Bacchus lived as a monk of Mar Saba for a time, but the abbot eventually became suspicious that unnamed individuals were "insinuating the apostasy of the venerable man to their godless ears," thereby placing Bacchus and the entire community in danger.[156] As a result, he asked the young convert to depart from the monastery. Bacchus began to wander, moving from monastery to monastery systematically in order to avoid detection. He eventually returned to Jerusalem and bumped into his mother there. Naturally, she was elated to find her former Muslim son now converted to Christianity and a monk, and she raced back to Maiouma to notify the family. It may be a hagiographic motif—or an indication of the family's half-hearted adhesion to Islam—but the text relates that Bacchus's siblings rejoiced when they heard the news. "Boiling over with love of God," as the *life* puts it, "they sold their property in Maiouma . . . and departed for a foreign land [*eis allodapē chōran aparantes*]."[157]

[154] *CMLT*, 81–82. Compare the *Life of Elias of Helioupolis*, which states that al-Mahdī issued a decree threatening to execute any convert to "the faith of the Arabs" who then returned to Christianity: *SPSH*, i, 52.

[155] *CMLT*, 83–84.

[156] *CMLT*, 89.

[157] *CMLT*, 96. On converts relocating to less threatening areas, see Goitein, *Mediterranean Society*, ii, 304.

There, they were baptized along with their spouses and children. One assumes they settled in a village where they were not known.

One of Bacchus's brothers, however, was furious with what had happened. The text tells us that he was married to an "inflexible, savage, and implacable woman, a kind of Jezebel . . . who refused to let him [join] the Christian faith."[158] This woman's family was also scandalized by the news and hired a bounty hunter to track down Bacchus and bring him to justice. This bounty hunter was also a convert from Christianity to Islam.[159] He eventually found Bacchus in Jerusalem, arrested him, and dispatched him to the governor in Fusṭāṭ (Gk. Phōsaton) in Egypt.[160] There, he was tried for apostasy and killed.

The *Life of Bacchus* provides an intimate portrait of the challenges facing religiously mixed families in early ʿAbbasid Palestine. Although filled with motifs meant to valorize the protagonist and appeal to the text's Constantinopolitan readers, it portrays a world not completely unmoored from historical reality. For example, Muslim sources of the period address many of the same concerns we find in the *life*, such as what to do if a Christian man converts to Islam and his wife refuses to follow him or whether a Muslim husband may ban his Christian wife from drinking wine, wearing a cross, or attending church.[161] In this period, it is safe to say that there were more incentives for men to convert to Islam than there were for women. As the taxpaying head of a household, a husband stood to benefit by liberating himself from the *jizya* (though of course, he would have taken on new Muslim taxes instead, including the *zakāt*). What is more, conversion provided him with access to the political and economic life of the upper classes. Of course, as Muslim society became bigger and more diverse, many converts probably remained in the same social classes into which they had been born. But following Richard Bulliet's observation that "no one willingly converts from one religion to another if by virtue of conversion he markedly lowers his social status,"[162] there must have been a great many who had little to gain by remaining Christian and at least something small to gain by becoming

[158] *CMLT*, 97. On the term *Jezebel* applied to another Muslim woman, see Binggeli, "Anastase le Sinaïte," 251 (Gk.), 566 (Fr.).

[159] *CMLT*, 97–98. On this bounty hunter, see chapter 5, sec. I.

[160] Scholars disagree about where Bacchus died. Given his origins in Palestine, some seem to suggest that he was executed in Jerusalem, but his *life* states that he was brought to "Phōsaton" for trial (e.g., *CMLT*, 101, 103, 105–6). The name "Phōsaton" (or "Phōssaton") appears frequently in Greek and Coptic documents of the period as a translation of the Arabic name "Fusṭāṭ" (modern Cairo). For discussion, see Dridi, "Fossaton and Babylon." I thank Audrey Dridi for sharing her unpublished work with me. Of course, *phossaton* can also mean an "army encampment," more generally.

[161] Abū Bakr al-Khallāl, *Aḥkām*, 176–78, 354–56; Fattal, *Statut légal*, 131–32.

[162] Bulliet, *Conversion to Islam*, 41.

Muslim. Such people must have traded their loyalties from church to mosque frequently.

Women, on the other hand, had less to gain by converting on their own or with their husbands.[163] Indeed, there is evidence that conversion among Christian and Jewish women was less common in the medieval period as a result. The reason for this is relatively simple: if a woman converted to Islam and her husband did not, their marriage was annulled, and she had to find a new Muslim spouse, leaving her in a socially precarious state.[164] On the other hand, if a husband converted to Islam and his wife did not, they remained legally married, and in fact, the entire family profited from the husband's new affiliation, improving their social standing as a whole. Of course, a husband's conversion to Islam had major consequences for the rest of the family. Provided they were still minors at the time of his apostasy, the children were henceforth considered Muslims. They were also more likely to marry Muslims and have Muslim children of their own. Thus, even if a husband's conversion had a salutary impact on his Christian family in the near term, it spelled the disappearance of Christianity from the family tree in the long term, probably within a generation or two. For this reason, intermarriage was among the most important ways in which the subject population of the caliphate came to be integrated with their Muslim rulers and neighbors over time.

Despite the economic incentives that drove conversion, we should not lose sight of the emotional toll it must have taken on individuals. The *Life of Bacchus* is probably not exaggerating when it portrays the martyr's mother as distraught and disappointed by her husband's conversion. It is tempting to imagine that there were many women like her in the seventh and eighth centuries, who dutifully prayed for the return of their Muslim husbands and for the conversion of their Muslim children. Although these women may have been powerless to overcome the allure of wealth and social security that compelled their husbands toward the mosque, they were not powerless to impart to their children a discreet interest, even belief, in Christianity.[165] In some

[163] Compare with Goitein, *Mediterranean Society*, ii, 299–303.

[164] Despite this, conversion was not always a bad option for a woman, especially if she wished to extricate herself from a bad marriage and her husband refused to grant her a writ of divorce. It could also be helpful if a non-Muslim woman wished to inherit from a Muslim relative. For legal views of women converting without their husbands, see Abū Bakr al-Khallāl, *Aḥkām*, 186–88, 205. Cf. the waiting period (*ʿidda*) for the wife of a Muslim man who converted to Christianity in the *dār al-ḥarb*: Abū Bakr al-Khallāl, *Aḥkām*, 432; ʿAbd al-Razzāq, *Muṣannaf*, vi, 82–83, nos. 10078–79; 105–6, nos. 10141, 10144; Khadduri, *Shaybānī's Siyar*, 198; Shatzmiller, "Women's Conversion," 240. I thank Oded Zinger for his suggestions on this matter.

[165] On the perception in Christian sources that wealth and power were the main reasons for converting, see chapter 5, sec. I.

instances, we even know this was allowed: Abū Bakr al-Khallāl speaks of mixed marriages in which the male offspring were raised as Muslims while the female offspring were raised as non-Muslims.[166] At a time when the social practices of Christianity and Islam were not as distinct as they would become in later periods, containing two religious identities in this way may have been a real option.[167]

Seen from this perspective, Bacchus's baptism is really not so surprising. If we believe the text, the religious instruction the martyr received from his mother—coupled with the visits he probably paid to churches and to his Christian relatives with her—nurtured in him a private spiritual identity as a Christian.[168] In the case of Bacchus, this private spiritual identity could not coexist with his public legal identity as a Muslim, as it probably did for many in his position. In the words of Thomas Sizgorich, it created a crisis that could only be resolved by the blood of martyrdom.[169]

Religiously Mixed Families in Egypt

In addition to the *Life of Bacchus*, there are several shorter texts that shed light on the experience of growing up in a religiously mixed household. One of the most intriguing is the *Life of George-Muzāḥim*. Muzāḥim was executed for apostasy in the Nile Delta, and this event is usually dated to 978. His biography was written in Arabic and survives in a number of unedited late medieval manuscripts, along with an Ethiopic translation studied by Osvaldo Raineri.[170] Although the text is short on historical details, it revolves around a familiar question stemming from a social reality: What happens to children when two religions coexist under the same roof?

The text refers to the martyr's father as Jāmiʿ and claims that he was of the "Ishmaelite, *ḥanīfī* race." The *Synaxarium of Alexandria* identifies him as a "Bedouin."[171] According to the story, this man forcibly married a Christian girl

166 Friedmann, *Tolerance and Coercion*, 112.

167 But even in late Ottoman times, the social frontier between the two religions could be very blurry: Grehan, *Twilight of the Saints*, 177–87, 190–96.

168 For parallel evidence from late medieval Egypt, see El-Leithy, "Coptic Culture," 240, 258–67; also Zorgati, *Hybrid Identities*, 71.

169 Sizgorich, "Accidental Conversion," 167.

170 MS Cairo, Coptic Museum—Hist. 469, 77r–87v; the summary that follows draws especially on 77v–78r. See also Raineri, *Giorgio il nuovo*. For references in liturgical calendars, see Basset, "Synaxaire arabe jacobite" (1923), 1120–23; Guidi, "Synaxaire éthiopien," 115–18; discussion in *CMR*, ii, 460–63; *BSO*, ii, 2–3; Anonymous, "Saint George the Egyptian"; Hoyland, *Seeing Islam*, 368 n. 101.

171 Basset, "Synaxaire arabe jacobite" (1923), 1120. The Ethiopic adds the *nisba* "al-ʿAṭāwī":

known as Mary and had seven children with her. The third of these was a boy named Muzāḥim. This Muzāḥim used to accompany his mother to church on Sundays and major feasts. He was so impressed by the piety of the Christians whom he met that he beseeched God to set him on "the straight path" (Ar. *al-ṭarīq al-mustaqīm*; cf. Q. *al-Fātiḥa* 1:6) and make him a Christian. He begged his mother to allow him to take Communion, but she refused, explaining that he first needed to be baptized. Instead, Muzāḥim took a piece of blessed unconsecrated bread—commonly known as the *antidōron*, per the Greek term—which the priests had reserved for catechumens and others who did not wish to partake of the Eucharist.[172] The text states that this bread tasted like honey, which only served to deepen Muzāḥim's Christian faith.

Muzāḥim's mother prayed that her son's growing interest in Christianity would rescue him from "the darkness of unbelief and oppression." But she also warned him against sharing his new beliefs in public, lest his Muslim father discover his secret and punish him. Nevertheless, Muzāḥim "distanced himself from the deeds of the Muslims [*al-ḥunafāʾ*]." His father eventually found out and flew into a rage, and in order to protect the boy, his mother hid him in a nearby village, where a priest agreed to baptize him. This was foiled, however, when the devil possessed the body of a local Muslim woman, who threatened to destroy the village and church unless Muzāḥim relented. Therefore, the priest dismissed the saint. Muzāḥim's efforts to receive baptism failed several times more before he managed to convince a priest to help. Thereafter, he took the Christian name "George" and married the daughter of a priest. Their happiness was short-lived, for George was constantly hounded by the Muslim authorities. After experiencing torture and witnessing several miracles, he was executed for apostasy.

If we push past the manifestly fictional elements in the story—such as the visits of angels and the repeated attempts at torturing and executing George—one realizes that the *life* was popular in its day precisely because it represented a phenomenon that must not have been entirely alien to its Egyptian readers. In fact, it was a phenomenon that would have been intelligible to Christians across the medieval Middle East. Like Bacchus, George was born into a religiously mixed household. Like Bacchus, George was the third of seven children.[173] Like Bacchus's, George's conversion took place through the secret

Raineri, *Giorgio il nuovo*, 3 n. 3. The Ethiopian *synaxarium* refers to him as "a Muslim from the Balaw," which may be a mistranslation of the *Synaxarium of Alexandria*'s "*muslim badawī*."

[172] Compare with the Muslim prince at the shrine of St. George of Diospolis: Aufhauser, *Miracula*, 69.

[173] Here, the tradition disagrees with itself; though the Arabic text I have consulted mentions seven, other sources mention three, six, or even nine children: Raineri, *Giorgio il nuovo*, 7 n. 1.

support of his Christian mother. Like Bacchus, George enjoyed informal access to the sacraments of the church before he was baptized. Bacchus's mother blessed her children with holy oil "as a foretaste of the divine baptism," while George consumed the unconsecrated bread of the mass with the support of his mother.[174]

It should not surprise us that Ḍaḥḥāk and Muzāḥim are represented as taking part in the ritual life of the church through "parallel sacraments" designed for Muslims. As David Taylor has recently discussed, a twelfth-century Syriac church canon ascribed to John of Marde outlines a baptism for Muslim children that was meant to fall short of full-on conversion. This was called the "Baptism of John," since John the Baptist was believed to have baptized without the full presence of the Holy Spirit.[175] Unlike a proper baptism, the "Baptism of John" conferred a blessing on Muslim children, a practice that is documented throughout the Ottoman period, too.[176] Whether it is the parallel chrismation of Bacchus, the parallel Eucharist of George, or the parallel baptism of John of Marde, it is easy to see how medieval churches developed strategies for incorporating certain Muslims into their ritual life. One suspects that these rituals targeted recent converts to Islam, who still had a toehold in their former Christian communities, or, as in the case of the martyrs, they targeted the children of Muslim fathers and Christian mothers. It is also possible that they catered to Muslims from entirely Muslim backgrounds who nonetheless wished to obtain the apotropaic powers of the Christian sacraments.

Christian mothers could exert a disruptive influence on the lives of their Muslim children. But as the *Synaxarium of Alexandria* makes clear, sisters could have an equally disruptive effect on their Muslim siblings. The *life* of the martyr Dioscorus is unknown outside this source.[177] What is more, it contains virtually no details about the martyr's historical context.[178] Still, as with the *Life of George*, the social reality it captures is intelligible given what we know about conversion and apostasy in Egypt in the medieval period.

[174] *CMLT*, 67–68.

[175] Taylor, "Syriac Baptism of St John"; text in Vööbus, *Synodicon*, ii, I, 246 (Syr.); ii, II, 259 (Eng.). For discussion, see Tannous, "Syria," 473–74; Freidenreich, "Muslims in Eastern Canon Law," 54; also chapter 2, sec. I.

[176] Vryonis, "Religious Changes," 173–74; Grehan, *Twilight of the Saints*, 178.

[177] Basset, "Synaxaire arabe jacobite" (1922), 845–47; discussion in *BSO*, i, 701–2; Hoyland, *Seeing Islam*, 338, 364 n. 89, 368 n. 101; MacCoull, "Rite of the Jar," 156; Mikhail, *From Byzantine to Islamic Egypt*, 69.

[178] The date of the martyrdom is unclear; the *Synaxarium of Alexandria* mentions a "king of Egypt" (Ar. *malik miṣr*) in connection with the saint, possibly a Fāṭimid caliph. The text also mentions that the martyrdom occurred "in the time of the Arabs," which could be any period until the reign of the Ayyūbids.

Dioscorus came from a Christian family in Alexandria but "left the religion of his fathers and joined the religion of the Arabs." When Dioscorus's sister in the Fayyūm learned of his apostasy, she wrote him a letter saying, "I would have rather that news reached me that you had died and remained a Christian, for I would have rejoiced at that. Instead, news has reached me that you have abandoned Christ your God." Henceforth, his sister wrote, she was suspending all contact: "From now on, do not show your face and do not exchange any letters with me!"

Dioscorus was overcome with regret as he read this, slapping his face and tearing at his beard. Convinced that his apostasy had been a mistake, he refastened his *zunnār* (Ar. *fa-shadda wasaṭahu bi-ʾl-zunnār*), beseeched God for forgiveness, and made the sign of the Cross. The Muslims in his area must have noticed the presence of the Christian belt, for they asked Dioscorus what had happened. "I am a Christian man," he said in reply, "and I shall die a Christian, too!" On the advice of an individual called "the king of Egypt," the Muslims had him tried, tortured, and killed.

Despite its brevity and lack of historical detail, the *Life of Dioscorus* is moving, indeed. It expresses the feelings of shock and disappointment that probably filled many Christian families when a loved one converted. It also reinforces the impression left by the biographies of Bacchus and George that women played an active role in trying to "reverse engineer" conversions. As we have seen, Christian women did not experience the same pressures to apostatize as men. Therefore, at least if the hagiography is to be trusted, they may have been less tolerant of male relatives who converted, including their husbands, sons, and brothers. The author of our text portrays Dioscorus's sister in a manner that more closely mirrors George's mother than Bacchus's. Both are represented as proactive agents of religious change, prompting their relatives to return or convert out of shame, in one case, and by directly subverting the wishes of a Muslim spouse, in another. The character of Bacchus's mother, by contrast, is portrayed as suffering silently as her family slips into unbelief. These women are dramatis personae, of course, but in representing stereotypical reactions to apostasy, the hagiographers present a range of possible coping mechanisms in the face of a common dilemma.

Religiously Mixed Families in al-Andalus

Al-Andalus offers the last and arguably most intriguing body of evidence about how religiously mixed families functioned in the early Islamic period. The most important texts are the Córdoba martyr acts (ca. 850–59), written by the priest Eulogius and his companion Paulus Alvarus.[179] As we have seen, Islamic law prohibited Muslim women from marrying non-Muslim men, and in general, this principle seems to have been honored. Of course, it must have happened from time to time,[180] and the martyrs Walabonsus and Maria (d. June 851) offer a clear example of the consequences of these unions.[181] According to Eulogius, their father was a Christian landowner from the city of Elche (Lat. Elepensus), located along the southeast coast of the Iberian Peninsula. He married a Muslim woman and converted her to Christianity. Together, they had two children. Because their marriage violated the norms of Islamic law, they were forced to flee Elche and settle in a remote village named Fronianus in the mountains northwest of Córdoba. While there, the mother died, and the father embarked on a life of asceticism. He entrusted Walabonsus to the monastery of St. Felix in Córdoba and Maria to a convent in the village of Cuteclara. Years later, the siblings were reunited when Walabonsus was appointed to serve as supervisor of this same convent. With the outbreak of violence in Córdoba in 851, both siblings confronted the *qāḍī* of the city, denounced the falsehoods of Islam, and were executed.[182]

The ninth-century Andalusī martyrs include a number of historically dubious saints, including the teenaged sisters Nunilo and Alodia, who allegedly came from the city of Bosca near Zaragoza and were killed in October 851 (Figure 1.2).[183] Even if the sisters are fictional, as Ann Christys has recently

[179] On religiously mixed marriages in al-Andalus, see Millet-Gérard, *Chrétiens mozarabes*, 31–32; Coope, *Martyrs of Córdoba*, 75–79; Safran, "Identity and Differentiation," 583–84; Safran, *Defining Boundaries*, 103–6, 125–67; Zorgati, *Hybrid Identities*, 92–128; Barton, *Conquerors, Brides, and Concubines*, esp. 13–44.

[180] E.g., the women of the Banū Qasī, a powerful family of *muwalladūn* (Muslims of local Iberian ancestry) based near Aragon, who were occasionally married to Christian lords in the north; see Barton, *Conquerors, Brides, and Concubines*, 32.

[181] *CSM*, ii, 412, lines 6–14 (marriage of Walabonsus and Maria's parents); discussion in *BS*, x, 867–68; Simonet, *Historia*, 339, 395–96, 413, 417–25; Colbert, *Martyrs of Córdoba*, 205–6, 225–35; Millet-Gérard, *Chrétiens mozarabes*, 31 n. 44, 56, 62, 82; Wolf, *Christian Martyrs*, 25–27, 32, 125 n. 17; Coope, *Martyrs of Córdoba*, 24–27, 71–72; Pochoshajew, *Märtyrer von Cordoba*, 174–78.

[182] On the martyrdom of Walabonsus, see *CSM*, ii, 403–4. Eulogius composed several accounts of the martyrdom of Maria, including one in the *Memoriale sanctorum* (*CSM*, ii, 408–15) and another in the *Documentum martyriale*, which Eulogius addressed to Maria and her companion Flora while they awaited execution (*CSM*, ii, 459–75). For discussion, see *CMR*, i, 682; Dozy, *Spanish Islam*, 291–93; Wolf, *Christian Martyrs*, 67–69; Christys, *Christians in al-Andalus*, 76–77.

[183] *CSM*, ii, 406–8. Eulogius did not know Nunilo and Alodia personally but learned about them from the bishop of Alcalá, Venerius. For the accounts of their martyrdom outside Eulogius's writings, see Christys, *Christians in al-Andalus*, 68–79; López, "Problemas históricos"; López, "La patria de las Santas Nunila y Alodia"; López, "Más sobre la problemática"; discussion in *BS*, ix, 1081–82; Simonet, *Historia*, 424–25; Colbert, *Martyrs of Córdoba*, 224–25; Millet-Gérard, *Chrétiens mozarabes*, 31 n. 44; Fierro, *Heterodoxia*, 55–56; Wolf, *Christian Martyrs*, 131 n. 41; Coope, *Martyrs of Córdoba*, 23–24, 28, 41, 75–77; Pochoshajew, *Märtyrer von Cordoba*, 176.

Figure 1.2. Nunilo and Alodia, Abbey Church of San Salvador, Leyre, Spain, twelfth century. Photo: Javier Miguel Martínez de Aguirre Aldaz.

argued, the general circumstances of their lives are consistent with what we know about the internal dynamics of mixed families. According to Eulogius, their father had been a Muslim but had permitted the girls to be raised in their mother's Christian faith. This liberally-minded man died prematurely, however, and their mother's second husband—an adherent of "an obstinate conquering paganism," as the text puts it—barred them from attending church. A sympathetic Christian aunt took custody of the girls and allowed them to worship as Christians once again. As adolescents, "like roses emerging from a patch of thorns" (Matthew 13:7), they were discovered for their apostasy and made known to a local prefect.[184] This official tried to entice them with offers of marriage to wealthy young men, but when they refused, he assigned them "to be instructed individually by common women [Lat. *mulierculis*] who possessed knowledge of their profane religion."[185] This catechesis failed to persuade Nunilo and Alodia, and after refusing to repent a second time, they were killed.

The most interesting part of the narrative is the discrepancy in the behavior of the mother's two husbands. According to the text, one was indifferent to his daughters' beliefs and even supported their being raised as Christians. The other was dogmatically opposed to Christianity and expected the girls to be raised as Muslims. Thus, if the *story of Nunilo and Alodia* reflects a social reality, it suggests that the implementation of Islamic family law could vary from one individual to the next. One wonders whether the girls' actual father was himself a convert from Christianity or was the product of a religiously mixed family and, therefore, had a more favorable view of the church. There is also indication from early legal sources and later Egyptian texts that Muslim fathers sometimes consented to raising their daughters according to their mothers' non-Muslim faith—or at least did not force their daughters to practice Islam like their brothers—given that inheritance and marriage could proceed as normal for girls without them having to become Muslims.[186] Though no brothers are mentioned in the story of Nunilo and Alodia, it may reflect a similar sex-specific tolerance of "apostasy" to Christianity (or of remaining Christian in situations of family-wide conversion).

[184] This was common language for describing Christians raised among Muslims: e.g., Harrak, "Martyrdom of Cyrus," 319; George-Muzāḥim: MS Cairo, Coptic Museum—Hist. 469, 77r.

[185] Apostates and heretics were often assigned catechists to teach them the ways of Islam. E.g., al-Ḥārith b. Saʿīd al-Kadhdhāb (d. 80/699): Ibn ʿAsākir, *Tārīkh*, xi, 431, cited in Judd, "Muslim Persecution of Heretics," 4; Vahan: Gatteyrias, "Martyre de saint Vahan," 204; Abo of Tiflīs: Lang, *Georgian Saints*, 125.

[186] Abū Bakr al-Khallāl, *Aḥkām*, 26; El-Leithy, "Coptic Culture," 91–97; cf. Friedmann, *Tolerance and Coercion*, 112.

The practice of intermarriage seems to have been widespread in al-Andalus in the ninth century.[187] This created a unique subculture in which the children of mixed families socialized together and even married one another, apparently drawn to a common hybrid upbringing. Aurelius and Sabigotho, who were executed in July 852, both had curious childhoods spent between Christianity and Islam.[188] Eulogius tells us that Aurelius was orphaned at a young age by his Muslim father and Christian mother. In their absence, he was raised by a Christian aunt within the church. His Muslim relatives, however, were not happy about this. They forced him to study "Arabic letters," probably including Muslim religious education. Unfortunately, "these vain figments were unable to change his understanding of the holy faith that had already been placed by heaven in his soul, for in his heart he always held fast to Christianity." His wife Sabigotho was born "Nathalia" to Muslim parents, but according to Eulogius, when her father died, her mother married another Muslim who was a secret Christian. They resolved to baptize the girl, bestowing on her the traditional Visigothic name "Sabigotho."

Years later, they were executed alongside Felix and Liliosa, another married couple with mixed loyalties: he a Christian who had converted to Islam and returned to Christianity, she the daughter of two secret Christians.[189] The phenomenon of "crypto-Christianity" that we observe in Córdoba is hard to detect in other parts of the early Muslim world, with the exception of Bacchus in Palestine, George in Egypt, and Anthony and Peter in North Africa. Some of the closest parallels outside the period come from early Ottoman Anatolia, where crypto-Christianity was widespread among recently converted Muslim populations.[190] Persecution was often an impetus for secret religious practices, as we see in Spain following the Christian conquest of the fifteenth century, when crypto-Islam and crypto-Judaism flourished among communities that

[187] For the opposite view, focusing on mixing among Arabs, Berbers, and the native population, see Guichard, *Al-Andalus*, 20–23, 55–85, 181–240; with a critique in Martinez-Gros, *Identité andalouse*, 115–66; discussion in Barton, *Conquerors, Brides, and Concubines*, 23.

[188] *CSM*, ii, 416–30, esp. 416–17, for their upbringing. For discussion, see *BS*, vi, 545–46; Simonet, *Historia*, 428–33; Colbert, *Martyrs of Córdoba*, 235–42; Millet-Gérard, *Chrétiens mozarabes*, 31 n. 44, 53–54, 91–92, 116; Fierro, *Heterodoxia*, 56; Wolf, *Christian Martyrs*, 27–29 (which claims that Aurelius received his Arabic education from his Christian aunt, whereas it more likely came from his Muslim relatives), 60, 69–70, 113–15; Coope, *Martyrs of Córdoba*, 19, 27–29, 53, 67, 71–72; Pochoshajew, *Märtyrer von Cordoba*, 179–81.

[189] *CSM*, ii, 417. For more on Felix, see sec. I above; discussion in Simonet, *Historia*, 428, 431–33; Colbert, *Martyrs of Córdoba*, 235–42; Millet-Gérard, *Chrétiens mozarabes*, 92, 120; Wolf, *Christian Martyrs*, 27–29; Coope, *Martyrs of Córdoba*, 27–28, 72, 76; Pochoshajew, *Märtyrer von Cordoba*, 179–81.

[190] Hasluck, "Crypto-Christians of Trebizond."

had been forced to join the Catholic Church.[191] Something similar occurred in Ottoman Salonica, where the followers of a messianic cabalist known as Sabbatai Sevi (d. 1676) converted to Islam to avoid persecution but carried on practicing Judaism in secret; they were known as the Dönme and still exist in small numbers in Turkey today.[192] The need to conform outwardly in a time of increased social tension may also explain the phenomenon in Córdoba. But the fact that individuals like Aurelius, Sabigotho, Felix, and Liliosa died together also suggests that they found solace in the company of others like them, also caught betwixt and between religions and family groups. Muslim jurists of the period were aware of this dissimulation and tried to suppress it; indeed, dissimulation of true religious beliefs seems to have been a special concern of Andalusī jurists, judging from the frequent accusations of hidden "Manichaeism" (Ar. *zandaqa*) levied against various individuals at this time.[193]

We should not regard mixed marriage as a custom of the socially or economically disenfranchised. In fact, mixed marriages happened at the very highest echelons of Andalusī society, including among the Umayyad rulers, whose mothers were overwhelmingly Christian girls from the north.[194] They were so mixed, in fact, that Ibn Ḥazm (d. 456/1054) once remarked that all but one of the Andalusī caliphs had blonde hair like their Iberian mothers.[195] A good example among the martyrs is Aurea, who was executed for apostasy in July 856 and was the daughter of a noble Muslim and a pious Christian woman.[196] Two of her brothers were reportedly executed for apostasy in 822, decades before the outbreak of violence in 850–59.[197] If we are to trust Eulogius, it seems that martyrdom was a family tradition for Aurea.

Eulogius describes Aurea as being "girded with garlands on account of her birth and adorned with honors on account of her Arab lineage" (Lat. *erat stemmatis ortu praecincta grandique fastu arabicae traducis exornabatur*), the only time a martyr is explicitly described as having "Arab" blood.[198] On the basis of

[191] García-Arenal, *Inquisición y moriscos*; García-Arenal and Rodríguez Mediano, *Orient in Spain*.

[192] Şişman, *Burden of Silence*.

[193] Fierro, "Accusations of '*Zandaqa*.'" It is important to note that this discourse was not deployed against Christians as such.

[194] Barton, *Conquerors, Brides, and Concubines*, 25–38.

[195] Ruggles, "Mothers of a Hybrid Dynasty," 69; also Lévi-Provençal, *Histoire*, iii, 174.

[196] *CSM*, ii, 456–59; discussion in *BS*, ii, 594–95; Simonet, *Historia*, 469–71; Colbert, *Martyrs of Córdoba*, 263–64; Wolf, *Christian Martyrs*, 32, 103; Coope, *Martyrs of Córdoba*, 12, 16–17, 71–72; Christys, *Christians in al-Andalus*, 78 (which speculates that Aurea never actually existed, though the author does not substantiate this claim).

[197] On the now-lost biography of these brothers by Eulogius's teacher, Speraindeo, see *CMR*, i, 633.

[198] Coope, *Martyrs of Córdoba*, 12.

this, she seems to have come from a prominent Muslim family. Eulogius states that Aurea's mother was a nun, though it is not clear whether her Muslim husband (or consort) was already dead. Aurea lived in a convent in the village of Cuteclara near Córdoba. Although she was legally a Muslim, "none of the outsiders [*nullus exterorum*, meaning Muslims] dared to protest her faith," that is, until Muslim relatives from Seville discovered her secret and notified the authorities.[199] Given how openly Aurea seems to have been living as a Christian, it is hard to believe that these family members did not know about her apostasy. Nevertheless, perhaps pressured by the sudden interest of Muslims outside the family fold, she was ordered to appear before a judge. She publicly repented of her crime but resumed practicing Christianity. When she was discovered a second time, she was apprehended, hauled before the judge, and sentenced to death.

Since Aurea was a member of the upper class, she was relatively free to flirt with Christianity—provided she was discreet about it. Because of her father, however, she remained a Muslim in the eyes of the law and was forced to balance the same public and private identities that bedeviled martyrs across the greater Middle East. As Jessica Coope has pointed out, the *qāḍī* (Lat. *iudex*) who tried Aurea was reportedly a relative: Eulogius states that "by right of birth, he belonged to the same lineage as the virgin."[200] The nature of the family connection is unclear, though judging from other Andalusī Muslims, such as the famous chronicler Ibn al-Qūṭīya (d. 367/977, lit. "Son of the Gothic Woman"), they were probably of mixed Arab and Iberian bloodlines.[201] For this reason, we can begin to understand the judge's angry question to Aurea during the interrogation: Why, "being so noble, did she defile herself out of obedience to the Christian faith, and [why] did she corrupt the badge of her lofty stock for this vile way of life?" Muslim sources identify the *qāḍī* of Córdoba at this time as Aḥmad b. Ziyād al-Lakhmī, whose family included other distinguished officials, including his brother Muḥammad, who was chief *qāḍī* under the *amīr* ʿAbd al-Raḥmān II (r. 206–38/822–52), and his nephew Aḥmad b. Muḥammad al-Lakhmī, who was chief *qāḍī* under ʿAbdallāh b. Muḥammad (r. 275–300/888–912).[202] If all these people were in fact related to each other, as Eulogius hints, it is a testament to the intense mixing in Córdoba that a single family could produce someone as exalted as a chief judge and someone as despised as a martyred nun.

[199] On the term *outsiders* for Muslims in Christian Arabic texts, see chapter 2, n. 39.

[200] *CSM*, ii, 456; discussion in Coope, *Martyrs of Córdoba*, 94–95 n. 5.

[201] Bosch-Vilá, "Ibn al-Ḳūṭiyya," *EI*², iii, 847–48; König, "Genealogie des Ibn al-Qūṭiyya."

[202] al-Khushanī, *Quḍāt qurṭuba*, 98–100; though there is nothing in al-Khushanī's report to indicate that this judge himself came from a religiously mixed family.

V. CONCLUSION

This chapter has explored Christian converts to Islam who then returned to Christianity, as well as martyrs who came from religiously mixed families. The next chapter will round out the story by examining a small but significant group of converts from entirely Muslim backgrounds. Broad conclusions about the nature of conversion in the early Islamic period will be postponed until then. Now, however, at the midway point through this tour of convert-martyrs, we would do well to ask whether their experience was in any way typical of the societies in which they lived. Can we regard their lives as representative of broader trends in the history of Muslim-Christian relations at the time?

In one sense, the martyrs were obviously outliers. The vast majority of Christians who converted to Islam in the Umayyad and early ʿAbbasid periods never returned to Christianity. Very few children of religiously mixed households opted for the Christian faith of their mothers over the Muslim faith of their fathers. Even if prohibitions on apostasy took time to crystallize, it is safe to say that most converts regarded Islam as a "religious Hotel California": there was plenty of room inside, but once you checked in, there was no checking out.[203] The threat of ostracism and death—to say nothing of the many benefits conferred by conversion—discouraged most new Muslims from ever leaving.

At the same time, despite their exceptionalism, the martyrs experienced dilemmas that were familiar to many Muslims and Christians in the postconquest period. While execution was an atypical outcome of these dilemmas, the contours of their lives were easily recognizable: they were Christians who worked as slaves in the households of wealthy Muslims, Christians who socialized and lived alongside Muslim friends and relatives, and children who were born into mixed unions of Muslim and Christian parents. Whereas most Christians responded to these pressures by acquiescing to Islam, the martyrs distinguished themselves by rejecting it. Thus, in the convert-martyrs, we catch a glimpse of both a culture and a counterculture, of a late antique Christian society slowly being transformed into a medieval Islamic society as well as an otherwise indivisible substratum of this society that stubbornly resisted change.

Finally, it has become fashionable in recent years to emphasize examples of conversions in the late ancient world that were fluid, ambiguous, and gradual and which point to some degree of hybrid religious belief.[204] Given the case

[203] Tannous, "Syria," 439.

[204] See esp. Sizgorich, "Accidental Conversion"; as well as other essays in Papaconstantinou,

studies in this chapter, it is hard to ignore the impression that for some early converts, the frontiers between Christianity and Islam were porous indeed. But by privileging "messiness" in this way, scholars perhaps fail to take seriously those aspects of conversion that were individual, doctrinal, and transformational. The *lives* of the neomartyrs, after all, hinge on scenes of decisive change, and to interpret them mainly as evidence for a lack of clear lines (acknowledging that such themes are sometimes present) is to render the category of "conversion" analytically somewhat useless. It is to imply that the very evidence we use to understand conversion in the early Islamic era—nearly all of which stresses the decisive shift between old and new—deliberately conceals an underlying world that was in fact quite the opposite. It is also to imply that the sources strive to create and impose on their readers an alternate reality chiseled by far clearer lines than what existed on the ground. Yet the *lives* of the martyrs succeeded as a genre precisely because they portrayed an experience that was familiar and intelligible to their readers. We should not underestimate this. We have much to learn from new approaches that stress hybridity and ambiguity, but we must be critical of them as well, asking ourselves whether they say more about religious belief (and unbelief) in the modern day than in the distant past.

McLynn, and Schwartz, *Conversion in Late Antiquity*; Donner, *Muhammad and the Believers*; Penn, *Envisioning Islam*. I owe these ideas to conversation with Luke Yarbrough.

2

Converting from Islam to Christianity

As we saw in chapter 1, conversion during the early Islamic period was not a one-way street from Christianity to Islam. There were many varieties of religious conversion, and no group demonstrates this better than the "true apostates"—individuals born to entirely Muslim families who then converted to Christianity.[1] Although this form of conversion was extremely important, it was also exceptionally rare. Not only did apostates face the death penalty if they were caught, but they probably enjoyed few material benefits because of their conversions, at least in comparison to their contemporaries who left the church for the mosque. To abandon Islam in this way was to voluntarily join the subjugated lower classes—not a conventional choice in any society, much less one in which religion played a central role in determining social and economic status, as it did in the early medieval Middle East. If converts managed to escape execution—and one supposes that some did—they faced a difficult road ahead, including ostracism by family and friends, loss of wealth, and even exile.

Given this, it is not surprising that true apostasy leaves such a faint trace in the annals of early Muslim history. It is also not surprising that scholars steeped in traditional Arabic sources ignore apostasy, downplay its significance, or deny that it was ever a problem.[2] Yet apostasy did occur, and the Christian hagiography of the early Islamic period sheds light on it in a way that virtually no other contemporary sources can do. To explore this phenomenon, the following chapter is divided into five sections: the first surveys the evidence for true apostasy in legal, historical, and ritual literature written by Muslims and Christians. The second discusses the *life* of the most famous of all the neomartyrs, Anthony al-Qurashī, who was executed in 799 after allegedly converting from Islam to Christianity. The third explores two instances of true apostasy from the early medieval Caucasus, while the fourth examines several examples from Iraq, Egypt, and al-Andalus. The fifth and final section revisits the *Life of Anthony* and investigates its connection to a cluster of leg-

[1] I borrow the phrase from Cook, "Apostasy from Islam," 260–66.

[2] Most egregiously, Ayoub, "Law of Apostasy," 90–91; also Ahmad, "Conversion from Islam"; O'Sullivan, "Death Penalty for Apostates."

ends about the conversion of the caliph and other high-ranking Muslim officials. The conclusion offers general reflections about the nature and portrayal of conversion, contending that we must see Islamization as a fragile, highly contingent process in the early period.

I. TRUE APOSTASY IN EARLY ISLAM: AN OVERVIEW

Classical Islamic law drew little meaningful distinction between the apostasy of recent converts to Islam and the apostasy of Muslims by birth. Both were subject to the same tradition ascribed to the Companion Ibn ʿAbbās: "Kill anyone who changes his religion!"[3] Despite this, certain medieval jurists were sensitive to distinctions between the two groups, including early authorities such as ʿAṭāʾ b. Abī Rabāḥ (d. ca. 114/732), al-Layth b. Saʿd (d. 175/791), Mālik b. Anas (d. 179/796), and al-Shāfiʿī (d. 204/820), along with a variety of Shīʿī scholars.[4] In general, they believed that apostates from non-Muslim backgrounds were entitled to avoid execution by making an act of repentance (Ar. *tawba*), while apostates from Muslim backgrounds were not—on the assumption that they should know better than to leave their natal faith. On balance, the archetypal apostate in early works of *ḥadīth* and *fiqh* was the Christian, Jewish, Zoroastrian, or pagan returnee (such as al-Mustawrid al-ʿIjlī, discussed in appendix 1), not the true apostate.[5] This may tell us something about which groups in early Muslim society were perceived to have a weaker, more tentative attachment to Islam. Still, even if Muslim scholars did not dwell on true apostasy as a distinct category of crime, they did fret about other forms of contact with Christians that could grease the way to conversion if left unchecked. These included practices such as praying in churches,[6] learning non-Arabic languages,[7] and celebrating

[3] For discussion, see chapter 1, sec. I.

[4] Ibn Qudāma, *Mughnī*, xii, 105–6; al-Shāfiʿī, *Kitāb al-umm*, ii, 570–72; Ḥurr al-ʿĀmilī, *Wasāʾil al-shīʿa*, xviii, 544–46. See also Heffening, "Murtadd," *EI²*, vii, 636; Kraemer, "Apostates, Rebels and Brigands," 42; Friedmann, *Tolerance and Coercion*, 134.

[5] See appendix 1.

[6] ʿAbd al-Razzāq, *Muṣannaf*, i, 411, no. 1610; x, 398, no. 19486. For discussion, see Bashear, "Qibla Musharriqa"; Hoyland, "Jacob and Early Islamic Edessa," 16; Guidetti, *In the Shadow of the Church*; Sahner, "First Iconoclasm in Islam," 53–54.

[7] ʿAbd al-Razzāq, *Muṣannaf*, i, 411, no. 1609, which warns against learning the "gibberish of the Persians" (Ar. *raṭānat al-aʿājim*). Compare with stories of the Prophet's secretary, Zayd b. Thābit, who is said to have learned Syriac and Hebrew in less than three weeks! See al-Mizzī, *Tahdhīb*, x, 28–29; Lecker, "Zayd b. Thābit"; Tannous, "Syria," 516–17.

Christian feasts, all of which brought the two groups into perilous proximity with one another.[8]

Much as Muslim jurists help confirm the reality of apostasy through the laws they formulated to prevent it, so Christian clergy confirm the reality of apostasy through the rituals they created to enable it. The Byzantine and Coptic Orthodox churches produced rites of abjuration of Islam during the ninth and fourteenth centuries, respectively.[9] Historians agree that these were mainly designed for converts returning to the Christian fold rather than Muslims converting to Christianity for the first time. Still, hagiographic sources hint that Muslim converts to Christianity were sometimes expected to renounce their beliefs in public, and these medieval formulas may provide templates of what this entailed.[10] The Greek rite, for example, calls on converts to abjure the Prophet Muḥammad, various members of the Prophet's family, the Companions, the Qur'an, and the Islamic belief that Jesus was a mere mortal. It also requires converts to renounce several Umayyad caliphs, including Muʿāwiya and Yazīd, suggesting that it may have been written with a Syrian audience in mind.

Muslim chronicles contain scattered references to true apostasy, often portraying it as a consequence of warfare and slavery. Al-Ṭabarī, for example, mentions that the ʿAbbasid envoy Naṣr b. al-Azhar visited Constantinople in 240/854–55 in order to negotiate the release of a large group of Muslim prisoners. He discovered that many of them had converted to Christianity in captivity, including a sizable contingent of soldiers from Egypt and North Africa.[11] Muslim jurists fretted about scenarios like this, devoting lengthy discussions to the treatment of Muslims who had apostatized in the Abode of War (Ar. *dār al-ḥarb*).[12] It is harder to find examples of truly voluntary conversions to Christianity in Muslim sources. If this did occur, Muslim authors were usually quick

[8] Abū Bakr al-Khallāl, *Aḥkām*, 51; de la Granja, "Fiestas cristianas"; Kassis, "Arabic-Speaking Christians," 407.

[9] On the Greek rite, see Montet, "Rituel d'abjuration"; complete text in *PG*, cxl, 123–36; for discussion, see Sahas, "Ritual of Conversion." For a related eleventh-century Greek rite, see Rigo, "Formula inedita d'abiura"; Aubineau, "Un recueil ‹De haeresibus›," 427; Eleuteri and Rigo, *Raccolta eresiologica*, 24–25, 53–57. For the Coptic rite, see MacCoull, "Rite of the Jar"; El-Leithy, "Coptic Culture," 132–34. On the twelfth-century Greek canonist Theodore Balsamon and his views on reconversion, see now Viscuso, *Guide for a Church under Islām*, 38–39.

[10] See discussion of the case of Ibn Rajāʾ, in sec. IV below.

[11] al-Ṭabarī, *Annales*, iii, 1349–52. I thank Luke Yarbrough for this reference. Compare the case of Salṭ b. al-ʿĀṣ, who was apprehended by the Byzantines at Nisibis, jailed at Constantinople, and converted to Christianity against his will: Ibn ʿAsākir, *Tārīkh*, viii, 387; discussion in Cook, "Apostasy from Islam," 260–61.

[12] Abū Bakr al-Khallāl, *Aḥkām*, 430–32, 440–44, 448–49; see also Ramaḍān, "Arab Prisoners of War in Byzantium," 166–71.

to dismiss it as a form of opportunism, as with Rabīʿa b. Umayya al-Qurashī, a notorious drunkard whom ʿUmar b. al-Khaṭṭāb exiled to Khaybar but who managed to flee to Byzantine Syria and convert to Christianity.[13] This is also the case with ʿAbd al-ʿAzīz b. Mūsā b. Nuṣayr, the son of the conqueror of al-Andalus, who was killed in 97/718 on suspicion of trying to grab power for himself—or, according to other traditions (designed to justify his violent death, no doubt), because he had converted to Christianity.[14] *Ḥadīth* about the end times cannot be considered records of real events, of course, but they do express real anxieties among Muslims in a given period. In this respect, it is telling that not a few early traditions that circulated in the Muslim East and West predicted the coming of a "mass apostasy" (Ar. *ridda shadīda*) near the Day of Judgment.[15] The geographer Ibn Ḥawqal expressed similar fears when he predicted that mass apostasy would descend on the Muslims of northern Syria following the Byzantine conquest of the tenth century.[16]

Aside from the *lives* of the martyrs, Christian sources are not particularly illuminating when it comes to understanding true apostasy. In one interesting report, the Armenian chronicler Sebeos states that fifteen thousand Muslim troops loyal to ʿAlī b. Abī Ṭālib were baptized as part of an agreement with the Byzantine emperor Constans II during the first Muslim civil war (36–41/656–61).[17] No other sources mention this event. Christian texts also claim that Muslims were sometimes baptized for medical and apotropaic purposes, as with the monk Rabban Khudhāwī, who reportedly baptized a daughter of the caliph Muʿāwiya in order to heal her broken arm.[18] As discussed in chapter 1, such baptisms were not usually for the purpose of conversion but were administered to confer a blessing; that being said, it is impossible to know what the

[13] Ibn ʿAsākir, *Tārīkh*, xviii, 51–52; discussion in Cook, "Apostasy from Islam," 261; Rowson, "Public Humiliation," 122. Another famous apostate who fled to Byzantium was the Ghassānid prince Jabala b. al-Ayham: Bray, "Christian King, Muslim Apostate."

[14] Fierro, *Heterodoxia*, 17–18; Fierro, "Castigo de los herejes," 287–88; Fierro, "Decapitation of Christians and Muslims," 147.

[15] For the east, see Nuʿaym b. Ḥammād, *Fitan*, 270; discussion in Cook, *Muslim Apocalyptic*, 10, 63; Cook, "Apostasy from Islam," 274. For the west, see ʿAbd al-Malik b. Ḥabīb, *Kitāb al-Tarīkh*, 155; discussion in Safran, "Identity and Differentiation," 577.

[16] Ibn Ḥawqal, *Aḥsan al-taqāsīm*, 172. See also the report of al-Muqaddasī (fl. fourth/tenth century) that many Muslims along the frontier with Byzantium had apostatized, while those who remained Muslim had to pay a tribute (Ar. *jizya*); Carlson, "Contours of Conversion," 803.

[17] Thomson, *Sebeos*, i, 154; ii, 287.

[18] Scher and Griveau, "Histoire nestorienne," 594; see also Hoyland, *Seeing Islam*, 189–90; Tannous, "Syria," 460. On the baptism of a Muslim governor in Iraq by another Syriac-speaking priest, see Budge, *Histories of Rabban Hôrmîzd the Persian and Rabban Bar ʿIdtâ*, i, 65–71 (Syr.); ii, 97–103 (Eng.); discussion in Hoyland, *Seeing Islam*, 189–92; Penn, *Envisioning Islam*, 136–37. Christians were sources of miraculous healing for Zoroastrians in Sasanian times, too; see Payne, *State of Mixture*, 68.

clergy (to say nothing of the Muslim recipients of baptism) made of what was happening.[19] Despite this, the overall evidence suggests that true apostasy did sometimes happen during the seventh, eighth, and ninth centuries, and even if it was limited in scope, it was a symptom of the wider culture of religious mobility at the time.

II. THE APOSTASY OF ANTHONY AL-QURASHĪ

One of the most fascinating and disputed cases of true apostasy is that of Anthony (né Rawḥ) al-Qurashī, an alleged member of the Prophet's tribe who converted to Christianity and was executed in Raqqa in 799.[20] Anthony is arguably the most famous neomartyr of the early Islamic period, and given the sensational details of his *life*, it is not hard to see why. An anonymous Arabic-speaking Melkite composed his *life* sometime in the early ninth century, shortly after his purported death, but his fame quickly spread to other communities and language groups. In addition to the Arabic evidence, there are Georgian and Ethiopic translations of the *life*, references to Anthony in three Syriac chronicles and a liturgical calendar, and a much-altered version of his *life* in Latin translation.[21] Anthony also has the distinction of being one of the only neomartyrs discussed by name in a Muslim source. The Iranian polymath al-Bīrūnī (d. ca. 440/1048) mentioned him in his *Kitāb al-āthār al-bāqiya* (commonly known as "The Chronology of Ancient Nations") in a section dealing with the feasts of the Melkites.[22]

We will turn to the authenticity of Anthony's *life* in a moment, but let us begin with an overview of what his biography says. The following summary

[19] See chapter 1, sec. IV.

[20] With extensive bibliography in *CMR*, i, 498–501. In addition to the literature cited below, see *BSO*, i, 210–11; Zayyāt, "Shuhadā' al-naṣrānīya," 462; Fiey, *Chrétiens syriaques*, 58; Fiey, *Saints syriaques*, 34–35; Bīṭār, *al-Qiddīsūn al-mansīyūn*, 188–95; Hoyland, *Seeing Islam*, 91 n. 122, 346–47 n. 3, 385–86; Griffith, "Christians, Muslims, and Neo-martyrs," 198–200; Vila, "Struggle over Arabisation" (which reiterates the chapter on Anthony in Vila's dissertation); Foss, "Byzantine Saints," 109–11; Tannous, "Syria," 467–68.

[21] For Georgian, see Kipshidze, "Zhitie i muchenichestvo sv. Antoniia Ravakha"; Peeters, "Autobiographie de S. Antoine." For Ethiopic, see Peeters, "S. Antoine le néo-martyr." For Syriac: Brooks, "Syriac Fragment," 225; Chabot, *Chronique*, iii, 18–19 (Fr.); iv, 487–88 (Syr.); Budge, *Chronography*, i, 121; Peeters, "Rabban Sliba," 171. For Latin variants, see Braida and Pelissetti, *Rawḥ al-Qurašī*, 49–63, 129–38. For more on the commemoration of Anthony in different Christian communities, see chapter 5, sec. III.

[22] Griveau, "Fêtes des Melchites," 299; for discussion, see Griffith, "Christians, Muslims, and Neo-martyrs," 204; Vila, "Christian Martyrs," 103–4; Braida and Pelissetti, *Rawḥ al-Qurašī*, 32; Binggeli, "Converting the Caliph," 78–79; Sizgorich, "Christian Eyes Only," 129–30; and appendix 1.

draws on one of the oldest recensions of his *life* in Sinai Arab. 513, a tenth-century manuscript.[23] As Juan Pedro Monferrer-Sala has recently argued, the oldest version may in fact be in an overlooked thirteenth-century manuscript, Sinai Arab. 445, which despite its late date preserves a much earlier recension of the text.[24] Monferrer-Sala's conclusions are convincing, but for the purposes of summarizing Anthony's biography, the differences between the two versions should be considered minor.

According to his *life*, Rawḥ al-Qurashī was a wealthy young Muslim from Damascus.[25] He lived in an abandoned monastery dedicated to Saint Theodore in a place called "Nayrab" on the slopes of Mount Qāsyūn. Next to this monastery stood a functioning church.[26] As the text reports, Rawḥ "was fond of the church and used to steal the blessed host and eat it." Sometimes, he would even "tear the crosses from their places, rip the altar cloths, and greatly harass the priest."[27] One day, Rawḥ found the church vacant, so he decided to amuse himself by grasping his bow and taking aim at the church's icon of Saint Theodore, which sat propped up on the altar (Figure 2.1). Upon firing, he witnessed his arrow come within a foot of the sacred image, but the arrow turned around in midair and flew back toward him, piercing his left hand. Terrified and reeling with pain, Rawḥ fell unconscious.

A few days later, Rawḥ witnessed another miracle when he observed the consecrated host transform into a lamb during the mass.[28] That night, Saint Theodore is said to have appeared to Rawḥ in a dream—armed with weapons and riding a horse—and chastised him for his belligerence. He then ordered Rawḥ to embrace Christ and repent. The young Muslim was so moved by the vision that he set off for Jerusalem the next day to be baptized.[29] The patriarch

[23] My citations follow the two main editions of the text: Dick, "Passion arabe," 119–26; and Braida and Pelissetti, *Rawḥ al-Qurašī*, 95–113, which corrects the errors in Dick.

[24] Monferrer Sala, "*Šahādat al-qiddīs Mār Anṭūniyūs*"; with English translation in Lamoreaux, "Hagiography," 117–23.

[25] Only Sinai 445 refers to Anthony as a "young man": Monferrer Sala, "*Šahādat al-qiddīs Mār Anṭūniyūs*," 258. According to the Ethiopic translation, Anthony is said to have lived in Aleppo but to have maintained a residence in al-Nayrab in Damascus; no other version of the *life* mentions Aleppo, and its inclusion here may reflect a minor claim on Anthony's cult among Christians in the city: Peeters, "S. Antoine le néo-martyr," 411, 422, 436; Binggeli, "Converting the Caliph," 85.

[26] Binggeli, "Converting the Caliph," 99–103.

[27] Dick, "Passion arabe," 119; Braida and Pelissetti, *Rawḥ al-Qurašī*, 95.

[28] The eighty-second canon of the Quinisext Council (ca. 692) banned representations of Christ as a lamb: Davis, *Ecumenical Councils*, 294. Rawḥ witnessed this miracle on the feast of St. Theodore, probably February 9, as in Garitte, *Calendrier palestino-géorgien*, 49.

[29] Rawḥ departed for Jerusalem via a village called Kiswa, twelve miles south of Damascus, the first stage on the caravan road between Syria and Egypt; see Yāqūt, *Muʿjam al-buldān*, iv, 461; Le Strange, *Palestine*, 488.

Figure 2.1. Icon of Saint Theodore, Mount Sinai, Egypt, ca. ninth–tenth centuries. Photo: St. Catherine's Monastery, Sinai, Egypt. Courtesy of Michigan-Princeton-Alexandria Expeditions to Mount Sinai.

at the time, Elias II (r. 770–97), expressed fear that by baptizing Rawḥ, he might incur the wrath of the Muslim authorities.[30] Therefore, he dispatched the young man to the River Jordan, where a group of monks submerged him in its chilly waters. They gave him a monastic cowl and a new Christian name: Anthony.[31]

Anthony went back to Damascus,[32] where his family mocked his coarse dress. After failing to persuade him to return to Islam, they handed him over to the *qāḍī*. "Shame on you, Rawḥ," the judge proclaimed: "Why have you left your religion into which you were born, not to mention the esteem and nobility you are owed [*ḥasabaka wa-sharafaka*]?"[33] When this, too, failed to persuade Anthony, the *qāḍī* threw him in prison (where he was jailed alongside other "Arabs and Qurashīs") and eventually dispatched him via the imperial post road to Raqqa, which was then the seat of the caliph Hārūn al-Rashīd (r. 170–93/786–809).[34] This method of transport—which the Muslim authorities used to move around other high-value captives—provides proof of Anthony's status and the danger he was seen to pose. The caliph also mocked the monk's ragged appearance, but after failing to persuade him, he ordered his execution.[35]

30 For Elias II, see Grumel, *Chronologie*, 452; also Fedalto, *Hierarchia Ecclesiastica Orientalis*, ii, 1002. For more on fear of baptizing Muslims, see chapter 5, sec. II.

31 The monastery beside the river may have been Dayr Fākhūr, which marked the site where John had baptized Jesus. The Companions Muʿādh b. Jabal and Kaʿb b. Murra were buried nearby: Yāqūt, *Muʿjam al-buldān*, ii, 525; Campbell, "Heaven of Wine," 181, 279.

32 In one recension, Anthony is said to have wandered in Egypt after his baptism: Pirone, "Martirio del nobile qurayshita Rawḥ," 498–99. Binggeli ("Converting the Caliph," 85) is inclined to see this as a literary motif connecting Anthony al-Qurashī to Anthony the Great. I am not convinced, given the historical discrepancy between the dates of patriarch Elias's death (797) and Anthony's martyrdom (December 799). Perhaps an Egyptian sojourn filled this gap.

33 Dick, "Passion arabe," 124; Braida and Pelissetti, *Rawḥ al-Qurašī*, 107. Compare to a similar exchange between Vahan and Hishām: Gatteyrias, "Martyre de saint Vahan," 201. The judge was either Yaḥyā b. Ḥamza al-Ḥaḍramī al-Ḥimyarī, chief *qāḍī* of Damascus until 183/799 (Ibn ʿAsākir, *Tārīkh*, lxiv, 125–35), or ʿUmar b. Abī Bakr al-ʿAdawī al-Mawṣilī, chief *qāḍī* of Damascus in 183–94/799–810 (Ibn ʿAsākir, *Tārīkh*, xliii, 547–51). I thank Mathieu Tillier for his help in identifying these figures.

34 Silverstein, *Postal Systems*, 53–89. The heretic al-Ḥārith b. Saʿīd al-Khadhdhāb (d. 80/699) was also conveyed to Damascus via the *barīd*: Ibn ʿAsākir, *Tārīkh*, xi, 431. Other versions of the *life* state that Anthony detoured to "New Khurāsān" (Peeters, "Autobiographie de S. Antoine," 63). I thank Stephen Shoemaker for his help with the Georgian here.

35 Anthony was greeted in Raqqa by the governor Harthama, probably the ʿAbbasid general of the same name who presided over the execution of Bacchus: Garitte, *Calendrier palestino-géorgien*, 59, 197 (the longer Greek *life* does not identify the governor by name). The identification with Harthama b. Aʿyan (e.g., Pirone, "Martirio del nobile qurayshita Rawḥ," 501; Vila, "Christian Martyrs," 293 n. 100; cf. Pellat, "Harthama b. Aʿyan," *EI*², iii, 231), who served as governor of Filasṭīn and Ifrīqiya under Hārūn al-Rashīd, is slightly problematic because Harthama had already been reposted from Ifrīqiya to Baghdad to serve as deputy of the guard at the time of Anthony's execution. Harthama was eventually killed because he slandered al-Faḍl b. Sahl—a trusted adviser of

Anthony welcomed this sentence, explaining that it would help to expiate his three greatest sins: having gone on pilgrimage to Mecca, having sacrificed on ʿĪd al-Aḍḥā, and having killed Christians during raids against the Byzantines.[36] With that, on Christmas Day, 799, Hārūn al-Rashīd ordered the saint to be decapitated. Some sources claim that he was buried in a nearby monastery (possibly one run by the West Syrians); another, in Persia; and another, in Baghdad.[37]

The story of Anthony al-Qurashī is gripping, but is it plausible? The answer is a combination of yes and no. The earliest dated reference to the martyr comes from a treatise on the veneration of icons written by Theodore Abū Qurra between 800 and 815, a few years after Anthony's alleged death. In it, Abū Qurra states:

> In our own day there was a well-known martyr, from a family of the highest nobility among the outsiders, whose story is widespread. May he remember us in his prayers, he is called St. Anthony. He used to tell everyone he met that he came to believe in Christianity only because of a miracle he saw in connection with an icon that belonged to St. Theodore, the martyr.[38]

Abū Qurra clearly regarded this martyr as a contemporary and as a real person. Indeed, his offhand comment has the quality of an eyewitness report or at least a report based on the hearsay of Christians who knew and remembered the saint.

Of all the facets of his *life*, it was Anthony's ancestry that left the deepest impression on his biographers. There were probably few true apostates in the generations after the conquests, but even fewer of them shared Anthony's sparkling pedigree. The sources describe him alternately as a member of the Prophet's tribe of Quraysh, a Muslim, a Hagarene, an Arab, a *ḥanīf*, a member of the nobility, and one of the "outsiders" (from Syr. *barrānāyē*, "nomads"), all

---

al-Maʾmūn—as being a Zoroastrian when he was in fact a convert in good standing: see al-Jahshiyarī, *al-Wuzarāʾ wa-ʾl-kuttāb*, 316–18.

[36] Sahner, "Old Martyrs, New Martyrs," 102–3.

[37] For the Monastery of the Column of the Olives, see Dick, "Passion arabe," 115, 126; Braida and Pelissetti, *Rawḥ al-Qurašī*, 47 n. 119, 112; also Peeters, "S. Antoine le néo-martyr," 413, 420, 439; Carlson and Michelson, "Monastery of Esṭona." For Persia: Chabot, *Chronique*, iv, 488. For Baghdad: Pirone, "Martirio del nobile qurayshita Rawḥ," 506–7 (which appears in an extended epilogue in the London recension; none of the manuscripts show any connection to Iraq despite this detail).

[38] Griffith, *Veneration of the Holy Icons*, 21, 74. For the original Arabic, see Dick, *Ikrām al-īqūnāt*, 173. The roughly contemporary Syriac *Chronicle of 813* also mentions Anthony: Brooks, "Syriac Fragment," 225–26.

of which emphasize his high social standing or his unique Muslim identity.[39] Some sources even identify him as a relative of various caliphs, including ʿUmar b. al-Khaṭṭāb and Hārūn al-Rashīd (who were themselves members of Quraysh).[40] Whatever the truth of these claims, which seem far-fetched indeed, in literary terms, they served to differentiate Anthony from most of the Christians who would have read his *life* and revered his memory (to say nothing of most of the Muslims who converted to Christianity at the time). Furthermore, as a literary device, they served to boost Christianity's prestige: the only reason an elite Muslim such as Rawḥ would leave the mosque for the church—and in the process, risk his own life—was that Christianity was indeed a "noble, true religion" (Ar. *dīn sharīf ṣaḥīḥ*), unlike Islam.[41]

Despite the abundance of references to Anthony in Christian sources, it is hard to identify him with any individual in Muslim texts, which is a cause for obvious suspicion.[42] Samir Khalil Samir came close to establishing a general profile of the martyr when he observed that a large number of Muslims in the postconquest period with the name "Rawḥ" lived in Syria and held important positions in the Umayyad administration and army.[43] The aristocratic martyr

[39] Respectively, (1) *hādhā ʾl-qurashī* (Dick, "Passion arabe," 119, 120, 122; Braida and Pelissetti, *Rawḥ al-Qurašī*, 95–97, 101; Pirone, "Martirio del nobile qurayshita Rawḥ," 485–86, 488) (for uses of the term *Qurashī* in Syriac, see Binggeli, "Converting the Caliph," 89 n. 46; for lucid discussion, see Vila, "Christian Martyrs," 127–28); (2) *muslim* (Budge, *Chronography*, i, 121); (3–4) *al-hājirī* and *rajul min ashrāf al-ʿarab* (Peeters, "S. Antoine le néo-martyr," 440; Braida and Pelissetti, *Rawḥ al-Qurašī*, 115); (5) *ḥanīf* (Dick, "Passion arabe," 126; Braida and Pelissetti, *Rawḥ al-Qurašī*, 111; Vat. ar. 175, 116v); (6) *li-mādhā tarakta dīnaka . . . wa-ḥasabaka wa-sharafaka* (e.g., Dick, "Passion arabe," 124); (7) *shahīd min al-barrānīyīn* (Dick, *Ikrām al-īqūnāt*, 173; with discussion in Griffith, "Venerating Images," 66; Payne Smith, *Thesaurus Syriacus*, i, 578 [*barrānāyā*]; Simonsohn, "Seeking Justice among the 'Outsiders' "). For the latter term in Latin sources, see chapter 1, n. 199.

It is unclear whether *ḥanīf* is being used in a positive or negative sense. Sizgorich ("Christian Eyes Only," 131–32) argued that Anthony's biographer wished to portray him as a pious Muslim (e.g., Q. *Āl ʿImrān* 3:67, *al-Nisāʾ* 4:125). Arabic Christian writers also used *ḥanīf* with neutral to negative connotations, as in the *Life of George-Muzāḥim*, where the meaning is closer to that of the Syriac *ḥanpā*, or "pagan." For more on the evolution of this term, see de Blois, "*Naṣrānī* (Ναζωραῖος) and *Ḥanīf* (ἐθνικός)"; for this term and Christian nomenclature for Muslims more generally, see Penn, *Envisioning Islam*, 53–101.

[40] ʿUmar: Peeters, "Rabban Sliba," 171 (Syr. *men sharbtā d-ʿumar*); and n. 42 below. Hārūn al-Rashīd: Griveau, "Fêtes des Melchites," 299 (*abū rawḥ ibn ʿamm hārūn al-rashīd*).

[41] Monferrer Sala, "*Šahādat al-qiddīs Mār Anṭūniyūs*," 258.

[42] The Ethiopic recension gives Rawḥ's full name as "Rāwx walda [= ibn] Ḥatm walda Bəḥērāwi walda ʿAmār walda Xaṭāb," corresponding to the Arabic "Rawḥ b. Ḥātim b. Bəḥērāwi [?] b. ʿUmar b. al-Khaṭṭāb" (Peeters, "S. Antoine le néo-martyr," 422). Interestingly, the Arabic text upon which the Ethiopic is based does not include a genealogy: Vatican ar. 175, 116v–117r. I am grateful to Luke Yarbrough for help with the Ethiopic and for acquiring images of the Vatican manuscript for me.

[43] Samir, "Rawḥ al-Qurašī," 348–53. The name "Rawḥ" is also attested in pre-Islamic inscriptions in Greek; e.g., de Vries, "Umm El-Jimal Project," 442.

seems to fit this onomastic profile. In the absence of hard evidence, one way to interpret Rawḥ may be to see him as a member of a minor Umayyad clan in Damascus or the descendant of Umayyad affiliates who survived the ʿAbbasid revolution of 750. In fact, as Wilferd Madelung has noted, Syrian texts of the period often use the name "Qurashī" interchangeably with "Umayyad."[44] Furthermore, various Umayyad caliphs are known to have inhabited the monastery of St. Theodore where Rawḥ also lived.

Arabic sources call this monastery "Dayr Murrān," and the geographer Yāqūt al-Ḥamawī (d. 626/1229) even states that its altar displayed a miraculous image (Ar. *wa-fī haykalihi ṣūra ʿajība daqīqat al-maʿānī*), possibly the same one mentioned in Anthony's *life*.[45] Interestingly, another martyr of the period—Peter of Capitolias—is said to have visited Dayr Murrān in 96/715, when he was sentenced to death by the caliph al-Walīd b. ʿAbd al-Malik, who was then on his deathbed in the monastery-palace.[46] According to another source, Hārūn al-Rashīd—who ordered Rawḥ's execution—is said to have visited Dayr Murrān and conversed with its abbot.[47] There are no clues about when or even if this encounter ever took place. Nonetheless, it is tempting to imagine Anthony's executioner alighting at his home only a few years before the martyrdom happened. In perhaps the most striking coincidence of all, Muslim sources report that al-Ḥārith b. Saʿīd al-Kadhdhāb—the notorious pseudo-prophet of Damascus, probably of Christian stock, whom the Umayyads had executed for heresy in 80/699—won converts by leading them to Dayr Murrān. There, they are said to have witnessed angels in the form of men on horseback (Ar. *rijāl ʿalā khayl*), exactly as Rawḥ received his vision of Saint Theodore.[48] Clearly, Dayr Murrān was a place of numinous power for Muslims and Christians alike.

Even if we cannot corroborate Rawḥ's existence using Islamic sources, we can place him on a spectrum of recognizable behavior among the Muslim aristocrats of his day. Medieval Arabic texts are filled with descriptions of encounters among Muslims, monks, and priests inside Christian monasteries. The most celebrated of these come from the "Books of Monasteries" (Ar. *kutub al-diyārāt*), the only surviving example of which is the one written by the Fāṭimid belletrist al-Shābushtī (d. ca. 388/988).[49] They describe amusing and

[44] Madelung, "Sufyānī between Tradition and History," 30; Madelung, "Apocalyptic Prophecies in Ḥimṣ," 148. David Cook ("Apostasy from Islam," 263) suggests that Rawḥ may have been a member of the tribe of Abū ʾl-Muʿayṭ but does not explain his reasoning.

[45] Yāqūt, *Muʿjam al-buldān*, ii, 533; for further references, see chapter 3, n. 63.

[46] Shoemaker, *Three Christian Martyrdoms*, 36–39; Peeters, "Passion de S. Pierre," 310.

[47] Hamilton, *Walid and His Friends*, 89 (no source given).

[48] Yāqūt, *Muʿjam al-buldān*, ii, 323; Ibn ʿAsākir, *Tārīkh*, xi, 427 (read *khayl* for *jabal*); with further references in Anthony, "Prophecy and Passion of al-Ḥāriṯ," 17, 22.

[49] al-Shābushtī, *Diyārāt*; discussion in Kilpatrick, "Monasteries through Muslim Eyes"; Camp-

occasionally racy gatherings in which Muslims enjoyed song, drink, and the company of Christian youths in monastic surroundings. These encounters could occasionally be very intense. A poem discussed by Elizabeth Key Fowden, for instance, speaks of a Muslim who was so overwhelmed by the beauty of a Christian he spied in a monastery that he wished to be transformed into the bread and wine of the Eucharist in order to become one with his beloved.[50] Of course, this imagery is poetic—not to mention profane—but it does highlight the porous boundaries between Muslims and Christians in mixed settings not unlike the one in which Rawḥ lived. Given this, it is not out of the question that such encounters sometimes led to conversion.

These meetings, however, were not always romantic; they could also be belligerent. Christian sources mention how Muslims sometimes spread mischief and havoc inside churches and monasteries. The parallels between these stories and Anthony's *life* are so close, in fact, that one suspects that they drew on a common reservoir of topoi then circulating among Christians in the Near East. The first author to spread these legends was Anastasius of Sinai (d. ca. 700), who recounted the visit of a group of Muslims to a church dedicated to Saint Theodore in the village of Karsatas near Damascus.[51] During the visit, one of the Muslims allegedly shot an arrow at an icon of Saint Theodore in the church, and the puncture produced a trickle of blood. None of the Muslims noticed this miracle, and needless to say, they did not repent of their crime either, so God struck them dead. The *Acts of the Council of Nicaea* in 787 reports a similar anecdote, in which a group of Muslim soldiers visited a church in Gabala (Ar. Jabala) along Syria's Mediterranean coast.[52] Having noticed a mosaic icon of the saint on the church's wall, one of the soldiers tried to gouge out its eye with the tip of his spear. As soon as he lifted his weapon, however, his own eye leapt out of its socket and onto the floor. Similar stories in Greek and Arabic will be discussed in the penultimate section of this chapter. Suffice it to say, it is obvious that the *Life of Anthony* recycles anecdotes found in earlier texts. At the same time, these stories are embedded in a social reality, as corroborated by the canons of Jacob of Edessa (d. 708), who advised one correspondent that he should wash and purify any altar on which Arabs

---

bell, "Heaven of Wine"; Sizgorich, "Monks and Their Daughters"; Bowman, "Christian Monasteries in the Early Islamic Period."

[50] Fowden, "Lamp and the Wine Flask," 16–17.

[51] Binggeli, "Anastase le Sinaïte," 220 (Gk.), 532 (Fr.). For the same story recycled by John of Damascus, see Kotter, *Contra imaginum calumniatores*, 184; and in much later Latin translation: Braida and Pelissetti, *Rawḥ al-Qurašī*, 138. For Jews attacking an icon in Tiberias, producing a trickle of miraculous blood, see Dick, *Ikrām al-īqūnāt*, 173.

[52] Mansi, *Sacrorum conciliorum nova et amplissima collectio*, xiii, 77–80; see also Aufhauser, *Miracula*, 8–12.

(Syr. *ṭayāyē*) had eaten and another to lock the doors of the church lest the "Hagarenes [*mhaggrāyē*] enter and mingle with the believers, and disturb them and laugh at the holy mysteries," just as in Anthony's *life*.[53] Thus, we see in the martyr's biography a kernel of lived experience surrounded by a casing of literary motifs.

The most valuable part of Anthony's *life* is what it reveals about the process of apostatizing from Islam—or at least how this process was represented by Christian authors. Many conversions in the early Islamic period were motivated by social and material concerns, but the *life* goes to great lengths to show how spiritual convictions might also play a role. Here, one is struck by the obvious and deliberate parallels between Anthony's *life* and that of another persecutor-turned-martyr, Paul of Tarsus, who likewise became a Christian after a miraculous encounter with the divine near Damascus (Acts 9:3–9). One suspects that the author of the text embellished the conversion scene to match the literary expectations of his readers, steeped as they were in biblical scenes of Saint Paul. We might compare the *Life of Anthony* with that of ʿAbd al-Masīḥ, who died several decades earlier and whose biography was also written in an Arabic-speaking Melkite milieu. As we saw in chapter 1, the *life* portrays ʿAbd al-Masīḥ's conversion as thoughtless and contingent but his reversion to Christianity as heartfelt and sincere—in other words, as quintessentially "Pauline." Likewise, the author of the *Life of ʿAbd al-Masīḥ* represents the saint's reversion in Baalbek using the conventions of late antique hagiography, specifically as a mirror image of the calling of Saint Anthony. According to this topos, God communicates with His holy ones by having them encounter random but significant passages in the Bible, especially during moments of crisis and conversion, a motif that famously surfaces in Augustine's *Confessions*, as well.[54]

Although the *Life of Anthony* is saturated with such topoi, we should not discount the possibility that some Muslims did indeed become Christians because of perceived miracles. If his biography is to be believed, therefore, not only did Anthony convert because of an intense encounter with the divine, but he then opted for the most demanding of spiritual paths, that of monasticism. Then, when faced with torture and death, he refused to renounce his Christianity. With Anthony and all the martyrs, we must be open to the possibility that religious change was not always a simple act of "adhesion," to use Arthur Darby Nock's expression.[55] It could also be a genuine act of "conversion," as the hagiographers strove to show.

[53] Vööbus, *Synodicon*, i, I, 237 (Syr.); i, II, 219 (Eng.). Discussion in Hoyland, "Jacob and Early Islamic Edessa," 16.

[54] For more, see chapter 1, n. 80.

[55] Nock, *Conversion*, 7.

III. TRUE APOSTASY IN THE CAUCASUS

David of Dwin

The next example of true apostasy brings us to the Caucasian frontier of the caliphate, to the Umayyad province of Armīniya, where David of Dwin was martyred in 703/705.[56] His *life* is preserved in two fifteenth-century manuscripts, but in all likelihood they are based on a much earlier composition. Indeed, there is strong internal evidence that the biography was written shortly after the martyr's death, and this is suggested by the role the Mamikonian royal family of Armenia is shown playing in promoting David's cult. The presence of these Christian nobles suggests that David became a prestige symbol for them in the eighth century, helping project an image of independence at a moment when the Umayyad authorities were cultivating and co-opting princely houses across the region.[57] In addition, there are several short passages about David in Armenian historical and liturgical sources.[58] His cult does not seem to have spread outside the Caucasus.

According to his *life*, David was born as "Surhan," an Arab (Arm. *tačik*) soldier of noble ancestry who arrived in Armenia sometime between 656 and 660.[59] He was part of a company of Arab troops stationed in the province of Ayrarat, north of Dwin (Ar. Dabīl), which was then the seat of the Muslim governor.[60] While traveling through the villages of the region, Surhan was

[56] I rely on the English translation by R. W. Thomson in the appendix of Hoyland, *Seeing Islam*, 672–76 (henceforth Thomson, "David of Dwin"). For the Armenian text, see Alishan, *Hayapatum*, i, 546–52; discussion in *CMR*, i, 719–20; *BHO*, 57–58; *BS*, iv, 518–19; *BSO*, i, 627; Grousset, *Histoire de l'Arménie*, 308; Hoyland, *Seeing Islam*, 370–73; Vacca, "Creation of an Islamic Frontier in Armīniya," 195–97; Anthony, *Crucifixion and Death*, 58–59.

[57] Thomson, "David of Dwin," 673, 676. On the princely families of Armenia and their interactions with the Muslim authorities, see Vacca, "Creation of an Islamic Frontier in Armīniya," 105–52.

[58] Maksoudian, *History of Armenia*, 107; Bayan, "Synaxaire arménien," 225–26.

[59] The original Arabic word underlying "Surhan" is not clear. "Ṣurḥān" is a possibility, but it is a relatively rare name in comparison to "Sirḥān" and "Ṣarḥān." Vowel shifts in colloquial Arabic are common, so the Armenian word could be any of the above. Hübschmann (*Armenische Grammatik*, 86–87) claims that *tačik* is a loanword from the Syriac *ṭayāyā*, "Arab," but it is clearly related to the Middle Persian *tāzīg*, also meaning "Arab" (MacKenzie, *Pahlavi Dictionary*, 83). In the late medieval period, Armenian colophons used the term *tačik* to denote various kinds of Muslims, including Tatars, Turkmen, Ottomans, and Mamlūks; see Sanjian, *Colophons of Armenian Manuscripts*, 438. I thank Thomas Carlson for his advice on this matter.

[60] On Arab tribal settlement in Armenia, see Vacca, "Creation of an Islamic Frontier in Armīniya," 141–44; and for the later period, see Ter-Ghewondyan, *Arab Emirates*; Vacca, "*Nisbas* of the North."

deeply impressed by the faith of the locals. He was so impressed, in fact, that "he separated himself from all his own in order to gain Christ."[61] From outside sources, it is clear that many Arab troops were leaving Armenia at this time in order to take part in the first Muslim civil war (35–41/656–61) between the partisans of ʿAlī b. Abī Ṭālib and Muʿāwiya b. Abī Sufyān.[62] Given this context, it seems likely that Surhan stayed behind in the Caucasus while many of his companions traveled south to fight.

Because Surhan was "much befriended and respected by many"—possibly a reference to his noble ancestry or to a position of leadership in the Arab army[63]—the local governor, or *ostikan*, Grigor Mamikonian (r. 661–85), presented him to the catholicos of the Armenian church, Anastas I (r. 662–68), for baptism. The Arab soldier was rechristened "David," and he eventually settled in a village beyond Dwin, where he married a local Christian girl.[64] They had several children. At the turn of the eighth century, when the story resumes, David was already an old man. At this time, the caliph ʿAbd al-Malik b. Marwān (r. 65–86/685–705) decided to reimpose direct rule on Armenia after decades of semiautonomy under Christian vassals.[65] Therefore, he dispatched a new governor, probably ʿAbdallāh b. Ḥātim al-Bāhilī, to subdue the province.[66] Soon after arriving in Dwin, ʿAbdallāh heard of David's conversion to Christianity. It is not clear how this information reached him, though the text hints that David may have leaked it himself, for it "was not right that the truth be hidden."[67] Therefore, ʿAbdallāh summoned the martyr to the capital for interrogation. David refused to repent and berated the governor in Arabic.[68] The Umayyad authorities then nailed him to a cross,[69] which they turned to face

[61] Thomson, "David of Dwin," 672.

[62] See chapter 1, sec. II.

[63] Thomson, "David of Dwin," 673. The text also states that Surhan was "famous and [descended] from great ancestors on his father's side."

[64] Intermarriage between Arab settlers and the local Christians was not uncommon; see Vacca, "Creation of an Islamic Frontier in Armīniya," 144.

[65] Garsoïan, "Rise of the Bagratuni," 125–26.

[66] The text refers to this figure as "Abdlay"; see Khalīfa b. Khayyāṭ, *Tārīkh*, 189. The chronology at this point is rather confused, and Hoyland (*Seeing Islam*, 373; cf. Anthony, *Crucifixion and Death*, 58) has suggested several other possibilities.

[67] Thomson, "David of Dwin," 674.

[68] Isaac, Perfectus, Emila, and Jeremiah of Córdoba (*CSM*, ii, 367, 398, 431–32) also berated their persecutors in Arabic. Bacchus refused to address them in Arabic, insisting on Greek instead: *CMLT*, 109–10.

[69] Reference to the nailing comes not from David's *life* but from John Catholicus in Maksoudian, *History of Armenia*, 107. Most crucifixions in this period involved binding the victim to the cross and not nailing. One wonders whether this detail is fictitious and meant to encourage comparison with Jesus's Crucifixion.

south, presumably in the direction of Mecca, the *qibla*.[70] His *life* tells us that the cross turned miraculously to face the east, the direction of the rising sun and of Christian worship (a motif that surfaces in Shīʿī martyrologies, too).[71] With the help of the nobleman Mushel Mamikonian, David's relics were collected and installed in a tomb inside the cathedral of Dwin.

Aside from the Sixty Martyrs of Gaza and George the Black, we have no neomartyrs executed as early as David. Indeed, the date of his martyrdom should prompt us to ask what kind of Muslim he was in the first place, given that "Islam" was still evolving in the mid-seventh century when David was initially dispatched to the Caucasus. It may not be a coincidence that his death coincided with the campaign of Islamization launched by ʿAbd al-Malik, which led to a rise in tensions between Muslims and Christians across the caliphate.[72] Furthermore, if the martyrdom indeed took place at the turn of the eighth century, it suggests that the Muslim authorities were policing apostasy laws at a very early date. It is hard to say how widely enforced the prohibition was at this time; indeed, one suspects that lower-profile apostates would not have suffered the fate that David did as a high-status convert. There is, of course, the possibility that David's biographer projected later developments into an earlier period so as to dramatize the martyrdom. But given the wealth of contextual details in the source, such deliberate anachronism seems unlikely. Rather, we are probably witnessing a very early account that corroborates the crystallization of apostasy laws during the middle Umayyad period.

The apostasy of David of Dwin also reflects the unique political circumstances that prevailed in the Caucasus over the course of the seventh and early eighth centuries. Unlike in Egypt, Syria, or Iraq, where Muslim control was relatively undisputed from the time of the conquests, the Umayyad caliphs struggled to project power in this far northern outpost of the empire. One consequence of this is that conversion to Islam in Armenia probably occurred at slower, more uneven rates than it did in the south, and indeed, Armenia stands out as one of the few regions under Muslim rule that fundamentally retained its Christian character throughout the Middle Ages. This mirrors the experience of other areas on the outskirts of the caliphate, such as Bukhārā in modern-day Uzbekistan, where locals are reported to have converted to and

[70] See the conclusion.

[71] Theodore, one of the Forty-Two Martyrs of Amorion, is said to have kneeled eastward as he was about to die: Vasil'evskii and Nikitin, *Skazaniia o 42 Amoriiskikh muchenikakh i tserkovnaia sluzhba im*, 32.

[72] Robinson, *ʿAbd al-Malik*, 113–19; Donner, *Muhammad and the Believers*, 194–224.

away from Islam in accord with the Arabs' shifting political fortunes during the seventh and early eighth centuries.[73]

Surhan probably arrived in Armenia at a time when Arab military might was building up, but this control seems to have evaporated as more pressing events spiraled out of control in the south. This probably created a power vacuum, such that the Muslim soldiers who remained behind—members of a rump force charged with keeping the peace or even deserters—had little supervision and found it tempting to "go native." In David, therefore, we have an example of what might have come to pass in the central lands of the empire had the earliest Arab troops not been sequestered in garrison cities (Ar. *amṣār*) such as Qayrawān, Fusṭāṭ, Kūfa, and Baṣra, which isolated them from the surrounding non-Muslim population.[74] If the establishment of garrison cities was a careful strategy aimed at countering assimilation, then it is not surprising that provincial soldiers like Surhan could convert after their Muslim companions left them in predominantly Christian lands such as Armenia. David is the quintessential example of a type of convert found in different periods and cultures: the individual who experiences religious change in the context of social vulnerability and dislocation.

Abo of Tiflīs

Another famous apostate from the Caucasus was Abo, who was executed in 786 in Tiflīs (Geo. Tbilisi), the capital of Georgia.[75] His *life* survives in several early Georgian manuscripts from the ninth to eleventh centuries, and there are claims that it was written within four years of his death by John Sabanisdze, a high-ranking clergyman who claims to have known Abo personally.[76] Georgian liturgical and historical texts also mention the saint in passing.[77] Unlike for the other neomartyrs from the Caucasus, Abo's cult seems to have

[73] al-Narshakhī, *Tārīkh-i Bukhārā*, 57. I am grateful to Uriel Simonsohn for this reference.

[74] On the dangers of non-Muslims infiltrating the *amṣār*, see ʿAbd al-Razzāq, *Muṣannaf*, vi, 60, nos. 10001–2; and chapter 1, n. 131.

[75] Georgian text in Abuladze, *Dzveli k'art'uli agiograp'iuli literaturis dzeglebi*, i, II, 46–81; English translation in Lang, *Georgian Saints*, 115–33. See also the Italian translation in Shurgaia, *Martirio di Abo*, 185–268; German translation in Schultze, "Abo von Tiflis," 11–41. For discussion, see *CMR*, i, 334–37; Kekelidze and Tarchnišvili, *Geschichte*, 94–95; *BS*, i, 86–87; Hoyland, *Seeing Islam*, 346, 685; Shurgaia, *Martirio di Abo*; Rayfield, *Literature of Georgia*, 49–54; Vacca, "Creation of an Islamic Frontier in Armīniya," 198–99.

[76] Shurgaia, *Martirio di Abo*, 77–85; for dating of the text, see 85–95. Rayfield (*Literature of Georgia*, 49) argues that it was completed by 787 because the text does not mention the martyrdom of the famous prince Arč'il (d. 787).

[77] Shurgaia, *Martirio di Abo*, 115; for liturgical sources: 115, 258–68.

spread outside the region, particularly among Georgian expatriates in Byzantium and the Holy Land, as suggested by the existence of manuscript copies of his *life* at Mt. Athos and Mt. Sinai.[78]

To understand the *Life of Abo*, it is important to first grasp the convoluted arc of Georgian history in the generations after the conquests.[79] The Arabs first entered the region through a series of sporadic and indecisive raids in the 640s. A treaty with the Byzantines led to a three-year truce and suspension of hostilities, after which a much larger Arab force invaded the area in 645–46 under the general Ḥabīb b. Maslama. This army eventually reached Tiflīs, where it obtained the submission of Stephen II, prince of K'art'li (as the region was known in Georgian). Thereafter, the Arabs governed Armenia, Georgia, and Caucasian Albania as territories of the larger province of Armīniya, with the primary capital at Dabīl (Dwin) and a secondary capital at Tiflīs. As we have seen, the Arabs ruled the region indirectly for much of the seventh century. The eighth century saw the restoration of Arab power, which was challenged again in the 770s when Armenian and Georgian aristocrats rebelled against the ʿAbbasid caliph al-Manṣūr (r. 136–58/754–75). The leader of this rebellion in Georgia was a Christian prince called Nerse (r. 760–72, 779–ca. 780), who was captured and imprisoned in Baghdad, where the story of Abo's martyrdom begins.

Abo was an Arab Muslim from Baghdad, around seventeen or eighteen years old. "He was born of the line of Abraham," his *life* states: "He had no foreign blood in him, nor was he born of a slave-woman, but of pure Arab stock on both his father's and his mother's side of the family."[80] Abo was a perfumer, adept at "preparing fragrant scent and lotions." He may have been educated, too, since he was reportedly "versed in the literature of the Saracens." In 158/775, with the death of al-Manṣūr and the accession of his son al-Mahdī, the duke Nerse was released from prison and permitted to return to Georgia.[81] Compelled by a "divine summons," the young Abo accompanied him northward. He lived with the duke, reportedly learning to speak, read, and write Georgian. Abo also discovered the Bible, attended church, and discussed the Christian faith with "many expert theologians." Before long, "he became estranged from the faith of Muhammad and abandoned the rites and beliefs of his native land." Given that the province of Georgia (Ar. Jurzān) remained under Muslim control, Abo could not profess his faith in public, so he

[78] *CMR*, i, 336.

[79] Minorsky and Bosworth, "Tiflīs," *EI²*, x, 478–79; Canard, "Armīniya," *EI²*, i, 635–38; Toumanoff, "Armenia and Georgia," esp. 605–11; Rayfield, *Edge of Empires*, 55–72.

[80] Lang, *Georgian Saints*, 117.

[81] On the release of prisoners with the accession of al-Mahdī, see Fiey, *Chrétiens syriaques*, 30.

fasted and prayed in secret. In the meantime, he searched for a discreet place to be baptized.

By 779, relations between Nerse and the ʿAbbasid authorities had soured once again. As a result, the court moved north through the Darial Pass to the land of the Khazars, a nomadic Turkic people who are purported to have converted to Judaism around the same time, and found sanctuary there.[82] Finally free from the scrutiny of Muslim officials, Abo was baptized in one of the Christian villages of the Khazars' realm. Soon the court moved again, this time to the small Christian kingdom of Abkhazia on the Black Sea.[83] Abo was moved by the piety of the locals, so he began practicing asceticism, "pass[ing] three months plunged in fasting and silent meditation."[84] The *life* then reports that al-Mahdī replaced Nerse with his more pliant nephew, Stephen III (r. ca. 779–86). In consequence, Abo felt free to return to Tiflīs, though he was warned by the Christians of Abkhazia that this would entail his all-but-certain death.

Back in Tiflīs, Abo "walked around openly professing the Christian faith." Muslims harassed him, pressuring him into returning to Islam, but he steadfastly refused. He carried on in this way for a time, supported and protected by the large Christian community of the city. This ended, however, with the arrival of a new hard-line *amīr* named Khuzayma b. Khāzim al-Tamīmī, who found out about Abo from local Muslims.[85] "He has abandoned this faith of ours," the crowds told the governor, "and declares himself a Christian and he walks fearlessly about the city teaching many of our people how to become Christians."[86] With that, Khuzayma had Abo tried for apostasy and thrown in prison. After he refused to repent, he was beheaded in January 786 (Figure 2.2).

As with David's, Abo's conversion was closely connected to the unique political scene in the Caucasus during the early Middle Ages. Abo's *life* does not explain why he left Baghdad with Nerse in 775 in the first place—perhaps to serve as a purveyor of perfumes at the reconstituted court in Tiflīs—though the move would prove to be propitious. In Abo, we find another young Muslim who found himself outside a Muslim social cocoon and had to adapt in a world dominated by the presence of Christianity. He provides an intriguing counterexample to the well-known story of Arabization and Islamization in the period,

[82] The *Life of Abo* seems to corroborate this conversion, which is a matter of some scholarly dispute; see Peeters, "Khazars dans la passion de S. Abo"; Pritsak, "Khazar Kingdom's Conversion"; Golden, "Conversion of the Khazars."

[83] For background, see Barthold and Minorsky, "Abkhāz," *EI²*, i, 100–102.

[84] Lang, *Georgian Saints*, 120.

[85] On Khuzayma, see al-Yaʿqūbī, *Tārīkh*, ii, 248; Khalīfa b. Khayyāṭ, *Tārīkh*, 304–5; al-Ṭabarī, *Annales*, iii, 648. For discussion of his activities in the Caucasus, see Toumanoff, *Christian Caucasian History*, 409–10.

[86] Lang, *Georgian Saints*, 123.

Figure 2.2. Chapel of Abo of Tiflīs (modern), with the Mtkvari (Kura) River in the foreground, Tbilisi, Georgia. Photo: Diego Delso/Wikicommons.

in which exposure to the language and culture of the conquerors often served as a precursor to conversion.[87] Here, however, the process unfolded in reverse: exposure to the Georgian language and culture brought about a Muslim's conversion to Christianity. There is ample evidence of Christian courtiers in the medieval Middle East and al-Andalus who converted to Islam in the hopes of ingratiating themselves with their Muslim masters.[88] By the same token, we must assume that there were Muslim courtiers who converted to Christianity for the same purpose, especially in places like the Caucasus, where Christians remained politically powerful after the conquests. As much is suggested by the medieval chronicler Thomas Artsruni, who mentions an anonymous "Muslim and a Persian by race" who was martyred during Bughā al-Kabīr's Armenian campaign (ca. 237/851–52) after converting to Christianity and working as a servant of the Christian nobleman Andzevats'i.[89]

[87] E.g., the *Apocalypse of Samuel of Qalamūn* from Egypt: Papaconstantinou, "Coptic after the Arab Conquest."

[88] Cheïkho, *Vizirs et secrétaires arabes chrétiens*. For a list of Nestorian secretaries in ʿAbbasid Baghdad, roughly a quarter of whom converted to Islam, see now Cabrol, *Secrétaires nestoriens*, 271–80; for further discussion of elite conversion, see El-Leithy, "Coptic Culture," 52–58; and chapter 5, sec. I.

[89] Thomson, *House of Artsrunik'*, 206–7; discussion in *CMR*, ii, 105. The text uses the term *tačik*, "Arab," in a religious sense, while it uses *parsik*, "Persian," in an ethnic sense.

Abo's conversion underscores the precarious place of Islam in this remote northern outpost of the caliphate. If we believe his *life*, therefore, there were clearly enough Muslims in Tiflīs in the late 770s to make Abo fearful about announcing his conversion in public. He felt free to be baptized only once he ventured into the lands of the Khazars, which lay outside the ʿAbbasids' control. It is striking, however, that upon his return to Tiflīs in 785, Abo spent a year living openly as an apostate. He experienced harassment, but it was not until the arrival of Khuzayma b. Khāzim—whose official remit included suppressing Christian resistance to Muslim rule, as indicated by the large number of executions he oversaw at the time[90]—that he felt truly unsafe living publicly as a renegade from Islam. This suggests a selective enforcement of the prohibition on apostasy, depending on political circumstances, as well as the officials in question. Not only did Abo carry on unmolested as a Christian for this period, but according to the crowds who handed him over to Khuzayma, he was even known to have proselytized Muslims.

It is significant that apostates such as David and Abo (as well as Vahan in chapter 1) came from the Caucasian frontiers of the caliphate and not from its central lands. One suspects that these dramatic and unusual acts of apostasy were less prevalent in areas where Muslim political power and social control were stronger. Nevertheless, they point to a phenomenon that could—and no doubt did—happen in any setting in which there was a significant imbalance between Christians and Muslims and weak mechanisms for keeping them apart. Left to chance, there could have been many more like David and Abo.

IV. TRUE APOSTASY IN IRAQ, AL-ANDALUS, AND EGYPT

Given this, what evidence exists for true apostasy in areas with an uninterrupted tradition of Muslim rule? The *Passion of the Twenty Martyrs of Mar Saba*, a late eighth- or early ninth-century Greek text, includes a curious note about an individual named Christopher, "a victory-bearing soldier and martyr of Christ, who just a few years ago was converted from unbelief to pious faith." According to the text, he was "grafted from a barren Persian olive [tree] onto a fruitful one" (cf. Psalm 52:8), eventually becoming a priest and monk.[91] Later,

[90] Cf. Arčʿil (d. 787), a Christian prince from Kakhetia, whom Khuzayma tried to co-opt as a vassal, in Thomson, *Rewriting Caucasian History*, 251–55; or Hamazasp and Sahak, Christian princes from the house of Artsruni, whom Khuzayma also tried to co-opt and convert, in Arzoumanian, *History of Lewond*, 144–47.

[91] *SPSH*, i, 40–41. For discussion, see Vailhé, "Monastère de Saint-Sabas," 24; Schick, *Christian Communities*, 175; Kazhdan, *Byzantine Literature*, 170; Hoyland, *Seeing Islam*, 346; Vila, "Christian Martyrs," 99–101, 323–26 (in which Vila claims that Christopher and Anthony al-Qurashī are the

he was slandered by a "God-denying man" and brought before the caliph al-Mahdī, who had him executed in 778.[92] Given the mention of al-Mahdī, Christopher may have died in or around Baghdad, though al-Mahdī's presence in the text may indicate a connection to Palestine and Mar Saba.

In light of the many examples of conversion from Córdoba, it is surprising that the Latin texts mention almost no true apostates. Most of the martyrs were killed for blasphemy, and among those killed for apostasy, nearly all were converts from Christianity to Islam and back, children of religiously mixed marriages, or products of secret Christian families—not ex-Muslims like Anthony, David, and Abo.[93] There was one martyr, however, who seems to have been the child of two practicing Muslims, and this was a young girl named Leocritia.[94] As her biographer Paulus Alvarus put it, she "was begotten from the dregs of the gentiles and brought forth from the flesh of wolves," typical language from Alvarus and Eulogius when speaking about individuals with Muslim ancestry.[95] Although both her parents seem to have been Muslims, her extended family was not entirely devoid of Christians; indeed, Leocritia gained exposure to Christianity through a relative named Litiosa, who was a nun. After practicing in secret for a time, Leocritia sought the counsel of Eulogius. Meanwhile, her parents were very worried by her religious interests, so to allay their concerns, Leocritia temporarily stopped her ascetic exercises and started dressing in lavish clothing. One day, she reportedly donned her finest outfit and announced that she was going to a friend's wedding. Instead, she fled to Eulogius for protection. Her parents contacted the *qāḍī* seeking his help, and this official initiated a manhunt to find her. Someone eventually notified the authorities of her whereabouts, which prompted her arrest and execution in March 859. Quite clearly, true apostasy was rare in Córdoba: from an Islamic perspective, attrition was more likely to come from the ranks of the

---

same person; I find this argument unconvincing given the very different circumstances of their lives and their names).

[92] The text states that Christopher was martyred on April 14, which was the Tuesday of Holy Week. Kazhdan (*Byzantine Literature*, 170) notes that during the reign of the patriarch Elias II, who is mentioned in the text, the only year in which April 14 fell on the Tuesday of Holy Week was 789. The entry for Christopher in the Palestinian Georgian calendar (Garitte, *Calendrier palestino-géorgien*, 60, 198–99), however, states that he was martyred under al-Mahdī, who reigned from 775 to 785. During that time, April 14 coincided with the Tuesday of Holy Week only once, in 778. This would seem a more plausible date than the one suggested by Kazhdan; see Grumel, *Chronologie*, 311.

[93] See chapter 1, sec. IV.

[94] The literature about Leocritia is extensive; for general comment, see Colbert, *Martyrs of Córdoba*, 94, 238, 344, 350–52, 357, 405, 444.

[95] *CSM*, i, 337–41, here 337; English translation in Sage, *Paul Albar*, 202–10. Discussion of this passage in Barton, *Conquerors, Brides, and Concubines*, 22 (which misidentifies Leocritia as the daughter of a mixed marriage).

recently converted or from Muslims of mixed ancestry than from Muslims of long standing.

One final example falls slightly outside the chronological scope of this book. Furthermore, the individual in question was not executed for apostasy, although Christian sources insist on calling him a *shahīd*, or "martyr."[96] Still, his path from Islam to Christianity closely mirrors that of other apostates, and therefore he merits consideration alongside them. This is Ibn Rajā᾽, later known as Paul, who lived in the late tenth and early eleventh centuries in Egypt.[97] In addition to his own voluminous writings against Islam, we know about his life thanks to a biography by Michael al-Damrāwī, the bishop of Tinnīs, in the *History of the Patriarchs of Alexandria*; this *life* was composed on the basis of an earlier recension by one Theodore b. Mīnā.[98] To my knowledge, Ibn Rajā᾽ was not considered a saint, and indeed, there are no references to him in liturgical sources of the period.

This apostate was born Yūsuf b. Rajā᾽. His father was a professional witness in the *qāḍī* court of Fāṭimid Cairo, and this seems to have given the young Ibn Rajā᾽ early exposure to Islamic law and theology. His biography states that he mastered the Qur᾽an, and given his Egyptian upbringing, one assumes that he was an adherent of the Mālikī or Shāfiʿī *madhhabs*.[99] During his youth, Ibn Rajā᾽ used to walk along the banks of the Nile River. One day, he came across a group of Fāṭimid soldiers preparing a pyre for a convicted apostate. As the crowds massed, Ibn Rajā᾽ approached the apostate and exhorted him to repent. The man refused, telling Ibn Rajā᾽ that he too would suffer for Christ one day. Furious at this prediction, Ibn Rajā᾽ beat the apostate with his shoe, and thereafter, the man was beheaded and burned.

Sometime later, perhaps between 980 and 985, Ibn Rajā᾽ embarked on a pilgrimage to Mecca.[100] During this trip, he received several nighttime visions in which a monk summoned Ibn Rajā᾽ to follow him. A Muslim friend told Ibn Rajā᾽ to ignore these dreams, which were the work of the devil, he claimed.

[96] Shenoda, "Lamenting Islam," 148 n. 252; cf. Atiya, Abd al-Masih, and Burmester, *History of the Patriarchs*, 101.

[97] For discussion, see *CMR*, ii, 541–46; *GCAL*, ii, 318–19; *BSO*, i, 120–24; Frederick, "Wāḍiḥ Ibn Rajā᾽," *CE*, vii, 2311; Shenoda, "Lamenting Islam," 135–50; Bertaina, "*Kalām* of Būluṣ Ibn Rajā᾽"; Bertaina, "Coptic Convert's Analysis of Islam." I am grateful to David Bertaina for sharing his articles with me and for his advice on various matters related to Ibn Rajā᾽. For a recently discovered Sicilian martyr from the same time period whose *life* was produced in Egypt, see Mandalà, "Martyrdom of Yūḥannā."

[98] For the life of Ibn Rajā᾽, see Atiya, Abd al-Masih, and Burmester, *History of the Patriarchs*, 101–13 (Ar.), 151–70 (Eng.).

[99] Atiya, Abd al-Masih, and Burmester, *History of the Patriarchs*, 101.

[100] Anthony al-Qurashī also claimed to have gone on pilgrimage to Mecca before his conversion: Dick, "Passion arabe," 126; Braida and Pelissetti, *Rawḥ al-Qurašī*, 111.

During his return to Egypt, Ibn Rajāʾ became separated from the caravan. He found himself wandering alone in the desert but encountered a mysterious man on horseback in the middle of the wilderness. This man rescued Ibn Rajāʾ by placing him on his mount and flying with him to the safety of the Church of St. Mercurius in Cairo. Waking up the next morning, Ibn Rajāʾ realized that the rider had been none other than Saint Mercurius (d. ca. 250) himself. The revelation was so stunning that Ibn Rajāʾ resolved to be baptized, and indeed, he asked for the help of the church's clergy. At first they refused to baptize the young Muslim, fearing the retribution of the authorities.[101] But after much pleading, they consented to Ibn Rajāʾ's request and immersed him in the baptismal font. He was christened "Paul" in a nod to the apostle who had also embraced Christianity after having persecuted it.

In the meantime, Ibn Rajāʾ's family feared that he had died. A friend spotted him leaving a church, noticing the Christian *zunnār* fastened around his waist, and notified the family that he was still alive.[102] These relatives apprehended Ibn Rajāʾ and returned him home. Enraged, his father exclaimed, "O my son! You have blighted my old age [Ar. *shaykhūkhatī*] among the judges and the witnesses! Perhaps you have done so because I did not marry you off?"[103] As a result, his father pledged to find him a bride of high social standing, that is, provided he promised to recant. Ibn Rajāʾ, however, refused. At first, the family contemplated killing him, "but their hearts were touched by pity," and they decided not to do this. Instead, they spirited him away to a remote area near Giza where he could live in anonymity and avoid bringing further dishonor upon the family. Ibn Rajāʾ had other plans, and instead of staying at Giza, he embarked for the Wādī ʾl-Naṭrūn, the great center of Egyptian monasticism northwest of Cairo, and there became a monk.

Several monks there told Ibn Rajāʾ that his conversion would be valid only if he abjured his Muslim faith in public—an unusual demand not attested in other accounts of apostasy from this period.[104] Therefore, he returned to Cairo to confront his father, who promptly imprisoned him in the cellar. Starvation had no effect, so Ibn Rajāʾ's father tried an even more brutal tactic, forcing his

[101] One priest at first wished to dispatch Ibn Rajāʾ to the Wādī ʾl-Ḥabīb (i.e., Wādī ʾl-Naṭrūn), away from the scrutiny of Muslim officials; compare with Anthony al-Qurashī, whom the patriarch of Jerusalem dispatched to the River Jordan (Dick, "Passion arabe," 123; Braida and Pelissetti, *Rawḥ al-Qurašī*, 103), or Bacchus, whom the abbot of Mar Saba baptized in a secret room (*CMLT*, 83–84).

[102] Atiya, Abd al-Masih, and Burmester, *History of the Patriarchs*, 106. For more on the *zunnār*, see chapter 1, sec. III.

[103] Atiya, Abd al-Masih, and Burmester, *History of the Patriarchs*, 107. Compare with the shaming of Anthony al-Qurashī at the hands of his Muslim family: Dick, "Passion arabe," 124; Braida and Pelissetti, *Rawḥ al-Qurašī*, 106–7.

[104] For what this abjuration may have entailed, see sec. I above.

son to watch as his brother raped his longtime concubine, with whom Ibn Rajāʾ had a son. To make matters worse, the father reportedly plotted to have the child drowned in the Nile by his own swimming instructor. Despite the relentless tortures, nothing could persuade Paul to give up his Christian faith. Therefore, according to his *life*, his father wrote directly to the Fāṭimid caliph al-Ḥākim (r. 386–411/996–1021), an Ismāʿīlī Shīʿī, requesting a sentence. The chief *qāḍī* of Cairo handled the case, but much to the father's surprise, no charges were handed down against Ibn Rajāʾ, and he was set free. For the rest of his life, he busied himself establishing a monastery and writing various apologetic works against Islam, some of which survive to the present.

By escaping execution, Ibn Rajāʾ diverges from the three main examples of apostasy in this chapter. He may have been tormented by his family, but neither these relatives nor the state officials who dealt with him imposed the death penalty. Scholars have attributed Ibn Rajāʾ's good luck to various factors, including the leniency of an Ismāʿīlī judge toward a virulent Christian polemicist (given that both Ismāʿīlīs and Christians looked upon Sunnī Muslims as their theological opponents),[105] as well as the erratic views of the caliph al-Ḥākim, whose reign vacillated between extreme tolerance and intolerance of his non-Muslim subjects.[106] Perhaps there were personal connections between Ibn Rajāʾ and the judicial establishment that protected him but are not reported in the sources. Whatever the case may be, Ibn Rajāʾ is indicative of the fact that death was not the only outcome in the event of apostasy, even when apostasy came to the attention of the state. His experience hints at the existence of a subculture of Muslim apostates in the Middle Ages who managed to avoid detection or were left unmolested by family and friends. Perhaps the best example of this is Moses Maimonides (d. 1204), the great Jewish theologian and physician, who is widely thought to have converted to Islam in order to escape persecution under the Almohads, only to return to Judaism later in life.[107]

If this is so, we must ask why "successful" apostates like Ibn Rajāʾ did not leave a deeper impression in the historical record of the period. Where are all the Muslims who converted to Christianity and got away with it? As David Cook has noted, the absence of such individuals is especially striking in Chris-

[105] Bertaina, "*Kalām* of Būluṣ Ibn Rajāʾ," 270–71.

[106] On al-Ḥākim's attitudes toward Christians, see Canard, "al-Ḥākim bi-Amr Allāh," *EI²*, iii, esp. 77–78; Lev, "Persecutions and Conversion"; Lev, "Fatimid Caliphs, the Copts, and the Coptic Church"; Walker, *Caliph of Cairo*, 205–14, 242–45. On the treatment of *dhimmīs* under the Fāṭimids, with special reference to the Jews, see Rustow, *Heresy and the Politics of Community*, 67–108.

[107] Stroumsa, *Maimonides*, 59.

tian texts, which were written with a Christian readership in mind.[108] Theoretically, at least, the authors of these sources should have had fewer qualms about discussing sensitive matters such as apostasy because their compositions rarely passed before the eyes of Muslims (though there is evidence to suggest that Muslims sometimes did comb through Christian books in search of offensive material).[109] Perhaps it is modern readers who believe that apostasy was rarer and more transgressive than it actually was in the medieval period. Therefore, the lacunae in the sources should prompt us to rethink whether apostasy was in fact rare or simply not a central concern in the struggle to define and maintain Christian identity in the early medieval Middle East.

V. A MUSLIM CONSTANTINE

In this penultimate section, I wish to ask a more straightforward literary question: What did hagiographic accounts of Muslim conversion mean for their authors and readers? If apostasy was a serious offense under any circumstances, then the apostasy of Muslims from entirely Muslim backgrounds was an offense of the very highest and most spectacular order. One way we can answer this question is by examining a smaller subset of texts: legends that describe the apostasy of the caliph and other high-ranking Muslim officials.[110] The *Life of Anthony al-Qurashī* is the most famous and historically plausible example of this genre—but it is not the most audacious. That distinction belongs to a still more fictional cluster of stories that speak of what I shall call a "Muslim Constantine."

Umayyad Palestine

One of the largest collections of such conversion stories was written in Greek and set at the shrine of St. George at Diospolis (Ar. Ludd) in Palestine.[111] The

[108] Cook, "Apostasy from Islam," 265.

[109] The *History of the Patriarchs of Alexandria* claims that al-Aṣbagh b. ʿAbd al-ʿAzīz, the son of the Umayyad governor of Egypt in the early 700s, investigated Christian sources and texts for possible insults against Islam; he had "the Gospel in Arabic," "books of alchemy," and "festal letters" read aloud to him. See Evetts, "History of the Patriarchs," 51.

[110] For overviews, see Swanson, "Christian al-Maʾmūn Tradition"; Binggeli, "Converting the Caliph"; Papaconstantinou, "Saints and Saracens."

[111] Discussion in Peeters, "S. Antoine le néo-martyr," 416–18; Vasiliev, "Life of St. Theodore," 199–200; Sahas, "Gregory Dekapolites (d. 842) and Islam"; Hoyland, *Seeing Islam*, 89–91, 383–86; Vila, "Christian Martyrs," 296–307; Braida and Pelissetti, *Rawḥ al-Qurašī*, 49–63; Binggeli, "Con-

surviving manuscripts are all late, ranging from the twelfth to the thirteenth century, though the texts seem to have been composed during the early ʿAbbasid period.[112] One account describes a Muslim who witnessed a priest venerating an icon of Saint George.[113] In a scene reminiscent of the *Life of Anthony*, this Muslim decided to fire an arrow at the icon, but the arrow turned around in midair and struck the man in his hand. Later, a priest explained that Saint George had performed the miracle. He then advised the Muslim to hang the icon over his bed, to light a candle before it, and the following morning, to anoint his hand with the oil. The Muslim did as he was told, and as predicted, his hand was healed. As a result of the miracle, he asked to be baptized, and the following day, he proclaimed his Christian faith "in the midst of all the Saracens." Upon hearing this, the crowd trampled the man to death.

Another version of the same story (attributed to Gregory of Dekapolis or a monk named Mark, depending on the recension) is more explicit about the apostate's Umayyad links.[114] This story is set in the new Muslim city of Ramla, just beside Diospolis, which allows us to date the legend's dramatic setting to during or shortly after the reign of the city's founder, the caliph Sulaymān b. ʿAbd al-Malik (r. 96–99/715–17).[115] According to one version, the caliph of Syria

verting the Caliph," 92–93. For more on the shrine of St. George at Diospolis and the environs, see Sharon, "Ludd," *EI²*, v, 798–803; Honigmann, "al-Ramla," *EI²*, viii, 423–24; Avni, *Byzantine-Islamic Transition*, 159–90. Christians and Muslims continued to share the ruined Byzantine church of St. George at Ludd until the late Ottoman period; see Grehan, *Twilight of the Saints*, 184–85.

112 On the dating of the manuscripts, see Aufhauser, *Miracula*, v–xv; Festugière, *Collections grecques de miracles*, 259–67. The first individual miracles attested outside the collection date to the eleventh century, and the first full collection in manuscript form dates to the sixteenth. For the dating of the composition of the texts to the ninth or tenth century, see Hoyland, *Seeing Islam*, 90; more generally, for the early history of the cult of St. George, see Walter, "Cult of Saint George," esp. 317.

113 Aufhauser, *Miracula*, 90–93; Festugière, *Collections grecques de miracles*, 308–10. The miracle collection contains several stories pertaining to Islam: drunken Muslims attacking an icon of Saint George with a spear (Aufhauser, *Miracula*, 8–12; cf. Mansi, *Sacrorum conciliorum nova et amplissima collectio*, xiii, 77–80), a Christian servant of a Muslim general refusing to convert to Islam (Aufhauser, *Miracula*, 13–18), Saint George reviving a Byzantine soldier after he was killed during a raid in Syria (Aufhauser, *Miracula*, 93–100), and a child from Mytilene being captured by Muslim pirates (Aufhauser, *Miracula*, 100–103).

114 For the version attributed to Gregory of Dekapolis, Vat. gr. 1130: Aufhauser, *Miracula*, 65–89 (odd pages); *PG*, c, 1201–12; Festugière, *Collections grecques de miracles*, 294–307 (6b); Sahas, "Gregory Dekapolites (d. 842) and Islam," 50–62. For the version attributed to Mark the Monk, Paris BNF gr. 1190: Aufhauser, *Miracula*, 64–88 (even pages, Gk.); Festugière, *Collections grecques de miracles*, 294–306 (6a, Fr.). See also the much later text from Iosaphaion 308 (1878): Aufhauser, *Miracula*, 66–88 (bottom of page). On the spurious attribution to Gregory, see now Binggeli, "Converting the Caliph," 92–93.

115 Vat. gr. 1130 states that the incident occurred in the place "which the Saracens call in their language *Ampelon*" (Aufhauser, *Miracula*, 65). Paris BNF gr. 1190 states that it took place near Jerusalem (Aufhauser, *Miracula*, 64). "Ampelon" is almost certainly a corruption of "al-Ramla," as

(Gk. *ameroumnēs*; from Ar. *amīr al-mu'minīn*, "commander of the faithful")[116] dispatched a nephew named "Malmeth" to attend to business in the city.[117] According to another, the caliph ordered a cousin (Gk. *anepsion*) to register for the army, but not wishing to do so, the cousin fled to Ramla.[118] While traveling, he came across an "old and miraculous church" dedicated to Saint George. In a scene reminiscent of reports found in Anastasius of Sinai, Theophanes Confessor, and Pseudo-Methodius, the man ordered his servants to place his twelve camels in the nave of the church.[119] The priest inside protested, but the Muslim nobleman refused to heed his complaints. Soon, a miraculous power struck the camels dead. Amazed, the Muslim lingered in the church for a while in order to observe the liturgy. Initially, the priest was apprehensive that this man would disrupt the service and snatch the host—a concern echoed in the *Life of Anthony* as well as the canons of Jacob of Edessa[120]—but he nevertheless allowed him to stay.

The Muslim then observed the priest holding a human child in his hands, pouring his blood into the chalice, and breaking his body over the paten. Realizing that he had observed a eucharistic miracle, the Muslim consumed the unconsecrated bread and begged the priest to baptize him.[121] The priest demurred, explaining that the caliph would kill him and burn his church if he ever discovered what had happened. Therefore, he dispatched the man to Mt. Sinai to be baptized in secret. There, he took the name "Pachomius" or "John," depending on the recension. After three years at Mt. Sinai, the apostate returned to Palestine and met the priest of the church once again. This man rejoiced "at seeing the former Arab wolf who had become the mildest of Christ's

evidenced by the late recension in Iosaphaion 308, which states that the martyrdom occurred "in Diospolis, the place the Saracens call Rempli" (Aufhauser, *Miracula*, 66). On this count, Hoyland (*Seeing Islam*, 383 n. 142) is correct but does not note the evidence from Iosaphaion 308, while Vila ("Christian Martyrs," 297–98 n. 109), Peeters ("S. Antoine le néo-martyr," 416–17), and Sahas ("Gregory Dekapolites [d. 842] and Islam," 50) overlook this.

[116]Compare this with Westernick, *Arethae archiepiscopi Caesarensis scripta minora*, i, 242; Sahas, "Gregory Dekapolites (d. 842) and Islam," 51 n. 17.

[117]Paris BNF gr. 1190 is the only version that identifies the martyr as "Malmeth"; Aufhauser, *Miracula*, 64.

[118]Different versions describe different degrees of relationship between the martyr and the caliph. Vat. gr. 1130 states that they were cousins (Aufhauser, *Miracula*, 65; *PG*, c, 1205c, 1208b–c); Paris BNF gr. 1190 states that they were uncle and nephew (Aufhauser, *Miracula*, 66).

[119]Binggeli, "Anastate le Sinaïte," 220 (Gk.), 532 (Fr.); de Boor, *Chronographia*, i, 404; Mango and Scott, *Theophanes*, 559, in which the caliph Hishām b. ʿAbd al-Malik is said to have left his camels "at St. Elijah's," where they were miraculously burned; Garstad, *Apocalypse, Pseudo-Methodius*, 48–49, which predicts that the Arabs "will stable their flocks in the tombs of the saints." I thank Uriel Simonsohn for this last reference.

[120]See n. 53 above.

[121]Aufhauser, *Miracula*, 69, 71. Compare with the *Life of George-Muzāḥim*; see chapter 1, sec. IV.

sheep."[122] The priest then advised the convert to profess his faith before the caliph. The new monk did as he was told, and the caliph greeted this news with bewilderment and rage. As in the *Life of Anthony*, the caliph asked him, "How did you give up your way of life and the royal scepter and go around as one of the poor, wearing these foul-smelling garments of hair?"[123] Although the caliph intended to be lenient, the other Muslims at court threatened that they would become Christians too unless he sentenced the apostate to death. Therefore, the ruler allowed a mob to drag the monk outside, where they tortured and killed him.

ʿAbbasid Baghdad

As evidence of just how widespread these legends became in the Middle Ages, we can track their evolution in a separate cluster of conversion stories centered on ʿAbbasid Baghdad. The first of these, written originally by Ibn Rajāʾ in Arabic and later incorporated into the *History of the Patriarchs of Alexandria*, describes a Muslim convert to Christianity named al-Hāshimī.[124] His generic-sounding name indicates that he was meant to be a member of the ʿAbbasid royal family, specifically the Banū Hāshim. Indeed, his father is described as being the "king" of the city. According to the text, al-Hāshimī used to ride through the streets of Baghdad with a company of soldiers. When he came across a church, he would order his troops to steal the Eucharist, break it apart, and mix it with dust. The priests of Baghdad were reportedly so frightened of al-Hāshimī that they abstained from celebrating the mass out of fear that he would barge in and disrupt the service.

One day, the Muslim prince entered a church and saw on the altar not a loaf of bread but a "beautiful and noble child." The priest then dismembered the child and distributed its flesh to the congregation, as in the story of the martyrdom of the Umayyad convert at Diospolis. Confused and angry, al-Hāshimī confronted the priest and demanded an explanation. When he realized that he had seen a miracle, he dismissed his Muslim companions and spent the night with the priest, who baptized him in secret. The following morning, al-

[122] Aufhauser, *Miracula*, 79; *PG*, c, 1208a. On similar language in contemporary Latin texts, see Barton, *Conquerors, Brides, and Concubines*, 22.

[123] Aufhauser, *Miracula*, 83. Compare with Dick, "Passion arabe," 124; Braida and Pelissetti, *Rawḥ al-Qurašī*, 107.

[124] Atiya, Abd al-Masih, and Burmester, *History of the Patriarchs*, 110–11 (Ar.), 165–67 (Eng.); discussion in *CMR*, ii, 544; Cook, "Apostasy from Islam," 263 n. 67 (which provides the wrong citation). David Bertaina, the recent editor of Ibn Rajāʾ's writing, tells me that the passage about al-Hāshimī does not appear in any of the manuscripts of the *Kitāb al-wāḍiḥ*.

Hāshimī's soldiers returned to check on him, and after discovering his baptism, they notified his father, the king. The king urged his son to renounce his Christianity, but he refused and was sentenced to death. According to the *History of the Patriarchs*, the Christians of Baghdad built a church in his honor, "which is now known as the Church of al-Hāshimī."[125]

The final legend comes from the *Life of Theodore of Edessa*, a hagiographic novel based loosely on the *life* of the famous Melkite churchman Theodore Abū Qurra. It was written in Greek in the ninth century in either Edessa, Palestine, or Constantinople and then translated into Arabic.[126] This Arabic version exists only in manuscript form and currently awaits further study.[127] The story revolves around Theodore, a bishop of Edessa, who went to Baghdad (Gk. Babylon) seeking the caliph's help in managing the affairs of his unruly diocese. The text identifies the caliph as "Mauias" (Ar. Muʿāwiya), though contextually, he is probably meant to be al-Ma'mūn (r. 198–218/813–33).[128] According to his *life*, Theodore found the caliph gravely ill and healed him with dust from the Church of the Holy Sepulcher.[129] Grateful for his help, the caliph agreed to intercede on Theodore's behalf in Edessa. They then engaged in a long discussion about Christian theology. The caliph was impressed by the bishop's arguments—not to mention his mastery of four languages, including Greek, Syriac, Arabic, and Persian.[130] Therefore, he asked to be baptized. Theodore led the caliph and a group of servants to the Tigris River, where they were immersed in the stream and converted. The caliph took the Christian name "John."[131]

For the remainder of the story, the caliph kept his Christian faith a secret, at one point even dispatching Theodore to Constantinople to obtain a relic of the True Cross on his behalf.[132] One day, after gathering his subjects (including

[125] The version of the *Life of Anthony* edited by Pirone ("Martirio del nobile qurayshita Rawḥ," 506–7) states that the martyr was buried in Baghdad, not Raqqa as in other recensions. One wonders whether there is a connection between this and the story of al-Hāshimī. See also Michael the Syrian, who writes that the relics of Anthony al-Qurashī went to Persia: Chabot, *Chronique*, iii, 19 (Fr.); iv, 488 (Syr.).

[126] On the martyrdom of the caliph Mauias-John, see *CMR*, ii, 585–93; Vasiliev, "Life of St. Theodore," 181, 188, 192, 195–97; Griffith, "*Life of Theodore*," 150–52, 156–60; Swanson, "Christian al-Ma'mūn Tradition"; Binggeli, "Converting the Caliph," 95–97. On the text more generally, see Abel, "Portée apologétique."

[127] I have consulted the version in Paris BNF ar. 147, 170r–179v. I thank Alexandre Roberts for providing me with the microfilm of this manuscript.

[128] Swanson, "Christian al-Ma'mūn Tradition," 82; Griffith, "Abū Qurrah in the Maǧlis of al-Ma'mūn." On al-Ma'mūn's record of treatment of Christians, see Fiey, *Chrétiens syriaques*, 63–75.

[129] Pomialovskij, *Zhitie izhe vo sviatykh ottsa nashego Feodora*, 72–79.

[130] Pomialovskij, *Zhitie izhe vo sviatykh ottsa nashego Feodora*, 84.

[131] Pomialovskij, *Zhitie izhe vo sviatykh ottsa nashego Feodora*, 80–88.

[132] Pomialovskij, *Zhitie izhe vo sviatykh ottsa nashego Feodora*, 88–94 (for Theodore's visit to Constantinople).

"Persians, Hagarenes, Hebrews, and Christians") on the plains of the "Adumenoi," the caliph decided to reveal his apostasy in public.[133] He mounted the rostrum and proclaimed, "I am a Christian and my name is John! I believe in the Father, the Son, and the Holy Spirit, the triune God of a single substance." Pulling a golden cross from his shirt and displaying it to the crowd, he bowed toward the east three times and said, "I adore your venerable cross, O Christ, and acknowledge you as my God, Lord, and Savior!" The crowd was dumbstruck by the spectacle and rushed against him, killing the caliph as well as his attendants in the process. The Christians of Baghdad reportedly fled in terror, but they managed to recover the caliph's body and install it in a nearby church, along with the remains of his servants. Their relics produced many miracles, "with the result that many Persians and Hagarenes abandoned the faith of their fathers and became Christians."

Interpreting Conversion Legends

Although none of these stories mimics the *Life of Anthony al-Qurashī* in its entirety, the parallels among them are obvious: the baptism of Muslim noblemen, miraculous icons, eucharistic visions, confrontations with Muslim relatives, and above all, martyrdom. With the exception of Ibn Rajāʾ's account of al-Hāshimī, they all emerge from a common Melkite milieu. The pressing question, therefore, is, Which came first: the *Life of Anthony* or the shorter legends set in Palestine and Iraq? A definitive answer must depend on close examination of the relevant manuscripts at a future time—especially those containing the *Miracles of St. George* and the *Life of St. Theodore*. For now, it is safe to say that the Diospolis and Baghdad legends are entirely fictional: there is no evidence of a caliph or a close relative of a caliph ever converting to Christianity and inspiring such myths.[134] The *Life of Anthony* contains fantastical elements

[133] Pomialovskij, *Zhitie izhe vo sviatykh ottsa nashego Feodora*, 113–15 (for the caliph's profession of faith and martyrdom).

[134] An older generation of scholars tried in vain to find a member of the Muslim ruling family who had become Christian; e.g., Vasiliev, "Life of St. Theodore," 199–210; with critique in Griffith, "*Life of Theodore*," 156–57. Some historical sources claim that high-ranking Muslims flirted with Christianity, but these should not be taken at face value; e.g., ʿAbd al-ʿAzīz b. Mūsā b. Nuṣayr (see n. 14 above). The Armenian translation of the *Chronicle of Michael the Syrian* claims that al-ʿAbbās b. al-Maʾmūn allied himself to the Byzantines and converted to Christianity during a rebellion against al-Muʿtasim (r. 218–27/833–42), but strangely the conversion is not attested in the Syriac version of Michael's work (Chabot, *Chronique*, iii, 101) or in Islamic historiography (al-Ṭabarī, *Annales*, iii, 1256–68); see Langlois, *Chronique*, 275, cited in Vasiliev, "Life of St. Theodore," 204–5.

too, but it also contains a wealth of contextual information that points to some basis in historical reality. This is also corroborated by the large number of nonhagiographic references to Anthony, including in the writing of Theodore Abū Qurra and various Syriac chronicles. The unusual circumstances of his life and death provided immediate grist for the hagiographic mill, it seems, and these traditions combined with stories about aristocratic Muslims converting in other cities throughout the empire. We may see the legend of the caliph's conversion as the apogee of this process of Christian mythmaking.

To understand the purpose of these stories, we must step back in time and consider their roots in the literature of late antiquity. If we search for pre-Islamic parallels in the Middle East, the closest we will find are Christian legends about the conversion of Zoroastrian aristocrats from the sixth and seventh centuries.[135] As Richard Payne has recently shown, Syriac-speaking Christians (mostly belonging to the Nestorian Church of the East) were a vital part of Sasanian society before the rise of Islam. Although scholars once imagined them as a beleaguered minority, Payne has argued that they formed a dynamic and growing portion of the population, one whose relationship with the ruling elite was defined by collaboration, compromise, and tolerance. In this world, Christians wrote stories about Zoroastrian nobles furtively converting to Christianity and being martyred, such as the famous Mar Qardagh (fl. fourth century).[136] Despite their fantastical elements, these hagiographic fantasies had some basis in reality: Zoroastrian aristocrats did indeed convert to Christianity, even if their numbers were in reality relatively small. What is more, while there is no evidence of a Sasanian monarch converting to Christianity outright,[137] Sasanian kings did lavish support on Christian institutions, including monasteries, churches, and saints' shrines, as well as on powerful Christian leaders, such as the catholicos of Seleucia-Ctesiphon (whose see was created with the help of the Sasanian monarch Yazdgird I in 410).[138] One way Christian authors explained this surprising cooperation was by claiming that the Three Magi of the Gospels had themselves converted the founder of the Sasanian dynasty, Ardashir I (r. 224–42, this despite the obvious problems of chronology).[139] It was with the arrival of Khusraw II at the court of the Byzantine emperor Maurice in 590, however, that claims of "true apostasy" reached a fever pitch. The alliance between these two men was

[135] Payne, *State of Mixture*, esp. 9, 164–66.

[136] Walker, *Mar Qardagh*; see also Morony, *Iraq*, 298–300; Payne, *State of Mixture*, 192–96.

[137] The son of the newly crowned Sasanian king Shahrbaraz (ca. 630) was reportedly a convert to Christianity: Hoyland, *In God's Path*, 12.

[138] Payne, *State of Mixture*, 164–98.

[139] Schilling, *Anbetung der Magier*, 91–96; Payne, *State of Mixture*, 164–65.

reportedly cemented by a rite known as *adoptio per arma*, and under normal circumstances, parties to this rite were both assumed to be Christians.[140]

In reality, Khusraw did not renounce Zoroastrianism to make his pact with Maurice, but that did not stop Christian writers from Armenia to Francia from composing dreamlike stories about his conversion.[141] John of Nikiu even modeled his account of Khusraw's baptism on older reports about the conversion of Constantine, underlining what must have been a widespread hope for the conversion of a second pagan empire.[142] The Christianization of Iran was never as advanced as hagiographic texts would have us believe: the Sasanian ruling elite was firmly committed to Zoroastrianism, as well as the social and political order that depended on it.[143] Nonetheless, stories about the conversion of Iranian monarchs tell us something important about the place of Christianity in a Zoroastrian empire and, in turn, can provide insight about the place of Christianity in a Muslim empire generations later.

As exercises in mythmaking, legends about the conversion of the caliph and the king of kings are remarkably similar. They reflect a common desire to establish the truth and prestige of Christianity in worlds in which the church was not on top. There was no better way of doing this than by claiming that Christianity had converted the most powerful of the unbelievers, that is, the caliph and king (much as Muslims claimed that Heraclius had entertained converting to Islam after his famous exchange of letters with Muḥammad).[144] Here, we are reminded of the words of Anthony al-Qurashī, who after witnessing a eucharistic miracle marveled that Christianity was indeed a "noble and true religion" (Ar. *dīn sharīf ṣaḥīḥ*).[145] Although it is left unsaid in Anthony's *life*, the obvious corollary of this statement is that Islam was an ignoble and false religion. Such a corollary would have been familiar to Christian hagiographers writing under Zoroastrian rule, who also used saints' *lives* to articulate the truth of their faith over that of their non-Christian sovereigns and competitors.

In addition, both sets of stories express a common eschatological hope, namely, a desire to see pagan society transformed from the top down by converting its ruler. We can liken this to how Christians in the Roman Empire

140 Schilling, *Anbetung der Magier*, 235–98; Payne, *State of Mixture*, 164.

141 Wallace-Hadrill, *Chronicle of Fredegar*, 7–9; Payne, *State of Mixture*, 164; more generally, Toral-Niehoff, "Constantine's Baptism Legend."

142 Charles, *Chronicle of John, Bishop of Nikiu*, 154; discussion in Schilling, *Anbetung der Magier*, 185–89; Payne, *State of Mixture*, 164.

143 Payne, "Cosmology"; Payne, *State of Mixture*, 23–58.

144 El Cheikh, *Byzantium Viewed by the Arabs*, 42–46.

145 Monferrer Sala, "*Šahādat al-qiddīs Mār Anṭūniyūs*," 258.

must have felt prior to the accession of Constantine: while they knew they could not topple a persecutory regime from without, they could aspire to transform it spiritually from within. This entailed winning elites for Christ, especially the emperor and his court. In the middle of the third century, the conversion of a Roman emperor must have seemed implausible—as implausible as the conversion of a king of kings in sixth-century Iran or the conversion of a caliph in ninth-century Iraq. But the Eusebian arc of salvation history teaches that Christianity is always one convert away from launching a spiritual revolution. All it took was a single "Constantine" to transform the church from a house of martyrs into a palace of princes and kings. Although Melkite Christians ceased to dream of baptizing the caliph after the ninth or tenth century, their Coptic counterparts in Egypt wrote similar narratives predicting the conversion of their Fāṭimid rulers, as did Jews in al-Andalus in the twelfth century.[146] It is interesting to note that Christians in the Church of the East—whose ancestors had pioneered the genre with stories about the conversion of Zoroastrian nobles—went silent on this matter after the rise of Islam.[147]

Finally, it is telling that when Christians imagined the end of times in the early Islamic period, they predicted the advent of a "scion of the mighty kings of the children of Ishmael" who would convert to Christianity and redeem the church, not unlike the motif examined in this section.[148] For their part, Muslims imagined similar things happening but looked upon these events with dread, not optimism: the *Kitāb al-fitan* of Nuʿaym b. Ḥammād (d. 228/843), an important collection of apocalyptic *ḥadīth* from the Umayyad and early ʿAbbasid periods, mentions the advent of a Muslim governor from the tribe of Umayya who would one day defect to the Byzantines and lead the reconquest of Syria, presumably converting to Christianity in the process.[149] Thus, the very scenario that inspired hope in Christians instilled fear in Muslims, a testament to how literary motifs could be recycled and reinterpreted across religious frontiers.

[146]For Copts in Fāṭimid Egypt, see Tropeau, "Traité christologique"; den Heijer, "Life of Afrahām Ibn Zurʿah"; Shenoda, "Lamenting Islam," 152–69. For Jews in twelfth-century al-Andalus, see Wasserstein, "*Fatwā* on Conversion," 180, 187 n. 46. See also Coptic hagiography claiming that Diocletian converted from his ancestral Christianity to paganism: Papaconstantinou, "Historiography, Hagiography," 80.

[147]For more on the Church of the East and its attitude toward the Muslim state, see chapter 5, sec. III.

[148]Mingana, "Apocalypse of Peter" (1930), 492–93; cited in Cook, *Muslim Apocalyptic*, 71.

[149]Nuʿaym b. Ḥammād, *Fitan*, 291, 295, 298; see also Ibn ʿAsākir, *Tārīkh*, xii, 444–45; cited in Cook, *Muslim Apocalyptic*, 70–71.

VI. CONCLUSION

This and the previous chapter have examined three groups of martyrs: Christians who converted to Islam and then returned to Christianity, Christians who were born into religiously mixed families, and Muslims who converted to Christianity. Given the literary motifs and religious biases that fill the texts, what do they reveal about the nature and meaning of conversion in the early medieval Middle East? First, apostasy was very rare. It was more common among recently converted Muslims than it was among Muslims of long standing. Still, apostates from both groups must have been uncommon, especially in comparison to the large numbers of permanent converts from Christianity to Islam. Regardless of how they left Islam, apostates faced stiff penalties if they were ever caught. Furthermore, they stood to gain little economically, socially, or politically from their conversions. Personal conviction must have played a powerful role for some apostates, but this does not seem to have overcome the staggering disincentives for most prospective converts. The Muslim community may have been small in its early years, but its long-term trajectory was always toward growth.

Second, apostasy seems to have occurred in practically every part of the caliphate where Muslims lived alongside Christian majorities—which in the early period meant most territories west of Iran. It is significant that two of the most detailed examples of true apostasy, David of Dwin and Abo of Tiflīs, took place along the Caucasian frontier, where a combination of a demographic imbalance between Christians and Muslims and the collapse of Muslim political authority made conditions ripe for "going native." This impression is confirmed by scholars of conversion in other cultural contexts, who stress the role of dislocation and relocation in catalyzing religious change.[150] By the same measure, Muslims in places such as al-Andalus, Syria, and Egypt could also "go native" by converting to Christianity, but apostasy was probably much harder in these regions because the coercive instruments of the state were much stronger. Aside from irregular cases like those of the martyrs, the only Muslims who did apostatize were probably inhabitants of majority-Christian areas, especially rural districts. In these places, conversion may have granted privileged access to Christian wives, Christian markets, and Christian inheritances that Muslims were otherwise barred from obtaining. Plus, the reach of the state in these areas was probably much weaker, so apostates could convert with far less fear of being punished.

[150] Kim, "Migration and Conversion of Korean American Christians."

Third, miracles play a role in many conversion stories, especially of Muslims converting to Christianity. We might be tempted to dismiss these reports of wonder-working icons and eucharistic visions as mere literary tropes, but they may reflect a real social context. Sociologists of religion, for example, have emphasized the importance of dreams in catalyzing conversion in many cultures around the world.[151] In a period closer to our own, Ramsay MacMullen observed that Christianity's success in late antiquity owed in large part to its perceived knack for exorcism and other supernatural feats.[152] Perceived miracles furnished proof of the power and truth of the Christian God—whether it was the third century or the eighth, it seems.

Fourth, clergy seem to have played a surprisingly peripheral role in the conversion of Muslims to Christianity. Though priests and monks appear in many saints' *lives*, it is usually to administer the sacrament of baptism at the end of the process—in other words, to formalize a conversion first brought about by a miracle, a vision, or the encouragement of friends much earlier. Priests and monks do not seem to have proselytized Muslims very aggressively, presumably because of the harsh penalties facing anyone found guilty of enabling conversions.[153] On balance, the initial impetus for many apostates seems to have come from without the institutional church, not from within it, at least if the *lives* of the martyrs are to be trusted.

Fifth, conversion from Islam was highly secretive. Baptisms were often conducted in discreet locations away from prying eyes. Some converts seem to have concealed their beliefs from Muslim relatives and friends, while others seem to have fled to the safety of majority-Christian areas or at least new areas where they could live anonymously. Most apostates probably avoided contact with Muslims or loose-lipped Christians who might betray them. Perhaps this explains the striking presence of upper-class Muslims in the sources, whose conversions (in addition to being prestigious) may have simply been too conspicuous to ignore. By contrast, apostates from the lower classes may have been able to fade into the background and avoid detection.

Sixth and finally, a disproportionate number of martyrs became monks after their conversions. This may be a narrative device designed to portray the apostates as the most exemplary converts, for ascetics were also the most exemplary Christians. If we push past the motif, however, they seem to have understood themselves as tapping into a richer and more demanding spiritual tradition than was available at the time in Islam. While it is true that this could reflect an anti-Muslim bias in the sources—the overwhelming majority of

[151] Bulkeley, "Dreaming and Religious Conversion."
[152] MacMullen, *Christianizing the Roman Empire*, 27–28.
[153] For more, see chapter 5, sec. II.

which were written by monks—it is striking to observe just how many martyrs became ascetics after their baptisms. Was every apostate a spiritual rigorist like Anthony al-Qurashī, who gave up his riches to don the monastic habit, or like Abo of Tiflīs, who abandoned his perfumes for a life of fasting and prayer? Probably not, yet, by the same token, not a small number of them were, and these are the ones who are apparent to us in the sources.

Around the same time that many martyrs were apostatizing and embracing monasticism, Islam was developing its own ascetic traditions. These were embodied by early spiritual authorities such as al-Ḥasan al-Baṣrī (d. 110/728), the great proto-Sufi, as well as ʿAbdallāh b. al-Mubārak (d. 181/797), the volunteer soldier (Ar. *mutaṭawwiʿ*) who combined a life of warfare, scholarship, and penance along the frontiers of the ʿAbbasid caliphate.[154] The rise of Muslim asceticism is a complicated phenomenon, but it is clear that it evolved as a result of, in conversation with, and in reaction to preexisting Christian practices.[155] Thus do we find many stories of Muslims seeking advice at the feet of Christian holy men. These monks were ecumenical symbols for Christians and Muslims alike, but they were also symbols of a spiritual path that was more developed in Christianity than in early Islam. As much is suggested by legends about the great ascetic Ibrāhīm b. Adham al-Balkhī (d. 161/777–78), who is said to have realized his calling through conversations with a Christian monk named Abba Simʿān.[156] Perhaps some apostates sensed this chasm and pursued baptism as a way of drawing closer to what they regarded as "original asceticism." By the same logic, perhaps conversions to Christianity trailed off with the advent of more mature forms of Muslim asceticism over the centuries, including Sufism.

As these two chapters have shown, conversion in the Umayyad and ʿAbbasid periods was not entirely a one-way street from Christianity to Islam. When we consider the demographic weight of Christianity, its relatively deeper roots in the societies of the Middle East where Muslims first settled, and the prevailing culture of religious change, it is remarkable that more did not follow the path of martyrs like ʿAbd al-Masīḥ and return to Christianity or of Anthony al-Qurashī and abandon their ancestral faith. Thus, if this tour through the convert-martyrs has accomplished anything, it is to show that

[154] For more on the *mutaṭawwiʿ* phenomenon, see Bonner, *Aristocratic Violence*, 107–34; Tor, *Violent Order*, 39–84.

[155] Beck, "Christliche Mönchtum"; Sviri, "Origin and Evaluation"; Livne-Kafri, "Early Muslim Ascetics"; Sahner, "Birth of Monasticism"; Sahner, "Monasticism of My Community Is Jihad."

[156] Abū Nuʿaym al-Iṣfahānī, *Ḥilyat al-awliyāʾ*, viii, 29–30, cited in Andrae, *In the Garden of Myrtles*, 12–13; Sizgorich, *Violence and Belief*, 174. For background, see Jones, "Ibrāhīm b. Adham," *EI*², iii, 985–86; Tor, *Violent Order*, 46–48.

Islamization was neither absolute nor inevitable in the early Middle Ages. Contrary to the views of the great Julius Wellhausen, "the increasing Islamisation of the conquered" peoples of the greater Middle East was not a "natural and inevitable process."[157] It could be a fragile, contested process in the mixed-up world that emerged in the wake of the conquests.

[157] Wellhausen, *Arab Kingdom*, 308.

3

Blaspheming against Islam

In his treatise on the judges of Córdoba, the Andalusī jurist al-Khushanī (d. ca. 371/981) recorded a striking event that took place at the start of the tenth century. In it, an unnamed Christian tried to provoke his own death by publically disparaging Islam.[1] His goal, it seems, was to attack the Muslim faith so viciously that the *qāḍī*—one Aslam b. ʿAbd al-ʿAzīz—would have no choice but to have him killed. Al-Khushanī states that the man was "moved by the idiocy and ignorance of the Christians." He even ascribed "a certain virtue" to his insults. The Christian challenged the judge to have him executed, but he prophesied that he would not succeed. "My likeness [Ar. *shabahī*] shall rest on one of the corpses," he proclaimed, "but that is all you shall kill. . . . As for me, from that hour, I shall be raised up to heaven," echoing the Qur'an's description of Jesus's Crucifixion (Q. *al-Mā'ida* 4:157–58). Dismissing this as the rant of a crazy man, Aslam had the Christian stripped and beaten. When he refused to repent, Aslam had him killed.

Unfortunately, al-Khushanī did not explain what the Christian said to make the judge so angry. He merely referred to it as an act of *takdhīb*, or "denial," another term with Qur'anic resonance (e.g., Q. *al-Burūj* 85:19). In any event, Muslim readers in tenth-century Córdoba probably did not need it spelled out explicitly. They had been living with blasphemers in their midst for more than a hundred years. The most famous of these were the forty-eight Christians who were executed in and around Córdoba between 850 and 859. These martyrs inspired great troves of hagiographic and apologetic texts on the Christian side, yet not so much as a whisper about them survives in Muslim sources. This imbalance makes al-Khushanī's report extremely precious.[2] Although set

[1] al-Khushanī, *Quḍāt qurṭuba*, 158–59; discussion in Wolf, *Christian Martyrs*, 34; Christys, *Christians in al-Andalus*, 81. Fierro ("Bāṭinism during the Umayyad Caliphate") has recently suggested that the scene shows the impact of Fāṭimid propaganda among Andalusī Christians at the time of the rebellion of ʿUmar b. Ḥafṣūn, a *muwallad* who converted from Islam to Christianity and had contact with Fāṭimid agents.

[2] Andalusī Muslim sources mention another Christian blasphemer named Dalja (also Dabḥa; Lat. Dulce?), who was executed under the chief *qāḍī* of Córdoba Aḥmad b. Muḥammad al-Lakhmī (r. 275–300/888–912). See Ibn Sahl, *Aḥkām*, 878–78; cf. al-Wansharīsī, *al-Miʿyar al-muʿrib*, ii, 344–45; discussion in Lévi-Provençal, *Histoire*, i, 231–32; García Gómez, "Dulce, mártir mozárabe";

half a century after the Córdoba martyrs incident, it describes a strikingly familiar scene. Not only does it help corroborate the general content of the stories we find in Christian hagiography, but it also underscores the fact that Muslims understood some of the motivations behind Christian blasphemy, even as they regarded them as utterly strange.[3]

This chapter investigates the history of Christian blasphemy against Islam. Although they were not as numerous as the apostate martyrs, there were many individuals who faced death for disparaging the Prophet. The greatest number of these came from al-Andalus, though there are several examples also from the Muslim East. Although most blasphemers did not undergo the religious transformations explored in chapters 1 and 2, their deaths were reactions to many of the same cultural and social pressures. The most important of these were the mounting threats of Islamization and Arabization and the need to oppose these through dramatic acts of resistance. This chapter argues that blasphemy emerged as a specific form of social and theological protest against Islam among heavily assimilated but unconverted Christians in the early Middle Ages. Furthermore, it contends that some of the Christians most likely to blaspheme were, paradoxically, those who were closest to Muslims. These included the children of religiously mixed families, Christian officials of the Muslim state, and residents of religiously mixed cities. Thus, it was precarious proximity to the religious other—coupled with the attendant feeling of suffocation and loss—that seems to have compelled some Christians to "take a stand" by blaspheming.

The chapter also argues that al-Andalus witnessed a relatively greater number of Christian blasphemers than other regions under Islamic rule due to a combination of specific social, religious, and political conditions. One was the especially acrimonious mix of old Muslims, new Muslims, and non-Muslims who jostled for power and influence on the peninsula through much of the early Middle Ages. The balance among these groups shifted as conversion increased, and this seems to have had an unsettling effect on the social order. This gave rise to tensions that burst forth in acts of blasphemy. Another factor was the sudden increase in the number of Muslim religious scholars (Ar. *ʿulamāʾ*) in al-Andalus from the second half of the ninth century onward, which entailed a heightened scrutiny of various forms of religious deviance, including heresy, apostasy, blasphemy, and intimate contact with non-Muslims. When it comes to the scholarly literature on Christian blasphemy,

---

Fierro, *Heterodoxia*, 121; Fierro, "Andalusian ‹Fatāwā›," 109–10; Wolf, *Christian Martyrs*, 34; Christys, *Christians in al-Andalus*, 80–81; Safran, *Defining Boundaries*, 96. For more on Aḥmad b. Muḥammad al-Lakhmī and his family, see chapter 1, sec. IV.

[3] Compare with al-Mustawrid al-ʿIjlī, in appendix 1.

the martyrs of Córdoba usually play a starring role. The reason for this is obvious: there is more evidence about blasphemy in ninth-century al-Andalus than in any other part of the early Islamic world. Given this, the basic goal of the chapter is to reframe our information by examining the Andalusī martyrs alongside contemporary examples from the Muslim East. In doing so, it seeks to challenge the aura of exceptionalism that usually surrounds the martyrs of Córdoba, who are often presented as "erratic blocks" in the history of al-Andalus and early Muslim-Christian relations more broadly.[4]

This chapter is divided into five sections. The first sets the stage by surveying the history of blasphemy in Islamic law and thought (amazingly, a subject that still awaits treatment in a book-length study).[5] It argues that blasphemy laws were slow to crystallize in the early period, and thus, martyrologies represent some of our best sources for tracking their development and implementation in real time. The second profiles several fictional or quasi-fictional narratives of blasphemy in Egypt, Syria, and Palestine and the role theological dispute played in the representation of blasphemy. The third discusses one of the most detailed but little-known accounts of blasphemy from the East, that of Peter of Capitolias, who was executed in Transjordan in 715. It argues that Christians understood anti-Muslim blasphemy through the lens of *parrhēsia*, or "audacious, candid speech." The fourth turns to the martyrs of Córdoba and explores the impact and meaning of blasphemy in Andalusī society in the mid-ninth century. The conclusion considers why Christians in al-Andalus turned to blasphemy to a seemingly greater extent than their counterparts in other parts of the greater Middle East.

I. BLASPHEMY IN EARLY ISLAM: AN OVERVIEW

Unlike the Bible (Leviticus 24:16), the Qur'an does not prescribe the death penalty for blasphemy, at least not explicitly.[6] In fact, the standard term for "blasphemy" as it came to be in later periods (Ar. *sabb*) almost never appears

[4] I borrow the phrase from Baynes, *Constantine the Great*, 3.

[5] For this reason, we eagerly await the completion of the following doctoral dissertations: Shobi Ahmed, "Erecting the Moral Imperium: Judgment of Blasphemy, Heresy, and Apostasy in Islam," Harvard University; Sarah Islam, "Blasphemy as a Legal Category in Early and Medieval Islamic History," Princeton University.

[6] For introductions to blasphemy in Islam, see Wiederhold, "Shatm," *EI*[2], xii, 725–27; Friedmann, *Tolerance and Coercion*, 149–52; Kamali, *Freedom of Expression*, 212–58; Ernst, "Blasphemy"; Stewart, "Blasphemy"; also Bercher, "Apostasie, le Blasphème et la Rébellion"; Santillana, *Diritto musulmano malichita*, i, 167–70; Turki, "Situation du ‹tributaire› qui insulte l'Islam"; Fierro, "Andalusian ‹Fatāwā›"; Wiederhold, "Blasphemy against the Prophet."

in the text, except once in a verse that commands Muslims not to blaspheme pagan deities (Q. *al-Anʿām* 6:108) lest the pagans use these insults as a pretense for disparaging God.[7] The absence of the term *blasphemy*, however, does not mean that the Qur'an tolerates blasphemous speech. To the contrary, it frequently states that questioning the Prophet or his revelation is an unacceptable and grave offense. There are several such passages that outline the Qur'an's views of blasphemy. Q. *al-Aḥzāb* 33:57 claims that whoever "hurts [*yu'dhūna*] God and His Messenger, God shall curse in this world and the next." A few verses later, at Q. *al-Aḥzāb* 33:60–61, the Qur'an states that "the hypocrites [*al-munāfiqūn*], those who bear disease in their hearts, and those who spread sedition [*wa-'l-murjifūn*] in Medina" shall be "accursed wherever they are found, seized and slaughtered completely." The famous *Ḥirāba* Verse—Q. *al-Mā'ida* 5:33, which commands a range of punishments for those who "wage war against God and spread corruption throughout the land"—does not mention blasphemy by name. Yet we know that early Muslim officials applied this verse to blasphemers, suggesting that "waging war against God" was thought to include insulting speech, at least in certain contexts.[8]

Lurking behind these verses are the taunts and insults visited upon the Prophet throughout his life. For example, the Qur'an states that Muḥammad's opponents accused him of being a sorcerer (*sāḥir*, Q. *Ṣād* 38:4), a poet (*shāʿir*, Q. *al-Ṣaffāt* 37:36), a soothsayer (*kāhin*, Q. *al-Ṭūr* 52:29, *al-Ḥāqqa* 69:42), and possessed (*majnūn*, Q. *al-Qalam* 68:2, *al-Takwīr* 81:22). It was in reaction to this defamation that the Qur'an nurtured an early discourse on blasphemy that would develop into legal and theological doctrines in later periods.[9] One of Muḥammad's greatest enemies in this respect was his uncle Abū Lahab, who so derided Muḥammad's prophecies that he and his wife became the subject of a short chapter of the Qur'an denouncing them for their insults (Q. *al-Masad* 111).[10] The Prophet is also reported to have had people killed for their insults, including Kaʿb b. al-Ashraf (d. ca. 3/624), a Jew from Medina who wrote verses inciting Quraysh to fight the Muslims and others that disparaged Muslim women. We also know that Muḥammad spared the lives of nearly everyone in Mecca when he finally took the city in 8/630, this despite the Meccans' early and fierce opposition to him; that being said, he specifically ordered the

[7] See also the Qur'anic term *takdhīb*, or "denial" of religiously revealed truths; Stewart, "Blasphemy," *EQ*, i, 235–36.

[8] See chapter 4, sec. II.

[9] Watt, *Muhammad at Mecca*, 123–31; Ammann, "Mockery," *EQ*, iii, 400–401; Bauer, "Insanity," *EQ*, ii, 539–41; discussion of these taunts and their relation to blasphemy in Ibn Taymīya, *al-Ṣārim al-maslūl*, 53–69.

[10] Watt, "Abū Lahab," *EI*², i, 136–37.

execution of a small group of individuals, including apostates and those who had slandered him during the previous years.[11] In general, fending off insults seems to have been a preoccupation of the earliest Muslims, even if these were not labeled as acts of "blasphemy" in the strict sense.

Given the lexical imprecision of the Qur'an, it is unsurprising that blasphemy did not become a technical preoccupation of the earliest Muslim jurists. For example, it is relatively hard to find chapters devoted to blasphemy (*sabb, shatm*) in early works of *ḥadīth* and *fiqh*, whereas these same texts are filled with discussions of apostasy (*irtidād, ridda*).[12] In the case of the Ḥanafī jurists of Kūfa (as well as some Shāfiʿīs), the explanation for this was obvious: blasphemy was considered a subcategory of apostasy and, therefore, did not need to be treated as a separate legal phenomenon.[13] By conflating apostasy and blasphemy in this way, the Ḥanafīs proved themselves to be more lenient: that is, they believed that blasphemers were entitled to the full suite of privileges and protections to which apostates were entitled, including repentance. They also decreed that punishment could be meted out at the discretion of a judge.[14] The three other main schools of Sunnī law were more severe, though on some level they collapsed the distinction between apostasy and blasphemy in similar ways.[15]

This is not to say that blasphemy is entirely missing from early works of *ḥadīth*:[16] a Prophetic tradition describes blasphemy as one of the main sins leading to damnation on Judgment Day.[17] Another condemns the practice of reviling the Prophet's Companions, including Abū Bakr and ʿAlī.[18] Still another states that blasphemy consists of claiming God to have a son.[19] These traditions highlight the fact that blasphemy could come in many forms. What is more, they underscore the existence of gradations of blasphemous speech: blasphemy against the Prophet (*sabb al-rasūl*), for instance, was generally re-

[11] Watt, "Kaʿb b. al-Ashraf," *EI²*, iv, 315; cf. al-Subkī, *al-Sayf al-maslūl*, 291–321. On the conquest of Mecca, see Guillaume, *Life of Muḥammad*, 550–51.

[12] There are exceptions: see ʿAbd al-Razzāq, *Muṣannaf*, v, 307–8 (no. 9706 deals with a Christian blasphemer).

[13] Friedmann, *Tolerance and Coercion*, 149–52, which surveys the phenomenon from a legal perspective; Kamali, *Freedom of Expression*, 213–16, 233–36; also Rabb, "Defamation and Blasphemy," 448–49.

[14] Fattal, *Statut légal*, 122–23.

[15] Wiederhold, "Shatm," *EI²*, xii, 726, remarking that neither al-Shaybānī (d. 189/805), nor al-Shāfiʿī (d. 204/820), nor Saḥnūn (d. 240/855) saw blasphemy as a distinct category of unbelief; with the correction in Friedmann, *Tolerance and Coercion*, 149 n. 149.

[16] Wensinck, *Concordances*, ii, 386–88 (*sabb*); iii, 64–65 (*shatm*).

[17] Muslim, *Ṣaḥīḥ*, iv, 1997, no. 2581.

[18] Muslim, *Ṣaḥīḥ*, iv, 1874–75, no. 2409; Aḥmad b. Ḥanbal, *Musnad* (1993), ii, 575, no. 9603; Abū Dāwūd, *Sunan* (1998), 706, no. 4650.

[19] al-Bukhārī, *Ṣaḥīḥ*, 790, no. 3193.

garded as the gravest offense, more serious than blasphemy against God Himself (*sabb allāh*).[20] Although some early authorities refrained from prescribing punishments for blasphemy, others took harsh stances against it. One popular *ḥadīth* describes how a man killed a female slave with whom he had several children after she had insulted the Prophet. Muḥammad allegedly praised the man for his actions.[21] Aḥmad b. Ḥanbal (d. 241/855), meanwhile, stated that blasphemers should be killed regardless of whether they were Muslims or non-Muslims.[22] Mālik b. Anas (d. 179/796) did not mention blasphemy as a capital offense in his *Muwaṭṭa*ʾ, but narrative sources indicate that he recommended the execution of blasphemers in practice. One of these was a Christian in Egypt who vilified the Prophet Muḥammad during the tenure of al-Mufaḍḍal b. al-Faḍāla (r. 169–71/786–87), chief *qāḍī* of Fusṭāṭ.[23]

Over the course of the Middle Ages, the Mālikīs developed a keen interest in blasphemy, and indeed, some of our richest discussions of the topic come from Egyptian, North African, and Andalusī jurists of the Mālikī *madhhab*. For instance, the Egyptian scholar Ibn Wahb (d. 197/813) was careful to differentiate among various targets of insulting speech, writing, "It is not lawful to kill a Muslim who vilifies anyone (e.g., the caliphs, the Companions, etc.) unless he vilifies the Prophet of God, for whoever vilifies the Prophet of God, [taking] his blood is licit."[24] This attitude hardened over time, such that all blasphemers were eventually understood to surrender their right to repent, regardless of who they were ridiculing, as indicated by the later Andalusī scholar al-ʿUtbī (d. ca. 254/868).[25]

The threat of blasphemy could come from within and without the Muslim community, and judicial views of non-Muslims who blasphemed varied widely. The Ḥanafīs of Kūfa, for example, believed that a *dhimmī* who blasphemed should not be killed automatically, because blasphemy did not necessarily violate the terms of the covenant between the Muslims and the People of the Book (Ar. *ʿahd al-dhimma*).[26] Ibn Ḥanbal, by contrast, held that Christians and Jews immediately relinquished their protected status when they reviled the Prophet and should therefore be killed. Interestingly, according to his disciple Abū Bakr al-Khallāl, Ibn Ḥanbal derived this principle from an anecdote involving a

[20] Friedmann, *Tolerance and Coercion*, 150; Kamali, *Freedom of Expression*, 231.

[21] Abū Dāwūd, *Sunan* (1998), 659, nos. 4361–62; al-Nasāʾī, *Sunan*, vii, 75, no. 4070; Ibn Taymīya, *al-Ṣārim al-maslūl*, 47–51; more generally, see Zayd b. ʿAlī, *Musnad*, 340–41.

[22] Abū Bakr al-Khallāl, *Aḥkām*, 255–58.

[23] al-Kindī, *Wulāt*, 382; al-Kindī, *Histoire des cadis égyptiens*, 145–46, cited in Tritton, *Non-Muslim Subjects*, 128–29; Fattal, *Statut légal*, 123.

[24] Ibn Wahb, *Kitāb al-muḥāraba*, 76.

[25] Ibn Rushd al-Jadd, *Bayān*, xvi, 420.

[26] Qāḍī ʿIyāḍ, *Shifāʾ*, ii, 565; cf. Kamali, *Freedom of Expression*, 236.

blaspheming monk, not unlike the martyrs discussed later in this chapter.[27] Al-Shāfiʿī made the same point in his description of a generic pact that Muslim rulers should contract with their non-Muslim subjects. Toward the beginning of this pact he states, "If any one of you speaks improperly of Muḥammad, the Book of God, or his religion, he forfeits the protection [*dhimma*] of God . . . his property and his blood are at the disposal of the Commander of the Faithful, like the property and lives of the people of the Abode of War."[28]

Other scholars took a slightly more lenient attitude toward non-Muslim blasphemy, distinguishing between the simple profession of faith in Judaism and Christianity—much of which implicitly challenged Islam—and direct attacks against Islam itself.[29] Thus, the aforementioned al-ʿUtbī quoted Mālik as claiming that Jews and Christians were perfectly free to say, "Muḥammad was sent not to us but to you." They were not free, however, to say that Muḥammad was a false prophet, which would entail the death penalty.[30] Al-ʿUtbī's discussion enshrines a simple but important legal principle governing debate between Muslims and non-Muslims in the early period: *dhimmīs* did not have to assent to specific Muslim beliefs, but they could not "weaponize" their disagreements by heaping scorn, insult, or ridicule on Islam itself. Put simply, they could speak subjectively about their own beliefs and experiences (within limits) but not objectively about those of their Muslim neighbors.

Despite this general hardening of sentiment, it took many years for Muslim scholars to think systematically about blasphemy as a specific category of crime. One important transitional work between the sparse early *ḥadīth* literature and later legal discussions is the *Shifāʾ* of the Almoravid jurist Qāḍī ʿIyāḍ b. Mūsā (d. 544/1149). In it, Qāḍī ʿIyāḍ includes several lengthy chapters pertaining to blasphemy against Muḥammad, God, angels, prophets, and divine scriptures.[31] It also contains detailed information on historical precedents in the life of Muḥammad, conditions for executing blasphemers, conditions for forgiving them, and advice on how to handle *dhimmīs* who insulted Islam.[32] Some of the earliest stand-alone treatises on blasphemy date from the fourteenth century and were produced in the Muslim East. The most famous of

[27] Abū Bakr al-Khallāl, *Aḥkām*, 256; cf. Ibn Wahb, *Kitāb al-muḥāraba*, 77.

[28] al-Shāfiʿī, *Kitāb al-umm*, v, 472.

[29] Kamali, *Freedom of Expression*, 217, 235–36.

[30] Ibn Rushd al-Jadd, *Bayān*, xvi, 414. See also Ibn Sahl, *Aḥkām*, 879; Abū Bakr al-Khallāl, *Aḥkām*, 292–302; discussion in Safran, *Defining Boundaries*, 97. For general discussion of al-ʿUtbī and his views of *dhimmīs*, see Fernández Félix and Fierro, "Cristianos y conversos"; Fernández Félix, *ʿUtbiyya y el proceso de formación de la sociedad islámica*, 433–92, esp. 459–80 for apostasy and blasphemy.

[31] Qāḍī ʿIyāḍ, *Shifāʾ*, ii, 465–660. I thank Matthew Anderson for drawing my attention to this source.

[32] For punishment of *dhimmīs* who blaspheme, see Qāḍī ʿIyāḍ, *Shifāʾ*, ii, 565–74.

these is Ibn Taymīya's (d. 728/1328) *al-Ṣārim al-maslūl ʿalā shātim al-rasūl* (*The Dagger Drawn against the One Who Vilifies the Messenger*), as well as Tāqī ʾl-Dīn al-Subkī's (d. 756/1355) *al-Sayf al-maslūl ʿalā man sabba ʾl-rasūl* (*The Sword Drawn against the One Who Blasphemes the Messenger*).[33] That it took Muslim jurists nearly seven hundred years to categorize blasphemy in this way is a testament to the slow process of systematization over time. This makes Christian hagiography—an independent witness to the evolution of blasphemy laws in the early period—extremely valuable.

II. THEOLOGICAL DISPUTE, BLASPHEMY, AND MARTYRDOM

Much as Muslim jurists dwelled on the difference between defamation and disagreement in matters of religion, Christian hagiographers explored how blasphemy could arise in the midst of spirited theological debate. Indeed, many martyrdom accounts hinge on the idea that one man's expression of religious truth was another man's expression of religious insult. Several of these accounts are hard to corroborate historically and may well be fictional. Nevertheless, they are grounded in a common social reality, in which the distinction between "free speech" and "disparaging speech" was often razor thin.

A good example comes from the *Synaxarium of Alexandria*, which contains a brief biography of a martyr named Menas, who died on February 11.[34] It is hard to date the story; the *synxarium* itself was compiled in the fourteenth century but drew on much older material in Coptic and Arabic. It is possible that the text represents the residue of a longer *life* that no longer survives, though to my knowledge, no information about Menas exists in outside sources. The account itself is set in the immediate postconquest period (ca. 640–50) as news of Egypt's new rulers was spreading throughout the country. Menas reportedly came from a family of farmers in Akhmīm (Gk. Panopolis), about 230 kilometers downstream from Luxor on the Nile. He embraced the monastic life when he was still young and inhabited several monasteries before settling in one near Ushmūnayn (Gk. Hermopolis).[35] According to the *synaxarium*, he resided there for sixteen years. Following the conquest, Menas

[33] Ibn Taymīya, *al-Ṣārim al-maslūl*, esp. 216–42 (for *dhimmī*s); discussion in Kamali, *Freedom of Expression*, 236–50; al-Subkī, *al-Sayf al-maslūl*, 233–402; for discussion of other blasphemy treatises, see al-Sāmarrāʾī, *Aḥkām al-murtadd*, 90–116, esp. 116.

[34] Basset, "Synaxaire arabe jacobite" (1915), 797–98; discussion in Coquin, "Menas," *CE*, v, 1589; Hoyland, *Seeing Islam*, 368–69; Sahner, "Old Martyrs, New Martyrs," 107.

[35] There was a famous monastery in this city dedicated to Saint Severus; see Grossman and Severin, "Ashmūnayn," *CE*, i, 285–88.

heard that the Muslims "denied that God has a Son, consubstantial and co-eternal with Him." This discovery pained him greatly, so he decided to confront the commander (Ar. *muqaddam*) of the Muslim army and set the record straight.

Menas challenged the general to explain why Muslims denied Christ's divinity. After hearing his unsatisfactory answer, the monk said, "You would not have to dissociate yourself from [this foul belief] if it turned out that Jesus was merely a son begotten of procreation and intercourse, but [in fact] he is light from light and God from God!" The Muslim was stunned by this outburst and told the monk to desist from his unbelief (Ar. *kufr*). The monk continued to goad the commander, however, reminding him that the Gospel promises life to anyone who believes in Jesus but threatens the wrath of God against anyone who denies him. Losing patience, the commander struck Menas with his sword and tossed his body into the river. Local Christians recovered his remains and venerated him as a saint.

The *Synaxarium of Alexandria* mentions a second martyr who was killed for blasphemy: Thomas, bishop of Damascus, whose feast falls on October 31 and whose death is undated.[36] According to the account, he was killed under "the king of the Arabs when they ruled these lands," which may hint at a date in the Umayyad period, but as in many of the biographies in the *synaxarium*, the details are vague. Thomas is said to have engaged in debate with one of the Muslim scholars (Ar. *ʿulamāʾ*) of Damascus and defeated him. Smarting from this loss, the scholar told the local *amīr* that Thomas had "cursed his religion" (*laʿana madhhabahu*), so the *amīr* summoned the bishop and asked for an explanation. Thomas said in reply, "As for this curse, nothing of the sort came from my mouth. I was merely insisting to him that Christ is the true God and that no other law [*sharīʿa*] came after his." The ruler reminded Thomas that he was subject to the rules of Islam and, therefore, had to be careful of what he said. But the bishop ignored this advice, and therefore he was beaten and executed.

It is hard to match Thomas with any figures known from Muslim or Christian sources.[37] The closest candidate is Peter of Damascus, a shadowy figure

[36] Basset, "Synaxaire arabe jacobite" (1909), 175; discussion in Hoyland, *Seeing Islam*, 368 n. 101; Sahner, "Old Martyrs, New Martyrs," 107.

[37] On a Chalcedonian patriarch of Antioch named "Thomas" who reigned during the time of ʿAbd al-Malik (65–86/685–705), see Eutychius, *Annales*, ii, 39–40; cf. Lequien, *Oriens christianus*, ii, 743. Despite the superficial similarities, we know that the Chalcedonian patriarchs of Antioch did not move to Damascus until around 1366, so they must be different; see Pahlitzsch, "Christians under Mamluk Rule," 36–37 n. 18, 40 n. 29; Todt, "Griechisch-orthodoxe (Melkitische) Christen," 85–87; Noble and Treiger, *Orthodox Church*, 32. I thank Johannes Pahlitzsch and Alexander Treiger for their help in this matter.

who according to Greek and Syriac chronicles was the Chalcedonian bishop of the city during the reign of al-Walīd b. Yazīd (r. 125–26/743–44).[38] He "proclaimed the impiety of the Arabs and Manicheans" and in punishment had his tongue cut out. The caliph then exiled him to Arabia Felix—that is, Yemen—where he carried on celebrating the mass "in a clear fashion" despite his missing tongue. Peter of Damascus is often conflated with another eighth-century blasphemer, Peter of Capitolias (d. 715), a village priest executed under al-Walīd b. ʿAbd al-Malik (whom we shall meet in the next section). Their biographies have many elements in common—including the martyrs' names, those of the caliphs who sentenced them, and, of course, their crimes. But their dates, hometowns, occupations, and ultimate fates were very different, suggesting that they may have been distinct historical personalities who were later conflated with one another. With this in mind, it is also possible that Peter of Damascus may have evolved from or been confused with Thomas of Damascus in medieval Copto-Arabic tradition.

A final example of a fictional blasphemy event is that of Michael of Mar Saba. His *life* is widely considered to be fictional, though there is no consensus about the precise history of the text. There are three relatively similar recensions of Michael's *life* in three different languages: a stand-alone Georgian biography, based on a now-lost Arabic or Greek *Vorlage* from Mar Saba, usually thought to be the oldest version; a nearly identical Greek account included in the *Life of Theodore of Edessa*, a hagiographic novel discussed in the previous chapter; and an Arabic translation of the same work.[39] The relationship among these texts has yet to be worked out satisfactorily, in my opinion. Therefore, I

[38] de Boor, *Chronographia*, i, 416; Mango and Scott, *Theophanes*, 577; Chabot, *Chronique*, ii, 506 ("patriarch" of Chalcedonians in Syria); Chabot, *Chronicon ad annum Christi 1234*, i, 314 ("bishop" of Chalcedonians in Damascus); Garitte, *Calendrier palestino-géorgien*, 47, 144; for discussion, see *CMR*, i, 290–92; Fedalto, *Hierarchia Ecclesiastica Orientalis*, ii, 729; *PMBZ*, i, III, 585; Todt, "Griechisch-orthodoxe (Melkitische) Christen," 69; Hoyland, *Theophilus*, 242–43; Johnson, "Social Presence of Greek," 65 n. 333.

[39] Georgian: Blanchard, "Martyrdom of Saint Michael." Greek: Pomialovskij, *Zhitie izhe vo sviatykh ottsa nashego Feodora*, 17–31. In what follows, direct quotations from the Greek are followed by references to matching passages in Georgian. For discussion, see *CMR*, i, 911–15; *CMR*, ii, 585–93; *BS*, ix, 448–49; *PMBZ*, i, III, 268–69; Peeters, "Passion de S. Michel"; Vasiliev, "Life of St. Theodore"; Schick, *Christian Communities*, 174–75; Griffith, "Michael, the Martyr"; Griffith, "Christians, Muslims, and Neo-martyrs," 172–83; Vila, "Christian Martyrs," 160–77; Swanson, "Christian al-Ma'mūn Tradition," 69–86. The main clue for the dating of the Georgian account is the reference to "burned martyrs" at Mar Saba (Blanchard, "Martyrdom of Saint Michael," 157), probably the Twenty Martyrs of Mar Saba, who were killed by suffocating on smoke in 788 or 797 (see *SPSH*, i, 1–41). Interestingly, the Greek account in the *Life of Theodore* does not mention this. It does, however, refer to ʿAbd al-Malik as a "Persian," suggesting perhaps that it was composed in the ʿAbbasid period when the caliphs were based in Iraq (Pomialovskij, *Zhitie izhe vo sviatykh ottsa nashego Feodora*, 17, 21–24, 26; see Griffith, "*Life of Theodore*," 155; Sahner, "Old Martyrs, New Martyrs," 103–4).

will sidestep the question of transmission and focus on the version of the text that until now has received the least attention: the Greek biography of Michael in the *Life of Theodore*. Regardless of the version we consult, however, it is clear that the historical Michael (if he ever existed) is completely disguised beneath layers of hagiography and polemic.[40]

The story of the martyrdom begins with the visit of ʿAbd al-Malik to Jerusalem. Around the same time, a young monk from Tiberias named Michael was dispatched to the Holy City to sell the wares of Mar Saba Monastery, including reed baskets.[41] While working in the market, Michael encountered the eunuch of ʿAbd al-Malik's wife, Seide (probably from Ar. *sayyida*, "mistress, lady"). The eunuch was struck by the monk's beauty and brought him to meet her. The caliph's wife tried to seduce him, but Michael found her "unshapely and foul-smelling."[42] Furious, she "shook like a hobgoblin" and turned the monk over to her husband, claiming that he had insulted her.

The text describes ʿAbd al-Malik as a "most gentle man" who "did not wish to harm a single Christian." He was impressed by Michael's intelligent answers to his questions, so he spared him from punishment. At the same time, he ordered the monk to convert to Islam. Michael refused, prompting a long discussion between the two men about Saint Paul and the Prophet Muḥammad. Their discussion quickly turned into a debate, and when the caliph could not persuade Michael that he was wrong, he summoned a Jewish deputy to take over.[43] Michael prevailed against this man too, proclaiming to the assembled audience of Persians and Arabs, "Muḥammad is most certainly not a prophet or an apostle but an imposter, a deceiver, and a forerunner of the anti-Christ!" Enraged, the crowd called for his blood, while the Christians present (including several scribes and doctors who were serving ʿAbd al-Malik) rejoiced. The caliph tried to win over Michael one last time, but when the monk refused to convert, he tried to kill him, first by poisoning him and then by burning him. At last, the caliph resorted to decapitation, and Michael was martyred.

[40] Griffith, "Michael, the Martyr," 147.

[41] On the relationship between the monk Theodore and Theodore Abū Qurra, see Lamoreaux, "Biography of Theodore," 26–32.

[42] Pomialovskij, *Zhitie izhe vo sviatykh ottsa nashego Feodora*, 20; Blanchard, "Martyrdom of Saint Michael," 151. Compare with the description of Potiphar's wife in Genesis 39. For other scenes of attempted sexual seduction, see chapter 5, n. 47.

[43] Jews often appear as dramatis personae in Christian dispute texts; see Penn, "*John and the Emir*," 89; Lamoreaux and Khairallah, "John of Edessa." Jews were also portrayed as collaborators with Muslims in the persecution of Christians, e.g., ʿUmar b. al-Khaṭṭāb, who removed a cross on the Mount of Olives under Jewish influence: de Boor, *Chronographia*, i, 342; Mango and Scott, *Theophanes*, 476. Jews were also present for the execution of Peter of Capitolias (see sec. III below) and for the execution of Bacchus (*CMLT*, 107, 112, 121). The same motif appeared in Syriac hagiography from the Sasanian world: Payne, *State of Mixture*, 40. On medieval European parallels, see Cutler and Cutler, *Jew as Ally of the Muslim*.

Michael's martyrdom is a much more detailed account of a scenario we have witnessed in comparably mythic form in the *lives* of Menas and Thomas: frank conversation between the followers of two religions devolving quickly into accusations of insult. As they are represented, the three martyrs deliberately provoked their interlocutors, goading them with ridicule until the only option left was violence. We should keep in mind that most theological debates between Muslims and Christians in the early Middle Ages did not descend into bloodshed. Indeed, we have numerous reports of exchanges between groups in which the tone of conversation remained academic and cordial. Luminaries such as Theodore Abū Qurra (d. post-816) and Timothy I (d. 823), for example, are well known for having debated high-ranking Muslims on a range of issues, including the divinity of Jesus, the nature of sacred scripture, and Muḥammad's status as a prophet.[44] The tradition even holds that Christian theologians debated the caliphs and their deputies, including al-Maʾmūn (r. 198–218/813–33). Of course, the accounts as they survive are as fictional and formulaic as the *Life of Michael of Mar Saba*. For this reason, Sidney Griffith has referred to the broader genre of dispute texts as "the monk in the emir's *majlis*": descriptions of religious disputes teeming with their own dramatis personae and literary motifs.

Far from being restricted to Christians, this genre was popular among other groups in the sectarian milieu of the medieval Middle East. A notable example is a Middle Persian text known as the *Mādayān ī Gizistag Abāliš*, or *The Book of the Accursed Abāliš*.[45] It was probably written in the ninth or tenth century and claims to record a debate between the Zoroastrian high priest Ādur-Farrōbāy son of Farroxzad and a "heretic" (M.P. *zandīk*) named Abāliš (whom Josef van Ess has identified with a "dualist" called Abū ʿAlī, who is well known from Muslim sources) at the court of al-Maʾmūn. It is better to read this text as a doctrinal manual for Zoroastrian priests concerned with the tenets of their own faith, rather than as a record of a real debate with Muslims and other outsiders. Still, works like the *Life of Michael* and the *Gizistag Abāliš* drew on a social reality in which theological debate among elites from different religions was very common.[46] In such debates, to point out a difference between Muslim and Christian doctrine was one thing, but to construe this difference as a deficiency or error in Islam was something entirely different. It was here

[44] Griffith, "Monk in the Emir's *Majlis*"; Griffith, *Church in the Shadow of the Mosque*, 77–81; Bertaina, *Christian and Muslim Dialogues*.

[45] Chacha, *Gajastak Abâlish*; Skjærvø, *Spirit of Zoroastrianism*, 243–47; discussion in Tafażżolī, "Abāliš," *EIr*, i, I, 58; de Jong, "Zoroastrians of Baghdad," 230–31. On the identification with Abū ʿAlī the *zindīq*, see van Ess, *Theologie und Gesellschaft*, iii, 203–4.

[46] For a famous account of such a debate, see Abū ʿAbdallāh al-Ḥumaydī, *Jadhwat al-muqtabis*, 161–62; discussion in Griffith, *Church in the Shadow of the Mosque*, 64.

that the line between disagreement and defamation could be negligible, and Christians might slip into the perilous realm of blasphemy. This seems to be the main lesson of these fanciful accounts.

III. THE MARTYRDOM OF PETER OF CAPITOLIAS

Whereas some Christians fell victim to charges of blasphemy unwittingly, others courted death voluntarily. The most interesting case of voluntary martyrdom in the Muslim East is that of Peter of Capitolias (Figure 3.1), who was executed in Transjordan in 715 on the orders of al-Walīd b. ʿAbd al-Malik (r. 86–96/705–15).[47] Despite the richness of his biography, the text itself has been largely inaccessible to scholars until recently. Thankfully, we can now rely on the complete edition and translation by Stephen Shoemaker rather than the partial and problematic French summary by Paul Peeters, which served as the standard reference work for many years.

Our ignorance of the text owes partly to its complicated history: the *Life of Peter* was probably composed in Greek in the southern Levant during the eighth century. Based on its intimate knowledge of local topography and personalities, there is reason to believe that it was written within a few years of Peter's death. The text claims to have been composed by John of Damascus—a claim corroborated by the Byzantine historian Theophanes—though this attribution may be fictional.[48] In this period, it was not uncommon to link texts to famous authors in order to endow them with authority and prestige.[49] What is certain is that its writer came from the same Greek-speaking Chalcedonian milieu as John, and if it was not John himself, the text may have been written under his name so as to draw attention to the martyr. We know that Peter's cult was commemorated by Chalcedonians (Melkites) in early medieval Pal-

[47] Peeters, "Passion de S. Pierre" (Fr. summary); Shoemaker, *Three Christian Martyrdoms*, 1–65 (Geo. text and Eng. trans. for this section); discussion in *CMR*, i, 419–22; *Acta sanctorum*, October, ii, 494–98; *BS*, x, 676–80; *BSO*, ii, 802; *PMBZ*, i, III, 582–84; Peeters, "Glanures martyrologiques," 123–25; Peeters, *Tréfonds oriental*, 211; Bīṭār, *al-Qiddīsūn al-mansīyūn*, 249–52, 256–57; Schick, *Christian Communities*, 173–74; Hoyland, *Seeing Islam*, 354–60; Griffith, "Christians, Muslims, and Neo-martyrs," 184–87; Vila, "Christian Martyrs," 252–60; Binggeli, "Converting the Caliph," 101–2; Sahner, "Old Martyrs, New Martyrs," 101; Anthony, *Crucifixion and Death*, 54, 56–58, 72.

[48] On the attribution to John, see Griffith, "Manṣūr Family," 37–38; Shoemaker, *Three Christian Martyrdoms*, xvi–xviii. Theophanes states that John of Damascus wrote a biography of "Peter of Maiouma," one of the doppelgängers of Peter of Capitolias with whom he was confused in later tradition; see de Boor, *Chronographia*, i, 416–17; Mango and Scott, *Theophanes*, 577–78; Hoyland, *Seeing Islam*, 354–60.

[49] On John's life and that of his family, see now Anthony, "Fixing John Damascene's Biography"; Griffith, "Manṣūr Family."

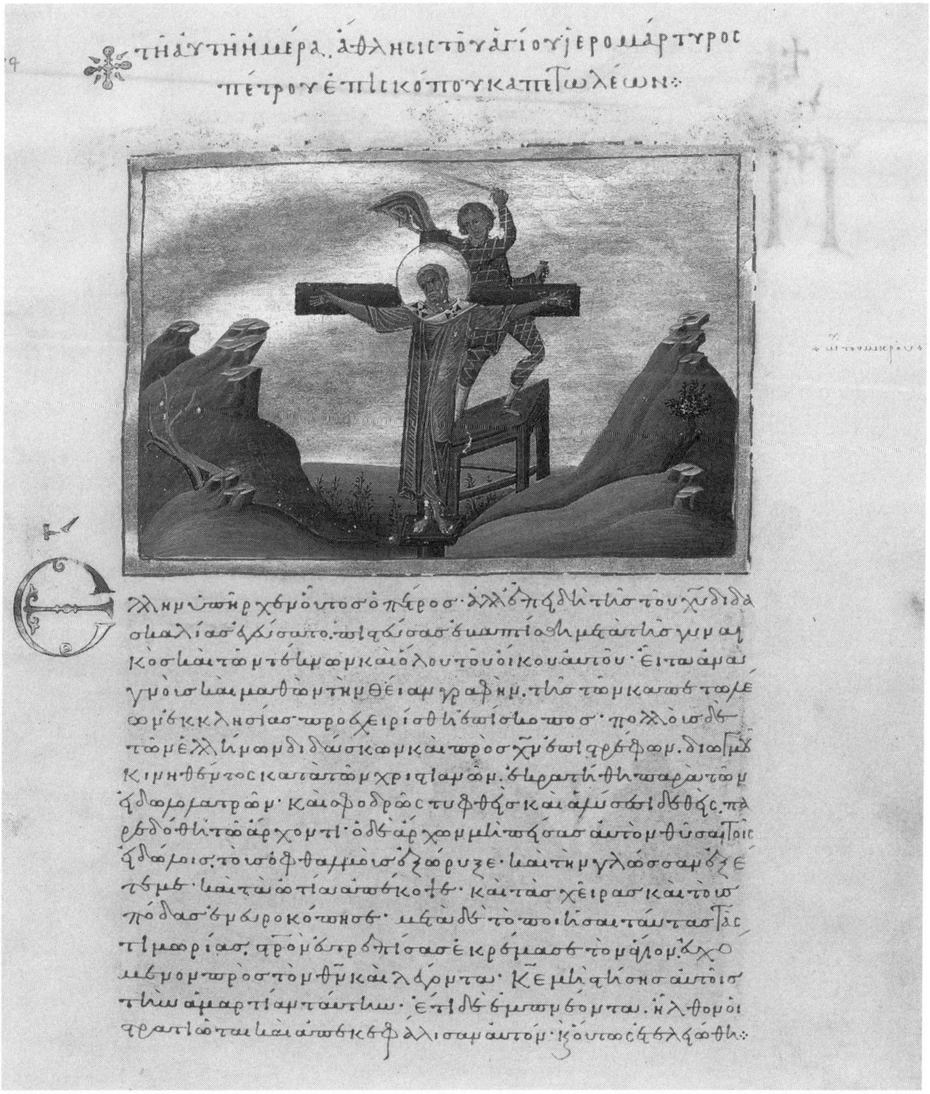

Figure 3.1. Peter of Capitolias, *Menologion of Basil II*, Vat. Gr. 1613 (11th c.), fol. 84r. Photo: Biblioteca Apostolica Vaticana.

estine and eventually spread to Constantinople.[50] The original Greek version no longer exists, though a Georgian translation does survive. This translation was probably completed during the ninth or tenth century during the great flowering of Georgian literature in the Chalcedonian monasteries of greater Syria, such as Mar Saba in Palestine and the Black Mountain near Antioch.[51] This version is contained in a unique sixteenth-century *menologion*, which provides the basis of Peeters's synopsis from 1939 and of Shoemaker's translation of 2016.[52]

According to his *life*, Peter came from Capitolias (Ar. Bayt Rās), one of the cities of the Decapolis, about five kilometers north of modern Irbid.[53] Classical Arabic poetry remembers Capitolias for its fine wines, which were traded as far south as the Ḥijāz in antiquity. It was not an insignificant site politically either: during the Umayyad period, the caliph Yazīd b. ʿAbd al-Malik (r. 101–5/720–24) is said to have established his court there and to have died nearby.[54]

Peter's *life* states that he was a village priest who was married with three children. Around the age of thirty, finding "this life less significant and more deceptive than shadows and dreams," Peter convinced his wife to embrace asceticism with him. She consented, and they placed their two daughters in a nearby convent. Peter, meanwhile, took charge of their son, who lived with him in a cell near the city center. Peter came to be considered a holy man among the local Christians, who "would come to him for the sake of spiritual benefit."[55] Ten years later, Peter's wife died. Around this time, he began to provide counsel to Christians who were being led away to martyrdom, "persuad[ing] them to choose death on behalf of Christ rather than this fleeting life," as the text puts it.

Peter's *life* does not identify who these martyrs were. There are relatively few examples of conversion by the sword in the Umayyad period—especially in a relatively out-of-the-way place like Capitolias—so these may have been Christians who converted to Islam and were contemplating returning to Christianity. Perhaps having rejected offers of repentance, they were now

[50] For Peter's feast in liturgical sources, see Garitte, *Calendrier palestino-géorgien*, 105, 393; Delehaye, *Synaxarium*, 105–6; *PG*, cxvii, 85–86 (*Menologion of Basil II*).

[51] See the introduction, nn. 52–55.

[52] MS Kutaisi—Gelati 4, 373–89.

[53] Sourdel-Thomine, "Bayt Rās," *EI²*, i, 1149; Yāqūt, *Muʿjam al-buldān*, i, 520; Schick, *Christian Communities* passim. For an introduction to the archaeology of the site, see Lenzen and Knauf, "Beit Ras/Capitolias."

[54] al-Ṭabarī, *Annales*, ii, 1463; Yāqūt, *Muʿjam al buldān*, i, 168; Ory, "Irbid," *EI²*, iv, 75–76; more generally, Sahner, "First Iconoclasm in Islam," 36–42.

[55] Shoemaker, *Three Christian Martyrdoms*, 14–15; Peeters, "Passion de S. Pierre," 302–3.

being executed as apostates. Whoever they were, the perceived decline of Christianity in Capitolias had a profound effect on Peter, and for the first time, he contemplated pursuing martyrdom himself. In this, he hoped that he might become a symbol of strength and resilience to the Christians around him who were being tempted to leave. The passage in question is worth quoting in full:

> For then he saw that the cloud of godlessness and the fog of seduction were widespread and that truth was violently oppressed by falsehood, when many who had vacillating thoughts were captivated by the ease of pleasures, by apostasy from the truth, and by falling willingly into falsehood. And some were attracted and won over through flattery, while others were stolen away by the promise of gifts. And once it happened that they broke some people through coercion by torture and beat them into exchanging light for darkness and made them renounce the name of our Lord Jesus Christ. Because of this he was enraged and distressed and forsaking life.[56]

Like many martyrologies, the *Life of Peter* is a polemical text. Therefore, we should take statements like this with a grain of salt. Indeed, it is impossible to say whether the Decapolis region was actually experiencing a wave of mass conversions; if anything, judging from Capitolias's rural location and the early date of the martyrdom, the claims of the text seem far-fetched. On the other hand, whether or not droves of Christians were actually apostatizing is immaterial. What is significant is that contemporary Christians plausibly represented it as a time of mass attrition, and it seems that this perception drove Peter to insult Islam in public.

According to his *life*, Peter fell seriously ill and was forced to postpone his planned martyrdom. When he felt strong enough to try again, he dispatched a servant named Qaiouma to the "temple of the Arabs"[57]—that is, the mosque—ordering him to convene the "noteworthy people."[58] When the wealthy Arabs

[56] Shoemaker, *Three Christian Martyrdoms*, 22–23; Peeters, "Passion de S. Pierre," 305.

[57] Hoyland (*Seeing Islam*, 359–60; cf. de Boor, *Chronographia*, i, 416–17) speculates that Qaiouma was the Muslim notable who betrayed Peter of Maiouma in Theophanes's garbled account of the episode. On the name Qayūmā/Qaium in Aramaic and Greek inscriptions of the period, see Hoyland, "Christian Palestinian Aramaic and Old Arabic," 32; Bowersock, *Mosaics as History*, 73.

[58] To explain the presence of Arabs and a mosque in the city at this early date, it may be significant that the inhabitants of Capitolias surrendered to the Arabs before the battle of Yarmūk in 15/636, possibly because of their commercial ties to communities in the Ḥijāz or because of the large Arab population that already lived there. This may have facilitated early Muslim settlement of the city; see Lenzen and Knauf, "Beit Ras/Capitolias," 38.

arrived at his house, Peter unleashed a torrent of insults. "Everyone who denies Christ and does not confess him as being God is deceived and heading for destruction," he proclaimed: "And anyone who calls someone else a prophet after the prophet John the Baptist places himself in error, 'for the Law and the Prophets were until John the Baptist' [Luke 16:16]!" The Arabs were furious with Peter. "Behold the astonishment," they cried: "O the extraordinary audacity! Do you see how he mocks us. . . . Should we not kill him?" Peter prayed that he would be martyred then and there, but the Arabs did not carry through with their plan, and his hopes for martyrdom were dashed.[59]

Despite being given a second chance, Peter's enthusiasm for death did not wane. He eventually recovered and started to prowl the streets of Capitolias vilifying Islam again. Family, friends, and neighbors pleaded with him to cease his insults, but he refused to heed their advice, dreaming of death "both day and night." The Arabs also complained to ʿUmar, the son of the caliph al-Walīd, who was then serving as governor of the *jund*, or military district, of al-Urdunn.[60] ʿUmar, in turn, deputized a local official named Zora (Ar. Zurʿa) to manage the situation.[61] Zora was instructed to question Peter and if he denied the charges, to release him. According to the text, the authorities suspected that Peter's outbursts were caused by illness, for "many people say such worthless things through delirium." If he refused to recant, however, Zora was ordered to place him in custody. When Zora eventually reached Capitolias, he made an offer of clemency, but Peter refused to acknowledge that he had blasphemed in the fog of sickness. Peter's friends and family likewise encouraged him to repent, but he ignored their pleas. "I am not lying," he proclaimed before the Christians of the city: "I do not ever recall any deception of the mind during the time of my illness, and what I said then is true." Zora then shackled Peter and led him away to Damascus.[62]

Even al-Walīd, who was then on his deathbed in the monastery-palace of Dayr Murrān (the very place where the martyr Anthony al-Qurashī lived decades later), tried to persuade Peter to recant.[63] He offered Peter the same exit strategy by suggesting that he had blasphemed in the throes of illness, but the martyr refused to accept this. "I will not cease to worship Christ, whom I

[59] Shoemaker, *Three Christian Martyrdoms*, 24–27; Peeters, "Passion de S. Pierre," 304.

[60] Khalīfa b. Khayyāṭ, *Tārīkh*, 199; Ibn ʿAsākir, *Tārīkh*, xlv, 354–60; Hoyland, *Seeing Islam*, 358 n. 74.

[61] On the identity of this figure, see Anthony, *Crucifixion and Death*, 56–57 n. 76.

[62] Shoemaker, *Three Christian Martyrdoms*, 30–35; Peeters, "Passion de S. Pierre," 306.

[63] Shoemaker, *Three Christian Martyrdoms*, 38–43; Peeters, "Passion de S. Pierre," 310. For al-Walīd at Dayr Murrān, see al-Ṭabarī, *Annales*, ii, 1270; for discussion of the site, see Sourdel, "Dayr Murrān," *EI²*, ii, 198; Zayyāt, *al-Diyārāt al-naṣrānīya*, 18, 21–22, 28, 33, 55, 59, 64, 107; Binggeli, "Converting the Caliph," 99–103; and chapter 2, sec. II.

call my God," he told the caliph: "But you, being blind in mind, believe in a false prophet and proclaim him as the messenger of God." Al-Walīd replied with exasperation, saying,

> So be it if you want to confess Jesus as God, even though he is a man and servant of the Creator. Why have you insulted our religion? Why have you said that our peaceful prophet is the master of deception and the father of lies?

No longer able to "tolerate the holy one's audacity," al-Walīd sentenced him to a gruesome death.[64] Fittingly, Peter had his tongue removed—"the organ of theology, the lyre of the harp of the spirit"—not unlike other neomartyrs, including Peter of Damascus and the Armenian apostate Mukat'l (d. ca. 851–52).[65] Peter died by crucifixion in Capitolias in January 715.

In the history of the Christian religion, it is axiomatic that a real martyr does not court death on his or her own.[66] Rather, a martyr suffers injustices inflicted by someone else. Given this, it was not hard for hagiographers in the early Islamic period to portray apostates as lambs being led to the slaughter: converts made the principled decision to reject Islam and embrace Christianity, while the Muslim authorities made their own decision to try, torture, and kill them. Although many apostates were in fact zealots who refused all offers of compromise, ultimately, it was not they who chose to confront the authorities and die but, rather, the authorities who chose to incarcerate and kill them. By contrast, it was very hard for hagiographers to portray blasphemers as victims of someone else's rage. Blasphemers were proactive in courting death; indeed, they recall the Circumcellions of late antique North Africa, extremist Christians who were so determined to follow in the footsteps of the early martyrs that they walked off cliffs and picked fights with judges in order to claim their mantle.[67] For hagiographers in the early Islamic period, there was a very thin line between martyrdom and suicide, especially when it came to blasphemers. Therefore, it was necessary to create legitimate pretenses for blasphemers to blaspheme—that is, circumstances of injustice against which a saint could

[64] Shoemaker, *Three Christian Martyrdoms*, 42–45; Peeters, "Passion de S. Pierre," 310–11.

[65] Shoemaker, *Three Christian Martyrdoms*, 46–47; Peeters, "Passion de S. Pierre," 311–13. On the removal of tongues in the Sasanian Empire, see Jullien, "Peines supplices," 261–62; for Peter of Damascus, see sec. II above; for Mukat'l (Ar. Muqātil), a Persian convert to Islam who was killed by Bughā al-Kabīr in Armīniya ca. 851–52, see Thomson, *House of Artsrunik'*, 250–51. Compare the Muslim heretic Mīthām al-Tammār (d. 60/671), who had his tongue removed: Sindawi, "Mīthām b. Yaḥyā al-Tammār," 275.

[66] Middleton, "Early Christian Voluntary Martyrdom."

[67] Gaddis, *There Is No Crime*, 111–19; more broadly, see Drees, "Sainthood and Suicide," 60–68.

react, thereby transforming his string of imprudent insults into a flood of holy outrage.

Thus, Peter's biographer was extremely careful to stress the perceived erosion of Christianity in Capitolias. Doing so provided the essential backdrop and justification for Peter's insults. If we trust the text, therefore, we know that Peter lived at a time when Christians were trading up to the religion of the ruling class due to a combination of coercion and opportunism. One suspects that there were many in Capitolias who shared Peter's melancholy, mourning the loss of their coreligionists to Islam. At the same time, many Christians may have resented Peter's confrontational style.[68] We can sense the presence of these individuals in the frightened exhortations of Peter's relatives and friends who begged him to stop blaspheming (and to stop rocking the boat for everyone else). Peter, however, was determined to speak truth to power. As his *life* put it, "O blessed tongue like the tongue of the chief of the apostles. . . . O thrice blessed voice which gladdens the angels and puts the devil to shame. . . . Behold the theologian, clearly proclaiming the truth to kings and princes!"[69]

In his blasphemy, Peter was exercising the ancient virtue of *parrhēsia*, or frank speech. In fact, the Georgian equivalent, *kardnierebai* (cf. Job 27:10; Hebrews 3:6; 2 Corinthians 7:4), appears several times in the text, including when Peter confronts al-Walīd with "audacity" and when the Arabs of Capitolias foam at the martyr's extreme "boldness."[70] The concept of *parrhēsia* had roots in classical Greek culture, in which it referred to the right of citizens to freely speak their minds.[71] The term also appeared in the New Testament at several points in order to express the idea of speaking with courage, assurance, or frankness before God. In late antiquity, *parrhēsia* was also regarded as a special gift of ascetics, martyrs, and bishops who rebuked the corrupt, the impious, and the powerful in the name of Christ.[72] The concept even had an Islamic analogue in the famous principle of "commanding the right and forbidding the wrong" (Ar. *al-amr bi-ʾl-maʿrūf wa-nahy ʿan al-munkar*).[73]

The Muslim conquest provided Christians with new opportunities for the exercise of *parrhēsia*. The word appears in several martyrologies, such as the

[68] For more on the theme of quietism in the *Life of Peter*, see chapter 5, sec. II.

[69] Shoemaker, *Three Christian Martyrdoms*, 40–41; Peeters, "Passion de S. Pierre," 310.

[70] Shoemaker, *Three Christian Martyrdoms*, 30–31, 38–39, 42–43, 46–47. I thank Stephen Shoemaker for helping me locate this term.

[71] Miquel, "Parrhèsia"; Spicq, *Lexicon of the New Testament*, iii, 56–62; Jeffreys, "Parrhesia."

[72] On the concept of *parrhēsia* in late antiquity and Byzantium, see Scarpat, *Parrhesia greca, parrhesia cristiana*; Brown, *Power and Persuasion*, 61–70, 106–8; Hatlie, "Martyrdom (*Martyrion*) and Speaking Out (*Parrhesia*)."

[73] Cook, *Commanding Right*, esp. 50–67.

legend of the Muslim prince of Diospolis, in which the martyr is shown confronting a group of Saracens and "boldly proclaiming [Gk. *parrhēsia*] that Christ is the true God."[74] Elias of Helioupolis is also said to have addressed his tormenters with *parrhēsia*.[75] Outside the canon of saints' *lives*, Thomas of Marga (fl. ninth century) describes a monk named Rabban Cyriacus who opposed a Muslim strongman who was reportedly plundering monasteries in northern Iraq. This Muslim was astonished when the monk rebuked him, for he knew that "this audacity [Syr. *parrehsiyā*] which his speech had acquired was out of the ordinary."[76] Likewise, Michael the Syrian recounts a debate during the 640s between a Muslim *amīr* named ʿAmr b. Saʿd and the West Syrian patriarch John II (r. 631–48) on the topic of sacred scripture. When the Muslim realized the patriarch's "audacity [Syr. *lbībūteh*] and the extent of his knowledge," he relented and accepted defeat.[77] The same virtue is ascribed to the martyr Anthony al-Qurashī during his confrontation with the caliph Hārūn al-Rashīd, according to Michael.[78] The term *parrhēsia* even appears in Arabized form (*barīsīyā*) in Christian texts of the early medieval period.[79]

As we consider the *Life of Peter of Capitolias*, it is worth recalling that the legal discourse on blasphemy in Islam was slow to crystallize. Although the Qurʾan contained ample warnings against disparaging speech, the early jurists sidestepped the issue of blasphemy as they focused on the more immediate threat of apostasy. What makes the *Life of Peter* so important, therefore, is that it provides an independent witness to the articulation and implementation of blasphemy laws before they materialized on a large scale in works of *ḥadīth* and *fiqh*. Here, it is interesting to note that the text never once refers to Peter's persecutors as "Muslims," to their faith as "Islam," or to their prophet as "Muḥammad." The most precise descriptor found anywhere in the text is *Arab*.[80] Of course, the *Life of Peter* cannot be taken as a record of the martyr's real words, yet his reported tirades match what scholars know about how Christians saw Islam at this time. Michael Penn, for instance, has recently documented the slippery terminology that Syriac-speaking Christians of the seventh and eighth

[74] Aufhauser, *Miracula*, 93.

[75] *SPSH*, i, 50; see also *CMLT*, 125; Pomialovskij, *Zhitie izhe vo sviatykh ottsa nashego Feodora*, 30.

[76] Budge, *Book of Governors*, i, 242.

[77] Chabot, *Chronique*, ii, 431–32 (Fr.); iv, 421–22 (Syr.). I thank Jack Tannous for sharing this reference with me.

[78] Chabot, *Chronique*, ii, 19 (Fr.); iv, 488 (Syr.).

[79] Oestrup, "Zwei arabische Codices sinaitici," 469. I thank Dmitry Morozov for sharing this reference with me.

[80] Shoemaker, *Three Christian Martyrdoms*, 24–27 ("temple of the Arabs," "best of the Arabs" in Capitolias), 32–33 ("Walid, the tyrant of the Arabs"). The *Life of Elias of Helioupolis* also avoids the term *Muslim* in favor of *Arab*; see *SPSH*, i, 48, 52 ("faith of the Arabs").

centuries applied to Muslims.[81] Muslims were called a variety of names, including *ṭayāyē* (Arabs), *ḥanpē* (pagans), *mhagrāyē* (Hagarenes; cf. Ar. *muhājirūn*, "emigrants"), and *ishmāʿelāyē* (Ishmaelites). The absence of a single overarching term in Syriac suggests that Christians had a rather fluid understanding of the people they were dealing with, more often than not seeing them in ethnic as opposed to religious terms. Here, it is telling that Syriac speakers did not use the words *Muslim* and *Islam* with an explicitly religious connotation until the 770s—nearly a century and a half after the conquest—when the equivalent terms *mashlmānā* and *mashlmānūtā* were first used.[82]

Peter's blasphemy contains the seeds of a theological critique that would mature and harden over time. It was a critique of Islam grounded in objections to Qurʾanic Christology and prophetology above all else.[83] That is to say, Christians argued against Muslims that Jesus was no mere man but God Himself and that the seal of the prophets was not Muḥammad but John the Baptist. One might rightly ask what level of theological literacy these arguments manifest: Can we take Peter—or more likely his learned biographer—as representative of what Christians understood about the doctrines of their rulers at this moment? Needless to say, the average Christian peasant in Peter's world did not converse with Muslim religious scholars or read the Qurʾan. Despite this, the average peasant was not totally ignorant about the beliefs of Muslims, and this base-level literacy seems to be reflected in the martyrology.

It is no coincidence that the dogmatic principles mentioned in the text were the same principles being articulated on Umayyad coins at this time. In clear Arabic script, these coins proclaimed that God "did not beget and He was not begotten" (cf. Q. *al-Ikhlāṣ* 112:3) and that Muḥammad was the "messenger of God" (Figure 3.2). In the majority-Christian world of Umayyad Syria, it was impossible not to read such legends as critiques of Christian doctrine. What is more, such coins sat in the pocket of every Christian man and woman in the *jund* of al-Urdunn. Thus, when we imagine the level of theological understand-

[81] Penn, *Envisioning Islam*, 53–101; see also Brock, "Syriac Views of Emergent Islam."

[82] Chabot, *Chronicon anonymum Pseudo-Dionysianum*, ii, 385, 391; for discussion and earlier, more ambiguous attestations of *mashlmānūtā*, probably for the concept of "tradition" rather than "Islam," see Penn, *Envisioning Islam*, 76–77, 209 n. 8; also Crone and Cook, *Hagarism*, 179 n. 7; Hoyland, *Seeing Islam*, 197, 340 n. 15, 378, 414 n. 88. For discussion of *mashlmānā*, meaning both "Muslim" and "traitor," see chapter 5, sec. I. Shaban ("Conversion to Early Islam," 24–25) provocatively asks whether the earliest Muslims may have been hesitant to use the word *muslimūn* because of the negative connotations of the root verb *aslama*, which before Islam primarily meant "to abandon something," "to give something up," "to let something loose entirely," "to leave or desert someone," etc. Could this theory also explain the Qurʾan's preference for the term *muʾminūn* over *muslimūn* (contra Donner, *Muhammad and the Believers*; cf. Ahmed, *What Is Islam?* 102 n. 249)?

[83] Shoemaker, *Three Christian Martyrdoms*, 26–27, 40–41.

Figure 3.2. Silver dirham, reign of al-Walīd b. ʿAbd al-Malik, Damascus mint, 92 AH (ca. AD 711). Obverse: "There is no god but God alone, He has no associate"; reverse: "God is one God, the eternal, He did not beget and He was not begotten, there is none like unto Him" (Qur'an *al-Ikhlāṣ* 112). Photo: Fitzwilliam Museum, Cambridge.

ing reflected in the *Life of Peter*—on the part of both its subject and his biographer—it may not have been that of a later Christian intellectual such as Theodore Abū Qurra. But it was sophisticated enough to rebut basic arguments about the most contentious issues.

To conclude this section, let us consider what Christian blasphemy may have meant for the Umayyad officials portrayed in the *Life of Peter*. While interrogating the martyr at Dayr Murrān, al-Walīd is reported as saying, "So be it if you want to confess Jesus as God, even though he is a man and servant of the Creator. Why have you insulted our religion?"[84] Like the Andalusī jurist al-ʿUtbī, al-Walīd did not object to the fact of disagreement between Muslims and Christians. What al-Walīd objected to was that Peter activated these disagreements as a pretense for disparaging Islam. Put differently, Peter was entitled to his negative views of Islam in private, but he was not entitled to express them in public, especially if he did so in a manner that undermined Muslim dogma.

Along these lines, one of the most striking features of the text is how leniently al-Walīd treated Peter. The caliph and his deputies are shown granting the martyr numerous chances to repent and save his life.[85] Of course, one way to interpret these scenes is as a series of hagiographic tropes meant to make

[84] Shoemaker, *Three Christian Martyrdoms*, 40–41; Peeters, "Passion de S. Pierre," 310.

[85] For more on the theme of repentance, see chapter 5, sec. I.

Peter look pious: here is a martyr more committed to defending his faith than to preserving his own life. It may also reflect legal conventions at the time, especially the practice of *istitāba*, whereby Muslim officials were obliged to offer apostates (and blasphemers) the opportunity to repent. There is a third possibility, however, that may explain their bewildered reaction, namely, that Christian blasphemy was something very new, perhaps even unprecedented for these officials. Even as Peter continued his insults, the Muslim authorities are shown clinging to the idea that Peter was simply ill: How else to explain his bizarre behavior other than as a consequence of sickness?[86] Reading between the lines, if the text has any basis in reality, one wonders whether the incredulity of the Umayyad officials may hint that in the early 700s, Peter's actions were not yet part of a familiar spectrum of behaviors through which Christians resisted their Muslim rulers. Non-Muslims might protest their subordination by tearing up tax registers or evicting state officials from their villages as other historical sources tell us, but they did not mock the beliefs of Muslims outright, at least not yet. Thus, al-Walīd and his subordinates may have reacted in this way precisely because Peter's offense was something novel. It is not inconceivable that he was among the first Christian blasphemers they had encountered. If this is true, Peter's behavior may track the general souring of Muslim-Christian relations that is thought to have followed the reign of ʿAbd al-Malik, when religious tensions between Muslims and Christians were on the rise. This was due to the caliph's well-known campaign of Islamizing the state and public space.[87] Within this constellation of flash points ignited by ʿAbd al-Malik, Christian blasphemy may have become a real issue for the first time.

IV. BLASPHEMY IN CÓRDOBA

Despite these examples, we should not forget that there are very few accounts of Christian blasphemy from the Muslim East. If the martyrs are any indication of overall numbers, it is telling that our evidence of blasphemy in the region amounts to a single detailed report in the *Life of Peter*, along with several fictionalized accounts in the *lives* of Menas, Thomas, and Michael. Put bluntly, the literary evidence for Christian blasphemy from the east is weak, especially in comparison to the evidence for apostasy in the same region from around

[86] Shoemaker, *Three Christian Martyrdoms*, 32–33, 38–39; Peeters, "Passion de S. Pierre," 306–8, 310.

[87] Robinson, *ʿAbd al-Malik*, 113–19; Donner, *Muhammad and the Believers*, 194–224.

the same time. Our portrait of blasphemy, however, does not look so incomplete if we expand our view to include the Muslim West. In Córdoba, the capital of the independent Umayyad emirate of al-Andalus, we have a great abundance of sources in Latin that discuss blasphemy.[88] In fact, these texts—which were written by Eulogius and Paulus Alvarus and which document the martyrdom of forty-eight Christians in and around Córdoba between 850 and 859—contain some of the very richest information about blasphemy anywhere in the medieval Middle East (information that Islamicists have not yet fully exploited).

Despite the potential of these sources, however, it is important to treat them with great caution. This is because there are essentially no medieval manuscripts of these works that have survived to the present. Instead, scholars must rely on printed copies of the texts as they were produced in the sixteenth century shortly before the originals disappeared.[89] But missing evidence is not the only problem; in some ways, even more troubling is that Christian sources present the martyrdoms as a great cataclysm in the life of the local church, whereas Muslim sources pass over the events in silence. How is it that one side of a conflict so assiduously documented the martyrdoms but the other side completely ignored them?

Given these problems, a certain degree of methodological skepticism has pervaded scholarship on the martyrs, especially in recent years. This has produced a great flurry of studies that attempt to disaggregate the goals of the martyrs from those of their biographers. We now possess a much more nuanced understanding of the literary, social, and theological agendas of the texts than we did fifty years ago, as exemplified by the work of Jessica Coope, Kenneth Wolf, Maria Jesús Aldana García and Pedro Herrera Roldán, Ann Christys, Charles Tieszen, and Jamie Wood.[90] This style of literary analysis, however, has led some scholars to the rather extreme conclusion that the martyrs' movement was basically made up—or if it did take place, it happened in a much more attenuated form than what the sources report. This view is especially pronounced in the work of Juan Pedro Monferrer-Sala and Sara Stroumsa.[91]

[88] For surveys of the events and the literature, see Colbert, *Martyrs of Córdoba*; Coope, *Martyrs of Córdoba*; Wolf, *Christian Martyrs*.

[89] Colbert, *Martyrs of Córdoba*, 435–53; Wolf, *Christian Martyrs*, 36–47; though medieval manuscripts of Paulus Alvarus's *Indiculus luminosus* do survive to the present: *CMR*, i, 648.

[90] Coope, *Martyrs of Córdoba*; Wolf, *Christian Martyrs*; Aldana García and Herrera Roldán, "Prudencio entre los mozárabes cordobeses"; Christys, *Christians in al-Andalus*, 52–107; Tieszen, *Christian Identity amid Islam*, 21–144; Wood, "Memorialising Martyrdom"; see also Duque, "Claiming Martyrdom."

[91] Monferrer Sala, "Mitografía hagiomartirial." This was also the subject of a public lecture

I am personally dubious of this skeptical approach: as we shall see in the coming pages, there are simply too many details in the writings of Eulogius and Paulus Alvarus that reflect a plausible social reality to discount them as *mitografía hagiomartirial*, in the words of Monferrer-Sala.

In this section, I wish to integrate literary and historical approaches in order to answer three main questions: How did Christians blaspheme against Islam? Why did individual martyrs blaspheme? And what social conditions led the martyrs to turn to this particular form of protest as a group? In asking these questions, I hope to avoid the myopic, totalizing questions that some historians have posed about the martyrs in the past. These include whether the martyrs were moved by an incipient Spanish nationalism,[92] by a desire to renew Latin Christian culture,[93] or by a subconscious Freudian death wish.[94] While elements of these questions may be attractive, they have limited explanatory power when we consider the varied identities of the martyrs and their biographers, not to mention the absence of corroborating evidence that might temper the sometimes wild claims of the sources. The analysis that follows will, I hope, be novel for two reasons: first, it will focus narrowly on the issue of blasphemy in Córdoba's Islamic context, and second, it will contextualize the martyrs alongside their counterparts from the east.[95]

John the Merchant

Modern historians have often seen the Christians of Córdoba as divided into two groups: the "accommodationists," who acquiesced to the Arab conquest and eagerly assimilated into Muslim culture, and the "rejectionists," who refused to surrender to the conquerors and clung jealously to their faith and

---

delivered by Sarah Stroumsa at the Institute for Advanced Study, Princeton, in February 2015 entitled "An Exercise in Methodological Skepticism: The Case of the Cordoban Voluntary Martyrs." I am grateful to Professor Stroumsa for discussing this matter with me at this conference and subsequently in written correspondence.

92 Notably Pérez de Urbel, *Saint under Moslem Rule*; cf. Levi-Provençal, *Histoire*, i, 225–39.

93 Waltz, "Significance of the Voluntary Martyrs"; Waltz, "Historical Perspective on the 'Early Missions.' "

94 Drees, "Sainthood and Suicide."

95 Astonishingly, most literature on the Córdoba martyrs shows no awareness that there were new martyrs in the Muslim East at the same time; for exceptions, see Coope, *Martyrs of Córdoba*, 39–40 (which acknowledges the existence of martyrs in Syria but misidentifies one of them as "Bishop" Peter of Maiouma); Monferrer Sala, "Mitografía hagiomartirial," 425–42; Christys, *Christians in al-Andalus*, 65–66, 69; Pochoshajew, *Märtyrer von Cordoba*, 144–45. More generally, for the eastern context, see Lapiedra Guttiérez, "Mártires de Córdoba."

identity. Within this dichotomy, the martyrs are often presented as "rejectionists" par excellence, and their deaths are presented as the ultimate form of protest against the perceived dwindling of Iberian Christian culture. As Isidro de la Cagigas put it, the martyrs expressed "the radical incompatibility" between the Christian faith and the ideas they had absorbed from their Muslim rulers.[96] A fault line did indeed run through the church of Córdoba in the ninth century, as will be discussed in chapter 5. But where Cagigas and others got it wrong, I think, was to assume that this dichotomy defined the martyrs throughout their entire lives. In fact, the evidence suggests that a great many martyrs kept a foot in both worlds, neither fully "accommodationists" nor fully "rejectionists." Even if through blasphemy they expressed their solidarity with the "rejectionist" view before their deaths, the circumstances that led to their executions indicate that they were deeply embedded in the very Muslim culture they allegedly despised.

To understand this contrast, let us examine the case of the confessor John, who was beaten for his blasphemous tirade in May 851.[97] According to Paulus Alvarus, John had been a merchant in the markets of Córdoba, and his business brought him into frequent contact with Muslim clients and friends. He was in the habit of swearing by the Prophet, and Paulus Alvarus reports that a group of Muslims—perhaps competitors in the market, who "burned with envy because of their love of merchandise"—one day approached John and asked why he always invoked Muḥammad's name given that he was a Christian. "Thinking little of our prophet," they said, "you always use his name in derision, and to ears that do not know you are a Christian, you often confirm your lying with oaths from our religion, false as they may seem to you." John took their question in "good faith" and resolved to set the record straight on what he really believed. "May God curse whoever wishes to invoke the name of your prophet," he exclaimed. Furiously, the Muslims surrounded John "like bees collected in a treacherous swarm," beating him and then escorting him to the chief *qāḍī* of the city.[98]

[96] Cagigas, *Mozárabes*, 179–211, esp. 195–96, for what Cagigas called *acomodaticios* and *intransigentes*; cf. Lévi-Provençal, *Histoire*, i, 236. For more on this theme, see chapter 5, sec. II. On the threat of assimilation, see especially Pérez de Urbel, *Saint under Moslem Rule*, 174; Lévi-Provençal, *Histoire*, i, 232; Chalmeta, "Mozarab," *EI*[2], vii, 247–48.

[97] There are two principal sources of information about John: the *Indiculus luminosus* of Paulus Alvarus (§ 5, in *CSM*, i, 277–78) and the *Memoriale sanctorum* of Eulogius (I, § 9, in *CSM*, ii, 377). For discussion, see Dozy, *Spanish Islam*, 282–83; Simonet, *Historia*, 389–91; Cagigas, *Mozárabes*, 212, 215, 489; Colbert, *Martyrs of Córdoba*, 42, 198–201; Cutler, "Spanish Martyrs' Movement," 324–25; Wolf, *Christian Martyrs*, 12, 28, 57, 102–3; Coope, *Martyrs of Córdoba*, 18, 27, 56; Safran, *Defining Boundaries*, 86, 94–95 n. 24, 151 n. 68.

[98] *CSM*, i, 277–78. For an Ottoman-era parallel, see Vaporis, *Witnesses for Christ*, 109–10, 150.

According to Eulogius's account, the Muslims told the judge,

> We have known this one to always persist in mocking our teacher and to attack him irreverently with words of imprecation. When he wants to stir up the sale of merchandise, he is not able to entice customers unless the most subtle mocker resorts to swearing our oath with careless words.

The judge then ordered John to be beaten. Thereafter, John refused to acknowledge the charges brought against him, so the authorities seated him backward on a horse and paraded him through the streets of Córdoba, a practice known in Islamic law as *tashhīr*, or "ignominious parading," which is portrayed in several other martyrologies of the period.[99] A herald at the head of the procession reportedly cried aloud, "This is the punishment which the detractor of our prophet and the mocker of our religion deserves!" John was not martyred but was thrown in prison and remained there over the coming decade, serving as an inspiration for other Christians who followed his path.[100]

The actual circumstances of John's blasphemy are very opaque. As Alvarus and Eulogius make it seem, John had been able to pass as a Muslim in the marketplace—a setting in which members of different religions mingled and transacted business constantly. In this world, social distinctions must have melted away or at least been very hard to perceive. The ninth-century Mālikī jurist al-Kinānī helps us imagine how this may have looked in a colorful treatise on the rules of the marketplace that is preserved in the *fatwā* collection of the latter-day scholar al-Wansharīsī (d. 914/1508). At one point, al-Kinānī was asked what to do with a Jew "who imitates the Muslims and drops the article of clothing [Ar. *ḥilyatahu*] by which he is known"—that is, one of the distinctive garments *dhimmīs* were obliged to wear in public. In reply, al-Kinānī advised jailing and beating the offender.[101] At another point, he was asked what the overseer of the market (*ṣāḥib al-sūq*) in Qayrawān should do with Jews and Christians who refused to don the *zunnār*. In reply, he said that they should be imprisoned, beaten, and then paraded through the neighborhoods where their coreligionists congregated, so that they might be a "warning and a rebuke" to others.[102]

99 Lange, "Ignominious Parading"; with parallels in the *Life of Peter of Capitolias*: Shoemaker, *Three Christian Martyrdoms*, 44–45, 54–55; and Anthony of Syracuse: Delehaye, *Synaxarium*, 72; see also Colbert, *Martyrs of Córdoba*, 42, 361; and chapter 4, nn. 68–69.

100 *CSM*, ii, 377.

101 al-Wansharīsī, *al-Miʿyār al-muʿrib*, vi, 69, cited in Safran, *Defining Boundaries*, 162–63.

102 al-Wansharīsī, *al-Miʿyār al-muʿrib*, vi, 421, cited in Safran, *Defining Boundaries*, 162–63.

John's story and al-Kinānī's judgments reflect a world in which identity could be exceptionally unclear in mixed settings, as the work of Janina Safran has shown.[103] In the marketplace, Muslims and non-Muslims dressed similarly, spoke similarly, and even invoked similar prophets and saints, thereby obscuring their religious loyalties.[104] Given that John's behavior was at one time so normal, what is striking about his story is how quickly his fortunes soured. Seemingly without warning, the offhand comments that had probably rolled off his tongue for years without comment from his Muslim friends landed him in hot water. What precipitated this violent change? The text hints that John's tormenters also worked in the markets, so perhaps jealousy or unequal profits caused the turnaround. Indeed, John's experience calls to mind the trial of Elias of Helioupolis, in which accusations of apostasy superimposed on financial grievances to start the machinery of state violence. Taken alone, neither religious offenses nor business grudges were enough to send these martyrs into the hands of the authorities. But taken together, they produced disastrous consequences for the accused. Whatever the case may be, John's initial blasphemy was not deliberate, it seems, but once he was cornered and called to account for his faith, his second blasphemy was very much planned.

Perfectus the Monk

In most cases, Eulogius does not provide transcripts of the martyrs' tirades, other than to note that they insulted the Prophet and his "godless religion." There is one case, however, in which Eulogius does furnish a great deal of information about how blasphemy worked in practice, and this is in the martyrdom of Perfectus, a monk who was the first of the Christians to be executed in April 850 (Figure 3.3).[105] As such, he sheds light on the method and

[103] Safran, "Identity and Differentiation"; Safran, "Pollution of the Christian"; Safran, "Sacred and the Profane"; Safran, *Defining Boundaries.*

[104] Eulogius and Alvarus complained of Christians who refused to make the sign of the cross after yawning and refused to call Jesus "God," referring to him instead as "a word and a spirit," echoing the Qur'an (e.g., Q. *al-Nisā'* 4:171); see *CSM*, i, 281; ii, 375–76, 487. For similar complaints in the east, see Sahas, *John of Damascus*, 133; Griffith, "First Christian *Summa Theologiae* in Arabic," 18–24.

[105] *CSM*, ii, 369, 377–78, esp. 397–401, from which the summary below draws. Discussion in *BS*, x, 488–89; Dozy, *Spanish Islam*, 278–81; Simonet, *Historia*, 385–91; Cagigas, *Mozárabes*, 212, 489; Colbert, *Martyrs of Córdoba*, 194–99; Millet-Gérard, *Chrétiens mozarabes*, 37, 54–57; Wolf, *Christian Martyrs*, 12, 24, 81–82, 102–3; Coope, *Martyrs of Córdoba*, 17–18; Pochoshajew, *Märtyrer von Cordoba*, 171–72; Safran, *Defining Boundaries*, 94, 99. Technically, the first martyrs to die were Adulphus and John, brothers of the martyr Aurea (d. 856). The monk Speraindeo wrote a biography

Figure 3.3. Perfectus of Córdoba (left), with Flora and Maria, Tabernacle Chapel, Mosque-Cathedral of Córdoba, ca. 1583–84. Photo: Juan Antonio Soto/ArtEnCórdoba.

portrayal of blasphemy in ninth-century al-Andalus in a way most other martyrs cannot. As a youth, Perfectus reportedly studied at the basilica of St. Acisclus—the patron saint of Córdoba, who was martyred under Diocletian in 304—located at the western end of the city.[106] The basilica was also home to an important monastic school. There, Perfectus was exposed "to a great many ecclesiastical subjects" and even acquired a talent and acquaintance with the Arabic language.[107] He remained at the basilica for most of his adult life.

The story of Perfectus's martyrdom begins when one day he left the monastery for "some household business." While on the road, he encountered a

of the brothers that no longer survives; see *CMR*, i, 633; Cagigas, *Mozárabes*, 211; Coope, *Martyrs of Córdoba*, xv.

[106] Castejón, "Cordoba Califal," 329–31. On Saint Acisclus, see *BS*, i, 160–61; on the representation of local Roman martyrs in the writings of Eulogius and Paulus Alvarus, see now Wood, "Memorialising Martyrdom," 52–55.

[107] On knowledge of Arabic among the martyrs and their biographers, see Millet-Gérard, *Chrétiens mozarabes*, 49–62, 71–76; for examples of Arabic phrases in the Latin texts, see *CSM*, i, 303; ii, 399, 709.

group of Muslims who peppered him with questions about Christianity. They also wanted to know his opinion about the Prophet Muḥammad. Perfectus happily "professed the power of Christ's divinity," but he was more reluctant to explain his views of Islam. "On the subject of your prophet," he told them, "I dare not explain how he is regarded among Catholics, for I have no doubt that you will be greatly insulted by this, causing you serious anxiety." Clearly aware of the risks of letting frank speech transform into blasphemy, Perfectus made a wager with his Muslim companions: he agreed to tell them his unvarnished opinions of their prophet if they agreed not to harm him. The Muslims were pleased by this and "falsely pledged their honor, forcing him to describe whatever the Christians believed with all fear having been suppressed."[108]

Per their agreement, Perfectus proceeded to state in Arabic his view that Muḥammad had been a false prophet who had "corrupted the malleable hearts of the masses with his deadly venom." He also explained that Muḥammad had been a carnal man, as evidenced by his lust for Zaynab—the wife of his adopted son, Zayd.[109] The episode is famous in Muslim lore, which claims that Muḥammad initially arranged the marriage of Zaynab and Zayd in order to showcase the egalitarian values of his new community. After all, Zaynab was a woman of noble birth, while Zayd was a former slave. Despite their disparity in status, they were absolute equals as Muslim believers. This plan backfired, however, when Muḥammad himself became attracted to Zaynab and had his adopted son divorce her. According to Islamic sources, the incident provided the context for the revelation of several Qurʾanic verses that forbade the old tribal practice of adoption, lest fathers and sons end up sharing the same wives, as Muḥammad and Zayd had done (Q. *al-Aḥzāb* 33:5, 33:37).[110] Whatever the story's significance for Muslims, Perfectus and other Christian polemicists of the early Middle Ages seized on it to prove how Muḥammad had been a "patron of lust and a slave to the pleasures of iniquity."

When Perfectus finished speaking, the Muslims permitted him to leave, "hold[ing] in their hearts the fury of revenge." Later, Perfectus met them again,

108 *CSM*, ii, 398.

109 Compare with Paulus Alvarus in the *Indiculus luminosus* (*CSM*, i, 296–98); discussion in Franke, "Freiwilligen Märtyrer," 40–41; Millet-Gérard, *Chrétiens mozarabes*, 129; Wasilewski, "Life of Muhammad," 343–45. The Zaynab-Zayd story is not often included in polemical accounts of the Prophet's life. It also appears in the writings of John of Damascus (Sahas, *John of Damascus*, 91) and the Egyptian Muslim convert Ibn Rajāʾ in the forthcoming edition and translation of the *Kitāb al-wāḍīḥ bi-ʾl-ḥaqq*, sec. 14, by David Bertaina. I am grateful to David Bertaina for allowing me to read this before its publication.

110 For background, see Lecker, "Zayd b. Ḥāritha," *EI*², xi, 475; Bosworth, "Zaynab bt. Djaḥsh," *EI*², xi, 484–85; Chaumont, "Tabannin," *EI*², xii, 768–69; Powers, *Zayd*, 30–48. For more on the representation of Muslims as carnal in the Córdoba martyr texts, see Tieszen, *Christian Identity amid Islam*, 87–88.

though this time, the Muslims decided to take revenge for his stinging insults. Therefore, like frenzied bees buzzing furiously around, they led him to the judge (Lat. *iudex*) and registered their complaint. Perfectus was thrown into prison and, according to Eulogius, remained there until "the paschal festivities of profane solemnity"—that is, ʿĪd al-Fiṭr, the holiday that marks the end of Ramadan.[111] On that occasion, Perfectus was invited to repent and go free, but instead, he merely reiterated his blasphemous tirade. "I have reviled and still do revile your prophet as the man of demons, a sorcerer, an adulterer, and a liar," he allegedly said. Furious, the Umayyad authorities had him executed in front of the "praetorium"—probably meaning the Umayyad *qaṣr* in the city center. His blood was so plentiful that it reportedly smeared the feet of his executioners.[112]

In some respects, the martyrdom of Perfectus closely resembles that of John the merchant. As their biographers portrayed them, both Christians failed to grasp the dangers of blaspheming during informal social encounters with Muslims. One suspects that neither man was as innocent as the sources make them appear. Indeed, it is hard to imagine that they did not foresee the likely consequences of their insults. At the same time, if there is any historical reality to the reports, it is telling that Perfectus seems to have grasped at least some of the dangers of excessive *parrhēsia*. After all, he initially demurred from the Muslims' offer to have a conversation about religion, and it was only after he had secured a promise of security that he finally unloaded his poisonous outburst.[113] From a narrative perspective, portraying their deaths in this way exonerates the martyrs of culpability for inciting Muslims.

The story suggests that Perfectus (or Eulogius) had a relatively good knowledge of the Prophet's life, and he was able to deploy this knowledge with devastating effects in conversation.[114] If we compare this incident with the blasphemy of Peter of Capitolias—which occurred nearly a century and a half earlier—we find that Christians had moved well beyond the simple polemic grounded in a critique of Qurʾanic Christology and prophetology. What we find in the Córdoba martyr texts is a slightly subtler, better-informed polemic that discredited the Prophet by calling his morals into question. As we shall see below, attacks like this reflect a world in which anti-Muslim apologetics formulated at the top of society were beginning to trickle down to the masses,

[111] Millet-Gérard, *Chrétiens mozarabes*, 38–39; Safran, "Sacred and the Profane," 27–28, which notes that the Umayyads sometimes granted clemency to criminals on this day. Perfectus was not so lucky, it seems. For more on executions on the feast of ʿĪd al-Aḍḥā, see Hawting, "Jaʿd b. Dirham"; Fierro, "Emulating Abraham"; Marsham, "Fire in Executions," 122–25.

[112] *CSM*, ii, 400.

[113] Contra Wolf, *Christian Martyrs*, 102.

[114] *CMR*, i, 721–22; Wasilewski, "Life of Muhammad."

who in turn mobilized them with devastating effects through ridicule. Regardless of what the martyrs said, their experiences call to mind the argument of the contemporary Andalusī jurist al-ʿUtbī, whom we met earlier in this chapter. On the topic of blasphemy, Christians were free to profess "the power of Christ's divinity"—to use Perfectus's words as reported by Eulogius. They were not free, however, to denounce Muḥammad as a "prophet of lust," as Perfectus is also alleged to have said.[115] Thus, if Eulogius's account bears any resemblance to what really happened, it shows a certain correspondence between the efforts of *dhimmīs* to insult Muslims and of Muslim jurists to police certain forms of speech and not others.

Christian Servants of the Umayyad Court

Even if many of the blasphemers in Córdoba did not undergo religious conversions, many of them experienced shifts in worldview that were just as profound. Among the most striking of these is a small group of martyrs who moved decisively from "accommodationist" to "rejectionist" views during the course of their lives. They never lived as Muslims per se, but as members of the Christian elite in the service of the Umayyad court they underwent a kind of "cultural conversion" to the habits, sensibilities, and customs of the Muslim rulers that was just as profound. Yet, according to their biographers, late in the game they seem to have experienced a change of heart—a kind of "cultural apostasy," in which they broke decisively with their Muslim patrons. In its place, they embraced what they imagined to be an undiluted Christian culture, and they announced this break through acts of blasphemy. The connection between blasphemy and "cultural apostasy," as I shall call it, is exceptionally clear in the cases of Isaac and Argimirus, two high-ranking Christian officials executed in June 851 and June 856, respectively. As two highly assimilated Christians, they reveal the paradox that enveloped many martyrs in Córdoba, who belonged to and profited from the very Muslim culture they so viciously attacked.

According to Eulogius, Isaac was among "the noble citizens of Córdoba," perhaps a descendant of the old Hispano-Gothic elite.[116] He reportedly enjoyed

[115] See n. 109 above.

[116] *CSM*, ii, 367–69, 402; English translation adapted from Colbert, "*Memoriale sanctorum*," 26–30. For discussion, see *BS*, vii, 919–20; Dozy, *Spanish Islam*, 283–85; Simonet, *Historia*, 391–96; Cagigas, *Mozárabes*, 212, 489; Colbert, *Martyrs of Córdoba*, 198, 210–11; Lévi-Provençal, *Histoire*, i, 235–36; Millet-Gérard, *Chrétiens mozarabes*, 58–61; Wolf, *Christian Martyrs*, 15, 23–25, 32, 54, 63, 102, 107–12, 117–19; Coope, *Martyrs of Córdoba*, 19–20, 73–75; Pochoshajew, *Märtyrer von Cordoba*, 173–74; Safran, *Defining Boundaries*, 95, 99, 112 n. 61, 211.

the gift of *parrhēsia* early in his life, having spoken from his mother's womb according to the sources. On another occasion when Isaac was only seven years old, a virgin of Córdoba is said to have received a vision in which she saw a great ball of light descending upon the boy, "who thrust it into his mouth and drank in all its brightness."[117] Here was a child destined to speak truth to power. As an adult, Isaac served as the *exceptor rei publicae*, meaning he was probably responsible for the affairs of Córdoba's Christian community, especially the collection of its taxes (Ar. *mustakhrij*).[118] As one of the most powerful Christians at court, he "became very skilled and learned in the Arabic language." Eulogius gives the impression that Isaac served the Umayyads for a long period. This came to an end, however, when he suddenly left office to become a monk, "inflamed with some unexpected spiritual desire." Isaac entered the monastic community of Tabanos, located seven miles from Córdoba, which had been founded shortly before by his cousin Jeremiah.[119] The former official passed three peaceful years in the monastery, but for unknown reasons in 851, he decided to descend to the city in order to blaspheme. He confronted the chief judge of Córdoba—most likely Saʿīd b. Sulaymān al-Ghāfiqī—whom he may have known through his prior service at the court.[120]

Whatever friendship the two men may have shared instantly melted away as Isaac assaulted the *qāḍī* with pointed questions. "O judge, I would like to become an ardent follower of the faith if only you would stop putting off explaining to me its logic and reason," he is reported to have said. The judge accepted this challenge, and with "cheeks puffed out and throat inflated, his lying tongue gave forth to him the words of instruction, which cackled in the hollows of his palette." The judge told Isaac how Muḥammad had received his revelation from the angel Gabriel, who taught him about God's law, the nature of paradise, and the throngs of beautiful women awaiting him there (the famous *ḥūrī*s; e.g., Q. *al-Ṭūr* 52:20, *al-Wāqiʿa* 56:36–37, *al-Naba* 78:33, etc.).[121] As he was in mid-sentence, however, Isaac interrupted him, crying aloud in Arabic, "He lied to you! May he waste away in the curses of heaven for this!" Confused by this outburst and "seized by some sort of mental stupidity," the judge began to weep.[122] He offered Isaac an opportunity to save himself by agreeing that he was "drunk with wine or overcome with madness," recalling

[117] *CSM*, ii, 368.

[118] *CSM*, ii, 402. On the role of the *exceptor*, see Chalmeta, "Ḳūmis," *EI²*, v, 376–77; Colbert, *Martyrs of Córdoba*, 246 n. 53; James, *History of Ibn al-Qūṭīya*, 75–76; Safran, *Defining Boundaries*, 42.

[119] On Tabanos, see Castejón, "Córdoba Califal," 335; Millet-Gérard, *Chrétiens mozarabes*, 58–61.

[120] al-Khushanī, *Quḍāt qurṭuba*, 92–97.

[121] Wensinck and Pellat, "Ḥūr," *EI²*, iii, 581–82.

[122] *CSM*, ii, 367.

the offer al-Walīd made to Peter of Capitolias.[123] Yet, like Peter, Isaac refused this and announced that he was "burning with the zeal of justice" and a desire to tell "the truth." When the *amīr* at the time, ʿAbd al-Raḥmān b. al-Ḥakam (r. 206–238/822–52), discovered what had happened, he became fearful that other Christians might follow Isaac and blaspheme. Therefore, he issued an edict threatening execution against anyone who lashed out against Islam.[124] A few days later, Isaac was hauled from prison and crucified on the banks of the Guadalquivir, the great river that flowed through the center of the city.

A few years later, a Christian official named Argimirus renounced his duties as *censor* (probably a judicial role) under the *amīr* Muḥammad b. ʿAbd al-Raḥmān (r. 238–73/852–86) and became a monk.[125] Eulogius tells us that unlike Isaac, who deliberately antagonized the Muslim authorities, Argimirus was "assailed by the trickery and hatred of certain pagans" and was wrongly accused of having blasphemed. At this point, nearly six years after the first martyrdoms, it must not have been hard to persuade a judge that another Christian was blaspheming—especially one like Argimirus, who had strangely abandoned a plum post in the Umayyad administration to become an ascetic. Whether or not Argimirus was guilty of blasphemy is unimportant, for when he appeared before the judge, he refused to repent of "deriding their prophet" and "professing the divinity of the Son of God." Eulogius states that he was placed on a small horse and impaled in punishment for these insults.

What compelled men like Isaac and Argimirus to give up positions of prestige and power in order to become monks? What compelled them to blaspheme against the Prophet? At a literary level, it is not hard to see in them echoes of a biblical figure such as Moses, who was raised alongside Pharaoh, only to leave the court in adulthood, wander in the desert, and eventually return to Egypt to confront his former friends. Of course, Isaac and Argimirus went one step further and got themselves killed. What is more, they led no "exodus" of Christians to the Promised Land, and indeed, one suspects that their efforts had little effect in stopping the forward march of conversion and assimilation.

Beneath these literary layers, it is clear that Isaac and Argmirus came from aristocratic Christian families who had collaborated with the Umayyads, per-

[123] See sec. III, above; on conversion in a state of intoxication, see Ibn Qudāma, *Mughnī*, xii, 148–50.

[124] *CSM*, ii, 368. On the edict of al-Mahdī against apostates in the *Life of Elias of Helioupolis*, see *SPSH*, i, 52.

[125] *CSM*, ii, 455–56; for discussion, see *BS*, ii, 405–6; Cagigas, *Mozárabes*, 219; Colbert, *Martyrs of Córdoba*, 42, 262–63; Millet-Gérard, *Chrétiens mozarabes*, 56, 87; Wolf, *Christian Martyrs*, 14, 32, 103; Coope, *Martyrs of Córdoba*, 21, 73–75; Pochoshajew, *Märtyrer von Cordoba*, 187; Safran, *Defining Boundaries*, 112 n. 61.

haps for generations, securing their status at court and at the head of the local Christian community. Eulogius presents us with an inverse doppelgänger of these martyrs in an unnamed nobleman whom he disparages for slavishly serving the Umayyads. Scholars usually identify this man as Ibn Antūnyān, a well-known figure in Muslim texts, who may have succeeded Isaac as *exceptor* yet later converted to Islam, possibly when the new *amīr* Muḥammad issued his decree dismissing Christians at court.[126] Isaac and Argimirus went in different directions, of course, abandoning their offices in order to become monks and, later, in order to air their grievances in blasphemous outbursts.

Throughout his work, Eulogius frames the martyrs' attacks as legitimate reactions to the Umayyads' assaults on Christian culture. However, we should not take these complaints necessarily to be those of the saints he eulogized (any more than we should take the complaints of Peter of Capitolias's biographer to be those of the martyr himself). Yet Isaac and Argimirus may have been protesting a system that was, in the words of Eulogius, perceived as responsible for "breaking down basilicas, disgracing priests, and [forcing us to] pay tribute with great affliction each month."[127] It was also a system they had played a role in perpetuating during their secular careers. Perhaps it was a sense of disgust with all they had accomplished through their work for the state; perhaps there were personal disputes between the martyrs and the Umayyad authorities that led to their resignations. Regardless, Eulogius here presents blasphemy as the handmaiden of ascetic renunciation. Asceticism allowed individuals like Isaac and Argimirus to extricate themselves from a culture they had once served but had come to despise. To blaspheme before the officials of the Umayyad state in this way was to tie the bow on a much longer-term process of "cultural apostasy" that began the day they left their posts.

What about the Rest?

Not all the blasphemers had such strong professional or personal relationships with Muslims, at least as the texts portray them. Despite this, the pressures of Islamization and Arabization affected each and every Christian in Córdoba. Eulogius and Paulus Alvarus described a spiritual torpor descending upon the church as a result of these forces. They complained especially that Christians were blunting their real convictions in order to fit in among Muslims, "stagnating in unrighteous silence about the dogmas of the heretics."[128] In consequence,

[126] *CSM*, ii, 440–41. For more on Ibn Antūnyān, see chapter 5, sec. I.
[127] *CSM*, ii, 385; trans. adapted from Colbert, "*Memoriale sanctorum*," 56.
[128] *CSM*, ii, 384; trans. adapted from Colbert, "*Memoriale sanctorum*," 55.

the church as a whole was living under siege, as they put it, "cast down by the carelessness of the negligent, beaten down wretchedly by the blows of some, and thrust down into the depths of sloth."[129] In this world, militant writers like Eulogius and Paulus Alvarus praised blasphemy as a means of drawing attention to the falsehoods of Islam and, more importantly, of calling on uncommitted Christians to choose sides.

In the case of John, Perfectus, Isaac, and Argimirus, biography and circumstance can help us explain what compelled the martyrs to blaspheme. With other Christians, however, there are no specific explanations underlying their insults other than perhaps the general zeitgeist. A good example involves four martyrs who were executed in September 852: Emila, Jeremiah, Rogelius, and Servusdei (Ar. ʿAbdallāh?). According to Eulogius, Emila was a young deacon at the basilica of St. Cyrian who came from noble stock.[130] Along with a friend, a lay aristocrat named Jeremiah, he uttered "such opprobrium against their Prophet" in Arabic that the "insults of the early martyrs were forgotten altogether." Eulogius does not tell us what they said, but it must have been unusually vituperative, for the Muslims of Córdoba "began to plot not only the deaths of the ones who had opposed them [i.e., Emila and Jeremiah], but they also considered the possibility of exterminating the entire church."[131] The next day, the city's Muslims faced another outburst when Rogelius, an elderly monk from near Granada, along with Servusdei, a Christian who had come "from the east across the sea as a pilgrim" (possibly from the Levant), walked into that temple of sacrileges (Lat. *fanum illud sacrilegorum*).[132] As they crossed the threshold of the building, "they proclaimed the Gospel, mocked the sect of impiety, and argued with the crowd."[133]

Eulogius's account of this episode is not especially detailed, but at the same time, it is not hard to imagine why this incident would have been especially

[129] *CSM*, ii, 369–70; trans. adapted from Colbert, "*Memoriale sanctorum*," 31.

[130] On the basilica of St. Cyprian, see Castejón, "Córdoba Califal," 332.

[131] On Emila and Jeremiah, see *CSM*, ii, 431–32; discussion in *BS*, iv, 1177–78; Simonet, *Historia*, 436–38; Cagigas, *Mozárabes*, 216, 491; Colbert, *Martyrs of Córdoba*, 242–43; Millet-Gérard, *Chrétiens mozarabes*, 57; Wolf, *Christian Martyrs*, 30, 82; Pochoshajew, *Märtyrer von Cordoba*, 182; Safran, *Defining Boundaries*, 99.

[132] Safran ("Sacred and the Profane," 26) assumes that this was the Great Mosque of Córdoba, but it also could have been one of several neighborhood mosques in the city; see Castejón, "Córdoba Califal," 279–87; González Gutiérrez, "Secondary Mosques in *Madinat Qurtuba*."

[133] *CSM*, ii, 432–33. On Rogelius and Servusdei, see discussion in *BS*, xi, 294–95; Simonet, *Historia*, 437–40; Cagigas, *Mozárabes*, 216, 491; Colbert, *Martyrs of Córdoba*, 204, 243–44; Millet-Gérard, *Chrétiens mozarabes*, 153; Wolf, *Christian Martyrs*, 30, 59 (which refers to Servusdei as a "Syrian," but there is no evidence for this in the text, which merely states that he came *ab orientis partibus ultra maria*; repeated in Cutler, "Spanish Martyrs' Movement," 328; Safran, *Defining Boundaries*, 93); Monferrer Sala, "Mitografía hagiomartirial," 441; Pochoshajew, *Märtyrer von Cordoba*, 182–83.

offensive to Muslims: not only did the martyrs disparage the Prophet in Arabic—the sacred language of Islam—but they also did so in a mosque. This took chutzpah of the highest order. Eulogius does not explain what motivated Rogelius and Servusdei. Given that they do not seem to have come from mixed families or necessarily worked alongside Muslims like other martyrs, perhaps their encounter with Islam was typical of the middle band of the church in the ninth century. Islam may not have been an intimate, personal reality in their households, but it was nonetheless ubiquitous in their city and therefore threatening. Like Eulogius and Alvarus, such individuals may have felt the hot breath of cultural change on their necks and lashed out in response.

V. CONCLUSION: DID AL-ANDALUS HAVE A "BLASPHEMY PROBLEM"?

When we consider what occurred in Córdoba in the mid-ninth century, what is most striking about the events is their suddenness: Eulogius and Paulus Alvarus portray the episode as a volcanic outburst, an unheralded explosion that occurred as quickly as it eventually subsided. Sadly, there are few corroborating texts that provide clues about the "actual" state of interreligious relations at the time. Was this wave of blasphemy really as unprecedented as the sources make it seem? Mostly when scholars explain what happened in Córdoba, they frame the martyrs' blasphemy as a response to Islamization and Arabization, which seem to have been intensifying in this period.[134] That is to say, the martyrs (and their biographers) were reacting to the perceived erosion of Christian faith and local Iberian culture and registered their displeasure through vicious outbursts in public. This theory is broadly persuasive, but it ultimately falls back on arguments made by Eulogius and Alvarus themselves, who, as we have seen, portrayed the situation to suit their specific apologetic goals. Can we step outside their hagiographic and polemical worlds to understand the martyrs' movement from another direction? What did their blasphemy mean, and why did blasphemy seem to take on greater significance in al-Andalus than in other areas under Muslim rule?

One of the most striking features of Andalusī society in this period was its extraordinary mix of peoples. As Maribel Fierro and Dolores Oliver Pérez have

[134]Notably, Colbert, *Martyrs of Córdoba*; Coope, *Martyrs of Córdoba*; Wolf, *Christian Martyrs*. On the intensification of conversion in al-Andalus in the mid-ninth century, see Bulliet, *Conversion to Islam*, 114–27; Barceló, "Estructura fiscal y procedimientos contables," 51; Kennedy, *Muslim Spain and Portugal*, 67. On the decline of Christians in al-Andalus more generally, see Epalza, "Mozarabs"; Aillet, *Mozarabes*, 45–93.

shown, Muslim scholars developed an extensive and precise vocabulary for classifying different groups and their relations with one another.[135] The specificity of these labels, however, belied a world in which racial, tribal, and religious affiliations were in fact overlapping and ambiguous. The Muslims of al-Andalus came in many shapes and colors: They were "Arabs," "Berbers," and local-born; they were old believers, *mawālī*, and new Muslims, sometimes called *musālima*. On top of this, there were the obvious cleavages between Muslims and non-Muslims. Yet, in an indication of just how slippery the vocabulary could be, one common term for indigenous Iberian converts to Islam—*muwalladūn*—was from time to time applied to Christians too, as in the case of local Hispano-Goths who came into contact with Arabic culture without necessarily converting.[136]

The specific meanings of these terms need not trouble us here. The significant takeaway is that they reveal an untidy mélange of peoples whom literate elites tried to order and understand as discrete groups—in what Fierro has called the "ethnic stratification" of Andalusī society.[137] More than in other areas, the management of ethnic and religious diversity seems to have been a particular concern in al-Andalus.[138] This is not because there was necessarily more diversity there than in Syria or Iraq, two regions of the eastern caliphate that in fact possessed a greater mix of languages and religions. It is because relations among different types of Muslims as well as between Muslims and non-Muslims seem to have been charged with a unique uncertainty in al-Andalus that one does not find to the same degree elsewhere. Although written from a Christian perspective, the Córdoba martyr texts are preoccupied with this same mixture and tension. Eulogius and Paulus Alvarus were interested in ordering and classifying society, too; like their Muslim counterparts, they strove to delineate the fuzzy frontiers between groups, not only as religious systems but as cultural orientations as well.

One reason that relations between communities may have been especially difficult in al-Andalus is that early Muslim settlement there occurred without the mediating institution of garrison cities, or *amṣār*.[139] These settlements,

135 Fierro, "Árabes, berbéres, muladíes"; Fierro, "*Mawālī* and *Muwalladūn* in al-Andalus"; Oliver Pérez, "Árabe, muladí y *mawla*."

136 Fierro, "*Mawālī* and *Muwalladūn* in al-Andalus," 228–31; see also Fierro, "Ibn Ḥafṣūn"; Fernández Féliz and Fierro, "Cristianos y conversos," 424–27. Arabized Christians are sometimes known as "Mozarabs" in the scholarly literature (from Ar. *mustaʿrab*), but this term is late, per Urvoy, "Vocable ‹mozarabe›."

137 Fierro, "*Mawālī* and *Muwalladūn* in al-Andalus," 227.

138 On the institution of *walāʾ* and how it differed between al-Andalus and other regions, see Crone, "Mawlā," *EI*², vi, 881.

139 Kennedy, "From Antiquity to Islam in the Cities of al-Andalus," 64; Manzano Moreno, "Iberian Peninsula and North Africa," 592.

which sprang up across places such as Iran, Iraq, Egypt, and North Africa, had the practical effect of sequestering Muslims from the surrounding non-Muslim populations, thereby limiting intimate contact between groups. By contrast, the Arabs and Berbers who conquered the Iberian Peninsula settled throughout the new territory in close, sometimes uncomfortable proximity to existing communities of Christians and Jews. This must have led to more constant interaction between conquerors and conquered than in other parts of the early Muslim empire, stoking tensions in the process. The encounter between Muslim and non-Muslim in al-Andalus may have been especially challenging considering the cultural chasm that divided the native Hispano-Gothic population from their new Arab and Berber overlords. Syria is another region that had few major garrison cities, but unlike in al-Andalus, many Christians there were already Arabic speakers, and therefore, they may have learned to live with their new rulers more easily than their Iberian counterparts a century later.

As for the apparent suddenness of the martyrs' movement, one way to explain this is by considering the changing demography of religious elites in al-Andalus in the early medieval period. Maribel Fierro and Manuela Marín have suggested that the late ninth century witnessed a decisive shift in the Islamic culture of the Iberian Peninsula; they have argued that for much of the previous hundred years, there were essentially no *ʿulamāʾ* in al-Andalus.[140] This is not to say that there were no Muslim scholars—indeed, the sources attest the existence of a *ṣāḥib al-ṣalāt* and a *qāḍī ʾl-ʿaskar* who were responsible for various religious functions in the first hundred years after the conquest and who were often recruited from the ranks of the army. Yet, for much of this period, there was not a permanent class of what we would recognize as Sunnī religious scholars, tasked with things such as promulgating Islamic law, transmitting *ḥadīth*, studying theology, or training others like them. The situation changed dramatically from the mid-800s onward. At this time, larger and larger numbers of *ʿulamāʾ* begin to appear in Muslim biographical dictionaries. What is more, Andalusī scholars started materializing in far-flung corners of the greater Middle East in pursuit of religious education, a phenomenon known in Arabic as *riḥla fī ṭalab al-ʿilm*, or "journeying in search of knowledge." Congregational mosques also started to appear in Iberian cities, while the Mālikī *madhhab* began to establish itself as the official school of law across al-Andalus.

If Fierro and Marín are correct that the second half of the ninth century witnessed an increase in the number of Sunnī *ʿulamāʾ*, then we might ask what

[140] Fierro and Marín, "Islamización de las ciudades"; Fierro, "Islamisation of al-Andalus"; see also Fierro, "Proto-Malikis, Malikis, and Reformed Malikis," 61–70. I am grateful to Maribel Fierro for discussing her ideas about this topic with me and for sharing unpublished work.

effect this had on the Muslim population as a whole, not to mention the non-Muslims they lived alongside. For one, the growing number of religious scholars in al-Andalus seems to have led to a new concern for doing things in accordance with the authoritative texts of the Islamic tradition, especially jurisprudence emanating from eastern cities. Thus early jurists such as ʿAbd al-Malik b. Ḥabīb (d. 238/853) began introducing new texts in al-Andalus that advocated for distinctively Muslim conduct on a range of "secular" issues, including the treatment of women and moneylending.[141] Another leading scholar was the Córdoban jurist al-ʿUtbī (d. ca. 255/869), whose large collection of legal *responsa*—studied ably by Ana Fernández Félix—allows us to peer into the daily concerns of Andalusī Muslims at this time of increasing Islamization.[142] It also may have manifested itself in heightened concerns about orthodoxy, heresy, apostasy, and blasphemy. These concerns were especially pronounced in the Mālikī *madhhab*, which across the medieval Islamic world presented itself as the defender of the traditions of Islam's first capital, Medina, which was home to the *madhhab*'s eponymous founder, Mālik b. Anas (d. 179/796). We can see this clearly in the manner in which the Mālikī clerical establishment boasted of having purged al-Andalus of all religious competitors, including scholars from other Sunnī *maddhab*s, along with Khārijīs, Shīʿīs, and Muʿtazilīs.[143]

In such a world, it is not hard to see how a new and assertive class of Muslim clergy may have started to scrutinize what they saw as inappropriate forms of contact between Muslims and Christians. Indeed, the Córdoba martyr texts give the impression of an older modus vivendi suddenly collapsing under the weight of changed circumstances and expectations in the mid-ninth century—of a society in which long-standing practices such as intermarriage, crypto-Christianity, and intercommunal fraternization were abruptly no longer permissible. If this is the case, the rise of an Islamic scholarly class in al-Andalus may explain how Muslims arrived at an ever more pronounced sense of their social and theological differences with Christians. The more hostile mood, in turn, may have antagonized Christians, turning them into what Manuel Cecilio Díaz y Díaz has called a "combative minority," for whom blasphemy emerged as a potent tool for registering their unhappiness.[144] Of course, there were plenty of ways to register one's unhappiness short of committing suicide,

[141] ʿAbd al-Malik b. Ḥabīb, *Adab al-nisāʾ*; ʿAbd al-Malik b. Ḥabīb, *Kitāb al-ribā*. I thank Maribel Fierro for drawing my attention to these texts.

[142] Fernández Féliz, *ʿUtbiyya y el proceso de formación de la sociedad islámica.*

[143] Fierro, "Heresy in al-Andalus," 895–98; Fierro, "Proto-Malikis, Malikis, and Reformed Malikis," esp. 58–59; see also Waltz, "Significance of the Voluntary Martyrs," 152–53; Wolf, *Christian Martyrs*, 16; Fierro, "Andalusian ‹Fatāwā›," 103–4; more generally, see Fierro, *Heterodoxia.*

[144] Díaz y Díaz, "Minoría combativa."

which is what the martyrs effectively did when they insulted the Prophet. But the perception of living in desperate times called for desperate measures, which the blasphemers embraced.

If Muslims were becoming more sensitive to these differences from the mid-ninth century onward, the same may have been true of Christians. Reading the Córdoba martyr texts alongside the *Life of Peter of Capitolias*, one is struck by the relative sophistication of anti-Muslim polemic on the Iberian Peninsula during the 850s versus its relative unsophistication in Transjordan during the early 700s. Indeed, scholars such as Franz Richard Franke, Dominique Millet-Gérard, Janna Wasilewski, Fernando González Muñoz, and Samir Khalil Samir have all shown the connections between the anti-Muslim attacks of Eulogius and Paulus Alvarus and those of Christian writers from the east, including important figures such as John of Damascus and ʿAbd al-Masīḥ al-Kindī.[145] In the 120 years between Peter's martyrdom and those of the blasphemers of Córdoba, the Christian critique of Islam became more pointed. Of course, this was a critique nurtured at the top of Christian society among theologians such as Theodore Abū Qurra, who debated Muslim scholars in salons filled with other elite clergy. But in essence their arguments on matters of history, scripture, and theology were now trickling down to the masses, who probably encountered them in sermons, street-corner catechesis, and popular literature.[146]

We can see this most clearly in Eulogius's account of the martyrdom of Perfectus, who was killed after mentioning the Prophet's "adulterous union" with Zaynab, the former wife of his adopted son, Zayd. It is unlikely that Perfectus knew the relevant Qurʾanic verses about this incident, but he almost certainly knew about it via polemical accounts of Muḥammad's life that were then circulating among Christians in al-Andalus, including the famous *Vita Mahumeti*.[147] Even if this polemical biography was often inaccurate about the details of the Prophet's biography, its effectiveness as ammunition for blasphemers lay in its knowledge and lampooning of basic facts and doctrines. Put simply, a more cogent critique of Islam at the top of Christian society in the years between Peter of Capitolias and the martyrs of Córdoba may have provided greater impetus for blasphemers down below.

[145] Franke, "Freiwilligen Märtyrer," 37–67; Millet-Gérard, *Chrétiens mozarabes*, 153–81; Wasilewski, "Life of Muhammad"; González Muñoz, "Conocimiento del Corán"; Samir, "Version latine de l'Apologie d'al-Kindī."

[146] On the dissemination of religious knowledge among the Muslim lower classes during the medieval period, see Berkey, *Popular Preaching*; Jones, *Power of Oratory*. We can imagine that something similar may have happened among Christians in al-Andalus and elsewhere.

[147] *CMR*, i, 721–22. See also Wolf, "Earliest Latin Lives of Muḥammad"; Hoyland, *Seeing Islam*, 512–15; Christys, *Christians in al-Andalus*, 62–68; Tieszen, *Christian Identity amid Islam*, 67–72.

Ultimately, whether it was assimilation, conversion, the *ʿulamāʾ*, or increasing theological literacy that sparked the new tensions, it is clear that the martyrs' movement was the fruit of a sudden and disorienting shift in the social and religious life of al-Andalus. The absence of a similar episode in Egypt, Syria, or Iraq suggests that these shifts may have been more gradual in the Muslim East than they were in the Muslim West. The only comparable cluster of martyrdoms in the east is that of the Melkite saints of greater Palestine, which occurred during the first fifty years of ʿAbbasid rule. Unlike with the Córdoba martyrs, however, it is difficult to connect these deaths to any one edict, ruler, or event, much less to each other. What is more, these martyrs were killed mostly for apostasy, not blasphemy. Still, if blasphemy did amount to a form of "cultural apostasy" among assimilated but unconverted Christians, as this chapter has argued, the absence of blasphemy trials in the east may suggest that there were fewer Christians there who felt under threat of losing their identity in the same way. Many Christians in the east shared the Arab culture of the conquerors and, therefore, may not have felt quite so alienated from Muslims as their counterparts in al-Andalus. There, the rise of Islam brought Latin-speaking Christians of Hispano-Gothic stock into close, sometimes unsettling contact with Arabs and Berbers. As Christians searched for a way to express their alienation from this culture, which was descending on them with sudden force in the mid-ninth century, they turned to blasphemy to protest and to draw a clear line around the church in an increasingly mixed-up world.

4

Trying and Killing Christian Martyrs

The previous chapters have examined behaviors that precipitated violence against Christians in the early Islamic period. In this chapter, I will turn to the nature of the violence itself: How did Muslim officials execute Christian martyrs, what were the social functions of capital punishment, and did the violence amount to a broad-based persecution of Christians by the Muslim state? Bloodshed is an unavoidable feature of Christian hagiography in the late antique and early medieval periods, and the *lives* of the neomartyrs are no exception. One saint was reportedly beaten so fiercely that his skin rotted away and filled with worms. Others were dismembered and blinded.[1] Still others were crucified and burned.

As always, we should be cautious about elements in the sources that smack of literary convention. Yet we should not be so quick to dismiss these details as simply motifs. As we shall see in the coming pages, there is good reason to believe that some accounts of trial, torture, and execution in Christian sources reflect a broader legal and social reality beyond the texts.[2] What is more, even if the *lives* of the martyrs stray into the realm of fiction, they tell us a great deal about how audiences in the medieval Middle East reacted to rituals of public punishment, something about which we know precious little.[3] As stylized records of actual events, therefore, the Christian hagiography of the early Islamic period provides a rich portrait of how the judicial system may have operated and was experienced by contemporaries.[4]

The central question of this chapter is why Umayyad and ʿAbbasid officials executed Christian martyrs. Their use of torture and capital punishment may strike the modern reader as cruel and unusual.[5] Yet we must not let contem-

[1] On rotten flesh and worms, see *SPSH*, i, 51; on amputation, blinding, and crucifixion, see chapter 5, sec. II; and on burning, see chapter 5, sec. III.

[2] Anthony, *Crucifixion and Death*, 55–56, affirming the parallels between the hagiography and early *fiqh* literature.

[3] Lange, "Ignominious Parading," 100; on the symbolic and ritual aspects of violence in early Islam, Lange, "Capital Punishment," *EI*^{3} (2011), ii, 104–10; Lange, *Justice, Punishment*; Lange and Fierro, "Public Violence in Islamic Societies"; Marsham, "Public Execution"; Marsham, "Fire in Executions"; Anthony, *Crucifixion and Death.*

[4] On the judicial system more broadly, see Tyan, *Organisation judiciaire*; Tillier, *Cadis d'Iraq.*

[5] On changes to the penal system of Western countries in the eighteenth and nineteenth cen-

porary assumptions about justice cloud our impression of how it was meted out in the past, for, in the astute words of Tamer El-Leithy, "horror disallows analysis."[6] In this world, the intensity of violence did not necessarily mean that it was arbitrary or indiscriminate. To the contrary, the violence of the Umayyad and ʿAbbasid states against Christian renegades was more often than not bureaucratic, contained, and aimed at two specific goals.

The first of these was to assert the primacy of Islam and the Islamic character of the ruling regime at a moment when Muslims were vastly outnumbered by their non-Muslim subjects. In theory, the postconquest society was meant to be structured around tidy hierarchies between rulers and ruled, which were based, in turn, on the dictates of the Qurʾan and emergent Islamic law. Yet it could be very hard to police or guarantee these hierarchies in practice, since Christians and other non-Muslims were numerically dominant in many parts of the empire. What is more, some of these non-Muslims were the aggrieved heirs of imperial and royal traditions that had been swept away by the conquests. Thus, the prospect of insubordination was never far off, and public displays of violence were designed to forestall the possibility of unrest ever boiling over. Christian dissidents were almost never militarized like the Shīʿī and Khārijī rebels who roiled the caliphate during the seventh and eighth centuries. Yet they posed a similar threat to an order that was premised on their subordination. In exploring these issues, this chapter will conclude by comparing the situation in the early medieval Middle East with what existed in high medieval Europe, especially through R. I. Moore's famous concept of "the persecuting society."

The second goal of the early Islamic state was to forge boundaries between groups at a time of exceptional mixing. As we have seen throughout this book, the martyrs were among the most public manifestations of a large but relatively invisible group of people who moved between Islam and Christianity. Social mobility and religious change were facts of life in the postconquest period, and seen from the perspective of the state, they were harmless provided they benefited the Muslim *umma*. They were damaging, however, when they led to attrition in the form of apostasy, as well as to protest in the form of blasphemy. In this world of porous borders, violence imposed clearer religious and social identities on those who wielded it and on those who experienced it. To quote Mary Douglas in her famous study of purity and pollution, "Ideas about separating, purifying, demarcating and punishing

turies, especially the abandonment of violence as a public spectacle and the emergence of a punitive culture geared toward rehabilitation and reform, see Foucault, *Discipline and Punish*, esp. 32–69.

[6]El-Leithy, "Sufis, Copts and the Politics of Piety," 77.

transgressions have as their main function to impose system on an inherently untidy experience."[7]

The *lives* of the martyrs describe discrete examples of violence against individuals, but did these amount to a broad-based persecution of Christians as a group? *Persecution*, of course, is a loaded term whose meaning depends on the perspective of the one who uses it. It also depends on scale, and it is impossible to know whether the neomartyrs discussed in this book are suggestive of a more general persecution of Christians across all of society. Indeed, if recent revisionist scholarship on martyrdom in the Roman period has anything to teach us, it is to be very cautious about imagining large-scale phenomena on the basis of small numbers of surviving texts.[8] In this chapter, I argue that there was no generalized persecution of Christians in early Islamic society. By that I mean there were no systematic efforts to extirpate Christians across the caliphate and, in fact, the state usually took a laissez-faire attitude toward governing *dhimmīs*. It allowed most non-Muslims to live as they wished provided they paid their taxes and accepted their subordination under the law. Conflict obviously occurred, but it took place against a backdrop of usually peaceful relations between communities. The fact that Muslim and Christian authors remarked on martyrdom at all tells us that it was something extraordinary, not something normal.

To be clear, the absence of generalized persecution—an argument that should come as no surprise to specialists of Islamic history—does not mean that there were no episodes of religious violence. The neomartyrs highlight an intolerant streak in the political and religious culture of the caliphate that affected many groups, Muslim and non-Muslim alike. That is, Muslim political leaders were sometimes keen to promote right belief and erase unbelief through bloodshed, coercion, and torture. In this, they behaved not so differently than the rulers of other late antique and medieval societies, who occasionally used the powers of the state to crush religious dissent.[9] This includes Christian states that marginalized pagans, Jews, and other outsiders. If anything, some medieval Islamic societies probably conducted themselves better than many contemporary Christian societies in Europe.[10]

The following chapter is divided into three sections, each of which describes a different stage of the martyr's journey through the judicial system. The first

[7] Douglas, *Purity and Danger*, 5.; cf. Sizgorich, *Violence and Belief*, 21–45, 231–71.

[8] See esp. Moss, *Myth of Persecution*.

[9] For intercommunal violence outside an Islamic context, see Gaddis, *There Is No Crime*; Drake, "Explaining Early Christian Intolerance"; Sizgorich, *Violence and Belief*; Frend, *Rise of the Monophysite Movement*; Moore, *Persecuting Society*; Stow, *Alienated Minority*; Nirenberg, *Communities of Violence*; Elukin, *Living Together, Living Apart*.

[10] Cohen, *Under Crescent and Cross*.

explores how martyrs came into the custody of the state and, once incarcerated, how they were tried and sentenced. The second examines the implementation of Qur'anic punishments—especially the "*Ḥirāba* Verse" (Q. *al-Mā'ida* 5:33)—against martyrs, showing that specifically Islamic forms of punishment were being used against apostates and blasphemers at a very early date. The third section highlights one of the most common forms of punishment against neomartyrs: punitive burning. Despite its frequent appearance in Christian sources, evidence from Muslim texts suggests that burning was very uncommon and, what is more, deeply controversial among the jurists of the day. This section compares the immolation of Christians with evidence from Muslim legal sources as well as historical examples of Shīʿīs and Khārijīs who were likewise burned. It also explores how Christian and Muslim authors employed shared literary tropes to portray the phenomenon of martyrdom. On the basis of this, the conclusion reconsiders why the state executed Christian martyrs so ferociously, including the threat of rebellion, heresy, and unbelief alongside concerns about social mixing.

I. PROSECUTING MARTYRS

One way we can gauge the absence of systematic persecution is by examining the manner in which the Umayyads and ʿAbbasids policed apostasy and blasphemy. Here, Christian sources often portray state officials as being downright passive in their pursuit of criminals. One searches in vain throughout the martyrologies for mention of police figures such as the *ṣāḥib al-sūq* or the *muḥtasib*, who were normally responsible for keeping tabs on *dhimmīs*, at least in later periods.[11] The sources occasionally refer to armed guards who arrested martyrs and conveyed them to prison, though their identity is usually left unclear.[12] Whoever they were, they are represented entering the scene only after having being tipped off by someone else outside the state apparatus.

One recurring theme in the martyrologies is that Christians were frequently betrayed by their relatives, friends, and neighbors. Indeed, if we trust the sources to provide a plausible snapshot of real experiences, it is striking how the state was so heavily dependent on private informants. There are several possible explanations for this. The most obvious is that "private individuals" (often animated by personal grievances) were in a better position to know

[11] Ibn Bassām, *Nihāyat al-rutba*, 207–8; Tyan, *Organisation judiciaire*, 617–50, esp. 642–43; Cahen and Talbi, "Ḥisba," *EI²*, iii, esp. 487; Lev, "Suppression of Crime."

[12] For example, guards (Ar. *aʿwān*) were dispatched to apprehend George-Muzāḥim: MS Cairo, Coptic Museum—Hist. 469, 79v, 81v, 85r.

about "private crimes." And provided it was concealed properly, apostasy was the ultimate private offense. While a conversion entailed interior change from one creed to another, this transformation usually manifested itself in certain changes visible to the naked eye, such as habits of prayer or styles of dress. At the same time, conversion did not necessarily manifest itself through a shift in routine. In fact, conversion could be kept very private, as in the case of the crypto-Christians of Córdoba, who practiced Christianity in secret while being perceived as Muslims in public. If a conversion did occur discreetly in this way, the people in the best position to report on it were those most intimately connected to the offenders, including family and friends.

The state's recourse to private informants also suggests that it was not always vigilant about enforcing the law. There are details in several martyrologies that seem to confirm this. The *Life of Elias of Helioupolis*, for example, states that the caliph al-Mahdī (r. 158–69/775–85) issued an order commanding the execution of Christians who had converted to Islam and then returned to Christianity and refused to repent. That al-Mahdī felt compelled to issue an edict affirming what was the opinion of most Muslim jurists at the time suggests that the official prohibition was not always enforced.[13] This confirms an impression left by the writings of the earlier Syriac churchman Jacob of Edessa (d. 708), who despite discussing conversion to Islam and conversion away from Islam never once suggested that apostates were in danger of being killed.[14] Along similar lines, the Umayyad *amīr* of Córdoba ʿAbd al-Raḥmān b. al-Ḥakam (r. 206–38/822–52) reportedly issued a decree in 851 threatening to execute anyone who committed blasphemy.[15] Once again, the promulgation of such an edict strongly hints either that the prohibition was new or that it existed on the books but was not usually enforced. Given that blasphemy laws were relatively slow to crystallize in this period, the former seems much more likely.

The tendency of intimates to betray their own is one of the most striking motifs in the hagiography of the early Islamic period.[16] Bacchus, for example, was reportedly imprisoned after his Muslim in-laws, furious about his conversion, hired a bounty hunter to track him down.[17] Flora of Seville, a martyr of

[13] *SPSH*, i, 52. Al-Mahdī also issued an edict ordering the dismissal of non-Muslims from state offices; see Yarbrough, "Islamizing the Islamic State," 283–84, 319. On anti-Christian edicts mentioned in Christian sources but not in Muslim sources, see Hoyland, *Seeing Islam*, 596; Sahner, "First Iconoclasm in Islam," 33–34.

[14] Penn, *Envisioning Islam*, 172.

[15] *CSM*, ii, 368.

[16] For comparison with Syriac material from the Sasanian period, see Payne, *State of Mixture*, 194.

[17] *CMLT*, 97–99.

mixed ancestry who was executed for apostasy in 851, was handed over to the authorities by her own Muslim brother.[18] The relatives of Anthony al-Qurashī, meanwhile, are said to have "quarreled and debated with [the martyr] for hours during the day." When he refused to reconsider his conversion, they dragged him to the *qāḍī* of Damascus for sentencing.[19]

According to Christian hagiographers, Muslim neighbors could be as ruthless as Muslim relatives. John of Córdoba, for instance, was beaten for blasphemy by his fellow merchants.[20] ʿAbd al-Masīḥ is said to have been outed by a former Muslim friend who recognized him during a chance encounter in a village called Ghaḍyān in southern Palestine. "This monk was with me raiding for years," his betrayer said: "He used to pray with us [Ar. *yuṣallī bi-nā*]. He is a man from among the Arabs and he used to be my friend."[21] The most detailed case of neighborly betrayal is that of Elias, whose Muslim boss initially promised to protect him from charges that he had apostatized. When Elias's family approached this man seeking unpaid wages, however, the Muslim threatened to expose him once and for all. The storm only subsided when Elias returned to his native city of Baalbek, but years later, he encountered the Muslim again and raised the matter of the unpaid wages. Furious, his former boss notified his own master, and together they reported Elias's apostasy to a judge.[22]

What led intimates to betray their own in this way? For one, as we saw in previous chapters, many apostasy and blasphemy cases came to the attention of the Muslim authorities due to a combination of an actual religious offense plus a superimposed social or economic grievance. This dynamic is most obvious in the stories of Elias and John of Córdoba, who were handed over to the authorities after first crossing swords with Muslim rivals (coworkers in both instances) who used their apostasy and blasphemy as pretenses for exacting revenge for other reasons. Beyond this, harboring an apostate in a family group or neighborhood probably carried high social costs. Apostasy may have been especially worrisome in the eyes of recent converts to Islam or Muslims of mixed ancestry who wished to show their commitment to their faith to the local authorities by proactively exposing religious deviancy around them. Their commitment may have been so intense that they were even willing to betray members of their own families and communities.

18 *CSM*, ii, 409–12.

19 Dick, "Passion arabe," 124; Braida and Pelissetti, *Rawḥ al-Qurašī*, 106.

20 *CSM*, i, 277–78.

21 Griffith, "ʿAbd al-Masīḥ," 367 (Griffith renders this as "He used to lead us in prayer," which seems to overinterpret the phrase). Yāqūt (*Muʿjam al-buldān*, iv, 206–7); Zayyāt, "Shuhadāʾ al-naṣrānīya," 464, which refers to the site as "Aṣyān."

22 *SPSH*, i, 46–48.

Islamic criminal law makes no provision for the punishment of families that harbor apostates. At the same time, it promises to punish anyone suspected of helping another person who has converted away from Islam.[23] Therefore, by preemptively exposing a relative or friend, Muslims might stave off suspicions that they had been involved in the crime themselves, even responsible for it. It is clear from the martyrologies that many Muslims looked to the state as the only legitimate authority for punishing religious offenses. Indeed, while family members and friends are shown handing over criminals to the authorities, they are almost never shown punishing criminals themselves. Indeed, mob violence is almost never attested in the *lives* of the martyrs, and even beatings prior to incarceration are rare. If these details capture an element of social reality, they testify to the close synergy between "citizen informants" and state officials. Both seem to have understood the limits of their resources and jurisdictions. As a result, they cooperated together to identify, punish, and discourage apostasy and blasphemy.

After they were captured, Christian martyrs were usually placed in jail and then presented for interrogation before high-ranking Muslim officials.[24] The martyrologies give the impression that the very highest echelons of the state oversaw the sentencing, which, if true, tells us the importance the state ascribed to crimes such as apostasy and blasphemy. Anthony al-Qurashī, for instance, was reportedly interrogated by the *qāḍī* of Damascus, who then referred his case to the governor (Ar. *wālī*) of Raqqa, a man named Harthama, who then referred it to the ʿAbbasid caliph Hārūn al-Rashīd.[25] Elias of Heliopolis encountered several officials in the course of his sentencing, beginning with an eparch named "Leithi,"[26] who referred his case to "a tetrarch and gov-

[23] Tritton, *Non-Muslim Subjects*, 6–7; Fattal, *Statut légal*, 61, 79; Cohen, "Pact of ʿUmar," 107; Noth, "Problems of Differentiation," 105; Jiménez Pedrajas, *Historia de los mozárabes*, 113–18, 224.

[24] Anthony al-Qurashī was held in an underground prison (Ar. *al-muṭbaq*; cf. Tillier, "Prisons et autorités urbaines," 403–6) that contained "brigands" (*quṭṭāʿ al-ṭarīq*, echoing the language of Islamic penal law, see below, n. 31). Later, he was transferred to a section reserved for "Qurashīs and Arabs"; see Dick, "Passion arabe," 124–25; Braida and Pelissetti, *Rawḥ al-Qurašī*, 107–8. Prisons for specific kinds of political and religious criminals are attested elsewhere, as in the prison for *zanādiqa* in Baghdad: Tillier, "Prisons et autorités urbaines," 401; Tillier, "Prisonniers dans la société musulmane," 196. For a Sasanian comparison, see Jullien, "Peines supplices," 250. Prisoners also depended on the charity of outsiders to survive (Tillier, "Vivre en prison"), a motif found in several martyrologies; e.g., *CMLT*, 105–6; MS Cairo, Coptic Museum—Hist. 469, 83r.

[25] Dick, "Passion arabe," 124–26; Braida and Pelissetti, *Rawḥ al-Qurašī*, 106–7, 109–10. For more on the identity of this judge, see chapter 2, n. 33.

[26] *SPSH*, i, 48–49. The identity of this figure is not clear. None of the *qāḍī*s of Damascus during the reign of al-Mahdī bear a name resembling "Leithi" (e.g., Layth, Laythī): Conrad, *Quḍāt Dimašq*, 614. One possibility suggested by McGrath ("Elias of Heliopolis," 88) is that he was the famed Egyptian jurist Layth b. Saʿd al-Fahmī (d. 175/791), who is known to have visited Damascus at this time but not to have worked as a *qāḍī*. He is reported to have traveled to Syria to visit Saʿīd b. ʿAbd

ernor" (Gk. *tetrarchēn kai . . . hēgoumena*) named "Mouchamad," who was "one of the cousins of Maadi, the king of the Arabs."[27] Peter of Capitolias was reportedly questioned by the governor of the *jund* of al-Urdunn, ʿUmar b. al-Walīd, then by his deputy Zora, and finally by the Umayyad caliph al-Walīd b. ʿAbd al-Malik.[28]

It is tempting to dismiss the presence of high-ranking officials as a literary motif designed to dramatize the martyr's encounter with the state. Indeed, they call to mind scenes of early Christian martyrs heroically standing before Roman governors and magistrates.[29] Yet close comparison between the Christian sources and Islamic law suggests that these were precisely the kinds of officials who would have presided over apostasy and blasphemy trials. Already in the eighth and ninth centuries, legal treatises detail a special category of punishment known as a *ḥadd* (pl. *ḥudūd*), named as such because it was specifically delineated in the Qurʾan and the *sunna*.[30] Since the *ḥudūd* were divinely ordained, the precipitating offenses were considered crimes against God Himself. Thus, it fell to the *imām*, or caliph—the plenipotentiary representative of God on earth—to implement them.[31] In classical Islamic law, the *ḥudūd* included several crimes, including theft (*sariqa*), brigandage (*ḥirāba*, *qaṭʿ al-ṭarīq*), adultery (*zinā*), false accusations of adultery (*qadhf*), the consumption of wine (*shurb al-khamr*), and for most legal schools, apostasy (*ridda*, *irtidād*), along with the subsidiary offense of blasphemy (*sabb*, *shatm*).[32] Given that the power to punish these offenses belonged to the caliph, it was logical that he would devolve his authority to an array of high-ranking deputies, as we see in the martyrologies. These officials, in turn, enjoyed wide leeway to pursue punishment as they deemed appropriate, a principle in Islamic law known as *taʿzīr*. Despite their draconian reputation in modern culture, the *ḥadd* penalties

al-ʿAzīz al-Tanūkhī, another famous jurist; see Ibn Manẓūr, *Mukhtaṣar*, xxi, 246; cf. Merad, "Layth b. Saʿd," *EI²*, v, 711–12; Tillier, "Cadis de Fusṭāṭ," 219; Ibn ʿAsākir, *Tārīkh*, l, 341–80. I thank Mathieu Tillier for his advice on this matter.

27 *SPSH*, i, 51. This was almost certainly Muḥammad b. Ibrāhīm al-Hāshimī; see Ibn ʿAsākir, *Tārīkh*, li, 227–32; McGrath, "Elias of Heliopolis," 88.

28 Shoemaker, *Three Christian Martyrdoms*, 30–35, 38–43; Peeters, "Passion de S. Pierre," 305–6, 310.

29 Shaw, "Judicial Nightmares."

30 Carra de Vaux, Schacht, and Goichon, "Ḥadd," *EI²*, iii, 20–21; Lange, "Capital Punishment," *EI³* (2011), ii, 104–5; Tyan, *Organisation judiciaire*, 567–71; Schacht, *Introduction to Islamic Law*, 175–87; Kraemer, "Apostates, Rebels and Brigands," 35. For the classical formulation, see al-Māwardī, *Aḥkām*, 248–69.

31 Ibn Abī Shayba, *Muṣannaf*, v, 506; Ibn Qudāma, *Mughnī*, xii, 165–66; see also Anthony, *Crucifixion and Death*, 28, 43–44.

32 Ibn Qudāma, *Mughnī*, xii, 112–15; Kraemer, "Apostates, Rebels and Brigands," 35 n. 5; more generally, Abou El Fadl, *Rebellion and Violence*, 47–60; Fierro, "Castigo de los herejes," 312.

do not seem to have been implemented very often in the medieval period. As Maribel Fierro and Intisar Rabb have shown, this is because jurists were urged to commute harsh sentencing in the presence of any legal doubt (*shubha*).[33]

The hagiography bears out the impression that the state was extremely cautious in sentencing Christians for apostasy and blasphemy. They portray a culture of deference in which lower-ranking officials were urged to refer challenging and potentially controversial cases to their superiors. This may mean that executions for apostasy and blasphemy were not normal, and therefore, when they did occur, they had to be handled with great care. Furthermore, they had to be seen as being treated with care, for the handling of these cases had a direct bearing on the public perception of the state—which wished to be seen as faithfully implementing the divine law. The governor responsible for jailing Dioscorus of Alexandria, for example, reportedly contacted the "king of Egypt" (possibly the Fāṭimid caliph) for advice about how to deal with apostasy.[34] Likewise, after Bacchus was turned over to the *amīr* of Jerusalem (possibly Harthama b. Aʿyan, who was also involved in the sentencing of Anthony al-Qurashī[35]), the *amīr* sought advice from a general (Gk. *stratēgos*, possibly the governor), who ordered the *amīr* to convey the prisoner to him.[36] Furthermore, the *qāḍī* of Córdoba who handled the trial of the blasphemer Isaac consulted with the *amīr* ʿAbd al-Raḥmān b. al-Ḥakam before sentencing him.[37] This set a precedent for future blasphemy trials in Córdoba, which were usually supervised by judicial officials, not by the Umayyad *amīrs* or their lieutenants.[38]

The most important symbol of the state's cautiousness was its use of *istitāba*, the practice of inviting apostates to repent and be reinstated as Muslims with full rights under the law.[39] Muslim jurists derived the practice of *istitāba* from a series of incidents occurring in the generations after the Proph-

[33] Fierro, "When Lawful Violence Meets Doubt"; Rabb, *Doubt in Islamic Law*, 69–98.

[34] Basset, "Synaxaire arabe jacobite" (1922), 846.

[35] *CMLT*, 100. The long biography of Bacchus does not mention the *amīr* (Gk. *amēran*) by name, but the Palestinian Georgian calendar identifies him as Harthama; see Garitte, *Calendrier palestino-géorgien*, 59, 197. For Harthama's tenure in Palestine, see al-Ṭabarī, *Annales*, iii, 630, 645; Pellat, "Harthama b. Aʿyan," *EI²*, iii, 231; Crone, *Slaves on Horses*, 177–79; see also chapter 2, n. 35.

[36] *CMLT*, 100–103, 122. This was possibly ʿAlī b. Sulaymān al-ʿAbbāsī, who ruled as governor of Egypt from 169/786 to 171/787; see al-Kindī, *Wulāt*, 131–32 (his successor, Mūsā b. ʿĪsā al-ʿAbbāsī, rebuilt the churches that Sulaymān had destroyed, 132); Kennedy, "Egypt," 79.

[37] *CSM*, ii, 368.

[38] But even among the Córdoba martyrs, there were exceptions; Columba (d. 853) was reportedly taken before "consuls" instead of a judge: *CSM*, ii, 451–52.

[39] ʿAbd al-Razzāq, *Muṣannaf*, x, 164–68; Abū Bakr al-Khallāl, *Aḥkām*, 416–24; Denny, "Tawba," *EI²*, x, 385; Griffel, "Toleration and Exclusion"; Kraemer, "Apostates, Rebels and Brigands," 41 n. 24.

et's death. These included the mass apostasy of Muslim soldiers from the tribe of Bakr b. Wā'il after the conquest of Tustar in southwestern Iran and the apostasy of a Christian convert to Islam known as al-Mustawrid al-ʿIjlī (discussed in appendix 1). Jurists disagreed about procedural details of *istitāba*, including the number of overtures an official was obliged to make (usually three), the length of time a criminal had to decide his or her fate (three days, three months, etc.), and the techniques officials could use to wring a recantation from an offender (starvation, torture, debate, etc.). Despite these disagreements, the general purpose of *istitāba* was clear: given the private, highly subjective quality of many conversions, *istitāba* helped determine whether an apostate had indeed converted compos mentis or whether he or she had done so because of peer pressure, mental illness, or another extenuating circumstance. Thus, *istitāba* guaranteed a high degree of certainty in criminal sentencing. Not only was this a matter of eliminating legal doubt, but it also reflected a pastoral concern deeply ingrained in Islamic criminal law. As Joel Kraemer put it, "Muslim authorities were more keen to recover the allegiance of a renegade than to dispatch his soul to eternal perdition."[40]

The hagiography confirms Kraemer's assertion. In fact, nearly every martyrology portrays Muslim officials as ostentatiously offering Christians a way out of the death penalty. Of course, the martyrs are also portrayed as refusing these offers. The martyrs' refusals may be a hagiographic device designed to make them appear more committed to upholding their faith than to protecting their lives.[41] But the sheer frequency of these overtures and the fact that they correspond in a general way to the principles of Islamic law suggest that we are dealing with stylized representations of actual legal proceedings.[42] The most dramatic examples of *istitāba* are in the *lives* of Peter of Capitolias and Elias of Helioupolis. According to these texts, Peter received overtures of forgiveness from three different officials, while Elias received six overtures from five people.[43] In the case of Elias, the state even dispatched an emissary to try to persuade him to change his mind, a "great old *logothete* who was honored by the entire Arab race for his skill in oratory."[44] It seems that the government kept catechists like this in reserve for emergency situations. Indeed, similar

[40] Kraemer, "Apostates, Rebels and Brigands," 43. See also Wasserstein, "*Fatwā* on Conversion," 179; Cook, "Apostasy from Islam," 278.

[41] On this motif in Syriac hagiography from the Sasanian period, see Payne, *State of Mixture*, 47,

[42] ʿAbd al-Masīḥ and David of Dwin were locked away for three days: Griffith, "ʿAbd al-Masīḥ," 368; Thomson, "David of Dwin," 674. The governor appealed to Bacchus three times: *CMLT*, 110. Al-Mutawakkil informed Constantine-Kakhay, "It is ordained with us to admonish unbelievers three times" (Abashidze and Rapp, "Kostanti-Kaxay," 156).

[43] For Peter, see chapter 3, sec. III; for Elias: *SPSH*, i, 48–51.

[44] *SPSH*, i, 54.

figures appear in the trials of the neomartyrs Vahan, Abo, Nunilo, and Alodia, and we know that the Umayyads dispatched catechists to try to persuade Muslim heretics to repent as well, including al-Ḥārith b. Saʿīd al-Kadhdhāb (d. 80/699).[45]

Thus, the sources suggest that the Umayyads and ʿAbbasids sentenced offenders only as a matter of last resort. We must keep in mind that the records that survive are of individuals who refused the offer of repentance and were killed. One assumes that there were some apostates and blasphemers who accepted forgiveness and went free, but they left behind no literary traces. Seen from the perspective of the hagiography and early Muslim law, the criminal justice system of the Umayyads and ʿAbbasids was hardly persecutory. If anything, it was enamored of procedure and quick to forgive, provided criminals were willing to return to Islam and renounce their outbursts. This, in turn, was done to maintain a semblance of fidelity to Islamic law, especially the requirement to act in a way that was perceived as just and lenient. This at least in part helps explain some of the foot-dragging evident in the sources.

II. QURʾANIC PUNISHMENTS AGAINST THE MARTYRS

If Umayyad and ʿAbbasid officials treated martyrs with caution and clemency before sentencing, they usually treated them with decisiveness and fury afterward. The tortures they employed were grisly and ferocious. They were designed not only to punish criminals but also to shock a public that might be tempted to mimic them. Although the punishments of the Umayyads and ʿAbbasids were unforgiving by modern standards, there was a clear method to them: in many instances, they followed the prescriptions of Islamic criminal law, which in turn were shaped by certain passages in the Qurʾan and *ḥadīth*.

One very detailed guide for capital punishment is the so-called *Ḥirāba* Verse (Q. *al-Māʾida* 5:33), which outlines a suite of penalties for those found guilty of *ḥirāba*, the crime of inciting war against God and His prophet. Khaled Abou El Fadl has argued that the ambiguity of the verse allowed for a wide array of offenses to be lumped together under the umbrella of "brigandage."[46] Among the most important of these were apostasy and blasphemy. The verse is worth quoting in full:

[45] Vahan: Gatteyrias, "Martyre de saint Vahan," 204. Abo: Lang, *Georgian Saints*, 125. Nunilo and Alodia: *CSM*, ii, 407–8. Al-Ḥārith b. Saʿīd: Ibn ʿAsākir, *Tārīkh*, xi, 431, cited in Judd, "Muslim Persecution of Heretics," 4.

[46] Abou El Fadl, *Rebellion and Violence*.

> The recompense of those who wage war against God [*yuḥāribūna ʾllāh*[a]] and His messenger and strive to spread corruption in the land [*wa-yasʿawna fī ʾl-arḍ fasād*[an]] is that they be killed or crucified or have their hands and feet cut off on alternate sides [*tuqaṭṭaʿ aydīhim wa-arjuluhum min khilāf*[in]], or they shall be expelled from the land. That shall be their degradation in this world, and in the hereafter, they shall have a terrible torment.

Medieval Muslim exegetes identified different historical contexts for the revelation of this verse.[47] One leading tradition states that it was revealed when a group of shepherds complained to Muḥammad that the sedentary life in Medina was no longer to their liking.[48] Therefore, the Prophet lent them several camels and his *mawlā* Yasār and bade them farewell into the desert. Instead of following his instructions, however, the shepherds stole the camels, killed Yasār, and apostatized from Islam. The Prophet reacted by exiling, amputating, blinding, crucifying, killing, and, according to some reports, burning them.[49]

During the medieval period, the *Ḥirāba* Verse was considered one locus classicus of Islamic penal law. Despite its prominence in Muslim legal sources, it is not clear from these texts how or even whether the verse was implemented in everyday life. Christian hagiography, however, provides underappreciated evidence that the verse was indeed used to punish religious dissidents and, what is more, that this began at an early date. The impact of the verse is clearest in the *Life of Peter of Capitolias*, in which Umayyad officials are shown applying an array of punishments lifted directly from the Qurʾan.[50] On the first day of his torture, Peter's tongue was removed. On the second day, his right hand and left foot were amputated, and after a day's rest, his left hand and right foot were cut off, seemingly in accordance with the *Ḥirāba* Verse. Finally, he was taken outside the city and crucified. Similar punishments also befell Rogelius and Servusdei, who committed blasphemy in a mosque in Córdoba in September 852.[51] According to Eulogius, their hands and feet were amputated, their heads were chopped off, and their bodies were affixed to racks (Lat.

47 Kraemer, "Apostates, Rebels and Brigands," 60–63; Abou El Fadl, *Rebellion and Violence*, 47–60; see also Anthony, *Crucifixion and Death*, 27–31.

48 Muqātil b. Sulaymān, *Tafsīr*, i, 472–73; al-Ṭabarī, *Jāmiʿ al-bayān*, iii, 206–15; al-Wāqidī, *Kitāb al-Maghāzī*, ii, 569–70; al-Bukhārī, *Ṣaḥīḥ*, 743, no. 3018; for discussion, see Wansbrough, *Quranic Studies*, 185–86; Marsham, "Public Execution," 107–8.

49 al-Ṭabarī, *Jāmiʿ al-bayān*, iii, 207–8.

50 Shoemaker, *Three Christian Martyrdoms*, 44–57; Peeters, "Passion de S. Pierre," 311–15.

51 *CSM*, ii, 433.

patibulis) overlooking the Guadalquivir River. Like Peter's, their outburst was particularly vicious, and perhaps for this reason state officials felt it appropriate to retaliate with equally vicious penalties (likewise, given the argument in the preceding section, perhaps they wished to be seen as adhering ostentatiously to the requirements of Islamic law, in this instance, the grisly particulars of the *Ḥirāba* Verse). Meanwhile, in Armenia, Bughā al-Kabīr is said to have killed a Muslim convert to Christianity named Muka'tl by removing his tongue and amputating his hands and feet.[52]

Among the martyrs, the most commonly implemented component of the *Ḥirāba* Verse was crucifixion.[53] As Andrew Marsham and Sean Anthony have recently shown, the punishment of crucifixion in early Islam drew on late antique precedents.[54] Roman magistrates continued to crucify criminals long after Constantine allegedly outlawed the practice due to Christian sensitivities. The Sasanians also crucified their criminals, though they targeted a fairly narrow range of offenders, including apostates and sorcerers.[55] The Umayyads employed crucifixion against an array of offenders, too—not just Christian martyrs. Indeed, nearly half of the fifty Muslim-on-Muslim executions tallied by Andrew Marsham in a recent article involved crucifixions.[56] The victims included a wide variety of rebels and heretics, including Shīʿīs and Khārijīs.[57] In effect, almost any offense against the Umayyads could be construed as a declaration of war against God Himself and, therefore, deserving of the punishments in the Qur'an. As Montgomery Watt and later Patricia Crone and Martin Hinds pointed out, the caliphs understood themselves as "deputies of God" (Ar. *khulafāʾ allāh*) on earth.[58] Therefore, they could punish acts of resis-

[52] Thomson, *House of Artsrunik'*, 250–51.

[53] For other references to crucifixion in the Qur'an, see Q. *Yūsuf* 12:41 (Pharaoh), *al-Aʿrāf* 7:124, *Ṭā-Hā* 20:71, *al-Shuʿarāʾ* 26:49 (crucifixion and amputation), *al-Nisāʾ* 4:157 (crucifixion of Jesus).

[54] Marsham, "Public Execution," 116–23; Anthony, *Crucifixion and Death*; Vogel, "Ṣalb," *EI*², viii, 935–36; Wensinck and Thomas, "Ṣalīb," *EI*², viii, 980–81; Robinson, "Crucifixion," *EQ*, i, 487–88; Spies, "Kreuzigung im Islam"; Ullmann, *Kreuzigung in der arabischen Poesie*; Fierro, "Violencia, política y religión," 55–63; Seidenstecker, "Responses to Crucifixion." In an interesting twist, a Christian named Tādhurus b. al-Ḥasan, who served as a vizier to Ṣāliḥ b. al-Mirdās (d. 420/1029), the founder of the Mirdāsid dynasty of Aleppo, crucified Muslims who had allegedly killed his Christian associate; see Ibn al-ʿAdīm, *Zubdat al-ḥalab*, 131–33. I thank Luke Yarbrough for this reference.

[55] Anthony, *Crucifixion and Death*, 15–26.

[56] Marsham, "Public Execution," 104, 126–36.

[57] For a list of these crucifixions, see Abū ʾl-ʿArab al-Tamīmī, *Kitāb al-miḥan*, 214–16; and other early Muslim crucifixions in Anthony, *Crucifixion and Death*, 38–39.

[58] Watt, "God's Caliph"; Crone and Hinds, *God's Caliph*, 24–42, 80–96; Abou El Fadl, *Rebellion and Violence*, 48.

tance against them through the provisions of the *Ḥirāba* Verse. Still, when we examine the wide array of crucifixions that occurred during the first centuries of Muslim rule, it is clear that an exceptional number of these were for apostasy. As much is suggested by the later poet Ibn Ḥamdīs al-Ṣiqillī (d. 527/1132), who described a crucified apostate as like a chameleon sunbathing on the branch of a tree, changing from one color to the next as the apostate swaps one religion for another.[59]

In the early Islamic period, crucifixion (Ar. *ṣalb*, *taṣlīb*) encompassed a far wider array of practices than what we typically imagine when we think of the death of Jesus in religious art.[60] Some martyrs were crucified in the "classic fashion," including David of Dwin, who was reportedly nailed to a cross.[61] Others were displayed on gallows, including Emila and Jeremiah of Córdoba, while others were hung on a device called a "fork" (Lat. *furca*), which secured the victim's head at a V-shaped juncture atop a wooden post.[62] Most martyrs were not killed by crucifixion but were crucified or hung on a rack once they were already dead, usually as a result of decapitation (as in the case of the martyr Columba; Figure 4.1). That being said, several were indeed killed as a direct consequence of crucifixion, including Peter of Capitolias.[63]

The early Muslim authorities seem to have favored crucifixion as a tool of political propaganda; by crucifying the bodies of rebels, the state conveyed a clear message about the impermissibility of apostasy, blasphemy, and other serious offenses such as rebellion. Indeed, most crucifixions were designed as public spectacles. Elias of Helioupolis, for example, was reportedly left hanging outside for fourteen days so the Christians of Damascus could inspect his mutilated body.[64] Many of the Córdoba martyrs were crucified on the south bank of the Guadalquivir River just opposite the Umayyad mosque and *qaṣr*, "in full view of the city," as Eulogius put it.[65] This was presumably so Christians could behold the consequences of the martyrs' treachery. Crucifixion was especially intertwined with the imperial ideology of the Umayyad caliphs. It

[59] Ullmann, *Kreuzigung in der arabischen Poesie*, 185, cited in Seidensticker, "Responses to Crucifixion," 205–6.

[60] Anthony, *Crucifixion and Death*, 6–14.

[61] Maksoudian, *History of Armenia*, 107; see also Anthony, *Crucifixion and Death*, 59. The longer version of David's *life* (Thomson, "David of Dwin," 675) simply states that he "spread himself on" the cross.

[62] *CSM*, ii, 432 (Lat. *equuleis*); compare with other crucifixions among the Córdoba martyrs: *CSM*, ii, 433 (*patibulis*, Rogelius and Serviusdei), 445 (*patibulo*, Fandila), 446 (*equuleo*, Anastasius, Felix, Digna), 456 (*patibulo*, Argimirus). For more on the *furca*, see Franchi de'Cavalieri, "*Furca*."

[63] Shoemaker, *Three Christian Martyrdoms*, 56–57; Peeters, "Passion de S. Pierre," 315.

[64] *SPSH*, i, 55.

[65] *CSM*, ii, 368.

Figure 4.1. Columba of Córdoba, choir stalls, Mosque-Cathedral of Córdoba, ca. 1748–57. Photo: Christian C. Sahner.

was so intertwined, in fact, that when the ʿAbbasids routed the last Umayyad ruler, Marwān b. Muḥammad, at the battle of the Zāb River in 132/750, they rushed to Damascus and other Syrian cities to exhume and crucify the remains of long-dead Umayyad family members.[66] There was no better way for a new

[66] Moscati, "Massacre des Umayyades"; Robinson, "Violence of the Abbasid Revolution"; Anthony, *Crucifixion and Death*, 1–2; Marsham, "Fire in Executions," 122.

revolutionary regime to assert itself than by co-opting the most potent weapon of its vanquished foes.

The martyrologies testify to the use of many other punishments not explicitly enumerated in the Qurʾan but which are well attested in Islamic law. Decapitation, for example, was extremely common; in contrast to the long, drawn-out process of torture associated with the *Ḥirāba* Verse, it was also relatively merciful.[67] Ignominious parading (Ar. *tashhīr*), the subject of an excellent article by Christian Lange, is depicted in several sources, including the *passions* of Anthony of Syracuse, John of Córdoba, and the Sixty Martyrs of Gaza.[68] The most detailed account of a *tashhīr* procession comes from the *Life of Peter of Capitolias*, who was "led about throughout the city on a litter, preceded by trumpets and heralds, who were proclaiming: 'This is what will happen to anyone who blasphemes against God and defames His prophet and messenger and derides our religion with insults.' "[69]

According to Muslim sources, these processions were often accompanied by an array of minor indignities, including head-shaving, hooding, and blackening of the face with charcoal (Ar. *taswīd al-wajh*; cf. Q. *Āl ʿImrān* 3:106, *al-Zumar* 39:60). Muslim sources also state that convicted criminals were sometimes pelted with rotten meat, dust, shoes, and even feces. This is borne out by certain Christian texts. Elias of Helioupolis, for instance, was showered with rubbish from the city's markets.[70] George-Muzāḥim was reportedly struck with bricks, pieces of wood, and dirt.[71] The scene of a convicted criminal being paraded around in this way must have left a deep impression on Christian bystanders. We do not know the size of the crowds that gathered to witness executions, though a report from the early twelfth century indicates that one hundred thousand people turned up in Iṣfahān to witness the *tashhīr* procession of a notorious Ismāʿīlī warlord.[72] Even if only a fraction of such a crowd assembled to watch the humiliation of martyrs in Capitolias, Córdoba, or Qayrawān, *tashhīr* processions must have succeeded in publicizing the charges against a criminal and in convincing a martyr's supporters not to follow suit.

[67] For background, see Fierro, "Decapitation of Christians and Muslims"; Zouache, "Têtes en guerre."

[68] Lange, "Ignominious Parading"; also Tyan, *Organisation judiciaire*, 611; Rowson, "Public Humiliation"; Anthony, *Crucifixion and Death*, 57–58. For Sasanian precedents, see Daryaee, *Sasanian Persia*, 64–65; Marsham, "Public Execution," 120. For Anthony of Syracuse, see Delehaye, *Synaxarium*, 72; John of Córdoba: *CSM*, i, 277–78; Sixty Martyrs of Gaza, esp. Florianus (Sophronius of Jerusalem?): Delehaye, "Passio sanctorum sexaginta martyrum," 306.

[69] Shoemaker, *Three Christian Martyrdoms*, 54–55; Peeters, "Passion de S. Pierre," 314.

[70] *SPSH*, i, 51.

[71] MS Cairo, Coptic Museum—Hist. 469, 86r–v.

[72] Lange, "Ignominious Parading," 83 n. 8.

III. THE PENALTY OF FIRE

The brutality of Umayyad and ʿAbbasid officials is nowhere clearer than in the practice of burning martyrs. Unlike crucifixion and amputation, which had strong justifications in the Qurʾan, immolation and cremation (that is, death by burning and the burning of already dead bodies) appear nowhere in Muslim sacred scripture. In fact, many Muslim jurists vigorously objected to their use. Despite this, punitive burning is mentioned frequently in Christian sources of the period. Indeed, it seems to have been implemented as a penalty for religious crimes such as apostasy and blasphemy. Yet it is not only Christian martyrs who were thrown to the flames. As Andrew Marsham has recently shown, immolation and cremation were also favored punishments against Shīʿī and Khārijī rebels in the late Umayyad period.[73] How can we understand the ambivalence of the legal tradition toward burning, on the one hand, and its widespread implementation against two such different groups, on the other?

It should be noted that early Muslims were not the first to burn criminals in the ancient Near East. Immolation is attested in the Hebrew Bible, such as Deuteronomy 13:16, which enjoins the burning of a town of idolaters.[74] The ancient Romans also burned their criminals, most famously under the emperor Nero, who threw Christians to the flames as scapegoats for the Great Fire of AD 64. Tacitus reports that on this occasion, many "were fastened to crosses, and when daylight faded, they were burned to serve as lamps by night."[75] The Romans would often dress bodies with tar to quicken the burning: indeed, the second-century poet Juvenal remarks that this produced a conflagration so intense that it left a furrow in the floor of the arena.[76] Some of our richest evidence about punitive burning comes from the Christians themselves. Writing in the early third century, Tertullian remarked that Christians were known as "faggot fellows" or "half-axle men" because they were fastened to wooden posts and set ablaze.[77] Eusebius of Caesarea described the execution of Christians in Lyons in 177, saying that their bodies were left outside to rot for six days and then burned and swept into the Rhône River, which flowed through the center of town.[78] As we shall see below, the disposal of bodies in rivers was

[73] Marsham, "Fire in Executions."

[74] See also Joshua 7:25; for disapproval of immolation, see Amos 2:1–2. For burning in the ancient Near East, see Westbrook, *Near Eastern Law*, 343, 423, 535, 963, 1028; Marsham, "Fire in Executions," 114–18.

[75] Tacitus, *Tacitus in Five Volumes*, v, 284–85, cited in Kyle, *Spectacles of Death*, 244. For a revisionist interpretation of the Great Fire, see Shaw, "Myth of the Neronian Persecution."

[76] Braund, *Juvenal and Persius*, 144–45, cited in Kyle, *Spectacles of Death*, 183 n. 109.

[77] Tertullian, *Apology*, 222–23, cited in Kyle, *Spectacles of Death*, 170.

[78] Eusebius, *Ecclesiastical History*, i, 436–37, cited in Kyle, *Spectacles of Death*, 250.

an important topos in Christian hagiography not only in late antiquity but also after the rise of Islam. Eusebius explained that the authorities disposed of bodies in this way to "overcome God and deprive the martyrs of their restoration," meaning resurrection on Judgment Day.[79]

Broadly speaking, the Romans were given to desecrating and mutilating the bodies of criminals. This was because, as Brent Shaw has put it, "denying proper burial [represented] the ultimate social penalty in the Roman world" and because it posed a hindrance to the soul's safe passage to the afterlife.[80] This continued under the Byzantines, whose punishments sometimes resembled those of Muslims. The emperor Heraclius, for example, is said to have executed the usurper Phocas (r. 602–10) by cutting off his right arm, removing his head, and then burning his corpse in the Forum Tauri of Constantinople.[81] Burning is attested elsewhere in Byzantine sources, though interestingly, it does not seem to have been applied to apostates and heretics, except in the case of Basil the Bogomil, who was burned in the hippodrome of Constantinople in 1118.[82] This may be because, as the earlier Syriac writer John of Ephesus (d. 588) indicated, total burning was not an appropriate form of punishment against baptized Christians, even if they were heretics.[83] While the Romans and Byzantines were enthusiastic immolators, the same cannot be said of their Sasanian counterparts. In fact, the Sasanians were doctrinally opposed to burning, for fire was considered the purest of substances in the Zoroastrian faith.[84] Therefore, to burn a criminal (much less any human body) was to desecrate the holy flame. If the early Muslims can be said to have adopted their penchant for burning from any of their predecessors, it was most likely from the Romans and the Byzantines, who themselves drew on older precedents.

Burning Bodies in Early Muslim Law

Early Muslim jurists expressed a wide variety of opinions about burning.[85] In fact, conflicting views are often ascribed to the same historical authorities. For

[79] See also Bynum, *Resurrection of the Body*, 58.

[80] Shaw, "Bandits," 5.

[81] Whitby and Whitby, *Chronicon Paschale*, 152. I thank Averil Cameron for this and the following reference.

[82] For Basil, see Anna Comnena, *Alexiad*, 502–4. More generally, see Burgmann, "Penalties," 1622; Patlagean, "Blason pénal du corps."

[83] John of Ephesus, *Third Part of the Ecclesiastical History*, 223–24. I am grateful to Peter Brown for this reference.

[84] Burning is not listed in Jullien's inventory of Sasanian punishments ("Peines supplices"). Yet the Sasanians did desecrate the bodies of Christians and Jews by subjecting them to excarnation; see Herman, "Zoroastrian Exhumation."

[85] For an overview, see Marsham, "Fire in Executions," 117–18; for early *ḥadith*, see ʿAbd

example, there are several reports claiming that the Prophet Muḥammad destroyed the bodies of his opponents with fire.[86] One states that he burned a group of Muslims who failed to attend the communal prayers in Medina.[87] Yet this same tradition ascribes to the Prophet an injunction against burning that states, "Kill anyone who changes his religion, but do not punish him with the punishment of God, meaning fire."[88] The injunction features in a number of other reports, including one in which the Prophet instructed his Companion Abū Hurayra (d. ca. 58/678) to locate and burn two pagans of Quraysh who had hindered the emigration of his daughter Zaynab from Mecca to Medina, thereby causing her to miscarry. Just as the search party was about to leave, however, the Prophet changed his mind, telling them to kill the Qurashīs but not to burn them, for "no one punishes with fire except for God."[89] Abū Bakr (r. 11–13/632–34) is also reported to have burned criminals and rebels, including al-Fujāʾa, a member of the Banū Sulaym who pretended to be a Muslim and even received weapons to fight during the Ridda Wars but who used these to harass the enemies of Islam and steal their money. When his ruse was discovered, he was executed at the Baqīʿ Cemetery in Medina.[90] Abū Bakr also instructed the general Khālid b. al-Walīd (d. 21/642) to burn two apostates. One of the apostates, however, objected to the sentence and reminded Khālid that no one punishes with fire except for God.[91]

ʿAlī b. Abī Ṭālib (r. 35–40/656–60) features in a number of the most common traditions about burning. The identity of his victims varies from one report to the next: Some mention Manichaeans (*zanādiqa*) from the Sawād of southern Iraq; others, idolaters among the Zuṭṭ; still others, Christian apostates such as al-Mustawrid al-ʿIjlī.[92] Ibn Abī Shayba's (d. 235/849) *Muṣannaf*, an important collection of precanonical *ḥadīth*, contains an especially interesting report

al-Razzāq, *Muṣannaf*, v, 212–15. The legal discourse on burning belongs to a still larger discourse about mutilation (Ar. *muthla*); see ʿAbd al-Razzāq, *Muṣannaf*, viii, 436; Lecker, "Burial of Martyrs"; Zouache, "Têtes en guerre," 207–10. On the famous mutilation of Ḥamza b. ʿAbd al-Muṭṭalib after the battle of Uḥud by Muʿāwiya's mother, Hind bt. ʿUtba, see al-Ṭabarī, *Annales*, i, 1415; El Cheikh, *Women, Islam, and Abbasid Identity*, 17–37.

[86] Wensinck, *Concordances*, i, 448–50; see also ʿAbd al-Razzāq, *Muṣannaf*, v, 212–15 (*bāb al-qatl bi-ʾl-nār*).

[87] al-Bukhārī, *Ṣaḥīḥ*, 164, no. 657; al-Tirmidhī, *Jāmiʿ*, i, 257, no. 217; Muslim, *Ṣaḥīḥ*, i, 451–52, nos. 251–52.

[88] ʿAbd al-Razzāq, *Muṣannaf*, x, 168, no. 18706; see also Lange, *Justice, Punishment*, 68–69.

[89] Guillaume, *Life of Muḥammad*, 314–16; al-Bukhārī, *Ṣaḥīḥ*, 729, no. 2954, also 743, no. 3016; Abū Dāwūd, *Sunan* (1998), 412, no. 2673; al-Tirmidhī, *Jāmiʿ*, iii, 230, no. 1571.

[90] al-Ṭabarī, *Annales*, i, 1903–4; discussion in Kraemer, "Apostates, Rebels and Brigands," 45; Marsham, "Public Execution," 126.

[91] Ibn Qudāma, *Mughnī*, xii, 108; see also ʿAbd al-Razzāq, *Muṣannaf*, v, 212, no. 9412; Juynboll, *Canonical Ḥadīth*, 280.

[92] *Zanādiqa*: Zayd b. ʿAlī, *Musnad*, 340, cited in Anthony, *Caliph and the Heretic*, 174. The Zuṭṭ

about ʿAlī and burning: it describes a group of men who took part in the Muslim prayers and collected the *ʿaṭāʾ* and the *rizq*—the salaries and allowances owed to Muslim soldiers.[93] Despite their outward conformity to Islam, they continued to worship idols in secret. When ʿAlī discovered their dissimulation, he had them imprisoned and asked the assembled Muslims for advice on what to do. The crowd urged ʿAlī to kill them, but he explained that he would not execute them immediately but would follow the example of Abraham and burn them alive.[94] As this and other traditions indicate, there was a strong connection in early Muslim belief between the crime of heresy and the penalty of fire.

Along with *ḥadīth* that praise ʿAlī for burning, there are others that criticize him for it, too. The most important of these is narrated on the authority of Ibn ʿAbbās, who reportedly said, "Were I in [ʿAlī's] place, I would not burn them, for the Prophet said, 'Do not punish with the punishment of God'!"[95] As time went on, Ibn ʿAbbās's statement was appended to longer historical reports about ʿAlī's encounters with heretics like the ones mentioned above. At other times, Ibn ʿAbbās's statement was listed as a tradition on its own.[96] Thus, in early Islamic law, ʿAlī and Ibn ʿAbbās emerged as advocates for two competing views of burning: ʿAlī became a staunch defender of burning, while Ibn ʿAbbās was presented as its greatest opponent. Josef van Ess has remarked that many of the burning *ḥadīth* first circulated in Baṣra following the reign of the brutal Umayyad governor Khālid al-Qasrī (d. 126/743–44).[97] As we shall see below, Khālid used burning to punish a number of prominent Shīʿī rebels in the region, including al-Mughīra b. Saʿīd al-ʿIjlī and Bayān b. Samʿān al-Nahdī, who were both executed in 119/737. Van Ess has suggested that the pro-burning traditions served to justify the state's actions against these men, whereas the anti-burning traditions buttressed the complaints of the rebels' sympathizers, who regarded the Umayyads as too heavy-handed.

(a people of Indian origin who were settled around the Persian Gulf): al-Nasāʾī, *Sunan*, vii, 73, no. 4065. On al-Mustawrid al-ʿIjlī, see appendix 1.

[93] Ibn Abī Shayba, *Muṣannaf*, v, 564, no. 29003, also no. 29004.

[94] This is a strange turn of phrase. If may refer to Genesis 22:8–9, in which Abraham intends to immolate Isaac as a sacrifice before being thwarted by God. It could also refer to Qurʾān *al-Anbiyāʾ* 21:51–73, in which Abraham smashes the pagan idols, and the pagans retaliate by trying to burn him, but God cools the flames and saves Abraham. Wherever it comes from, other Muslim rulers seem to have had similar ideas: e.g., Hawting, "Jaʿd b. Dirham"; Fierro, "Emulating Abraham."

[95] ʿAbd al-Razzāq, *Muṣannaf*, v, 213, no. 9413; al-Bukhārī, *Ṣaḥīḥ*, 743, no. 3017; Abū Dāwūd, *Sunan* (1998), 657, no. 4351; al-Nasāʾī, *Sunan*, vii, 72, no. 4060; for discussion, see Kraemer, "Apostates, Rebels and Brigands," 44–45 n. 39; Juynboll, *Canonical Ḥadīth*, 146; Hawting, "Jaʿd b. Dirham," 36; Marsham, "Public Execution," 127; Anthony, *Caliph and the Heretic*, 174 n. 39.

[96] E.g., Wensinck, *Concordances*, iv, 164.

[97] van Ess, *Kitāb an-Nakt des Naẓẓām*, 50–57; see also Anthony, *Caliph and the Heretic*, 176; Tucker, *Mahdis and Millenarians*, 13.

Burning Christian Martyrs

Needless to say, burning was a controversial form of punishment in early Muslim society. What is more, historical sources suggest that it occurred rarely. Andrew Marsham, for example, records only eight instances of public burnings during the Umayyad period, in comparison to twenty-four of crucifixion.[98] There is one group not recorded in Marsham's tally that was punished in this way very frequently, and these were Christian apostates and blasphemers. The earliest example of a martyr being burned is Peter of Capitolias in 715.[99] His biography states that Zora, the subgovernor of the Trichora, ordered "the multitude of the city" to gather. He then commanded his deputies "to light a fire in the oven near the venerable monastery of Sabinian, the nobly victorious martyr, in which the daughters of the now-praised Peter had been placed."[100] The *life* reports that a group of Jews took custody of the body (a motif with deep roots in Christian polemical literature in late antiquity), while several horsemen surrounded the oven, lest local Christians try to steal the body.[101] The authorities then "threw [the corpse] into the furnace, together with the wood, the bloodstained rags, the severed limbs, and all the clothes and shoes," reducing them to a pile of ash. They then placed the incinerated remains in a bag, "sealed [it] with the seal of the rulers in order to take extra care," and scattered these in the Yarmūk River, which lay several kilometers away. Peter's executioners were so determined to eliminate all traces of his demise—presumably given that his relics could become potent symbols for any Christians who tried to collect them—that they even cleansed the oven with water and wiped it down with rags. These they disposed of in a "waterless desert cave."

The martyr ʿAbd al-Masīḥ endured a similar fate when he was executed in Palestine decades later.[102] Following his decapitation, the authorities brought his body to a place called Bāligha, where there was an abandoned well.[103] They tossed the body inside, filled the well with firewood, and set it ablaze. Nine

[98] Marsham, "Public Execution."

[99] Shoemaker, *Three Christian Martyrdoms*, 56–57; Peeters, "Passion de S. Pierre," 315. On the burning of blasphemers in later Mālikī *fiqh*, see Qāḍī ʿIyāḍ, *Shifāʾ*, ii, 572–73.

[100] On Saint Sabinian, martyred under Maximus and Maximinian, see *BS*, x, 309–10; Delehaye, *Synaxarium*, 77; Griveau, "Fêtes des Melchites," 312.

[101] On Jewish efforts to destroy the body of the Virgin Mary in early Christian polemics, see Shoemaker, "Let Us Go and Burn Her Body," 798–812; on Jews as dramatis personae in the *lives* of the new martyrs, see chapter 3, n. 43; on Jews assisting in the burning of Polycarp's body, see Ehrman, *Apostolic Fathers*, i, 384–85.

[102] Griffith, "ʿAbd al-Masīḥ," 368.

[103] Another version of the *life* identifies the village as "Bāligha" (Zayyāt, "Shuhadāʾ al-naṣrānīya," 465), though the tenth-century Muslim geographer al-Muqaddasī refers to the site as

months later, a group of monks from Mt. Sinai returned to Bāligha to claim the body. They lowered one of the monks into the well in a basket, and when he reached the bottom, he found himself wading up to his knees in ash. Much to his surprise, he discovered ʿAbd al-Masīḥ's skull intact, "gleaming like snow."[104] Several years later in Damascus, the body of Elias of Helioupolis was also burned after being decapitated and crucified.[105] The judge ordered his remains and the cross to be incinerated. When the executioners lit the fire, however, the martyr's body refused to burn. They threw even more wood onto the pyre, but like the Jewish youths in the fiery furnace in the book of Daniel, Elias would not combust.[106] In the end, the weary executioners resigned themselves to chopping up his corpse and scattering its pieces in the Baradā River, which ran through central Damascus.

After the execution of the Georgian martyr Abo in 786, his body was reportedly stuffed into a box, along with his clothing and the blood-soaked earth on which he had perished.[107] The ʿAbbasid authorities then collected "firewood, straw, and oil" and incinerated the pile. The ash was reportedly swept into a sheepskin and tossed into a river. The same governor who killed Abo, Khuzayma b. Khāzim al-Tamīmī, also ordered the execution of the Armenian nobles Hamazasp and Sahak (Figures 4.2 and 4.3). The chronicler Łewond states that after Khuzayma had them whipped, decapitated, and hung from the gallows, he ordered them to be burned and for their ashes to be thrown into a river.[108] Sometimes bodies were not burned but merely thrown into the water, as in the case of the Forty-Two Martyrs of Amorion, who were killed in Baghdad and then dumped directly in the Tigris.[109]

Burning was also a common form of punishment in Umayyad Córdoba. Isaac, the former *exceptor* who was executed for blasphemy in June 851, was reportedly killed, hung from a rack, and then tossed on "a most rapacious fire" until his body was "reduced to ash, and thereafter, thrown into the river so they would be submerged."[110] Only four days later, the martyrs Peter, Walabonsus, Sabinianus, Wistremundus, Habentius, and Jeremiah were crucified

---

"Bāliʿa," which possessed a church and may be the biblical "Baalah" (cf. Joshua 15:9): Le Strange, *Palestine*, 306; Avni, *Byzantine-Islamic Transition*, 185 (not mentioned in Yāqūt).

104 Griffith, "ʿAbd al-Masīḥ," 369.

105 *SPSH*, i, 57–58.

106 Compare with the incorruptibility of the bodies of Muslim martyrs in Cook, *Martyrdom in Islam*, 118.

107 Lang, *Georgian Saints*, 131.

108 Arzoumanian, *History of Lewond*, 147.

109 Vasil'evskii and Nikitin, *Skazaniia o 42 Amoriiskikh muchenikakh i tserkovnaia sluzhba im*, 35.

110 *CSM*, ii, 402.

Figure 4.2. Sahak, Church of the Holy Cross, Aght‘amar, Lake Van, Turkey, ca. 915–21. Photo: Christian Mathis.

Figure 4.3. Hamazasp, Church of the Holy Cross, Aght‘amar, Lake Van, Turkey, ca. 915–21. Photo: Christian Mathis.

for blasphemy. Eulogius states that the authorities "finished them off in a vast fire then handed over their ashes into the river, where they were lost."[111] It took another two years for a burning to occur in Córdoba, when in June 853 Benildis was reportedly "burned in a giant fire and thrown into the depths of the river and dispersed."[112] The burning of Christian martyrs carried on sporadically outside al-Andalus over the coming two centuries. Anthony and Peter of Syracuse, for example, are said to have been dismembered, castrated, and tossed into a fire.[113] Christopher, a Melkite bishop of Antioch who was killed in 967 for allying himself with the Ḥamdānid *amīr* Sayf al-Dawla, was reportedly decapitated, and then his head was burned "in the furnace of the bathhouse" (Ar. *atūn al-ḥammām*) located beside the home of his killer, one Ibn Mānik, in Aleppo.[114] The undated martyrdom of Dioscorus states that the saint was burned in a specially constructed pit on the outskirts of Alexandria.[115] Meanwhile, in the thirteenth century, the Mamlūk sultan Baybars (r. 658–76/1260–77) is said to have dug a ditch outside the Bāb Zuwayla in Cairo, where he incinerated the body of Mary the Armenian, a Christian slave who refused her master's order to convert.[116]

Despite the sheer abundance of information about punitive burning, it is important to keep in mind that immolation and cremation were stock motifs in Christian hagiography of the period and that this may have influenced the representation of martyrdom after the rise of Islam. One of the most famous martyrs of all time, Polycarp of Smyrna (d. ca. 155), was reportedly burned twice by his Roman tormenters. What is more, his *life* states that his followers tried to steal the bones and ash that were left over once the conflagration died down. In turn, they stored these relics in a safe place where they could be venerated, for they were "more valuable than precious stones."[117] Candida Moss doubts the authenticity of this section of Polycarp's *life*, partly because it reflects the practices of latter-day Christians living at a time when relics were extremely popular.[118] These same customs did not exist in the second century when Polycarp actually died, underscoring how immolation and relic recovery emerged as hagiographic motifs only in later centuries. Similar accounts of

[111] *CSM*, ii, 404.

[112] *CSM*, ii, 447.

[113] Delehaye, *Synaxarium*, 73.

[114] Zayyāt, "Vie du patriarche melkite," 350.

[115] Basset, "Synaxaire arabe jacobite" (1922), 846–47.

[116] Basset, "Synaxaire arabe jacobite" (1923), 1296–97. In another Egyptian example, the Fāṭimid caliph al-Ḥākim threatened to burn his Christian and Jewish scribes in a silo: al-Nābulusī, *Sword of Ambition*, 64–65.

[117] Ehrman, *Apostolic Fathers*, i, 392–93.

[118] Moss, "On the Dating of Polycarp," 565–68; Moss, *Myth of Persecution*, 103.

burning can also be found in the *Passion of the Forty Martyrs of Sebaste* (d. 320)—whose remains were cremated and thrown into a river—and the Martyrs of Najrān (d. 523)—whose immolation at the hands of the Jewish king of Ḥimyar, Dhū Nuwās, is famously mentioned in the Qurʾan (Q. *al-Burūj* 85:1–10).[119]

Burning Muslim Heretics

The fact that burning was a common motif in Christian hagiography does not mean that reports of immolation were made up. While burning was a recurring trope in texts, there is strong evidence to suggest that the immolation of apostates and blasphemers was part of a wider strategy aimed at suppressing religious dissent in the early Islamic period.[120] One way we know this is through reports about the incineration of various Shīʿī and Khārijī rebels during the final decades of Umayyad rule in Iraq. At first blush, it may come as a surprise that state officials punished such different groups by such similar means. After all, parity in punishment often suggests equivalence in crime, and there are few obvious similarities between Muslim heretics and Christian martyrs.

As with Christian hagiography, we must be sensitive to the existence of literary motifs in accounts of Muslim-on-Muslim violence. Indeed, Andrew Marsham has recently shown that reports about burning Muslim rebels are layered compositions in their own right that draw heavily on one another. In a more general sense, they are also dependent on older late antique literary models. They are a reminder that Christians and Muslims in the early medieval Middle East shared a common heritage for depicting martyrdom. Their language sprang from a common wellspring of late antique hagiographic norms that passed between the communities as a consequence of conversion, social interaction, and the exchange of texts. Thus, while many accounts of burning may have a basis in reality, we must keep in mind that many are highly stylized as well, molded to suit the conventions of a genre. Despite this caveat, Marsham concludes that reports about burning in Muslim sources "probably do provide glimpses of Umayyad responses to specific ideological challenges."[121] Therefore, we would do well to contextualize these reports alongside the

[119]Leemans et al., *Greek Homilies on Christian Martyrs*, 74; Shahîd, *Martyrs of Najrân*, 44–47, 49, 61, cited in Marsham, "Fire in Executions," 117, 121. On the Najrān martyrs in early Islamic lore, see Sizgorich, "Martyrs of Najrān."

[120]For an overview of punitive burning in Islamic history, see al-Shāljī, *Mawsūʿat al-ʿadhāb*, vi, 187–204; for examples of burning from the Umayyad period other than the ones listed here, see Marsham, "Fire in Executions," 108 n. 4.

[121]Here, Marsham, "Fire in Executions," 109, more generally, 118–22.

Christian evidence to grasp what punitive burning meant in early Islamic society more broadly.

One of the earliest alleged cases of burning is that of ʿAbdallāh b. Sabaʾ, the semilegendary partisan of ʿAlī b. Abī Ṭālib, whom later sources denounced as the founder of extreme Shīʿism (Ar. *ghulūw*).[122] He was reportedly captured, interrogated, and burned for his radical beliefs, including that ʿAlī was the divinely appointed executor of the Prophet (*waṣī*). Several years later in 60/680, Mītham al-Tammār, another extreme partisan of ʿAlī, was crucified in Kūfa. His killers planned to burn his body, but at the last minute a group of his fellow date-sellers rescued his remains and buried them beside a local stream.[123] They then disposed of his cross on a garbage heap. In the same year, al-Mukhtār al-Thaqafī, a prominent Shīʿī rebel based in Kūfa, burned a group of men whom he accused of taking part in the assassination of al-Ḥusayn at Karbalāʾ.[124] Al-Mukhtār would suffer the same fate when he was captured by ʿAbdallāh b. al-Zubayr and burned in Kūfa in 67/686. Al-Mukhtār's deputy, Ibrāhīm b. al-Ashtar, was also captured and burned.[125]

The most important accounts of burning from the early Islamic period are set in Iraq in the 730s and 740s. Iraq was a famously restive province at this time, and the burnings took place in the midst of the tumult that proceeded—and would ultimately give rise to—the ʿAbbasid Revolution. Early Islamic historical sources, nearly all of which were written in ʿAbbasid times with a pro-ʿAbbasid agenda, dwell on this tumult as a way of telling the prehistory of the coming golden age. In fact, many ʿAbbasid writers such as al-Masʿūdī (d. 345/956) combined accounts of Umayyad burnings with stories of how victorious ʿAbbasid soldiers took revenge on the Umayyads by exhuming and burning the corpses of dead caliphs and their family members in Syria.[126] Thus, the two episodes were yoked together in a morality tale about justice, injustice, and extreme violence. In 119/737, for instance, al-Mughīra b. Saʿīd and Bayān b. Samʿān took part in an abortive revolt against the Umayyads in Kūfa. Like ʿAbdallāh b. Sabaʾ, these men were described as *ghulāt*, that is, extreme Shīʿīs who preached the divinity of ʿAlī and a host of other heterodox ideas, including prophecy, sorcery, anthropomorphism, and the transmigration of souls. Reports about their deaths vary widely (and are often conflated with other

[122] Anthony, *Caliph and the Heretic*, 161–94.

[123] al-Ṭūsī, *Rijāl*, 81; Sindawi, "Mītham b. Yaḥyā al-Tammār"; Modarressi, *Early Shīʿite Literature*, 42–44, cited in Anthony, *Crucifixion and Death*, 54–55.

[124] al-Ṭabarī, *Annales*, ii, 670–71, cited in Marsham, "Public Execution," 129.

[125] Ibn ʿAsākir, *Tārīkh*, xiv, 388.

[126] al-Masʿūdī, *Prairies d'or*, v, 471–73; cf. Marsham, "Fire in Executions," 108, 122.

martyrdom episodes). According to one, the Umayyad governor of Iraq, Khālid al-Qasrī, tied their bodies to bundles of reeds, dressed them with naphtha, and burned them near the congregational mosque of Kūfa.[127]

In the same year, Khālid captured the Khārijī rebel Wazīr al-Sakhtiyānī at the old Lakhmid capital of Ḥīra. At first, Khālid was impressed by the man's piety and learning, but the caliph Hishām (r. 105–25/724–43) ordered Khālid to burn him.[128] Interestingly, one of the principal transmitters of the anti-burning *ḥadīth* mentioned above—in which the Prophet proclaims, "No one punishes with fire except for God"—was the famous Baṣran scholar Ayyūb al-Sakhtiyānī (d. 131/748–49; no relation to the above).[129] He belonged to a circle well known for its anti-Umayyad, anti-Murjiʾī views, which accords well with the content of the *ḥadīth*. This confirms van Ess's impression that the *ḥadīth* first circulated among Iraqis displeased with the Umayyads' heavy-handed suppression of rebellion.

The most famous rebel to be immolated was Zayd b. ʿAlī, a grandson of al-Ḥusayn, a great-grandson of ʿAlī, and a great-great-grandson of the Prophet Muḥammad. Zayd led an abortive anti-Umayyad revolt in Kūfa that was suppressed in 121/738–39. According to Muslim sources, the governor of Iraq, Yūsuf b. ʿUmar, had him beheaded, crucified, and burned. His ashes were then scattered in the Euphrates. Another account states that Zayd's corpse was left hanging outside for five years. It was eventually taken down to be burned in retaliation for the rebellion of his son, Yaḥyā b. Zayd, in 125/743.[130] Later that year, traditions (possibly fabricated) claim that Yaḥyā met the same fate when he, too, was beheaded, crucified, and burned, and his ashes were scattered from a boat in the Euphrates.[131] After the ʿAbbasid Revolution, Abū Muslim (d. 137/755) is said to have gathered Yaḥyā's remains and buried them at Jūzjān in Afghanistan, where they became the focus of a local pilgrimage. Abū Mus-

[127] al-Ṭabarī, *Annales*, ii, 1620; Ibn ʿAsākir, *Tārīkh*, xvi, 142–43; Hawting, "Jaʿd b. Dirham," 36, 41 n. 29; Marsham, "Public Execution," 134; Marsham, "Fire in Executions," 109–11, 122–25; also Tucker, "Rebels and Gnostics"; Tucker, *Mahdis and Millenarians*, 52–70.

[128] al-Ṭabarī, *Annales*, ii, 1628–29; Hawting, "Jaʿd b. Dirham," 36; Marsham, "Public Execution," 134; Marsham, "Fire in Executions," 111, 118–19.

[129] al-Mizzī, *Tahdhīb*, iii, 457–64; Madelung, "Murdjiʾa," *EI²*, vii, 607. Al-Ṭabarī's source for this execution was the Baṣran philologist and alleged Khārijī Abū ʿUbayda Maʿmar b. Muthannā (Marsham, "Fire in Executions," 111, 118), which hints that the Khārijīs played a role in preserving the memory of the martyrdom; see Weipert, "Abū ʿUbayda," *EI³* (2007), i, 24–25.

[130] al-Yaʿqūbī, *Tārīkh*, ii, 326; Abū ʾl-Faraj al-Iṣfahānī, *Maqātil*, 82–94; see also Abou El Fadl, *Rebellion and Violence*, 53–54 n. 92, 72–73; Marsham, "Public Execution," 134–35; Marsham, "Fire in Executions," 111–12, 120–22; Anthony, *Crucifixion and Death*, 46–51.

[131] al-Ṭabarī, *Annales*, ii, 1774, cited in Marsham, "Public Execution," 135; Marsham, "Fire in Executions," 112–13, 120–22.

lim is also reported to have tracked down Yaḥyā's executioners and punished them by burning.[132]

When we step back and consider this evidence, several things jump out as significant. Burning was closely associated with the projection of power under the Umayyad caliphs, as evidenced by their execution of Shīʿī and Khārijī rebels. Burnings also seem to have taken place almost exclusively in Iraq. One obvious explanation for this is that Iraq was more restive than other provinces of the caliphate and, thus, there were more revolts for the Umayyads to suppress there. Gerald Hawting and Andrew Marsham have also suggested that burning a body may have held special significance in this region, given that it had once been the heartland of Sasanian power and the Zoroastrians who had once ruled from the Iraqi city of Ctesiphon considered fire to be sacred.[133] It may have been that the Umayyads burned criminals in order to offend and infuriate elements of the subject population—both Zoroastrians and Muslim converts from Zoroastrian backgrounds who clung to the old taboos.[134]

Finally, although punitive burning was closely associated with the Umayyads, it did not die out with the dynasty's collapse. Not only do we have abundant evidence of Christian martyrs being burned under the ʿAbbasids, but we also have examples of Muslims being burned. For instance, after being accused of practicing Zoroastrianism (or Buddhism or Manichaeism) in secret, the governor and general al-Afshīn (d. 226/841) was crucified and incinerated, and his ashes were scattered in the Euphrates.[135] The same fate befell the mystic and martyr of Baghdad al-Ḥallāj (d. 309/922), who famously proclaimed, "I am the truth."[136] Later, in 494/1101, the Saljūqs burned a large group of Ismāʿīlīs at Iṣfahān. The official who oversaw the fire pits was reportedly named "Mālik," which is also the name of the angel who guards the gates of hell, according to Muslim tradition (cf. Q. *al-Zumar* 39:71, *al-Muddaththir* 74:31).[137] This underlines the fact that burning probably had eschatological connotations in different periods, since the fires of this world were seen to prefigure the fires of the next.

[132] Madelung, "Yaḥyā b. Zayd," *EI²*, xi, 250.

[133] Hawting, "Jaʿd b. Dirham," 36; Marsham, "Fire in Executions," 124. It is important to keep in mind that even if the Sasanians maintained a large bureaucratic and military presence in Iraq, the Zoroastrian heartlands lay farther east on the Iranian Plateau. This mitigates the argument to some extent. If the Zoroastrian connection is true, one wonders whether future research might yield evidence of punitive burning in Iran, too.

[134] On the Zoroastrian population of early Islamic Iraq, see Morony, *Iraq*, 280–305.

[135] al-Ṭabarī, *Annales*, iii, 1317–18; Bosworth, "Afšīn," *EIr*, i, II, 590; Abou El Fadl, *Rebellion and Violence*, 54 n. 92.

[136] Massignon and Gardet, "al-Ḥallādj," *EI²*, iii, 101.

[137] Lange, "State Punishment and Eschatology," 162.

Destroying Saints' Relics

What led Muslim officials to burn martyrs and rebels in this way? In both cases, it seems that they hoped to forestall the creation of cult sites around the graves of dead criminals. Al-Balādhurī, for example, states that the governor Yūsuf b. ʿUmar assigned four hundred men to protect the body of Zayd b. ʿAlī, working in shifts of one hundred at a time to fend off his supporters, who plotted to snatch the body.[138] This is a hagiographic trope, of course, which also appears in Christian sources, but it probably relies on elements of historical fact.[139] Muslim and Christian sources also mention the theft of bodies at night and the furtive collection of martyrs' remains after being dumped in a river, as with Mītham al-Tammār, Menas, Elias, and Sisenandus and Columba.[140] Christians were especially assiduous about collecting the physical residue of executions—including ash, chunks of flesh, crosses, clothing, and even bloodied soil and stones—as we see in the cases of Peter of Capitolias and Abo of Tiflīs in Christian sources and al-Mustawrid al-ʿIjlī in Muslim sources.[141] The *Life of Peter* also includes a poignant scene in which the martyr's son crosses himself with his father's blood as it pools on the ground; echoes of this can be found in Michael Synkellos's account of the Forty-Two Martyrs of Amorion.[142]

Two hagiographic works express the anxiety about recovering bodies very explicitly. The *Life of Abo* reports an exchange between the ʿAbbasid governor Khuzayma and certain "foes of Christ" who came to him with a warning about the trickery of Christians:

> We know that the Christians have a custom that if someone is executed for this Christ of theirs, they steal his body and give it honourable burial. And with fraudulent intent they publicly declare it to have miraculous healing powers and distribute the garments and the hair from its head

[138] Anthony, *Crucifixion and Death*, 47.

[139] Michael Synkellos states that guards were stationed along the banks of the Tigris River after the ʿAbbasids threw the bodies of the Forty-Two Martyrs of Amorion into the river; Vasil'evskii and Nikitin, *Skazaniia o 42 Amoriiskikh muchenikakh i tserkovnaia sluzhba im*, 35.

[140] Mītham: al-Ṭūsī, *Rijāl*, 81. Menas: Basset, "Synaxaire arabe jacobite" (1915), 798. Elias: *SPSH*, i, 53–54, 58. Sisenandus and Columba: *CSM*, ii, 405, 452.

[141] Peter: Shoemaker, *Three Christian Martyrdoms*, 56–57; Peeters, "Passion de S. Pierre," 314–15. Abo: Lang, *Georgian Saints*, 131–32. Al-Mustawrid: Abū Bakr al-Khallāl, *Aḥkām*, 419–20, inter alia.

[142] Shoemaker, *Three Christian Martyrdoms*, 46–49; Peeters, "Passion de S. Pierre," 312–13; Vasil'evskii and Nikitin, *Skazaniia o 42 Amoriiskikh muchenikakh i tserkovnaia sluzhba im*, 32–33.

> as well as its bones as talisman against sickness, and in this way they deceive a lot of ignorant people. Now order his body to be handed over for us to take out and burn with fire and scatter to the wind and confound the fraud of the Christians, so that they may all see and be afraid, and some of them be converted to our faith.[143]

The *Life of Elias* includes an even more concise explanation of the Muslims' behavior at a point in the story when the martyr's remains were beginning to attract the attention of local Christians. They reported witnessing miracles around the body, and these reports made the ʿAbbasid authorities very nervous:

> Having heard the report, [Leithi the eparch] ordered that the body of the saint be brought down from the cross and burned with fire before stories of these visions spread, so that the Christians, seizing [the saint's body] would not build churches or celebrate religious festivals in praise of his memory.[144]

These two passages can help us understand both social reality and the literary aims of the texts. At a social level, it is clear that the authorities wished to crush the apostates' "charismatic power . . . to survive beyond the grave," in the words of Andrew Marsham.[145] The same applies to the Umayyads' treatment of Iraqi heretics, who posed an equal threat of inspiring civil disobedience after their deaths. At the same time, as hagiographic discourse, stories about the miraculous survival of relics show how a persecuted class in early Muslim society—Christian martyrs as well as anti-Umayyad rebels—could survive in the face of terrible persecution. The relics of martyrs were physical manifestations of their supporters' will to survive and keep on resisting. Given this, it is not surprising that the same motif appears in such disparate bodies of evidence.

Stepping outside the canon of martyrologies for a moment, we realize that the treatment of relics was a major concern in the early encounter between Muslims and Christians. The *Disputation between a Monk of Bēt Ḥālē and a Muslim Amīr*—written in Syriac and traditionally dated to the early eighth century (though recently redated to the late eighth or early ninth)—contains a significant passage about relics. In it, the Muslim asks the monk whether Christians confuse their worship of the Creator with worship of created things

[143] Lang, *Georgian Saints*, 130.
[144] *SPSH*, i, 57–58.
[145] Marsham, "Fire in Executions," 122.

when they venerate the bones of martyrs, echoing the Qur'anic discourse about *shirk*.[146] The monk replied by staunchly defending relics, explaining that the bones of martyrs were a direct conduit to Christ himself. Relics were also a topic of discussion in a letter the patriarch Timothy I (r. 780–823) wrote to a clergyman named Mār Naṣr. In it, Timothy mentioned several pastoral concerns arising from contact between Christians and Muslims, at one point giving Naṣr advice on how to respond to people who denigrated and ignored the bones of saints—perhaps under Muslim influence.[147] Theophanes states that the iconoclastic emperor Leo III's hostility to images came directly from the Arabs, and so did his hatred of relics.[148] The ʿAbbasid caliph al-Hādī (r. 169–70/785–86) was reportedly passing near Mosul when he was seized by a sudden urge to throw the bones of several Christian martyrs into the Tigris.[149] As soon as the thought crossed his mind, however, he was overwhelmed with pain and forced to stop. The *Synaxarium of Constantinople* mentions something similar when it recounts the efforts of a group of Muslims to burn the relics of a bishop named John of Polybotos (fl. ca. 813–20) during a siege of Amorion.[150] The dead bishop, however, stopped them in their tracks, and the relics went unharmed.

In terms of narrative goals, these stories attempt to demonstrate Muslims' hostility to Christian sacred objects. More than this, Muslims are portrayed as tacitly acknowledging their numinous power: Why else would they seek to destroy them so viciously? Thus, relics became powerful symbols of Christian identity and resistance to Muslim rule but also proof of the truth of their faith, even in the eyes of their enemies.

IV. CONCLUSION: FORMATION OF A PERSECUTING SOCIETY?

If parity in punishment can be taken to imply equivalence in crime, how can we explain the similarities between the deaths of Christian martyrs and

[146] Taylor, "Disputation between a Muslim and a Monk of Bēt Ḥālē," 232–35. I am grateful to Professor Gerrit Reinink for sending me his unpublished edition of this text prior to the appearance of Taylor's article. For further discussion, see Reinink, "Veneration of Icons, the Cross, and the Bones of the Martyrs"; Griffith, "Crosses, Icons," 63–65; also Penn, *Envisioning Islam*, 134–35.

[147] Braun, *Timothei patriarchae 1 epistulae*, i, 261–64 (Syr.); ii, 181–83 (Lat.); also Griffith, "Syriac Letters," 130.

[148] de Boor, *Chronographia*, i, 406; Mango and Scott, *Theophanes*, 561, cited in Crone, "Islam, Judeo-Christianity and Byzantine Iconoclasm," 64 n. 19.

[149] Fiey, *Chrétiens syriaques*, 40.

[150] Delehaye, *Synaxarium*, 279–80.

Muslim heretics? What common threats did these pose to the established order? At least among Muslim rebels, the danger they posed to the state was clear: men such as al-Mughīra b. Saʿīd and Zayd b. ʿAlī challenged the very foundations of Umayyad legitimacy by offering a menacing counternarrative about who was meant to rule the *umma* and what "true Islam" was all about. For these men, it was the Umayyads who were the usurpers; they were the ones who had toppled the Prophet's family from its place at the head of the Muslim community and replaced it with a system of despotism. Over time, the cause of the Shīʿīs came to be connected with that of another marginalized group, non-Arab Muslims (*mawālī*), who, despite their growing numbers, were often treated as second-class citizens by the tribal elites who dominated the state. Both groups sought to restore an imagined egalitarianism from the days of the Prophet by purging the *umma* of tyranny, impiety, and chauvinism.[151] Thus, the revolts that rocked Umayyad Iraq were no mere civil disturbances. They were threatening because they sought nothing less than to reshape the ruling elite in a radical way.

Seen in this light, it is not surprising that the Umayyads turned to such brutal tactics as crucifixion and burning to suppress their foes. By destroying the corpses of rebel leaders, the Umayyads hoped to eliminate the physical residue of the revolts themselves. What better way to discourage rebellion than by denying potential insurgents symbols for inspiration? Although the revolts of men like al-Mughīra b. Saʿīd and Zayd b. ʿAlī failed in the near term, they paved the way for the ʿAbbasid Revolution, which ended up realizing many of their original goals. These included elevating the Prophet's family to a position of preeminence in the Muslim community and improving the status of non-Arab Muslims—at least in theory. In a brutal twist of fate, the ʿAbbasids announced their victory over the Umayyads by exhuming, crucifying, and burning the remains of Umayyad family members—co-opting the tactics of the very regime they had worked to overturn.

If the Umayyads crucified and burned proto-Shīʿī rebels because they posed a challenge to the state, how can we explain the use of the same punishments against Christian martyrs, who did not enjoy the same political power? Furthermore, how can we explain the persistence of these practices against Christians well into the ʿAbbasid period, after the Umayyads had disappeared? Put differently, what did an individual like Zayd b. ʿAlī have in common with Elias of Helioupolis, Abo of Tiflīs, or Benildis of Córdoba, all of whom were punished in remarkably similar ways? Here, it is important to remember that Christian martyrs generally came from the lower and middling classes. There

[151] The classic treatment remains Wellhausen, *Arab Kingdom*, esp. 492–566.

were some—such as Anthony al-Qurashī and Hamazasp and Sahak of Armenia—who hailed from the aristocracy. But almost none of the martyrs were plausible organizers of social unrest, with none of the ability to arm and lead disgruntled Christians into rebellion. Indeed, one measure of the martyrs' relative insignificance in the eyes of contemporary Muslims is that Islamic sources almost completely ignore them as we have seen. On the one hand, this is in keeping with the studied uninterest of Muslim writers in the affairs of non-Muslims. But on the other hand, it also reflects the unimportance that chroniclers and jurists ascribed to these Christian dissidents. Why bother recording the misdeeds of a peasant who had apostatized or blasphemed?

Despite this, the deliberate and ferocious manner in which Muslim officials punished martyrs time and time again suggests something different about the threat they posed. Although members of the lower classes, Christian martyrs were not exactly treated like flies, carelessly swatted away and squashed. There was a method, precision, and intensity to their executions, suggesting that they meant something very important to the Umayyad and ʿAbbasid officials who killed them. The abundant and striking parallels between their deaths and those of Muslim rebels confirm the impression. Like the Shīʿīs, Christian martyrs told a dangerous counternarrative about subservience and obedience, challenging basic assumptions about who in Islamic society stood on top and who sat below. Although the Qurʾan and Islamic law imposed hierarchies on the mixed population of the Middle East, martyrs rejected this stratification by challenging Islam's basic dominance over them, pledging their fealty to a higher power instead, that is, God.

The Muslim authorities claimed that no converts could go back to their original faith, but in the martyrs, we see a class of people who shifted between Christianity and Islam. The Muslim authorities also claimed that no Muslims born to Muslim parents could leave their ancestral religion, but in the martyrs, we see a group of apostates who rejected their adherence to the ruling religion. Finally, the Muslim authorities claimed that *dhimmī*s could not denigrate or challenge Muḥammad in public, but in the martyrs, we see a group of blasphemers who denounced him as a false prophet, thereby undermining the very basis of Islamic rule. Of course, the martyrs were not large in number. But even if the martyrs were few and their deaths were uncoordinated, they constituted the exposed tip of a vast iceberg: they were public manifestations of a largely invisible form of social unrest that was at constant risk of surfacing. Killing disruptive Christians was the state's way of containing this unrest, of preventing a few signal acts of protest from becoming social movements unto themselves.

It can be hard to appreciate the threat that non-Muslims were seen to pose to the Islamic order. After all, some scholars of the postconquest period would see Christians as passive, servile actors, having slumped into a state of "dhimmitude," to use the phrase of Bat Ye'or.[152] We would do well, however, to see the Christian population of the Muslim empire as many Umayyad and ʿAbbasid officials did: not as sheep to be corralled behind a fence of laws but as threats to a political order premised on their religious and social inferiority. Nuʿaym b. Ḥammād, a collector of early apocalyptic traditions, expressed these fears explicitly when he predicted that the non-Muslims (Ar. *al-aʿājim*) of Ḥimṣ would one day lock the gates of the city while the Muslims were away campaigning and violate their women.[153] The tradition tells us something about the large number of Christians in Ḥimṣ in the eighth century, but it also conveys the Muslims' fear that Christians might rise up against them at a moment's notice.

Although Muslim-Christian relations in the postconquest period were generally nonviolent, this did not mean that Christians were always happy with Muslim rule. Not only were Christians more numerous than Muslims in many areas, but in places such as Egypt, Palestine, Syria, and al-Andalus, Christians were the dispossessed heirs of imperial and royal traditions that had been swept away by the coming of Islam. It is amazing that this combination of factors did not lead to greater social upheaval. In fact, if we zoom out and search for turmoil in the early medieval Middle East, the most obvious manifestations of it were not among Christians or Zoroastrians who had lost their states but among non-Arab converts to Islam.[154] Despite notionally joining the ruling elite, these *mawālī* found themselves treated as despised second-class citizens. Still, they had access to military and political power—the kinds of power that were mostly denied to *dhimmīs*—and therefore could express their grievances in the form of revolt.

Although they pale in comparison with the number and impact of Muslim revolts, the largely overlooked Christian rebellions of the postconquest period were not insignificant either. Among the most famous were the revolts of the Mardaites—known as the Jarājima in Arabic sources—who occupied the mountains of coastal Syria and managed to resist the direct imposition of Muslim rule for decades after the conquests.[155] In 751, the Arabs of Mayyāfāriqīn in northern Mesopotamia rebelled against the ʿAbbasids, providing an opening for a local Christian named John to organize his own militia, which wreaked

[152] Bat Ye'or, *Decline of Eastern Christianity*; Bat Ye'or, *Islam and Dhimmitude*.

[153] Nuʿaym b. Ḥammād, *Fitan*, 280; discussion in Cook, *Muslim Apocalyptic*, 69–70—on fears of Christians as a "fifth column" in the wars with the Byzantines, see generally 69–71, 74, 311, 316, 366.

[154] Hoyland, *In God's Path*, 201–6.

[155] Canard, "Djarādjima," *EI*², ii, 456–58.

havoc throughout the region.[156] Taxation was often the root cause of Christian unrest, as indicated by the Coptic tax revolts in Egypt during the 720s.[157] The same grievances drove the more famous Bashmuric Rebellion in Egypt in 214–15/829–30, in which Christians of the lower Nile Delta joined forces with Muslim peasants to protest the collapse of irrigation systems and the rising taxes.[158] Muslim sources also mention a tax rebellion in Ḥimṣ in 241/855 involving the city's Christians, which the caliph al-Mutawakkil brutally suppressed by burning the city's churches, expelling its Christian population, and whipping and crucifying the leaders.[159] Perhaps the most curious case of a non-Muslim uprising is the one that occurred in al-Andalus under ʿUmar b. Ḥafṣūn, who rallied Christians and indigenous Iberian converts to Islam (Ar. *muwalladūn*) against the Umayyads between 267/880 and 303/916. Ibn Ḥafṣūn, himself a *muwallad*, is even said to have converted to Christianity during the third decade of the revolt.[160] The geographer Ibn Ḥawqal (fl. fourth/tenth century) describes the social world of these rebels in the rural reaches of al-Andalus, where thousands of Christian peasants were reportedly given to rising up against their Muslim rulers, retreating to fortresses, and risking extermination in an effort to throw off Umayyad rule.[161]

A fascinating but overlooked case of Christian uprising occurred in the Iraqi city of Takrīt during the 810s, and this incident typifies the threat non-Muslim unrest posed to the social order. Michael the Syrian and Bar Hebraeus both report that the local metropolitan, a man named Basilius, took control of the city, levied a special tribute on Muslims, tolerated blasphemy against the Prophet, and allowed pigs to run amok through the city's mosques.[162] The Muslims of Takrīt rushed to Baghdad and registered their complaints at the court, accusing the Christians of essentially upending the *dhimmī* code. Although Basilius managed to escape punishment, the caliph al-Maʾmūn killed another of the uprising's leaders, a Christian nobleman named ʿAbdūn, who was later remembered as a martyr. The impulse to violently upend the *dhimmī* system was not restricted to Christians. Indeed, Muslim sources describe a

[156] Chabot, *Chronicon anonymum Pseudo-Dionysianum*, ii, 196–99; discussion in Hoyland, *In God's Path*, 211.

[157] al-Maqrīzī, *Khiṭaṭ* (2002–13), iv, II, 999–1000; discussion in Mikhail, *From Byzantine to Islamic Egypt*, 118–27.

[158] Ohta, "Social Context of the Bashmūric Revolt"; Mikhail, *From Byzantine to Islamic Egypt*, 75–76, 189–91.

[159] al-Ṭabarī, *Annales*, iii, 1422–24; discussion and further references in Gil, *History of Palestine*, 296–97.

[160] See esp. Acién Almansa, *Entre el feudalismo y el Islam*; Fierro, "Ibn Ḥafṣūn."

[161] Ibn Ḥawqal, *Viae et regna*, 76; discussion in Fierro, "Islamisation of al-Andalus."

[162] Chabot, *Chronique*, iii, 48–49 (Fr.); iv, 506–7 (Syr.); Abbeloos and Lamy, *Chronicon*, iii, 183–84; discussion in Fiey, "Tagrît," 314; Morony, "History and Identity," 20.

similar incident that took place in the Iranian city of Kāzarūn in Fārs, where the famous Sufi Abū Isḥāq al-Kāzarūnī (d. 426/1033) tried to convert the local Zoroastrian population.[163] Many Zoroastrians were furious at his efforts and tried to drive him away by stoning him and destroying the *miḥrāb* of his new mosque. Tensions continued to mount, with al-Kāzarūnī's followers returning to sack the Zoroastrians' fire temples. The Zoroastrians retaliated by trying to assassinate al-Kāzarūnī, but they failed, and the *shaykh*'s followers finally plundered the Zoroastrian quarter of the city.[164]

The takeaway from these examples is clear: non-Muslims contested Muslim rule in the postconquest period to a much greater extent than is usually acknowledged. The resistance of Christian martyrs never amounted to a broad-based social movement, but we can see their acts of apostasy and blasphemy as belonging to a common spectrum of insubordinate behavior that the authorities tried to crush. In many respects the social functions of violence mirrored what would happen centuries later in Western Europe, where, as R. I. Moore argued, Jews (and a host of other outsider groups) became the targets of state persecution not because they were socially, politically, and economically weak but precisely because they were strong on all three counts. This, in turn, was threatening to large groups of Christian elites. Although treated as theologically and socially backward, Jews wielded outsized power in the royal courts of Europe and among the merchant class. In this world, persecution emerged as a way of closing the gap between their "low status" in theory and their "high value" in practice, of fortifying a social order built on the premise of their impotence.[165]

In a recent revised edition of his book, Moore has downplayed the role of economic and social competition between Christian elites and Jews. Instead, he has emphasized the theological and historical threat that Jews were seen to pose to the Catholic Church as a reason for their persecution. Still, the point stands that Jews had to be given a new subordinate identity to offset their actual clout in society.[166] The Christians of the early medieval Middle East were not a demographic minority like the Jews. Furthermore, their numbers were too great and their divisions were too abundant for them to fill the same specific political and economic niche as Jews in medieval European society. It also goes without saying that non-Muslims—particularly in the early period—

[163] Maḥmūd b. ʿUthmān, *Vita des Scheich Abū Ishāq al-Kāzarūnī*, 20–22, 24–29, 155, cited in Choksy, *Conflict and Cooperation*, 81–82; Yavari, "Abū Isḥāq Kāzarūnī."

[164] On Zoroastrian unrest in this period more generally, see Crone, *Nativist Prophets*, esp. 31–188.

[165] Moore, *Persecuting Society*, 95.

[166] Moore, *Persecuting Society*, 167–69.

experienced nothing like the sheer volume and ferocity of persecution visited upon Jews in Europe centuries later. Yet they suffered from a similar disparity in belonging to a theoretical lower class yet constituting a major force in society. In Moore's words, "Persecution itself served to ward off the actual or imagined threats that might be represented by those whose real importance and potential power was not reflected in their condition and status."[167] That Muslims might be easily overwhelmed or assimilated by their non-Muslim subjects was a "truth too dangerous for propaganda," to borrow a nice turn of phrase from Moore. On the contrary, "it [had to] be concealed as completely as possible," and public spectacles of violence served to maintain rigid distinctions between rulers and ruled.[168]

We can sense the fear of disappearing in a sea of non-Muslims in a sermon that the Andalusī theologian and jurist al-Mundhir b. Saʿīd al-Ballūṭī (d. 355/966) delivered before the caliph of Córdoba, ʿAbd al-Raḥmān b. Muḥammad, more than two hundred years after the conquest of the Iberian Peninsula. "O assembly of Muslims," al-Mundhir proclaimed:

> You know that here on this peninsula you are surrounded by all kinds of polytheists and all types of heretics [Ar. *ḍurūb al-mushrikīn wa-ṣunūf al-mulḥidīn*] who strive to sow dissension among you and break your community apart, to cause you to forsake your religion, to dishonor your women, and undermine the call of the Prophet![169]

Muslims across the early medieval Mediterranean harbored similar feelings, born of a sense that their power—while considerable—was precarious indeed. At least in the early period, Islamization and Arabization were constantly challenged and were much more fragile than we typically imagine. As a result, in the war over symbolic capital, the Muslim state had to demonstrate its power over the very individuals who did the most to undermine it—namely, apostates and blasphemers who publicly repudiated Islam.

This leads us to the second function of violence against Christian martyrs, which was to erect boundaries between Muslims and Christians at a time of social and religious mixing. Some martyrs were highly visible "shape-shifters," crossing boundaries that elites assiduously worked to maintain. To reiterate the words of Mary Douglas, "Ideas about separating, purifying, demarcating

[167] Moore, *Persecuting Society*, 131.

[168] Moore, *Persecuting Society*, 143.

[169] al-Nubāhī, *Quḍāt al-andalus*, 68, cited in Safran, *Defining Boundaries*, 35 (which cites the wrong page number). For an eschatological *ḥadīth* urging Muslims to abandon al-Andalus for fear that it would be reconquered by Christians, see Fierro and Faghia, "Nuevo texto de tradiciones escatológicas," 106.

and punishing transgressions have as their main function to impose system on an inherently untidy experience."[170] Porosity and transformation were acceptable provided they benefited the Muslim *umma* in the form of conversion. They were unacceptable, however, when they led to attrition from the *umma* in the form of apostasy. By crucifying a martyr in full view of a city or by burning his or her remains in a town square, the Umayyad and ʿAbbasid authorities communicated the impermissibility of these crimes in graphic and brutal detail. In the long run, establishing and enforcing the prohibition on apostasy was one crucial factor in transforming Islam from the religion of a ruling minority into the religion of a demographic majority. This transformation owed much to the promise of prosperity converts could expect to find once inside the *umma*. But it also owed much to the threat of loss and punishment that new Muslims could expect if they ever left it.

[170] Douglas, *Purity and Danger*, 5.

5

Creating Saints and Communities

"And that one," the boy said, "they shot today. Was he a hero, too?"

"Yes."

"The one that stayed with us that time?"

"Yes. He was one of the martyrs of the Church."

"He had a funny smell," one of the girls said.

"You must never say that again," the mother said. "He may be one of the saints."

"Shall we pray to him then?"

The mother hesitated. "It would do no harm. Of course, before we know he is a saint, there will have to be miracles. . . ."

"Did he call '*Viva Cristo Rey*'?" the boy asked.

"Yes, he was one of the heroes of the faith."

—Graham Greene, *The Power and the Glory* (1940)

This book has attempted to demonstrate how we can use the *lives* of the martyrs as sources of information about the social history of Muslims and Christians in the postconquest Middle East. In this final chapter, I wish to examine the *lives* of the martyrs explicitly as a genre of literature. Who wrote them? Who read them? Why were they created? And what can they tell us about changing ideas of community among Christians in the early medieval Middle East and al-Andalus?

As we have seen, the interpretation of hagiography is not simply about recovering the "when" and "where" of a saint's *life*. It is also about recovering the motivations of its author, and here, literary conventions need not be our enemy. In fact, the literary qualities of the texts can provide important clues about the goals of those who produced them and the expectations of those who read them. This is especially true when it comes to understanding how memories of violence configured communal identity in the postconquest period.[1] Still, we must constantly reckon with the gap between record and representation. Graham Greene put his finger on this gap when he wrote about

[1] For an earlier period, see Castelli, *Martyrdom and Memory*.

the transformation of a drunken, philandering priest in revolutionary Mexico into a symbol of strength and resilience to the poor around him. In so doing, he asked where history ends and cult begins: Were the martyrs actual heroes who died witnessing to their faith, or were they ordinary people unwittingly transformed into extraordinary symbols by their biographers and the communities that revered them? The question Greene posed in *The Power and the Glory* also applies to the Christians of the early medieval Middle East.

To answer this question, the following chapter is organized into three sections. The first examines the social and religious backdrop of martyrology-writing, namely, the perceived threat of Islamization and Arabization. It highlights one of the most important recurring characters in the sources, the unrepentant apostate, whom Christian authors included as a way of demonizing converts to Islam. The second section discusses the authors of the texts and their motives. It argues that the *lives* of the martyrs were written largely by monks and priests who were eager to advance an anti-assimilationist agenda. This view, emanating primarily but not exclusively from rural monastic communities, clashed with more accommodating attitudes toward Muslims emanating from Christians in cities. The third section explores how these attitudes mapped onto Christian sectarianism in the early medieval Middle East. It explains why Melkites—the Chalcedonian Christians who remained in communion with Constantinople after the conquest—embraced martyrdom as a central aspect of their identity, whereas their counterparts in other communities, such as the West Syrians (Miaphysites), East Syrians (Nestorians), and Copts, were more tepid in their embrace of new martyrs. It argues that the Melkites—onetime beneficiaries of Byzantine imperial patronage—found the experience of living as a subject community especially difficult and enshrined their frustrations in stories of resistance to Islam.

I. MARTYROLOGIES AS RESPONSES TO CONVERSION: THE MARTYR AND THE APOSTATE

Like all saints, the new martyrs were meant to be emulated. The *Life of Peter of Capitolias* makes this clear when it states, "We set him before all as one to be imitated for the sake of those who would attain the good and for the glorification of God," or later in the text, "Let us wonder at his patience; let us imitate his faith; let us emulate his yearning."[2] Paulus Alvarus of Córdoba ex-

[2] Shoemaker, *Three Christian Martyrdoms*, 4–5, 64–65. See also *CMLT*, 90–91 (Bacchus is said to emulate the ascetics of the Palestinian desert); Lang, *Georgian Saints*, 120 (Abo emulates local

pressed the same sentiment when he described Eulogius as a "lamp placed on a pedestal and like a city on a mountaintop," giving light and inspiration to those who read his biography, particularly on his feast day.[3] The power of emulation is spelled out mostly clearly in the *Life of Abo*, in which the ʿAbbasid governor Khuzayma is urged to kill Abo for fear that the local Christians will emulate him.[4]

Not all martyrs were the same, of course, and each biography conveyed a slightly different message to its readers. The *lives* of martyrs who returned to Christianity were designed to encourage other recent converts to abandon Islam. In the process, they communicated a message of unconditional forgiveness to those contemplating returning to the church, especially given the risks involved. Far from facing stigmatization or rejection, returnees could expect to be absolved of their sins and celebrated as heroes if they ended up dying for their faith. This message is especially pronounced in the preface to the *Life of Elias of Helioupolis*, which uses the biblical story of the sinful woman anointing the feet of Jesus (Luke 7:36–50) as a metaphor for the unconditional forgiveness awaiting sinners, presumably meaning ex-Muslims in this context.[5]

As for biographies of Muslim converts to Christianity, especially those written in Arabic, Thomas Sizgorich has gone so far as to argue that they were composed with Muslim audiences in mind.[6] By drawing on motifs, themes, and key words familiar to Muslim readers, the texts aimed to provide support and succor to individuals considering the risky leap from the mosque to the church. We cannot rule out this possibility, of course, but what is even more likely is that biographies of apostates such as Anthony al-Qurashī were designed to assert the superiority of Christianity over Islam, specifically by showcasing high-status Muslims debasing themselves and embracing Christianity out of sheer conviction. In so doing, these biographies inverted the story line of religious change in the postconquest Middle East: instead of portraying Islam as the leading faith, which snatched believers from Christianity, it portrayed Christianity as the leading faith, which snatched believers from Islam.

Finally, the *lives* of blasphemers were designed to articulate the perceived falsehoods of Islam and to encourage Christians to stick up for their beliefs at

---

Christians and Saint Anthony); *CSM*, ii, 367 (Eulogius writes about the martyrs to provide an example to Christians); more generally, Swanson, "ʿAbd al-Masīḥ," 122–25.

[3] *CSM*, i, 336; trans. adapted from Sage, *Paul Albar*, 201. For general remarks on the audience of saints' *lives*, see Efthymiadis and Kalogeras, "Audience, Language and Patronage."

[4] Lang, *Georgian Saints*, 123.

[5] *SPSH*, i, 43. Also Griffith, "ʿAbd al-Masīḥ," 364 (Ar.), 371 (Eng.; cf. Luke 15:7, 10); *CMLT*, 75–76; Peeters, "S. Romain le néomartyr," 423.

[6] Sizgorich, "Christian Eyes Only," 121.

a time when they felt besieged by conversion and assimilation. Resistance lay at the heart of the message in the *lives* of blasphemers; as Eulogius put it, "The adversaries of justice must be resisted by all means," and there was no better way of doing this than by disparaging the Prophet before the powerful.[7]

The Unrepentant Apostate

Hagiographers offered their readers models to emulate. They also offered them models to avoid, and these came in the form of an extremely common dramatis persona in the texts, "the unrepentant apostate." This was a character who began life as a Christian and converted to Islam but, unlike the martyr, refused to admit his or her error. The apostate and the martyr stood on opposite sides of a fault line that divided non-Muslims across the caliphate, who were split about how to cope with friends and family members switching sides. Should they be tolerated in the interest of keeping them close to the church? Or should they be stigmatized in the interest of discouraging others from imitating them? As this chapter will argue, the two characters expressed the anxieties of a small but vocal camp of Christians, mostly clergy, who refused accommodation to Muslim faith and culture and condemned anyone seen as being too close to them.

Before profiling these characters, it is worth understanding how Christian writers of the period made sense of apostasy more generally. It goes without saying that most regarded conversion as an unalloyed evil. This view is summed up in the *Chronicle of Zuqnīn*, which mentions a deacon who went to the provincial capital of Edessa to convert.[8] There, an unnamed Arab told him to renounce baptism, the cross, and the Eucharist and then to affirm his belief in Muḥammad, the Qur'an, and Jesus as "word and spirit of God" (cf. Q. *al-Nisā'* 4:171). The deacon then removed his *zunnār* and prayed toward Mecca. As he bowed down, however, "a beautiful white object in the shape of a dove went out from his mouth and ascended to heaven." As the deacon watched his soul escape from his body, he cried out in anguish and regret. The message of the story is clear: Christians who traded up to the religion of the ruling class were committing spiritual suicide. Although repentance was possible, few availed themselves of the opportunity, preferring the short-term gains of conversion and ignoring the eternity of suffering that followed apostasy.

Given this, it is not surprising that Christian writers refused to acknowledge that anyone might adopt Islam voluntarily or for reasons other than

[7] *CSM*, ii, 391; trans. adapted from Colbert, "*Memoriale sanctorum*," 66.

[8] Chabot, *Chronicon anonymum Pseudo-Dionysianum*, ii, 389–91.

demonic possession, laziness, or material gain.[9] The acquisition of riches as a reason for conversion is an especially common theme in the hagiography of the period. Elias of Helioupolis, for example, was allegedly offered "a horse, a chariot, gold, and a beautiful girl as a wife" if he agreed to convert.[10] The Georgian prince Arč'il was told he could become "general over the land of K'art'li [i.e., Georgia], and king and lord over the peoples of K'art'li" if he apostatized.[11] In the *Life of Michael of Mar Saba*, the caliph tells the martyr that Muḥammad managed to persuade the Arabs and Persians to convert through promises of "eating good things, soft garments, banquets, and marriage."[12] Finally, the martyr Romanus pointedly rejected these offers of worldly comfort when he told the caliph, "The honor and gifts that you promise me and all the glory of your kingdom are like dry grass to me, and like a passing dream and a vanished shadow."[13]

Christians in the early medieval Middle East favored a range of social and economic explanations for mass conversion. In a general sense, their views do not differ significantly from those of modern historians who regard the pursuit of status as among the main drivers of conversion in the early medieval period. Interestingly, many scholarly explanations hinge on the specific issue of taxation, namely, the idea that non-Muslims converted to avoid paying the *jizya* and the *kharāj* (even if the meaning and religious connotations of these taxes changed over time).[14] What is fascinating about the hagiography is that despite harping on various material incentives for conversion, it never once mentions the avoidance of taxation as a factor. How can this be?

It is important to remember that taxation of non-Muslims was neither consistent nor crippling during the early period, despite the impression given by latter-day ʿAbbasid jurists to the contrary. The chronicler al-Balādhurī (d. ca. 279/892), for example, mentions an array of idiosyncratic practices which existed in the seventh century and which belie our image of a mono-

[9] Demons: Binggeli, "Anastase le Sinaïte," 233 (Gk.), 548–49 (Fr.); see also Flusin, "Démons et Sarrasins"; Reinink, "Doctrine of the Demons." Laziness: *CSM*, ii, 369. Wealth and power: Delehaye, "Passio sanctorum sexaginta martyrum," 305; Gatteyrias, "Martyre de saint Vahan," 189, 202; *CMLT*, 110; Arzoumanian, *History of Lewond*, 145–46; *PG*, c, 1209c–d; Vasil'evskii and Nikitin, *Skazaniia o 42 Amoriiskikh muchenikakh i tserkovnaia sluzhba im*, 34.

[10] *SPSH*, i, 52.

[11] Thomson, *Rewriting Caucasian History*, 253.

[12] Blanchard, "Martyrdom of Saint Michael," 154. See also Eulogius's comment that Muḥammad offered his followers "not paradise but a brothel" (*CSM*, ii, 376).

[13] Shoemaker, *Three Christian Martyrdoms*, 192–93; Peeters, "S. Romain le néomartyr," 425.

[14] On taxation and Islamization, see esp. Dennett, *Conversion and the Poll Tax*; Løkkegaard, *Islamic Taxation*, 128–43; Fattal, *Statut légal*, 264–91; Robinson, "Neck-Sealing in Early Islam." On the Umayyad tax system more generally, Robinson, *ʿAbd al-Malik*, 71–72, 75–77; Papaconstantinou, "Administering the Early Islamic Empire"; Hoyland, *In God's Path*, 97, 198–201.

lithic tax regime. The Samaritans of Palestine and Jordan are said to have paid a special tax rate in exchange for serving as spies and guides in the Muslim army; the powerful Christian tribe of Taghlib paid a tax normally reserved for Muslims—the *ṣadaqa* instead of the *jizya*—though at double the normal rate because they demanded to remain Christian; and the Christian Jarājima of coastal Syria avoided the *jizya* altogether by fighting in the Muslim army.[15] There is no question that taxation played a major role in Islamization, and indeed, Muslim and Christian sources detail its punishing effects on the subject population.[16] As the *History* of al-Ṭabarī remarks of prospective converts (possibly Zoroastrians) in Khurāsān: "You only have to let a herald announce that whoever converts will be free of taxes [Ar. *al-kharāj*] and 50,000 people shall come pray with you!"[17] But the lesson of the martyrologies may be that taxation was not the singular threat to non-Muslims that historians often imagine it to be (taxes on Muslims were also heavy). Rather, it may be more accurate to see taxation as one of a great variety of carrots and sticks that prompted Christians to convert but not necessarily the most important.

As a figure susceptible to these material temptations, the character of the unrepentant apostate was as old as the character of the martyr. In fact, the apostate appears in the earliest martyrdom account set after the conquests. This is the *Life of George the Black* as told in the *Narrationes* of Anastasius of Sinai—the tale of a Christian slave in Damascus who renounced his faith when he was eight years old, only to resume practicing it in secret later. George was eventually found out by a fellow slave, whom Anastasius calls a "Christ-hating apostate."[18] This individual reported George's secret to their Muslim master, who had the young slave killed after he refused to pray alongside him in the mosque. Later martyrologies were even more explicit in portraying apostates as agents of violence. As we have seen, Elias of Helioupolis was betrayed by his own boss—a Syrian Christian who had converted to Islam and managed a workshop on behalf of a wealthy Arab Muslim.[19] The *Passion of the Twenty Martyrs of Mar Saba* states that the first of the monks to be killed was decapitated by "one of the apostates."[20] The text provides no further context, though

[15] al-Balādhurī, *Liber expugnationis regionum*, 158 (Samaritans), 159–61 (Jarājima), 181–83 (Taghlibites).

[16] For a particularly vivid description of violence against the Christian population of northern Mesopotamia at the hands of ʿAbbasid agents, see Chabot, *Chronicon anonymum Pseudo-Dionysianum*, ii, 314–17, 343; discussion in Sahner, "Old Martyrs, New Martyrs," 89–90.

[17] al-Ṭabarī, *Annales*, ii, 1024, cited in Hoyland, *In God's Path*, 166.

[18] Binggeli, "Anastase le Sinaïte," 252 (Gk.), 567 (Fr.).

[19] *SPSH*, i, 45.

[20] *SPSH*, i, 19. Michael Synkellos's account of the Forty-Two Martyrs of Amorion also refers to Muslims as "apostates" (Vasil'evskii and Nikitin, *Skazaniia o 42 Amoriiskikh muchenikakh i tserkovnaia sluzhba im*, 29), though this seems to be a straightforward term of opprobrium rather

Figure 5.1. Mar Saba Monastery, West Bank, Palestine, view ca. 1900. Photo: Adoc-photos/ Art Resource, New York.

he may have been a Christian who had become a Muslim. Given the setting, it is possible that he belonged to one of the Bedouin tribes of the Judean Desert near Mar Saba (Figure 5.1) that had been interacting with the monastery for centuries and which at this very time were beginning to Islamize.[21] The text makes clear that the Muslims who attacked Mar Saba were not strangers to the monastery but in fact neighbors who had "long thirsted to take control of it and its property."[22]

than a reference to converts. On the Twenty Martyrs of Mar Saba more generally, see *CMR*, i, 393–96; *BHG*, ii, 96; *BS*, xi, 536–37; *BSO*, ii, 915; Blake, "Deux lacunes comblées"; Blake, "Littérature grecque en Palestine"; Grumel, "Vingt moines sabaites"; Auzépy, "Étienne le Sabaïte et Jean Damascène"; Schick, *Christian Communities*, 103, 174–75; Gil, *History of Palestine*, 474; Hoyland, *Seeing Islam*, 366–67; Kazhdan, *Byzantine Literature*, 169–81; Vila, "Christian Martyrs," 308–30. For English translation, see Shoemaker, *Three Christian Martyrdoms*, 67–147.

[21] On the tribes of the Judean Desert and their relationship with the local monasteries, see Cyril of Scythopolis, *Lives of the Monks of Palestine*, 72–73; Avni, *Byzantine-Islamic Transition*, 154–57. For the literary background in late antiquity, see now Klein, "Perceptions of Arab Nomads in Late Antique Hagiography"; and for the situation in the Sinai, Ward, *Mirage of the Saracen*.

[22] *SPSH*, i, 5.

The *life* of the martyr Bacchus contains an especially interesting portrait of an apostate. When Bacchus was baptized, nearly all of his siblings followed suit except for one brother, who was prevented from converting by his wife and her staunchly Muslim family. The text states that they were so incensed by Bacchus's transformation that they hired a bounty hunter to track him down and deliver him to the authorities. This bounty hunter was "one of the most hated and wicked apostates" in the entire region: "He belonged to the same race as us," Bacchus's biographer laments, "but he despised our faith." This man was also called a "second Judas," for he received "ample silver" from Bacchus's Muslim relatives in compensation for his services, just as Judas received silver from the chief priests of the Temple in order to trap Jesus.[23] Apostates like this bounty hunter were frequently compared with Judas. Indeed, the author of the *Chronicle of Zuqnīn* seized on the fact that in Syriac, the words for "traitor" and "Muslim" are in fact homonyms (*mashlmānā*).[24] When it came to Christian converts to Islam, they were *mashlmānē* in both senses of the term.

One final text in which an apostate catalyzes violence against Christians is the *Life of Romanus*, who was killed in 780.[25] The text was written by Stephen Manṣūr the Hymnographer at the monastery of Mar Saba, probably in Greek, and was then translated into Arabic. Neither of these recensions exists today, though we can detect traces of an Arabic *Vorlage* in the Georgian version that does survive. The text is contained in two manuscripts of the tenth and eleventh centuries, one in Georgia and the other at the Iviron Monastery on Mount Athos. In addition to the hagiographic tradition, there is a reference to Romanus in the tenth-century Georgian Palestinian calendar.[26] Romanus began life as a monk in Galatia in central Anatolia. One day he was captured by a band of marauding Arabs and brought to Baghdad, where he sat in captivity for nine

[23] *CMLT*, 97–98. Here, "same race" (Gk. *homophylos*) probably means that the man was a non-Arab Christian. For discussion of this figure and whether he was a Muslim or a Christian, see Chrysostomides, "Religious Code-Switching," 124–25.

[24] For *mashlmānā*, see Payne Smith, *Thesaurus Syriacus*, i, 4192; Sokoloff, *Syriac Lexicon*, 849; see also the Pshitta's use of the term at 3 Maccabees 3:24, Matthew 27:3, Mark 14:44, etc. For a possible conflation of "traitor" and "Muslim" in a Syriac text, see Chabot, *Chronicon anonymum Pseudo-Dionysianum*, ii, 385, 391; with discussion in Harrak, *Chronicle of Zuqnīn*, 328 n. 2. On the related term *mashlmānūtā* (tradition, but possibly also translated as "Islam"), see chapter 3, sec. III.

[25] On Romanus generally, see Peeters, "S. Romain le néomartyr"; *CMR*, i, 390–93; *BS*, xi, 324–25; *BSO*, ii, 882; *PMBZ*, i, IV, 53–54; Bīṭār, *al-Qiddīsūn al-mansīyūn*, 360–65; Hoyland, *Seeing Islam*, 365–67; Griffith, "Christians, Muslims, and Neo-martyrs," 193–96; Kazhdan, *Byzantine Literature*, 172–75, 180, 187; Vila, "Christian Martyrs," 278–87; Nanobashvili, "Literary Contacts," 272–73. English translation in Shoemaker, *Three Christian Martyrdoms*, 149–97.

[26] Garitte, *Calendrier palestino-géorgien*, 64, 213–14.

years. During his imprisonment, Romanus encountered a monk by the name of Jacob, who is said to have abjured Christianity and embraced Islam, though curiously, he continued to wear monastic garb.[27] Jacob tried to ingratiate himself with the caliph al-Mahdī (r. 158–69/775–85) by claiming that Romanus was in fact a notorious Christian from Ḥimṣ of the same name who was known for shuttling back and forth to Byzantium carrying secrets to help the Romans in their wars against the Arabs. Al-Mahdī summoned Romanus for interrogation, though the monk denied these charges vigorously. Eventually, it became clear that he was telling the truth, so the caliph had the apostate Jacob expelled, and Romanus was set free. Despite this, al-Mahdī could not escape his suspicion that Romanus actually was a Byzantine spy. After having him transferred to Raqqa in eastern Syria, the caliph discovered Romanus ministering to Greek prisoners who had converted to Islam. Since proselytizing Muslims was considered a capital offense under Islamic law, al-Mahdī ordered him to be killed.

The *Life of Romanus* features a rogues' gallery of sinners and criminals, including Muslims and iconoclasts who made life difficult for the future martyr.[28] Yet the text reserves a special hatred for the monk Jacob, who is portrayed as the proximate cause of Romanus's meeting with al-Mahdī. Indeed, if Jacob had not whispered in the ear of the caliph, one suspects that Romanus might not have died. Interestingly, the martyr's biographer describes Jacob in similar language as Bacchus's betrayers: another Judas.[29] A related motif surfaces in Michael Synkellos's account of the Forty-Two Martyrs of Amorion, in which a group of Paulician troops—derisively labeled "Manichaeans"—betray their commander Kallistos to the Arabs, prompting comparison with Judas.[30] In the same text, one of the forty-two would-be martyrs—a man who "suffered from the heresy of the holy icons"—is shown converting to Islam under duress. His iconophile companions, meanwhile, remain steadfast, showing how heretical Christian beliefs were understood to make men susceptible to betrayal and apostasy.[31] As a dramatis persona, therefore, this figure conveyed a clear message of condemnation of anyone who might likewise be tempted to be-

[27] Shoemaker, *Three Christian Martyrdoms*, 178–81; Peeters, "S. Romain le néomartyr," 420–21.

[28] Shoemaker, *Three Christian Martyrdoms*, 156–57, 162–65; Peeters, "S. Romain le néomartyr," 412, 414.

[29] Shoemaker, *Three Christian Martyrdoms*, 178–79; Peeters, "S. Romain le néomartyr," 420.

[30] Vasil'evskii and Nikitin, *Skazaniia o 42 Amoriiskikh muchenikakh i tserkovnaia sluzhba im*, 29, with further discussion of "Manichaeans" at 30; cf. Efthymiadis, "Hagiography from the 'Dark Age,'" 111.

[31] Vasil'evskii and Nikitin, *Skazaniia o 42 Amoriiskikh muchenikakh i tserkovnaia sluzhba im*, 34. This is a motif borrowed from the *Passion of the Forty Martyrs of Sebaste*, and in fact, the author acknowledges the parallel; see Leemans et al., *Greek Homilies on Christian Martyrs*, 70.

come Muslim. Hagiographers did so by equating the sin of apostasy with the greatest sin in salvation history, Judas's betrayal of Jesus.

Aristocratic Apostates

Christian hagiographers of the early Islamic period tried to stem the tide of conversion at all levels of society, though they were especially concerned to halt the tide among the elite. To understand this, we must remember that the authors of our texts were educated clergy. In this world, monastic communities thrived in tandem with lay elites—including tribal chiefs and local princes—and together, they acted as the leaders and protectors of the Christian community. Specifically, they often worked as brokers between the Muslim state and the Christian population (much as clerical and lay elites did for Jewish and Zoroastrian communities at the same time). Nobles also provided financial support to churches and encouraged their sons to serve as abbots and bishops. As time went on, however, more and more of these lay elites converted to Islam, usually as a way of preserving their high status in the new political order.[32] Depending on the individual, this process could be more or less voluntary.

In response to the shrinking of the Christian lay elite, clergy developed an important variation on the figure of the unrepentant apostate, and this was the unrepentant aristocratic apostate. A good example comes from the *Memoriale sanctorum* of Eulogius, who disparages an anonymous Christian whom scholars usually associate with Qūmis b. Antūnyān (from Lat. *comes*, or "count"), a high-ranking official known from Muslim texts. Ibn Antūnyān, whom Eulogius calls the *exceptor rei publicae*, served as one of the heads of the Christian community in al-Andalus and was probably responsible for the collection of taxes (Ar. *qūmis, mustakhrij*).[33] Around the time the martyrs started to die, the *amīr* Muḥammad b. ʿAbd al-Raḥmān (r. 238–73/852–86) issued a series of edicts punishing Christians in an effort to suppress blasphemers. One of these edicts is said to have barred Christians from serving in public office. As a non-Muslim, Ibn Antūnyān would have been an obvious casualty of the new policy, and his conversion—well documented in Muslim sources—may have been connected to this. Naturally, Eulogius and the other Christian hard-

[32]Kennedy, "Syrian Elites"; Mikhail, *From Byzantine to Islamic Egypt*, 37–50. On the state of monasteries in this period, see Pahlitzsch, "Christian Pious Foundations."

[33]For Arabic Muslim accounts of Ibn Antūnyān, see al-Khushanī, *Quḍāt qurṭuba*, 110–12; Ibn al-Qūṭīya, in James, *History of Ibn al-Qūṭīya*, 110–11, 115. For discussion, see Dozy, *Spanish Islam*, 287–88, 300; Simonet, *Historia*, 400–402, 411, 434–35, 443–44; Cagigas, *Mozárabes*, 188, 203; Colbert, *Martyrs of Córdoba*, 104–8, 245, 307, 363; Lévi-Provençal, *Histoire*, i, 290–91; Wolf, *Christian Martyrs*, 14; Coope, *Martyrs of Córdoba*, 74, 87–89; Safran, *Defining Boundaries*, 111–13. On the office of the *exceptor*, see chapter 3, n. 118. The martyr Isaac also served as *exceptor*: *CSM*, ii, 402.

liners resented this deeply: the very man who had been entrusted with protecting their interests had abandoned his faith at the first sign of hardship. As Eulogius put it, the former Christian secretary had put "the pomp of earthly honor before heavenly things . . . choosing to die to God than not to live in the world."[34]

Another text that harps on the cowardice of aristocratic converts is the *Apologeticus martyrum*, written in Latin in 864 by the abbot Samson, who was head of several prominent monasteries in Córdoba and who worked as a translator for the Umayyad *amīrs*.[35] After several years of service, his relations with the court soured, and he was accused of having incited Christians to commit blasphemy. His accusers seem to have been both Muslims and Christians, including several noblemen and bishops who were part of the *amīr*'s entourage. In the text, Samson accused these men of prostituting themselves to the authorities for the sake of power and wealth. One of these turncoat Christians was Hostegesis of Málaga, who squandered the money his diocese had earmarked for the care of the poor by lavishing gifts on the *amīr*'s sons.[36] Samson also denounced Hostegesis's uncle, a bishop from Granada, who had been deposed from his office but managed to obtain a comfortable position at court, which he exploited to harass Christians and imprison priests. Echoing the diatribes in the *lives* of Bacchus and Romanus, Samson referred to the bishop as a "new Judas."[37] Samson took special issue with Hostegesis's elderly uncle, Auvurnus, who was so eager to ingratiate himself with the Muslims at court that he converted to Islam at a very old age. Samson described in graphic and grotesque detail how this Auvurnus had himself circumcised; indeed, he took perverse delight in recounting how the surgeon's scalpel sliced painfully through the man's tough old foreskin.[38]

Zooming out from Córdoba, it seems that circumcision (or the lack thereof) was an important marker of communal identity in the early Islamic period.[39] Dionysius of Tel Maḥrē condemned Christians who underwent the "Jewish and Muslim [Syr. *ḥanpē*] custom" of circumcision.[40] Likewise, the Egyptian Mālikī scholar Ibn Wahb (d. 197/813) was asked what to do if someone could

[34] *CSM*, ii, 440; trans. adapted from Colbert, "*Memoriale sanctorum*," 88. See also *CSM*, i, 333; Sage, *Paul Albar*, 195–96.

[35] *CSM*, ii, 505–658. On Samson and his work, see *CMR*, i, 691–94; Simonet, *Historia*, 487–502; Casado Fuente, *El abad Samsón*; Coope, *Martyrs of Córdoba*, 58–62. He served as abbot of the monastery of Pinna Mellaria, which had strong connections to several martyrs: Castejón, "Córdoba Califal," 334; Millet-Gérard, *Chrétiens mozarabes*, 64–65.

[36] *CSM*, ii, 548–50, cited in Coope, *Martyrs of Córdoba*, 57–58.

[37] *CSM*, ii, 550, cited in Coope, *Martyrs of Córdoba*, 58.

[38] *CSM*, ii, 550, cited in Coope, *Martyrs of Córdoba*, 58.

[39] Wensinck, "Khitān," *EI*², v, 20–22; for Egypt, Sijpesteijn, *Shaping a Muslim State*, 166–67.

[40] Vööbus, *Synodicon*, ii, I, 30 (Syr.); ii, II, 33 (Eng.), cited in Penn, *Envisioning Islam*, 166.

not determine whether an unclaimed corpse belonged to a Muslim or a Christian. He recommended checking the penis and if it was circumcised, to perform a proper Muslim burial. But if it was uncircumcised, he recommended burying the body quickly.[41] Despite the importance of circumcision, some new Muslims—especially those flocking to Islam for tax relief or political expedience—tried to avoid the procedure altogether, which provoked the ire of officials who doubted the sincerity of their conversions.[42] Likewise, it seems that Christians such as Auvurnus practiced circumcision as a way of drawing closer to Muslim friends, much as Hellenized Jews had once performed "reverse circumcisions" to disguise their faith in mixed settings such as the bath or gymnasium.[43] As Paulus Alvarus wrote, invoking the teaching of Saint Paul (cf. Romans 2:29), a Christian who had himself circumcised took on the mark of the anti-Christ, for he rejected the circumcision of the heart in favor of the circumcision of the flesh.[44]

The image of the aristocratic apostate was especially prevalent in Christian writings from the Caucasus.[45] There, the Arabs managed to establish control partly by co-opting ancient princely families as viceroys. Though conversion to Islam was not required of them, numerous nobles converted anyway. Many of the texts that denounce these individuals—usually chronicles, as opposed to saints' *lives*—were written at a time when local princely houses were ascendant and wished to project an aura of independence from Muslim rule. The *Royal Georgian Annals*, for example—a compilation of historical and hagiographic texts from the eighth and ninth centuries—mentions a martyr named Arč'il who was head of the Chosroid royal house that ruled K'art'li during the late eighth century.[46] In 785–86, a new ʿAbbasid governor—the famous Khuzayma b. Khāzim al-Tamīmī—was dispatched to the Caucasus to suppress the nobles. According to the chronicler, Khuzayma became infatuated with Arč'il's

[41] Ibn Rushd al-Jadd, *Bayān*, ii, 289; Fernández Félix, *ʿUtbiyya y el proceso de formación de la sociedad islámica*, 454, 550. I owe this reference to Maribel Fierro.

[42] Wellhausen, *Arab Kingdom*, 451; Hawting, *First Dynasty*, 80. The Afshīn (d. 226/841), an ʿAbbasid general and governor originally from Ushrūsana in Transoxania, fell from grace in a famous trial in which he was accused of harboring secret Zoroastrian (or Buddhist or Manichaean) beliefs. As evidence of this, his accusers pointed to the fact that he remained uncircumcised despite professing to be a Muslim: al-Ṭabarī, *Annales*, iii, 1312–13.

[43] Rubin, "Celsus's Decircumcision Operation."

[44] *CSM*, i, 313–14. See discussion of circumcision in al-Andalus in Simonet, *Historia*, 369; Millet-Gérard, *Chrétiens mozarabes*, 47; Coope, *Martyrs of Córdoba*, 58; Safran, *Defining Boundaries*, 114.

[45] On the representation of aristocrats in pre-Islamic hagiography from the same region, see Payne, *State of Mixture*, 143.

[46] For the martyrdom of Arč'il, see Thomson, *Rewriting Caucasian History*, 251–55. For discussion, Kekelidze and Tarchnišvili, *Geschichte*, 415; Toumanoff, "Medieval Georgian Historical Literature," 171–73; Toumanoff, *Christian Caucasian History*, 394–97; Rapp, *Medieval Georgian Historiography*, 469–80.

beauty (a polemical trope used against Khuzayma elsewhere, as well as generally against powerful Muslims, who were sometimes accused of homosexuality).[47] He offered him the chance to convert, but Arčʿil refused and was thrown into jail. There, he was recognized by another nobleman who had converted to Islam and was now collaborating with the Muslim authorities. The man remembered that Arčʿil's family had been involved in the death of an uncle of his years before. Filled with rage, the man whispered incriminating lies about Arčʿil to the governor. As a result of their collusion, Arčʿil was executed.

A similar scene unfolds in the *Life of Constantine-Kakhay*, a Georgian prince who was executed in Iraq in 853.[48] Like Arčʿil in the century before, he refused to convert to Islam and be co-opted by the ʿAbbasids. Therefore, he was captured and dispatched to the capital at Sāmarrāʾ, where he met the caliph al-Mutawakkil (r. 232–47/847–61). For a second time Constantine refused to convert, and therefore, he was thrown into jail. The authorities then dispatched two soldiers to try to persuade him to abjure his Christianity. The men had originally come to Iraq as captives years earlier, having been seized in the border region between Armenia and Georgia. Unlike Constantine, however, they had repudiated their faith and become Muslims. Thus, they "were honored by the king" and endowed with wealth and power. "We know you are sensible," they told the martyr: "We too were Christians, but we could not withstand the command of the king, and for this we have received honors from him. As for eternal life, who knows what is better."[49]

Most Christian writers were quick to condemn apostates like these. But some showed flashes of tolerance—even understanding—about their dilemmas. A good example is the Armenian chronicler Łewond—a priest whose history has been dated to the eighth or ninth century—who lamented the apostasy of a Christian prince named Mehruzhan. Although Łewond referred to this man

[47] On Khuzayma's lust for the Armenian noblemen Hamazasp, Sahak, and Mehruzhan, see Arzoumanian, *History of Lewond*, 145; compare with similar themes in the *Life of Pelagius* (d. ca. 925, Córdoba): Rodríguez Fernández, *S. Pelayo*, 54–62; Bowman, "*Martyrdom of St. Pelagius*," 232; and discussion in Christys, *Christians in al-Andalus*, 88–101. See the same theme in the *Life of Elias of Helioupolis*, highlighted recently in Sizgorich, "Dancing Martyr," 23–25. While sexual themes are indeed present in the text, in my opinion Sizgorich goes too far in emphasizing their centrality.

[48] Abashidze and Rapp, "Kostanti-Kaxay." For discussion, *CMR*, i, 852–56; *BS*, iv, 249–50; *BSO*, i, 568; Peeters, "De S. Constantino"; Rayfield, *Literature of Georgia*, 51–52.

[49] Abashidze and Rapp, "Kostanti-Kaxay," 156. The apostates came from "Somkhetʿi"—Armenia—and Abashidze and Rapp ("Kostanti-Kaxay," 169–70) take this to mean that they were probably adherents of the anti-Chalcedonian creed. The pro-Chalcedonian Georgian author may be implying that the Armenians' heterodox Christian theology made them susceptible to conversion to Islam.

as a "wolf," he also acknowledged that his conversion may not have been genuine. After all, "since . . . such an apostasy was committed unwillingly and under the threat of an apparent death, perhaps Christ will show him mercy on account of his sincere repentance."[50]

II. A HOUSE DIVIDED

Why is the unrepentant apostate so important for understanding notions of community among Christians after the Arab conquests? In one obvious sense, the apostate and the martyr sat on opposite sides of a question that vexed churches from al-Andalus to the Caucasus: How should Christians understand conversion to Islam and interact with the large numbers of their brethren who were switching sides? This raises a second question: Who is the enemy in the *lives* of the martyrs? At first glance, Muslims would seem to be the obvious answer. Yet, surprisingly, Christian hagiography does not polemicize against Islam as robustly as one would expect. If anything, the Muslim antagonists of the stories are often portrayed as exhausting all options before resorting to execution.[51] Sometimes they are even depicted in a positive light, especially in contrast to heretical Christians, such as iconoclasts.[52] This is not to deny that the sources denounce Muslims as godless, impious, cruel, bloodthirsty, tyrannical, lustful, drunkards, or barbarians.[53] Instead, it is to observe that the

[50] Arzoumanian, *History of Lewond*, 145, also 194 (the death of Mehruzhan). On the relief sculptures of Hamazasp and Sahak from a famous tenth-century church at Lake Van, see Der Nersessian, *Church of the Holy Cross*, 14–15. Vacca ("Creation of an Islamic Frontier in Armīniya," 159) remarks that Łewond drafted his history at the peak of Arab-Armenian cooperation. Yet Łewond shows a clear antagonism toward Islam that is more typical of Armenian authors writing in times of hostility between Arabs and Armenians, such as Sebeos and Thomas Artsruni.

[51] Contrast with the portrayal of pagan magistrates in late antique hagiography: MacMullen, "Judicial Savagery"; Shaw, "Judicial Nightmares."

[52] For example, the Greek-speaking Saracen who saved Romanus from the plots of the iconoclastic monks by rallying other Muslims to his side: "And so the Saracens, foreign in their faith, seemed to be better than those who considered themselves Christians, and they showed more reverence for the monastic schema than those who thought of themselves as servants" (Shoemaker, *Three Christian Martyrdoms*, 174–77; Peeters, "S. Romain le néomartyr," 419). Michael Synkellos's account of the Forty-Two Martyrs of Amorion also condemns the iconoclasm of the emperor Theophilus (r. 829–40), but it does not spare Muslims of criticism, either; Vasil'evskii and Nikitin, *Skazaniia o 42 Amoriiskikh muchenikakh i tserkovnaia sluzhba im*, 25.

[53] Godless: Shoemaker, *Three Christian Martyrdoms*, 22–23, 26–27; Abashidze and Rapp, "Kostanti-Kaxay," 154; Vasil'evskii and Nikitin, *Skazaniia o 42 Amoriiskikh muchenikakh i tserkovnaia sluzhba im*, 30. Impious: Delehaye, "Passio sanctorum sexaginta martyrum," 300, 305; Thomson, "David of Dwin," 674. Cruel: Delehaye, "Passio sanctorum sexaginta martyrum," 303; Peeters, "S. Romain le néomartyr," 412. Bloodthirsty: Shoemaker, *Three Christian Martyrdoms*, 34–35; Vasil'evskii and Nikitin, *Skazaniia o 42 Amoriiskikh muchenikakh i tserkovnaia sluzhba im*,

martyrologies as a whole take little interest in Muslim belief as such, with notable exceptions such as the *lives* of Peter of Capitolias and Michael of Mar Saba and some of the Córdoba martyr texts.[54]

The real enemy in many sources is not the "outside outsiders"—that is, the Muslim persecutors. Rather, it is the "inside outsiders"—that is, the bad Christians who convert to Islam and refuse to go back, the bad Christians who ingratiate themselves with Muslims at court, the bad Christians who refuse to protest the apostasy of their family and friends, and the bad Christians who show too great an interest in the culture of their Muslim neighbors. It is these individuals, caught betwixt and between worlds, whom hagiographers attacked most frequently and viciously.

Monks as Impresarios of the Martyrs

It is important to note that a large number of martyrologies came from monasteries and, what is more, from a relatively small number of specific institutions, including Mar Saba in Palestine, St. Catherine's in the Sinai, and several foundations in and around Córdoba.[55] Even when it is not obvious where a given text was produced, it is striking that nearly all of them valorize asceticism. This seems to reflect the monastic milieu in which they were written. There were several laymen and -women among the martyrs, but a plurality were monks and nuns.[56] How can we explain the ascetic backgrounds of the texts and their writers?

The authors of the sources advocated a position of "no compromise" with Muslim culture. In fact, we might think of the writers as advocates of a "resistance" or "anti-assimilationist" view that was beginning to spread among Christians in the generations after the conquests. Partisans of this view were committed to preserving the Christian community at all costs, even if it meant antagonizing the authorities and ostracizing friends and family who crossed

32 ("bloodstained"). Tyrannical: Papadopoulos-Kerameus, "Muchenichestvo shestidesiati novykh sviatykh muchenikov postradavshikh," 2; Gatteyrias, "Martyre de saint Vahan," 204. Lustful, see chapter 3, n. 42; and n. 47 above. Drunken: *SPSH*, i, 6. Barbarians: Vasil'evskii and Nikitin, *Skazaniia o 42 Amoriiskikh muchenikakh i tserkovnaia sluzhba im*, 23, 31–32.

[54] See chapter 2, secs. II–III.

[55] For Mar Saba and the monasteries of Palestine, see the *lives* of Bacchus, Anthony, the Twenty Martyrs of Mar Saba, Michael of Mar Saba, and Romanus. For Mt. Sinai, see the *lives* of ʿAbd al-Masīḥ, Abo (ancient manuscripts at Sinai: *CMR*, i, 336), and Pachomius-Joachim (sojourns at Mt. Sinai; *PG*, c, 1205c; Aufhauser, *Miracula*, 76).

[56] For lay martyrs, see the *lives* of Elias, Dioscorus, the martyrs of Syracuse, and many of the Córdoba martyrs, such as the soldier Sanctius (*CSM*, ii, 402).

sides. We might compare the situation in the early medieval Middle East and al-Andalus with what occurred in the Balkans in the early Ottoman period. There, as Tijana Krstić has shown, monks played an important role not only in encouraging Christians to pursue martyrdom but also, once they were dead, in memorializing the martyrs through hagiography.[57] When it comes to the medieval Middle East, it is harder to identify the beliefs of their opponents, advocates of what we might call the "accommodationist" or "pro-assimilationist" view. We have no texts that were obviously written by Christians championing compromise and understanding with the religious other.

At the same time, we can take stock of their views—or at least a caricatured version of their views—in the complaints and critiques of their opponents. Through the attacks of the "resisters," the "accommodationists" emerge as a group eager to fashion a positive modus vivendi for living alongside Muslims: a modus vivendi predicated not on antagonism toward and isolation from the religious other but on submission to the law and good relations with the Muslim authorities. These positions never gave rise to formal schisms in the early Middle Ages, as theological disputes over Christ's nature had once done in late antiquity. What is more, there were probably many shades of gray between these two extremes. In fact, it may be helpful to think of these less as static groups and more as fluid orientations that ebbed and flowed depending on circumstance.

There are a few areas where we can sense the tension between partisans of "rejection" and "accommodation" in high relief, and the most important of these is the controversy surrounding proselytizing Muslims. As is well known, Muslims were forbidden from converting to Christianity, and what is more, Christians were banned from encouraging Muslims to convert. Indeed, they could face the death penalty if they were discovered. This did not stop some from trying to baptize Muslims anyway, nor did it stop hagiographers from commemorating their efforts in saints' *lives*. There is a recurring scene in the sources in which one group of clergy—usually urban priests and bishops—is depicted as refusing to baptize Muslims out of fear of retaliation by the authorities. This prompts the martyrs to seek help from another group of clergy—usually rural monks, who gladly embrace the task despite the obvious risks. Variations on this scene can be found in the *lives* of figures as diverse as Anthony al-Qurashī, the Muslim nobleman of Diospolis, Bacchus, George the New, and Ibn Rajāʾ.[58] There are also general scenes of clergy trying

[57] Krstić, *Contested Conversions to Islam*, 125–32.

[58] Anthony: Dick, "Passion arabe," 123–24; Braida and Pelissetti, *Rawḥ al-Qurašī*, 103–5. Muslim nobleman: *PG*, c, 1205b–c; Aufhauser, *Miracula*, 74, 76. Bacchus: *CMLT*, 81–84. George-Muzāḥim:

to convert Muslims in the *passions* of the Sixty Martyrs of Gaza, Vahan, and Romanus.[59]

These scenes obviously harness hagiographic tropes. But they trade on a significant element of truth, namely, that the existence of divisions between clergy over the requirement and prudence of engaging in missionary work among Muslims. These divisions are corroborated by certain outside sources. The East Syrian churchman John bar Penkāyē (d. ca. late seventh–early eighth century) criticized his Christian rivals for failing in what he saw as their basic duty to baptize Muslims (Syr. *ḥanpē*).[60] Given this context, we might read scenes of prospective converts being turned away from baptism as a soft critique of clergy who did not wish to engage in that most Christian of duties (cf. Matthew 28:19), which was considered illegal under the law of Islam. This critique never manifested itself forcefully, but it hums in the background of many stories about thwarted baptisms, and it may be connected to the wider rift between the supporters of "resistance" and "accommodation."

Another area where we can detect a chasm between worldviews is in Christian reactions to martyrs: Did they support their protests against Islam, or did they try to stop them? In several sources, including the *lives* of Peter of Capitolias, Vahan of Gołtʿn, and Cyrus of Ḥarrān, family and friends are shown pleading with the martyrs to stop their provocations.[61] They were concerned to spare the martyrs a grisly death, of course, but also to spare family or community members the retribution of Muslim officials, who might be tempted to impose collective punishment on them. Syriac hagiography from the pre-Islamic period contains striking parallels to this in scenes of martyrs destroying Zoroastrian fire temples without the approval of their communities, much as Christian vigilantes razed pagan temples and synagogues in the Roman Empire without the consent of their bishops.[62]

That many Christians preferred quietism is most obvious in the *Life of Peter of Capitolias*. In one striking scene, the caliph al-Walīd is said to have ordered

MS Cairo, Coptic Museum—Hist. 469, 78v, etc. Ibn Rajāʾ: Atiya, Abd al-Masih, and Burmester, *History of the Patriarchs*, 105.

[59] Sixty Martyrs: Delehaye, "Passio sanctorum sexaginta martyrum," 306; on the bishop Florianus, who proselytizes Muslims, and his connection to Sophronius of Jerusalem, see Woods, "60 Martyrs of Gaza," 136–37. Vahan: Gatteyrias, "Martyre de saint Vahan," 195 ("il allait . . . pour arracher les païens à leurs erreurs"). Romanus: Peeters, "S. Romain le néomartyr," 423; Shoemaker, *Three Christian Martyrdoms*, 184–89.

[60] Mingana, *Sources syriaques*, ii, 147.

[61] Peter: Shoemaker, *Three Christian Martyrdoms*, 30–31, 34–35; Peeters, "Passion de S. Pierre," 303–6. Vahan: Gatteyrias, "Martyre de saint Vahan," 196. Cyrus: Harrak, "Martyrdom of Cyrus," 326–27.

[62] Payne, *State of Mixture*, 48.

his son ʿUmar to "gather a crowd for him of fathers and mothers, citizens and foreigners, lords and those bearing the yoke of servitude with women and virgins, the old and the young, and above all the children and relatives of the all-praised martyr" to witness Peter's execution. Within this diverse group, al-Walīd knew who posed the greatest threat: the monks, who were not only prominent members of the Christian church but also the most likely to protest conversion and assimilation. Therefore, the caliph specially instructed his son to convene the ascetics "so that they will be witness to the savagery of the martyr's unbearable tortures."[63] In other words, the Umayyads knew that by inculcating quietism at the top of Christian society, they could guarantee obedience at its lower levels. There was no better way of doing this than by cowing the normally strident and rigorous monks. If the *Life of Peter* has any basis in reality, therefore, this tactic must have ended up reinforcing—if not itself creating—the split between those Christians who protested subjugation and those who quietly acquiesced in it.

The Church of Córdoba as a Model

The rift between supporters of "resistance" and "accommodation" can be hard to detect in the sources, though it was extremely pronounced in one location, the city of Córdoba.[64] Most of what we know about the situation there comes from the champions of the resistance view, Eulogius, Paulus Alvarus, and Samson. The voices of their opponents do not survive, though we can reconstruct their views thanks to the sheer volume of material left behind by their enemies. The sources leave the clear impression that many Christians in Córdoba abhorred the martyrs and their brazen outbursts in front of Umayyad officials. Many regarded the blasphemers as little more than rabble-rousers, "unwilling for them to be received into the roll of the saints."[65] What is more, their critics argued that the martyrs had produced no miracles, proof positive in their view that they were not real saints.[66]

For their part, Eulogius and Paulus Alvarus accused these skeptics of turning a blind eye to the abuses of the Muslim authorities. They "considered it nothing," lamented Eulogius, "the razing of basilicas, the taunting of priests,

[63] Shoemaker, *Three Christian Martyrdoms*, 42–43; Peeters, "Passion de S. Pierre," 310–11.

[64] Cagigas, *Mozárabes*, 179–209; Coope, *Martyrs of Córdoba*, 55–69; Tieszen, *Christian Identity amid Islam*, 45–97. On the theme of traitors and collaborators in Andalusī chronicles more generally, see Clarke, *Muslim Conquest of Iberia*, 102–17.

[65] *CSM*, ii, 382; trans. adapted from Colbert, "*Memoriale sanctorum*," 51.

[66] See esp. Wolf, *Christian Martyrs*, 77–85.

the paying of the tribute with great affliction each month."[67] If we peer past these statements, we will recognize Eulogius's opponents as quietists who saw little to gain by challenging Muslim rule through blasphemous tirades. If anything, many in this group were convinced that assimilation had brought the Christians of Córdoba great prosperity and peace: Why rock the boat?

But for Eulogius and his allies, the passivity of the assimilationists was a sure step along the road to outright disappearance. As Eulogius wrote in the *Memoriale sanctorum*, the group biography of the martyrs that he completed around 856:

> Our holy church is cast down by the carelessness of the negligent, beaten down wretchedly by the blows of some, and thrust down to the depths by the sloth of others. . . . Now, at last, with everyone content in torpid silence or plunging headlong in the deepest abyss of vices, "There is no one to redeem or to save" (Ezekiel 13:5).[68]

Eulogius did not believe that Córdoba's Christians would disappear overnight. But he did believe that through many minor, almost unconscious steps, openness to Muslims would lead to an erosion of Christian culture. There were already signs of this happening. For instance, Eulogius complained that Christians no longer made the sign of the cross after they yawned. He also objected to Christians calling Jesus a "Word of God and a Spirit and a prophet," echoing the language of the Qur'an (Q. *al-Nisāʾ* 4:171).[69] Eventually, this lukewarm Christian culture would lead to a complete vanishing of Christian faith.

Through this context we can begin to understand Eulogius and Paulus Alvarus's striking and strange obsession with language. Indeed, the protection and promotion of *Latinitas* were essential parts of their mission as stalwart "resisters." As Michel Banniard and others have shown, the Latin style of Eulogius and Alvarus was among the very densest and most florid in medieval Europe.[70] They filled their treatises with archaic vocabulary, labyrinthine syntax, and allusions to great classical authors such as Vergil, Cato, and Horace.[71] Eulogius is even said to have composed in a style resembling that of Livy,

[67] *CSM*, ii, 385; trans. adapted from Colbert, "*Memoriale sanctorum*," 56.

[68] *CSM*, ii, 369–70; trans. adapted from Colbert, "*Memoriale sanctorum*," 31.

[69] *CSM*, ii, 375–76, 487.

[70] Banniard, *Viva voce*, 423–84; see also Pérez de Urbel, *Saint under Moslem Rule*, 88–98; Wright, *Late Latin and Early Romance*, 145–207; Aillet, *Mozarabes*, 133–52. On Latin, Arabic, and language change in al-Andalus more generally, see van Koningsveld, *Latin-Arabic Glossary*; Kassis, "Arabic-Speaking Christians"; Kassis, "Arabization and Islamization"; Collins, "Literacy and the Laity"; Sahner, "From Augustine to Islam."

[71] For a list of these quotations, see Sage, *Paul Albar*, 56–59.

Cicero, and Quintillian.[72] One hesitates to accept such comparisons at face value. But Eulogius was a voracious reader and strove to emulate his literary heroes, stalwarts of a Latin culture that was equal parts Christian and pagan. Indeed, Alvarus boasted that Eulogius had acquired copies of "Augustine's *City of God*, Vergil's *Aeneid*, the metrical works of Juvenal, the satirical writings of Horace, the ornate treatises of Porphyry, the collection of Aldhelm's epigrams, [and] Avienus's fables in meter" during a visit to the Christian-controlled Pyrenees in 848–49.[73] Thanks to this reading, he became "a master of [Latin] metrics, which until then Spanish scholars did not know."[74]

Eulogius and his friends were not simply antiquarians. They strove to mimic a high Latin style because they saw themselves as standing on the precipice of a major cultural shift. Terrified that Latin might disappear as a language of literature and everyday life and be eclipsed by Arabic once and for all, they strove to express themselves in what they imagined to be a pure and undiluted Latin tongue. Of course, their style was in reality anything but pure and undiluted. In the words of Roger Wright, it was downright "recondite and recherché."[75] In fact, their Latin was so convoluted one wonders who was able to actually read their works outside a small circle of highly educated clergy.[76] Yet their "back-to-basics" campaign called for a self-consciously conservative mode of expression, one that harkened back to an imagined golden age, much as English speakers today might write in the style of the King James Bible so as to sound somber or authoritative. It did not matter that their Latin was clunky and eccentric: what mattered was that it seemed real, for Latin was about all things Arabic was not. It was an ancient tongue and more than this, a Christian tongue. We have hints that Greek speakers in the Levant may have done the same at a similar moment of rapid Arabization in the region.[77]

For Eulogius and Alvarus, the perceived erosion of Latin was above all a sign of the ongoing assimilation of Christians into Arab Muslim culture. This,

[72] *CSM*, ii, 365.

[73] *CSM*, i, 335–36; trans. adapted from Sage, *Paul Albar*, 200. Comment in Millet-Gérard, *Chrétiens mozarabes*, 65–67.

[74] *CSM*, i, 333; trans. adapted from Sage, *Paul Albar*, 195.

[75] Wright, "End of Written Ladino," 28. Also, Wasserstein, "Language Situation in al-Andalus."

[76] Eulogius at times condemned the *rusticitas* of his contemporaries' Latin but at other times praised *rusticitas* and expressed a desire to speak simply and directly: see Banniard, *Viva voce*, 439; *CSM*, ii, 370.

[77] The *Passion of the Twenty Martyrs of Mar Saba* is an exceptionally florid text; its author was a proud Greek speaker and included a striking account of a miracle that implicitly disparaged Syriac and praised Greek: *SPSH*, i, 36 (for an earlier example of a miracle involving Syriac and Greek, see Lampadaridi, *Vie de S. Porphyre*, 148–49). On the Greek vocabulary of the text, see Vila, "Christian Martyrs," 315 n. 158, 321 n. 173, 321–22, 327; compare this with the archaizing vocabulary of the Córdoba martyr texts: Daniel, *Arabs and Mediaeval Europe*, 33–35.

in turn, threatened the very foundations of the church. As Alvarus put it in an oft-quoted passage in the *Indiculus luminosus*:

> What trained person, I ask, can be found today among our laity who with a knowledge of Holy Scripture looks into the Latin volumes of any of the doctors? . . . Do not all the Christian youths, handsome in appearance, fluent of tongue, conspicuous in their dress and action, distinguished for their knowledge of gentile [i.e., Muslim] lore, highly regarded for their ability to speak Arabic, do they not all eagerly use the volumes of the Chaldeans, read them with greatest interest, discuss them ardently, and, collecting them with great trouble, make them known with every praise of their tongue, the while, they are ignorant of the beauty of the Church and look with disgust upon the Church's rivers of paradise as something vile. Alas! Christians do not know their own law, and Latins do not use their own tongue.[78]

That a compromised command of Latin was seen to imply a compromised commitment to Christianity is also clear from the *Apologeticus martyrum* of Samson. In it, Samson attacks the corrupt bishop Hostegesis of Málaga for being unable to differentiate between the dative and nominative cases, as well as for the *rusticitas* of his speech.[79] Of course, Samson was a translator of Latin and Arabic and therefore must have observed high linguistic standards. But in the background of his taunts and those of Alvarus was a deep-seated conviction that the sorry state of a man's Latin reflected the sorry state of his Christian faith. It was a conviction shared by other Christian populations in the early Islamic world, especially those in Egypt, who saw the erosion of Coptic as a precursor of mass conversion to Islam.[80] Interestingly, it was not a worry restricted to Christians either: the Mālikī jurist of al-Andalus al-ʿUtbī was once asked whether it was appropriate for Muslims to read a book written in a non-Arabic language—*kitāb al-ʿajam*—in this context, probably meaning Latin.[81] Anxieties about the language of the religious other cut both ways.

[78] *CSM*, i, 314; trans. adapted from Colbert, *Martyrs of Córdoba*, 301. The passage is widely discussed: e.g., Waltz, "Significance of the Voluntary Martyrs," 153–54; Wasserstein, "Language Situation in al-Andalus," 5; Coope, *Martyrs of Córdoba*, 8; Christys, *Christians in al-Andalus*, 10 ("too much has been made of this passage"); Glick, *Islamic and Christian Spain*, 197–98; Griffith, *Church in the Shadow of the Mosque*, 152; Tieszen, *Christian Identity amid Islam*, 35.

[79] *CSM*, ii, 569–70; discussion in Coope, *Martyrs of Córdoba*, 59–60.

[80] See esp. the tenth-century *Apocalypse of Samuel of Qalamūn*, with discussion of the relevant passage in Papaconstantinou, "Coptic after the Arab Conquest."

[81] Ibn Rushd al-Jadd, *Bayān*, viii, 452; ix, 337–38, cited in Fernández Felix and Fierro, "Cristianos y conversos," 420. Worries about reading non-Muslim books surface elsewhere, e.g., ʿAbd al-Razzāq, *Muṣannaf*, vi, 110–14, which deals with the larger question of asking *dhimmīs* for information of a religious nature.

Ultimately, the "rejectionists" of Córdoba were worried about purity and corruption. They were convinced that the church was being polluted by its failure to halt assimilation and so set out to protest these changes, to call the faithful to repent, and to encourage the steadfast to speak up.[82] Eulogius, for one, was so outraged by the accommodationists of Córdoba that he refused to celebrate mass as long as the city's bishop—one Reccafred, whom he regarded as being too close to Muslims—remained in power.[83] In this, Eulogius was not only registering a complaint; he was also trying to avoid sin and corruption, for by celebrating mass on the bishop's watch, he might become "entangled in his error."[84] Eulogius was eventually reconciled with the church hierarchy, but there were other Christians who broke with it permanently over the Muslim question.[85] Another bishop of Córdoba, Saul, alluded to such groups in a letter that he sent to Alvarus in the early 850s. In it, he referred to two mysterious factions of the local church known as "Donatists" and "Migetians."[86] The Donatists, well known from the writings of Saint Augustine (d. 430), were a schismatic sect in Roman North Africa that had split from the Catholic Church in the wake of the Great Persecution. They hereticized anyone who had complied with the imperial edicts requiring Christians to hand over their sacred scriptures. As such, they were remembered down the ages as the quintessential hard-liners of early Christianity, a group that looked upon compromise with the outside world as inherently evil.[87] The Migetians are less well known, but they would have been immediately recognizable in ninth-century al-Andalus. A local heterodox movement, they believed that the Trinity was revealed successively in the persons of David, Jesus, and Paul. Due to their sensitivity to the pollutants of outsiders, they also refused to eat with anyone who opposed their doctrines.[88] The use of the terms *Donatist* and *Migetian*, therefore, underscores the existence of a group of Christians who refused the authority of bishops whom they saw as being tainted by collusion with Muslims.

Talk of "resistance" and "accommodation" should not blind us to the likelihood that most Christians in Córdoba supported neither view entirely. The

[82] *CSM*, ii, 392, in which Eulogius writes, "In the midst of a crooked and perverse generation: among whom you shine as lights in the world" (Philippians 2:15).

[83] *CSM*, i, 332.

[84] *CSM*, i, 333; trans. adapted from Sage, *Paul Albar*, 196.

[85] *CSM*, i, 224; discussion in Colbert, *Martyrs of Córdoba*, 182.

[86] *CSM*, i, 222–24; discussion in Coope, *Martyrs of Córdoba*, 62–63; also Daniel, *Arabs and Mediaeval Europe*, 34.

[87] Frend, *Donatist Church*; see now Miles, *Donatist Schism*.

[88] Cavadini, *Last Christology of the West*, 10–23; Urvoy, "Pensée religieuse des mozarabes"; Tieszen, *Christian Identity amid Islam*, 147–68.

majority probably stood somewhere in between, and we have occasional hints of how this middle may have looked. The bishop Saul, for instance, staked out a moderate position for much of the 850s that ended up infuriating many different groups. On the one hand, Saul was denounced by Eulogius and Alvarus for being too cooperative with the Umayyads and their crackdown on Christians. On the other hand, Saul was also harassed by the Umayyads for not doing more to extinguish the martyrs' protests. The state was so angry with him, in fact, that he was imprisoned on two separate occasions. Life in Córdoba was apparently so intolerable that Saul eventually went into hiding.[89] Even if the majority of Christians resembled Saul—enthusiastic partisans of neither orientation—his story makes clear how this majority may have been easily overwhelmed by voices at the extremes, calling for either radical protest against Muslims or radical cooperation with them. The enmity between rival Christian views was exacerbated by the meddling of the Umayyad authorities. Throughout much of the decade, the court leaned on church leaders to publicly denounce martyrs. This pressure led to a major meeting in 852 in which a group of bishops anathematized the renegades and a second in 853 in which an assembly of bishops, abbots, priests, and nobles swore a public oath denouncing martyrs.[90] In such an environment, polarization was inevitable, but polarization may not have swayed the uncommitted middle, whose true size is impossible to measure but which must have been large indeed.

The Contours of Division

As we saw in chapter 3, what happened in Córdoba between 850 and 859 was sui generis. Despite the violence of the moment, it was seemingly over as soon as it began. What is more, nothing like it occurred in any other region under Muslim rule. In the words of Manuel Cecilio Díaz y Díaz, the Christian factions of al-Andalus seem to have been exceptionally "combative": combative toward their Muslim neighbors and combative toward each other.[91] Our impressions of the moment are colored by the prolific output of writers such as Eulogius, Alvarus, and Samson, who dramatized the minute details of the tumultuous decade. They have no counterparts in other regions of the greater Middle East. Given all this, we should be cautious about importing models from al-Andalus to make sense of Christian-Muslim interaction in other cor-

[89] *CSM*, ii, 436, 445; also i, 223–24. Discussion in Colbert, *Martyrs of Córdoba*, 31, 230–31; Coope, *Martyrs of Córdoba*, 61.

[90] *CSM*, ii, 433–35; discussion in Colbert, *Martyrs of Córdoba*, 244–50.

[91] Díaz y Díaz, "Minoría combativa."

ners of the Muslim-ruled world, where relations between the groups may have been more peaceful. Still, it is not hard to imagine how Christian communities in Egypt, Palestine, Syria, or Iraq could have become divided in similar, if less rancorous ways, split between an intransigent group that rejected Muslim culture and a more tolerant group that accepted conversion and assimilation as facts of daily life.

If this is so, such a divide provides a ready context for understanding the origins and purpose of Christian martyrologies from the early Islamic period. The martyr and the apostate were not merely dramatis personae. As a type and antitype, they embodied a powerful stream of thought in certain communities who divided the world into "good Christians" and "bad Christians." The good Christians resembled the martyrs: unflinching in their loyalty to the church and their opposition to Islam. The bad Christians resembled the apostates: acquiescent to the changes sweeping through the region and open to embracing the religion of the conquerors. For clerical authors, one group offered a model for survival; the other group, a path to disappearance. We can sense the extent to which martyrs became mainstream in the east by their inclusion in various liturgical calendars; indeed, even if their biographies championed extremist positions, it is telling that the cults found their way into the life of the mainstream church, which cannot be said of their counterparts in al-Andalus around the same time.[92]

What types of people were attracted by these two worldviews? As we observed earlier in the chapter, monks played a central role in promoting the cults of the martyrs in practically every area. As Edward Malone famously remarked, there was a natural affinity between the spirituality of monks and the spirituality of martyrs, a tradition that went back to late antiquity.[93] This connection was made explicit in the Córdoban martyr texts, in which a great many martyrs were monks themselves or laypeople connected to monastic foundations. As Franz Richard Franke argued, Eulogius and Alvarus strove to present these martyrdoms as the final stage of a process of spiritual purification that had begun inside the cloister.[94] Sources from the east make similar

[92] Christys, *Christians in al-Andalus*, 125, which notes the inclusion of several martyrs' feasts in the Latin version of the Calendar of Córdoba, which are missing from the Arabic version; more generally, see Forcada, "Calendar of Córdoba," *EI*³ (2011), i, 145–46. For martyrs in liturgical calendars in the east, see sec. III below.

[93] Malone, *Monk and the Martyr*.

[94] Franke, "Freiwilligen Märtyrer," 19–20; compare with Eulogius's own statement that the initial outbreak of violence "caused many enjoying the ease of a safe confession in the contemplation of God in the deserts of the mountains and the groves of the wilderness to go forth to curse willingly and publicly" (*CSM*, ii, 401; trans. adapted from Colbert, "*Memoriale sanctorum*," 82).

claims about the connection between martyrdom and monasticism.[95] In fact, these texts not only heap praise on the monastic life but also subtly disparage competing forms of Christian spirituality, namely, the life of secular clergy. This critique is most obvious in accounts of urban clergy who refuse to baptize Muslims. Such stories are extremely telling in that they reveal a wider constellation of differences between these two intertwined but distinct branches of the Christian elite, some of which manifested themselves in the texts. Indeed, several Melkite saints' *lives* of the period—including the biographies of Romanus and Timothy of Kākushtā—feature angry confrontations between monks and patriarchs. At least in the case of Timothy, the attack centers on the patriarch's ostentatious display of wealth—and thus implicitly his proximity to Muslim power.[96]

If there was indeed a rift between monks and secular clergy over the proper response to Islamization, it is not hard to imagine why. Patriarchs, bishops, and priests were representatives of the institutional church and had to interact with the Muslim state in order to survive. We know, for example, that the Muslim authorities often influenced the outcome of patriarchal and episcopal elections.[97] They intervened in intra-Christian disputes, picking winners and losers.[98] They tasked church leaders with the collection of taxes and other administrative responsibilities.[99] Given this relationship of mutual dependency, overt hostility to Islam or to conversion would have been socially taboo,

[95] E.g., the *Life of Peter of Capitolias*: Shoemaker, *Three Christian Martyrdoms*, 10–19; Peeters, "Passion de S. Pierre," 302–3. *Life of Bacchus*: *CMLT*, 90–91.

[96] Wood, "Christian Authority under the Early Abbasids," 263–70. The *Life of Romanus* contains a scene in which a monk and a patriarch of Jerusalem engage in a dispute. John the Baptist materializes and sides with the monk, underscoring the pro-monastic view of the author: Peeters, "S. Romain le néomartyr," 417–18; Shoemaker, *Three Christian Martyrdoms*, 170–73.

[97] On the situation in Mesopotamia, see Morony, *Iraq*, 341, 353–54; Conrad, "Nestorian Diploma of Investiture." In Egypt, see Mikhail, *From Byzantine to Islamic Egypt*, 184–91.

[98] First, the *Maronite Chronicle* states that West Syrian bishops paid twenty thousand *denarii* annually to Muʿāwiya to protect them from their Maronite rivals: Brooks, *Chronica minora*, ii, 70; Palmer, *West Syrian Chronicles*, 30. Second, in 695, the Umayyad governor of Egypt, ʿAbd al-ʿAzīz b. Marwān, suspended all Christian liturgies partly because he objected to the lack of consensus among the sects about basic points of theology: Evetts, "History of the Patriarchs," 35. Third, around 745, Marwān II attempted to stamp out Monothelitism and enforce Dyothelitism through violence and financial penalty: Chabot, *Chronique*, ii, 511 (Fr.); iv, 467 (Syr.); discussion in Tannous, "In Search of Monothelitism," 31–32, 35. Fourth, in the eighth century, the Muslim *amīr* of Aleppo settled a dispute between the two leading sects in the city—the Maronites and the Maximianists—by splitting the cathedral in two and granting the larger portion to the Maronites: Chabot, *Chronique*, ii, 495 (Fr.); iv, 460–61 (Syr.). In this, the caliphs followed the example of the Sasanian kings, who also intervened in intra-Christian disputes; see Payne, *State of Mixture*, 187.

[99] *CMR*, i, 152; Simonsohn, *Common Justice*, 99–119; Payne, *State of Mixture*, 40–42; and the classic study of the Jews under Muslim rule, Goitein, "Minority Selfrule."

to say nothing of politically imprudent. These church leaders were often (but not exclusively) based in cities, where the pace of Islamization and Arabization was much faster than in the countryside. Indeed, Islam was an essentially urban phenomenon during its first three centuries, if not for much longer.[100]

Monks, on the other hand, lived largely but not exclusively in rural areas where fewer Muslims could be found. Over the centuries, the Islamization of the countryside proceeded slowly: Richard Bulliet has suggested that the countryside of Iraq became heavily Muslim only in the tenth and eleventh centuries—though even this timing seems too early a conjecture and may have varied based on the subregion in question.[101] In his recent survey of archaeology in early Islamic Palestine, Gideon Avni paints a picture of a rural world almost completely untouched by Muslims through at least the ninth century. With the exception of a few Umayyad palaces, defensive structures such as *ribāṭ*s, and the occasional farm, Muslims do not seem to have built—must less occupied—anything outside urban areas for much of the postconquest period.[102] In a world like this—in which Islam was not a day-to-day reality for most Christians but a distant threat—the need for religious and cultural compromise was probably less pressing. Familiarity usually exercises a moderating influence on people, but rural monks, cut off from Muslims to a greater extent than urban clergy, may have taken to anti-Muslim polemic more enthusiastically. These feelings of hostility toward the religious other would have only intensified as a result of the monks' natural sense of separation from society and desire to cleanse themselves from its corrupting influence. Ascetics may have seen Islam as simply one of a variety of worldly pollutants to keep at bay.

Given all this, it is easy to see why the "accommodationist" orientation—if it ever existed as such—may have found favor among Christians in urban centers who were attached to large metropolitan dioceses. By contrast, the "resistance" view may have taken root among Christians in rural areas, especially those that depended on monasteries for spiritual and economic sustenance. The example of Córdoba complicates this dichotomy, of course, for there we have an urban movement that also drew support from semirural monasteries. But just as distance from the religious other could breed hostility, proximity to the other could also inculcate suspicion, and the Córdoba martyrs' movement represents a chimeric blend of these two impulses. Regardless, we must note once again that we lack a clearly articulated view from the "accommodationist" side. The martyrologies strongly hint that such a group did

[100] For the classic statement of this view, see von Grunebaum, "Structure of the Muslim Town"; with caveat in Bulliet, *Conversion to Islam*, 54.

[101] Bulliet, *Conversion to Islam*, 87; for Egypt, see Sijpesteijn, *Shaping a Muslim State*, 91–111.

[102] Avni, *Byzantine-Islamic Transition*, esp. 210, 247, 335.

exist, even if it was not as coherent a phenomenon in Egypt, Syria, and Iraq as it would one day become in al-Andalus.

III. DID THE MELKITES CREATE THE CULT OF THE NEW MARTYRS?

So far, this chapter has investigated the role of institutions and geography in the formation of Christian communities under Muslim rule. In this final section, I wish to explore the effects of intra-Christian sectarianism on the cult of the neomartyrs. Why did certain Christian denominations take to martyrology-writing (or preserve what they had already written) more enthusiastically than others? Do disparities in the numbers of saints and texts suggest different social realties behind the representation of violence? In general, it is hard to find intra-Christian polemics in hagiography from the early medieval Middle East. The authors of martyrologies were more focused on the outside threat of Islam than on the inside threat of Christian factionalism. Although sectarian rancor did not disappear after the conquests, to an extent, Christian rivalries were eclipsed by the shared menace of the new religion, especially when it came to writing saints' *lives*.[103]

Imbalances among the Sects

Despite the general absence of sectarian polemics, it is often possible to reconstruct the loyalties of a text's author or subject. The Melkites of Syria and Palestine—the Chalcedonian Christians who remained in communion with Constantinople after the Arab conquest—were the most prolific writers of martyrologies in the greater Middle East.[104] Although Melkite authors rarely trumpeted their allegiances explicitly, they often signaled them in subtle and implicit ways. These included references to bishops and patriarchs who are known to have served in the Melkite hierarchy;[105] allusions to famous Melkite theologians such as John of Damascus or Theodore Abū Qurra;[106] and discussions of Melkite institutions and holy sites, such as the monasteries of Mar

[103] Griffith, "Christological Controversies in Arabic"; for a good overview of these communities, see Griffith, *Church in the Shadow of the Mosque*, 129–40.

[104] For an introduction to the Melkites, see Griffith, "Church of Jerusalem and the 'Melkites.'"

[105] For instance, the patriarch of Jerusalem, Elias II (r. 770–97), who appears in the *Life of Anthony al-Qurashī*: Dick, "Passion arabe," 122–23; Braida and Pelissetti, *Rawḥ al-Qurašī*, 103.

[106] The *Life of Peter of Capitolias* is ascribed to John of Damascus: Shoemaker, *Three Christian*

Saba, Choziba, or Mt. Sinai.[107] Language can also shed light on the confessional background of a saint's *life*: although some languages, including Arabic and Syriac, were shared by different communities, there were other languages that were exclusively used by Melkites. This is especially true of the small but significant collection of Georgian saints' *lives*, which were translated from Greek and Arabic during the ninth and tenth centuries. These translations were produced due to contacts between the Melkite churches of the Levant and their ecclesiastical counterparts in the Caucasus, who subscribed to the same Chalcedonian creed.[108]

The most important measure of Melkite support for the neomartyrs is the number of saints commemorated in their liturgical calendars. The earliest such document comes from a ninth-century Syriac manuscript at Mt. Sinai that has been studied by André Binggeli. Along with a host of biblical and pre-Constantinian saints, this calendar mentions three neomartyrs: Bacchus, Christopher the Persian, and Anthony al-Qurashī. Their inclusion testifies to the institutionalization of their cults at a very early date.[109] A tenth-century Georgian calendar from Mt. Sinai studied by Gérard Garitte mentions thirteen different neomartyrs of Palestinian and Georgian origin. These include Abo of Tiflīs, Elias of Helioupolis, the Twenty Martyrs of Mar Saba, Romanus, and Peter of Capitolias.[110] Finally, Jean-Marie Sauget's compilation of Melkite Arabic calendars produced between the tenth and fourteenth centuries mentions six neomartyrs, among them the Sixty Martyrs of Jerusalem, ʿAbd al-Masīḥ, and Christopher of Antioch.[111] In addition to sources from inside the caliphate, there are also *synaxaria* from Constantinople that mention neomartyrs. These calendars reveal the transfer of Melkite cults from greater Syria to the church

Martyrdoms, 2–3. Theodore Abū Qurra is mentioned in the *Life of Michael of Mar Saba*, in Blanchard, "Martyrdom of Saint Michael," 149, 158.

[107] For Mar Saba, see the *Life of Michael*: Blanchard, "Martyrdom of Saint Michael"; *Life of Bacchus*: *CMLT*, 77–90; *Passion of the Twenty Martyrs*: *SPSH*, i, 1–41. For St. George of Choziba, see the *Life of Anthony al-Qurashī*: Dick, "Passion arabe," 123; Braida and Pelissetti, *Rawḥ al-Qurašī*, 104. For Mt. Sinai, see the *Life of ʿAbd al-Masīḥ*: Griffith, "ʿAbd al-Masīḥ"; *life* of the Muslim nobleman at Diospolis-Ramla: *PG*, c, 1205c–d.

[108] For more on Georgian and the Melkites of Syria-Palestine, see the introduction, sec. II.

[109] Binggeli, "Calendrier melkite de Jérusalem," esp. 190–92.

[110] Garitte, *Calendrier palestino-géorgien*, 44/126–27 (Abo of Tiflīs), 44/131–32 (Arčʿil), 45/136 (Anthony al-Qurashī), 47/144 (Peter of Damascus), 48/151 (Elias of Helioupolis), 54/172 (Forty-Two Martyrs of Amorion), 55/179–80 (Twenty Martyrs of Mar Saba), 59/196 (Epiphanius?), 59/197 (Bacchus), 60/198–99 (Christopher the Persian), 64/213–14 (Romanus), 92/340 (Michael of the Zobē Monastery), 98/363–64 (Sixty Martyrs of Jerusalem), 105/393 (Peter of Capitolias), 110/410 (Eleutherius?).

[111] Sauget, *Synaxaires melkites*, 310–11 (Sixty-Three [Sixty] Martyrs of Jerusalem), 332–34 (Anthony al-Qurashī), 344–45 (Rizqallāh of Tripoli, Mamlūk), 366–67 (ʿAbd al-Masīḥ), 377–78 (Ephrem of Damascus?), 380–83 (Christopher of Antioch), 411–14 (Michael of Mar Saba), 427–29 (Isaac of Ḥamā?).

of Byzantium, including those of Peter of Capitolias and Bacchus.[112] All told, there are twelve saints whose cults can be securely connected to Melkite circles, not counting the saints mentioned in historical and literary texts who were not obviously commemorated in the Melkite liturgy.[113]

The abundance of Melkite saints stands in sharp contrast to the dearth of martyrs from other denominations.[114] Despite their large numbers in this period, especially in northern Syria and Mesopotamia, the West Syrians (Miaphysites) seem to have venerated only one new martyr of their own, Cyrus of Ḥarrān (d. 769), whose biography is found in the epilogue of a longer historical work, the *Chronicle of Zuqnīn*.[115] West Syrian chronicles mention several other martyrs—including Muʿādh the Taghlibite (d. 709), Layth b. Maḥatta of the Banū Tanūkh (d. 780), and ʿAbdūn of Takrīt (d. 820)—but none of these saints became the subjects of stand-alone hagiographies, nor did they find their way into *synaxaria*.[116] The *Martyrology of Rabban Ṣlībā*, a thirteenth-century West Syrian calendar, mentions three groups of new martyrs, but surprisingly, two of these (Anthony al-Qurashī and the Forty-Two Martyrs of Amorion) were originally Melkite or Byzantine saints who entered the liturgical life of rival churches.[117] The dearth of West Syrian martyrs is even more striking given that this community did not stop writing hagiography after the conquests. Indeed, there are several prominent West Syrian saints who lived during the seventh and eighth centuries, including Gabriel of Qarṭmīn (fl. seventh century), Theodota of Āmid (d. 698), and Symeon of the Olives (d. 734).[118] Though their biographies all mention Muslims, none of them were actually martyred by Muslims. Jean-Maurice Fiey's inventory of Syriac saints, meanwhile, contains dozens of saints who lived after the Arab conquests, but almost none of these died as martyrs.[119] What is more, we know that the West Syrians

[112] Delehaye, *Synaxarium*, 105–6, 310–12.

[113] These include (in chronological order of death) the Sixty Martyrs of Gaza, Michael of Mar Saba, Peter of Capitolias, the Sixty Martyrs of Jerusalem, ʿAbd al-Masīḥ, Elias of Helioupolis, Christopher the Persian, Bacchus, the Twenty Martyrs of Mar Saba, Anthony al-Qurashī, and Christopher of Antioch.

[114] On the absence of Syriac neomartyrologies, see Hoyland, *Seeing Islam*, 376; Binggeli, "Converting the Caliph," 78; Tannous, "Hagiographie syro-occidentale," 229.

[115] See chapter 1, sec. II.

[116] Muʿādh: Chabot, *Chronique*, ii, 480–81 (Fr.); iv, 451–52 (Syr.). Layth: Chabot, *Chronique*, iii, 1 (Fr.); iv, 478–79 (Syr.). ʿAbdūn: Chabot, *Chronique*, iii, 48–49 (Fr.); iv, 506–7 (Syr.); Abbeloos and Lamy, *Chronicon*, iii, 183–84.

[117] Peeters, "Rabban Sliba," 171 (Anthony al-Qurashī), 177 (Forty-Two Martyrs of Amorion), 180 (Cyrus of Ḥarrān); on the Forty-Two Martyrs in other West Syrian calendars, see Nau, "Martyrologe et douze ménologes," 73.

[118] Tannous, "Hagiographie syro-occidental," 233–41; Tannous, "Simeon of the Olives."

[119] Fiey, *Saints syriaques*, e.g., 38–39 (Athanasius Sandalāyā, d. 758), 72 (Elias, patriarch of Antioch, r. 709–23), 187–88 (Theodore of Kashkar, fl. seventh century).

carried on writing and copying old martyrologies after Islam.[120] Clearly, the community was not averse to venerating new saints or to composing new literature about old saints. The problem seems to have been new martyrs specifically.

The situation is remarkably similar among the Copts of Egypt. Only a few full martyrologies emanated from this community, including the *Life of George-Muzāḥim* (d. 979) and the *lives* of a number of later saints from the Mamlūk and Ottoman periods.[121] The *Synaxarium of Alexandria* mentions several neomartyrs, but with the exception of George, we have no independent information about these figures. In several cases, all we know is that they died under the Arabs.[122] What is more, many of their *lives* smack of fiction. As with the West Syrians, the silence of the Copts is striking given that the postconquest period witnessed a flowering of other kinds of hagiographic writing in their community. Indeed, the great martyrological cycles of the Coptic Church—which describe the suffering of early Christians at the hands of Roman officials[123]—derive mostly from the early Islamic period.[124] The Copts even began to date their history according to the "era of the martyrs" at this time.[125] Therefore, why is it that this community so eagerly commemorated the violence of bygone years while virtually ignoring the violence of the present, at least in hagiographic form?

The most conspicuous silence comes from the Church of the East, also known as the East Syrians or Nestorians, the leading Christian sect in much of Iraq and Iran. To my knowledge, there is not a single saint's *life*, chronicle,

[120] E.g., the Syriac *Passion of the Forty Martyrs of Sebaste* (d. 320) survives in manuscripts from the ninth, tenth, twelfth, thirteenth, and seventeenth centuries but none from late antiquity: Baumstark, *Geschichte*, 93–94.

[121] For George-Muzāḥim, see chapter 1, sec. IV. For the later material, see Zaborowski, *John of Phanijōit*; Labib, "Būlus al-Ḥabīs, Saint," *CE*, ii, 424–25. See the Mamlūk saints discussed in El-Leithy, "Coptic Culture," 101–39; Shenoda, "Lamenting Islam," 121–71; and the Ottoman saints discussed in Armanios, *Coptic Christianity in Ottoman Egypt*, 41–90.

[122] Basset, "Synaxaire arabe jacobite" (1909), 175 (Thomas of Damascus), 360 (Barsanuphius), 376 (Symeon); (1915), 797–98 (Menas); (1922), 845–47 (Dioscorus); (1923), 1120–23 (George-Muzāḥim), 1296–97 (Mary the Armenian).

[123] For a list of Coptic martyrs, nearly all of whom died in the Roman period, see O'Leary, *Saints of Egypt*; Atiya, "Martyrs, Coptic," *CE*, v, 1550–59.

[124] On the Coptic martyrs cycle and composition, see the overviews in Orlandi, "Cycle," *CE*, iii, 666–68; Orlandi, "Hagiography," *CE*, iv, 1191–97; Papaconstantinou, "Hagiography in Coptic," 331–35; also Baumeister, "Historia Monachorum in Aegypto"; Baumeister, "Ägyptische Märtyrerhagiographie"; Papaconstantinou, "Historiography, Hagiography"; Sahner, "Old Martyrs, New Martyrs," 108–11. For an example of Copto-Arabic hagiography of this period, set during the reign of Diocletian and translated into Arabic, see Monferrer-Sala, "Greek Christian Martyr of Persian Origin."

[125] Mikhail, *From Byzantine to Islamic Egypt*, 131–35; Papaconstantinou, "Historiography, Hagiography."

or *synaxarium* from this community that mentions a neomartyr.[126] The silence is deafening considering that the Church of the East had for centuries produced martyrologies set inside the Sasanian Empire, including accounts of conflict between Christian community leaders and Zoroastrian elites.[127] In fact, many of these Sasanian martyrologies continued to be copied after the Arab conquest.[128] Despite their frenetic efforts to record the deeds of old martyrs, the East Syrians were mute about the deeds of new martyrs. How can we explain this?

Before offering an interpretation of the evidence, it is worth noting that not all neomartyr cults bear a clear sectarian stamp. In fact, there is a small but significant group of saints who were venerated by many different communities. The best example is Anthony al-Qurashī, who despite starting out as a Melkite saint found his way into the *Martyrology of Rabban Ṣlībā*, the *Chronicle of 819*, and the *Chronicle of Michael the Syrian*, all West Syrian works.[129] A version of Anthony's *life* was even translated into Geʿez, the language of the non-Chalcedonian Ethiopian Orthodox Church.[130] Paul Peeters also states that Anthony was featured in a Maronite calendar.[131] Another saint who was especially proficient at transcending sectarian divisions was Vahan of Gołtʿn. According to his *life*, several communities in the Syrian city of Ruṣāfa vied for custody of his relics, including "Greeks, Jacobites, and Nestorians," that is, Melkites, West Syrians, and East Syrians.[132] These warring factions ultimately agreed to bury Vahan in a neutral space known as the "cemetery of the foreigners." Later, a proper church was also built in his honor, and his body was entombed inside. A Christian courtier named Theophilus allegedly stole his body and hid it in his private rooms. This Theophilus was a "Greek," probably meaning a Melkite, and he is said to have given a "story of the martyrdom of the courageous confessor in the Greek language" to Vahan's Armenian biographer Abraham, who had traveled to Ruṣāfa to learn about the martyr's fate.[133] Thus, in Vahan, we have an example of a single saint who

[126] For example, see a fourteenth-century *Synaxarium* with many local saints but no neomartyrs: Fiey, "Dyptiques nestoriens," esp. 402–4.

[127] For an overview, see Brock, *Guide to the Persian Martyr Acts.*

[128] Payne, *State of Mixture*, 48–49; the most fascinating examples are the Persian martyr acts translated from Syriac into Sogdian: Sims-Williams, *Christian Sogdian Manuscript C2*, 137–64. See also the recent study of the martyr ʿAbdā da-Mshīḥā of Sinjar, set in the fourth century but thought to have been written between 650 and 850 after the conquests: Butts and Gross, *Slave of Christ.*

[129] Peeters, "Rabban Sliba," 171; Brooks, *Chronica minora*, iii, 253–54; Chabot, *Chronique*, iii, 18–19 (Fr.); iv, 487–88 (Syr.).

[130] Peeters, "S. Antoine le néo-martyr."

[131] Peeters, "Autobiographie de S. Antoine," 63.

[132] Gatteyrias, "Martyre de saint Vahan," 209–12.

[133] Gatteyrias, "Martyre de saint Vahan," 213.

was revered in four different churches. It was possible for some martyrs to become truly ecumenical symbols.

At the same time, we have hints that Christian sectarianism did interfere in the creation of other saints' cults. It is telling that while the *Chronicle of 819* and *Michael the Syrian* mention Anthony al-Qurashī, neither of these sources calls him a "saint" or a "martyr."[134] The clearest case of a sectarian dispute is that of Eustathius, son of the Byzantine nobleman Marianus, who was a prisoner of war killed by the Umayyads at Ḥarrān in 739–40. Two different versions of his *life* survive in Chalcedonian and non-Chalcedonian works. The Byzantine historian Theophanes, for example, reports that Eustathius was offered the chance to convert to Islam and go free but he refused to apostatize and was killed. Theophanes makes clear that he died a saint, for his "venerable and holy remains performed countless cures."[135] The West Syrian chronicler Michael and the anonymous author of the *Chronicle of 1234*, meanwhile, state that Eustathius died under distinctly political circumstances: after the caliph Hishām b. ʿAbd al-Malik discovered that the emperor Leo III had been killing Arab prisoners of war (the two historians claim that this was not true), he started killing Byzantine prisoners in retaliation, and Eustathius was one casualty of this purge. Interestingly, as Michael and the *Chronicle of 1234* also state, "There was uncertainty among many as to whether [Eustathius and his companions] should be regarded as real martyrs [Syr. *sāhdē sharīrē*]."[136] Neither clarifies the nature of this uncertainty—whether it owed to the political circumstances of Eustathius's death or to the fact that he was a Chalcedonian Christian and did not deserve to be venerated by his theological rivals.

A Social Reality behind the Imbalance?

The imbalance of evidence among competing Christian sects prompts us to ask several basic questions: Why did the Melkites venerate more neomartyrs than their counterparts in other Christian churches? Was this because martyrdom resonated as a symbol to a greater extent among Melkites than among other groups? Or was it because Melkites experienced higher levels of violence and therefore came to possess more martyrs? Finally, if the Melkites were responsible for the lion's share of our texts, was neomartyrdom in fact a broad phenomenon stretching across the Middle East or simply the creation of one

[134] See chapter 2, n. 21.

[135] de Boor, *Chronographia*, i, 414; Mango and Scott, *Theophanes*, 573.

[136] Chabot, *Chronique*, ii, 501 (Fr.); iv, 463 (Syr.); Chabot, *Chronicon ad annum Christi 1234*, i, 313; see also Binggeli, "Converting the Caliph," 86.

community? The third of these four questions is the easiest to address, so let us tackle it first.

There is little evidence that the Muslim authorities treated Christian denominations differently purely on the basis of their beliefs as opposed to their political connections. By and large, the Umayyads and ʿAbbasids regarded the Christian communities of their realm as an undifferentiated mass of *naṣārā* (the Qurʾan's term for Christians). There were exceptions to this rule, of course: Muslim potentates sometimes intervened on behalf of one sect or another in theological and political disputes.[137] In Egypt, for example, the turn of the eighth century witnessed a shift in government patronage away from Melkites to Copts and West Syrians, especially among lay ministers.[138] Meanwhile, Muslim theologians arrived at ever more nuanced understandings of the theological differences among the sects, as we see in the works of Abū ʿĪsā ʾl-Warrāq (d. 247/861), ʿAbd al-Jabbār al-Hamadhānī (d. 415/1025), Ibn Ḥazm (d. 456/1064), and al-Shahristānī (d. 548/1153).[139] But when it came to the politics of intra-Christian sectarianism, the Muslims were relatively indifferent to who was right, provided the Christians paid their taxes and obeyed the law.

Despite the overall picture of neutrality, there is some indication that the Umayyads and ʿAbbasids may have treated the Melkites slightly differently than other Christians, though not on the basis of theology but, rather, on the basis of politics. The Melkites remained in communion with the Byzantine emperor and, at least in principle, also remained loyal to him, despite the emperor's being the sworn enemy of the caliph. There is evidence to suggest that the Melkites were essentially ignorant of what was happening in Constantinople, but their titular connections to a foreign power made them suspect in the eyes of the state.[140] This is corroborated by a group of Melkite martyrs who were killed on suspicion of being Byzantine agents, including the Sixty Martyrs of Jerusalem (d. 724/725), Romanus (d. 780), and Christopher of Antioch (d. 969).[141] The *History of the Patriarchs of Alexandria* provides

[137] See n. 98 above.

[138] Mikhail, *From Byzantine to Islamic Egypt*, 41; on the Gūmāyē of Edessa, who served in Egypt under the Umayyads, see Debié, "Christians in the Service of the Caliph."

[139] Thomas, *Anti-Christian Polemic in Early Islam*; Reynolds, *Muslim Theologian in the Sectarian Milieu*; Pulcini, *Exegesis as Polemical Discourse*; al-Shahrastānī, *Milal wa-ʾl-niḥal*, 262–72; more generally, Griffith, *Church in the Shadow of the Mosque*, 140–42; Seleznyov, "Denominations of Syrian Christianity."

[140] Eutychius (d. 458/1066) reports that between the reigns of the ʿAbbasid caliphs al-Manṣūr (r. 136–58/754–75) and al-Rāḍī (r. 322–29/934–40) the Melkites did not know the names of the patriarchs of Constantinople: Eutychius, *Annales*, ii, 49, 87–88; discussion in Griffith, "Venerating Images," 71.

[141] Sixty Martyrs: Papadopoulos-Kerameus, "Muchenichestvo shestidesiati novykh sviatykh muchenikov postradavshikh," 4. Romanus: Shoemaker, *Three Christian Martyrdoms*, 178–81, 182–

further evidence of this when it reports that a Coptic bishop named Pachomius took advantage of the government's paranoia about Christian espionage to falsely accuse the Melkite patriarch of Alexandria of spying for the Byzantines. The authorities reacted by arresting the patriarch and cutting off two of his fingers.[142] Theophanes tells a similar story about Theodore, the Melkite patriarch of Antioch, who was banished to Moab around 755–56 after allegedly relaying sensitive information about the Arabs to the emperor Constantine V.[143] A few years later, the Melkite population of the Vale of Marʿash (Gk. Germanikeia) was deported to Palestine, and Michael the Syrian explains that this was done because they were suspected of having spied for the Byzantines.[144] From all these reports, it is clear that the Arabs sometimes regarded their Melkite subjects as a fifth column, especially at times of heightened tension with Byzantium. Given this, it is possible that they harassed them more intensely than other Christian groups.[145]

It is also possible that the Melkites produced more martyrs because they were the single biggest Christian denomination in the Levant. Michael the Syrian states that the Maronites were once the biggest Chalcedonian group in Syria (the Chalcedonians having been split into two parties, Maronites and Melkites), but in the early eighth century, an influx of captives from Byzantium tipped the balance in favor of the Melkites.[146] The rise in the number of Melkites was also connected to the prestige and influence of the Byzantine Empire, which remained powerful despite the territorial losses of the conquest. Indeed, Melkites continued to control the major sees of Jerusalem, Antioch, and Edessa, much as they had done in Roman times. Another factor in the Melkites' favor was the persecutory campaigns of powerful Christian officials such as Sergius b. Manṣūr. The same passage in the *Chronicle of Michael the Syrian* that mentions Melkite captives claims that Sergius oppressed the Orthodox—that is, non-Chalcedonian, West Syrian Christians—in Damascus and Ḥimṣ, forcing them to erase their distinctive addition to the Trisagion prayer. These cam-

85, 190–91; Peeters, "S. Romain le néomartyr," 420–22, 424. Christopher: Zayyāt, "Vie du patriarche melkite," 348.

[142] Mikhail, *From Byzantine to Islamic Egypt*, 199.

[143] de Boor, *Chronographia*, i, 430; Mango and Scott, *Theophanes*, 594.

[144] de Boor, *Chronographia*, i, 444–45; Mango and Scott, *Theophanes*, 614; Chabot, *Chronique*, ii, 526 (Fr.); iv, 476 (Syr.).

[145] Fiey, *Chrétiens syriaques*, 27–28, 48–50; Hoyland, *In God's Path*, 197–98. In this sense, their plight may not have been so different from that of East Syrian Christians under the Sasanians, who were also sometimes suspected of being a fifth column: Brock, "Christians in the Sasanian Empire."

[146] Chabot, *Chronique*, ii, 492 (Fr.); iv, 457–58 (Syr.). Discussion in Tannous, "In Search of Monothelitism," 34.

paigns, in turn, prompted many West Syrians to switch sides and become Melkites.[147]

That this produced a long-lasting demographic shift in the Levant is suggested by the twelfth-century West Syrian theologian Dionysius bar Ṣalībī, who wrote a polemical treatise against Melkites couched as a rebuttal to a West Syrian convert to the Melkite creed. The convert defended his decision partly by pointing out that the Melkites were more numerous than the West Syrians.[148] In his eyes, at least, the numerical dominance of this community was proof that God regarded them as the true Christians. If Melkites were more numerous than other Christian denominations at the time, it also stands to reason that they were interacting with Muslims more frequently and, therefore, may have experienced more episodes of violence. The West Syrians were an increasingly rural community too, concentrated in the countryside of northern Mesopotamia where their monasteries and patriarchs resided. Given that Islam was largely an urban phenomenon, it stands to reason that interreligious conflict was less common in the areas where West Syrians predominated, and therefore, martyrdom may have been less common there, too. Though the situation in Egypt in this period is murky, it is often thought that Coptic communities were more numerous in the countryside than Melkite communities. Melkites may have predominated in cities, where the legacy of Byzantine rule was much stronger and where there were also more Muslims.

Ultimately, it is hard to prove definitively that the Melkites took to martyrology-writing more enthusiastically than their rivals because of political pressures or demographic circumstances. What we can say with certainty is that martyrdom helped configure the identity of this community in a way it simply did not for competing sects. Here, it is not hard to see why they may have promoted tales of protest and suffering. As heirs to the Byzantine legacy in the Islamic Middle East, the Melkites arguably fell the farthest and hardest because of the Arab conquest.[149] At the start of the seventh century, they enjoyed the patronage and protection of the emperor himself, but after, they were transformed into one of a variety of second-class citizens in the new Muslim *oikoumene*. Whereas the Copts, West Syrians, and East Syrians had extensive experience living without access to power, the Melkites knew little but a tradition of dominance, and therefore, they struggled to make sense of their new predicament. What is more, they suddenly had to compete with rival Christian denominations as equals, not as superiors. Their rivals took advantage of this

[147] Debié ("Christians in the Service of the Caliph," 63–64) refers to this process as the "re-Chalcedonianization of Syria."

[148] Mingana, *Woodbrooke Studies*, i, 22.

[149] Crone, "Islam, Judeo-Christianity and Byzantine Iconoclasm," 61–62.

new situation to expand their reach beyond their traditional geographic bases of power.[150]

The collapse of Roman authority was difficult for all Christian churches. Despite the entrenched myth that some sects welcomed the conquerors with open arms because of their theological enmity toward the Byzantines, there is very little evidence that this animosity motivated "heterodox" Christian to collaborate with the Muslims on a large scale.[151] Most Christians in the early medieval Middle East preferred the rule of a Christian emperor—even if they regarded his interpretation of Chalcedon as errant—to the suzerainty of a Muslim caliph. This feeling must have been especially pronounced among Melkites. Given their unique predicament as heirs to an imperial tradition that had suddenly vanished, tales of martyrdom expressed a deep-seated desire to protest and resist their newfound subjugation. In stories of the conversion of Muslim aristocrats and caliphs to Christianity, the Melkites went one step further by expressing their most audacious desire of all: not only to conserve their flock by fending off conversion but to restore the old imperial system by winning a new pagan empire for Christ.[152] It was this tragic sense of loss that fed a desire for stories about combat, survival, and death. Better to suffer a martyr's fate in defense of Christianity than to go silently into the night, accepting the indignities of Muslim rule. It may be no coincidence that outside the Levant, the Christians most attracted to tales of martyrdom were, like the Melkites, also heirs to vanquished royal traditions. These included the Hispano-Goths of al-Andalus, along with the Armenians and Georgians, who were ruled by quasi-independent aristocratic houses during late antiquity and the Middle Ages. This observation also applies to the neomartyrs of later periods—such as the ones commemorated in the Ottoman Balkans and Communist Russia—where the loss of Christian empire at the hands of "godless kings" also created conditions ripe for stories of martyrdom.

The Melkites' predicament can also help us understand why other Christian communities produced virtually no new martyrs in the early medieval period.

[150] Kennedy, "Islam," 227. On the expansion of non-Melkite communities in Jerusalem after the conquests, see Avni, *Byzantine-Islamic Transition*, 127; Penn, *Envisioning Islam*, 139. On the expansion of East Syrians outside of Iraq after the conquest, Meinardus, "Nestorians in Egypt," 116–21; Meinardus, "Nestorians in Jerusalem"; Walker, "Church of the East," 1016–17.

[151] Many scholars have suggested that there was sympathy or collaboration to one degree or another; see Levtzion, "Conversion to Islam in Syria and Palestine," 302; Kennedy, *Great Arab Conquests*, 148–49. Others have argued against it: Butler, *Arab Conquest of Egypt*, 439–46; Palme, "Political Identity versus Religious Distinction?"; Mikhail, *From Byzantine to Islamic Egypt*, 16–36; Hoyland, *In God's Path*, 73–74. On the representation of Copts in early Muslim historiography from Egypt, which portrays them as acquiescent in the conquest, see Coghill, "Minority Representation."

[152] See chapter 2, sec. V.

As the West Syrians, Copts, and East Syrians had long been seen as heretical in the eyes of the people who ruled them, one suspects that they had an easier time adjusting to the presence of another religiously alien state (albeit one that was even more alien than the Byzantines). The playbook that had enabled them to flourish under the Byzantines and Sasanians would help them to flourish under the Umayyads and ʿAbbasids, too. This was especially true of the Church of the East, which, as the research of Richard Payne and others has shown, thrived in the centuries before the conquests thanks to a close, almost symbiotic relationship with the Sasanian court.[153] The Arab conquests and the resultant shift of power away from Iraq altered the relationship between the church and its non-Christian masters. Indeed, the Church of the East lay outside the orbit of the Muslim elite through much of the Umayyad period, when the community's rural monasteries first rose to prominence.[154] But with the return of political power to Iraq under the ʿAbbasids, the church again managed to secure its place as the leading Christian institution of the realm, largely by ingratiating itself among the powerful. So strong was the collaboration between the Muslim and East Syrian elite that we might regard the Church of the East as the "second religion" of the ʿAbbasid state, to use the apt words of Jean-Maurice Fiey.[155]

A particularly significant moment in this respect was the transfer of the seat of the catholicos to Baghdad during the reign of patriarch Timothy I (r. 780–832).[156] This restored an arrangement that had existed between the catholicoi and the Sasanian kings before the conquest and which had bestowed on the church so much power and wealth.[157] An institution like this that flour-

[153] Payne, *State of Mixture.*

[154] Wood, "Christians in Umayyad Iraq." Even during the conquests, it seems that the East Syrians were eager to accommodate Muslim rule, possibly given their long experience dealing with the Sasanians. Mār Emmeh, the East Syrian bishop of Nineveh, reportedly gave provisions and land to Muslim armies. In reward, he received a letter of investiture as catholicos from none other than ʿAlī b. Abī Ṭālib, which he showed to Muslim officers as a sign of his authority; see Landron, "Chrétiens de l'Est (nestoriens) et musulmans," 198; Robinson, *Empire and Elites*, 18.

[155] Fiey, *Chrétiens syriaques*, 29. The foundation of a new capital at Baghdad shifted the administration of many churches to the east, not just for the East Syrians. In the *life* of the martyr Christopher of Antioch, all the candidates for the Melkite patriarchate of Antioch are said to have come from Iraq, not Syria; see Zayyāt, "Vie du patriarche melkite"; Wood, "Christian Authority under the Early Abbasids." On tensions between the East Syrians and the Copts in Egypt during the ʿAbbasid period as a result of the East Syrians' privileged relationship with the Muslim state, see Meinardus, "Nestorians in Egypt," 117.

[156] On Timothy, see Berti, *Timoteo I*, 170–93.

[157] On continuities in the church's interactions with the state between the Sasanian and Islamic periods, see Morony, *Iraq*, 332–72; also the useful if flawed overview in Young, *Patriarch, Shah, and Caliph.* On the Sasanian experience as providing good preparation for the East Syrians under Islam, see Frenschkowski, "Christianity," 466.

ished through partnerships with the religious other was not likely to promote the cult of neomartyrs—though it bears repeating that the Church of the East produced many martyrologies in Sasanian times. The decline in enthusiasm for martyrologies despite the constant experience of living under non-Christian rulers is difficult to understand and deserves further reflection.

At their core, the neomartyrs were symbols of protest against Muslim power: symbols of a Christian society that was alienated from its rulers and wished to keep the floodgates of change firmly shut. At least among the clerical elite who were responsible for writing saints' *lives*, there was little utility in promoting ideas that might upset the balance of power between church and empire. In this sense, one suspects that the response of the Church of the East in Iraq to the rise of Islam was very much opposite to that of the Melkites in Syria and Palestine. What is more, the history of Muslim settlement in Iraq—in which most new emigrants sequestered themselves in new cities such as Kūfa, Baṣra, Wāsiṭ, and Mosul—guaranteed that social mixing between Muslims and non-Muslims was less common.[158] Indeed, in Syria—the heartland of the Melkite Church—there were virtually no garrison towns, and the Muslims by and large settled in existing communities, often side by side with Christians.[159] By contrast, in Iraq—the heartland of the Church of the East—the two groups were more segregated and, therefore, may have avoided the kinds of routine social interaction that stirred violence and provoked martyrdom, particularly in the seventh and early eighth centuries.

One final factor may have made the neomartyrs especially popular among the Melkites as opposed to other communities. It is important to remember that monasteries such as Mar Saba and St. Catherine's were very cosmopolitan places, even in the early Middle Ages (Figure 5.2). Although they were no longer in the political orbit of Byzantium, they continued to attract large numbers of Byzantine monks, who prayed, studied, and lived alongside local Arabic- and Syriac-speaking Christians. It is hard to know the precise balance between foreigners and locals in these places, but the medieval *typikon*, or monastic rule, of Mar Saba gives an impression of how things may have been. It states that the head of the monastery had to be a Greek speaker, while his stewards had to be Syriac speakers.[160] The *typikon* was compiled centuries after the conquests at a time when the only native Greek speakers in Palestine were

[158]On Arab settlement in Iraq, see Bulliet, *Conversion to Islam*, 80–91; Morony, *Iraq*, 236–53; Hoyland, *In God's Path*, 161. I owe this insight to conversation with Patricia Crone.

[159]Whitcomb, "Amṣār in Syria?"; on al-Ṭabarīya, founded as a *miṣr* according to the sources but with no archaeological evidence of this: Avni, *Byzantine-Islamic Transition*, 72.

[160]Kurtz, "Review of A. Dmitrijevskij. *Die Klosterregeln des hl. Sabbas*," 170; discussion in McCormick, *Survey of the Holy Land*, 142–43.

probably imports from abroad. One assumes, therefore, that their numbers at Mar Saba were not insignificant. Unlike the local brethren, these Byzantine monks did not hail from communities where Christians and Muslims rubbed shoulders, spoke the same languages, and intermarried as they did in the cities of the Levant. They came from across the frontier in the Byzantine Empire where Muslims were not a day-to-day reality but, rather, treated as bitter enemies lurking in the distance.[161] Such monks may have had a harder time perceiving the virtues of accommodation—that is, a worldview predicated on the pursuit of *convivencia* in religiously mixed environments. These were precisely the kinds of monks who probably found the messages of the martyrologies most appealing and may have been responsible for writing some of our texts. Indeed, expatriate monks may have even spread the cults of the neomartyrs outside the caliphate. There are countless examples of such monks—including Michael Synkellos and the Graptoi brothers—who moved between Palestine and Byzantium in this period. These monks were probably active in introducing saints such as Peter of Capitolias into the *Synaxarium of Constantinople* or rewriting texts such as the *Life of Bacchus* in Byzantine manuscripts.[162]

The cult of the neomartyrs was a truly cosmopolitan affair, and the monks who promoted it forged connections that spanned the caliphate and beyond. In addition to ties between Palestine and Constantinople, there were networks connecting greater Syria and the Caucasus. The oldest surviving manuscript of the *Life of Abo of Tiflīs*, for example, written in the tenth century, does not come from Georgia where Abo died and where his biography was first written. Rather, it comes from Mt. Sinai, where Georgian monks are known to have been acticve throughout late antiquity and the Middle Ages.[163] A smaller but extremely significant network is the one that connected Palestine to al-Andalus, as we see in the *life* of the Sabaite monk George, who was martyred

[161] For Byzantine views of Islam, see Khoury, *Théologiens byzantins*; Sahas, "Byzantine Anti-Islamic Literature." Michael Penn (*Envisioning Islam*, 55–56, 112–13, 119, etc.) has suggested that Syriac-speaking Christians held nuanced, tolerant views of Islam because they lived alongside Muslims, whereas Byzantine Christians tended to have simplistic, intolerant views of Islam because they did not. Franke ("Freiwilligen Märtyrer"; cf. Colbert, *Martyrs of Córdoba*, 15) remarked that the Córdoba martyrs became more famous in the north of Iberia because churches in Christian-controlled areas could more freely polemicize against the Muslim enemy than churches in Muslim-controlled areas in the south. In other words, geography matters deeply for understanding the appeal of the cults of the neomartyrs.

[162] For the feast of Peter in Constantinople: Delehaye, *Synaxarium*, 105–6; *PG*, cxvii, 85–86. On the Byzantine manuscripts of the *Life of Bacchus*: *CMR*, i, 599; and Byzantine hymns in Bacchus's honor: Dēmētrakopoulos, "Hagios Bakchos," 351–62.

[163] Garitte, *Catalogue des manuscrits géorgiens littéraires du Mont Sinaï*, 41–42; *CMR*, i, 366; on Georgians at Sinai, Johnson, "Social Presence of Greek," 81–84.

Figure 5.2. St. Catherine's Monastery, Mount Sinai, Egypt, sixth century. Photo: Christian C. Sahner.

in Córdoba in 852.[164] According to Eulogius, George first ventured west from Palestine ("a celestial dwelling on a foreign shore") in order to seek donations for his beleaguered community from the Christians of Africa.[165] Unfortunately, he found the church in Africa "beaten by the blow of tyrants," so he headed to Spain in pursuit of greener pastures. Fluent in Arabic and Greek (though not in Latin, as scholars once thought), George did not find the money he was looking for in Córdoba, but he did find friendship with several local Christians, including Aurelius, Sabigotho, Felix, and Litiosa, with whom he perished.

[164] *CSM*, ii, 416–30, esp. 425–30; for discussion, see Jiménez Pedrajas, "Jorge, Aurelio y Natalia"; Levy-Rubin and Kedar, "Neglected Sabaite Martyr"; Kedar, "Latin in Ninth-Century Mar Sabas?" More generally, *BS*, vi, 544–45; Dozy, *Spanish Islam*, 303; Simonet, *Historia*, 428–33, 477–80; Cagigas, *Mozárabes*, 215, 490; Colbert, *Martyrs of Córdoba*, 142, 235–42, 345; Millet-Gérard, *Chrétiens mozarabes*, 159–66; Wolf, *Christian Martyrs*, 29; Coope, *Martyrs of Córdoba*, 21–22, 28, 39–40, 53, 67, 71–72; Pochoshajew, *Märtyrer von Cordoba*, 179–81; McCormick, *Origins of the European Economy*, 928.

[165] On earlier Greek-speaking monks on the Iberian Peninsula, see Maya Sánchez, *Vitas sanctorum patrum Emeretensium*, 25, 31. I am grateful to Juan Pedro Monferrer-Sala for drawing this to my attention.

George was not the only martyr in the early Islamic period whose travels brought him into contact with far-flung Christian communities: Vahan of Gołt'n spent his formative years in Armenia before dying in Ruṣāfa; Romanus hailed from Anatolia but was incarcerated in Baghdad and killed in Raqqa; and Constantine-Kakhay was reared in Georgia but imprisoned and executed in Sāmarrā'. Yet George of Mar Saba was unique for the distance he traveled en route to his death, as well as the connections he forged between two famous hotbeds of martyrology-writing: Mar Saba in Palestine and the church of Córdoba. There is no written evidence from Mar Saba itself about George. But it is not inconceivable that news of George's death eventually made its way to Palestine. Eulogius states that George

> composed for his brothers, his relatives, and all the citizens of his country a brief account of his own martyrdom among his comrades, which he sent to me to polish, lest its rather rough style diminish faith in his actions among those to whom he sent it.[166]

Eulogius claims to quote verbatim from George's account in the *Memoriale sanctorum*, and indeed, he leads us to believe that the text was eventually dispatched to the east. If George's story did indeed reach Palestine, this would prove in dramatic and definitive fashion that the cult of the neomartyrs was a phenomenon that truly stretched across the early Islamic world.[167]

Although the Melkites of greater Syria played a starring role in creating neomartyr cults, the phenomenon of martyrdom itself existed in many parts of the Muslim *oikoumene*. It was created not only by a common legal regime that treated diverse groups of Christians in a similar way, especially when it came to apostasy and blasphemy. It was also created by a common set of texts, ideas, liturgical practices, and people flowing from al-Andalus to the Caucasus.

IV. CONCLUSION

To sum up, what types of Christian communities were most likely to be drawn to the cults of neomartyrs? It goes without saying that the cults themselves are inseparable from the clergy who promoted them, especially monks. Even if the laity are depicted in the sources, we have no explicitly lay eyewitnesses to the martyrs that could help us measure the gap between their views and

[166] *CSM*, ii, 426. For George's account as redacted by Eulogius, see *CSM*, ii, 426–28.
[167] Monferrer-Sala, "Mitografía hagiomartirial," 429.

those of their "shepherds." We must assume that some lay Christians disapproved of the messages enshrined in the texts. These may have included Christians who lived alongside Muslims in mixed cities, Christian aristocrats who profited from high-level collaboration with the Muslim authorities, or Christians who belonged to religiously mixed families and were not particularly unsettled by intimate contact with Islam. By the same token, there must have been other lay Christians who enthusiastically embraced the messages of the martyrologies. These may have included individuals in rural areas with little practical experience of Islam; elites who witnessed their status diminished by the coming of a new Muslim order; or those who simply saw in Islam a false, competing faith. At the same time, as I argued in the case of Córdoba, there must have been many lay Christians who did not fit neatly into either group, who saw both positive and negative elements in the message of the martyrs.

The same applies to clergy more generally: ascetics in rural areas may have found these harrowing tales of apostates and blasphemers more appealing by dint of their own psychological orientation—especially their commitment to spiritual warfare—and their geographic isolation. Secular clergy in urban areas, meanwhile, may have seen in these stories a threat to a social order they were responsible for upholding: that is, a culture that traded tribute for security and subservience for prosperity under their Muslim rulers. They had little time for rabble-rousing behavior like that which is lionized in the texts. These differences may have also mapped onto Christian sects as a whole. Some communities such as the East Syrians had little interest in new martyrs. This may have been because of their unique capacity to thrive under non-Christian imperial powers, first the Sasanians and later the ʿAbbasids. Other communities such as the Melkites promoted new martyrs with gusto. This may have been because of their ties to the Byzantine emperor and imperial church and the attendant sense of disorientation that followed when these ties were put under strain or cut altogether by the conquests. For such a community, tales of combat, resistance, and triumph over Islam must have held a special appeal. This helps explain why, in a sense, the Melkites did indeed "invent" the cult of the neomartyrs, even as other Christian communities produced new saints, albeit in more modest numbers.

CONCLUSION

Making of the Muslim World

In these final pages, let us turn to the chronology of the martyrdoms. As we have seen, it is exceptionally difficult to date the composition of most texts. This is not only because most authors are anonymous but also because the manuscript traditions of many texts are patchy and opaque. It is often possible, however, to identify when a martyr died thanks to details in the sources or to contextual information furnished by Muslim literature. On the basis of these, we can plot a rough history of Christian martyrdom during the early Islamic period. What does this reveal about the ebb and flow of bigger processes, including religious and cultural change?

Very few Christians who died during the seventh century were venerated as saints. This small group includes the Sixty Martyrs of Gaza and George the Black. This is striking, since there was no shortage of violence against Christians at this time, especially in the midst of the conquest. But when the dust of the campaigns settled and the Arabs turned their attention to the business of governing, relations between Muslims and non-Muslims proved to be generally peaceful. This is because for most of the seventh century, the Muslim elite was preoccupied with prosecuting civil wars against itself, as well as wars of conquest against foreign neighbors. In these trying and distracted times, the Arab rulers of the Middle East were usually content to allow the subject population to live as it wished, provided it paid tribute in the form of taxes and recognized the general authority of the Muslim regime. Given this laissez-faire approach, religious tensions were not particularly pronounced, and this probably led to lower levels of violence relative to later periods.

In some respects, interreligious contact was actually quite common at this time, since many non-Muslims came to live among Muslims after the conquests had ended. In other respects, however, these non-Muslims were cut off from their old kinship networks when they settled in Muslim areas, and therefore, they were more likely to embrace Islam and assimilate into Arab culture. This was especially true of certain socially vulnerable populations, including the massive numbers of slaves and concubines who found their way into Muslim homes, as well as male migrants who flocked to Muslim-dominated cities in search of work. Most Christians had more limited interactions with the conquerors. These were mediated by the presence of garrison cities (Ar. *amṣār*) where the emigrants put down roots, particularly in places such as Iraq, Iran, Egypt, and North Africa. Such settlements were designed to quarantine Muslims from the surrounding non-Muslim populations, lest they lose their distinctive social identity amid a sea of difference. There were certain parts of the caliphate where *amṣār* did not exist—such as the Marw Oasis in modern Turkmenistan—and in these places, Arab Muslims mixed freely with non-Arab non-Muslims. Their interactions gave rise to hybrid cultures, languages, and even religious practices that would have a profound impact on the development of Islamic civilization down the centuries. But in predominantly Christian areas of the empire where garrison cities and other Muslim settlements often separated the conquerors from the conquered, segregation ruled the day. Lower levels of intimate contact in the seventh century probably reduced the number of violent encounters between the two communities. Not only did this lead to fewer martyrdoms, but it also created social conditions in which Christians did not necessarily feel as drawn to stories of protest and resistance as they would in later years.

The turn of the eighth century is often regarded as an inflection point in Islamic history, and this seems to have had profound consequences for relations between the Muslim ruling class and the Christian subject population. After decades of internal tumult, the Muslim elite under ʿAbd al-Malik (r. 65–86/685–705) focused its energies for the first time on fashioning a distinctively Islamic empire out of the diverse realms they had seized over the preceding decades. The signs of this political and religious shift are well known: the demolition of Christian and Jewish holy sites and the erection of extravagant Muslim sanctuaries (such as the Dome of the Rock; Figure C.1); the minting of new dirhams, which banished old Byzantine and Sasanian iconography in favor of the aniconic Muslim creed; the alleged expulsion of Greek and Persian speakers from state service; and the proliferation of new, overtly antagonistic laws against non-Muslims.[1] This was an elite program imposed from the top down, but it seems to have sensitized all levels of society to basic religious and cultural differences that had not existed before or were not considered as important. One consequence of this zeitgeist was new concerns about apostasy and, to a lesser extent, blasphemy.

Given the changes under ʿAbd al-Malik and his successors, it is not surprising to detect an uptick in the reported cases of martyrdom after the year 700. These were scattered across the eastern realms of the caliphate, including the martyrdoms of David of Dwin, Muʿādh the Taghlibite, Peter of Capitolias, the

[1] On these new laws, see now Sahner, "First Iconoclasm in Islam," 27–34.

Figure C.1. Dome of the Rock, Jerusalem, ca. 691–92. Photo: Christian C. Sahner.

Sixty Martyrs of Jerusalem, Vahan of Gołt'n, Eustathius son of Marianus, and ʿAbd al-Masīḥ. Fred Donner has described the beginning of the eighth century as a time of transition from a community of "believers" with capacious and relatively inchoate ideas about who belonged inside the *umma* to a community of "Muslims" with a much firmer sectarian identity and higher standards of belonging.[2] Many of these ideas were formulated in direct opposition to Islam's religious competitors, including Christianity, Judaism, and Zoroastrianism. Thus, what it meant to be a "Muslim" was increasingly defined in opposition to what it meant to be a "non-Muslim." That this process of negative self-definition should have also manifested itself in increased rates of violence against non-Muslims is not out of the question. Likewise, if we assume that some martyrologies were written not long after the events they purport to describe, it is not unusual that Christians felt compelled to commemorate the victims of the new culture of religious tension. Indeed, martyrs' cults may have helped Christians make sense of their situation at a moment when interreligious tensions were on the rise and the state was using its coercive power to

[2]Robinson, *ʿAbd al-Malik*, 113–19; Donner, *Muhammad and the Believers*, 194–224.

subjugate non-Muslims in a way it had not done previously during the seventh century.

The largest number of new martyrs died during the first fifty years of ʿAbbasid rule. The majority of these hailed from greater Syria, particularly Palestine, though outliers also came from the Caucasus and Anatolia. These included Cyrus of Ḥarrān, Christopher the Persian, Elias of Helioupolis, the women martyrs of Ḥimṣ, Layth b. Maḥatta of the tribe of Tanūkh, Romanus, Abo of Tiflīs, Arčʿil, Hamazasp and Sahak, the Twenty Martyrs of Mar Saba, and Anthony al-Qurashī. One of these died under al-Manṣūr (r. 136–58/754–75), six under al-Mahdī (r. 158–69/775–85), three under al-Hādī (r. 169–70/785–86), and twenty-two under Hārūn al-Rashīd (r. 170–93/786–809, including the Twenty Martyrs). Despite the large concentration of saints during the second half of the eighth century, it is important to stress that there was nothing systematic about their deaths. Indeed, a campaign to execute apostates and blasphemers was no more apparent under the ʿAbbasids than it had been under the Umayyads. What is more, we have ample evidence of ʿAbbasid caliphs selectively patronizing and promoting Christianity, alongside examples of extreme violence.[3] Therefore, how can we explain the apparent uptick in martyrdom at this time?

Even if it is impossible to pin the martyrdoms on any one official or piece of legislation, it is clear that the surge in violence reflected the changing position and perception of Christians in early ʿAbbasid society. Several explanations may provide context. First, Jean-Maurice Fiey once suggested that the harsh treatment of Christians began in earnest under al-Manṣūr in response to the ongoing wars between the Arabs and the Byzantines.[4] That is, Christians were increasingly regarded as a fifth column in ʿAbbasid society, as a source of potential treason that had to be checked and suppressed. Robert Hoyland has suggested something similar with respect to the middle Umayyad period, when certain discriminatory laws against non-Muslims came into existence in reaction to the failed siege of Constantinople, at least according to one claim in the *Chronicle of Michael the Syrian*.[5] These anxieties lingered on in early Islamic apocalyptic tradition, in which Christians were often portrayed as potential backstabbers of their Muslim neighbors.[6]

Whatever the actual merits of these fears, the anxieties they provoked were real. These, in turn, may have fueled violence. It is no coincidence that several

[3] To name but one of many examples, al-Manṣūr is said to have erected a church in Damascus: Bashear, "Qibla Musharriqa," 267.

[4] Fiey, *Chrétiens syriaques*, 27–28; and chapter 5, sec. III.

[5] Hoyland, *In God's Path*, 198; cf. Chabot, *Chronique*, ii, 488 (Fr.); iv, 456 (Syr.).

[6] Cook, *Muslim Apocalyptic*, 69–71, 74, 311, 316, 366.

martyrs were killed on suspicion of having been Byzantine spies. The situation under the early ʿAbbasids mirrored what existed under the Sasanians centuries before, who sporadically accused Christians of sympathizing with the Byzantine Empire. Christian elites were quick to disavow any loyalty to a power other than the Sasanian court, but the king of kings—like the caliph—found it hard to believe that local Christians were not working to support their coreligionists in a rival state. This was especially true during times of heightened tensions between Ctesiphon and Constantinople.[7]

The apparent increase in martyrdoms during the second half of the eighth century may also reflect a new campaign aimed at implementing laws against apostasy and blasphemy. Even if such laws existed in the Umayyad period, they may not have been enforced as vigorously. In fact, it may be the case that formal death penalty prohibitions on apostasy and blasphemy—neither of which are mentioned explicitly in the Qur'an—were products of the ʿAbbasid period and only later projected into the distant past. Luke Yarbrough has recently suggested something similar regarding prohibitions on non-Muslims serving in the Muslim state, which jurists dated to the first Islamic century in order to fashion an aura of antiquity and authority around them.[8] Through careful analysis of the relevant *ḥadīth*, he has traced these rules not to the reign of ʿUmar b. al-Khaṭṭāb (r. 13–23/634–44) or ʿUmar b. ʿAbd al-ʿAzīz (r. 99–101/717–20), as the Islamic tradition often claims, but to late Umayyad and early ʿAbbasid times.

Underlying the apparent surge in martyrdom may have been even deeper changes in the fabric of Middle Eastern society. It may be no coincidence that violence against Christians was on the rise at precisely the moment when Muslims and non-Muslims first came into contact and competition as members of an integrated society with vertical divisions, rather than as a ruling class of conquerors and a complex taxpaying base with horizontal divisions.[9] Muslims and Christians around the year 800 were no longer mainly distinguished from each other as Arabs and non-Arabs, as city dwellers and village dwellers, as soldiers and peasants, as they had been through much of the Umayyad period. In fact, these tidy divisions were collapsing as non-Muslims entered the *umma* in droves, as Muslim settlement of the countryside increased, and as Islam reached ever more into the peasantry and subelites. In this world, contact and competition among old Muslims, new Muslims, and non-Muslims was on the rise and must have had an irritant effect on the social order. This seems to have led to new concerns about social and religious differentiation,

[7] Brock, "Divided Loyalties."
[8] Yarbrough, "Upholding God's Rule."
[9] I owe this language to Luke Yarbrough.

and these, in turn, may have led to higher rates of violence. We can see this especially in the martyrdom accounts of Arab Christians such as Muʿādh the Taghlibite, ʿAbd al-Masīḥ, and Layth b. Maḥaṭṭa of the Tanūkh, who fell victim to changing ideas about the possibility of remaining fully Arab and at the same time fully Christian. Maintaining this identity, which, as Henri Lammens argued long ago, was very possible during the seventh century, became a more significant and perilous balancing act in the eighth century, when Arabs were increasingly expected to convert.[10]

What is more, the ʿAbbasids seem to have adopted a more brazenly Islamic style of rule than their Umayyad predecessors. This may reflect the bias of the mainstream Arab Muslim historiography, some of which was written in ʿAbbasid times with the goal of demonizing the vanquished Umayyad foe.[11] But even taking this into account, it is clear that the ʿAbbasids came to power pledging to purge the empire of impiety and corruption. This campaign may also have manifested itself in harsher attitudes toward non-Muslims. Indeed, what it meant to be a good Muslim ruler was increasingly correlated with the suppression and humiliation of those who refused to embrace "true religion"—whether their unbelief lay inside or outside the Islamic tent. If this is so, it accords well with the recent argument of John Turner, who has suggested that "Islamic orthodoxy" was established and asserted in the early ʿAbbasid period through certain forms of religious and social exclusion.[12] Within the Muslim community, the *miḥna* of al-Maʾmūn and his successors (218–37/833–52) was the most prominent example of this strategy in action. But persecutory behavior toward Christians and other non-Muslims may have been another. Christians responded to this experience by commemorating the most pious of their dead brethren as martyrs.

It is easy to imagine how the hagiographers' message of protest and resistance might have gained traction among Christians at this time. The *lives* of the martyrs provided a portrait of a world that appealed to churches facing tougher circumstances. The texts vilified Muslims, condemned converts as turncoats, and urged their readers to withdraw into Christian cocoons. At a moment when the faithful were taxed but left alone—as was largely the case during the seventh century—new martyrs had limited symbolic appeal. But at a moment when Christians not only were taxed but also imagined themselves to be living under the threat of mass conversion and assimilation—as was the case from the late eighth century onward—martyrs took on greater signifi-

[10] Lammens, *Moʿâwiya*, 419–42.

[11] Indeed, the Umayyads also employed religious rhetoric to justify their rule: Crone and Hinds, *God's Caliph*, 24–42.

[12] Turner, *Inquisition in Early Islam*. I owe this language to Luke Yarbrough.

cance. This, in turn, encouraged the commemoration of new saints and the composition of new hagiographic texts.

Martyrdom declined precipitously in the mid-ninth century, which is surprising for several reasons. For one, the reign of the ʿAbbasid caliph al-Mutawakkil (r. 232–47/847–61) is often regarded as having been an exceptionally difficult time for *dhimmīs*.[13] His reign is remembered for the imposition of strict Sunnī orthodoxy, which led to the marginalization of a wide range of religious competitors, including Muʿtazilīs and Shīʿīs, not to mention Jews and Christians. Yet the written evidence suggests that only one martyr died during al-Mutawakkil's reign: the Georgian saint Constantine-Kakhay, who was executed at Sāmarrāʾ in 853. The Córdoba martyrs were also executed at this time, but al-Andalus lay far beyond the reach of the ʿAbbasid court, and it is unlikely that the caliph's policies exerted any direct influence there. If there is a connection between the reign of al-Mutawakkil and what happened in Córdoba, this owes to a widespread zeitgeist—stemming from parallel experiences of Islamization and Arabization in two different regions under Muslim control—rather than a single law.[14]

Second, the majority of these later martyrs were killed along the western fringe of the Muslim-controlled world, including the martyrs of Córdoba and Syracuse.[15] There were also several cases of martyrdom in the east in the tenth century, including Christopher of Antioch and George the New. Chapter 3 considered the timing of the Córdoba martyrs incident in relation to demographic changes in al-Andalus like those that had unsettled relations between Muslims and non-Muslims in the east a century earlier. Indeed, we must remember that the Iberian Peninsula was conquered only in 92/711, a full seventy years after the capture of Palestine, Syria, and Egypt. Thus, it may have been decades behind in experiencing the same kinds of shifts that had brought old Muslims, new Muslims, and non-Muslims into competition in the east between 750 and 800. Al-Andalus had its own martyrdom moment like Palestine and Syria, but it occurred on "tape delay" due to the later onset of Islamization and Arabization.

Despite their early success, the cults of the new martyrs seem to have petered out during the tenth century and beyond. Although Christian scribes continued to copy biographies of martyrs (indeed, many of our manuscripts date from the central and high Middle Ages), and although churches continued

[13]Fiey, *Chrétiens syriaques*, 83–105; Cohen, *Under Crescent and Cross*, 63; Levy-Rubin, *From Surrender to Coexistence*, 103–12; Penn, *Envisioning Islam*, 94.

[14]Lapiedra Gutiérrez, "Mártires de Córdoba."

[15]The Forty-Two Martyrs of Amorion, who died in 845, are an exception, though they were captured inside Byzantium.

to include new martyrs in liturgical calendars, they created very few new martyrs after 800. The major exception to this rule was the new martyrs in Egypt under the Mamlūks and Ottomans, but there was nothing comparable to the scale of what occurred earlier in Syria or al-Andalus.[16] The decline is also apparent across the border in Byzantium, where the foreign neomartyrs were rapidly overshadowed by local neomartyrs of Iconoclasm. Not until the early modern period did Christians under Muslim rule write biographies of new martyrs in large numbers once again, though this time with the Ottomans in place of the Umayyads and ʿAbbasids. How can we explain the apparent shift?

For one, it is possible that Christians and Muslims achieved a more stable, peaceful modus vivendi over time. While conversion from Christianity to Islam continued throughout the centuries—probably accelerating during spasms of social unrest and violence[17]—Christians may have become more despondent toward this threat. While they certainly did not smile on the changes happening around them, they probably saw religious and cultural change as unavoidable realities of daily life. The routinization of these processes, in turn, may have made them less appealing subjects for hagiography and polemic. By the tenth century, there was no point in praying for the complete disappearance of Islam, for the apostasy of the countless Christians who had traded their churches for mosques, or for the conversion of the caliph to Christianity. To one degree or another, those were real desires in the earliest Islamic period, but as time went on, the pressing question for Christian elites shifted from conversion and assimilation to theological differentiation. Although the earliest Christian dialogues about Islam were written around the time of the first martyrologies, as martyrology disappeared, dialogue and debate took over as the dominant literary response to the new religion. Especially in the salon culture of ʿAbbasid Baghdad, the pressing task turned to discrediting Islam by critiquing its fundamental doctrines—not protesting the social consequences of conversion and assimilation. The disappearance of martyrology is not unlike what happened to apocalyptic literature, which was once a vital genre among the Christians of the caliphate but more or less petered out after the passage of the first Islamic century.[18]

[16] El-Leithy, "Coptic Culture," 101–39; Zaborowski, *Coptic Martyrdom of John of Phanijōit*; Shenoda, "Lamenting Islam," 121–71; Armanios, *Coptic Christianity in Ottoman Egypt*, 41–90.

[17] See esp. introduction, n. 29; chapter 1, n. 4; and the rebellions mentioned in chapter 4, sec. IV.

[18] Sahner, "Old Martyrs, New Martyrs," 112; for the Syriac material, see Penn, *Envisioning Islam*, 33. There are several tenth-century apocalypses from Egypt that complicate the picture: Papaconstantinou, "Coptic after the Arab Conquest"; Mikhail, *From Byzantine to Islamic Egypt*, 99–103.

One also wonders whether the cults of the neomartyrs became a liability for Christians over time. In moments of increased mixing, a socially subversive saint's cult was more likely to attract negative attention from lower-class Muslims, who lived cheek-to-jowl with their non-Muslim neighbors. They might be tempted to notify a fellow Muslim official, who in turn might be tempted to suppress the cult. No Muslim would have been pleased to discover that churches were venerating criminals who had converted from Christianity to Islam and back, apostates who had abandoned Islam for Christianity, or blasphemers who had viciously attacked the Prophet. Indeed, we know that Muslims of the period were not entirely indifferent to the writings of their Christian subjects, especially when it came to the representation of the Islamic faith. The *History of the Patriarchs of Alexandria* states that an Umayyad governor of Egypt investigated Christian books for possible insults against Islam, including a Gospel translated into Arabic, books of alchemy, and festal letters.[19] Given this and given that the biographies of martyrs were by definition antagonistic toward Islam, Christians may have started to pursue less aggressive genres of literature that were conducive to living alongside Muslims. Christians were free to air their grievances in private, of course, but airing them in public through hagiography, on feast days, and in pilgrimages may have been too great a risk to their own security.

Today, the new martyrs of the early medieval period are all but invisible in the spiritual life of most Middle Eastern churches. For the Melkites, the process may have begun as early as the tenth century, when their liturgical customs were brought in line with those of Constantinople, as the work of Daniel Galadza has recently shown.[20] This seems to have caused many local feasts to disappear from the calendar and to be replaced by feasts imported from the imperial capital. In the modern day, it is telling that new martyrs generally do not appear in *synaxaria*; their cult sites are no longer active; and their relics are nearly impossible to track down. Living memory of the martyrs carries on in a few places—such as the Cathedral of Córdoba, whose choir stalls and tabernacle chapel are adorned with images of the saints from the sixteenth and eighteenth centuries, and Tbilisi, where the martyr Abo is still celebrated as the city's patron saint. As for nearly everyone else, we can gauge their anonymity using a book published by the Antiochene Orthodox archimandrite Tūmā Bīṭār in 1995: *al-Qiddīsūn al-mansīyūn fī 'l-turāth al-anṭākī* (*The Forgotten Saints in the Antiochene Tradition*).[21] The title of Bīṭār's book sums up the

[19] Evetts, "History of the Patriarchs," 51.
[20] Galadza, *Liturgy and Byzantinization in Jerusalem.*
[21] Bīṭār, *al-Qiddīsūn al-mansīyūn*, 188–95 (Anthony al-Qurashī), 249–52 (Peter of Capitolias),

dwindling of the martyrs' cults in the present and the fact that their message failed to resonate among Middle Eastern Christians down the ages.

Throughout this book, we have seen the manner in which martyrs helped the Christians of the Middle East, al-Andalus, and the Caucasus create new forms of identity following the Arab conquests. It is worth noting that Christians were not the only group that relied on memories of violence to make sense of their situation. Around the same time that Christian hagiographers were composing biographies of martyrs, Shīʿīs and other sympathetic Muslims were narrating stories about the deaths of their own saints. These martyrs were members of the Prophet's family—often descendants of his cousin and son-in-law ʿAlī b. Abī Ṭālib—who had been killed in the political tumult of the seventh and eighth centuries.[22] Like the Christians, the Shīʿīs believed that their saints had been unjustly executed for their beliefs. They too saw them as victims of persecution at the hands of a godless state, one that was bent on dethroning the true leaders of the *umma*. Several classic examples of Muslim martyrology in this vein include the *Maqātil al-ṭālibīyīn* of the Sunnī Abū ʾl-Faraj al-Iṣfahānī (d. 356/967), a collection of stories about the death of ʿAlī and his descendants; the *Kitāb al-rijāl* of al-Kishshī (d. ca. 360/970), a biographical dictionary of individuals who transmitted *ḥadīth* from the Shīʿī imams, including many who were martyred; and the *Kitāb al-miḥan* of Abū ʾl-ʿArab al-Tamīmī (d. 333/945), another Sunnī who took an interest in the deaths of pious Muslims, some of them members of the Prophet's family.[23]

This tradition of Muslim hagiography did not emerge out of thin air. It drew on a long-standing tradition of martyrological writing in the Middle East that went back to late antiquity. When educated Christians converted to Islam, they did not forget this pre-Islamic literary heritage. Rather, they adapted it to suit their new beliefs and communal norms. This generated striking parallels between the hagiographic literatures of Christians and Muslims, parallels that are sometimes so precise that a common source is impossible to ignore. Sean Anthony has recently identified a good example of this in the Armenian *Life of David of Dwin*.[24] The text states that when the Umayyads crucified David, they erected his cross facing south, presumably in the direction of the *qibla* to symbolize his submission to Islam. Miraculously, however, David's cross turned to the east in the direction of the rising sun and Christian worship,

264–77 (Elias of Helioupolis), 293–300 (ʿAbd al-Masīḥ), 350–51 (Bacchus), 360–65 (Romanus), 373–80 (Christopher of Antioch), 537–38 (George the Black).

[22] Cook, *Martyrdom in Islam*, 52–62.

[23] Abū ʾl-Faraj al-Iṣfahānī, *Maqātil*; al-Ṭūsī, *Rijāl*; Abū ʾl-ʿArab al-Tamīmī, *Kitāb al-miḥan*.

[24] Anthony, *Crucifixion and Death*, 59.

thereby redeeming his death for Christ.[25] In recounting the martyrdom of the ʿAlid rebel Zayd b. ʿAlī in 121/738–39, the Syrian historian Ibn ʿAsākir (d. 571/1176) states that the Umayyads initially crucified him facing the Euphrates. But the following morning, Zayd's cross miraculously turned to the south and faced the *qibla*. His horrific death was thereby redeemed for Islam.[26] It is all but certain that the author of David's biography and the transmitters of Zayd's martyrdom story never knew each another. Yet both groups of storytellers had recourse to the same hagiographic motifs in order to lionize their martyred heroes. A more thorough analysis would doubtless reveal other examples of this scene popping up in Christian and Muslim sources. For now, suffice it to say, the parallels between the martyrdoms of David and Zayd reveal how Christians and Muslims employed a shared religious vocabulary in the early Middle Ages. This, in turn, reflected a consensus about how memories of suffering shored up and even created sectarian identities.

The notion that emergent sects in the medieval Middle East relied on martyrs to configure a sense of community is not so far-fetched. Here, a comparison with the modern period may be helpful. Anyone who walks the streets of Beirut today will know that the city is filled with memorials to different martyrs.[27] They are found in practically every neighborhood, whether Christian, Sunnī, Shīʿī, or Druze. The martyrs, most of whom died during the Lebanese Civil War of 1975 to 1990, are men and women who perished trying to protect their communities' interests, as well as their particular notion of political and religious truth. Despite the preponderance of martyrs, there is no consensus among the Lebanese as to who counts as a "saint." In a city of deep internal divisions—in which entire neighborhoods and city blocks are Balkanized by sect—martyrs play an essential role in reinforcing grievances of the past. These, in turn, shore up the identity of communities in the present, guaranteeing that no one forgets the bloodshed that created them.

One is tempted to imagine that something similar happened in the medieval period, when Christians and Shīʿīs rallied around martyrs in order to accomplish similar goals. Martyrs served many purposes, but in religiously mixed cities such as Córdoba, Damascus, and Baghdad, where differentiation and competition ruled the day, martyrs delimited and fortified the borders of the community. The third-century church father Tertullian once remarked that "the blood of the martyrs is the seed of the church," a statement that could be usefully applied to the "Shīʿī mosque" as well.

[25] Thomson, "David of Dwin," 676.

[26] Ibn ʿAsākir, *Tārīkh*, xix, 479.

[27] Sahner, *Among the Ruins*, 75–76, 180, and for contemporary Damascus, 75–76.

APPENDIX 1

Comparing Christian and Muslim Accounts of Martyrdom

Despite abundant information about the neomartyrs in Christian sources, Muslim texts say virtually nothing about them. How, then, can we measure the chasm between record and representation in the *lives* of the saints when practically all our evidence comes from one side? To help answer this question, this appendix introduces the limited but important information about Christian martyrdom in medieval Muslim sources.

The most famous reference to a Christian neomartyr in a Muslim source is from the *Chronology of Ancient Nations* (Ar. *Kitāb al-āthār al-bāqiya fī ʾl-qurūn al-khāliya*) of the Iranian polymath al-Bīrūnī (d. 442/1050). The goal of his work was to compare the calendars of various ethnic and religious groups in the greater Middle East, including the Melkites of Khwārazm near the Aral Sea.[1] According to al-Bīrūnī, the Melkites celebrated the following feast on December 29:

> The commemoration of Anthony the Martyr: [The Christians] allege that he is Abū Rawḥ, the cousin of Hārūn al-Rashīd, and that he converted to Christianity after having been a Muslim. As a result, Hārūn crucified him. [The Christians] have a long and incredible tale [*qiṣṣa ṭawīla ʿajība*] about him. We have not heard it or read it, or anything like it in the books of reports and histories [*kutub al-akhbār wa-ʾl-tawārīkh*] [which is unsurprising] given that the Christians are a credulous people overly trusting of such things, most especially [stories] connected to their beliefs, not endeavoring in any way to correct the reports or verify the traditions [*taṣḥīḥ al-akhbār wa-ʾl-taḥqīq al-āthār*].[2]

[1] On the history of this community, see Nasrallah, "L'Église melchite," 323–24; and for al-Bīrūnī's description of his sources, see Griveau, "Fêtes des Melchites," 294.

[2] Griveau, "Fêtes des Melchites," 299. Discussion in Griffith, "Christians, Muslims, and Neomartyrs," 204; Vila, "Christian Martyrs," 103–4; Braida and Pelissetti, *Rawḥ al-Qurašī*, 32; Binggeli, "Converting the Caliph," 78–79; Sizgorich, "Christian Eyes Only," 129–30. Al-Bīrūnī mentions one other neomartyr, though without discussing the circumstances of his death. Peter, patriarch of Damascus (Griveau, "Fêtes des Melchites," 302), here commemorated on January 15. For general comment, see Galadza, "al-Biruni's Melkite Calendar."

This is a remarkable anecdote. Not only is it one of a small handful of Muslim references to a Christian neomartyr, but it also makes clear that Muslims and Christians clung to different standards of historical evidence (at least in al-Bīrūnī's eyes). The author contrasts supposedly reliable sources of information—including classical genres of Islamic literature (*akhbār, tawārīkh*)—with supposedly unreliable sources of information—including Christian hagiography. The fundamental question al-Bīrūnī poses—about the possibility of sifting fact from fiction, of corroborating the information with outside sources—still confronts any historian working on the *lives* of the saints.

Despite its importance, al-Bīrūnī's calendar does little to help us establish whether the historical Anthony ever actually lived. Other Muslim sources, however, give us fairly unvarnished reports about individuals who are normally known only through Christian texts. These sources, in turn, can help us verify and contextualize accounts on the Christian side. The single best example is that of Layth b. Maḥaṭṭa, the chief of the Christian tribe of Tanūkh, who was martyred by the caliph al-Mahdī in 780.[3] Information about his death comes from multiple sources, which are translated below:

1. Michael the Syrian, *Chronicle* (d. 1199, Syr.):

> In the year 1090 [= A.D. 780], al-Mahdī came to Aleppo and the Tanūkh who were living in tents around Aleppo came out to meet him. He saw that they were riding Arab horses and were richly decorated. Then someone said to him, "All these people are Christians."[4] He fumed with rage and ordered that they become Muslims. When he threatened them with tortures, around five thousand men became Muslims, but the women were spared. Until now, some of them are found in the churches of the west. One of them, a venerable man by the name of Layth, was martyred [*ashed*].[5]

[3] Nau, *Arabes chrétiens*, 107–8; Tritton, *Non-Muslim Subjects*, 130, which erroneously states that seven thousand Christians were put to death; Fattal, *Statut légal*, 171; Fiey, *Chrétiens syriaques*, 35; Shahîd, *Byzantium and the Arabs in the Fourth Century*, 400–407, 418–32; Shahîd, "Tanūkh," *EI²*, x, 191; Hoyland, *Seeing Islam*, 353; Penn, *Envisioning Islam*, 115–16. For more on al-Mahdī's campaigns against the Christians of Syria, see chapter 1, sec. I.

[4] Palmer ("Messiah and the Mahdi," 72–73) assumes the Tanūkh were mostly non-Chalcedonians (Miaphysites).

[5] Chabot, *Chronique*, iii, 1 (Fr.); iv, 478–79 (Syr.). The report is copied in the slightly later chronicle of Bar Hebraeus: Bedjan, *Chronicon*, 127–32. Before mentioning the Tanūkh, Bar Hebraeus states that al-Mahdī tore down churches that had been built after the Arab conquest—presumably because this was forbidden under the Pact of ʿUmar—including a Chalcedonian church in Aleppo. Bar Hebraeus then mentions that al-Mahdī persecuted Manichaeans in northern Syria. Were his actions against the Tanūkh part of a wider campaign against non-Muslims? See Bedjan, *Chronicon*, 126. Compare this with the *Chronicle of Zuqnīn*'s account of persecution in the Jazīra

2. Inscription on the wall of the Church of St. Sergius, Ehnesh, southwestern Turkey (ca. late eighth century, Syr.):

And in the year 1091, the commander of the faithful, Mahdī came and entered as far as Giḥūn and he returned, ordering that the churches be destroyed and the Tanūkh become Muslims.[6]

3. al-Balādhurī, *Futūḥ al-buldān* (d. 279/892, Ar.):

The camp [*ḥāḍir*] of Qinnasrīn belonged to the tribe of Tanūkh, since they had first come to Syria and settled in tents of goat's hair and later built [permanent] abodes there. Abū ʿUbayda summoned them to Islam, and some of them converted, while the Banū Salīḥ b. Ḥulwān b. ʿImrān b. al-Ḥāf b. Quḍāʿa remained Christians. Certain sons of Yazīd b. Ḥunayn al-Ṭāʾī from Antioch told me that according to their elders, some of the inhabitants of the camp converted to Islam during the caliphate of the commander of the faithful al-Mahdī, and it was written on their hands in green, "Qinnasrīn."[7]

4. al-Yaʿqūbī, *Tārīkh* (d. 284/897, Ar.):

[Al-Mahdī] departed until he reached the frontier, then set out for Jerusalem where he remained for several days, then left. When he reached the *jund* of Qinnasrīn, the Tanūkh greeted him with gifts saying, "We are your maternal uncles, O Commander of the Faithful!" He said in response, "Who are these people?" It was said to him, "The Tanūkh, ultimately belonging to the Quḍāʿa," and their situation and great numbers were described to him. It was also said, "All of them are Christians." Al-Mahdī replied, "I do not accept your [professed] kinship with me!" A single man among them apostatized [*wa-irtadda minhum rajul*], so al-Mahdī beheaded him. The rest became frightened and stuck with Islam.[8]

around the same time, including "Christians, pagans [*ḥanpē*], Jews, Samaritans, worshippers of fire and the sun, Zoroastrians [*magūshē*], Muslims [*mashlmānē*], Sabaeans [*ḥarranāyē*, "Ḥarrānians"], and Manichaeans" (Chabot, *Chronicon anonymum Pseudo-Dionysianum*, ii, 316).

[6] Chabot, "Notes d'épigraphie," 286–87 (when Chabot visited in 1897, the village was still majority Christian, mostly Armenian). Palmer, "Messiah and the Mahdi"; Palmer, *West Syrian Chronicles*, 71–74.

[7] al-Balādhurī, *Liber expugnationis regionum*, 144–45. The anecdote jumps in time from Abū ʿUbayda in the seventh century to al-Mahdī in the eighth. The meaning of writing in green is unclear. There are other examples of Christians being marked in similar ways, as when Christians in Egypt were reportedly branded with an image of a lion: al-Maqrīzī, *Khiṭaṭ* (1853), ii, 493; and neck-sealing: Robinson, "Neck-Sealing in Early Islam."

[8] al-Yaʿqūbī, *Tārīkh*, ii, 398–99. For interpretation of the phrase "We are your maternal uncles," see Shahîd, *Byzantium and the Arabs in the Fourth Century*, 429–30.

The circumstances of Layth's martyrdom become clear only after consulting these four reports together. Taken as a whole, they suggest that al-Mahdī was on his way north from Jerusalem when he encountered the tribe of Tanūkh near Qinnasrīn, the ancient city of Chalcis, located southwest of Aleppo. The land between Qinnasrīn and Aleppo formed part of the Tanūkh's historic domains. It appears that the entire tribe was Christian. Members of the tribe greeted al-Mahdī on horseback and were dressed in beautiful clothing for the occasion. One of the caliph's attendants notified him that the Tanūkh were Christians, and this news—coupled with the tribesmen's ostentatious display of wealth—caused him to fly into a rage.[9] Al-Mahdī then ordered the Tanūkh to convert to Islam, whereupon the men of the tribe abandoned Christianity. The women, meanwhile, were allowed to carry on as Christians, presumably in accordance with Islamic law, under which Muslim men were free to keep non-Muslim wives. Despite this provision, some of the women in the tribe fled west, possibly to Byzantium. In his anger, al-Mahdī ordered the destruction of the Tanūkh's churches.

Christian and Muslim sources both state that a single individual resisted the forced conversion and was killed. Michael the Syrian and Bar Hebraeus refer to this man as "Layth," while an unpublished Islamic manuscript discovered by Irfan Shahîd gives the man's patronymic as "Ibn Maḥaṭṭa."[10] Layth b. Maḥaṭṭa was the leader of the tribe, and it seems that the ʿAbbasids targeted him as a way of pressuring the rest of his kinsmen to submit to Islam. He may have resisted as a final show of strength against the caliph or because he felt an obligation to uphold the tribe's ancient religion. Although the Syriac sources claim that he was "martyred," there is no evidence that he was ever commemorated in the liturgy or had a cult site of his own. If he were, one assumes that this would have been among the West Syrians (Miaphysites), given the confessional background of the Syriac texts and the church at Ehnesh that bears the inscription about the incident. Regardless, the story of the Tanūkh and al-Mahdī underscores the potential payoff of knitting together Christian and Muslim sources.

We can perform a similar exercise with two members of the Christian tribe of Taghlib, Muʿādh and Shamʿālā, who were tortured in 709 during the reign

[9] The caliph's anger in reaction to the ostentatious dress of the Tanūkh may be a literary motif. The Prophet is said to have reacted in the same way to the sumptuous dress of a Christian delegation from Kinda: Kennedy, *Prophet and the Age of the Caliphates*, 38. Muʿādh b. Jabal is said to have scoffed at the luxuries and the pretenses of Byzantine generals: al-Azdī, *Futūḥ al-shām*, 115–16. The point in these anecdotes is to emphasize the austerity and otherworldliness of Islam in contrast to the decadence and worldliness of Christianity.

[10] Shahîd, *Byzantium and the Arabs in the Fourth Century*, 431 n. 61.

of the Umayyad caliph al-Walīd b. ʿAbd al-Malik.[11] Though the written evidence about them is less diverse than the evidence about Layth, their story highlights the possibility of verifying and enriching a Christian martyrdom account through comparison with Muslim texts. The main sources for the torture of the Taghlibite Christians are the *Chronicle of Michael the Syrian* and the *Kitāb al-aghānī* of Abū ʾl-Faraj al-Iṣfahānī (d. 360/971).[12] Michael states that Muḥammad b. Marwān, the Umayyad governor of Mesopotamia, forced Muʿādh, who was then leader of the Banū Taghlib (like the Tanūkh, another famous Christian tribe), to "apostatize and convert to Islam" (*nahgar w-naḥnef*).[13] Muʿādh reportedly resisted this order and in punishment was thrown into a pit of mud and later killed. Muḥammad then exposed his corpse atop a dung heap, but Michael states that the body did not decay. He then reports that a Christian from Dara known as Eustathius obtained Muʿādh's relics and transferred them to a purpose-built monastery.[14] Sometime later, the new leader of the Banū Taghlib, a man named Shamʿālā, ran afoul of the caliph al-Walīd, who was allegedly upset to see an Arab chieftain worshipping the cross. The caliph's objection is intelligible in the context of early eighth-century Arab politics, in which it was increasingly expected that Arab tribesmen would convert. Like Muʿādh before him, Shamʿālā refused, and therefore, al-Walīd had a chunk of flesh removed from his thigh. This he allegedly cooked and force-fed to the Christian. Though Shamʿālā was not executed, Michael the Syrian persists in calling him a "martyr" (*sāhdā*) as well as "confessor" (*mawdyānā*). We might be tempted to dismiss this queer story of cannibalism as a hagiographic fiction, but the Muslim writer Abū ʾl-Faraj al-Iṣfahānī mentions the same detail, including the anecdote about al-Walīd eating Shamʿālā's flesh, followed by several lines of poetry about the incident. Quite clearly, the encounter may have actually happened, and due to the gruesome circumstances of Shamʿālā's torture, it became common knowledge among Christians and Muslims alike. In fact, we may be witnessing a common historiographical

[11] Nau, *Arabes chrétiens*, 109–10; Tritton, *Non-Muslim Subjects*, 90–91; Fattal, *Statut légal*, 171; Shahîd, *Byzantium and the Arabs in the Fourth Century*, 432; Hoyland, *Seeing Islam*, 352–53; Morony, "History and Identity," 18. ʿUmar b. al-Khaṭṭāb allowed the Taghlibites to remain Christians and avoid paying the *jizya* provided they paid double the rate of the Muslim tax, the *ṣadaqa*. This arrangement is discussed frequently in Islamic legal literature: e.g., ʿAbd al-Razzāq, *Muṣannaf*, iv, 485–86; vi, 72; Ibn Qayyim al-Jawzīya, *Aḥkām*, i, 206–22; and general discussion in Tritton, *Non-Muslim Subjects*, 89–92; Fattal, *Statut légal*, 36–37; Lecker, "Taghlib b. Wāʾil," *EI*², x, 89–93; Friedmann, *Tolerance and Coercion*, 63–68.

[12] Chabot, *Chronique*, ii, 480–82 (Fr.); iv, 451–52 (Syr.); Abū ʾl-Faraj al-Iṣfahānī, *Aghānī*, x, 99, which gives his full name in Arabic as Shamʿala b. ʿĀmir b. ʿAmr b. Bakr al-Taghlibī.

[13] For biographical information about Muḥammad b. Marwān, see Hoyland, *Theophilus*, 184–85, 246.

[14] Carlson and Michelson, "Dara": Gk. Daras, Turk. Oğuz. To my knowledge, there is no record of a monastery dedicated to Muʿādh in Dara.

strand woven into two disparate bodies of evidence, as was not uncommon for Muslim and Christian authors at this time.[15]

Such parallels between Christian and Muslim sources are not meant to diminish the basic source gap that bedevils any history of the neomartyrs. Yet they instill confidence that Christian tales of martyrdom may have a basis in reality. When Muslims did bother to write about individual Christians who were venerated as saints, they ended up recounting some of the same information. This was especially true of martyrs from prominent social and political backgrounds. Indeed, it is no coincidence that the only martyrs who attracted the attention of Muslim writers—including Layth b. Maḥaṭṭa and Shamʿālā—were individuals of high standing in Arab society and therefore merited discussion in the annals of Islamic history.

Even if Muslim sources were generally ignorant of neomartyrs by name, they were not ignorant of the phenomenon of martyrdom itself. The most important set of traditions in this respect revolve around a figure known as al-Mustawrid b. Mushammit b. Kaʿb b. Adana al-ʿIjlī, a Christian who was executed for apostasy under ʿAlī b. Abī Ṭālib, presumably while he was caliph in 35–40/656–61.[16] In these traditions, which are narrated on the authority of Abū ʿAmr al-Shaybānī (d. ca. 101/719 in Kūfa), al-Mustawrid is represented as the quintessential Christian apostate, yet curiously, Christian sources do not mention him. This may mean that we are dealing with a literary representation of a general social phenomenon or if al-Mustawrid did exist, that Christians did not know about him or wish to remember him. The story of al-Mustawrid belongs to a larger genre of reports in which ʿAlī is shown interrogating and killing different groups of apostates and heretics.[17] Jurists frequently presented al-Mustawrid's death as a legal precedent for the practice of *istitāba*, that is, the act of offering criminals a chance to repent before killing them.[18] Offenders such as apostates were supposed to receive three chances to repent, though early sources suggest that a much wider array of practices existed in real life.[19]

One of the most interesting discussions of al-Mustawrid and *istitāba* comes from the *Aḥkām ahl al-milal* of Abū Bakr al-Khallāl (d. 311/923), a

[15] Debié, *Écriture de l'histoire en syriaque*, 382–87. For the eating of flesh in another martyrdom incident, see Mandalà, "Martyrdom of Yūḥannā," 75–81, 94.

[16] Caskel, *Ǧamharat an-nasab*, i, 160; Ibn Makūlā, *Ikmāl*, vi, 167; van Ess, *Kitāb an-Nakt des Naẓẓām*, 51; Kraemer, "Apostates, Rebels and Brigands," 45 n. 41; Morony, *Iraq*, 443 (which mistakes al-Mustawrid for a member of the Banū Nājiya, another tribe that was divided between Muslims and Christians at the time; see below, n. 24).

[17] For example, Ibn Abī Shayba, *Muṣannaf*, v, 564, nos. 29003–4.

[18] On al-Mustawrid and *istitāba*, see ʿAbd al-Razzāq, *Muṣannaf*, x, 170, nos. 18710–11; Abū Yūsuf, *Kitāb al-kharāj*, 181–82; al-Ṭaḥāwī, *Sharḥ*, iii, 266; Kraemer, "Apostates, Rebels and Brigands," 47 n. 49.

[19] See chapter 4, n. 39.

collection of *responsa* by Aḥmad b. Ḥanbal (d. 241/855) on the topic of non-Muslims:

> ʿAbdallāh—his father—Muḥammad b. Abī ʿAdī—Sulaymān—Abū ʿAmr al-Shaybānī, who said: A man from the tribe of ʿIjl converted to Christianity, and ʿUtba b. Farqad wrote about that to ʿAlī b. Abī Ṭālib. He commanded with respect to it [to bring the man to him]. So he brought him until a hairy man with clothes of wool [*thiyāb al-ṣūf*] shackled in iron was thrown before him. ʿAlī addressed him at great length, but the man was silent. Then the man uttered something that entailed his destruction, saying, "I do not know what you are talking about, other than that Jesus Christ is God." When he said this, ʿAlī stood up and trampled on him. When the people saw ʿAlī [do this], they trampled the man, too. ʿAlī said to them, "Desist!" But they did not desist until they had killed him. He commanded that his body be burned. The Christians began to come and they took of his flesh and blood. One of them dropped coins and bent over as if to pick them up, but took pieces of his flesh instead. The Christians proclaimed, "Martyr [*shahīdā*]," with a *dāl*."[20]

The *Tahdhīb al-āthār* of al-Ṭabarī (d. 310/923) contains two similar reports that are also worth quoting in full:

> Muḥammad b. ʿAbd al-Aʿlā al-Ṣanʿānī—Muʿtamir b. Sulaymān—his father—Abū ʿAmr al-Shaybānī, who said: ʿUtba b. Farqad sent to ʿAlī a man who had converted to Christianity and apostatized from Islam. Before him came a man on an ass, hairy, and covered in wool. ʿAlī called on him to repent for a long time, but the man remained silent. Then he uttered a word that entailed his destruction, saying, "I do not know what you are talking about, other than Jesus is this and that," and he mentioned some heretical thing [*shirk*]. Therefore, ʿAlī trampled on the man, and the people trampled on him too. Then ʿAlī said, "Restrain him" or "Desist!" But they did not stop until they had killed him. ʿAlī ordered that he be burned in the fire. Then the Christians began to proclaim, "*Shahīdhā, shahīdhā*," by which they meant, "*Shahīd*" [that is, "Martyr"]. One of them brought a dinar or dirham that he dropped,

[20] Abū Bakr al-Khallāl, *Aḥkām*, 419–20. *Isnād*: ʿAbdallāh b. Aḥmad b. Ḥanbal (d. 290, Baghdad), son of Aḥmad b. Ḥanbal (d. 241, Baghdad). Muḥammad b. Ibrāhīm b. Abī ʿAdī al-Sulamī (d. 194, Baṣra), in al-Mizzī, *Tahdhīb*, xxiv, 321–24; Sulaymān b. Ṭarkhān al-Taymī (d. 143, Baṣra), in al-Mizzī, *Tahdhīb*, xii, 5–12; Saʿd b. Iyās Abū ʿAmr al-Shaybānī (d. 101, Kūfa), in al-Mizzī, *Tahdhīb*, x, 258–60.

then came as if searching for it, meanwhile, covering it with ashes or blood.[21]

Yaʿqūb b. Ibrāhīm—Ibn ʿUlayya—Sulaymān al-Taymī—Abū ʿAmr al-Shaybānī, who said: A man from the tribe of ʿIjl waged *jihād* for a long time [*kāna ṭawīl al-jihād*] and then converted to Christianity. ʿUtba b. Farqad wrote to ʿAlī about him. He instructed ʿUtba to dispatch the man to him. So a man was brought before him and placed in front of ʿAlī. ʿAlī began addressing him and circling him until the man uttered a word that entailed his destruction, saying, "I do not know what you are talking about, except that Jesus is the son of God." So ʿAlī pounced on him and trampled him. Then the people trampled him. ʿAlī told them, "Desist," so they desisted. But lo, the man had already died. Therefore, he ordered that he be burned. The Christians began to proclaim, "Martyr [*shahīdā*]," and they began to pick up what they found of his bones and blood."[22]

There are other reports about al-Mustawrid al-ʿIjlī, but for our purposes, these constitute the most important. They describe an encounter between ʿAlī and an apostate from the tribe of ʿIjl b. Lujaym, one of the most powerful clans from the confederation of Bakr b. Wāʾil. Along with the Banū Shaybān, the Banū ʿIjl are known to have inhabited the right bank of the Euphrates River in Iraq, with territory stretching from the town of ʿAyn al-Tamr to the Persian Gulf. Christianity spread widely among the Bakrī tribes in late antiquity, thanks mostly to the efforts of Syriac-speaking non-Chalcedonian missionaries. Due to their position along the frontiers of the Sasanian Empire, they also had extensive dealings with Lakhmids of Ḥīra, another group of Arab Christians. Some ʿIjlī tribesmen took part in the conquest of Iraq, and this may have owed to the tribe's long-standing hostility toward the Sasanians. But over time, the group became divided between a faction that supported the Muslims—presumably leading to their own conversion to Islam—and a group that remained aligned with the Persians and their Lakhmid allies, and this faction seems to have remained heavily Christian.[23] This was typical of many Arab tribes in

[21] al-Ṭabarī, *Tahdhīb*, iv, 78–79, no. 139. *Isnād*: Muḥammad b. ʿAbd al-Aʿlā al-Ṣanʿānī al-Qaysī (d. 245, Baṣra), in al-Mizzī, *Tahdhīb*, xxv, 581–83; Muʿtamir b. Sulaymān b. Ṭarkhān al-Taymī (d. 187, Baṣra), in al-Mizzī, *Tahdhīb*, xxviii, 250–56. Sulaymān b. Ṭarkhān al-Taymī and Saʿd b. Iyās Abū ʿAmr al-Shaybānī, see n. 20 above.

[22] al-Ṭabarī, *Tahdhīb*, iv, 79, no. 140. *Isnād*: Yaʿqūb b. Ibrāhīm b. Kathīr al-Qaysī (d. 252, Baghdad? cf. Ibn Ḥajar, *Tahdhīb*, xi, 381–82), in al-Mizzī, *Tahdhīb*, xxxii, 311–14; Ismāʿīl b. Ibrāhīm al-Asadī (d. 193, Kūfa, Baṣra), in al-Mizzī, *Tahdhīb*, iii, 23–33. Sulaymān b. Ṭarkhān al-Taymī and Saʿd b. Iyās Abū ʿAmr al-Shaybānī, see n. 20 above.

[23] For discussion, see Watt, "ʿIdjl," *EI²*, iii, 1022–23; Donner, "Bakr b. Wāʾil Tribes"; al-Qāḍī,

Syria and Mesopotamia, which found themselves divided between Christianity and Islam as a result of the conquests.[24] This experience may have been especially taxing for the Banū ʿIjl, for the tribe became a hotbed of religious dissidents in the eighth century and beyond.[25] It is in the context of these internal divisions that we can begin to understand the alleged martyrdom of al-Mustawrid.

The sources state that al-Mustawrid al-ʿIjlī converted to Christianity or that he apostatized from Islam. It is not clear, therefore, whether he was born a Christian, converted to Islam, and then returned to Christianity or whether he was born a Muslim and then converted (likely the former). ʿAlī learned about al-Mustawrid's crime from ʿUtba b. Farqad al-Sulamī, a wealthy Companion and general who served as governor of Mosul and later of Azerbaijan.[26] The sources state that al-Mustawrid apostatized after waging *jihād* with the Muslims. After he was arrested, he appeared before the caliph dressed like a monk, with woolen clothes and chains, and seated on an ass. ʿAlī threatened him, seeking his return to Islam, but the man refused and professed his Christian faith. Disgusted, ʿAlī beat al-Mustawrid, and then the crowd joined him. Eventually, his body was thrown into the fire.

The most interesting part of the traditions is what is said about the fate of al-Mustawrid's body. These details transform the story from simply another execution narrative into a proper martyrology. Groups of Christians reportedly collected al-Mustawrid's remains, including pieces of his flesh, bone, ash, and blood. One Christian reportedly wished to avoid the scrutiny of Muslim officials, so he dropped coins onto the ground in order to discreetly collect the saint's relics as he bent over. The Christians instantly proclaimed al-Mustawrid a martyr, or *shahīd*. Curiously, the traditions also remark on the Christians' mispronunciation of this Arabic word: instead of calling al-Mustawrid a *shahīd*, they called him a *shahīdhā*.

At first glance, this detail is perplexing, but it seems that the transmitters wanted to convey the idea that the Christian tribesmen had a very poor command of the Arabic language. Specifically, it seems to reflect how a native

"Non-Muslims in the Muslim Conquest Army," 88–93.

[24] Another tribe, the Banū Nājiya, were reportedly divided into Muslims, Christians, and apostates from Islam after the battle of Ṣiffīn (37/657). They then rebelled against Muʿāwiya: al-Ṭabarī, *Annales*, i, 3434–40; ʿAbd al-Razzāq, *Muṣannaf*, x, 171–72, no. 18715; Ibn Abī Shayba, *Muṣannaf*, v, 564, no. 29008.

[25] Several prominent extremist Shīʿīs were members of the Banū ʿIjl, e.g., al-Mughīra b. Saʿīd al-ʿIjlī (d. 119/737; see chapter 4, sec. III) and Abū Manṣūr al-ʿIjlī. Apparently the tribesmen did not forget their Christian roots completely, since Abū Manṣūr claimed that God spoke to him in Syriac! See Madelung, "al-Mughīriyya," *EI²*, vii, 347–48; Madelung, "al-Manṣūriyya," *EI²*, vi, 441–42; Tucker, "Rebels and Gnostics"; Tucker, "Manṣūriyya" (for the Syriac reference, 66).

[26] Ibn Saʿd, *Biographien Muhammeds*, vi, 26–27.

speaker of Aramaic might have mispronounced or modified the Arabic word, especially at a time when ever larger numbers of Aramaic-speaking Christians were converting to Islam and embracing Arabic culture.[27] To harp on their weak Arabic, therefore, was to criticize these Christians for continuing to practice Christianity; indeed, the idea seems to be that Christian Arabs were not full Arabs, unlike their Muslim counterparts, who fortified their Arabness by embracing Islam.

As a historical incident, the martyrdom of al-Mustawrid al-ʿIjlī is highly dubious. The major Muslim chroniclers pass over it in silence, and as we have already noted, there is no record of al-Mustawrid on the Christian side. The *isnāds* suggest that the story began to circulate in Iraq during the early to mid-eighth century, long after the event had allegedly taken place in the mid-seventh century. What is more, it seems to belong to a larger corpus of *ḥadīth* narrated by Abū ʿUmar al-Shaybānī concerning encounters between ʿAlī and various converts to Christianity.[28] The biggest reason for skepticism, however, is the contents of the reports themselves. They describe an apostasy trial unlike anything that would have happened during the caliphate of ʿAlī b. Abī Ṭālib, if they ever happened so early at all. Rather, they describe an encounter typical of the late Umayyad or early ʿAbbasid period, and we know this through the many parallels between the martyrology of al-Mustawrid and those of various Christian neomartyrs.

For example, al-Mustawrid seems to have become a monk after apostatizing from Islam, judging from the woolen garments mentioned in the texts. Several neomartyrs followed a similar path, including ʿAbd al-Masīḥ and Bacchus, who also turned from Islam to a life of monasticism. Al-Mustawrid's conversion most closely resembles that of ʿAbd al-Masīḥ, who not only embraced asceticism after returning to Christianity but did so after a period of waging *jihād* with Muslims.[29] Al-Mustawrid's entrance before ʿAlī also recalls reports of *tashhīr* processions in Christian hagiography: John of Córdoba and Anthony of Syracuse, for example, were also chained, seated on donkeys, and paraded around as a form of public humiliation.[30] Meanwhile, as we saw in chapter 4, the bodies of Christian martyrs were frequently burned, just like the body of al-Mustawrid. The authorities also struggled to prevent the martyrs' support-

[27] In Syriac, a terminal *dālath* that is preceded by a vowel is usually pronounced like an Arabic *dhāl*; thus, the Syriac word *talmīdā* (pupil, disciple) passes into Arabic as *talmīdh*. The long *alif* at the end of the word is typical of eastern Aramaic pronuciation. For discussion of a Coptic official who converted to Islam and could not pronounce Arabic properly, see al-Nābulusī, *Sword of Ambition*, 161–77.

[28] E.g., ʿAbd al-Razzāq, *Muṣannaf*, x, 169–70, no. 18709.

[29] Griffith, "ʿAbd al-Masīḥ," 362.

[30] *CSM*, i, 277–78; Delehaye, *Synaxarium*, 72; see chapter 4, nn. 68–69.

ers from collecting their physical remains, a trope that appears in reports about al-Mustawrid.

What we have in Abū Bakr al-Khallāl, al-Ṭabarī, and other sources, therefore, is essentially an antihagiography of a Christian martyr. In form and content, it closely resembles stories Christians were writing about their own martyrs at the time. But unlike its Christian counterparts, this tradition was designed with a legal goal in mind, namely, to exemplify best practices for trying and killing apostates. Implicit in this was also a desire to demonize individuals who left Islam. Thus, the very figure whom Christians lionized as a saint the Muslims condemned as a criminal. How can we explain the striking similarities between the two bodies of evidence?

Even if al-Mustawrid al-ʿIjlī was not a historical martyr, the Muslims who narrated his traditions were familiar with Christian martyrdom more generally. The parallels between the two sets of texts are simply too abundant and too precise to account for otherwise. What seems most likely is that the eighth-century Muslim transmitters of the report were well aware of the apostasy trials happening around them. What is more, they may have been sensitive to the surge in violent episodes that was occurring at this time, as discussed in the conclusion of this book. In turn, they circulated fictionalized accounts of a contemporary social reality, though setting them in the time of ʿAlī b. Abī Ṭālib as a way of creating a patina of antiquity and authenticity around them.

Yet it was not only the trial and execution of martyrs that caught the eye of Muslim traditionists. It was also the establishment of martyrs' cults. They signaled their understanding of this process by having al-Mustawrid's supporters proclaim him a *shahīd* and by having them collect his relics, presumably for a church somewhere offstage. There is no evidence that Muslims were reading Christian hagiography at this time, so the only way to account for the parallels is as a result of eyewitness observation.[31] That Christians and Muslims represented martyrdom in such similar ways reinforces the overall argument of this book that Christian hagiography was grounded in a social reality. Al-Mustawrid al-ʿIjlī may not prove the existence of any new martyrs by name, but he helps us see how their biographies may be historically plausible.

[31] Sizgorich ("Christian Eyes Only," 121) argues that some Christian martyrologies were written with a Muslim audience in mind, though his argument is weak, since there is minimal evidence that these texts circulated outside Christian contexts and because Muslims show limited knowledge about the broader phenomenon.

APPENDIX 2

Glossary of Names and Key Words

ʿAbbasids: Dynasty of caliphs based in Iraq; ruled 132–656/750–1258

ʿAbd al-Malik b. Marwān (r. 65–86/685–705): Fifth Umayyad caliph; launched campaign to Islamize public spaces, state administration, and coinage; constructed the Dome of the Rock in Jerusalem

ʿAbd al-Masīḥ (d. mid-eighth century): Arab Christian who converted to Islam while fighting with Muslims against the Byzantines; later returned to Christianity and became abbot of Mt. Sinai; executed for apostasy in Palestine

ʿAbd al-Raḥmān b. al-Ḥakam (r. 206–38/822–52): Fourth Umayyad *amīr* of al-Andalus

ʿAbd al-Razzāq al-Ṣanʿānī (d. 211/827): Yemeni scholar and early compiler of *ḥadīth*; his collection contains extensive discussion of relations between Muslims and non-Muslims and other topics that are less covered in the later canonical collections

ʿAbdūn of Takrīt (d. ca. 820): Christian noblemen who was executed after taking part in a local rebellion against Muslim rule (see Basilius of Takrīt)

Abo of Tiflīs (d. 786): Muslim of Baghdad who converted to Christianity in Georgia; later executed for apostasy (see John Sabanisdze)

Abraham (fl. mid-eighth century): Armenian monk and biographer of Vahan of Gołtʿn

Abū Bakr al-Khallāl (d. 311/923): Muslim jurist of Baghdad and adherent of the Ḥanbalī school of law; compiled the legal *responsa* of Aḥmad b. Ḥanbal, a lengthy section of which concerns the treatment of non-Muslims survives

Abū Bakr al-Ṣiddīq (r. 11–13/632–34): First Rightly Guided Caliph; led Wars of Apostasy against Arab tribes who had pledged loyalty to the Prophet but rescinded this upon his death

Aghlabids: Independent dynasty that governed Ifrīqiya nominally on behalf of the ʿAbbasid caliphs; ruled 184–296/800–909

Aḥmad b. Ḥanbal (d. 241/855): Native of Baghdad and founder of the Ḥanbalī school of law in Sunnī Islam

ʿAlī b. Abī Ṭālib (r. 35–40/656–61): Fourth Rightly Guided Caliph; cousin and son-in-law of the Prophet Muḥammad; revered as the first imam in Shīʿism

amṣār (sing. *miṣr*): Garrison cities established by Arab armies during the conquests, especially in Iraq, Egypt, and North Africa; designed to segregate Muslim settlers from the surrounding non-Muslim population

Anastasius of Sinai (d. ca. 700): Greek-speaking monk from Mt. Sinai who traveled throughout the eastern Mediterranean after the Arab conquest; composed early accounts of Muslim-Christian interaction, including the first accounts of neomartyrdom (see George the Black, Euphemia, Moses of Klysma)

al-Andalus: Muslim province on the Iberian Peninsula, encompassing most of modern Spain and Portugal; conquered ca. 92/711

Anthony al-Qurashī (d. 799): Muslim convert to Christianity from Damascus who apostatized after witnessing a eucharistic miracle in a church; killed by Hārūn al-Rashīd in Raqqa

Anthony of Syracuse (d. ca. 875–86): See Martyrs of Syracuse

antidōron: In the eastern churches, leavened bread that is blessed but not consecrated like the Eucharist; occasionally given to Muslims in the early Middle Ages

Arčʿil of Kakhetia (d. 786): Georgian prince who was executed after refusing to convert to Islam and be co-opted as an ʿAbbasid vassal

Argimirus of Córdoba (d. 856): Christian official of the Umayyad state who became a monk and was executed after being falsely accused of blasphemy

Aurea of Córdoba (d. 856): Christian nun born to a Muslim father and Christian mother in a family of high social standing; eventually executed for apostasy

Aurelius of Córdoba (d. 852): Orphaned by his Muslim father and Christian mother and raised by Christian relatives; his Muslim relatives objected and forced him to practice Islam; continued as a secret Christian and was eventually killed for blasphemy. Married to Sabigotho, another crypto-Christian; executed with Sabigotho, Felix, Liliosa, and George

Bacchus (d. 787–88): Born to a Muslim father and Christian mother in Maiouma in Palestine; eventually converted to Christianity and became a monk of Mar Saba; killed for apostasy

Basilius of Takrīt (fl. 810s): West Syrian (Miaphysite) metropolitan of Takrīt who led a short-lived uprising against Muslim rule; his collaborator, the Christian layman ʿAbdūn, was killed

Bughā al-Kabīr (d. 248/862): Turkish military commander under the

ʿAbbasids; led a campaign in Armenia (ca. 237/851–52) that produced several Christian martyrs

catholicos: Title of the patriarch of the Church of the East; also title of the head of the Armenian Orthodox Church

Christopher of Antioch (d. 967): Melkite bishop originally from Iraq who was killed after becoming embroiled in an intra-Muslim dispute at the time of the Byzantine conquest of northern Syria

Christopher the Persian (d. 778): Muslim convert to Christianity who later became a priest and monk; executed for apostasy, possibly in Iraq

Companions (Ar. *ṣaḥāba*): Technical term for the generation of early Muslims who knew the Prophet personally

Constantine-Kakhay (d. 853): Georgian prince who refused to be co-opted as an ʿAbbasid vassal; imprisoned and executed in Sāmarrāʾ after refusing to convert

Copts: Non-Chalcedonian Christians of Egypt who broke with the church of Constantinople after 451; also known as Monophysites, Miaphysites; primary languages: Coptic, Arabic, and Greek

Córdoba: Capital of the independent Umayyad emirate of al-Andalus from 138/756; capital of the independent Umayyad caliphate of al-Andalus from 316/929; site of the famous martyrdom incident between 850 and 859

Cyrus of Ḥarrān (d. 769): Christian layman, possibly a soldier, who was executed in northern Mesopotamia after being falsely accused of apostatizing from Islam; venerated among the West Syrians (Miaphysites)

David of Dwin (d. 703/705): Muslim soldier stationed in Armenia who converted to Christianity; later executed for apostatizing from Islam

dhimmī: A protected non-Muslim living under Muslim rule; principally Jews and Christians ("People of the Book") but Zoroastrians and other non-Muslims as well

Dioscorus of Alexandria (d. unknown): Christian convert to Islam from Egypt; returned to Christianity after being shamed by his Christian sister; executed for apostatizing from Islam

East Syrians–Church of the East: Syriac-speaking denomination concentrated in Iraq, with large populations in Iran, Central Asia, and China; separated from the church of Constantinople after the Council of Ephesus in 431; beneficiaries of imperial patronage under the Sasanian kings; also known as Nestorians; primary languages: Syriac, Greek, and Arabic

Elias of Helioupolis (d. 779): Christian peasant from Baalbek; executed in

Damascus after being falsely accused of apostatizing from Islam during the course of a party with Muslim guests

Emila of Córdoba (d. 852): A young deacon of noble stock who was executed for blasphemy along with the martyr Jeremiah

Eulogius of Córdoba (d. 859): Priest and biographer of the martyrs of Córdoba; executed for assisting in the conversion of a Muslim girl to Christianity (see Leocritia); author of many hagiographic and polemical works in Latin

Euphemia of Damascus (fl. mid-seventh century): Christian slave who was tortured by her Muslim master; although she was not executed, her biographer Anastasius of Sinai called her a "neomartyr," making her the first saint after the conquest to bear this title

Eustathius (d. 739–40): Son of a Byzantine nobleman who became a prisoner of war under the Umayyads at Ḥarrān; later executed after refusing to convert to Islam

Fāṭimids: Dynasty of Shīʿī Ismāʿīlī caliphs in North Africa and Egypt; established the city of Cairo; ruled 297–567/909–1171

Felix of Córdoba (d. 853): Christian layman who converted to Islam and returned to Christianity; married to Liliosa, a crypto-Christian; executed for blasphemy

fiqh: Islamic jurisprudence, law

Forty-Two Martyrs of Amorion (d. 845): Byzantine soldiers captured during an Arab attack in Anatolia in 838, later executed in Iraq; widely venerated among Christians in Byzantium and the caliphate alike

George of Mar Saba (d. 852): Palestinian monk who traveled to Córdoba seeking funds to support his home community at Mar Saba; executed for blasphemy along with Aurelius, Sabigotho, Felix, and Liliosa

George the Black (d. mid-seventh century): Christian youth who was taken captive and converted to Islam while a slave; later practiced Christianity in secret and was executed for apostasy in Damascus; first recorded instance of a martyr's cult after the conquest

George the New, né Muzāḥim (d. 979): Born to a Muslim father and Christian mother in Egypt; after attending mass, converted to Christianity and later killed for apostatizing from Islam

ḥadd (pl. *ḥudūd*): Punishments delineated in the Qurʾan and *ḥadīth* for especially grievous crimes, including apostasy and blasphemy

al-Hādī (r. 169–70/785–86): Fourth ʿAbbasid caliph

ḥadīth (pl. *aḥādīth*): Accounts of what the Prophet and his Companions said and did; these acquired legal force in later periods and were often subject to falsification

Hamazasp and Sahak (d. 786): Armenian noblemen who were executed after refusing to convert to Islam

Hārūn al-Rashīd (r. 170–93/786–809): Fifth ʿAbbasid caliph

al-Hāshimī: Fictional Muslim prince who converted to Christianity in ʿAbbasid Baghdad; later executed for apostatizing from Islam; biography originally written by the Muslim convert to Christianity Ibn Rajāʾ

hēgoumenos: Abbot or superior of a monastery

ḥirāba: Brigandage, plundering, waging war; as in Q. *al-Māʾida* 5:33

Hishām b. ʿAbd al-Malik (r. 105–25/724–43): Tenth Umayyad caliph

Ibn ʿAbbās (d. 68/688): Companion of the Prophet Muḥammad and prolific narrator of *ḥadīth*

Ibn Antūnyān (fl. mid-ninth century): High-ranking Christian official in the Umayyad court of Córdoba; converted to Islam and reviled by Christians as a traitor

Ibn Rajāʾ (fl. late tenth–early eleventh centuries): Muslim convert to Christianity from Egypt who later became a monk and polemicist against Islam

irtidād, ridda: Terms for apostasy in Islamic law and theology

Isaac of Córdoba (d. 851): Christian official of the Umayyad state who became a monk and was later executed for blasphemy

istitāba: The act of offering criminals repentance before executing them; required by Islamic law in cases of apostasy and blasphemy

Jacob of Edessa (d. 708): West Syrian (Miaphysite) bishop of Edessa in northern Mesopotamia; prolific theologian, historian, and canonist; composed early accounts of Muslim-Christian interactions

Jazīra: The northern part of the territory stretching between the Tigris and the Euphrates rivers; northern Mesopotamia

Jeremiah of Córdoba (d. 852): Aristocratic Christian executed for blasphemy along with Emilas

jizya: Poll tax paid by non-Muslims, allegedly in commutation for military service, though its early history remains unclear; many converted to Islam in the early period to escape this and other religiously affiliated financial burdens (see *kharāj*)

John of Córdoba (fl. mid-ninth century): Christian merchant who used to curse the Prophet in public; later imprisoned and beaten for blasphemy

John of Damascus (d. ca. 749): Chalcedonian (Melkite) monk and theologian from Syria known for his influential treatises on icons, among other topics; member of a prominent Christian family that included several high-ranking servants of the Umayyad state; alleged author of the *Life of Peter of Capitolias*

John Sabanisdze (fl. late eighth century): Georgian churchman; contemporary and biographer of the martyr Abo of Tiflīs

jund (pl. *ajnād*): Term for a military district of the early Muslim state

kharāj: Land tax paid by non-Muslims, though its early history remains unclear; many converted to Islam in the early period to escape this and other religiously affiliated financial burdens; often conflated with the *jizya*

Khārijī (pl. Khawārij): Member of a Muslim sect that emerged in the first century after the Prophet's death that rejected the authority of the caliphs; believed that piety—not tribal lineage—was the main qualification for serving as the *imām*; renowned for their violence and their practice of denouncing other Muslims as unbelievers; many Khārijīs rebelled in Iraq and Iran

Khuzayma b. Khāzim al-Tamīmī: ʿAbbasid governor of the Caucasus, involved in several martyrdom episodes in the late 780s

Layth b. Maḥaṭṭa (d. 780): Chief of the Christian tribe of Tanūkh; executed after refusing to comply with the orders of the caliph al-Mahdī to convert to Islam

Leocritia of Córdoba (d. 859): Muslim girl who converted to Christianity with the help of a Christian relative and the priest Eulogius; executed for apostasy with Eulogius

Łewond (fl. eighth–ninth centuries): Armenian chronicler who discussed the period of early Arab rule in the Caucasus

Liliosa of Córdoba (d. 852): Born to two Muslims who practiced Christianity in secret; married to Felix, who converted to Islam and back to Christianity; executed for blasphemy with Felix, Aurelius, Sabigotho, and George

madhhab (pl. *madhāhib*): Term for a school of law in Islam; in Sunnism, these include the Ḥanbalī, Ḥanafī, Mālikī, and Shāfiʿī schools, though there were other schools that died out in the early period

al-Mahdī (r. 158–69/775–85): Third ʿAbbasid caliph

Mālik b. Anas (d. 179/796): A native of Medina and founder of the Mālikī school of law; Mālikism later became the leading legal school in al-Andalus

al-Maʾmūn (r. 198–218/813–33): Seventh ʿAbbasid caliph; subject of Christian legends claiming that he converted from Islam to Christianity (see Theodore of Edessa)

al-Manṣūr (r. 136–58/754–75): Second ʿAbbasid caliph and founder of Baghdad

Mar Saba Monastery: Famous Chalcedonian (Melkite) monastery founded in the fifth century and located between Jerusalem and the Dead Sea;

major center of martyrology-writing after the Arab conquest; home to Greek-, Syriac-, Arabic-, and Georgian-speaking monks

Maria of Córdoba (d. 851): Born to a Christian father and a Muslim mother who converted to Christianity in order to be married; lived in a convent and was executed for blasphemy; killed with Flora of Córdoba; her brother Walabonsus was also executed

Maronites: Chalcedonian Christians of Syria who held to the doctrine that Christ possessed a single will, in contrast to the church of Constantinople, which held that Christ possessed two wills; originating in a group of monasteries around Ḥamā, eventually spreading to the mountains of Lebanon; also known as Monothelites and today part of the Roman Catholic Church; languages: Syriac, Arabic, and Greek

Martyrs of Córdoba (d. 850–59): Forty-eight Christians executed for blasphemy and apostasy in the capital of the independent Umayyad emirate of al-Andalus

Martyrs of Syracuse (d. ca. 875–86): Christians from Sicily who were taken captive and brought to the Aghlabid court in Ifrīqiya (modern-day Tunisia), probably Qayrawān; two of them, the brothers Anthony and Peter, were converted to Islam and trained to serve as government officials, but they continued to practice Christianity in secret; executed for apostasy

mawlā (pl. *mawālī*): Non-Arab convert to Islam who joins an Arab tribe as a client to secure his status as a Muslim; considered second-class citizens in most early Islamic societies; widely reviled but formed an ever larger portion of the Muslim population as time went on

Melkites: Chalcedonian Christians of the Middle East (especially the Levant) who remained in communion with Constantinople after the conquest; prolific writers of martyrologies, particularly in Palestine; also known as Arab Orthodox, Antiochene Orthodox, Rūm; primary languages: Greek, Arabic, Syriac, and Georgian

Menas of Ushmūnayn (d. 640s?): Egyptian monk who denounced Islam at the time of the conquests and was executed

Michael of Mar Saba (d. ca. 700): Monk of Mar Saba Monastery killed by ʿAbd al-Malik after refusing to convert to Islam; probably fictional

Michael the Syrian (d. 1199): Patriarch of the Syrian Orthodox Church and author of an important chronicle of world history

Moses of Klysma (fl. mid-seventh century): Young Christian from Egypt who converted back and forth between Christianity and Islam (see Anastasius of Sinai)

Mt. Sinai (Monastery of St. Catherine): Famous Chalcedonian (Melkite)

monastery founded in the sixth century and located on the site of the Burning Bush; center of martyrology-writing after the conquest; home to Greek-, Syriac-, Arabic-, and Georgian-speaking monks

Muʿādh al-Taghlibī (d. 709): Chief of the Christian tribe of Taghlib who was executed after refusing an order of an Umayyad governor in Iraq to convert to Islam

Muʿāwiya b. Abī Sufyān (r. 41–60/661–80): First Umayyad caliph and founder of the Umayyad dynasty; previously governor of Syria

Muḥammad (d. 11/632): Prophet of Islam

Muḥammad b. ʿAbd al-Raḥmān (r. 238–73/852–86): Fifth Umayyad *amīr* of al-Andalus

Muslim nobleman of Diospolis (Lydda): Fictional Umayyad prince who converted to Christianity after witnessing a miracle at the shrine of St. George; later martyred for apostasy from Islam

al-Mustawrid al-ʿIjlī: Arab tribesman who converted from Islam to Christianity and was killed by ʿAlī b. Abī Ṭālib; a quasi-fictional character mentioned in Muslim legal texts on apostasy

Muʿtazilī: A school of Islamic theology that flourished in Iraq during the ʿAbbasid period known for rationalist speculation and the belief that the Qurʾan was uncreated and, thus, not coeternal with God

Nuʿaym b. Ḥammād (d. 228/843): Muslim scholar who compiled a large collection of apocalyptic *ḥadīth* from the Umayyad and ʿAbbasid periods

Nunilo and Alodia (d. 851): Sisters born to a Muslim father and Christian mother; raised as Christians until their mother's second husband, also a Muslim, objected to their Christian beliefs; killed for apostasy; possibly fictional

Pact of ʿUmar: Body of laws regulating contact between Muslims and non-Muslims; based on the peace treaties allegedly contracted between the caliph ʿUmar b. al-Khaṭṭāb and the Christians of the Middle East during the conquests; dating to a much later period in its final form

parrhēsia: Frank or audacious speech

Paulus Alvarus (d. mid-ninth century): Christian layman of Córdoba who wrote several apologetic works about the martyrs of his city as well as a biography of his friend the priest Eulogius

Perfectus of Córdoba (d. 850): Monk executed for blasphemy after engaging in a frank discussion about Islam with Muslims whom he met on the road; first of the Córdoba martyrs to be executed

Peter of Capitolias (d. 715): Priest from northwestern Transjordan who was executed for blasphemy

Peter of Syracuse (d. ca. 875–86): See Martyrs of Syracuse

Rogelius of Córdoba (d. 852): Elderly monk from Granada who was executed after committing blasphemy in a mosque with Serviusdei

Romanus (d. 780): Anatolian monk taken captive and later killed by al-Mahdī on suspicions of serving as a Byzantine spy and reconverting Christian converts to Islam

sabb, *shatm*: Terms for blasphemy, defamation, in Islamic law and theology

Sabigotho of Córdoba (d. 852): Born to Muslim parents who practiced Christianity in secret; married Aurelius, another crypto-Christian; eventually executed for blasphemy, along with Aurelius, Felix, Liliosa, and George

Samson of Córdoba (fl. mid-ninth century): Prominent Christian abbot who worked as a translator for the Umayyad court of al-Andalus; later wrote a polemical treatise attacking Muslims and their corrupt Christian supporters

Sasanians: Dynasty of Zoroastrian Persian kings who ruled Iran, Iraq, and much of Central Asia between 224 and 651; cultivated close ties with the Church of the East; originated in Fārs in Iran but ruled from Ctesiphon in Iraq

Servusdei of Córdoba (d. 852): A Christian, possibly from the Middle East, who was executed after committing blasphemy in a mosque with Rogelius

shahāda: The Muslim profession of faith, "There is no God but God, Muḥammad is the messenger of God"

Shamʿālā (fl. early eight century): Chief of the Christian tribe of Taghlib who was tortured after refusing the order of the caliph al-Walīd b. ʿAbd al-Malik to convert to Islam

Shīʿī: Adherents of a sect of Islam that believed that leadership of the Muslim community should have passed from the Prophet Muḥammad to members of his family, especially his cousin ʿAlī and ʿAlī's male descendants, known as the *imāms*; the Umayyads suppressed several early Shīʿī revolts in Iraq before the ʿAbbasids succeeded in toppling them and establishing their own quasi-Shīʿī dynasty; today consisting of several distinct branches, including Imāmī, Ismāʿīlī, and Zaydī Shīʿism

Sixty Martyrs of Gaza (d. late 630s): Byzantine soldiers executed following the Arab conquest of Palestine

Sixty Martyrs of Jerusalem (d. 724–25): Byzantine soldiers executed during an alleged Christian pilgrimage to Muslim-controlled Palestine

Stephen Manṣūr: Monk of Mar Saba Monastery responsible for writing the *passions* of Romanus and the Twenty Martyrs of Mar Saba

Sulaymān b. ʿAbd al-Malik (r. 96–99/715–17): Seventh Umayyad caliph

synaxarium (pl. *synaxaria*): A liturgical calendar containing feasts commemorated in the course of the church year; often contains biographical information about individual saints

al-Ṭabarī (d. 310/923): Muslim polymath and author of an important chronicle of world history in Arabic

Taghlib: Prominent Arab Christian tribe of the pre- and early Islamic periods, concentrated in Iraq

Tanūkh: Prominent Arab Christian tribe of the pre- and early Islamic periods, concentrated in Syria, Iraq, and northern Mesopotamia

Theodore Abū Qurra (d. post-816): Melkite churchman and scholar from Edessa; the first known Christian theologian to have written in Arabic

Theodore of Edessa: Fictional Melkite monk and bishop responsible for converting the caliph al-Maʾmūn to Christianity; possibly modeled on Theodore Abū Qurra

Theophanes Confessor (d. 818): Byzantine chronicler of the ancient and medieval Near East

Thomas Artsruni (d. ca. 904–8): Armenian chronicler who described early Arab rule in the Caucasus

Thomas of Damascus (d. ca. eighth century?): Bishop who engaged in a debate with a Muslim scholar and was later executed for blasphemy

Timothy I (d. 823): Long-reigning catholicos of the Church of the East; responsible for moving the seat of the church to Baghdad; presided over a network of dioceses stretching from the Mediterranean to China

Twenty Martyrs of Mar Saba (d. 788/797): Palestinian monks killed during a Bedouin raid on their monastery

ʿulamāʾ (sing. *ʿālim*): Muslim religious scholars

ʿUmar b. ʿAbd al-ʿAzīz (r. 99–101/717–20): Eighth Umayyad caliph

ʿUmar b. al-Khaṭṭāb (r. 13–23/634–44): Second Rightly Guided Caliph; oversaw the conquest of Syria, Egypt, Iraq, and parts of Iran

Umayyads: Dynasty of caliphs based in Syria; ruled 41–132/661–750; after the ʿAbbasid revolution, a branch of the Umayyad family carried on in al-Andalus, initially as independent *amīr*s (138–316/756–929) and then as independent caliphs (316–422/929–1031)

umma: The Muslim community or nation

Vahan of Gołtʿn (d. 737): Armenian prince who was taken captive and sent to Syria and converted to Islam; eventually returned to Armenia and converted back to Christianity; executed for apostasy in Ruṣāfa in Syria

Walabonsus of Córdoba (d. 851): Born to a Christian father and a Muslim mother who converted to Christianity; eventually became a deacon and was executed for blasphemy; his sister Maria was also killed

al-Walīd b. ʿAbd al-Malik (r. 86–96/705–15): Sixth Umayyad caliph

al-Walīd b. Yazīd (r. 125–26/743–44): Eleventh Umayyad caliph

West Syrians: Non-Chalcedonian Christians of Syria and Mesopotamia who established an independent hierarchy after breaking with the church of Constantinople in 451; also known as Syrian Orthodox, Miaphysites, Monophysites, Jacobites; primary languages: Syriac, Greek, and Arabic

Women Martyrs of Ḥimṣ (d. 779–80): The wife of an archdeacon and the wife of a nobleman who converted from Islam to Christianity; executed after refusing to return to Islam by an ʿAbbasid general

Yazīd b. ʿAbd al-Malik (r. 101–5/720–24): Ninth Umayyad caliph

Zāb River: In northern Mesopotamia; site of a famous battle in 132/750 when ʿAbbasid forces routed the Umayyads, leading to the toppling of the Umayyad dynasty

Zayd and Zaynab: Zayd was the Prophet's adopted son and was married to Zaynab until Muḥammad forced him to divorce her so that he could marry her himself; their divorce was apparently controversial in its own time and became the target of Christian polemics in the early Middle Ages

Zayd b. ʿAlī (d. 121/737–38): Grandson of the Shīʿī *imām* al-Ḥusayn who led an abortive anti-Umayyad revolt in Kūfa; beheaded, crucified, and burned in punishment

zunnār (pl. *zanānīr*): Under the terms of Islamic law, a special girdle Christians were obliged to wear in order to distinguish them from Muslims

Bibliography

Abashidze, Medea D., and Stephen H. Rapp Jr. "The Life and Passion of Kostanti-Kaxay." *Le Muséon* 117 (2004), 137–73.

Abbeloos, Joannes Baptista, and Thomas Josephus Lamy, eds. *Gregorii Barhebræi chronicon ecclesiasticum*. 3 vols. Louvain: Peeters, 1872–77.

ʿAbd al-Malik b. Ḥabīb. *Kitāb al-Tarīkh (La Historia)*. Jorge Aguadé, ed. Madrid: Consejo Superior de Investigaciones Científicas, 1991.

——. *Kitāb adab al-nisāʾ*. ʿAbd al-Majīd Turkī, ed. Beirut: Dār al-Gharb al-Islāmī, 1992.

——. *Kitāb al-ribā*. Nadhīr Awhab, ed. Dubai: Markaz Jumʿa al-Majīd lil-Thaqāfa wa-ʾl-Turāth, 2012.

ʿAbd al-Razzāq al-Ṣanʿānī. *al-Muṣannaf*. 12 vols. Ḥabīb al-Raḥmān al-Aʿẓamī, ed. Beirut: al-Maktab al-Islāmī, 1970–(?).

Abel, A. "La portée apologétique: La ‹vie› de St. Théodore d'Edesse." *Byzantinoslavica* 10 (1949), 229–40.

Abou El Fadl, Khaled. *Rebellion and Violence in Islamic Law*. Cambridge: Cambridge University Press, 2001.

Abū ʿAbdallāh al-Ḥumaydī. *Jadhwat al-muqtabis fī tārīkh ʿulamāʾ al-andalus*. Bashshār ʿAwwād Maʿrūf and Muḥammad Bashshār ʿAwwād, eds. Tunis: Dār al-Gharb al-Islāmī, 2008.

Abū Bakr al-Khallāl. *Aḥkām ahl al-milal*. Sayyid Kisrawī Ḥasan, ed. Beirut: Dār al-Kutub al-ʿIlmīya, 1994.

Abū Dāwūd. *Sunan Abī Dāwūd*. Beirut: Dār Ibn Ḥazm, 1998.

——. *Sunan Abī Dāwūd*. 7 vols. Shuʿayb al-Arnaʾūṭ and Muḥammad Kāmil Qarah Balilī, eds. Damascus: Dār al-Risāla al-ʿAlamīya, 2009.

Abū ʾl-ʿArab al-Tamīmī. *Kitāb al-miḥan*. Yaḥyā Wahīb al-Jabbūrī, ed. Beirut: Dār al-Gharb al-Islāmī, 2006.

Abū ʾl-Faraj al-Iṣfahānī. *Kitāb al-aghānī*. 21 vols. Būlāq, Cairo: Dār al-Kutub, 1868.

——. *Maqātil al-ṭālibīyīn*. Beirut: Manshūrāt al-Fajr, 2009.

Abū Nuʿaym al-Iṣfahānī. *Ḥilyat al-awliyāʾ*. 10 vols. Muḥammad Amīn al-Khānjī, ed. Cairo: Maktabat al-Khānjī, 1932–38.

Abū Yūsuf. *Kitāb al-kharāj*. Beirut: Dār al-Maʿrifa, 1979.

Abuladze, Ilia, ed. *Dzveli kʿartʿuli agiograpʿiuli literaturis dzeglebi*. 6 vols. Tbilisi: Mecniereba, 1963–89.

Acién Almansa, Manuel. *Entre el feudalismo y el Islam: ʿUmar Ibn Ḥafṣūn en los historiadores, en las fuentas y en la historia*. Jaén: Universidad de Jaén, 1997.

Acta sanctorum octobris tomus secundus. Antwerp: Apud Petrum Joannem vander Plassche, 1768.

Agha, Saleh Said. *The Revolution which Toppled the Umayyads: Neither Arab nor ʿAbbāsid*. Leiden: Brill, 2003.

Ahmad, Syed Barakat. "Conversion from Islam." In *The Islamic World from Classical to Modern Times: Essays in Honor of Bernard Lewis*. C. E. Bosworth, Charles Issawi, Roger Savoy, and A. L. Udovitch, eds. Princeton: Darwin Press, 1989, 3–25.

Aḥmad b. Ḥanbal. *Musnad aḥmad b. ḥanbal.* 6 vols. Beirut: al-Maktab al-Islāmī and Dār al-Ṣādir, 1969.

——. *Musnad al-imām aḥmad b. ḥanbal.* 8 vols. Ṭāhā al-Majdhūb and Muḥammad Salīm Ibrāhīm Samāra, eds. Beirut: al-Maktab al-Islāmī, 1993.

Ahmed, Shahab. *What Is Islam? The Importance of Being Islamic.* Princeton: Princeton University Press, 2015.

Aillet, Cyrille. *Les mozarabes: Christianisme, islamisation et arabisation en péninsule ibérique (IXe–XIIe siècle).* Madrid: Casa de Velázquez, 2010.

Akasoy, Anna. "*Convivencia* and Its Discontents: Interfaith Life in al-Andalus." *International Journal of Middle East Studies* 42 (2010), 489–99.

Akhbār al-dawla al-ʿabbāsīya wa-fīhi akhbār al-ʿabbās wa-waladihi. ʿAbd al-ʿAzīz al-Dūrī and ʿAbd al-Jabbār al-Muṭṭalibī, eds. Beirut: Dār al-Ṭalīʿa lil-Ṭibāʿa wa-ʾl-Nashr, 1971.

Aldana García, Maria Jesús, and Pedro Herrera Roldán. "Prudencio entre los mozárabes cordobeses: Algunos testimonios." *Latomus* 56 (1997), 765–83.

Ali, Kecia. *Marriage and Slavery in Early Islam.* Cambridge, MA: Harvard University Press, 2010.

Alishan, Ghewond, ed. *Hayapatum: Patmich'k' ew patmut'iwnk' hayots'.* 3 vols. Venice: S. Ghazar, 1901.

Alkhateeb, Firas. *Lost Islamic History: Reclaiming Muslim Civilisation from the Past.* London: Hurst, 2014.

Amari, Michele. *Storia dei Musulmani di Sicilia.* 3 vols. Florence: Felice le Monnier, 2002–3.

Anastasius of Sinai. *Anastasii Sinaitae quaestiones et responsiones.* Marcel Richard and Joseph A. Munitiz, eds. Turnhout: Brepols, 2006.

Andrae, Tor. *In the Garden of Myrtles: Studies in Early Islamic Mysticism.* Birgitta Sharpe, trans. Albany: State University of New York Press, 1987.

Anna Comnena. *The Alexiad.* E.R.A. Sewter, trans. London: Penguin, 1969.

Anonymous. "A New Martyr: Saint George the Egyptian." *Coptic Church Review* 3 (1982), 75–77.

Anthony, Sean W. "The Prophecy and Passion of al-Ḥāriṯ b. Saʿīd al-Khaḏḏāb: Narrating a Religious Movement from the Caliphate of ʿAbd al-Malik b. Marwān." *Arabica* 57 (2010), 1–29.

——. *The Caliph and the Heretic: Ibn Sabaʾ and the Origins of Shīʿism.* Leiden: Brill, 2012.

——. "Who Was the Shepherd of Damascus? The Enigma of Jewish and Messianist Responses to the Islamic Conquests in Marwānid Syria and Mesopotamia." In *The Lineaments of Islam: Studies in Honor of Fred McGraw Donner.* Paul M. Cobb, ed. Leiden: Brill, 2012, 21–59.

——. *Crucifixion and Death as Spectacle: Umayyad Crucifixion in Its Late Antique Context.* New Haven: American Oriental Society, 2014.

——. "Fixing John Damascene's Biography: Historical Notes on His Family Background." *Journal of Early Christian Studies* 23 (2015), 607–27.

Armanios, Febe. *Coptic Christianity in Ottoman Egypt.* New York: Oxford University Press, 2011.

Arnold, T. W. *The Preaching of Islam: A History of the Propagation of the Muslim Faith.* London: Archibald Constable and Co., 1896.

Arzoumanian, Zaven, trans. *History of Lewond the Eminent Vardapet of the Armenians.* Wynnewood, PA: St. Sahag and St. Mesrob Armenian Church, 1982.
[*CE*] Atiya, Aziz S., ed. *The Coptic Encyclopedia.* 8 vols. New York: Macmillan, 1991.
Atiya, Aziz S. "Martyrs, Coptic." *CE*, v, 1550–59.
———. "Synxarion, Copto-Arabic: The List of Saints." *CE*, vii, 2173–90.
Coquin, René-Georges. "Menas of al-Ashmūnayn, Saint." *CE*, v, 1589.
———. "Synaxarion, Copto-Arabic: Editions of the Synaxarion." *CE*, vii, 2172–73.
Frederick, Vincent. "Wāḍiḥ ibn Rajāʾ, al-." *CE*, vii, 2311.
Grossman, Peter, and Hans-Georg Severin. "Ashmūnayn, al-." *CE*, i, 285–88.
Labib, Subhi Y. "Būlus al-Ḥabīs, Saint." *CE*, ii, 424–25.
Orlandi, Tito. "Cycle." *CE*, iii, 666–68.
———. "Hagiography." *CE*, iv, 1191–97.
Atiya, Aziz S., Yassa Abd al-Masih, and O.H.E. Burmester, eds. and trans. *History of the Patriarchs of the Egyptian Church. Volume 2,2: Khaël III–Šenouti II (A.D. 880–1066).* Cairo: Publications de la Société d'Archéologie Copte, 1948.
Aubineau, Michel. "Un recueil ‹De haeresibus›: Sion College, Codex Graecus 6." *Revue des études grecques* 80 (1967), 425–29.
Aufhauser, Joannes B., ed. *Miracula S. Georgii.* Leipzig: Teubner, 1913.
Augustine of Hippo. *Confessions.* Henry Chadwick, trans. Oxford: Oxford University Press, 1991.
Auzépy, Marie-France. "De la Palestine à Constantinople (VIIIe–IXe siècles): Étienne le Sabaïte et Jean Damascène." *Travaux et mémoires* 12 (1994), 183–218.
———. *L'hagiographie et l'iconoclasme byzantin: Le cas de la "Vie d'Étienne le Jeune."* Aldershot: Ashgate, 1999.
Avni, Gideon. *The Byzantine-Islamic Transition in Palestine: An Archaeological Approach.* Oxford: Oxford University Press, 2014.
Ayalon, David. "Regarding Population Estimates in the Countries of Medieval Islam." *Journal of the Economic and Social History of the Orient* 28 (1985), 1–19.
Ayoub, Mahmoud. "Religious Freedom and the Law of Apostasy in Islam." *Islamochristiana* 20 (1994), 75–91.
al-Azdī. *Tārīkh futūḥ al-shām.* ʿAbd al-Munʿim ʿAbdallāh ʿĀmir, ed. Cairo: Muʾassasat Sijil al-ʿArab, 1970.
Al-Azmeh, Aziz. *The Emergence of Islam in Late Antiquity: Allāh and His Peoples.* New York: Cambridge University Press, 2014.
Baer, Marc. "Dönme (Maʾaminim, Minim, Shabbetaim)." In *Encyclopedia of Jews in the Islamic World.* 5 vols. Norman Stillman, executive ed. Leiden: Brill, 2010, ii, 89–90.
al-Balādhurī. *Liber expugnationis regionum auctore Imámo Ahmed ibn Jahya ibn Djábir al-Beládsorí, quem e codice Leidensi et codice Musei Brittanici.* M. J. de Goeje, ed. Leiden: Brill, 1866.
Banniard, Michel. *Viva voce: Communication écrite et communication orale du IVe au IXe siècle en Occident latin.* Paris: Institut des Études Augustiniennes, 1992.
Barceló, Miquel. "Un estudio sobre la estructura fiscal y procedimientos contables del emirato omeya de Córdoba (138–300/755–912) y del califato (300–366/912–976)." *Acta historica et archæologica mediævalia* 5–6 (1984–85), 45–72.
Barnes, T. D. "Legislation against the Christians." *Journal of Roman Studies* 58 (1968), 32–50.

Bartlett, Robert. *Why Can the Dead Do Such Great Things? Saints and Worshippers from the Martyrs to the Reformation.* Princeton: Princeton University Press, 2013.
Barton, Simon. *Conquerors, Brides, and Concubines: Interfaith Relations and Social Power in Medieval Iberia.* Philadelphia: University of Pennsylvania Press, 2015.
Bashear, Suliman. "Qibla Musharriqa and Early Muslim Prayer in Churches." *Muslim World* 81 (1991), 267–82.
——. *Arabs and Others in Early Islam.* Princeton: Darwin Press, 1997.
Basset, René. "Le synaxaire arabe jacobite (rédaction copte)." *Patrologia Orientalis* 1 (1904), 1–166 (217–379).
——. "Le synaxaire arabe jacobite (rédaction copte)." *Patrologia Orientalis* 3 (1909), 167–469 (243–545).
——. "Le synaxaire arabe jacobite (rédaction copte)." *Patrologia Orientalis* 11 (1915), 470–825 (505–859).
——. "Le synaxaire arabe jacobite (rédaction copte)." *Patrologia Orientalis* 16 (1922), 826–1066 (185–424).
——. "Le synaxaire arabe jacobite (rédaction copte)." *Patrologia Orientalis* 17 (1923), 1067–1324 (525–782).
Bat Ye'or. *The Dhimmi: A Historical Survey of Jews and Christians under Islam.* David Maisel, Paul Fenton, and David Littman, trans. Rutherford, NJ: Farleigh Dickinson University Press, 1984.
——. *The Decline of Eastern Christianity under Islam: From Jihad to Dhimmitude.* Miriam Kochan and David Littman, trans. Madison, NJ: Farleigh Dickinson University Press, 1996.
——. *Islam and Dhimmitude: Where Civilizations Collide.* Miriam Kochan and David Littman, trans. Madison, NJ: Farleigh Dickinson University Press, 2002.
Baumeister, Theofried. "Die Historia Monachorum in Aegypto und die Entwicklung der koptischen Hagiographie." In *Coptic Studies on the Threshhold of a New Millennium: Proceedings of the Seventh International Congress of Coptic Studies, Leiden, 27 August–2 September 2000.* 2 vols. Mat Immerzeel and Jacques Van der Vliet, eds. Leuven: Peeters, 2004, i, 269–80.
——. "Ägyptische Märtyrerhagiographie im frühen Mönchtum Palästinas." In *Martyrdom and Persecution in Late Antique Christianity: Festschrift Boudewijn Dehandschutter.* J. Leemans, ed. Leuven: Peeters, 2010, 33–45.
Baumstark, Anton. *Geschichte der syrischen Literatur.* Bonn: A. Marcus und E. Webers Verlag, 1922.
Bayan, G. "Le synaxaire arménien de Ter Israel." *Patrologia Orientalis* 21 (1930), 1–879.
Baynes, Norman H. *Constantine the Great and the Christian Church.* London: Oxford University Press, 1972.
[*EI*^{2}] Bearman, Peri, Thierry Bianquis, C. E. Bosworth, E. van Donzel, and Wolfhart P. Heinrichs, eds. *The Encyclopaedia of Islam. Second Edition.* 13 vols. Leiden: Brill, 1954–2009.

Barthold, W., and V. Minorsky. "Abkhāz." *EI*^{2}, i, 100–102.
Bosch-Vilá, J. "Ibn al-Ḳūṭiyya." *EI*^{2}, iii, 847–48.
Bosworth, C. E. "Zaynab bt. Djaḥsh." *EI*^{2}, xi, 484–85.
Brockett, A. "al-Munāfiḳūn." *EI*^{2}, vii, 561–62.
Cahen, Cl., and M. Talbi. "Ḥisba." *EI*^{2}, iii, 485–93.
Canard, M. "Armīniya." *EI*^{2}, i, 634–50.

——. "Djarādjima." *EI²*, ii, 456–58.
——. "al-Ḥākim bi-Amr Allāh." *EI²*, iii, 76–82.
Carra de Vaux, Barron, Joseph Schacht, and A.-M. Goichon. "Ḥadd." *EI²*, iii, 20–22.
Chalmeta, P. "Ḳūmis." *EI²*, v, 376–77.
——. "Mozarab," *EI²*, vii, 246–49.
Chaumont, E. "Tabanniⁱⁿ." *EI²*, xii, 768–69.
Crone, Patricia. "Mawlā." *EI²*, vi, 874–82.
Denny, F. M. "Tawba." *EI²*, x, 385.
Heffening, W. "Murtadd." *EI²*, vii, 635–36.
Honigmann, E. "al-Ramla." *EI²*, viii, 423–24.
Jones, Russell. "Ibrāhīm b. Adham." *EI²*, iii, 985–86.
Lecker, M. "Taghlib b. Wā'il." *EI²*, x, 89–93.
——. "Zayd b. Ḥāritha." *EI²*, xi, 475.
Madelung, Wilferd. "al-Manṣūriyya." *EI²*, vi, 441–42.
——. "al-Mughīriyya." *EI²*, vii, 347–48.
——. "Murdji'a." *EI²*, vii, 605–7.
——. "Yaḥyā b. Zayd." *EI²*, xi, 249–50.
Massignon, L., and L. Gardet. "al-Ḥallādj." *EI²*, iii, 99–104.
Merad, A. "Layth b. Sa'd." *EI²*, v, 711–12.
Minorsky, V., and C. E. Bosworth. "Tiflīs." *EI²*, x, 478–79.
Morony, Michael G. "Madjūs." *EI²*, v, 1110–18.
Ory, S. "Irbid." *EI²*, iv, 75–76.
Pellat, Ch. "Harthama b. A'yan." *EI²*, iii, 231.
Shahîd, Irfan. "Tanūkh." *EI²*, x, 190–92.
Sharon, Moshe. "Ludd." *EI²*, v, 798–803.
Sourdel, D. "Dayr Murrān." *EI²*, ii, 198.
Sourdel-Thomine, J. "Bayt Rās." *EI²*, i, 1149.
Stillman, Y. K., N. A. Stillman, and T. Majda. "Libās." *EI²*, v, 732–53.
Tritton, A. S. "Zunnār." *EI²*, xi, 571–72.
Vogel, F. E. "Ṣalb." *EI²*, viii, 935–36.
Watt, W. Montgomery. "Abū Lahab." *EI²*, i, 136–37.
——. "'Idjl." *EI²*, iii, 1022–23.
——. "Ka'b b. al-Ashraf." *EI²*, iv, 315.
Wensinck, A. J. "Khitān." *EI²*, v, 20–22.
Wensinck, A. J., and Ch. Pellat. "Ḥūr." *EI²*, iii, 581–82.
Wensinck, A. J., and D. Thomas. "Ṣalīb." *EI²*, viii, 980–81.
Wiederhold, Lutz. "Shatm." *EI²*, xii, 725–27.
Beaucamp, Joëlle, Françoise Briquel-Chatonnet, and Christian Julien Robin, eds. *Juifs et chrétiens en Arabie au Ve et VIe siècles: Regards croisés sur les sources.* Paris: Association des amis du Centre d'histoire et civilisation de Byzance, 2010.
Beck, Edmund. "Das christliche Mönchtum im Koran." *Studia Orientalia* 13, no. 3 (1946), 1–29.
Bedjan, Paul, ed. *Gregorii Barhebræi Chronicon Syriacum e codd. mss. emendatum ac punctis vocalibus adnotationibusque locupletatum.* Paris: Maisonneuve, 1890.
Bennison, Amira K. *The Great Caliphs: The Golden Age of the 'Abbasid Empire.* London: I. B. Tauris, 2009.

Bercher, L. "L'Apostasie, le Blasphème et la Rébellion en droit Musulman malékite." *Revue tunisienne* 30 (1923), 115–30.

Berkey, Jonathan P. *Popular Preaching and Religious Authority in the Medieval Islamic Near East.* Seattle: University of Washington Press, 2001.

Bernards, Monique, and John Nawas, eds. *Patronate and Patronage in Early and Classical Islam.* Leiden: Brill, 2005.

Bertaina, David. *Christian and Muslim Dialogues: The Religious Uses of a Literary Form in the Early Islamic Middle East.* Piscataway, NJ: Gorgias Press, 2011.

——. "*Ḥadīth* in the Christian Arabic *Kalām* of Būluṣ Ibn Rajāʾ (c. 1000)." *Intellectual History of the Islamicate World* 2 (2014), 267–86.

——. "A Medieval Coptic Convert's Analysis of Islam: The *Kitāb al-wāḍiḥ bi-l-ḥaqq* of Būluṣ ibn Rağāʾ." *Parole de l'Orient* 39 (2014), 181–201.

Berti, Vittorio. *Vita e studi di Timoteo I patriarca cristiano di Baghdad.* Paris: Association pour l'avancement des études iraniennes, 2009.

[*BS*] *Bibliotheca sanctorum.* 16 vols. Rome: Istituto Giovanni XXIII nella Pontificia Università lateranense, 1961–2013.

[*BSO*] *Bibliotheca sanctorum orientalium. Enciclopedia dei santi: Le chiese orientali.* 2 vols. Rome: Città nuova, 1998–99.

Binggeli, André. "Anastase le Sinaïte: *Récits sur le Sinaï* et *Récits utiles à l'âme.* Édition, traduction, commentaire." Ph.D. dissertation, Université Paris IV, 2001.

——. "L'Hagiographie du Sinaï en arabe d'après un recueil du IXe siècle (*Sinaï arabe 542*)." *Parole de l'Orient* 32 (2007), 163–80.

——. "Converting the Caliph: A Legendary Motif in Christian Hagiography and Historiography of the Early Islamic Period." In *Writing "True Stories": Historians and Hagiographers in the Late Antique and Medieval Near East.* Arietta Papaconstantinou with Muriel Debié and Hugh Kennedy, eds. Turnhout: Brepols, 2010, 77–103.

——. "Un ancien calendrier melkite de Jérusalem (Sinai Syr. M52N)." In *Sur le pas des Araméens chrétiens. Mélanges offerts à Alain Desreumaux.* Françoise Briquel-Chatonnet and Muriel Debié, eds. Paris: Geuthner, 2010, 181–94.

——. "La réception de l'hagiographie palestinienne à Byzance après les conquêtes arabes." In *Byzantine Hagiography: Texts, Themes and Projects.* Antonio Rigo, Michele Trizio, and Eleftherios Despotakis, eds. Turnhout: Brepols, 2017.

Bīṭār, Tūmā. *al-Qiddīsūn al-mansīyūn fī ʾl-turāth al-anṭākī.* Douma, Syria: ʿĀʾilat al-Thālūth al-Quddūs, Dayr Mār Yuḥannā, 1995.

Blake, Robert P., ed. *Catalogue des manuscrits géorgiens de la Bibliothèque de la Laure d'Iviron au mont Athos.* Paris: A. Picard, 1932.

——. "Deux lacunes comblées dans *Passio XX monachorum sabitarum.*" *Analecta Bollandiana* 68 (1950), 27–43.

——. "La littérature grecque en Palestine au VIIIe siècle." *Le Muséon* 78 (1965), 367–80.

Blanchard, Monica. "The Georgian Version of the Martyrdom of Saint Michael, Monk of Mar Sabas Monastery." *ARAM* 6 (1994), 149–63.

Blankinship, Khalid Yahya. *The End of the Jihâd State: The Reign of Hishām Ibn ʿAbd al-Malik and the Collapse of the Umayyads.* Albany: State University of New York Press, 1994.

Bonner, Michael. "Some Observations Concerning the Early Development of Jihad on the Arab-Byzantine Frontier." *Studia Islamica* 75 (1992), 5–31.

——. *Aristocratic Violence and Holy War: Studies in the Jihad and the Arab-Byzantine Frontier.* New Haven: American Oriental Society, 1996.

Bowersock, G. W. *Martyrdom and Rome.* Cambridge: Cambridge University Press, 1995.

——. *Mosaics as History: The Near East from Late Antiquity to Islam.* Cambridge, MA: Belknap Press of Harvard University Press, 2006.

——. *The Crucible of Islam.* Cambridge, MA: Harvard University Press, 2017.

Bowersock, G. W., Peter Brown, and Oleg Grabar, eds. *Late Antiquity: A Guide to the Postclassical World.* Cambridge, MA: Belknap Press of Harvard University Press, 1999.

Bowman, Bradley. "The Status of Christian Monasteries in the Early Islamic Period: An Examination of Early Muslim Attitudes toward Monastic Communities and Its Relevance to the Formative Period of Islam." Ph.D. dissertation, University of Chicago, 2013.

Bowman, Jeffrey, trans. "Raguel, *The Martyrdom of St. Pelagius.*" In *Medieval Hagiography: An Anthology.* Thomas Head, ed. New York: Garland Publishing Inc., 2000, 227–35.

Boyarin, Daniel. *Dying for God: Martyrdom and the Making of Christianity and Judaism.* Stanford, CA: Stanford University Press, 1999.

Braida, Emanuela, and Chiara Pelissetti. *Storia di Rawḥ al-Qurašī: Un discendente di Maometto che scelse di divenire cristiano.* Turin: Silvio Zamorani, 2001.

Braun, Oskar, ed. *Timothei patriarchae 1 epistulae.* 2 vols. Louvain: Imprimerie Orientaliste, 1953.

Braund, Susanna Morton, ed. and trans. *Juvenal and Persius.* Loeb Classical Library. Cambridge, MA: Harvard University Press, 2004.

Bray, Julia. "Christian King, Muslim Apostate: Depictions of Jabala Ibn al-Ayham in Early Arabic Sources." In *Writing "True Stories": Historians and Hagiographers in the Late Antique and Medieval Near East.* Arietta Papaconstantinou with Muriel Debié and Hugh Kennedy, eds. Turnhout: Brepols, 2010, 175–203.

Bréhier, Elias. "La situation des chrétiens de Palestine à la fin du VIIIe siècle et l'établissement du protectorat de Charlemagne." *Le moyen âge,* sèr. 2, 21 (1919), 67–75.

Brett, Michael. "The Spread of Islam in Egypt and North Africa." In *Northern Africa: Islam and Modernization.* Michael Brett, ed. London: Frank Cass, 1973, 1–12.

Brock, Sebastian P. "Christians in the Sasanian Empire: A Case of Divided Loyalties." *Studies in Church History* 18 (1982), 1–19.

——. "Syriac Views of Emergent Islam." In *Studies on the First Century of Islamic Society.* G.H.A. Juynboll, ed. Carbondale, IL: Southern Illinois University Press, 1982, 9–21.

——. *The History of the Holy Mar Maʿin with a Guide to the Persian Martyr Acts.* Piscataway, NJ: Gorgias Press, 2008.

——. "Syriac Hagiography." In *The Ashgate Research Companion to Byzantine Hagiography. Volume I: Periods and Places.* Stephanos Efthymiadis, ed. Farnham, UK: Ashgate, 2011, 259–83.

Brooks, E. W. "Byzantines and Arabs in the Time of the Early Abbasids." *English Historical Review* 15 (1900), 728–47.

——. "A Syriac Fragment." *Zeitschrift der Deutschen Morgenländischen Gesellschaft* 54 (1900), 195–230.

Brooks, E. W., ed. *Chronica minora.* 3 vols. Paris: E Typographeo Reipublicae, 1903–5.

Brown, Peter. “The Rise and Function of the Holy Man in Late Antiquity.” *Journal of Roman Studies* 61 (1971), 80–101.

——. *The World of Late Antiquity: From Marcus Aurelius to Muhammad.* London: Thames and Hudson, 1971.

——. *The Cult of the Saints: Its Rise and Function in Latin Christianity.* Chicago: University of Chicago Press, 1981 (with a new preface, 2014).

——. *Power and Persuasion in Late Antiquity: Towards a Christian Empire.* Madison, WI: University of Wisconsin Press, 1992.

——. *The Rise of Western Christendom: Triumph and Diversity, A.D. 200–1000.* 2nd ed. Malden, MA: Blackwell Publishers, 2003.

Budge, E. A. Wallis, ed. and trans. *The Book of Governors: The “Historia monastica” of Thomas Bishop of Margâ, A.D. 840.* 2 vols. London: Kegan Paul, Trench, Trübner and Co. Ltd., 1893.

——, ed. and trans. *The Histories of Rabban Hôrmîzd the Persian and Rabban Bar ʿIdtâ.* 2 vols. London: Luzac and Co., 1902.

——, ed. and trans. *The Chronography of Gregory Abû'l-Faraj, the Son of Aaron, the Hebrew Physician Commonly Known as Bar Hebraeus, Being the First Part of His Political History of the World.* 2 vols. London: Oxford University Press, 1932.

al-Bukhārī. *Ṣaḥīḥ al-bukhārī.* Damascus: Dār Ibn Kathīr lil-Ṭibāʿa wa-ʾl-Nashr, 2002.

Bulkeley, Kelly. “Dreaming and Religious Conversion.” In *The Oxford Handbook of Religious Conversion.* Lewis R. Rambo and Charles E. Farhadian, eds. Oxford: Oxford University Press, 2014, 256–70.

Bulliet, Richard W. *Conversion to Islam in the Medieval Period: An Essay in Quantitative History.* Cambridge, MA: Harvard University Press, 1979.

——. “Conversion Stories in Early Islam.” In *Conversion and Continuity: Indigenous Christian Communities in Islamic Lands, Eighth to Eighteenth Centuries.* Michael Gervers and Ramzi Jibran Bikhazi, eds. Toronto: Pontifical Institute of Mediaeval Studies, 1990, 123–33.

——. “Conversion-Based Patronage and Onomastic Evidence.” In *Patronate and Patronage in Early and Classical Islam.* Monique Bernards and John Nawas, eds. Leiden: Brill, 2005, 246–62.

——. “Conversion and Law: A Muslim-Christian Comparison.” In *Law and Tradition in Classical Islamic Thought: Studies in Honor of Professor Hossein Modarressi.* Michael Cook, Najam Haider, Intisar Rabb, and Asma Sayeed, eds. New York: Palgrave Macmillan, 2013, 279–90.

——. “The Conversion Curve Revisited.” In *Islamisation: Comparative Perspectives from History.* A.C.S. Peacock, ed. Edinburgh: University of Edinburgh Press, 2017, 69–79.

Burgmann, Ludwig. “Penalties.” In *Oxford Dictionary of Byzantium.* 3 vols. Alexander Kazhdan, ed. Oxford: Oxford University Press, 1991, iii, 1622.

Butler, Alfred J. *The Arab Conquest of Egypt and the Last Thirty Years of Roman Dominion.* Oxford: Clarendon Press, 1902.

Butts, Aaron Michael, and Simcha Gross. *The History of the “Slave of Christ”: From Jewish Child to Christian Martyr.* Piscataway, NJ: Gorgias Press, 2016.

Bynum, Caroline Walker. *The Resurrection of the Body in Western Christianity, 200–1336.* New York: Columbia University Press, 1995.

Cabrol, Cécile. *Les secrétaires nestoriens à Bagdad (762–1258 AD).* Beirut: CERPOC, 2012.

Cagigas, Isidro de las. *Los mozárabes.* 2 vols. Madrid: Instituto de Estudios Africanos, 1947–48.

Cahen, Claude. "Fiscalité, propriété, antagonismes sociaux en Haute-Mésopotamie au temps des premiers ʿAbbāsides d'après Denys de Tell-Maḥré." *Arabica* 1 (1954), 136–52.

———. "An Introduction to the First Crusade." *Past and Present* 6 (1954), 6–30.

Cameron, Averil. "The Long Late Antiquity: A Late Twentieth-Century Model." In *Classics in Progress: Essays on Ancient Greece and Rome.* T. P. Wiseman, ed. Oxford: Oxford University Press for the British Academy, 2002, 165–91.

Cameron, Averil, Lawrence I. Conrad, G.R.D. King, and John Haldon, eds. *The Byzantine and Early Islamic Near East: Papers of the Workshop on Late Antiquity and Early Islam.* 4 vols. Princeton: Darwin Press, 1992–2004.

Campbell, Elizabeth. "A Heaven of Wine: Muslim-Christian Encounters in Monasteries in the Early Islamic Middle East." Ph.D. dissertation, University of Washington, 2009.

Carlson, Thomas A. "The Contours of Conversion: The Geography of Islamization in Syria, 600–1500." *Journal of the American Oriental Society* 135 (2015), 791–816.

Carlson, Thomas A., and David A. Michelson. "Dara—ܕܪܐ." *Syriac Gazetteer,* June 30, 2014. Thomas A. Carlson and David A. Michelson, eds. *Syriaca.org: The Syriac Reference Portal.* David A. Michelson, ed. http://syriaca.org/place/67.html.

———. "Monastery of Esṭona—ܕܝܪܐ ܕܐܣܛܘܢܐ." *Syriac Gazateer,* June 30, 2014. Thomas A. Carlson and David A. Michelson, eds. *Syriaca.org: The Syriac Reference Portal.* David A. Michelson, ed. http://syriaca.org/place/371.html.

Casado Fuente, Genadio. *Estudios sobre el latín medieval español: El abad Samsón. Edición crítica y comentario filológico de su obra.* Madrid: Facultad de Filosofía y Letras, 1964.

Caskel, Werner, ed. *Ǧamharat an-nasab; das genealogische Werk des Hišām Ibn Muḥammad al-Kalbī.* 2 vols. Leiden: Brill, 1966.

Castejón, Rafael. "Córdoba Califal." *Boletín de la Real Academia de Ciencias, Bellas Letras y Nobles Artes de Córdoba* 8 (1929), 253–339.

Castelli, Elizabeth A. *Martyrdom and Memory: Early Christian Culture Making.* New York: Columbia University Press, 2004.

Cavadini, John C. *The Last Christology of the West: Adoptionism in Spain and Gaul, 785–820.* Philadelphia: University of Pennsylvania Press, 1993.

Cavallo, Guglielmo. "Qualche riflessione sulla continuità della cultura greca in oriente tra i secoli VII e VIII." *Byzantinische Zeitschrift* 88 (1995), 13–22.

Cereti, Carlo G. "Myths, Legends, Eschatologies." In *The Wiley Blackwell Companion to Zoroastrianism.* Michael Stausberg and Yuhan Sohrab-Dinshaw Vevaina, with Anna Tessmann, eds. Malden, MA: Wiley Blackwell, 2015, 259–72.

Chabot, J.-B., ed. *Chronique de Michel le Syrien: Patriarche jacobite d'Antioche (1166–1199).* 4 vols. Paris: Ernest Leroux, 1899–1910.

———. "Notes d'épigraphie et d'archéologie orientale." *Journal asiatique,* sèr. 9, 16 (1900), 249–88.

———, ed. *Chronicon anonymum Pseudo-Dionysianum vulgo dictum.* 4 vols. CSCO 91, 104, 121, 507. Louvain: L. Durbecq, 1949–89.

———, ed. *Anonymi auctoris chronicon ad annum Christi 1234 pertinens.* 3 vols. Louvain: L. Durbecq, 1952–53.

Chacha, Homi F. *Gajastak Abâlish: Pahlavi Text with Transliteration, English Translation, Notes and Glossary*. Bombay: Trustees of the Parsi Punchayet Funds and Properties, 1936.

Charanis, Peter. "The Transfer of Population as a Policy in the Byzantine Empire." *Comparative Studies in Society and History* 3 (1961), 140–54.

Charles, R. H. *The Chronicle of John, Bishop of Nikiu*. London: Williams and Norgate, 1916.

Cheïkho, Louis. *Les vizirs et secrétaires arabes chrétiens en Islam, 622–1517*. Camille Hechaïmé, ed. Rome: Pontificio Istituto Orientale, 1987.

Choksy, Jamsheed K. *Purity and Pollution in Zoroastrianism: Triumph over Evil*. Austin: University of Texas Press, 1989.

———. *Conflict and Cooperation: Zoroastrian Subalterns and Muslim Elites in Medieval Iranian Society*. New York: Columbia University Press, 1997.

———. "Hagiography and Monotheism in History: Doctrinal Encounters between Zoroastrianism, Judaism, and Christianity." *Islam and Christian-Muslim Relations* 14 (2003), 407–21.

Christys, Ann. *Christians in al-Andalus (711–1100)*. Richmond, UK: Curzon, 2002.

Chrysostomides, Anna. " 'There Is No God but God': Islamisation and Religious Code-Switching, Eighth to Tenth Centuries." In *Islamisation: Comparative Perspectives from History*. A.C.S. Peacock, ed. Edinburgh: Edinburgh University Press, 2017, 118–33.

Clarke, Nicola. *The Muslim Conquest of Iberia: Medieval Arabic Narratives*. London: Routledge, 2012.

Cobb, Paul M. *White Banners: Contention in ʿAbbāsid Syria, 750–880*. Albany: State University of New York Press, 2001.

Coghill, Edward P. Z. "Minority Representation in the *Futūḥ Miṣr* of Ibn ʿAbd al-Ḥakam." In *The Late Antique World of Early Islam: Muslims among Christians and Jews in the East Mediterranean*. Robert G. Hoyland, ed. Princeton: Darwin Press, 2015, 9–35.

Cohen, Mark R. "At the Origins of the Distinctive Dress Regulation for Non-Muslims in Islam: The *Zunnār*, Discrimination or Reinforcement of Communal Identity?" Unpublished MS, 1993.

———. "What Was the Pact of ʿUmar? A Literary-Historical Study." *Jerusalem Studies in Arabic and Islam* 23 (1999), 100–157.

———. *Under Crescent and Cross: The Jews in the Middle Ages*. Revised ed. with new introduction and afterword. Princeton: Princeton University Press, 2008.

Colbert, Edward P. "The *Memoriale sanctorum* of Eulogius of Cordova: A Translation with Critical Introduction." M.A. thesis, Catholic University of America, 1956.

———. *The Martyrs of Córdoba (850–859): A Study of the Sources*. Washington, DC: Catholic University of America Press, 1962.

Collins, Roger. "Literacy and the Laity in Early Mediaeval Spain." In *The Uses of Literacy in Early Mediaeval Europe*. Rosamond M. McKitterick, ed. Cambridge: Cambridge University Press, 1990, 109–33.

[*CMLT*] Combefis, Franciscus, ed. *Christi martyrum lecta trias Hyacinthus Amastrensis, Bacchus et Elias novi-martyres*. Paris: Apud Fredericum Leonard, 1666.

Conrad, Gerhard. *Die Quḍāt Dimašq und der Maḏhab al-Auzāʿī*. Beirut: Franz Steiner Verlag, 1994.

Conrad, Lawrence I. "A Nestorian Diploma of Investiture from the Tadhkira of Ibn Ḥamdūn: The Text and Its Significance." In *Studia Arabica et Islamica: Festschrift for Iḥsān ʿAbbās on His Sixtieth Birthday*. Wadād al-Qāḍī, ed. Beirut: American University of Beirut, 1981, 83–104.

Cook, David. *Studies in Muslim Apocalyptic*. Princeton: Darwin Press, 2002.

——. "Apostasy from Islam: A Historical Perspective." *Jerusalem Studies in Arabic and Islam* 31 (2006), 248–88.

——. *Martyrdom in Islam*. Cambridge: Cambridge University Press, 2007.

Cook, Michael. *Commanding Right and Forbidding Wrong in Islamic Thought*. Cambridge: Cambridge University Press, 2000.

Coope, Jessica A. *The Martyrs of Córdoba: Community and Family Conflict in an Age of Mass Conversion*. Lincoln, NE: University of Nebraska Press, 1995.

Cowe, S. Peter. "Armenian Hagiography." In *The Ashgate Research Companion to Byzantine Hagiography. Volume I: Periods and Places*. Stephanos Efthymiadis, ed. Farnham, UK: Ashgate, 2011, 299–322.

Crone, Patricia. "Islam, Judeo-Christianity and Byzantine Iconoclasm." *Jerusalem Studies in Arabic and Islam* 2 (1980), 59–95.

——. *Slaves on Horses: The Evolution of the Islamic Polity*. Cambridge: Cambridge University Press, 1980.

——. " 'No Compulsion in Religion': Q. 2:256 in Mediaeval and Modern Interpretation." In *Le Shīʿisme imāmite quarante ans après: Hommage à Etan Kohlberg*. Mohammad Ali Amir-Moezzi, Meir M. Bar-Asher, and Simon Hopkins, eds. Turnhout: Brepols, 2009, 131–78.

——. *The Nativist Prophets of Early Islamic Iran: Rural Revolt and Local Zoroastrianism*. Cambridge: Cambridge University Press, 2012.

Crone, Patricia, and Michael Cook. *Hagarism: The Making of the Islamic World*. Cambridge: Cambridge University Press, 1977.

Crone, Patricia, and Martin Hinds. *God's Caliph: Religious Authority in the First Centuries of Islam*. Cambridge: Cambridge University Press, 1986.

Cutler, Allan. "The Ninth-Century Spanish Martyrs' Movement and the Origins of Western Christian Missions to the Muslims." *Moslem World* 55 (1965), 321–39.

Cutler, Allan, and Helen Elmquist Cutler. *The Jew as Ally of the Muslim: Medieval Roots of Anti-Semitism*. Notre Dame, IN: University of Notre Dame Press, 1986.

Cyril of Scythopolis. *The Lives of the Monks of Palestine*. R. M. Price, trans., with John Binns. Kalamazoo, MI: Cistercian Publications, 1991.

Dalrymple, William. *From the Holy Mountain: A Journey in the Shadow of Byzantium*. London: HarperCollins Publishers, 1997.

Dan, Joseph. "Hagiography." In *Encyclopaedia Judaica*. 22 vols. Fred Skolnik, with Michael Berenbaum, eds. Detroit: Thomson Gale, 2007, viii, 224–26.

Daniel, Norman. *The Arabs and Mediaeval Europe*. London: Longman, 1975.

Daryaee, Touraj. *Sasanian Persia: The Rise and Fall of an Empire*. London: I. B. Tauris, 2009.

——. "Zoroastrianism under Islamic Rule." In *The Wiley Blackwell Companion to Zoroastrianism*. Michael Stausberg and Yuhan Sohrab-Dinshaw Vevaina, with Anna Tessmann, eds. Malden, MA: Wiley Blackwell, 2015, 103–18.

Davis, Leo Donald. *The First Seven Ecumenical Councils (325–787): Their History and Theology*. Collegeville, MN: Liturgical Press, 1983.

de Blois, François. "*Naṣrānī* (Ναζωραῖος) and *Ḥanīf* (ἐθνικός)." *Bulletin of the School of Oriental and African Studies* 65 (2002), 1–30.

de Boor, Carolus, ed. *Theophanis chronographia.* 2 vols. Leipzig: Teubner, 1883–85.

de Jong, Albert. "The *Dēnkard* and the Zoroastrians of Baghdad." In *The Zoroastrian Flame: Exploring Religion, History, and Tradition.* Alan Williams, Sarah Stewart, and Almut Hintze, eds. London: I. B. Tauris, 2016, 223–38.

de la Granja, Fernando. "Fiestas cristianas en al-Andalus." *al-Andalus* 34 (1969), 1–53; *al-Andalus* 35 (1970), 119–42.

De Ste. Croix, G.E.M. "Aspects of the 'Great' Persecution." *Harvard Theological Review* 47 (1954), 75–113.

——. "Why Were the Early Christians Persecuted?" *Past and Present* 26 (1963), 6–38.

——. *Christian Persecution, Martyrdom, and Orthodoxy.* Michael Whitby and Joseph Streeter, eds. Oxford: Oxford University Press, 2006.

de Vries, Bert. "The Umm El-Jimal Project, 1981–1991." *Annual of the Department of Antiquities of Jordan* 27 (1993), 433–60.

Debié, Muriel. "Writing History as 'Histories': The Biographical Dimension of East Syriac Historiography." In *Writing "True Stories": Historians and Hagiographers in the Late Antique and Medieval Near East.* Arietta Papaconstantinou, with Muriel Debié and Hugh Kennedy, eds. Turnhout: Brepols, 2010, 43–75.

——. *L'écriture de l'histoire en syriaque. Transmissions interculturelles et constructions identitaires entre hellénisme et islam.* Leuven: Peeters, 2015.

——. "Christians in the Service of the Caliph: Through the Looking Glass of Communal Identities." In *Christians and Others in the Umayyad State.* Antoine Borrut and Fred M. Donner, eds. Chicago: Oriental Institute of the University of Chicago, 2016, 53–71.

Delehaye, Hippolyte, ed. *Synaxarium ecclesiae Constantinopolitanae e Codice Sirmondiano.* Brussels: Apud Socios Bollandianos, 1902.

——. "Passio sanctorum sexaginta martyrum." *Analecta Bollandiana* 23 (1904), 289–307.

——. *Les légendes hagiographiques.* Brussels: Bureaux de la Société des Bollandistes, 1905.

——. *A travers trois siècles: L'œuvre des Bollandistes 1615–1916.* Brussels: Bureaux de la Société des Bollandistes, 1920.

Dēmētrakopoulos, Phōtios. "Hagios Bakchos ho neos." *Epistēmonikē epetēris tēs philosophikēs scholēs tou panepistēmiou Athēnōn* 26 (1977–79), 331–63.

den Heijer, Johannes. "Apologetic Elements in Copto-Arabic Historiography: The Life of Afrahām Ibn Zurʿah, 62nd Patriarch of Alexandria." In *Christian Arabic Apologetics during the Abbasid Period (750–1258).* Samir Khalil Samir and Jørgen S. Nielsen, eds. Leiden: Brill, 1994, 192–202.

Dennett, Daniel C. *Conversion and the Poll Tax in Early Islam.* Cambridge, MA: Harvard University Press, 1950.

Der Nersessian, Sirarpie. *Aght'amar: Church of the Holy Cross.* Cambridge, MA: Harvard University Press, 1965.

Detoraki, Marina. "Greek *Passions* of the Martyrs in Byzantium." In *The Ashgate Research Companion to Byzantine Hagiography. Volume II: Genres and Contexts.* Stephanos Efthymiadis, ed. Farnham, UK: Ashgate, 2014, 61–101.

Devos, Paul. "Le R. P. Paul Peeters (1870–1950): Son œuvre et sa personnalité de Bollandiste." *Analecta Bollandiana* 69 (1951), i–lix.

Devreese, Robert, ed. *Le fonds Coislin.* Paris: Imprimerie nationale, 1945.

Díaz y Díaz, Manuel Cecilio. "Los mozárabes. Una minoría combativa." In *¿Existe una identidad mozárabe? Historia, lengua y cultura de los cristianos de al-Andalus (siglos IX–XII).* Cyrille Aillet, Mayte Penelas, and Philippe Roisse, eds. Madrid: Casa de Velázquez, 2008, 1–8.

Dick, Ignace. "La passion arabe de S. Antoine Ruwaḥ néo-martyr de Damas († 25 déc. 799)." *Le Muséon* 74 (1961), 109–33.

——, ed. *Maymar fī ikrām al-īqūnāt li-thāwdhūrus abī qurra.* Jounieh, Lebanon: al-Maktaba al-Būlusīya, 1986.

Donner, Fred M. "The Bakr b. Wāʾil Tribes and Politics in Northeastern Arabia on the Eve of Islam." *Studia Islamica* 51 (1980), 5–38.

——. *Muhammad and the Believers: At the Origins of Islam.* Cambridge, MA: Belknap Press of Harvard University Press, 2010.

Douglas, Mary. *Purity and Danger: An Analysis of the Concept of Pollution and Taboo.* London: Routledge, 2002.

Dozy, Reinhart. *Spanish Islam: A History of the Moslems in Spain.* Francis Griffin Stokes, trans. London: Chatto and Windus, 1913.

Drake, H. A. "Lambs into Lions: Explaining Early Christian Intolerance." *Past and Present* 153 (1996), 3–36.

Drees, Clayton J. "Sainthood and Suicide: The Motives of the Martyrs of Córdoba, A.D. 850–859." *Journal of Medieval and Renaissance Studies* 20 (1990), 59–89.

Dridi, Audrey. "Toponyms in Multilingual Contexts: The Case of Fossaton and Babylon during the First Century of Islamic Egypt." Unpublished MS.

Dussaud, René. *Topographie historique de la Syrie antique et médiévale.* Paris: Librairie Orientalist Paul Geuthner, 1927.

Duque, Adriano. "Claiming Martyrdom in the Episode of the Martyrs of Córdoba." *Collectanea Christiana Orientalia* 8 (2011), 23–48.

Dvornik, Francis. *La vie de saint Grégoire le Décapolite et les Slaves macédoniens au IXe siècle.* Paris: Champion, 1926.

Efthymiadis, Stephanos, ed. *The Ashgate Research Companion to Byzantine Hagiography. Volume I: Periods and Places.* Farnham, UK: Ashgate, 2011.

——. "Hagiography from the 'Dark Age' to the Age of Symeon Metaphrastes (Eighth–Tenth Centuries)." In *The Ashgate Research Companion to Byzantine Hagiography. Volume I: Periods and Places.* Stephanos Efthymiadis, ed. Farnham, UK: Ashgate, 2011, 95–142.

——, ed. *The Ashgate Research Companion to Byzantine Hagiography. Volume II: Genres and Contexts.* Farnham, UK: Ashgate, 2014.

Efthymiadis, Stephanos, and Nikos Kalogeras. "Audience, Language and Patronage in Byzantine Hagiography." In *The Ashgate Research Companion to Byzantine Hagiography. Volume II: Genres and Contexts.* Stephanos Efthymiadis, ed. Farnham, UK: Ashgate, 2014, 247–84.

Ehrman, Bart D., trans. *The Apostolic Fathers.* 2 vols. Loeb Classical Library. Cambridge, MA: Harvard University Press, 2003.

El Cheikh, Nadia Maria. *Byzantium Viewed by the Arabs.* Cambridge, MA: Harvard University Press, 2004.

El Cheikh, Nadia Maria. *Women, Islam, and Abbasid Identity.* Cambridge, MA: Harvard University Press, 2015.

Eleuteri, Paolo, and Antonio Rigo. *Eretici, dissidenti, musulmani ed ebrei a Bisanzio: Una raccolta eresiologica del XII secolo.* Venice: Il Cardo, 1993.

El-Leithy, Tamer. "Coptic Culture and Conversion in Medieval Cairo, 1293–1524 A.D." Ph.D. dissertation, Princeton University, 2005.

——. "Sufis, Copts and the Politics of Piety: Moral Regulation in Fourteenth-Century Upper Egypt." In *Le développement du soufisme en Égypte à l'époque mamelouke.* Richard McGregor and Adam Sabra, eds. Cairo: Institut français d'archéologie orientale, 2006, 75–119.

Ellenblum, Ronnie. *Frankish Rural Settlement in the Latin Kingdom of Jerusalem.* Cambridge: Cambridge University Press, 1998.

Elukin, Jonathan M. *Living Together, Living Apart: Rethinking Jewish-Christian Relations in the Middle Ages.* Princeton: Princeton University Press, 2007.

Epalza, Miguel de. "Mozarabs: An Emblematic Christian Minority in Islamic al-Andalus." In *The Legacy of Muslim Spain.* Salma Khadra Jayyusi, ed. Leiden: Brill, 1992, 149–70.

Ernst, Carl W. "Blasphemy: Islamic Concept." In *Encyclopedia of Religion.* 2nd ed. 15 vols. Lindsay Jones, ed. Detroit: Macmillan Reference, 2005, ii, 974–77.

Eusebius. *The Ecclesiastical History.* Loeb Classical Library. 2 vols. J.E.L. Oulton, trans., with H. J. Lawlor. London: William Heinemann Ltd., 1942.

Eutychius. *Eutychii patriarchae Alexandrini annales.* 2 vols. L. Cheikho, B. Carra de Vaux, and H. Zayyat, eds. Beirut: E Typographeo Catholico, 1906–9.

Evans, Helen C., with Brandie Ratliff, eds. *Byzantium and Islam: Age of Transition, 7th–9th Century.* New York: Metropolitan Museum of Art; and New Haven: Yale University Press, 2012.

Evetts, B. "History of the Patriarchs of the Coptic Church of Alexandria, III: Agathon to Michael I (766)." *Patrologia Orientalis* 5 (1910), 1–215.

Fargues, Philippe. "Demographic Islamization: Non-Muslims in Muslim Countries." *SAIS Review* 21 (2001), 103–16.

Fattal, Antoine. *Le statut légal des non-musulmans en pays d'Islam.* Beirut: Imprimerie catholique, 1958.

Fedalto, Giorgio. *Hierarchia Ecclesiastica Orientalis: Series episcoporum ecclesiarum Christianarum orientalium.* 2 vols. Padua: Edizioni Messaggero, 1988.

Feissel, D. "Bulletin épigraphique: Inscriptions chrétiennes et byzantines." *Revue des études grecques* 100 (1987), 347–87.

Fernández Félix, Ana. "Children on the Frontiers of Islam." In *Conversions islamiques: Identités religieuses en Islam méditerranéen.* Mercedes García-Arenal, ed. Paris: Maisonneuve et Larose, 2001, 61–72.

——. *Cuestiones legales del islam temprano: La 'Utbiyya y el proceso de formación de la sociedad islámica andalusí.* Madrid: Consejo Superior de Investigaciones Científicas, 2003.

Fernández Félix, Ana, and Maribel Fierro. "Cristianos y conversos al Islam en al-Andalus bajo los Omeyas. Una aproximación al proceso de islamización a través de una fuente legal Andalusí del s. III/X." *Anejos de Archivo Español de Arqueología* 13 (2000), 415–27.

Fernández-Morera, Darío. *The Myth of the Andalusian Paradise: Muslims, Christians, and Jews under Islamic Rule in Medieval Spain.* Wilmington, DE: Intercollegiate Studies Institute Books, 2016.

Festugière, A.-J., ed. and trans. *Collections grecques de miracles. Sainte Thècle, saints Côme et Damien, saints Cyr et Jean (extraits), saint Georges.* Paris: Picard, 1971.

Fierro, Maribel. *La heterodoxia en al-Andalus durante el período omeya.* Madrid: Instituto Hispano-Arabe de Cultura, 1987.

——. "Accusations of '*Zandaqa*' in al-Andalus." *Quaderni di Studi Arabi* 5/6 (1987–88), 251–58.

——. "Andalusian ‹Fatāwā› on Blasphemy." *Annales islamologiques* 25 (1991), 103–17.

——. "Heresy in al-Andalus." In *The Legacy of Muslim Spain.* Salma Khadra Jayyusi with Manuel Marín, eds. Leiden: Brill, 1992, 895–908.

——. "Árabes, beréberes, muladíes y *mawālī.* Algunas reflexiones sobre los datos de los diccionarios biógraficos andalusíes." *Estudios onomástico-biográficos de al-Andalus* 7 (1995), 41–54.

——. "Four Questions in Connection with Ibn Ḥafṣūn." In *The Formation of al-Andalus. Part I: History and Society.* Manuela Marín, ed. and trans. Aldershot: Ashgate, 1998, 291–328.

——. "Violencia, política y religión en al-Andalus durante el S. IV/X: El reinado de ʿAbd al-Raḥmān III." In *De muerte violenta. Política, religión y violencia en al-Andalus.* Maribel Fierro, ed. Madrid: Consejo Superior de Investigaciones Científicas, 2004, 37–101.

——. "*Mawālī* and *Muwalladūn* in al-Andalus (Second/Eighth–Fourth/Tenth Centuries)." In *Patronate and Patronage in Early Classical Islam.* Monique Bernards and John Nawas, eds. Leiden: Brill, 2005, 195–245.

——. "Proto-Malikis, Malikis, and Reformed Malikis in al-Andalus." In *The Islamic School of Law: Evolution, Devolution, and Progress.* Peri Bearman, Rudolph Peters, and Frank E. Vogel, eds. Cambridge, MA: Islamic Legal Studies Program, Harvard University, 2005, 57–76.

——. "*Idraū l-ḥudūd bi-l-shubuhāt*: When Lawful Violence Meets Doubt." *Hawwa* 5 (2007), 208–38.

——. "Decapitation of Christians and Muslims in the Medieval Iberian Peninsula: Narratives, Images, Contemporary Perceptions." *Comparative Literature Studies* 45 (2008), 137–64.

——. "El castigo de los herejes y su relación con las formas del poder político y religioso en al-Andalus (SS. II/VIII–VII/XIII)." In *El cuerpo derrotado: Cómo trataban musulmanes y cristianos a los enemigos vencidos (Península Ibérica, SS. VIII–XIII).* Maribel Fierro and Francisco García Fitz, eds. Madrid: Consejo Superior de Investigaciones Científicas, 2008, 283–316.

——. "Emulating Abraham: The Fāṭimid al-Qāʾim and the Umayyad ʿAbd al-Raḥmān III." In *Public Violence in Islamic Societies: Power, Discipline, and the Construction of the Public Sphere, 7th–19th Centuries CE.* Christian Lange and Maribel Fierro, eds. Edinburgh: Edinburgh University Press, 2009, 130–55.

——. "Conversion, Ancestry and Universal Religion: The Case of the Almohads in the Islamic West (Sixth/Twelfth–Seventh/Thirteenth Centuries)." *Journal of Medieval Iberian Studies* 2 (2010), 155–73.

——. "Plants, Mary the Copt, Abraham, Donkeys and Knowledge: Again on Bāṭinism during the Umayyad Caliphate in al-Andalus." In *Differenz und Dynamik im Islam. Festschrift für Heinz Halm zum 70. Geburtstag*. Hinrich Biesterfeldt and Verena Klemm, eds. Würzburg: Ergon-Verlag, 2012, 125–44.

Fierro, Maribel. "The Islamisation of al-Andalus: Recent Studies and Debates." In *Islamisation: Comparative Perspectives from History*. A.C.S. Peacock, ed. Edinburgh: Edinburgh University Press, 2017, 199–220.

Fierro, Maribel, and Saadia Faghia. "Un nuevo texto de tradiciones escatológicas sobre al-Andalus." *Sharq al-Andalus* 4 (1990), 99–111.

Fierro, Maribel, and Manuela Marín. "La islamización de las ciudades andalusíes a través de sus ulemas (s. II/VIII–comienzos s. IV/X)." In *Genèse de la ville islamique en al-Andalus et au Maghreb occidental*. Patrice Cressier and Mercedes García-Arenal, with Mohamed Méouak, eds. Madrid: Casa de Velázquez and Consejo Superior de Investigaciones Científicas, 1998, 65–97.

Fiey, Jean Maurice. "Diptyques nestoriens du XIVe siècle." *Analecta Bollandiana* 81 (1963), 371–413.

——. "Tagrît. Esquisse d'histoire chrétienne." *L'Orient Syrien* 8 (1963), 289–342.

——. *Chrétiens syriaques sous les Abbassides surtout à Bagdad (749–1258)*. Louvain: Secrétariat du CorpusSCO, 1980.

——. "Conversions à l'Islam de juifs et chrétiens sous les Abbasides d'après les sources arabes et syriaques." In *Rapports entre juifs, chrétiens et musulmans*. Johannes Irmscher, ed. Amsterdam: Verlag Adolf M. Hakkert, 1995, 13–28.

——. *Saints syriaques*. Lawrence I. Conrad, ed. Princeton: Darwin Press, 2004.

Fisher, Greg. *Between Empires: Arabs, Romans, and Sasanians in Late Antiquity*. Oxford: Oxford University Press, 2011.

Fisher, Linford D. *The Indian Great Awakening: Religion and the Shaping of Native Cultures in Early America*. New York: Oxford University Press, 2012.

[*EI*^{3}] Fleet, Kate, Gudrun Krämer, Denis Matringe, John Nawas, and Everett Rowson, eds. *Encyclopaedia of Islam Three*. Leiden: Brill, 2007–present.

Forcada, Miguel. "Calendar of Córdoba." *EI*^{3} (2011), i, 145–46.

Griffel, Frank. "Apostasy." *EI*^{3} (2007), i, 131–34.

Lange, Christian. "Capital Punishment." *EI*^{3} (2011), ii, 104–10.

Weipert, Reinhard. "Abū ʿUbayda." *EI*^{3} (2007), i, 24–25.

Flusin, Bernard. "Démons et Sarrasins: L'auteur et le propos des *Diègèmata stèriktika* d'Anastase le Sinaïte." *Travaux et mémoires* 11 (1991), 381–409.

——. "Palestinian Hagiography (Fourth–Eighth Centuries)." In *The Ashgate Research Companion to Byzantine Hagiography. Volume I: Periods and Places*. Stephanos Efthymiadis, ed. Farnham, UK: Ashgate, 2011, 199–226.

Foss, Clive. "Byzantine Saints in Early Islamic Syria." *Analecta Bollandiana* 125 (2007), 93–119.

Foucault, Michel. *Discipline and Punish: The Birth of the Prison*. Alan Sheridan, trans. New York: Vintage Books, 1979.

Fowden, Elizabeth Key. *The Barbarian Plain: Saint Sergius between Rome and Iran*. Berkeley: University of California Press, 1999.

——. "The Lamp and the Wine Flask: Early Muslim Interest in Christian Monasticism." In *Islamic Crosspollinations: Interactions in the Medieval Middle East*. Anna Akasoy, James E. Montgomery, and Peter E. Pormann, eds. Exeter: Gibb Memorial Trust, 2007, 1–28.

Fowden, Garth. *Empire to Commonwealth: Consequences of Monotheism in Late Antiquity.* Princeton: Princeton University Press, 1993.

——. *Before and after Muḥammad: The First Millennium Refocused.* Princeton: Princeton University Press, 2014.

Franchi de'Cavalieri, P. "Della *furca* e della sua sostituzione alla croce nel diritto penale romano." *Nuovo bulletino di archeologia cristiana* 13 (1907), 63–113.

Franke, Franz Richard. "Die freiwilligen Märtyrer von Cordova und das Verhältnis der Mozaraber zum Islam." *Gesammelte Aufsätze zur Kulturgeschichte Spaniens* 13 (1958), 1–170.

Frantz-Murphy, Gladys. "Conversion in Early Islamic Egypt: The Economic Factor." In *Documents de l'Islam médiéval: Nouvelles perspectives de recherche.* Yūsuf Rāġib, ed. Cairo: Institut français d'archéologie orientale, 1991, 11–17.

Freidenreich, David M. *Foreigners and Their Food: Constructing Otherness in Jewish, Christian, and Islamic Law.* Berkeley: University of California Press, 2011.

——. "Muslims in Eastern Canon Law, 1000–1500." In *Christian-Muslim Relations: A Bibliographic History. Volume 4: 1200–1350.* David Thomas and Alex Mallett, eds. Leiden: Brill, 2012, 45–57.

Frend, W.H.C. *The Donatist Church: A Movement of Protest in Roman North Africa.* Oxford: Clarendon Press, 1952.

——. *Martyrdom and Persecution in the Early Church. A Study of a Conflict from the Maccabees to Donatus.* Oxford: Blackwell, 1965.

——. *The Rise of the Monophysite Movement: Chapters in the History of the Church in the Fifth and Sixth Centuries.* Cambridge: Cambridge University Press, 1972.

Frenschkowski, Marco. "Christianity." In *The Wiley Blackwell Companion to Zoroastrianism.* Michael Stausberg and Yuhan Sohrab-Dinshaw Vevaina, with Anna Tessmann, eds. Malden, MA: Wiley Blackwell, 2015, 457–75.

Friedmann, Yohanan. "A Note on the Conversion of Egypt to Islam." *Jerusalem Studies in Arabic and Islam* 3 (1981–82), 238–40.

——. *Tolerance and Coercion in Islam: Interfaith Relations in the Muslim Tradition.* Cambridge: Cambridge University Press, 2003.

Gaddis, Michael. *There Is No Crime for Those Who Have Christ: Religious Violence in the Christian Roman Empire.* Berkeley: University of California Press, 2005.

Galadza, Daniel. "Liturgical Byzantinization in Jerusalem: al-Biruni's Melkite Calendar in Context." *Bollettino della badia greca di Grottaferrata,* 3rd ser., 7 (2010), 69–85.

——. *Liturgy and Byzantinization in Jerusalem.* Oxford: Oxford University Press, 2017.

García Gómez, Emilio. "Dulce, mártir mozárabe de comienzos del siglo X." *al-Andalus* 19 (1954), 451–54.

García-Arenal, Mercedes. *Inquisición y moriscos: Los procesos del Tribunal de Cuenca.* Madrid: Siglo XXI de España, 1978.

García-Arenal, Mercedes, and Fernando Rodríguez Mediano. *The Orient in Spain: Converted Muslims, the Forged Gospels of Granada, and the Rise of Orientalism.* Consuelo Lopez-Morillas, trans. Leiden: Brill, 2013.

Garitte, Gérard, ed. *Catalogue des manuscrits géorgiens littéraires du Mont Sinaï.* Louvain: L. Durbecq, 1956.

Garitte, Gérard. *Le calendrier palestino-géorgien du Sinaiticus 34 (Xe siècle).* Brussels: Société des Bollandistes, 1958.

Garsoïan, Nina. "The Arab Invasions and the Rise of the Bagratuni (640–884)." In *The*

Armenian People from Ancient to Modern Times. 2 vols. Richard G. Hovannisian, ed. New York: St. Martin's Press, 1996, i, 117–42.

Garstad, Benjamin, ed. and trans. *Apocalypse, Pseudo-Methodius; An Alexandrian World Chronicle.* Cambridge, MA: Harvard University Press, 2012.

Gatteyrias, M.J.A. "Élégie sur les malheurs de l'Arménie et le martyre de saint Vahan de Koghten. Épisode de l'occupation arabe en Arménie, traduit pour la première fois de l'arménien littéral, sur l'édition des RR. PP. Méchitaristes." *Journal asiatique* 16 (1880), 177–214.

Geary, Patrick J. "Saints, Scholars, and Society: The Elusive Goal." In *Living with the Dead in the Middle Ages.* Patrick J. Geary, ed. Ithaca, NY: Cornell University Press, 1994, 9–29.

Gero, Stephen. *Byzantine Iconoclasm during the Reign of Leo III with Particular Attention to the Oriental Sources.* Louvain: Secrétariat du Corpus, 1973.

Gervers, Michael, and Ramzi Jibran Bikhazi, eds. *Conversion and Continuity: Indigenous Christian Communities in Islamic Lands, Eighth to Eighteenth Centuries.* Toronto: Pontifical Institute of Mediaeval Studies, 1990.

Gibb, H.A.R. "The Fiscal Rescript of ʿUmar II." *Arabica* 2 (1955), 1–16.

[*CSM*] Gil, Ioannes, ed. *Corpus scriptorum Muzarabicorum.* 2 vols. Madrid: Instituto Antonio de Nebrija, 1973.

Gil, Moshe. *A History of Palestine, 634–1099.* Cambridge: Cambridge University Press, 1992.

Glick, Thomas F. *Islamic and Christian Spain in the Early Middle Ages.* 2nd ed. Leiden: Brill, 2005.

Goitein, S. D. *A Mediterranean Society: The Jewish Communities of the Arab World as Portrayed in the Documents of the Cairo Geniza.* 6 vols. Berkeley: University of California Press, 1967–93.

——. "Minority Selfrule and Government Control in Islam." *Studia Islamica* 31 (1970), 101–16.

Golden, Peter B. "The Conversion of the Khazars to Judaism." In *The World of the Khazars: New Perspectives. Selected Papers from the Jerusalem 1999 International Khazar Colloquium.* Peter B. Golden, Haggai Ben Shammai, and András Roná-Tas, eds. Leiden: Brill, 2007, 123–62.

Goldziher, Ignaz. *Muslim Studies.* 2 vols. C. R. Barber and S. M. Stern, eds. London: Allen and Unwin, 1966–71.

González Gutiérrez, C. "Secondary Mosques in *Madinat Qurtuba*: Islamization and Suburban Development through Minor Religious Spaces." *Papers from the Institute of Archaeology* 25 (2015), 1–18.

González Muñoz, Fernando. "El conocimiento del Corán entre los Mozárabes del siglo IX." In *Sub luce florentis calami: Homenaje a Manuel C. Díaz y Díaz.* Santiago de Compostela: Universidade de Santiago de Compostela, 2002, 390–409.

[*GCAL*] Graf, Georg, ed. *Geschichte der christlichen arabischen Literatur.* 5 vols. Vatican City: Biblioteca Apostolica Vaticana, 1944–53.

Greene, Graham. *The Power and the Glory.* New York: Penguin Books, 2003.

Greene, Molly. *The Edinburgh History of the Greeks, 1453 to 1768: The Ottoman Empire.* Edinburgh: Edinburgh University Press, 2015.

Greenfield, Richard P. H. *The Life of Lazaros of Mt. Galesion: An Eleventh-Century Pillar Saint.* Washington, DC: Dumbarton Oaks Research Library and Collection, 2000.

Gregory, Brad S. *Salvation at Stake: Christian Martyrdom in Early Modern Europe*. Cambridge, MA: Harvard University Press, 1999.

Grehan, James. *Twilight of the Saints: Everyday Religion in Ottoman Syria and Palestine*. Oxford: Oxford University Press, 2014.

Griffel, Frank. *Apostasie und Toleranz im Islam: Die Entwicklung zu al-Ġazālīs Urteil gegen die Philosophie und die Reaktionen der Philosophen*. Leiden: Brill, 2000.

——. "Toleration and Exclusion: al-Shāfiʿī and al-Ghazālī on the Treatment of Apostates." *Bulletin of the School of Oriental and African Studies* 64 (2001), 339–54.

Griffith, Sidney H. "The Arabic Account of ʿAbd al-Masīḥ al-Naǧrānī al-Ghassānī." *Le Muséon* 98 (1985), 331–74.

——. "Stephen of Ramlah and the Christian Kerygma in Arabic in Ninth-Century Palestine." *Journal of Ecclesiastical History* 36 (1985), 23–45.

——. "Theodore Abū Qurrah's Arabic Tract on the Christian Practice of Venerating Images." *Journal of the American Oriental Society* 105 (1985), 53–73.

——. "Greek into Arabic: Life and Letters in the Monasteries of Palestine in the Ninth Century; the Example of the *Summa Theologiae Arabica*." *Byzantion* 56 (1986), 117–38.

——. "Anastasios of Sinai, the *Hodegos*, and the Muslims." *Greek Orthodox Theological Review* 32 (1987), 341–58.

——. "The Monks of Palestine and the Growth of Christian Literature in Arabic." *Muslim World* 78 (1988), 1–28.

——. "The First Christian *Summa Theologiae* in Arabic: Christian *Kalām* in Ninth-Century Palestine." In *Conversion and Continuity: Indigenous Christian Communities in Islamic Lands, Eighth to Eighteenth Centuries*. Michael Gervers and Ramzi Jibran Bikhazi, eds. Toronto: Pontifical Institute of Mediaeval Studies, 1990, 15–31.

——. "Michael, the Martyr and Monk of Mar Sabas Monastery, at the Court of the Caliph ʿAbd al-Malik; Christian Apologetics and Martyrology in the Early Islamic Period." *ARAM* 6 (1994), 115–48.

——. "From Aramaic to Arabic: The Languages of the Monasteries of Palestine in the Byzantine and Early Islamic Periods." *Dumbarton Oaks Papers* 51 (1997), 11–31.

——, trans. *Theodore Abu Qurrah: A Treatise on the Veneration of the Holy Icons*. Louvain: Peeters, 1997.

——. "Christians, Muslims, and Neo-martyrs: Saints' Lives and Holy Land History." In *Sharing the Sacred: Religious Contacts and Conflicts in the Holy Land, First–Fifteenth Centuries CE*. Arieh Kofsky and Guy G. Stroumsa, eds. Jerusalem: Yad Izhak Ben Zvi, 1998, 163–207.

——. "The Monk in the Emir's *Majlis*: Reflections on a Popular Genre of Christian Literary Apologetics in Arabic in the Early Islamic Period." In *The Majlis: Interreligious Encounters in Medieval Islam*. Hava Lazarus-Yafeh, Mark R. Cohen, Sasson Somekh, and Sidney H. Griffith, eds. Wiesbaden: Harrassowitz Verlag, 1999, 13–65.

——. "The Qurʾān in Arab Christian Texts: The Development of an Apologetic Argument: Abū Qurrah in the Maǧlis of al-Maʾmūn." *Parole de l'Orient* 24 (1999), 203–33.

——. "The *Life of Theodore of Edessa*: History, Historiography, and Religious Apologetics in Mar Saba Monastery in Early Abbasid Times." In *The Sabaite Heritage in the Orthodox Church from the Fifth Century to the Present*. Joseph Patrich, ed. Leuven: Peeters, 2001, 147–69.

Griffith, Sidney H. "'Melkites,' 'Jacobites' and the Christological Controversies in Arabic in Third/Ninth-Century Syria." In *Syrian Christians under Islam: The First Thousand Years.* David Thomas, ed. Leiden: Brill, 2001, 9–55.

——. *The Beginnings of Christian Theology in Arabic: Muslim-Christian Encounters in the Early Islamic Period.* Aldershot: Ashgate, 2002.

——. "The Church of Jerusalem and the 'Melkites': The Making of an 'Arab Orthodox' Christian Identity in the World of Islam (750–1050 CE)." In *Christians and Christianity in the Holy Land: From the Origins to the Latin Kingdoms.* Ora Limor and Guy G. Stroumsa, eds. Turnhout: Brepols, 2006, 175–204.

——. "The Syriac Letters of Patriarch Timothy I and the Birth of Christian *Kalām* in the Muʿtazilite Milieu of Baghdad and Baṣrah in Early Islamic Times." In *Syriac Polemics: Studies in Honour of Gerrit Jan Reinink.* Wout Jac. van Bekkum, Jan Willem Drijvers, and Alex C. Klugkist, eds. Leuven: Peeters, 2007, 103–32.

——. *The Church in the Shadow of the Mosque: Christians and Muslims in the World of Islam.* Princeton: Princeton University Press, 2008.

——. "Crosses, Icons and the Image of Christ in Edessa: The Place of Iconophobia in the Christian-Muslim Controversies of Early Islamic Times." In *Transformations of Late Antiquity: Essays for Peter Brown.* Philip Rousseau and Manolis Papoutsakis, eds. Farnham, UK: Ashgate, 2009, 63–84.

——. *The Bible in Arabic: The Scriptures of the "People of the Book" in the Language of Islam.* Princeton: Princeton University Press, 2013.

——. "The Manṣūr Family and Saint John of Damascus: Christians and Muslims in Umayyad Times." In *Christians and Others in the Umayyad State.* Antoine Borrut and Fred M. Donner, eds. Chicago: Oriental Institute of the University of Chicago, 2016, 29–51.

Griveau, Robert. "Martyrologes et ménologes orientaux, XVI–XVIII; Les fêtes des Melchites, par al-Birouni." *Patrologia Orientalis* 10 (1915), 289–312.

Grousset, René. *Histoire de l'Arménie des origines à 1071.* Paris: Payot, 1973.

Grumel, Venance. "L'ère mondiale dans la date du martyre des vingt moines sabaites." *Revue des études byzantines* 14 (1956), 207–8.

——. *Traité d'études byzantines. I. La chronologie.* Paul Lemerle, ed. Paris: Presses universitaires de France, 1958.

Guichard, Pierre. *Al-Andalus: Estructura antropológica de una sociedad islámica en occidente.* Barcelona: Barral Editores, 1976.

Guidetti, Mattia. *In the Shadow of the Church: The Building of Mosques in Early Medieval Syria.* Leiden: Brill, 2017.

Guidi, Ignazio. "La synaxaire éthiopien: Les mois de Sanê, Hamtê et Nahasê." *Patrologia Orientalis* 1 (1907), 1–187.

Guillaume, A., trans. *The Life of Muḥammad: A Translation of Ibn Isḥāq's "Sīrat Rasūl Allāh."* London: Oxford University Press, 1955.

Guillou, André. "Prise de Gaza par les Arabes au VIIe siècle." *Bulletin de correspondence hellénique* 81 (1957), 396–404.

Haldon, John. "The Works of Anastasius of Sinai: A Key Source for the History of Seventh-Century East Mediterranean Society and Belief." In *The Byzantine and Early Islamic Near East. Volume I: Problems in the Literary Source Material.* Averil Cameron and Lawrence I. Conrad, eds. Princeton: Darwin Press, 1992, 107–47.

Haldon, John, and Hugh Kennedy. "The Arab-Byzantine Frontier in the Eighth and

Ninth Centuries: Military Organization and Society in the Borderlands." *Zbornik Radova Vizantološkog Instituta* 19 (1980), 79–116.

[*BHG*] Halkin, François, ed. *Bibliotheca hagiographica graeca.* 3 vols. Brussels: Société des Bollandistes, 1957.

Hamilton, Robert. *Walid and His Friends: An Umayyad Tragedy.* Oxford: Oxford University Press, 1988.

Harrak, Amir. "Christianity in the Eyes of the Muslims of the Jazīrah at the End of the Eighth Century." *Parole de l'Orient* 20 (1995), 337–56.

——. "Arabisms in Part IV of the Syriac Chronicle of Zuqnīn." In *Symposium Syriacum VII: Uppsala University, Department of Asian and African Languages, 11–14 August 1996.* René Lavenant, ed. Rome: Pontificio Istituto Orientale, 1998, 469–98.

——, trans. *The Chronicle of Zuqnīn Parts III and IV, A.D. 488–775.* Toronto: Pontifical Institute of Mediaeval Studies, 1999.

——. "Piecing Together the Fragmentary Account of the Martyrdom of Cyrus of Ḥarrān." *Analecta Bollandiana* 121 (2003), 297–328.

Harrison, Alwyn. "Behind the Curve: Bulliet and Conversion to Islam in al-Andalus Revisited." *Al-Masāq* 24 (2012), 35–51.

Harvey, Susan Ashbrook. "Martyr Passions and Hagiography." In *The Oxford Handbook of Early Christian Studies.* Susan Ashbrook Harvey and David G. Hunter, eds. Oxford: Oxford University Press, 2008, 603–27.

Hasluck, F. W. "The Crypto-Christians of Trebizond." *Journal of Hellenic Studies* 41 (1921), 199–202.

Hatlie, Peter. "The Politics of Salvation: Theodore of Stoudios on Marytrdom (*Martyrion*) and Speaking Out (*Parrhesia*)." *Dumbarton Oaks Papers* 50 (1996), 263–87.

Hawting, Gerald. *The First Dynasty of Islam: The Umayyad Caliphate AD 661–750.* 2nd ed. London: Routledge, 2000.

——. "The Case of Jaʿd b. Dirham and the Punishment of 'Heretics' in the Early Caliphate." In *Public Violence in Islamic Societies: Power, Discipline, and the Construction of the Public Sphere, 7th–19th Centuries CE.* Christian Lange and Maribel Fierro, eds. Edinburgh: Edinburgh University Press, 2009, 27–41.

Herman, Geoffrey. " 'Bury My Coffin Deep!' Zoroastrian Exhumation in Jewish and Christian Sources." In *Tiferet Leyisrael: Jubilee Volume in Honor of Israel Francus.* Joel Roth, Menahem Schmelzer, and Yaacov Francus, eds. New York: Jewish Theological Seminary, 2010, 31–59.

Hindmarsh, Bruce. "Religious Conversion as Narrative and Autobiography." In *The Oxford Handbook of Religious Conversion.* Lewis R. Rambo and Charles E. Farhadian, eds. Oxford: Oxford University Press, 2014, 343–68.

Hinterberger, Martin. "The Byzantine Hagiographer and His Text." In *The Ashgate Research Companion to Byzantine Hagiography. Volume II: Genres and Contexts.* Stephanos Efthymiadis, ed. Farnham, UK: Ashgate, 2014, 211–46.

——. "Byzantine Hagiography and Its Literary Genres. Some Critical Observations." In *The Ashgate Research Companion to Byzantine Hagiography. Volume II: Genres and Contexts.* Stephanos Efthymiadis, ed. Farnham, UK: Ashgate, 2014, 25–60.

Ḥitti, Philip K. "The Impact of the Crusades on Eastern Christianity." In *Medieval and Middle Eastern Studies in Honor of Aziz Suryal Atiya.* Sami A. Hanna, ed. Leiden: E. J. Brill, 1972, 211–17.

Hoyland, Robert G. *Seeing Islam as Others Saw It: A Survey and Evaluation of Christian, Jewish, and Zoroastrian Writings on Early Islam.* Princeton: Darwin Press, 1997.

———. "Language and Identity: The Twin Histories of Arabic and Aramaic (and: Why Did Aramaic Succeed Where Greek Failed?)." *Scripta Classica Israelica* 23 (2004), 183–99.

———. "Jacob and Early Islamic Edessa." In *Jacob of Edessa and the Syriac Culture of His Day.* Bas ter Haar Romeny, ed. Leiden: Brill, 2008, 11–24.

———. "Mount Nebo, Jabal Ramm, and the Status of Christian Palestinian Aramaic and Old Arabic in Late Roman Palestine and Arabia." In *The Development of Arabic as a Written Language.* M.C.A MacDonald, ed. Oxford: Archaeopress, 2010, 29–46.

———, trans. *Theophilus of Edessa's Chronicle and the Circulation of Historical Knowledge in Late Antiquity and Early Islam.* Liverpool: Liverpool University Press, 2011.

———. *In God's Path: The Arab Conquests and the Creation of an Islamic Empire.* New York: Oxford University Press, 2015.

Hübschmann, H. *Armenische Grammatik.* Leipzig: Druck und Verlag von Bretkopf und Härtel, 1897.

Humphreys, R. Stephen. "Christian Communities in Early Islamic Syria and Northern Jazira: The Dynamics of Adaptation." In *Money, Power and Politics in Early Islamic Syria: A Review of Current Debates.* John Haldon, ed. Farnham, UK: Ashgate, 2010, 45–56.

Ḥurr al-ʿĀmilī. *Wasāʾil al-shīʿa.* 20 vols. Muḥammad al-Rāzī, ed. Beirut: Dār al-Iḥyāʾ al-Turāth al-ʿArabī, n.d.

Ibn ʿAbd al-Ḥakam. *The History of the Conquest of Egypt, North Africa and Spain, Known as the "Futūḥ Miṣr" of Ibn ʿAbd al-Ḥakam.* Charles C. Torrey, ed. New Haven: Yale University Press, 1922.

Ibn ʿAbd Rabbih al-Andalusī. *Kitāb al-ʿiqd al-farīd.* 6 vols. Aḥmad Amīn, Aḥmad al-Zayn, and Ibrāhīm al-Ibyārī, eds. Cairo: Maṭbaʿat Lajnat al-Talīf wa-ʾl-Tarjama wa-ʾl-Nashr, 1940–49.

Ibn Abī Shayba. *Kitāb al-muṣannaf fī ʾl-aḥādīth wa-ʾl-āthār.* 7 vols. Kamāl Yūsuf al-Ḥūt, ed. Beirut: Dār al-Tāj, 1989.

Ibn al-ʿAdīm. *Zubdat al-ḥalab min tārīkh ḥalab.* Khalīl al-Manṣūr, ed. Beirut: Dār al-Kutub al-ʿIlmīya, 1996.

Ibn ʿAsākir. *Tārīkh madīnat dimashq.* 80 vols. ʿAlī Shīrī, ed. Beirut: Dār al-Fikr lil-Ṭibāʿa wa-ʾl-Nashr wa-ʾl-Tawzīʿ, 1995–2000.

Ibn Bassām. *Nihāyat al-rutba fī ṭalab al-ḥisba.* Ḥusām al-Dīn al-Sāmarrāʾī, ed. Baghdad: Maktabat al-Maʿārif, 1968.

Ibn Ḥajar al-ʿAsqalānī. *Tahdhīb al-tahdhīb.* 12 vols. Hyderabad: Maṭbaʿat Majlis Dāʾirat al-Maʿārif al-Niẓāmīya al-Kāʾina fī ʾl-Hind, 1907–9.

Ibn Ḥawqal. *Viae et regna descriptio ditionis moslemicae auctore Abu'l-Kásim Ibn Haukal.* M. J. de Goeje, ed. Leiden: Brill, 1873.

———. *Kitāb aḥsan al-taqāsīm fī maʿrifat al-aqālīm.* Beirut: Dār Maktabat al-Ḥayāt, 1964.

Ibn Hishām. *al-Sīra al-nabawīya.* 4 vols. Muṣṭafā al-Saqqā, Ibrāhīm al-Abyārī, and ʿAbd al-Ḥafīẓ al-Shalabī, eds. Cairo: Maṭbaʿat Muṣṭafā al-Bābī al-Ḥalabī, 1936.

Ibn Makūlā. *Ikmāl fī rafʿ al-irtiyāb ʿan al-muʾtalif wa-ʾl-mukhtalif min al-asmāʾ wa-ʾl-kunā wa-ʾl-ansāb.* 7 vols. ʿAbd al-Raḥmān b. Yaḥya al-Muʿallimī al-Yamānī, ed. Hyderabad: Dāʾirat al-Maʿārif al-ʿUthmānīya, 1962–67.

Ibn Manẓūr. *Mukhtaṣar tārīkh madīnat dimashq li-ibn ʿasākir.* 29 vols. Rawḥīya al-Naḥḥāṣ, Riyāḍ ʿAbd al-Ḥamīd Murād, Muḥammad Muṭīʿ al-Ḥāfiẓ, et al., eds. Damascus: Dār al-Fikr, 1984–96.

Ibn Qayyim al-Jawzīya. *Aḥkām ahl al-dhimma.* 3 vols. Abū Barāʾ Yūsuf b. Aḥmad al-Bakrī and Abū Aḥmad Shākir b. Tawfīq al-ʿĀrūrī, eds. al-Dammām: Ramādī lil-Nashr, 1997.

Ibn Qudāma. *al-Mughnī.* 16 vols. Muḥammad Sharaf al-Dīn Khaṭṭāb, Muḥammad al-Sayyid, and Ibrāhīm Ṣādiq, eds. Cairo: Dār al-Ḥadīth, 1996.

Ibn Qutayba. *Kitāb ʿuyūn al-akhbār.* 4 vols. Cairo: Dār al-Kutub al-Miṣrīya, 1925–30.

Ibn Rushd al-Jadd. *al-Bayān wa-ʾl-taḥṣīl.* 20 vols. Muḥammad Ḥajjī, ed. Beirut: Dār al-Gharb al-Islāmī, 1984–87.

Ibn Saʿd. *Ibn Saad Biographien Muhammeds, seiner Gefährten under späteren Träger des Islam bis zum Jahre 230 der Flucht.* 9 vols. Eduard Sachau, ed. Leiden: Brill, 1904–30.

Ibn Sahl. *al-Aʿlām bi-nawāzil al-aḥkām al-maʿrūf bi-ʾl-aḥkām al-kubrā.* Nūra Muḥammad ʿAbd al-ʿAzīz al-Tuwayjirī, ed. N.p., 1995.

Ibn Taymīya. *al-Ṣārim al-maslūl ʿalā shātim al-rasūl.* Ibrāhīm Shams al-Dīn, ed. Beirut: Dār al-Kutub al-ʿIlmīya, 2009.

Ibn Wahb. *Kitāb al-muḥāraba min al-muwaṭṭaʾ.* Miklos Muranyi, ed. Beirut: Dār al-Gharb al-Islāmī, 2002.

al-Jahshiyarī. *Kitāb al-wuzarāʾ wa-ʾl-kuttāb.* Muṣṭafā al-Saqqā, Ibrāhīm al-Abyārī, and ʿAbd al-Ḥafīẓ al-Shalabī, eds. Cairo: Maṭbaʿat Muṣṭafā al-Bābī al-Ḥalabī wa-Awlādihi, 1938.

James, David, trans. *Early Islamic Spain: The "History" of Ibn al-Qūṭīya: A Study of the Unique Arabic Manuscript in the Bibliothèque Nationale de France, Paris.* London: Routledge, 2009.

Janin, Raymond. "Les géorgiens à Jérusalem." *Echos d'orient* 16 (1913), 32–38, 211–19.

Jeffery, Arthur. *The Foreign Vocabulary of the Qurʾān.* Gerhard Böwering and Jane Dammen McAuliffe, eds. Leiden: Brill, 2007.

Jeffreys, Elizabeth M. "Parrhesia." In *Oxford Dictionary of Byzantium.* 3 vols. Alexander Kazhdan, ed. Oxford: Oxford University Press, 1991, iii, 1591.

Jiménez Pedrajas, Rafael. "San Eulogio de Córdoba, autor de la Pasión francesca de los mártires mozárabes cordobeses Jorge, Aurelio y Natalia." *Anthologica Annua* 17 (1970), 465–583.

———. *Historia de los mozárabes en Al Ándalus: Mozárabes y musulmanes en Al Ándalus: ¿Relaciones de convivencia? ¿O de antagonismo y lucha?* Córdoba, Spain: Almuzara, 2013.

John of Ephesus. *The Third Part of the Ecclesiastical History of John Bishop of Ephesus.* R. Payne Smith, trans. Oxford: Oxford University Press, 1860.

Johnson, Scott Fitzgerald, ed. *The Oxford Handbook of Late Antiquity.* Oxford: Oxford University Press, 2012.

———. "Introduction: The Social Presence of Greek in Eastern Christianity, 200–1200 CE." In *Languages and Cultures of Eastern Christianity: Greek.* Scott Fitzgerald Johnson, ed. Farnham, UK: Ashgate, 2014, 1–122.

Jones, Linda G. *The Power of Oratory in the Medieval Muslim World.* New York: Cambridge University Press, 2012.

Joseph, Zeki. *Beth Qustan: Ein aramäisches Dorf im Wandel der Zeiten.* Glane, the Netherlands: Bar Hebräus Verlag, 2010.

Judd, Steven. "Ghaylan al-Dimashqi: The Isolation of a Heretic in Islamic Historiography." *International Journal of Middle East Studies* 31 (1999), 161–84.
——. "Muslim Persecution of Heretics during the Marwānid Period (64–132/684–750)." *al-Masāq* 23 (2011), 1–14.
Jullien, Christelle. "Peines supplices dans les *Actes des martyrs persans* et droit sassanide: Nouvelles prospections." *Studia Iranica* 33 (2004), 243–69.
Juynboll, G.H.A., ed. *Encyclopedia of Canonical Ḥadīth.* Leiden: Brill, 2007.
Kamali, Mohammad Hashim. *Freedom of Expression in Islam.* Revised ed. Cambridge: Islamic Texts Society, 1997.
Kaplan, Michel, and Eleonora Kountoura-Galaki. "Economy and Society in Byzantine Hagiography: Realia and Methodological Questions." In *The Ashgate Research Companion to Byzantine Hagiography. Volume II: Genres and Contexts.* Stephanos Efthymiadis, ed. Farnham, UK: Ashgate, 2014, 389–418.
Kashouh, Hikmat. *The Arabic Versions of the Gospels: The Manuscripts and Their Families.* Berlin: De Gruyter, 2012.
Kassis, Hanna. "Arabic-Speaking Christians in al-Andalus in an Age of Turmoil (Fifth/Eleventh Century until A.H. 478/A.D. 1085)." *al-Qanṭara* 15 (1994), 401–22.
——. "The Arabization and Islamization of the Christians of al-Andalus: Evidence of Their Scriptures." In *Languages of Power in Islamic Spain.* Ross Brann, ed. Bethesda, MD: CDL Press, 1997, 136–55.
Kazhdan, Alexander. "Constantinopolitan Synaxarium as a Source for Social History of Byzantium." In *The Christian East: Its Institutions and Its Thought—A Critical Reflection.* Robert F. Taft, ed. Rome: Pontificio Istituto Orientale, 1996, 485–515.
——. *A History of Byzantine Literature (650–850).* With Lee F. Sherry and Christine Angelidi. Athens: National Hellenic Research Foundation, 1999.
Kazhdan, Alexander, and Alice-Mary Talbot. "Hagiography." In *The Oxford Dictionary of Byzantium.* 3 vols. Alexander Kazhdan, ed. Oxford: Oxford University Press, 1991, i, 897–99.
Kedar, Benjamin Z. "Latin in Ninth-Century Mar Sabas?" *Byzantion* 65 (1995), 252–54.
Kekelidze, K., and Michael Tarchnišvili. *Geschichte der kirchlichen georgischen Literatur.* Vatican City: Biblioteca Apostolica Vaticana, 1955.
Kennedy, Hugh. *Muslim Spain and Portugal: A Political History of al-Andalus.* London: Longman, 1996.
——. "Egypt as a Province in the Islamic Caliphate, 641–868." In *The Cambridge History of Egypt. Volume 1: Islamic Egypt, 640–1571.* Carl F. Petry, ed. Cambridge: Cambridge University Press, 1998, 62–85.
——. "From Antiquity to Islam in the Cities of al-Andalus and the Mashriq." In *Genèse de la ville islamique en al-Andalus et au Maghreb occidental.* Patrice Cressier, Mercedes García-Arenal, and Mohamed Meouak, eds. Madrid: Casa de Velázquez—Consejo Superior de Investigaciones Científicas, 1998, 53–64.
——. "Islam." In *Late Antiquity: A Guide to the Post-classical World.* G. W. Bowersock, Peter Brown, and Oleg Grabar, eds. Cambridge, MA: Belknap Press of Harvard University Press, 1999, 219–37.
——. *The Great Arab Conquests: How the Spread of Islam Changed the World We Live In.* Philadelphia: Da Capo, 2007.
——. "Syrian Elites from Byzantium to Islam: Survival or Extinction?" In *Money, Power*

and Politics in Early Islamic Syria: A Review of Current Debates. John Haldon, ed. Farnham, UK: Ashgate, 2010, 181–200.

——. *The Prophet and the Age of the Caliphates.* 3rd ed. London: Routledge, 2015.

Khadduri, Majid, trans. *The Islamic Law of Nations: Shaybānī's Siyar.* Baltimore: Johns Hopkins Press, 1966.

Khalek, Nancy. *Damascus after the Muslim Conquest: Text and Image in Early Islam.* Oxford: Oxford University Press, 2011.

Khalīfa b. Khayyāṭ. *Tārīkh khalīfa b. khayyāṭ.* Muṣṭafā Najīb Fawwāz and Ḥikmat Kishlī Fawwāz, eds. Beirut: Dār al-Kutub al-ʿIlmīya, 1995.

Khoury, Adel Théodore. *Les théologiens byzantins et l'Islam. Textes et auteurs, VIIIe–XIIIe s.* Louvain: Éditions "Nauwelaerts"; and Paris: Beatrice-Nauwelaerts, 1969.

Khuraysāt, M. A. "Dawr al-ʿarab al-mutanaṣṣira fī ʾl-futūḥāt." In *Bilād al-shām fī ṣadr al-islām: 24–30 jumādā ʾl-ākhira 1405 H, 16–22 ādhār 1985: al-Nadwa al-thānīya min al-muʾtamar al-dawlī al-rābiʿ li-tārīkh bilād al-shām.* 2 vols. Amman: University of Jordan, 1987, ii, 135–64.

al-Khushanı. *Quḍāt qurṭuba wa ʿulamāʾ ifrīqiya.* ʿIzzat al-ʿAṭṭār al-Ḥusaynī, ed. Cairo: Maktabat al-Khānjī, 1953.

Kiel, Yishai, and Prods Oktor Skjærvø. "Apostasy and Repentance in Early Medieval Zoroastrianism." *Journal of the American Oriental Society* 137 (2017), 221–43.

Kilpatrick, Hilary. "Monasteries through Muslim Eyes: The Diyarat Books." In *Christians at the Heart of Islamic Rule: Church Life and Scholarship in ʿAbbāsid Iraq.* David Thomas, ed. Leiden: Brill, 2003, 19–37.

Kim, Rebecca Y. "Migration and Conversion of Korean American Christians." In *The Oxford Handbook of Religious Conversion.* Lewis R. Rambo and Charles E. Farhadian, eds. Oxford: Oxford University Press, 2014, 190–208.

al-Kindī. *Kitāb al-wulāt wa-kitāb al-quḍāt.* Rhuvon Guest, ed. Leiden: Brill, 1912.

——. *Histoire des cadis égyptiens.* Aḫbār quḍāt Miṣr. Mathieu Tillier, trans. Cairo: Institut français d'archéologie orientale, 2012.

King, Daniel. "Why Were the Syrians Interested in Greek Philosophy?" In *History and Identity in the Late Antique Near East.* Philip Wood, ed. Oxford: Oxford University Press, 2013, 61–82.

Kipshidze, I. "Zhitie i muchenichestvo sv. Antoniia Ravakha." *Khristianskij Vostok* 2 (1911[?]), 54–104.

Kister, M. J. ". . . *Illā bi-ḥaqqihi* . . . : A Study of an Early *Ḥadīth*." *Jerusalem Studies in Arabic and Islam* 5 (1984), 33–52.

——. " 'Do Not Assimilate Yourselves . . .': *Lā tashabbahū*." *Jerusalem Studies in Arabic and Islam* 12 (1989), 321–71.

Klein, Konstantin M. "Marauders, Daredevils, and Noble Savages: Perceptions of Arab Nomads in Late Antique Hagiography." *Der Islam* 92 (2015), 13–41.

König, Daniel. "Rückbindung an die westgotische Vergangenheit. Zur Interpretation der Genealogie des Ibn al-Qūṭiyya." In *Integration und Disintegration der Kulturen im europäischen Mittelalter.* Michael Borgolte, Julia Dücker, Marcel Müllerburg, and Bernd Schneidmüller, eds. Berlin: Akademie Verlag, 2011, 127–37.

Kotter, Bonifatius, ed. *Die Schriften des Johannes von Damaskos. III: Contra imaginum calumniatores orationes tres.* Berlin: Walter de Gruyter, 1975.

Kraemer, Joel L. "Apostates, Rebels and Brigands." *Israel Oriental Studies* 10 (1980), 34–73.

Kreiner, Jamie. *The Social Life of Hagiography in the Merovingian Kingdom.* Cambridge: Cambridge University Press, 2014.

Krstić, Tijana. *Contested Conversions to Islam: Narratives of Religious Change in the Early Modern Ottoman Empire.* Stanford, CA: Stanford University Press, 2011.

Krusch, Bruno. "Zur Florians- und Lupus-Legende: Eine Entgegnung." *Neues Archiv der Gesellschaft für Ältere Deutsche Geschichtskunde* 24 (1899), 533–70.

Kurtz, Eduard. "Review of A. Dmitrijevskij. *Die Klosterregeln des hl. Sabbas.*" *Byzantinische Zeitschrift* 3 (1894), 167–70.

Kyle, Donald G. *Spectacles of Death in Ancient Rome.* London: Routledge, 1998.

Lammens, Henri. *Études sur le règne du calife omaiyade Moʿâwiya Ier.* Paris: Paul Geuthner, 1908.

Lamoreaux, John C., ed. and trans. *The Life of Stephen of Mar Saba.* Louvain: Peeters, 1999.

——. "The Biography of Theodore Abū Qurrah Revisited." *Dumbarton Oaks Papers* 56 (2002), 25–40.

——. "Hagiography." In *The Orthodox Church in the Arab World 700–1700: An Anthology of Sources.* Samuel Noble and Alexander Treiger, eds. De Kalb, IL: Northern Illinois University Press, 2014, 112–35.

Lamoreaux, John C., and Hassan Khairallah. "The Arabic Version of the Life of John of Edessa." *Le Muséon* 113 (2000), 439–60.

Lampadaridi, Anna, ed. *La conversion de Gaza au christianisme. La Vie de S. Porphyre de Gaza par Marc le Diacre.* BHG 1570. Brussels: Société des Bollandistes, 2016.

Landron, M. Benedicte. "Les relations originelles entre chrétiens de l'Est (nestoriens) et musulmans." *Parole de l'Orient* 10 (1981–82), 191–222.

Lane, Edward William, ed. *An Arabic-English Lexicon.* 8 pts. Beirut: Librairie du Liban, 1968.

Lang, David Marshall, trans. *Lives and Legends of the Georgian Saints.* London: George Allen and Unwin Ltd.; and New York: Macmillan Company, 1956.

Lange, Christian. "Legal and Cultural Aspects of Ignominious Parading (*Tashhīr*) in Islam." *Islamic Law and Society* 14 (2007), 81–108.

——. *Justice, Punishment and the Medieval Muslim Imagination.* Cambridge: Cambridge University Press, 2008.

——. "Where on Earth Is Hell? State Punishment and Eschatology in the Islamic Middle Period." In *Public Violence in Islamic Societies: Power, Discipline, and the Construction of the Public Sphere, 7th–19th Centuries CE.* Christian Lange and Maribel Fierro, eds. Edinburgh: Edinburgh University Press, 2009, 156–78.

Lange, Christian, and Maribel Fierro. "Introduction: Spatial, Ritual and Representational Aspects of Public Violence in Islamic Societies (7th–19th Centuries CE)." In *Public Violence in Islamic Societies: Power, Discipline, and the Construction of the Public Sphere, 7th–19th Centuries CE.* Christian Lange and Maribel Fierro, eds. Edinburgh: Edinburgh University Press, 2009, 1–23.

——, eds. *Public Violence in Islamic Societies: Power, Discipline, and the Construction of the Public Sphere, 7th–19th Centuries CE.* Edinburgh: Edinburgh University Press, 2009.

Langlois, Victor, trans. *Chronique de Michel le grand, patriarche des syriens jacobites, traduite pour la première fois sur la version arménienne du prêtre Ischôk.* Venice: Typographie de l'académie de Saint-Lazare, 1868.

Lapidus, Ira. "The Conversion of Egypt to Islam." *Israel Oriental Studies* 2 (1972), 248–62.

Lapiedra Gutiérrez, Eva. "Los mártires de Córdoba y la política anticristiana contemporánea en oriente." *Al-Qanṭara* 15 (1994), 453–63.

Le Strange, Guy. *Palestine under the Moslems: A Description of Syria and the Holy Land from A.D. 650 to 1500.* London: Alexander P. Watt, 1890.

Lecker, Michael. "Zayd b. Thābit, 'A Jew with Two Sidelocks': Judaism and Literacy in Pre-Islamic Medina (Yathrib)." *Journal of Near Eastern Studies* 56 (1997), 259–73.

——. "On the Burial of Martyrs in Islam." In *The Concept of Territory in Islamic Law and Thought.* Yanagihashi Hiroyuki, ed. London: Kegan Paul International, 2000, 37–49.

——. "Najrān Inc.: The Najrānī Exiles in Iraq, Syria and Baḥrayn from ʿUmar ibn al-Khaṭṭāb to Hārūn al-Rashīd." In *Juifs et chrétiens en Arabie au Ve et VIe siècles: Regards croisés sur les sources.* Joëlle Beaucamp, Françoise Briquel-Chatonnet, and Christian Julien Robin, eds. Paris: Association des amis du Centre d'histoire et civilisation de Byzance, 2010, 293–302.

Leemans, Johan, Wendy Mayer, Pauline Allen, and Boudewijn Dehandschutter. *"Let Us Die That We May Live": Greek Homilies on Christian Martyrs from Asia Minor, Palestine and Syria (c. AD 350–450).* London: Routledge, 2003.

Lenzen, C. J., and E. A. Knauf. "Beit Ras/Capitolias: A Preliminary Evaluation of the Archaeological and Textual Evidence." *Syria* 64 (1987), 21–46.

Leppin, Hartmut. "Christianity and the Discovery of Religious Freedom." *Rechtsgeschichte* 22 (2014), 62–78.

Lequien, Michel. *Oriens christianus, in quatuor patriarchatus digestus quo exhibentur ecclesiae, patriarchae, caeterique praesules totius Orientis.* 3 vols. Paris: Ex typographia regia, 1740.

Leslau, Wolf, ed. *Comparative Dictionary of Geʿez (Classical Ethiopic).* Wiesbaden: Harrassowitz, 1987.

Lev, Yaacov. "Persecutions and Conversion to Islam in Eleventh-Century Egypt." *Asian and African Studies* 22 (1988), 73–91.

——. "The Suppression of Crime, the Supervision of Markets, and Urban Society in the Egyptian Capital during the Tenth and Eleventh Centuries." *Mediterranean Historical Review* 3 (1988), 71–95.

——. "The Fatimid Caliphs, the Copts, and the Coptic Church." *Medieval Encounters* 21 (2015), 390–410.

Lévi-Provençal, Évariste. *Histoire de l'Espagne musulmane.* 3 vols. Paris: Maisonneuve, 1953.

Levtzion, Nehemia. "Toward a Comparative Study of Islamization." In *Conversion to Islam.* Nehemia Levtzion, ed. New York: Holmes and Meier Publishers, Inc., 1979, 1–23.

——. "Conversion to Islam in Syria and Palestine and the Survival of Christian Communities." In *Conversion and Continuity: Indigenous Christian Communities in Islamic Lands, Eighth to Eighteenth Centuries.* Michael Gervers and Ramzi Jibran Bikhazi, eds. Toronto: Pontifical Institute of Mediaeval Studies, 1990, 289–311.

Levy-Rubin, Milka. "Arabization versus Islamization in the Palestinian Melkite Community during the Early Muslim Period." In *Sharing the Sacred: Religious Contacts and Conflicts in the Holy Land, First–Fifteenth Centuries CE.* Arieh Kofsky and Guy G. Stroumsa, eds. Jerusalem: Yad Izhak Ben Zvi, 1998, 149–62.

Levy-Rubin, Milka. "New Evidence Relating to the Process of Islamization in the Early Muslim Period: The Case of Samaria." *Journal of the Economic and Social History of the Orient* 43 (2000), 257–76.

———. *Non-Muslims in the Early Islamic Empire: From Surrender to Coexistence.* Cambridge: Cambridge University Press, 2011.

Levy-Rubin, Milka, and Benjamin Kedar. "A Spanish Source on Mid-Ninth Century Mar Saba and a Neglected Sabaite Martyr." In *The Sabaite Heritage in the Orthodox Church from the Fifth Century to the Present.* Joseph Patrich, ed. Leuven: Peeters, 2001, 63–72.

Lewis, Bernard. *Semites and Anti-Semites: An Inquiry into Conflict and Prejudice.* London: Phoenix, 1997.

Lifshitz, Felice. "Beyond Positivism and Genre: 'Hagiographical' Texts as Historical Narrative." *Viator* 25 (1994), 95–114.

Little, Donald P. "Coptic Conversion to Islam under the Baḥrī Mamlūks, 692–755/1293–1354." *Bulletin of the School of Oriental and African Studies* 39 (1976), 552–69.

Livne-Kafri, Ofer. "Early Muslim Ascetics and the World of Christian Monasticism." *Jerusalem Studies in Arabic and Islam* 20 (1996), 105–29.

Løkkegaard, Frede. *Islamic Taxation in the Classical Period with Special Reference to Circumstances in Iraq.* Copenhagen: Branner & Korch, 1950.

López, Carlos María. "Problemas históricos en torno a las Santas Nunila y Alodia." *Principe de Viana* 24 (1964), 155–63.

———. "En torno a la patria de las Santas Nunila y Alodia." *Principe de Viana* 26 (1965), 395–404.

———. "Más sobre la problemática en torno a las Santas Nunilo y Alodia." *Principe de Viana* 28 (1970), 101–32.

Lowry, Heath W. *The Shaping of the Ottoman Balkans, 1350–1500: The Conquest, Settlement and Infrastructural Development of Northern Greece.* Istanbul: Bahçeşehir University Publications, 2008.

Luzzi, Andrea. "Synaxaria and the Synaxarion of Constantinople." In *The Ashgate Research Companion to Byzantine Hagiography. Volume II: Genres and Contexts.* Stephanos Efthymiadis, ed. Farnham, UK: Ashgate, 2014, 197–208.

MacCoull, L.S.B. "The Rite of the Jar: Apostasy and Reconciliation in the Medieval Coptic Orthodox Church." In *Peace and Negotiation: Strategies for Coexistence in the Middle Ages and Renaissance.* Diane Wolfthal, ed. Turnhout: Brepols, 2000, 145–62.

MacKenzie, D. N., ed. *A Concise Pahlavi Dictionary.* London: Oxford University Press, 1971.

MacMullen, Ramsay. *Christianizing the Roman Empire (A.D. 100–400).* New Haven: Yale University Press, 1984.

———. "Judicial Savagery in the Roman Empire." *Chiron* 16 (1986), 147–66.

Madelung, Wilferd. "Apocalyptic Prophecies in Ḥimṣ in the Umayyad Age." *Journal of Semitic Studies* 31 (1986), 141–85.

———. "The Sufyānī between Tradition and History." *Studia Islamica* 63 (1986), 5–48.

Maḥmūd b. ʿUthmān. *Die Vita des Scheich Abū Isḥāq al-Kāzarūnī in der persischen Bearbeitung.* Fritz Meier, ed. Leipzig: Kommissionsverlag F. A. Brockhaus, 1948.

al-Makhṭūṭāt al-ʿarabīya fī abrashīyāt ḥimṣ wa-ḥamāh wa-ʾl-lādhaqīya lil-rūm al-

urthūdhuks. Beirut: Qism al-Tawthīq wa-ʾl-Dirāsāt al-Anṭākīya-Jāmiʿat al-Balamand, 1994.

Maksoudian, Krikor H., trans. and ed. *Yovhannēs Drasxanakertcʿi: History of Armenia.* Atlanta: Scholars Press, 1987.

Malone, Edward. *The Monk and the Martyr: The Monk as the Successor of the Martyr.* Washington, DC: Catholic University of America Press, 1950.

Mandalà, Giuseppe. "Political Martyrdom and Religious Censorship in Islamic Sicily: A Case Study during the Age of Ibrāhīm II (261–289/875–902)." *Al-Qanṭara* 35 (2014), 151–86.

———. "The Martyrdom of Yūḥannā, Physician of Ibn Abī 'l-Ḥusayn Ruler of the Island of Sicily. Editio Princeps and Historical Commentary." *Journal of Transcultural Medieval Studies* 3 (2016), 33–118.

Mango, Cyril. "Greek Culture in Palestine after the Arab Conquest." In *Scritture, libri e testi nelle aree provinciali di Bisanzio: Atti del seminario di Erice (18–25 settembre 1988).* 2 vols. Guglielmo Cavallo, Giuseppe De Gregorio, and Marilena Maniaci, eds. Spoleto: Centro italiano di studi sull'alto Medioevo, 1991, i, 149–60.

———. "Saints." In *The Byzantines.* Guglielmo Cavallo, ed., with Thomas Dunlap, Teresa Lavender Fagan, and Charles Lambert, trans. Chicago: University of Chicago Press, 1997, 255–80.

Mango, Cyril, and Roger Scott, trans. *The Chronicle of Theophanes Confessor: Byzantine and Near Eastern History, A.D. 284–813.* Oxford: Clarendon Press, 1997.

Mansi, J. D., ed. *Sacrorum conciliorum nova et amplissima collectio.* 56 vols. Paris: H. Welter, 1758–98.

Manzano Moreno, Eduardo. "The Iberian Peninsula and North Africa." In *The New Cambridge History of Islam. Volume 1: The Formation of the Islamic World, Sixth to Eleventh Centuries.* Chase F. Robinson, ed. Cambridge: Cambridge University Press, 2010, 581–621.

al-Maqrīzī. *Kitāb al-mawāʿiẓ wa-ʾl-iʿtibār bi-dhikr al-khiṭaṭ wa-ʾl-āthār.* 2 vols. Būlāq, Cairo: Dār al-Ṭibāʿa al-Miṣrīya, 1853.

———. *al-Mawāʿiẓ wa-ʾl-iʿtibār fī dhikr al-khiṭaṭ wa-ʾl-āthār.* 7 vols. Ayman Fuʾād Sayyid, ed. London: Muʾassasat al-Furqān lil-Turāth al-Islāmī, 2002–13.

Marcone, Arnoldo. "A Long Late Antiquity? Considerations of a Controversial Periodization." *Journal of Late Antiquity* 1 (2008), 4–19.

Mardirossian, Aram. "Les canons du synode de Partaw (768)." *Revue des études arméniennes* 27 (1998–2000), 117–34.

Marlow, Louise. *Hierarchy and Egalitarianism in Islamic Thought.* Cambridge: Cambridge University Press, 1997.

Marsham, Andrew. "Public Execution in the Umayyad Period: Early Islamic Punitive Practice and Its Late Antique Context." *Journal of Arabic and Islamic Studies* 11 (2011), 101–36.

———. "Attitudes to the Use of Fire in Executions in Late Antiquity and Early Islam: The Burning of Heretics and Rebels in Late Umayyad Iraq." In *Violence in Islamic Thought from the Qurʾān to the Mongols.* Robert Gleave and István T. Kristó-Nagy, eds. Edinburgh: Edinburgh University Press, 2015, 106–27.

Martin-Hisard, Bernadette. "Brebis, boucs/loups, et chiens: Une hagiographie géorgienne anti-arménienne du début du Xe siècle." *Révue des études arméniennes* 23 (1992), 209–35.

Martin-Hisard, Bernadette. "Georgian Hagiography." In *The Ashgate Research Companion to Byzantine Hagiography. Volume I: Periods and Places.* Stephanos Efthymiadis, ed. Farnham, UK: Ashgate, 2011, 285–98.

Martinez-Gros, Gabriel. *Identité andalouse.* Paris: Sinbad, 1997.

al-Masʿūdī. *Les prairies d'or.* 9 vols. C. Barbier de Meynard, ed. and trans. Paris: Imprimerie impériale, 1861–1917.

Mavroudi, Maria. "Greek Language and Education under Early Islam." In *Islamic Cultures, Islamic Contexts: Essays in Honor of Professor Patricia Crone.* Behnam Sadeghi, Asad Q. Ahmed, Adam Silverstein, and Robert Hoyland. Leiden: Brill, 2015, 295–342.

al-Māwardī. *al-Aḥkām al-sulṭānīya wa-ʾl-wilāyat al-dīnīya.* Muḥammad Fahmī al-Sirjānī, ed. Cairo: al-Maktaba al-Tawfīqīya, 1978.

Maya Sánchez, A., ed. *Vitas sanctorum patrum Emeretensium.* CCSL 116. Turnhout: Brepols, 1992.

[*EQ*] McAuliffe, Jane Dammen, ed. *Encyclopaedia of the Qurʾān.* 5 vols. Leiden: Brill, 2001–6.

Adang, Camilla P. "Hypocrites and Hypocrisy." *EQ*, ii, 468–72.

Ammann, Ludwig. "Mockery." *EQ*, iii, 400–401.

Bauer, Thomas. "Insanity." *EQ*, ii, 539–41.

Hallaq, Wael. "Apostasy." *EQ*, i, 119–22.

Robinson, Neal. "Crucifixion." *EQ*, i, 487–89.

Stewart, Devin. "Blasphemy." *EQ*, i, 235–36.

McCormick, Michael. *Origins of the European Economy: Communication and Commerce, A.D. 300–900.* Cambridge: Cambridge University Press, 2001.

——. *Charlemagne's Survey of the Holy Land: Wealth, Personnel, and Buildings of a Mediterranean Church between Antiquity and the Middle Ages.* Washington, DC: Dumbarton Oaks Research Library and Collection, 2011.

McGrath, Stamatina. "Elias of Heliopolis: The Life of an Eighth-Century Syrian Saint." In *Byzantine Authors: Literary Activities and Preoccupations. Texts and Translations Dedicated to the Memory of Nicolas Oikonomides.* John W. Nesbitt, ed. Leiden: Brill, 2003, 85–107.

Meinardus, Otto. "The Nestorians in Egypt." *Oriens Christianus* 51 (1967), 112–22.

——. "A Note on the Nestorians in Jerusalem." *Oriens Christianus* 51 (1967), 123–29.

Menocal, María Rosa. *The Ornament of the World: How Muslims, Jews, and Christians Created a Culture of Tolerance in Medieval Spain.* Boston: Little, Brown, 2002.

Mgaloblishvili, Tamila. "The Georgian Sabaite (Sabatsminduri) Literary School and the Sabatsmindian Version of the Georgian *Mravaltavi* (Polykephalon)." In *The Sabaite Heritage in the Orthodox Church from the Fifth Century to the Present.* Joseph Patrich, ed. Leuven: Peeters, 2001, 229–33.

——. "An Unknown Georgian Monastery in the Holy Land." *ARAM* 18–19 (2006–7), 527–39.

Middleton, Paul. "Early Christian Voluntary Martyrdom: A Statement for the Defence." *Journal of Theological Studies* 64 (2013), 556–73.

[*PG*] Migne, J. P., ed. *Patrologia Cursus Completus, Series Graeca.* 161 vols. Paris: Imprimerie Catholique, 1857–66.

Mikhail, Maged S. A. *From Byzantine to Islamic Egypt: Religion, Identity and Politics after the Arab Conquest.* London: I. B. Tauris, 2014.

Miles, Richard, ed. *The Donatist Schism: Controversy and Contexts.* Liverpool: Liverpool University Press, 2016.

Miller, Patricia Cox. *Biography in Late Antiquity: A Quest for the Holy Man.* Berkeley: University of California Press, 1983.

Millet-Gérard, Dominique. *Chrétiens mozarabes et culture islamique dans l'Espagne des VIIIe–IXe siècles.* Paris: Études Augustiniennes, 1984.

Mingana, Alphonse, ed. *Sources syriaques.* 2 vols. Leipzig: O. Harrassowitz, 1907.

———. *Woodbrooke Studies: Christian Documents in Syriac, Arabic, and Garshūni, Edited and Translated with a Critical Apparatus.* 7 vols. Cambridge: W. Heffer and Sons Limited, 1927–34.

———. "Apocalypse of Peter." *Bulletin of the John Rylands Library* 14 (1930), 182–297, 423–562; and 15 (1931), 179–279.

Miquel, Pierre. "Parrhèsia." In *Dictionnaire de spiritualité ascétique et mystique, doctrine et histoire.* 17 vols. Marcel Viller, general ed. Paris: G. Beauchesne et ses fils, 1937–95, xii, I, 260–67.

al-Mizzī. *Tahdhīb al-kamāl fī asmāʾ al-rijāl.* 35 vols. Bashshār ʿAwwād Maʿrūf, ed. Beirut: Muʾassasat al-Risāla, 1992.

Modarressi, Hossein. *Tradition and Survival: A Bibliographic Survey of Early Shīʿite Literature.* Oxford: Oneworld, 2003.

Monferrer Sala, Juan Pedro. "Mitografía hagiomartirial. De nuevo sobre los supuestos mártires cordobeses del siglo IX." In *De muerte violenta. Política, religión y violencia en al-Andalus.* Maribel Fierro, ed. Madrid: Consejo Superior de Investigaciones Científicas, 2004, 415–50.

———. "*Šahādat al-qiddīs Mār Anṭūniyūs.* Replanteamiento de la 'antigüedad' de las versiones sinaíticas a la luz del análisis textual." *Miscelánea de estudios árabes y hebraicos* 57 (2008), 237–67.

———. "A Greek Christian Martyr of Persian Origin: Anatolius' Martyrdom in an Arabic Fragment from 'the Mingana Collection' (*Chr. Arab.* 236)." *Le Muséon* 124 (2011), 125–48.

Montet, Edouard. "Un rituel d'abjuration des musulmans dans l'église grecque." *Revue de l'histoire des religions* 53 (1906), 145–63.

Moore, R. I. *The Formation of a Persecuting Society.* 2nd ed. Oxford: Basil Blackwell, 2007.

Morales, Ambrosio de, ed. *Divi Eulogii Cordubensis, martyris, doctoris et electi Archiepiscopi Toletani opera.* Alcalá, 1574.

Morony, Michael G. *Iraq after the Muslim Conquest.* Princeton: Princeton University Press, 1984.

———. "The Age of Conversions: A Reassessment." In *Conversion and Continuity: Indigenous Christian Communities in Islamic Lands, Eighth to Eighteenth Centuries.* Michael Gervers and Ramzi Jibran Bikhazi, eds. Toronto: Pontifical Institute of Mediaeval Studies, 1990, 135–50.

———. "History and Identity in the Syrian Churches." In *Redefining Christian Identity: Cultural Interaction in the Middle East since the Rise of Islam.* J. J. van Ginkel, H. L. Murre-van den Berg, and T. M. van Lint, eds. Leuven: Peeters, 2005, 1–33.

Morrow, John Andrew. *The Covenants of the Prophet Muhammad with the Christians of the World.* Hillsdale, NY: Sophia Perennis, 2013.

Moscati, Sabatino. "Le massacre des Umayyades dans l'histoire et dans les fragments poétiques." *Archív orientální* 18 (1950), 88–115.

Moss, Candida R. "On the Dating of Polycarp: Rethinking the Place of the *Martyrdom of Polycarp* in the History of Christianity." *Early Christianity* 1 (2010), 539–74.

———. *The Myth of Persecution: How Early Christians Invented a Story of Martyrdom.* New York: Harper One, 2013.

Mourad, Suleiman. "Christian Monks in Islamic Literature: A Preliminary Report on Some Arabic *Apophthegmata Patrum.*" *Bulletin of the Royal Institute for Inter-faith Studies* 6 (2004), 81–98.

Munt, Harry. " 'No Two Religions': Non-Muslims in the Early Islamic Ḥijāz." *Bulletin of the School of Oriental and African Studies* 78 (2015), 249–69.

———. "What Did Conversion to Islam Mean in Seventh-Century Arabia?" In *Islamisation: Comparative Perspectives from History.* A.C.S. Peacock, ed. Edinburgh: Edinburgh University Press, 2017, 83–101.

Muqātil b. Sulaymān. *Tafsīr muqātil b. sulaymān.* 5 vols. ʿAbdallāh Maḥmūd Shiḥāta, ed. Cairo: al-Hayʾa al-Miṣrīya al-ʿAmma lil-Kitāb, 1979–89.

Muslim. *Ṣaḥīḥ muslim.* 5 vols. Muḥammad Fuʾād ʿAbd al-Bāqī, ed. Beirut: Dār al-Fikr, 1999.

Musurillo, Herbert, trans. *The Acts of the Christian Martyrs.* Oxford: Clarendon Press, 1972.

al-Nābulusī, Abū ʿAmr ʿUthmān b. Ibrāhīm. *The Sword of Ambition: Bureaucratic Rivalry in Medieval Egypt: Abū ʿAmr ʿUthmān ibn Ibrāhīm al-Nābulusī al-Miṣrī.* Luke B. Yarbrough, ed. and trans. New York: New York University Press, 2016.

Nanobashvili, Mariam. "The Development of Literary Contacts between the Georgians and the Arabic Speaking Christians in Palestine from the 8th to the 10th Century." *ARAM* 15 (2003), 269–74.

al-Narshakhī. *Tārīkh-i Bukhārā.* Mudarris Riḍawī, ed. Tehran: Bunyād-i Farhang-i Īrān, 1972.

al-Nasāʾī. *Sunan al-nasāʾī.* 8 vols. ʿAbd al-Wārith ʿAlī, ed. Beirut: Dār al-Kutub al-ʿIlmīya, 1995.

Nasrallah, Joseph. "L'Église melchite en Iraq, en Perse et dans l'Asie centrale. II. Le catholicosat de Bagdad." *Proche-Orient Chrétien* 26 (1976), 319–53.

Nau, François. "Littérature canonique syriaque inédite." *Revue de l'orient chrétien* 14 (1909), 113–30.

———. "Un martyrologe et douze ménologes syriaques." *Patrologia Orientalis* 10 (1915), 1–162.

———. *Les arabes chrétiens de Mésopotamie et de Syrie du VIIe au VIIIe siècle.* Paris: Imprimerie Nationale, 1933.

Nef, Annliese. "Violence and the Prince: The Case of the Aghlabid Amīr Ibrāhīm II (261–89/875–902)." In *Public Violence in Islamic Societies: Power, Discipline and the Construction of the Public Sphere, 7th–19th Centuries CE.* Christian Lange and Maribel Fierro, eds. Edinburgh: Edinburgh University Press, 2009, 217–37.

Nirenberg, David. *Communities of Violence: Persecution of Minorities in the Middle Ages.* Princeton: Princeton University Press, 1996.

Noble, Samuel, and Alexander Trei4ger, eds. *The Orthodox Church in the Arab World, 700–1700: An Anthology of Sources.* De Kalb, IL: Northern Illinois University Press, 2014.

Nock, A. D. *Conversion: The Old and the New in Religion from Alexander the Great to Augustine of Hippo.* Oxford: Clarendon Press, 1933.

Noth, Albrecht. "Problems of Differentiation between Muslims and Non-Muslims: Re-

reading the 'Ordinances of 'Umar' (*al-Shurūṭ al-'Umariyya*)." In *Muslims and Others in Early Islamic Society*. Robert G. Hoyland, ed. and trans. Farnham, UK: Ashgate, 2004, 103–24.

Nu'aym b. Ḥammād. *Kitāb al-fitan*. Suhayl Zakkār, ed. Beirut: Dār al-Fikr, 1994.

al-Nubāhī. *Tārīkh quḍāt al-andalus*. É. Lévi-Provençal, ed. Cairo: Scribe Egyptien, 1948.

Oestrup, J. "Uber zwei arabische Codices sinaitici der Strassburger Universitäts- und Landesbibliothek." *Zeitschrift der Deutschen Morgenländischen Gesellschaft* 51 (1897), 453–71.

Ohta, Keiko. "The Coptic Church and Coptic Communities in the Reign of al-Ma'mūn: A Study of the Social Context of the Bashmūric Revolt." *Annals of the Japan Association for Middle East Studies* 19 (2004), 87–116.

O'Leary, De Lacy. *The Saints of Egypt*. London: Society for Promoting Christian Knowledge, 1937.

Oliver Pérez, Dolores. "Una nueva interpretacíon de árabe, muladí y *mawla* como voces representativas de grupos sociales." In *Proyección histórica de España en sus tres culturas: Castilla y León, América y el Mediterráneo*. 3 vols. Eufemio Lorenzo Sanz, ed. Valladolid: Junta de Castilla y León, Consejería de Cultura y Turismo, 1993, III, 143–55.

O'Sullivan, Declan. "The Interpretation of Qur'anic Text to Promote or Negate the Death Penalty for Apostates and Blasphemers." *Journal of Qur'anic Studies* 3 (2001), 63–93.

Pahlitzsch, Johannes. "Mediators between East and West: Christians under Mamluk Rule." *Mamlūk Studies Review* 9, no. 2 (2005), 31–47.

——. "Christian Pious Foundations as an Element of Continuity between Late Antiquity and Islam." In *Studien zur Geschichte und Kultur des islamischen Orients*. Miriam Frenkel and Yaacov Lev, eds. Berlin: Walter de Gruyter, 2009, 125–51.

Palme, Bernhard. "Political Identity versus Religious Distinction? The Case of Egypt in the Later Roman Empire." In *Visions of Community in the Post-Roman World: The West, Byzantium and the Islamic World, 300–1100*. Walter Pohl, Clemens Ganter, and Richard Payne, eds. Farnham, UK: Ashgate, 2012, 81–98.

Palmer, Andrew. "The Messiah and the Mahdi: History Presented as the Writing on the Wall." In *Polyphonia Byzantina: Studies in Honour of Willem J. Aerts*. Hero Hokwerda, Edmé R. Smits, and Marinus M. Woesthuis, eds. Groningen: Egbert Forsten, 1993, 45–84.

——, trans. *The Seventh Century in the West Syrian Chronicles*. With Sebastian Brock and Robert Hoyland. Liverpool: Liverpool University Press, 1993.

Papaconstantinou, Arietta. "Historiography, Hagiography, and the Making of the Coptic 'Church of the Martyrs' in Early Islamic Egypt." *Dumbarton Oaks Papers* 60 (2006), 65–86.

——. " 'They Shall Speak the Arabic Language and Take Pride in It': Reconsidering the Fate of Coptic after the Arab Conquest." *Le Muséon* 120 (2007), 273–99.

——. "Between *Umma* and *Dhimma*: The Christians of the Middle East under the Umayyads." *Annales islamologiques* 42 (2008), 127–56.

——. " 'What Remains Behind': Hellenism and *Romanitas* in Christian Egypt after the Arab Conquest." In *From Hellenism to Islam: Cultural and Linguistic Change in the Roman Near East*. Hannah M. Cotton, Robert G. Hoyland, Jonathan J. Price, and David J. Wasserstein, eds. Cambridge: Cambridge University Press, 2009, 447–66.

——. "Administering the Early Islamic Empire: Insights from the Papyri." In *Money,*

Power and Politics in Early Islamic Syria: A Review of Current Debates. John Haldon, ed. Farnham, UK: Ashgate, 2010, 57–74.

Papaconstantinou, Arietta. "Hagiography in Coptic." In *The Ashgate Research Companion to Byzantine Hagiography. Volume I: Periods and Places.* Stephanos Efthymiadis, ed. Farnham, UK: Ashgate, 2011, 323–43.

——. "Saints and Saracens: On Some Miracle Accounts of the Early Arab Period." In *Byzantine Religious Culture: Studies in Honor of Alice-Mary Talbot.* Denis Sullivan, Elizabeth Fisher, and Stratis Papaioannou, eds. Leiden: Brill, 2012, 323–38.

——. "Introduction." In *Conversion in Late Antiquity: Christianity, Islam, and Beyond: Papers from the Andrew W. Mellon Foundation Sawyer Seminar, University of Oxford, 2009–2010.* Arietta Papaconstantinou, with Neil McLynn and Daniel L. Schwartz, eds. Burlington, VT: Ashgate, 2015, xv–xxxvii.

Papaconstantinou, Arietta, with Neil McLynn and Daniel L. Schwartz, eds. *Conversion in Late Antiquity: Christianity, Islam, and Beyond: Papers from the Andrew W. Mellon Foundation Sawyer Seminar, University of Oxford, 2009–2010.* Burlington, VT: Ashgate, 2015.

Papadogiannakis, Yannis. "Christian Identity in Seventh-Century Byzantium: The Case of Anastasius of Sinai." In *Motions of Late Antiquity: Essays on Religion, Politics, and Society in Honour of Peter Brown.* Jamie Kreiner and Helmut Reimitz, eds. Turnhout: Brepols, 2016, 249–67.

Papadopoulos-Kerameus, Athanasios. "Muchenichestvo shestidesiati novykh sviatykh muchenikov postradavshikh vo Sviatom grade Khrista Boga nashego pod vladichestvom Arabov." *Pravoslavnyi palestinskii sbornik* 12 (1892), 1–25.

[*SPSH*] ——, ed. *Syllogē Palaistinēs kai Syriakēs hagiologias.* 3 vols. St. Petersburg: Tipografiia Kirshbaum, 1907–13.

Pargoire, J. "Les LX soldats martyrs de Gaza." *Echos d'orient* 8 (1905), 40–43.

Patlagean, Évelyne. "Ancienne hagiographie byzantine et histoire sociale." *Annales. Histoire, Sciences Sociales* 23 (1968), 106–26.

——. "Byzance et le blason pénal du corps." In *Du châtiment dans la cité. Supplices corporels et peine de mort dans le monde antique. Table ronde organisée par l'École française de Rome avec le concours du Centre national de la recherche scientifique (Rome 9–11 novembre 1982).* Rome: L'École française de Rome, 1984, 405–27.

Payne, Richard. "Cosmology and the Expansion of the Iranian Empire, 502–628 CE." *Past and Present* 220 (2013), 3–33.

——. *A State of Mixture: Christians, Zoroastrians, and Iranian Political Culture in Late Antiquity.* Oakland, CA: University of California Press, 2015.

Payne Smith, R., ed. *A Compendious Syriac Dictionary.* J. Payne Smith, ed. Oxford: Ex typographeo Clarendoniano, 1903.

——, ed. *Thesaurus Syriacus.* 2 vols. Hildesheim: G. Olms, 1981.

Peacock, A.C.S., ed. *Islamisation: Comparative Perspectives from History.* Edinburgh: Edinburgh University Press, 2017.

Peeters, Paul. "Le martyrologe de Rabban Sliba." *Analecta Bollandiana* 27 (1908), 129–200.

[*BHO*] ——, ed. *Bibliotheca hagiographica orientalis.* Brussels: Apud editores, 1910.

——. "S. Romain le néomartyr († 1 mai 780) d'après un document géorgien." *Analecta Bollandiana* 30 (1911), 393–427.

——. "S. Antoine le néo-martyr." *Analecta Bollandiana* 31 (1912), 410–50.

——. "L'autobiographie de S. Antoine le néomartyr." *Analecta Bollandiana* 33 (1914), 52–63.
——. "Les traductions orientales du mot Martyr." *Analecta Bollandiana* 39 (1921), 50–64.
——. "De S. Constantino, martyre in Babilonia." In *Acta sanctoroum, Novembriis*, vol. 6. Louvain, 1925, 541–63.
——. "La passion de S. Michel le Sabaïte." *Analecta Bollandiana* 48 (1930), 65–98.
——. "Les Khazars dans la passion de S. Abo de Tiflis." *Analecta Bollandiana* 52 (1934), 21–56.
——. "La passion de S. Pierre de Capitolias († 13 janvier 715)." *Analecta Bollandiana* 57 (1939), 299–333.
——. "Glanures martyrologiques." *Analecta Bollandiana* 58 (1940), 104–25.
——. *Orient et Byzance: Le tréfonds oriental de l'hagiographie byzantine*. Brussells: Société des Bollandistes, 1950.
Penelas, Mayte. "Some Remarks on Conversion to Islam in al-Andalus." *Al-Qanṭara* 23 (2002), 193–200.
Penn, Michael. "*John and the Emir*: A New Introduction, Edition and Translation." *Le Muséon* 121 (2008), 65–91.
——. *Envisioning Islam: Syriac Christians and the Early Muslim World*. Philadelphia: University of Pennsylvania Press, 2015.
Pentz, Peter. *The Invisible Conquest: The Ontogenesis of Sixth and Seventh Century Syria*. Copenhagen: National Museum of Denmark, Collection of Near Eastern and Classical Antiquities, 1992.
Pérez de Urbel, Justo. *A Saint under Moslem Rule*. Anonymous Benedictine of Stanbrook Abbey, Worcester, England, trans. Milwaukee, WI: Bruce Publishing Company, 1937.
Peters, Rudolph, and Gert J. J. de Vries. "Apostasy in Islam." *Die Welt des Islams* 17 (1976), 1–25.
Piccirillo, Michele. *The Mosaics of Jordan*. Patricia M. Bikai and Thomas A. Dailey, eds. Amman: American Center of Oriental Research, 1993.
Pirone, Bartolomeo. "Un altro manoscritto sulla vita e sul martirio del nobile qurayshita Rawḥ." In *Biblica et semitica: Studi in memoria di Francesco Vattioni*. Luigi Cagni, ed. Naples: Istituto universitario orientale, 1999, 479–509.
Pochoshajew, Igor. *Die Märtyrer von Cordoba: Christen im muslimischen Spanien des 9. Jahrhunderts*. Frankfurt am Main: Verlag Otto Lembeck, 2007.
Pomialovskij, I. *Zhitie izhe vo sviatykh ottsa nashego Feodora, arkhiepiskopa Edesskago, po dvum rukopisiam Moskovskoi sinodal'noi biblioteki izdal*. St. Petersburg: Tipografiia Imp. Akademii nauk, 1892.
Posener, Georges. "L'ἀναχώρησις dans l'Égypte pharaonique." In *Le monde grec: Pensée, littérature, histoire, documents. Hommages à Claire Préaux*. Jean Bingen, Guy Cambier, and Georges Nachtergael, eds. Brussels: Éditions de l'Université de Bruxelles, 1975, 663–69.
Powers, David S. *Zayd*. Philadelphia: University of Pennsylvania Press, 2014.
Pritsak, Omeljan. "The Khazar Kingdom's Conversion to Judaism." *Harvard Ukranian Studies* 2 (1978), 261–81.
[*PMBZ*] *Prosopographie der mittelbyzantinischen Zeit*. 16 vols. Berlin: de Gruyter, 1998–2013.

Pulcini, Theodore. *Exegesis as Polemical Discourse: Ibn Ḥazm on Jewish and Christian Scriptures.* Atlanta: Scholars Press, 1998.

al-Qāḍī, Wadād. "Non-Muslims in the Muslim Conquest Army in Early Islam." In *Christians and Others in the Umayyad State.* Antoine Borrut and Fred M. Donner, eds. Chicago: Oriental Institute of the University of Chicago, 2016, 83–127.

Qāḍī ʿIyāḍ b. Mūsā. *Kitāb al-shifāʾ.* 2 vols. Muḥammad Amīn Qarah ʿAlī, Usāma al-Rifāʿī, Jamāl al-Sayrawān, Nūr al-Dīn Qarah ʿAlī, and ʿAbd al-Fattāḥ al-Sayyid, eds. Damascus: Dār al-Wafāʾ lil-Ṭibāʿa wa-ʾl-Nashr, 1972.

Rabb, Intisar. *Doubt in Islamic Law: A History of Legal Maxims, Interpretation, and Islamic Criminal Law.* New York: Cambridge University Press, 2015.

———. "Society and Propriety: The Cultural Construction of Defamation and Blasphemy as Crimes in Islamic Law." In *Accusations of Unbelief in Islam: A Diachronic Perspective on* Takfīr. Camilla Adang, Hassan Ansari, Maribel Fierro, and Sabine Schmidtke, eds. Leiden: Brill, 2016, 434–64.

Raineri, Osvaldo, ed. *Gli atti etiopici del martire egiziano Giorgio il nuovo († 978).* Vatican City: Biblioteca Apostolica Vaticana, 1999.

Ramaḍān, ʿAbd al-ʿAzīz M. A. "The Treatment of Arab Prisoners of War in Byzantium, 9th–10th Centuries." *Annales islamologiques* 43 (2009), 155–94.

Rambo, Lewis R., and Charles E. Farhadian, eds. *The Oxford Handbook of Religious Conversion.* Oxford: Oxford University Press, 2014.

Rapp, Stephen H., Jr. *Studies in Medieval Georgian Historiography: Early Texts and Eurasian Contexts.* Leuven: Peeters, 2003.

Rayfield, Donald. *The Literature of Georgia: A History.* 3rd ed. London: Garnett Press, 2010.

———. *Edge of Empires: A History of Georgia.* London: Reaktion, 2012.

Reinink, Gerrit J. "Following the Doctrine of the Demons: Early Christian Fear of Conversion to Islam." In *Cultures of Conversions.* Jan N. Bremmer, Wout J. van Bekkum, and Arie L. Molendijk, eds. Leuven: Peeters, 2006, 127–38.

———. "The Veneration of Icons, the Cross, and the Bones of the Martyrs in an Early East-Syrian Apology against Islam." In *Bibel, Byzanz und Christlicher Orient: Festschrift für Stephen Gerö zum 65. Geburtstag.* D. Bumazhnov, E. Grypeou, T. B. Sailors, and A. Toepel, eds. Leuven: Peeters, 2011, 329–42.

Renard, John. *Friends of God: Islamic Images of Piety, Commitment, and Servanthood.* Berkeley: University of California Press, 2013.

Reynolds, Gabriel Said. *A Muslim Theologian in the Sectarian Milieu: ʿAbd al-Jabbār and the Critique of Christian Origins.* Leiden: Brill, 2004.

Rigo, Antonio. "Una formula inedita d'abiura per i musulmani (fine X–inizi XI secolo)." *Rivista di studi bizantini e neoellenici* 29 (1992), 163–73.

Robinson, Chase F. *Empire and Elites after the Muslim Conquest: The Transformation of Northern Mesopotamia.* Cambridge: Cambridge University Press, 2000.

———. *ʿAbd al-Malik.* Oxford: Oneworld Publications, 2005.

———. "Neck-Sealing in Early Islam." *Journal of the Economic and Social History of the Orient* 48 (2005), 401–41.

———. "The Violence of the Abbasid Revolution." In *Living Islamic History: Studies in Honour of Professor Carole Hillenbrand.* Yasir Suleiman, ed. Edinburgh: Edinburgh University Press, 2010, 226–51.

Rodríguez Fernández, Celso. *La Pasión de S. Pelayo: Edición crítica, con traducción y comentarios*. Santiago de Compostela: Monografías de Universidade de Santiago de Compostela, 1991.

Rossi Taibbi, Giuseppe, ed. *Vita di Sant 'Elia il Giovane*. Palermo: Istituto siciliano di studi bizantini e neoellenici, 1962.

Rousseau, Philip, ed. *A Companion to Late Antiquity*. Chichester: Wiley-Blackwell, 2009.

Rowson, Everett K. "Reveal or Conceal: Public Humiliation and Banishment as Punishments in Early Islamic Times." In *Public Violence in Islamic Societies: Power, Discipline, and the Construction of the Public Sphere, 7th–19th Centuries CE*. Christian Lange and Maribel Fierro, eds. Edinburgh: Edinburgh University Press, 2009, 119–29.

Rubin, Jody P. "Celsus's Decircumcision Operation." *Urology* 16 (1980), 121–24.

Ruggles, D. Fairchild. "Mothers of a Hybrid Dynasty: Race, Genealogy, and Acculturation in al-Andalus." *Journal of Medieval and Early Modern Studies* 34 (2004), 65–94.

Russell, Gerard. *Heirs to Forgotten Kingdoms: Journeys into the Disappearing Religions of the Middle East*. London: Simon and Schuster, 2015.

Rustow, Marina. *Heresy and the Politics of Community: The Jews of the Fatimid Caliphate*. Ithaca, NY: Cornell University Press, 2008.

Safran, Janina M. "Identity and Differentiation in Ninth-Century al-Andalus." *Speculum* 76 (2001), 573–98.

——. "Rules of Purity and Confessional Boundaries: Maliki Debates about the Pollution of the Christian." *History of Religions* 42 (2003), 197–212.

——. "The Sacred and the Profane in Islamic Corboba." *Comparative Islamic Studies* 1 (2005), 21–41.

——. *Defining Boundaries in al-Andalus: Muslims, Christians, and Jews in Islamic Iberia*. Ithaca, NY: Cornell University Press, 2013.

Sage, Carleton M. *Paul Albar of Cordoba: Studies on His Life and Writings*. Washington, DC: Catholic University of America Press, 1943.

Sahas, Daniel J. *John of Damascus on Islam: The "Heresy of the Ishmaelites."* Leiden: Brill, 1972.

——. "What an Infidel Saw that a Faithful Did Not: Gregory Dekapolites (d. 842) and Islam." *Greek Orthodox Theological Review* 31 (1986), 47–67.

——. "Ritual of Conversion from Islam to the Byzantine Church." *Greek Orthodox Theological Review* 36 (1991), 57–69.

——. "Eighth-Century Byzantine Anti-Islamic Literature." *Byzantino-Slavica* 57 (1996), 229–38.

Sahner, Christian C. "From Augustine to Islam: Translation and History in the Arabic Orosius." *Speculum* 88 (2013), 905–31.

——. *Among the Ruins: Syria Past and Present*. London: Hurst; and New York: Oxford University Press, 2014.

——. "Old Martyrs, New Martyrs and the Coming of Islam: Writing Hagiography after the Conquests." In *Cultures in Motion: Studies in the Medieval and Early Modern Periods*. Adam Izdebski and Damian Jasiński, eds. Kraków: Jagiellonian University Press, 2014, 89–112.

——. "Islamic Legends about the Birth of Monasticism: A Case Study on the Late Antique Milieu of the Qur'ān and Tafsīr." In *The Late Antique World of Early Islam: Muslims among Christians and Jews in the East Mediterranean*. Robert G. Hoyland, ed. Princeton: Darwin Press, 2015, 393–435.

Sahner, Christian C. "The First Iconoclasm in Islam: A New History of the Edict of Yazīd II (AH 104/AD 723)." *Der Islam* 94 (2017), 5–56.
——. " 'The Monasticism of My Community Is Jihad': A Debate about Asceticism, Sex, and Warfare in Early Islam." *Arabica* 64 (2017), 1–35.
al-Sāmarrā'ī, Nu'mān 'Abd al-Razzāq. *Aḥkām al-murtadd fī 'l-sharī'a al-islāmīya*. Beirut: Dār al-'Arabīya and al-Maktab al-Islāmī, 1968.
Samir, Samir Khalil. "Les plus anciens homélaires géorgiens et les versions patristiques arabes." *Orientalia Christiana Periodica* 42 (1976), 217–31.
——. "Saint Rawḥ al-Qurašī. Étude d'onomastique arabe et authenticité de sa passion." *Le Muséon* 105 (1992), 343–59.
——. *Foi et culture en Irak au XIe siècle: Elie de Nisibe et l'Islam*. Aldershot: Variorum, 1996.
——. "La version latine de l'Apologie d'al-Kindī (vers 830 ap. J.-C.) et son original arabe." In *¿Existe una identidad mozárabe? Historia, lengua y cultura de los cristianos de al-Andalus (siglos IX–XII)*. Cyrille Aillet, Mayte Penelas, and Philippe Roisse, eds. Madrid: Casa de Velázquez, 2008, 33–81.
Sanjian, Avedis K. *Colophons of Armenian Manuscripts, 1301–1480: A Source for Middle Eastern History*. Cambridge, MA: Harvard University Press, 1969.
Santillana, David. *Istituzioni di diritto musulmano malichita con riguardo anche al sistema sciafiita*. 2 vols. Rome: Istituto per l'Oriente, 1925–38.
Al Sarhan, Saud. "The Responsa of Aḥmad Ibn Ḥanbal and the Formation of Ḥanbalism." *Islamic Law and Society* 22 (2015), 1–44.
Sauget, Joseph-Marie. *Premières recherches sur l'origine et les caractéristiques des synaxaires melkites (XIe–XVIIe siècles)*. Brussels: Société des Bollandistes, 1969.
Savant, Sarah Bowen. *The New Muslims of Post-conquest Iran: Tradition, Memory, and Conversion*. Cambridge: Cambridge University Press, 2013.
Scarpat, Giuseppe. *Parrhesia greca, parrhesia cristiana*. Brescia: Paideia Editrice, 2001.
Schacht, Joseph. *An Introduction to Islamic Law*. Oxford: Clarendon Press, 1964.
Schaefer, Richard T. *Racial and Ethnic Groups*. 13th ed. Boston: Pearson, 2012.
Scher, Addaï, and Robert Griveau. "Histoire nestorienne (Chronique de Séert), seconde partie (II)." *Patrologia Orientalis* 13 (1919), 433–639.
Schick, Robert. *The Christian Communities of Palestine from Byzantine to Islamic Rule: A Historical and Archaeological Study*. Princeton: Darwin Press, 1995.
Schilling, Alexander Markus. *Die Anbetung der Magier und die Taufe der Sāsāniden: Zur Geistesgeschichte der iranischen Christentums in der Spätantike*. Louvain: Peeters, 2008.
Schultze, K. "Das Martyrium des heiligen Abo von Tiflis." *Texte und Untersuchungen zur Geschichte der altchristlichen Literatur, Neue Folge* 28 (1905), 2–41.
Schütz, Edmond. "Armenia: A Christian Enclave in the Islamic Near East in the Middle Ages." In *Conversion and Continuity: Indigenous Christian Communities in Islamic Lands, Eighth to Eighteenth Centuries*. Michael Gervers and Ramzi Jibran Bikhazi, eds. Toronto: Pontifical Institute of Mediaeval Studies, 1990, 217–36.
Schwartz, Daniel L. *Paideia and Cult: Christian Initiation in Theodore of Mopsuestia*. Washington, DC: Center for Hellenic Studies; and Cambridge, MA: Harvard University Press, 2013.
Seidensticker, Tilman, "Responses to Crucifixion in the Islamic World (1st–7th/7th–13th Centuries)." In *Public Violence in Islamic Societies: Power, Discipline, and the*

Construction of the Public Sphere, 7th–19th Centuries CE. Christian Lange and Maribel Fierro, eds. Edinburgh: Edinburgh University Press, 2009, 203–16.

Seleznyov, Nikolai N. " 'For They Ascend to Three *Maḏāhib* as Their Roots': An Arabic Medieval Treatise on Denominations of Syrian Christianity." In *"Rassypannoe" i "sobrannoe": Strategii organizatcii smyslovogo prostranstva v arabo-musul'manskoi kul'ture.* A. V. Smirnov, ed. Moscow: Sadra, 2015, 122–35.

Sennott, Charles M. *The Body and the Blood: A Reporter's Journey through the Holy Land.* Oxford: PublicAffairs, 2001.

Shaban, M. "Conversion to Early Islam." In *Conversion to Islam.* Nehemia Levtzion, ed. New York: Holmes and Meier Publishers, Inc., 1979, 24–29.

al-Shābushtī. *al-Diyārāt.* Kūrkīs ʿAwwād, ed. Baghdad: Maktabat al-Muthannā, 1966.

al-Shāfiʿī. *Kitāb al-umm.* 11 vols. Rifʿat Fawzī ʿAbd al-Muṭṭalib, ed. El Mansûra: Dār al-Wafāʾ lil-Ṭibāʿa wa-ʾl-Nashr wa-ʾl-Tawzīʿ, 2001.

Shahîd, Irfan. *The Martyrs of Najrân: New Documents.* Brussels: Société des Bollandistes, 1971.

——. *Byzantium and the Arabs in the Fourth Century.* Washington, DC: Dumbarton Oaks Research Library and Collection, 1984.

al-Shahrastānī. *al-Milal wa-ʾl-niḥal.* Amīr ʿAlī Muhannā and ʿAlī Ḥasan Fāʿūr, eds. Beirut: Dār al-Maʿrifa, 1993.

al-Shāljī, ʿAbbūd. *Mawsūʿat al-ʿadhāb.* 2nd ed. 7 vols. Beirut: Dār al-ʿArabīya lil-Mawsūʿāt, 1999.

Shatzmiller, Maya. "Marriage, Family, and the Faith: Women's Conversion to Islam." *Journal of Family History* 21 (1996), 235–66.

Shaw, Brent D. "Bandits in the Roman Empire." *Past and Present* 105 (1984), 3–52.

——. "Judicial Nightmares and Christian Memory." *Journal of Early Christian Studies* 11 (2003), 533–63.

——. "The Myth of the Neronian Persecution." *Journal of Roman Studies* 105 (2015), 73–100.

Shenoda, Maryann Magdalen. "Lamenting Islam, Imagining Persecution: Copto-Arabic Opposition to Islamization and Arabization in Fatimid Egypt (969–1171 CE)." Ph.D. dissertation, Harvard University, 2010.

Sherwin-White, A. N. "The Early Persecutions and Roman Law Again." *Journal of Theological Studies* 3 (1952), 199–213.

Shoemaker, Stephen J. " 'Let Us Go and Burn Her Body': The Image of the Jews in Early Dormition Traditions." *Church History* 68 (1999), 775–823.

——. *The Death of a Prophet: The End of Muhammad's Life and the Beginnings of Islam.* Philadelphia: University of Pennsylvania Press, 2012.

——, trans. *Three Christian Martyrdoms from Early Islamic Palestine: Passion of Peter of Capitolias, Passion of the Twenty Martyrs of Mar Saba, Passion of Romanos the New-Martyr.* Provo, UT: Brigham Young University Press, 2016.

Shurgaia, Gaga. *La spiritualità georgiana: Martirio di Abo, santo e beato martire di Cristo di Ioane Sabanisze.* Rome: Edizioni Studium, 2003.

Sijpesteijn, Petra M. "Landholding Patterns in Early Islamic Egypt." *Journal of Agrarian Change* 9 (2009), 120–33.

——. *Shaping a Muslim State: The World of a Mid-Eighth-Century Egyptian Official.* Oxford: Oxford University Press, 2013.

Silverstein, Adam J. *Postal Systems in the Pre-modern Islamic World.* Cambridge: Cambridge University Press, 2007.

Simonet, Francisco Javier. *Historia de los Mozárabes de España deducida de los mejores y más auténticos testimonios de los escritores cristianos y arabes.* Madrid: Establecimiento tipográfico de la viuda é hijos de M. Tello, 1897–1903.

Simonsohn, Uriel I. "Seeking Justice among the 'Outsiders': Christian Recourse to Non-ecclesiastical Judicial Systems under Early Islam." *Church History and Religious Culture* 89 (2009), 191–216.

——. *A Common Justice: The Legal Allegiances of Christians and Jews under Early Islam.* Philadelphia: University of Pennsylvania Press, 2011.

——. "Conversion to Islam: A Case Study for the Use of Legal Sources." *History Compass* 11 (2013), 647–62.

——. " 'Halting between Two Opinions': Conversion and Apostasy in Early Islam." *Medieval Encounters* 19 (2013), 344–72.

——. "Conversion, Apostasy, and Penance: The Shifting Identities of Muslim Converts in the Early Islamic Period." In *Conversion in Late Antiquity: Christianity, Islam, and Beyond: Papers from the Andrew W. Mellon Foundation Sawyer Seminar, University of Oxford, 2009–2010.* Arietta Papaconstantinou, with Neil McLynn and Daniel L. Schwartz, eds. Burlington, VT: Ashgate, 2015, 197–215.

——. "The Legal and Social Bonds of Jewish Apostates and Their Spouses according to Gaonic Responsa." *Jewish Quarterly Review* 105 (2015), 417–39.

——. "Communal Membership despite Religious Exogamy: A Critical Examination of East and West Syrian Legal Sources of the Late Sasanian–Early Islamic Periods." *Journal of Near Eastern Studies* 75, no. 2 (2016), 1–18.

Sims-Williams, Nicholas. *The Christian Sogdian Manuscript C2.* Berlin: Akademie-Verlag, 1985.

Sindawi, Khalid. "Mīthām b. Yaḥyā al-Tammār: An Important Figure in Early Shīʿism." *al-Qanṭara* 29 (2008), 269–91.

Şişman, Cengiz. *The Burden of Silence: Sabbatai Sevi and the Evolution of the Ottoman-Turkish Dönmes.* New York: Oxford University Press, 2015.

Sizgorich, Thomas. "For Christian Eyes Only? The Intended Audience of the Martyrdom of Antony Rawḥ." *Islam and Christian-Muslim Relations* 20 (2009), 119–35.

——. *Violence and Belief in Late Antiquity: Militant Devotion in Christianity and Islam.* Philadelphia: University of Pennsylvania Press, 2009.

——. " 'Become Infidels or We Will Throw You into the Fire': The Martyrs of Najrān in Early Muslim Historiography, Hagiography, and Qurʾānic Exegesis." In *Writing "True Stories": Historians and Hagiographers in the Late Antique and Medieval Near East.* Arietta Papaconstantinou, with Muriel Debié and Hugh Kennedy, eds. Turnhout: Brepols, 2010, 125–47.

——. "Monks and Their Daughters: Monasteries as Muslim-Christian Boundaries." In *Muslims and Others in Sacred Space.* Margaret Cormack, ed. Oxford: Oxford University Press, 2013, 193–216.

——. "Mind the Gap: Accidental Conversion and the Hagiographic Imaginary in the First Centuries A.H." In *Conversion in Late Antiquity: Christianity, Islam, and Beyond: Papers from the Andrew W. Mellon Foundation Sawyer Seminar, University of Oxford, 2009–2010.* Arietta Papaconstantinou, with Neil McLynn and Daniel L. Schwartz, eds. Burlington, VT: Ashgate, 2015, 163–74.

——. "The Dancing Martyr: Violence, Identity, and the Abbasid Postcolonial." *History of Religions* 57 (2017), 2–27.

Skjærvø, Prods Oktor. *The Spirit of Zoroastrianism*. New Haven: Yale University Press, 2011.

Smith, Kyle. *Constantine and the Captive Christians of Persia: Martyrdom and Religious Identity in Late Antiquity*. Oakland, CA: University of California Press, 2016.

Soifer, Maya. "Beyond *Convivencia*: Critical Reflections on the Historiography of Interfaith Relations in Christian Spain." *Journal of Medieval Iberian Studies* 1 (2009), 19–35.

Sokoloff, Michael, ed. and trans. *A Syriac Lexicon: A Translation from the Latin; Correction, Expansion, and Update of C. Brockelmanns's "Lexicon Syriacum."* Winona Lake, IN: Eisenbrauns; and Piscataway, NJ: Gorgias Press, 2009.

Spencer, Robert. *The Truth about Muhammad: Founder of the World's Most Intolerant Religion*. Washington, DC: Regnery Publishing, 2006.

——. *Religion of Peace? Why Christianity Is and Islam Isn't*. Washington, DC: Regnery Publishing, 2007.

Spicq, Ceslas. *Theological Lexicon of the New Testament*. 3 vols. James D. Ernest, ed. and trans. Peabody, MA: Hendrickson Publishers, 1994.

Spies, Otto. "Über die Kreuzigung im Islam." In *Religion und Religionen: Festschrift für Gustav Mensching zu seinem 65. Geburtstag*. Bonn: Ludwig Rohrscheid Verlag, 1967, 143–56.

Stausberg, Michael, and Yuhan Sohrab-Dinshaw Vevaina, with Anna Tessmann, eds. *The Wiley-Blackwell Companion to Zoroastrianism*. Malden, MA: Wiley Blackwell, 2015.

Stewart, Devin J. "Blasphemy." In *The Princeton Encyclopedia of Islamic Political Thought*. Gerhard Bowering with Patricia Crone, Wadad Kadi, Devin J. Stewart, Muhammad Qasim Zaman, and Mahan Mirza, eds. Princeton: Princeton University Press, 2013, 71–73.

Stow, Kenneth R. *Alienated Minority: The Jews of Medieval Latin Europe*. Cambridge, MA: Harvard University Press, 1992.

Stromberg, Peter G. "The Role of Language in Religious Conversion." In *The Oxford Handbook of Religious Conversion*. Lewis R. Rambo and Charles E. Farhadian, eds. Oxford: Oxford University Press, 2014, 117–39.

Stroumsa, Sarah. *Maimonides in His World: Portrait of a Mediterranean Thinker*. Princeton: Princeton University Press, 2009.

al-Subkī, Tāqī ʾl-Dīn. *al-Sayf al-maslūl ʿalā man sabba ʾl-rasūl*. Iyād Aḥmad al-Ghawj, ed. Amman: Dār al-Fatḥ, 2000.

Sullivan, Donald. "Jean Bolland (1596–1665) and the Early Bollandists." In *Medieval Scholarship: Biographical Studies on the Formation of a Discipline. Volume 1: History*. Helen Damico and Joseph Zavadil, eds. New York: Garland, 1995, 3–14.

Sviri, Sara. "*Wa-rahbānīyatan ibtadaʿūhā*: An Analysis of Traditions Concerning the Origin and Evaluation of Christian Monasticism." *Jerusalem Studies in Arabic and Islam* 13 (1990), 195–208.

Swanson, Mark N. "The Martyrdom of ʿAbd al-Masīḥ, Superior of Mount Sinai (Qays al-Ghassānī)." In *Syrian Christians under Islam: The First Thousand Years*. David Thomas, ed. Leiden: Brill, 2001, 107–29.

——. "The Christian al-Maʾmūn Tradition." In *Christians at the Heart of Islamic Rule:*

Church Life and Scholarship in ʿAbbasid Iraq. David Thomas, ed. Leiden: Brill, 2003, 63–92.

Swanson, Mark N. "Arabic Hagiography." In *The Ashgate Research Companion to Byzantine Hagiography. Volume I: Periods and Places.* Stephanos Efthymiadis, ed. Farnham, UK: Ashgate, 2011, 345–67.

al-Ṭabarī. *Annales quos scripsit Abu Djafar Mohammed ibn Djarir at-Tabari cum aliis.* 15 vols. in 3 pts. M. J. de Goeje, ed. Leiden: Brill, 1879–1901.

——. *Tahdhīb al-āthār wa-tafṣīl ʿan rasūl allāh min al-akhbār.* 4 vols. Maḥmūd Muḥammad Shākir, ed. Cairo: Maṭbaʿat al-Madanī, 1982.

——. *Tafsīr al-ṭabarī: Jāmiʿ al-bayān ʿan tawīl āy al-qurʾān.* 7 vols. Ṣalāḥ ʿAbd al-Fattāḥ al-Khālidī and Ibrāhīm Muḥammad al-ʿAlī, eds. Damascus: Dār al-Qalam; and Beirut: al-Dār al-Shāmīya, 1997.

Tacitus. *Tacitus in Five Volumes.* 5 vols. Loeb Classical Library. Cambridge, MA: Harvard University Press, 1969–70.

al-Ṭaḥāwī. *Sharḥ maʿānī ʾl-āthār.* 5 vols. Muḥammad Zuhrī al-Najjār, Muḥammad Sayyid Jād al-Ḥaqq, and Yūsuf ʿAbd al-Raḥmān al-Marʿashlī, eds. Beirut: ʿĀlam al-Kutub, 1994.

Talbi, Mohamed. *L'émirat aghlabide, 184–296, 800–909: Histoire politique.* Paris: Librairie d'Amérique et d'Orient, 1966.

Tannous, Jack. "Syria between Byzantium and Islam: Making Incommensurables Speak." Ph.D. dissertation, Princeton University, 2010.

——. "L'hagiographie syro-occidentale à la période islamique." In *L'hagiographie syriaque.* André Binggeli, ed. Paris: Geuthner, 2012, 225–45.

——. "You Are What You Read: Qenneshre and the Miaphysite Church in the Seventh Century." In *History and Identity in the Late Antique Near East.* Philip Wood, ed. Oxford: Oxford University Press, 2013, 83–102.

——. "In Search of Monothelitism." *Dumbarton Oaks Papers* 68 (2014), 29–68.

——. "The Life of Simeon of the Olives: A Christian Puzzle from Islamic Syria." In *Motions of Late Antiquity: Essays on Religion, Politics, and Society in Honour of Peter Brown.* Jamie Kreiner and Helmut Reimitz, eds. Turnhout: Brepols, 2016, 309–29.

Taylor, David G. K. "The Disputation between a Muslim and a Monk of Bēt Ḥālē: Syriac Text and Annotated English Translation." In *Christsein in der islamischen Welt. Festschrift für Martin Tamcke zum 60. Geburtstag.* Sidney H. Griffith and Sven Grebenstein, eds. Wiesbaden: Harrassowitz Verlag, 2015, 187–242.

——. "The Syriac Baptism of St John: A Christian Ritual of Protection for Muslim Children." In *The Late Antique World of Early Islam: Muslims among Christians and Jews in the East Mediterranean.* Robert Hoyland, ed. Princeton: Darwin Press, 2015, 437–60.

Ter-Ghewondyan, Aram. *The Arab Emirates in Bagratid Armenia.* Nina G. Garsoïan, trans. Lisbon: Livraria Bertrand, 1976.

Tertullian. *Apology; De spectaculis. Minucius Felix Octavius.* Loeb Classical Library. T. R. Glover and Gerald H. Rendall with W.C.A. Kerr, trans. London: William Heinemann Ltd., 1953.

Thomas, David. *Anti-Christian Polemic in Early Islam: Abū ʿĪsā al-Warrāq's "Against the Trinity."* Cambridge: Cambridge University Press, 1992.

[*CMR*, ii] Thomas, David, and Alex Mallett, eds. *Christian-Muslim Relations: A Bibliographical History. Volume 2 (900–1050).* Leiden: Brill, 2010.

[*CMR*, i] Thomas, David, and Barbara Roggema, eds. *Christian-Muslim Relations: A Bibliographical History. Volume 1 (600–900).* Leiden: Brill, 2009.

Thomson, Robert W., trans. *History of the House of Artsrunik'*. Detroit: Wayne State University Press, 1985.

——. *Rewriting Caucasian History: The Medieval Armenian Adaptation of the Georgian Chronicles. The Original Georgian Texts and the Armenian Adaptations.* Oxford: Clarendon Press, 1996.

——, trans. "The Passion of David of Dwin." In *Seeing Islam as Others Saw It: A Survey and Evaluation of Christian, Jewish, and Zoroastrian Writings on Early Islam.* Robert G. Hoyland. Princeton: Darwin Press, 1997, 672–76.

——, trans. *The Armenian History Attributed to Sebeos.* 2 vols. With James Howard-Johnston and Tim Greenwood. Liverpool: Liverpool University Press, 1999.

Tieszen, Charles L. *Christian Identity amid Islam in Medieval Spain.* Brill: Leiden, 2013.

Tilley, Maureen A., trans. *Donatist Martyr Stories: The Church in Conflict in Roman North Africa.* Liverpool: Liverpool University Press, 1996.

Tillier, Mathieu. "Prisons et autorités urbaines sous les Abbassides." *Arabica* 55 (2008), 387–408.

——. *Les cadis d'Iraq et l'état abbasside (132/750–335/945).* Damascus: L'Institut français du Proche-Orient, 2009.

——. "Vivre en prison à l'époque abbasside." *Journal of the Economic and Social History of the Orient* 52 (2009), 635–59.

——. "Les prisonniers dans la société musulmane (IIe/VIIIe–IVe/Xe siècle)." In *Dynamiques sociales au Moyen Âge en Occident et Orient.* Elisabeth Malamut, ed. Aix-en-Provence: Publications de l'Université de Provence, 2010, 191–212.

——. "Les ‹premiers› cadis de Fusṭāṭ et les dynamiques régionales de l'innovation judiciaire (750–833)." *Annales islamologiques* 45 (2011), 213–42.

al-Tirmidhī. *al-Jāmiʿ al-kabīr.* 6 vols. Bashshār ʿAwwād Maʿrūf, ed. Beirut: Dār al-Gharb al-Islāmī, 1996.

Todt, Klaus-Peter. "Griechisch-orthodoxe (Melkitische) Christen im zentralen und südlichen Syrien." *Le Muséon* 119 (2006), 33–88.

Tor, D. G. *Violent Order: Religious Warfare, Chivalry, and the ʿAyyār Phenomenon in the Medieval Islamic World.* Würzburg: Ergon, 2007.

Toral-Niehoff, Isabel. "Constantine's Baptism Legend: A 'Wandering' Story between Byzantium, Rome, the Syriac and the Arab World." In *Negotiating Co-existence: Communities, Cultures and* Convivencia *in Byzantine Society.* Barbara Crostini and Sergio La Porta, eds. Trier: Wissenschaftlicher Verlag Trier, 2013, 131–43.

Toumanoff, Cyril. "Medieval Georgian Historical Literature (VIIth–XVth Centuries)." *Traditio* 1 (1943), 139–82.

——. *Studies in Christian Caucasian History.* Washington, DC: Georgetown University Press, 1963.

——. "Armenia and Georgia." In *The Cambridge Medieval History. Volume 4: The Byzantine Empire.* 2 vols. J. M. Husey, ed. Cambridge: Cambridge University Press, 1966, i, 593–637.

Tritton, A. S. *The Caliphs and Their Non-Muslim Subjects: A Critical Study of the Covenant of ʿUmar.* London: Oxford University Press, 1930.

Tropeau, Gérard. "Un traité christologique attribué au calife fatimide al-Muʿizz." *Annales islamologiques* 15 (1979), 11–24.

Tsafrir, Nurit. "The Attitude of Sunnī Islam toward Jews and Christians as Reflected in Some Legal Issues." *al-Qanṭara* 36 (2005), 317–36.

Tucker, William F. "Rebels and Gnostics: al-Muġīra Ibn Saʿīd and the Muġīriyya." *Arabica* 22 (1975), 33–47.

——. "Abū Manṣūr al-ʿIjlī and the Manṣūriyya: A Study in Medieval Terrorism." *Der Islam* 54 (1977), 66–76.

——. *Mahdis and Millenarians: Shīʿite Extremists in Early Muslim Iraq.* Cambridge: Cambridge University Press, 2008.

Turki, Abdelmagid. "Situation du ‹tributaire› qui insulte l'Islam, au regard de la doctrine et la jurisprudence musulmanes." *Studia Islamica* 30 (1969), 39–72.

Turner, John P. *Inquisition in Early Islam: The Competition for Political and Religious Authority in the Abbasid Empire.* London: I. B. Tauris, 2013.

al-Ṭūsī. *Ikhtiyār maʿrifat al-rijāl al-maʿrūf bi rijāl al-kishshī.* Jawād al-Qayyūmī al-Iṣfahānī, ed. Qom: Muʾassasat al-Nashr al-Islāmī al-Tābiʿa li-Jamāʿat al-Mudarrisīn bi-Qum al-Musharrafa, 2006.

Tyan, Émile. *Histoire de l'organisation judiciaire en pays d'Islam.* Leiden: Brill, 1960.

Ullmann, Manfred. *Das Motiv der Kreuzigung in der arabischen Poesie des Mittelalters.* Wiesbaden: Harrassowitz, 1995.

Urvoy, Dominique. "La pensée religieuse des mozarabes face à l'Islam." *Traditio* 39 (1983), 419–32.

——. "Les aspects symboliques du vocable ‹mozarabe›: Essai de réinterprétation." *Studia Islamica* 78 (1993), 117–53.

Vacca, Alison Marie. "From K'usti Kapkoh to al-Ğarbī: Sasanian Antecedents, the Sectarian Milieu, and the Creation of an Islamic Frontier in Armīniya." Ph.D. dissertation, University of Michigan, 2013.

——. "*Nisbas* of the North: Muslims from Armenia, Caucasian Albania, and Azerbaijan in Arabic Biographical Dictionaries (4th–7th Centruries AH)." *Arabica* 62 (2015), 521–50.

——. "The Fires of Naxčawan: In Search of Intercultural Transmission in Arabic, Armenian, Greek, and Syriac." *Le Muséon* 129 (2016), 323–62.

——. *Non-Muslim Provinces under Early Islam: Islamic Rule and Iranian Legitimacy in Armenia and Caucasian Albania.* Cambridge: Cambridge University Press, 2017.

Vailhé, Siméon. "Le monastère de Saint-Sabas (Suite.)." *Échos d'Orient* 3 (1899), 18–28.

van Ess, Josef. *Das Kitāb an-Nakt des Naẓẓām und seine Rezeption im Kitāb al-Futyā des Ğāḥiẓ.* Göttingen: Vandenhoeck und Ruprecht, 1972.

——. *Theologie und Gesellschaft im 2. und 3. Jahrhundert Hidschra: Eine Geschichte des religiösen Denkens im frühen Islam.* 6 vols. Berlin: Walter de Gruyter, 1991–97.

van Koningsveld, P.S.J.. *The Latin-Arabic Glossary of the Leiden University Library: A Contribution to the Study of Mozarabic Manuscripts and Literature.* Leiden: New Rhine Publishers, 1977.

Vaporis, Nomikos. *Witnesses for Christ: Orthodox Christian Neomartyrs of the Ottoman Period, 1437–1860.* Crestwood, NY: St. Vladimir's Seminary Press, 2000.

Vasil'evskii, V., and P. Nikitin, eds. *Skazaniia o 42 Amoriiskikh muchenikakh i tserkovnaia sluzhba im.* St. Petersburg: Akademiia, 1906.

Vasiliev, Alexander. "The Life of St. Theodore of Edessa." *Byzantion* 16 (1942–43), 165–225.

Vila, David H. "Christian Martyrs in the First Abbasid Century and the Development of an Apologetic against Islam." Ph.D. dissertation, Saint Louis University, 1999.

———. "The Struggle over Arabisation in Medieval Arabic Christian Hagiography." *al-Masāq* 15 (2003), 35–46.

Viscuso, Patrick Demetrios, trans. *Guide for a Church under Islām: The Sixty-Six Canonical Questions Attributed to Theodōros Balsamōn*. Brookline, MA: Holy Cross Orthodox Press, 2014.

von Grunebaum, G. E. "The Structure of the Muslim Town." In *Islam: Essays in the Nature and Growth of a Cultural Tradition*. Abingdon, UK: Routledge, 2008, 141–58.

Vööbus, Arthur. *The Synodicon in the West Syrian Tradition*. 2 vols. in 4 pts. Louvain: Secrétariat du Corpus, 1975.

Vryonis, Speros, Jr. "Religious Changes and Patterns in the Balkans, 14th–16th Centuries." In *Aspects of the Balkans: Continuity and Change. Contributions to the International Balkan Conference Held at UCLA, October 23–28, 1969*. Henrik Birnbaum and Speros Vryonis Jr., eds. The Hauge: Mouton, 1972, 151–76.

Walker, Joel Thomas. *The Legend of Mar Qardagh: Narrative and Christian Heroism in Late Antique Iraq*. Berkeley: University of California Press, 2006.

———. "From Nisibis to Xi'an: The Church of the East in Late Antique Eurasia." In *The Oxford Handbook of Late Antiquity*. Scott Fitzgerald Johnson, ed. Oxford: Oxford University Press, 2012, 994–1052.

Walker, Paul E. *Caliph of Cairo: Al-Hakim bi-Amr Allah, 996–1021*. Cairo: American University of Cairo Press, 2009.

Wallace-Hadrill, J. M., trans. *The Fourth Book of the Chronicle of Fredegar with Its Continuations*. London: Thomas Nelson and Sons Ltd., 1960.

Walmsley, Alan. *Early Islamic Syria: An Archaeological Assessment*. London: Duckworth, 2007.

Walter, Christopher. "The Origins of the Cult of Saint George." *Revue des Études Byzantines* 53 (1995), 295–326.

Waltz, James. "The Significance of the Voluntary Martyrs of Ninth-Century Córdoba." *Muslim World* 60 (1970), 143–59.

———. "Historical Perspective on the 'Early Missions' to Muslims: A Response to Allan Cutler." *Muslim World* 61 (1971), 170–86.

Wansbrough, John. *Quranic Studies: Sources and Methods of Scriptural Interpretation*. Oxford: Oxford University Press, 1977.

———. *The Sectarian Milieu: Content and Composition of Islamic Salvation History*. Oxford: Oxford University Press, 1978.

al-Wansharīsī. *al-Miyʿār al-muʿrib wa-ʾl-jāmiʿ al-mughrib*. 13 vols. Muḥammad Ḥajjī, ed. Rabat: Nashr Wizārat al-Awqāf wa-ʾl-Shuʾūn al-Islāmīya lil-Mamlaka al-Maghribīya, 1981–83.

al-Wāqidī. *The "Kitāb al-Maghāzī" of al-Wāqidī*. 3 vols. Marsden Jones, ed. London: Oxford University Press, 1966.

Ward, Walter D. *Mirage of the Saracen: Christians and Nomads in the Sinai Peninsula in Late Antiquity*. Berkeley: University of California Press, 2014.

Wardrop, O. "Georgian Manuscripts at the Iberian Monastery on Mount Athos." *Journal of Theological Studies* 12 (1911), 593–607.

Wasilewski, Janna. "The 'Life of Muhammad' in Eulogius of Córdoba: Some Evidence for the Transmission of Greek Polemic to the Latin West." *Early Medieval Europe* 16 (2008), 333–53.

Wasserstein, David J. "A *Fatwā* on Conversion in Islamic Spain." In *Studies in Muslim-Jewish Relations.* 4 vols. New York: Harwood Academic Publishers, 1993–98, i (1993), 177–88.

——. "The Language Situation in al-Andalus." In *The Formation of al-Andalus. Part 2: Language, Religion, Culture and the Sciences.* Maribel Fierro and Julio Samsó, eds. Aldershot: Ashgate, 1998, 3–17.

——. "Why Did Arabic Succeed Where Greek Failed? Language Change in the Near East after Muhammad." *Scripta Classica Israelica* 22 (2003), 257–72.

——. "Conversion and the *Ahl al-dhimma.*" In *The New Cambridge History of Islam. Volume 4: Islamic Cultures and Societies to the End of the Eighteenth Century.* Robert Irwin, ed. Cambridge: Cambridge University Press, 2010, 184–208.

Watt, W. Montgomery. *Muhammad at Mecca.* Oxford: Clarendon Press, 1953.

——. "God's Caliph. Qur'ānic Interpretations and Umayyad Claims." In *Iran and Islam in Memory of the Late Vladimir Minorsky.* C. E. Bosworth, ed. Edinburgh: Edinburgh University Press, 1971, 565–74.

Wellhausen, Julius. *The Arab Kingdom and Its Fall.* Margaret Graham Weir, trans. Calcutta: University of Calcutta Press, 1927.

Wensinck, A. J. *Concordances et indices de la tradition musulmane.* 8 vols. Leiden: Brill, 1936–88.

Westbrook, Raymond, ed. *A History of Near Eastern Law.* 2 vols. Leiden: Brill, 2003.

Westernick, L. G., ed. *Arethae archiepiscopi Caesarensis scripta minora.* 2 vols. Leipzig: Teubner, 1968–72.

Whitby, Michael, and Mary Whitby. *Chronicon Paschale 284–628 AD.* Liverpool: Liverpool University Press, 1989.

Whitcomb, Donald. "Amṣār in Syria? Syrian Cities after the Conquest." *ARAM* 6 (1994), 13–33.

White, Carolinne, trans. *Early Christian Lives.* London: Penguin Books, 1998.

Wiederhold, Lutz. "Blasphemy against the Prophet Muḥammad and His Companions (*Sabb al-Rasūl, Sabb al-Ṣaḥābah*): The Introduction of the Topic into Shāfiʿī Legal Literature and Its Relevance for Legal Practice under Mamluk Rule." *Journal of Semitic Studies* 42 (1997), 39–70.

Wolf, Kenneth Baxter. *Christian Martyrs in Muslim Spain.* Cambridge: Cambridge University Press, 1988.

——. "The Earliest Latin Lives of Muḥammad." In *Conversion and Continuity: Indigenous Christian Communities in Islamic Lands, Eighth to Eighteenth Centuries.* Michael Gervers and Ramzi Jibran Bikhazi, eds. Toronto: Pontifical Institute of Mediaeval Studies, 1990, 89–101.

Wood, Jamie. "Persecution, Past and Present: Memorialising Martyrdom in Late Antique and Early Medieval Córdoba." *al-Masāq* 27 (2015), 41–60.

Wood, Philip. "Christian Authority under the Early Abbasids: The *Life of Timothy of Kakushta.*" *Proche-Orient Chrétien* 61 (2011), 258–74.

——. "Christians in Umayyad Iraq: Decentralisation and Expansion (600–750)." In *Power, Patronage and Memory in Early Islam: Perspectives on Umayyad History.* Andrew Marsham and Alain George, eds. Edinburgh: Edinburgh University Press, 2017, 255–74.

Woods, David. "The 60 Martyrs of Gaza and the Martyrdom of Bishop Sophronius of Jerusalem." *ARAM* 15 (2003), 129–50.

Wright, Roger. *Late Latin and Early Romance in Spain and Carolingian France*. Liverpool: F. Cairns, 1982.

———. "The End of Written Ladino in al-Andalus." In *The Formation of al-Andalus. Part 2: Language, Religion, Culture and the Sciences*. Maribel Fierro and Julio Samsó, eds. Aldershot: Ashgate, 1998, 19–35.

al-Yaʿqūbī. *Tārīkh*. 2 vols. Beirut: Dār Ṣādir, 1960.

Yāqūt. *Muʿjam al-buldān*. 5 vols. Beirut: Dār Ṣādir, 1977.

Yarbrough, Luke B. "Islamizing the Islamic State: The Formulation and Assertion of Religious Criteria for State Employment in the First Millennium AH." Ph.D. dissertation, Princeton University, 2012.

———. "Upholding God's Rule: Early Muslim Juristic Opposition to State Employment of Non-Muslims." *Islamic Law and Society* 19 (2012), 11–85.

———. "Origins of the *Ghiyār*." *Journal of the American Oriental Society* 134 (2014), 113–21.

———. " 'I'll Not Accept Aid from a *Mushrik*.' " In *The Late Roman and Early Islamic Mediterranean and Near East: Authority and Control in the Countryside*. Alain Delattre, Marie Legendre, and Petra Sijpesteijn, eds. Princeton: Darwin Press, forthcoming.

[*EIr*] Yashater, Ehsan, ed. *Encyclopædia Iranica*. London: Paul Kegan and Routledge, 1982–present.

Bosworth, C. E. "Afšīn." *EIr*, i, II, 589–91.

Shahbazi, A. Shapur, Erich Kettenhofen, and John R. Perry. "Deportations." *EIr*, vii, 297–312.

Sundermann, Werner. "Mani." *EIr*, http://www.iranicaonline.org/articles/mani-founder-manicheism.

Tafażżolī, Aḥmad. "Abāliš." *EIr*, i, I, 58.

Yavari, Neguin. "The Conversion Stories of Shaykh Abū Isḥāq Kāzarūnī." In *Christianizing Peoples and Converting Individuals*. Guyda Armstrong and Ian N. Wood, eds. Turnhout: Brepols, 2000, 225–46.

Young, William G. *Patriarch, Shah, and Caliph: A Study of the Relationships of the Church of the East with the Sassanid Empire and the Early Caliphates Up to 820 A.D. with Special Reference to Available Translated Syriac Sources*. Rawalpindi: Christian Study Centre, 1974.

Zaborowski, Jason R. *The Coptic Martyrdom of John of Phanijōit: Assimilation and Conversion to Islam in Thirteenth-Century Egypt*. Leiden: Brill, 2005.

al-Zamakhsharī. *al-Kashshāf ʿan ḥaqāʾiq ghawāmiḍ al-tanzīl wa-ʿuyūn al-aqāwīl fī wujūh al-taʾwīl*. 4 vols. Beirut: Dār al-Kitāb al-ʿArabī, 1965.

Zayd b. ʿAlī. *Musnad al-imām zayd*. Beirut: Dār Maktabat al-Ḥayāt, 1966.

Zayyāt, Ḥabīb. "Shuhadāʾ al-naṣrānīya fī ʾl-islām." *al-Machreq* 36 (1938), 459–65.

———. "Simāt al-naṣārā wa-ʾl-yahūd fī ʾl-islām." *al-Machreq* 43 (1949), 161–252.

———. "Vie du patriarche melkite d'Antioche Christophore († 967) par le protospathaire

Ibrahîm b. Yuhanna. Document inédit du Xe siècle." *Proche-Orient Chrétien* 2 (1952), 11–38, 333–66.
Zayyāt, Ḥabīb. *al-Diyārāt al-naṣrānīya fī 'l-islām*. Beirut: Dar al-Machreq, 1999.
Zorgati, Ragnhild Johnsrud. *Pluralism in the Middle Ages: Hybrid Identities, Conversion, and Mixed Marriages in Medieval Iberia*. New York: Routledge, 2012.
Zouache, Abbès. "Têtes en guerre au Proche-Orient, mutilations et décapitations, Ve–VIe/XIe–XIIe siècles." *Annales islamologiques* 43 (2009), 195–244.

Index

conversion to Islam (*cont.*)
natural experiences, 32; ease of, 35; emotional toll of, 67–68; external *versus* interior, 52–53; fluid and ambiguous of, 78–79; to gain riches, 202–3; martyrologies as response to, 200–212; mass, 203–4, 246–47; as means of improving life, 45; multiple forms of, 31–79; in Muslim-Christian tensions, 149–51, 159; privacy of, 164; social and economic explanations for, 202–4; with spiritual, emotional, or intellectual change, 33; through coercion and captivity, 38–45; usual conception of, 29–30; while intoxicated, 56–59; works on, 13n.29
converts: ambivalence toward, 38–39; taxing of, 39
Cook, David, 104–5
Cook, Michael, 12
Coope, Jessica, 77
Coptic Christians: martyrologies of, 228; myths of rulers' conversion, 113
Córdoba: voluntary martyrs of, 3–4; blasphemy in, 118–19, 140–54; literary analysis of martyrdom stories of, 141–42; mixed marriages in, 77; resisters *versus* accommodationists in, 216–21; true apostasy in, 101–2
Córdoba martyr acts, 71–72; manuscripts of, 21–22
Córdoba martyrs, 3–4, 247; flip-floppers among, 38; scholarly literature on, 119–20
corruption, worries about, 217–20
Crone, Patricia, 12, 34–35, 172
crucifixions, 94n.69, 172–75, 181–83; of Christian martyrs, 192–96; as response to challenge to state, 192
crypto-Christianity, 75–76
cult sites, preventing creation of, 189–91
Cyprian of Carthage, 2
Cyrus of Ḥarrān, 15, 49–53, 227

Ḍaḥḥāk. *See* Bacchus
Dalja, 118n.2
Damrāwī, Michael al-, 102
David of Dwin, 93–96, 242; crucifixion of, 173; martyrology of, 250–51
Dayr Fākhūr monastery, 87n.31
Dayr Murrān monastery, 90, 134
Debié, Muriel, 39
decapitation, 88, 128, 173, 175, 180–81, 184, 204–5
Delehaye, Hippolyte, 9
Devşirme, 43n.62
dhimmīs: forbidden to denigrate Islam, 124, 149, 193; laissez-faire attitude toward, 5–6, 162; oppression of, 144, 194, 247
Dhū Nuwās, 185
Díaz, Manuel Cecilio Díaz y, 157, 221
Dionysius bar Ṣalībī, 233
Dionysius of Tel Maḥrē, 209
Dioscorus, 70–71, 184
Disputation between a Monk of Bēt Ḥālē and a Muslim Amīr, 190–91
Donatists, 220; martyrs, 2
Donner, Fred, 243
Douglas, Mary, 161–62, 197–98

East Syrians (Nestorians): accommodation of to Muslim rule, 200, 228–29, 235n.154, 240; lack of martyrologies of, 228–29
Egypt: religiously mixed families in, 68–71; true apostasy in, 100–105
Elias of Helioupolis, 53–59; betrayal of, 165, 204; date of execution of, 54n.104; offer of riches to convert, 203; offers to repent, 169; on *parrhēsia,* 137; passion of, 20; protecting body of, 190; trial of, 145
Emila, 153; crucifixion of, 173
Emulation, power of, 200–201
end of times: Christian beliefs about, 112–13, 188; Muslim beliefs about, 83
Ess, Josef van, 129
eucharistic miracle, 107
Eulogius of Córdoba, 19; on accommodationists of Córdoba, 220, 221; on Andulusī martyrs, 71–77; on assimilationists, 216–17; call to emulate, 201; on Córdoba blasphemers, 152–54; on Córdoba martyrs, 141, 158; on crucifixion and burning of blasphemers, 184; on George of Mar Saba, 238; on Isaac story, 150–51; on John the Merchant, 144; Latin style of, 217–19; on martyrdom as spiritual purification, 222; *Memoriale sanctorum* of, 208–9, 217, 239; on Perfectus the Monk, 145–46, 149; on Qur'anic punishments, 171–72; on Umayyad martyrs, 150–52
Euphemia of Damascus, first labeled "new martyr," 40n.52
Eusebius of Caesarea, 176–77
Eustathius, 242–43; sectarian dispute over, 230; uncertainty of death of, 230